Uncertain Spatiotemporal Data Management for the Semantic Web

Luyi Bai
Northeastern University, China

Lin Zhu
Northeastern University, China

A volume in the Advances in Systems Analysis, Software Engineering, and High Performance Computing (ASASEHPC) Book Series

Published in the United States of America by
IGI Global
Engineering Science Reference (an imprint of IGI Global)
701 E. Chocolate Avenue
Hershey PA, USA 17033
Tel: 717-533-8845
Fax: 717-533-8661
E-mail: cust@igi-global.com
Web site: http://www.igi-global.com

Library of Congress Cataloging-in-Publication Data

CIP PENDING

TITLE: Uncertain Spatiotemporal Data Management for the Semantic Web
ISBN: 9781668491089
eISBN: 9781668491096

This book is published in the IGI Global book series Advances in Systems Analysis, Software Engineering, and High Performance Computing (ASASEHPC) (ISSN: 2327-3453; eISSN: 2327-3461)

British Cataloguing in Publication Data
A Cataloguing in Publication record for this book is available from the British Library.

Advances in Systems Analysis, Software Engineering, and High Performance Computing (ASASEHPC) Book Series

Vijayan Sugumaran
Oakland University, USA

ISSN:2327-3453
EISSN:2327-3461

Mission

The theory and practice of computing applications and distributed systems has emerged as one of the key areas of research driving innovations in business, engineering, and science. The fields of software engineering, systems analysis, and high performance computing offer a wide range of applications and solutions in solving computational problems for any modern organization.

The **Advances in Systems Analysis, Software Engineering, and High Performance Computing (ASASEHPC) Book Series** brings together research in the areas of distributed computing, systems and software engineering, high performance computing, and service science. This collection of publications is useful for academics, researchers, and practitioners seeking the latest practices and knowledge in this field.

Coverage

- Network Management
- Enterprise Information Systems
- Metadata and Semantic Web
- Software Engineering
- Storage Systems
- Computer Graphics
- Virtual Data Systems
- Distributed Cloud Computing
- Human-Computer Interaction
- Engineering Environments

IGI Global is currently accepting manuscripts for publication within this series. To submit a proposal for a volume in this series, please contact our Acquisition Editors at acquisitions@igi-global.com or visit: https://www.igi-global.com/publish/.

The Advances in Systems Analysis, Software Engineering, and High Performance Computing (ASASEHPC) Book Series (ISSN 2327-3453) is published by IGI Global, 701 E. Chocolate Avenue, Hershey, PA 17033-1240, USA, www.igi-global.com. This series is composed of titles available for purchase individually; each title is edited to be contextually exclusive from any other title within the series. For pricing and ordering information please visit https://www.igi-global.com/book-series/advances-systems-analysis-software-engineering/73689. Postmaster: Send all address changes to above address.

Titles in this Series

For a list of additional titles in this series, please visit:
www.igi-global.com/book-series/advances-systems-analysis-software-engineering/73689

ODE, BVP, and 1D PDE Solvers for Scientific and Engineering Problems With MATLAB Basics
Leonid Burstein (ORT Braude College of Engineering, Israel (Retred))
Engineering Science Reference • © 2024 • 300pp • H/C (ISBN: 9781668468500) • US $245.00

Digital Technologies in Modeling and Management Insights in Education and Industry
GS Prakasha (Christ University, India) Maria Lapina (North-Caucasus Federal University, Russia) and Deepanraj Balakrishnan (Prince Mohammad Bin Fahd University, Saudi Aabia)
Information Science Reference • © 2024 • 320pp • H/C (ISBN: 9781668495766) • US $250.00

The Software Principles of Design for Data Modeling
Debabrata Samanta (Rochester Institute of Technology, Kosovo)
Engineering Science Reference • © 2023 • 318pp • H/C (ISBN: 9781668498095) • US $270.00

Investigations in Pattern Recognition and Computer Vision for Industry 4.0
Chiranji Lal Chowdhary (Vellore Institute of Technology, Vellore, India) Basanta Kumar Swain (Government College of Engineering, Bhawanipatna, India) and Vijay Kumar (Dr B R Ambedkar National Institute of Technology Jalandhar, India)
Engineering Science Reference • © 2023 • 276pp • H/C (ISBN: 9781668486023) • US $270.00

Cyber-Physical System Solutions for Smart Cities
Vanamoorthy Muthumanikandan (Vellore Institute of Technology, Chennai, India) Anbalagan Bhuvaneswari (Vellore Institute of Technology, Chennai, India) Balamurugan Easwaran (University of Africa, Toru-Orua, Nigeria) and T. Sudarson Rama Perumal (Rohini College of Engineering and Technology, India)
Engineering Science Reference • © 2023 • 182pp • H/C (ISBN: 9781668477564) • US $270.00

Cyber-Physical Systems and Supporting Technologies for Industrial Automation
R. Thanigaivelan (A.K.T. Memorial College of Engineering and Technology, India) S. Kaliappan (Velammal Institute of Technology, India) and C. Jegadheesan (Kongu Engineering College, India)
Engineering Science Reference • © 2023 • 444pp • H/C (ISBN: 9781668492673) • US $270.00

Perspectives and Considerations on the Evolution of Smart Systems
Maki K. Habib (American University in Cairo, Egypt)
Engineering Science Reference • © 2023 • 419pp • H/C (ISBN: 9781668476840) • US $325.00

701 East Chocolate Avenue, Hershey, PA 17033, USA
Tel: 717-533-8845 x100 • Fax: 717-533-8661
E-Mail: cust@igi-global.com • www.igi-global.com

Table of Contents

Preface

Spatial and temporal information plays an important role in many applications. Since a considerable amount of spatiotemporal data emerges in spatiotemporal applications, the requirement of managing spatiotemporal data has attracted much attention both from academia and industry. The data types of spatiotemporal data are numerous and the structure is complex. Therefore, studies on spatiotemporal data management need good models to represent spatiotemporal features so that operations on spatiotemporal data can be carried out.

On the other hand, Semantic Web is a kind of intelligent network. It can not only understand words and concepts, but also understand the logical relationship between them. It can make communication more efficient and valuable. RDF (Resource Description Framework) and XML (Extensible Markup Language) are two important parts in the architecture of Semantic Web. RDF, as a standard metadata description framework proposed by the World Wide Web Consortium (W3C), is suitable for modeling and querying Web data. With the rapid development of the Internet, XML is increasingly accepted as a medium for integrating and exchanging data, gradually becoming the mainstream and de facto standard for information exchange and coding format. As a result, studies on spatiotemporal data management on the basis of RDF and XML becomes crucial.

Most information is uncertain and imprecise, which is one of the inherent features of spatiotemporal data. Uncertainty is either measurement error or imprecision due to incomplete knowledge. The researches on uncertain spatiotemporal data focus on how to model and query uncertain spatiotemporal data, which are attracting an increased attention.

This book goes to concerning the topic of uncertain spatiotemporal data management for the Semantic Web. The topics of this book include 20 chapters: spatiotemporal data modeling based on RDF; algebraic operations on spatiotemporal RDF data; pattern match query for spatiotemporal RDF data; ranking properties of spatiotemporal RDF data; path-based approximate matching of spatiotemporal RDF data; subgraph matching of spatiotemporal RDF data; spatiotemporal data modeling based on XML; transformation of spatiotemporal data between object-oriented database and XML; querying spatiotemporal data based on XML twig pattern; fast leaf-to-root holistic twig query on spatiotemporal XML data; interpolation and prediction of spatiotemporal XML data integrated with grey dynamic model; keyword coupling query of spatiotemporal XML data; uncertain spatiotemporal data modeling based on XML; schema of uncertain spatiotemporal XML data; determining topological relations of uncertain spatiotemporal data; predicting uncertain spatiotemporal XML data integrated with grey dynamic model; querying uncertain spatiotemporal data based on XML twig pattern; keyword query of uncertain spatiotemporal XML data; flexible query of uncertain spatiotemporal XML data; query relaxation for uncertain spatiotemporal XML data.

Concerning spatiotemporal data modeling based on RDF, we propose a spatiotemporal data model based on RDF to achieve its functionality by labeling properties with spatiotemporal feature tags and determining the topological relations among different spatiotemporal entities. Concerning algebraic operations on spatiotemporal RDF data, we explore an algebraic operational framework to represent the content of spatiotemporal data and support RDF graphs. Concerning pattern match query for spatiotemporal RDF data, we present a spatiotemporal RDF representation model. Based on this model, algorithms are proposed to obtain some candidate isomorphic graph of the query graph, and the process of pattern matching is given. Concerning ranking properties of spatiotemporal RDF data, we discuss the ranking of spatiotemporal RDF data properties and attempt to improve the query efficiency of large RDF datasets. Concerning path-based approximate matching of spatiotemporal RDF data, we propose an algorithm for path-based approximate matching of spatiotemporal RDF data, which includes the decomposition graph algorithm and the combination query path algorithm. Concerning subgraph matching of spatiotemporal RDF data, we propose an algorithm for subgraph matching of spatiotemporal RDF data. This algorithm can quickly determine whether the query result is empty for queries whose temporal or spatial range exceeds a specific range by adopting a preliminary query filtering mechanism in the query process.

Concerning spatiotemporal data modeling based on XML, we propose a framework for representing spatiotemporal data in XML, specifically addressing the spatiotemporal changes of multiple objects. Concerning transformation of spatiotemporal data between object-oriented database and XML, we focus on exploring a set of mapping functions and rules to identify the most suitable XML schema that describes the existing object-oriented database. Concerning querying spatiotemporal data based on XML twig pattern, we propose an algorithm for matching a spatiotemporal XML query twig pattern by extending region coding scheme to filter the nodes. Concerning fast leaf-to-root holistic twig query on spatiotemporal XML data, we use streams to store leaf nodes in XML corresponding to leaf query node and filter the streams to delete unmatched nodes. Concerning interpolation and prediction of spatiotemporal XML data integrated with grey dynamic model, we extract the corresponding position information of each time interval and propose an algorithm for constructing an AVL tree to store them. Concerning keyword coupling query of spatiotemporal XML data, we study the intra-coupling logic relationship and the inter-coupling logic relationship separately. Then, a calculation method of keyword similarity is proposed.

Concerning uncertain spatiotemporal data modeling based on XML, we establish an uncertain spatiotemporal data model based on XML. Then, we provide a set of algebraic operations for capturing and handling uncertain spatiotemporal data. Concerning schema of uncertain spatiotemporal XML data, XML Schema normalization is used to obtain generalized XML Schema constraint documents for uncertain spatiotemporal data. Concerning determining topological relations of uncertain spatiotemporal data, we adopt polygon approximation and triangulation to represent uncertain spatiotemporal data and to determine topological relation of uncertain spatiotemporal data. Concerning predicting uncertain spatiotemporal XML data integrated with grey dynamic model, the approach is unique in the predicting element nodes which are integrated into the position element node in uncertain spatiotemporal XML data tree. Concerning querying uncertain spatiotemporal data based on XML twig pattern, the proposed algorithm can query uncertain spatiotemporal data. By extending interval coding, spatiotemporal elements of uncertain data to represent uncertain spatiotemporal information is added. Uncertain spatiotemporal data document tree is established, and the relationship between father and son and ancestor-descendant among nodes is redefined. Concerning keyword query of uncertain spatiotemporal XML data, the approach includes the data structure of a dynamic keyword data warehouse, probability calculation, keyword query algorithm, as well as pruning and sorting algorithms for keyword query. Concerning flexible query of uncertain spatiotemporal XML data, we propose a Single-Relaxation algorithm for single attribute relaxation and a Multiple-Relaxation algorithm for combining attribute relaxation. Concerning query relaxation for uncertain spatiotemporal XML data, we give *SingleRelaxation* algorithm and *MultipleRelaxation* algorithm according to the different number of relaxing attributes. In addition, a *T-List* structure is designed to quickly locate the nodes' positions, and *RSort* algorithm is proposed to sort accurate query results and extended query results.

This book aims to provide a single record of current research in the uncertain spatiotemporal data management for the Semantic Web. The objective of the book is to provide state-of-the-art information to researchers and graduate students of the (uncertain) spatiotemporal data management based on RDF and XML. Researchers and graduate students interested in (uncertain) spatiotemporal data management for the Semantic Web will find this book a starting point and a reference for their study, research, and development.

We would like to acknowledge the researchers in the area of spatiotemporal databases, RDF, XML, and uncertain databases. Based on both their publications and the many discussions with some of them, their influence on this book is profound. The materials in this book are the outgrowth of research conducted by the authors in recent years. The research work was supported by the National Natural Science Foundation of China (61402087), the Natural Science Foundation of Hebei Province (F2022501015), and the Fundamental Research Funds for the Central Universities (2023GFYD003). Special thanks go to Nina Eddinger and Angelina Olivas for their advice and help to propose, prepare, and publish this book. This book will not be completed without support from them.

Luyi Bai
Northeastern University, China

Lin Zhu
Northeastern University, China

Chapter 1
Spatiotemporal Data Modeling Based on RDF

ABSTRACT

In semantic web, modeling knowledge graphs based on RDF is becoming more and more popular. Existing efforts are mainly to add spatiotemporal labels to RDF, which expand RDF triple into quad or quintuple. However, extra labels often cause additional overhead and lead to inefficient information organization management. Accordingly, the authors propose a spatiotemporal data model based on RDF, called stRDFS. This model achieves its functionality by labeling properties with spatiotemporal feature tags and determining the topological relations among different spatiotemporal entities. stRDFS considers spatiotemporal attributes as a part of the RDF model, which can record spatiotemporal information without changing the current RDF standard. This approach improves the ability to record and linking spatiotemporal data. More importantly, depending on the formatting of spatiotemporal attributes, it will improve the semantic inferring ability, and the users are not required to be familiar with the underlying representations of spatiotemporal data.

1 INTRODUCTION

With the prompt development of the Internet, knowledge graph is rapidly emerging, which contributes a lot to the knowledge organization and intelligent applications on the Internet (Qian et al., 2019; Song et al., 2018), and has significant meanings for artificial intelligence. Knowledge graph (Zhang et al., 2020) is a knowledge base that represents objective concepts/entities and their relationships in the form of graph. It constitutes a huge semantic network diagram where nodes represent entities or concepts, and edges are composed of attributes or relationships.

In Semantic Web, entities can be mainly divided into general entities and spatiotemporal entities. As for general data, the knowledge graph can be expressed as RDF (Chakkarwar et al., 2016; Elzein et al., 2018; McBride, 2004). RDF (Resource Description Framework), a language proposed by the World Wide Web Consortium (W3C), which can express the semantics of knowledge graph formally. RDF is inclusive, exchangeable, and easy to extend, control, and integrate in data processing, so Tong (Tong,

DOI: 10.4018/978-1-6684-9108-9.ch001

2018) maps object-oriented database models into RDF, and Takama et al. (Takama & Hattori, 2007) study the mining association rules for adaptive search engine based on RDF. For spatiotemporal data, there have been some achievements in representing spatiotemporal entities, such as the temporal data model, spatial data model (Pfoser & Tryfona, 2008), and spatiotemporal data model (Zhu et al, 2020).

In the representation of temporal data, some researchers try to take temporal data as linked data and establish the corresponding temporal models (Crouch & Kalouli, 2018; Fossati et al., 2018; Ho et al., 2017; Lutz et al., 2008; Peng et al., 2017). For example, Lutz et al. (Lutz et al., 2008) study the TDL (Temporal Description Logic) model representing temporal entities and temporal description logic. However, TDL model is not compatible well with the current mainstream Semantic Web editing tools, which leads to the inability to be widely used in the representation of large-scale temporal information. Batsakis et al. (Batsakis & Petrakis, 2011) establish standards of the Semantic Web and the 4D-fluents approach for representing the evolution of temporal information in entities. Based on the 4D-fluents approach, the 4-Fluents Plug-In (a tool for handling temporal ontology in Protégé) has been proposed. But the complexity and inflexibility of the 4-Fluents plug-in bring great challenges to temporal semantics and data self-updating. Peng et al. (Peng et al., 2017) explore a general relation extraction framework based on graph LSTMs (graph long short-term memory networks). It can be easily extended to cross-sentence n-ary temporal relation extraction. Unfortunately, the complexity of temporal relations makes this model weak, so the model is unsuitable for recording large-scale temporal data. There are also some unstructured models of temporal information. For instance, SWRL (de Farias et al., 2017) (The Semantic Web Rule Language) provides a standard method for representing temporal data. Watkins et al. (Watkins & Nicole, 2006) demonstrate the use of named graphs. In (Tappolet & Bernstein, 2009), Tappolet et al. present a syntax and storage format based on named graphs to express temporal RDF. However, researchers seldom pay attention to the extension of RDF model to represent temporal entities. Since all entities and relations can link to each other by labels, Hernández et al. (Hernández et al., 2015) add temporal qualifiers and values to the RDF model representation in the form of labels. Then RDF triples are expanded into a quintuple (s, p, o, q, v), where (s, p, o) refers to the primary relation, q is the temporal qualifier property, and v is the temporal qualifier value. Besides, there are some models that label properties with the time interval (Gutierrez et al., 2005; Pugliese et al., 2008).

In addition to temporal data, prior works also focus on the representation of spatial data (Ademaj et al., 2019; Cui et al., 2018; Jiang, 2020). Spatial information in the RDF data model is usually represented as serializations of geometries accompanied by a Coordinate Reference System (CRS). CRS, it defines how to relate these serializations to real geometries on the surface of Earth. W3C GEO (Lieberman et al., 2007), an RDF vocabulary, can represent simple location information in RDF. W3C GEO provides the basic terminology for serializing point geometries. It represents latitude, longitude, and other information about spatially-located things by a namespace. GeoRDF (Consortium et al, 2012; Brodt et al., 2010; Consoli et al., 2015) is an RDF compatible profile for geometric information (points, lines, and polygons) and can be used for representing any point on the earth. GeoMetadataOverSvg is a geographic information notation for GeoRDF, which plays a significant role in the spatial data connection in the Semantic Web. Unfortunately, GeoMetadataOverSvg can only represent three-dimensional geospatial metadata and it fails to link to temporal data. Then, Batsakis et al. (Batsakis & Petrakis, 2010; Batsakis & Petrakis, 2011) put forward SOWL, which Builds upon well-established standards of the Semantic Web and the 4D-fluents approach for representing the evolution of temporal information in ontologies. SOWL illustrates how spatial and spatiotemporal information and evolution in space and time can be efficiently represented in OWL.

With the development of spatial models and temporal models, some researchers try to combine spatial data with temporal data to form spatiotemporal data and establish the corresponding models (Hoffart et al., 2013; Koubarakis & Kyzirakos, 2010; Li et al., 2019; Lu et al., 2019; Wang et al., 2014; Xu et al., 2017). Among them, the researchers take fuzziness (Lu et al., 2019) into account, and also focus on cloud detection (Xu et al., 2017) and practical application (Li et al., 2019). The most mature spatiotemporal models are the YAGO2 (Hoffart et al., 2013), gst-Store (Wang et al., 2014), and stRDF (Koubarakis et al., 2010), the first two expand RDF triple into quintuple and the last one is quad. In fact, both quintuple and quad methods may bring additional overhead to the system, leading to inefficient connection of large amounts of spatiotemporal data. This chapter focuses on stRDF model, a structured spatiotemporal RDF developed from the spatial model GeoRDF, which is proposed by Koubarakis et al. (Koubarakis et al., 2010) and extended to the RDF. However, stRDF model is inflexible that it is weak in recording dynamically changing multistate data. When the knowledge graph is updated, the changes in spatiotemporal attribute values cannot be captured in time. Even worse, it is also not good at dealing with flexible relations among spatiotemporal entities. Thus, it is important to improve the model to record changing data and relations and capture changes in massive dynamic spatiotemporal attribute values. Motivated by such an observation, this chapter aims to provide a spatiotemporal knowledge graph model on the basis of RDF without changing the current RDF standard. Our solution relies on the effort of the RDF triple to record spatiotemporal data. In this case, we can divide the entities into spatiotemporal entities and non-spatiotemporal entities according to attribute names. Spatiotemporal entities describe the evolution of relations and objects in spatiotemporal dimensions, and non-spatiotemporal entities describe static relations and objects without temporal attributes, spatial attributes, or spatiotemporal attributes. In order to describe the relations between different spatiotemporal entities, we construct the determination methods of topological relations in stRDFS.

To summarize, the contributions of this chapter are the following:

- We propose a spatiotemporal data model based on RDF, called stRDFS, which can record spatiotemporal data without changing the current RDF standard. In the meantime, it solves the problem of synchronous updates successfully.
- We explore the determination methods of topological relations between different spatiotemporal entities.

The rest of the chapter is organized as follows. We introduce the related work in Section 2. The modeling approach is proposed in Section 3. Section 4 is dedicated to the determination methods of topological relations, Section 5 makes a comparison and Section 6 concludes the chapter.

2 RELATED WORK

The recent research results presented in this section mainly include spatiotemporal data models based on RDF, such as temporal data model, spatial data model, and spatiotemporal data model.

2.1 Temporal Data Model on RDF

When the temporal concept is not included in many Semantic Web tools and techniques, the most important step is to identify models that can introduce time. These temporal models can be roughly divided into two categories. The first category is an ontology method that obtains no temporal data from the users. Temporal concepts and temporal relations are later added to the ontology and these operations are transparent to the users, for example, Wangni (Wangni, 2017) adopts this model. The second category is that the users create temporal entities rather than adding them later. This approach is adopted in most models and will be discussed in detail in the following.

TDL (Temporal Description Logic) model (Lutz et al., 2008) combines standard DLs with temporal data. It is a relatively primitive model whose main operators are 'since', 'until', 'always in the past', 'sometime in the future' and 'in the next moment in future'. Ho et al. (Ho et al., 2017) study how to represent fuzzy temporal data based on this model. Unfortunately, TDL is not compatible well with the current mainstream Semantic Web editing tools. Within a time interval, the entities of 4D-Fluents (Batsakis & Petrakis, 2011; Debruyne & O'sullivan, 2017; Zhu et al., 2020) are represented by the temporal part of the entity. However, in practical applications, the model is not only complicated but also inflexible. The N-ary relation (Fossati et al., 2018; Mandya et al., 2018; Peng et al., 2017) suggests properties of two objects and a new object which occurs during time intervals. Compared to other methods, this method results in the smallest time unit being useless and the structure is complicated. The named graph (Crouch & Kalouli, 2018) is a subgraph of the ontology RDF attributes graph, which can be specified by distinct names. However, many platforms do not support this model. In (Dautov & Distefano, 2018), the SWRL provides a standard method for representing temporal data. Then Wlodarczyk et al. (Wlodarczyk et al., 2011) develop SWRL-F based on the above rules to describe fuzzy temporal data and relations. Besides, Treur (Treur, 2018) proposes an approach on the basis of Reification. Reification can represent the N-element temporal relationship, but its semantic express ability is limited and scalability is not strong. There are also some other models that use temporal tags to extend RDF. For example, Gutierrez et al. (Gutierrez et al., 2005) and Pugliese et al. (Pugliese et al., 2008) introduce time into RDF. In (Hernández et al., 2015), temporal qualifiers and values are added to the RDF model. The RDF triple is expanded into a quintuple (s, p, o, q, v), where s denotes the subject, p represents the predicate, o expresses the objects, q depicts a temporal qualifier property, and v is a temporal qualifier value. Yet the quintuple or quad representation method may bring additional overhead to the system, leading to inefficient connection of large amounts of temporal data.

With the improvement of theory and advancement of technology, temporal RDF models are still developing. The spatiotemporal model proposed in this chapter absorbs the advantages of the above models in temporal data representation, improves the scalability and self-renewal ability of the model, and contributes to correlating a large amount of temporal data.

2.2 Spatial Data Model on RDF

In order to represent the spatial information (e.g. longitude, latitude, and altitude) of the entities, several models improved on traditional RDF are proposed. Among spatial models, one of the most mature developments is GeoRDF. Therefore, we will focus on GeoRDF (Consortium et al, 2012; Brodt et al., 2010; Consoli et al., 2015) in this section.

RDFIG defines a simple vocabulary for expressing points on the earth in WGS84 form. Based on the spatial vocabulary, a more mature model GeoRDF is established. GeoRDF defines three main classes: geo: SpatialObject, geo: Feature, and geo: Geometry. At present, the GeoRDF model has been applied to the project and has corresponding processing platforms and tools. For example, the project LinkedGeo-Data focuses on publishing OpenStreetMap data as linked data. Besides, Sparqlify has taken advantage of the GeoRDF. Toward the geospatial information resides in a spatially enabled relational database, Geometry2RDF is the first tool to allow users to convert geospatial data into an RDF graph. In addition to the above tools, TripleGeo is developed in the GeoKnow. The GeoRDF model achieves remarkable results in the representation of spatial data and can record various points on the earth. At the same time, the tools that support GeoRDF can absorb different forms of data sets and have been widely used.

2.3 Spatiotemporal Data Model on RDF

An ever-increasing number of real-life applications produce spatiotemporal data that record the position of moving objects. So some researchers are focusing on spatiotemporal data modeling. For example, Chang et al. (Chang et al., 2011) propose a temporospatial model on the basis of MML and software framework, which encourages reusability, sharing, and storage.

At present, spatiotemporal data are usually provided as relational tables (Kim et al., 2000) or XML documents (Bai et al., 2016), which can be mapped into the RDF data model using R2RML (Vaisman & Chentout, 2019). R2RML is a standard language that allows defining customized mappings from relational databases to RDF datasets. In (Vaisman & Chentout, 2019), data are spatiotemporal in nature and R2RML can produce spatiotemporal Linked Open Data. Data generated in this way are used to populate a SPARQL endpoint. This endpoint is implemented using Strabon, a spatiotemporal RDF triple store built by extending the RDF store Sesame. Di et al. (Di et al., 2019) combine spatiotemporal information with RDF and present a novel representation model of spatiotemporal RDF. Besides, in order to study the efficient spatiotemporal RDF query processing, Vlachou et al. (Vlachou et al., 2019) represent spatiotemporal data in RDF and store it in knowledge bases with the following notable features: (a) the data is dynamic, since new spatiotemporal data objects are recorded every second, and (b) the size of the data is vast and can easily lead to scalability issues. As a result, this raises the need for efficient management of large-scale, dynamic, spatiotemporal RDF data. There are also some studies on modeling uncertain spatiotemporal data based on RDF (Wang et al., 2019).

2.4 Algebra of RDF Graphs

In order to represent the spatiotemporal information of the entities such as longitude, latitude and altitude, several extended models of traditional RDF are proposed (Amjadi & Soroudi, 2018; Arenas et al., 2018; Consoli et al., 2015). stRDF (Arenas et al., 2018; Koubarakis & Kyzirakos, 2010; Nikitopoulos et al., 2021) is the most mature development among this works and we will introduce it in this section.

Although the GeoRDF model is widely used for the expression of geographic information, since the GeoRDF dataset does not have temporal properties, it cannot represent spatiotemporal data. Now, there are some studies on querying temporal RDF (Zhang et al., 2019). Therefore, the link of spatiotemporal data has attracted the attention of many scholars. For example, Cheng et al. (Cheng & Ma, 2017) propose a kind of fuzzy spatiotemporal description logic. Nikitopoulos et al. (Nikitopoulos et al., 2021) explore distributed spatiotemporal RDF queries on Spark. Besides, the stRDF model (Koubarakis &

Kyzirakos, 2010; Tran et al., 2018; Velayutham et al., 2018) has been proposed and established. stRDF model is an extension of the W3C standard RDF. It can represent geospatial data that changes over time. The stRDF model has been recognized by most scholars in the representation of spatiotemporal data. Although the stRDF model seems to be perfect, there are still many problems. For example, stRDF uses spatiotemporal datasets to record entities whose spatiotemporal attributes are changing with time and space. However, there is no one-to-one correspondence between spatiotemporal data and spatiotemporal attributes, which may result in a large number of spatiotemporal relationships expressing ambiguity. Due to the above features, the stRDF model can only link a small amount of spatiotemporal data and cannot record changing data accurately.

In this chapter, we propose an stRDFS model that solves the above two problems: The first point is to establish the correspondence between attributes and spatiotemporal entities. The second point is that the stRDFS model can capture varying spatiotemporal attribute values. In particular, we establish a class set that describes spatiotemporal attributes for the stRDFS model.

2.5 Discussion

In order to illustrate the novelity of stRDFS proposed in this chapter clearly, we set a comparative study on modeling spatiotemporal data based on RDF.

As shown in Table 1, Temporal RDF(Gutierrz et al., 2005; Tappolet & Bernstein, 2009), Named graph(Crouch & Kalouli, 2018) and tRDF(Pugliese et al., 2008) are focus on temporal data modeling; GEO(Lieberman et al., 2007) and GeoRDF(Consortium et al, 2012; Brodt et al., 2010; Consoli et al., 2015) are the representation of spatial data; stRDF(Koubarakis & Kyzirakos, 2010), YAGO2(Hoffart et al., 2013), g^{st}-Store(Wang et al., 2014) and stRDFS devote to modeling spatiotemporal data. Among the spatiotemporal models, stRDF expands RDF triples into quad, and YAGO2 and g^{st}-Store expand RDF triples into quintuple. The expansion of triples could easily solve the express of spatiotemporal features. However, the extra labels often cause data redundancy and lead to additional overhead for the system. stRDFS is an extending RDF by labeling properties with spatiotemporal features without expanding RDF triples, which meets the needs of the purpose in this chapter.

Table 1. Comparative study on spatiotemporal data modeling

	Spatial feature	Temporal feature	Spatial (S) or Temporal (T) Expansion	Spatial (S) or Temporal (T) labeling of properties
Temporal RDF		√		T
Reifying RDF		√	T	
Named graph		√		
tRDF		√		T
GEO	√			
GeoRDF	√			
YAGO2	√	√	S and T	
g^{st}-Store	√	√	S and T	
stRDF	√	√	T	
Our work	√	√		S and T

3 DATA MODEL

In this section, we will propose a spatiotemporal model based on RDF. In order to distinguish it from stRDF model, we will propose stRDFS data model which is good at recording dynamically changing data and flexible relations of spatiotemporal data at first. Then, we will define the main classes of stRDFS and describe them.

For the description of spatiotemporal data, there has been stRDF Koubarakis & Kyzirakos, 2010 quad (s, p, o, τ), where s represents subject, p represents property name, o represents a spatial object with spatial data, and τ represents temporal data. For example, the stRDF graph is shown in Figure 1 which represents the temporal data and spatial data of mobile receivers. In the graph, the attribute HasGeometry represents geometric coordinates of the receiver position; the attribute TimeSlice represents temporal data of the signal which is propagated by the receiver. As shown in Figure 1, temporal data of stRDF model is stored together in the form of a set, such as T = {[8t, 15t], 17t}, which causes that temporal data is difficult to correspond to a certain part of the object. At the same time, T = {[8t, 15t], 17t} has no correspondence with spatial position, that is, cannot describe temporal data of the receiver's signal at a certain location, resulting in the fuzzy information indicating time and space. When we use stRDF model to describe changing relations among spatiotemporal entities, spatial data, and temporal data are separated, which leads to the uncertainty of information representation. To solve this problem, this chapter extends RDF model and proposes stRDFS model. stRDFS model establishes the relations between spatial data and temporal data of the same object, and better describes the changing spatiotemporal state in four-dimensional space.

3.1 The stRDFs Data Model

By extending RDF data model (s, p, o), stRDFS model can be formed. The specific representation of stRDFS is defined as follows:

Definition 1. Given a URI set R, empty vertex set B, text description set K, temporal data set I, and spatial data set S, an stRDFS expression is g (s, p: <t, l>, o) where:

- s is a resource name and $s \in R \cup B$.
- p is a property name and $p \in R$.
- is a value and $o \in R \cup B \cup K \cup I \cup S$.
- $t \in I$ is temporal data.
- $l \in S$ is spatial data.

In Definition 1, stRDFS uses attributes to associate temporal data with spatial data, linking attributes with spatiotemporal data to form spatiotemporal attributes p. When spatiotemporal data changes, spatiotemporal attributes associated with them will change as well. Therefore, the upper layer processing mechanism only needs to perceive the changes of spatiotemporal attributes instead of understanding the changes of spatiotemporal data accurately.

Definition 2. A mapping from x to y is denoted as fx-y, where x represents s or p and y represents t, l or o.

For example, fs-o represents the mapping relationship from s to o and fs-t is the mapping relationship from s to t.

Definition 3. Given an stRDFS expression g (s, p: <t, l>, o), U = {fs-o, fs-t, fs-l, fp-t, fp-l} is a mapping set of g.

In Definition 3, fs-o represents the mapping, whose function is expressed as an attribute name, from s to o. The mapping fs-t indicates that s has linked with temporal data, and the formed triple is (s, p, t). In (s, p, t), the property represents "temporal information" and the attribute value t represents temporal data. The mapping fs-l indicates that s has linked with spatial data and the expression is (s, p, l). In the triple, the attribute represents "spatial information" and the attribute value l represents spatial data. The fp-t indicates that p has linked with temporal data and combines with other mappings to form an stRDFS tuple. When fp-t is combined with fs-o, the tuple is formed as (s, p: t, o), indicating that the temporal data describes the valid time of (s, p, o). When fp-t is combined with fs-t, the formed tuple is (s, p: t2, t1), indicating that the valid time of s is t1, and the valid time of the tuple (s, p, t1) is t2. When fp-t is combined with fs-l, a tuple (s, p: t, l) is formed, indicating that s has linked with spatial data l, and the valid time of tuple (s, p: t, l) is t. The mapping fp-l represents that p has linked with spatial data and combines with other mappings to form an stRDFS tuple. When fp-l is combined with fs-o, the tuple is formed as (s, p: l, o), indicating that the spatial data l describes (s, p, o). When fp-l is combined with fs-t, the formed tuple is (s, p: l, t), indicating that the valid time of s is t, and the spatial data of (s, p, t) is l. When fp-l is combined with fs-l, a tuple (s, p: l2, l1) is formed, indicating that s has linked with spatial data of l1, and spatial data of (s, p, l1) is l2. The mapping fp-o is illegal. The fo-t and fo-l logically represent temporal data and spatial data of o, respectively. In the stRDFS structure, fo-t and fo-l are converted into fs-t and fs-l, and they can appear as tuple mappings alone. For instance, (s1, p, o: t) can be converted into two tuples (s1, p1, o) and (s2, p2, t), where s2 = o and p2 represents "temporal information". Similarly, (s1, p, o: l) can be converted into two tuples (s1, p1, o) and (s2, p2, l), where s2 = o and p2 represents "spatial information".

We will give the definition of stRDFS graph in the following. Before this, we define the value range at first.

Definition 4. The value range of the mapping fx-y is denoted as Range (fx-y) where Range (fx-y) = y.

Definition 5. Given an stRDFS expression g (s, p: <t, l>, o), an stRDFS graph for g is a labeled graph G (V, E, F, λ, T, L) where:

- V = s ∪ Range (U) is the set of vertices.
- E = {(r, r')} is the set of edges from r to r' where ∀r, r' ∈ V
- F (r, r') = {f | (r, f: <t, l>, r') ∈ G} is the mappings set of E where ∀r, r' ∈ V*.
- is the set of labels given by vertices or edges.
- T ∈ Range (fs-t ∪ fp-t).
- L ∈ Range (fs-l ∪ fp-l).

According to Definition 5, there are two cases: the first one is that stRDFS graph vertices contain spatiotemporal information, in this case T ∈ Range (fs-t) and L ∈ Range (fs-l), as shown in Figure 2(a), the second is that the stRDFS graph edges contain spatiotemporal information, in this case T ∈ Range (fp-t) and L ∈ Range (fp-l), as shown in Figure 2. The expression of T and L will be defined in the following.

Figure 1. The stRDF graph of the mobile receiver (a)T ∈ Range (f_{s-t}) and L ∈ Range (f_{s-l}) (b) T ∈ Range (f_{p-t}) and L ∈ Range (f_{p-l})

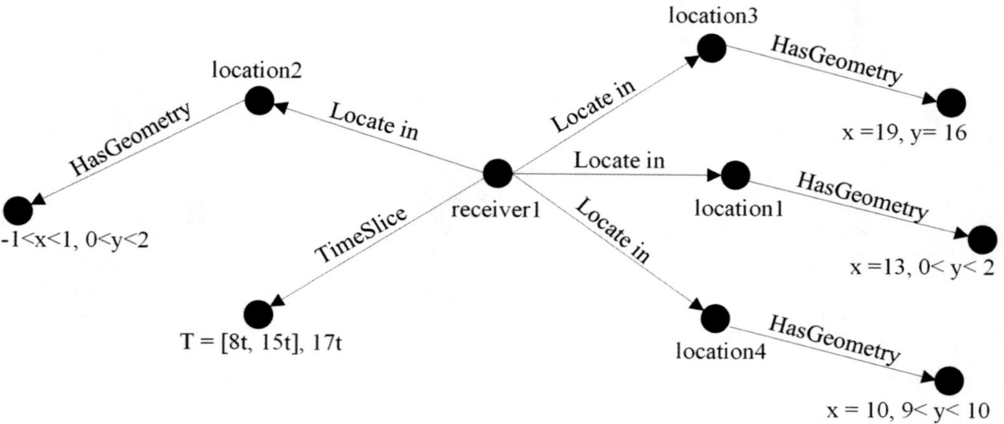

Figure 2. Representation of spatiotemporal information in stRDFS (a)T' ∈ Range (f_{s-t}) (b) T' ∈ Range (f_{p-t})

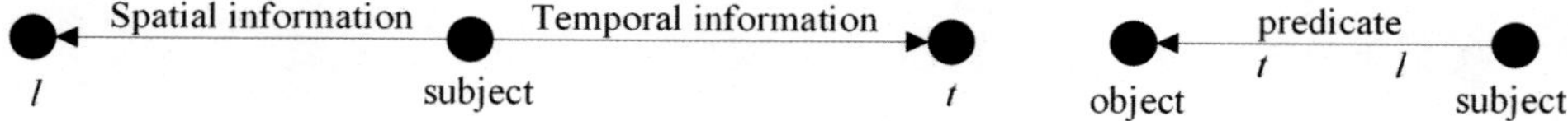

Figure 3 Representation of temporal information in tRDFS graph

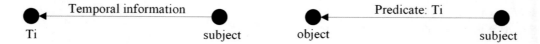

Figure 4. The (s, p, o, t) model graph of example 1

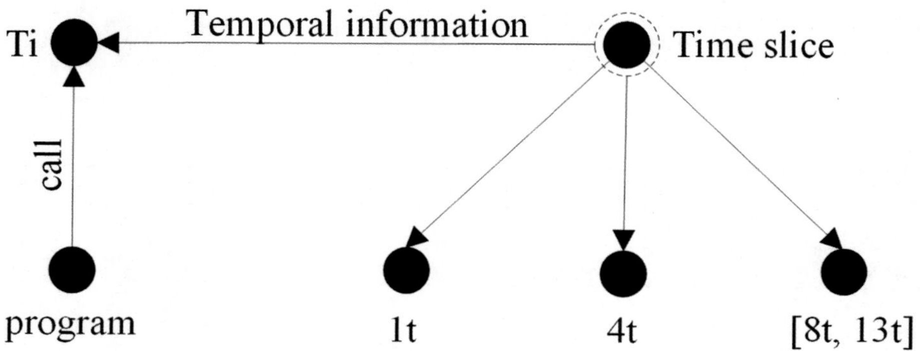

Figure 5. The tRDFS graph of example 1 (a)L' ∈ Range (f_{s-l}) (b) L' ∈ Range (f_{p-l})

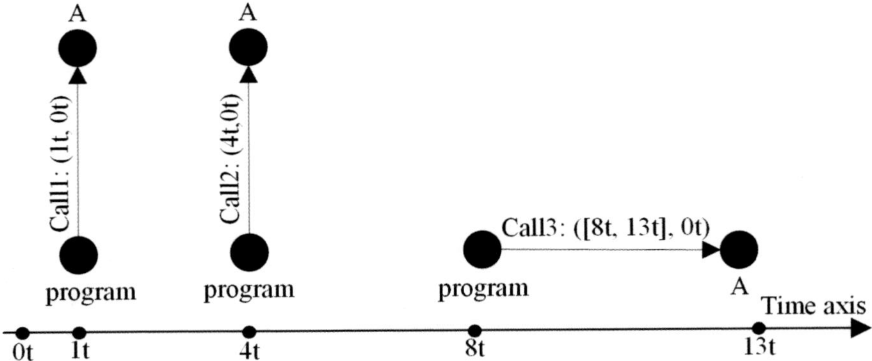

Figure 6. Representation of spatial information in sRDFS graph

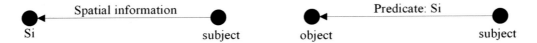

Definition 6. Given an stRDFS expression g (s, <p: <t, l>, o) and (vi, fvi-vj, vj) ∈ g, the temporal data of (vi, fvi-vj, vj) is represents by Ti = f (N, k) where:

- N = [ts(f), te(f)] is valid time where ts(f) represents start time of mapping fvi-vj, and te(f) represents terminal time of mapping fvi-vj.
- k = tr(f) is reference time recorded as now.

In Definition 6, N represents the valid time of the spatiotemporal data. If the valid time is a time point, then ts(f) = te(f). If the valid time is a time period, then ts(f) < te(f). The reference time, which is a measure of the valid time at the time axis position, is denoted by k. In stRDFS model, k is set to "now" and temporal states of the model (s, < p: <t, l>, o) are determined by k.

The relationship is as follows:

Box 1.

	Before	After	Now
ts(f) < te(f)	te(f) < k	k < ts(f)	ts(f) < k < te(f)
ts(f) = te(f)	te(f) = te(f) < k	k < ts(f) = te(f)	ts(f) = te(f) = k

If there is no spatial data, stRDFS model becomes a tRDFS model (s, p: Ti, o) with only temporal data, where s is a resource name, p is a property name with temporal data Ti, and o ∈ R ∪ B ∪ K ∪ I is the value of p. In tRDFS model, there are three mappings of fs-o, fs-t and fp-t. When only fs-o exists, that is, when there is no temporal data, the formed expression is (s, p, o). When only fs-t exists, it indicates that temporal data of s is Ti and the formed expression is (s, p, Ti) where the property represents "temporal information" and the attribute value is the temporal data of s. When fp-t and fs-o are present at the same time, the resulting tRDFS model is (s, p: Ti, o), indicating that temporal data of the model is Ti. When only fp-t and fs-t are formed, the expression is (s, p: Ti1, Ti2), indicating that temporal data of the model expression is Ti1, and temporal data of s is Ti2. If given a tRDFS model m (s, p: Ti, o), a tRDFS graph form is a labeled graph M (V', E', F', λ', T') where:

- V' = s ∪ Range (fs-o ∪ fs-t) is the set of vertices.
- E' = {(r, r')} is the set of edges where ∀r, r' ∈ V'.
- F' (r, r') = {f | (r, f: Ti, r') ∈ M} is the mappings set of E' where ∀r, r' ∈ V'.
- λ' is the label given by vertices or edges.
- T' ∈ Range (fs-t ∪ fp-t).

In tRDFS graph, there are two cases: the first one is that vertices contain temporal information, in this case T' ∈ Range (fs-t), as shown in Figure 3(a), the second is that tRDFS graph edges contain temporal information, in this case T' ∈ Range (fp-t), as shown in Figure 3(b).

In order to illustrate the practical application of tRDFS clearly, we put forward the following examples:

Example 1. When data set A in the database is called by the program, the time slice is 1t, 4t and [8t, 13t] (current time is represented by 0t), then tRDFS model is expressed as: (program, call1: (1t, 0t), A), (program, call2: (4t, 0t), A) and (program, call3: ([8t, 13t], 0t), A). Without the form of (program, call, A, [1t, 4t, [8t, 13t]]), tRDFS model links temporal data and attributes to form temporal properties. When the temporal data changes, the corresponding temporal properties change. For example, (program, call1: (1t, 0t), A) and (program, call2: (4t, 0t), A) are different model expressions and call1, call2 and call3 are different temporal properties. Next, we use the (s, p, o, t) model to represent temporal data in Figure 4 and use tRDFS model in Figure 5. By comparing these two figures, we can conclude that tRDFS model can show temporal information more clearly and accurately than the (s, p, o, t) model does.

Definition 7. Given an stRDFS expression g (s, p: <t, l>, o) and (vi, fvi- vj, vj) ∈ g, the spatial data of (vi, fvi-vj, vj) is represented by Si = f (L, D, H) where:

- L ∈ (0°, 90°N) ∪ (0°, 90°S) which stands for latitude.
- D ∈ (0°, 180°E) ∪ (0°, 180°W) which stands for longitude.
- H is the height above the sea level.

In real life, there may be situations that stRDFS model that describes the spatial data of large areas. Therefore, in stRDFS model, longitude, latitude, and altitude may be intervals rather than certain values. In stRDFS model, we use x ~ C to describe the range, where x represents L, D or H, ~ denotes a set of {<, ≤, ≥, =, >, ≠} and C stands for rational numbers with unit. For example, AreaA has a latitude range of (30°N, 40°N), a longitude range of (116°E, 118°E), and its average elevation is 50 m. In stRDFS model, Si is expressed as ((30°N, 40°N), (116°E, 118°E), 50m).

The stRDFS description of spatial data is shown as the following:

Box 2.

ex: areaA strdfs: hasGeometry
"(30°N < L < 40°N) and (116°E < D < 118°E) and (H = 50m)" ^^ strdfs: SemiLinearPointSet.

Definition 8. Given an stRDFS model g (s, p: <t, l>, o) and (x, fx-y: <t, l>, y) ∈ g, then for (x, fx-y: <t, l>, y), t = Ti (fx-y) and l = Si (fx-y) which is represented as Definition 6 and Definition 7, respectively.

Figure 7. The knowledge graph by sRDF model

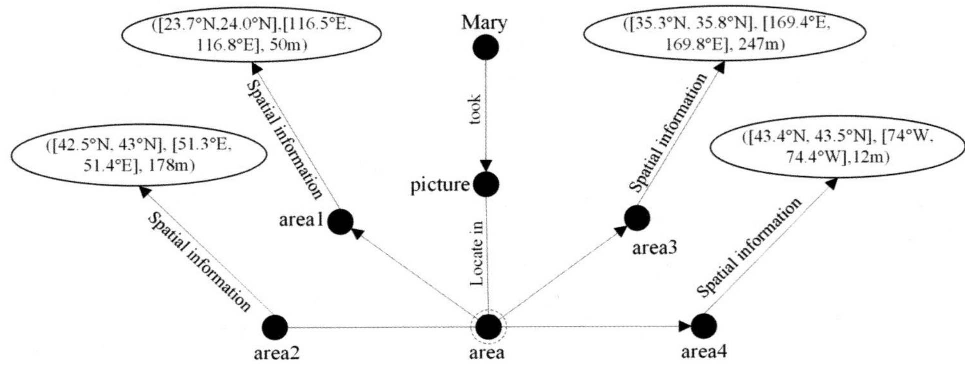

Figure 8. The knowledge graph by sRDFS model

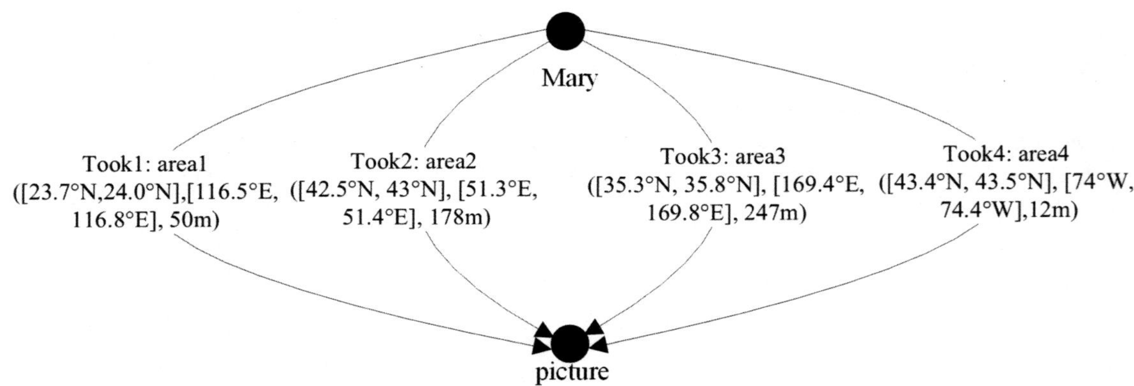

If there is no temporal data in stRDFS model, it turns into an sRDFS model (s, p: Si, o) where s is a resource name, p is a property name with spatial data Si, and o ∈ R ∪ B ∪ K ∪ S is the value of p. The model sRDFS, which is an stRDFS model with only spatial data, is based on RDF model and better than sRDF model (s, p, o, l). In sRDFS model, there are three types of mappings: fs-o, fs-l and fp-l. When only fs-o exists, that is, when there is no spatial data in sRDFS, the formed expression is (s, p, o). When only fs-l exists, it indicates that the spatial data of s is Si. The formed expression is (s, p, Si) where the property represents "spatial information" and the property value is the spatial data of s. When fp-l and fs-o are present, the resulting sRDFS model is (s, p: Si, o), indicating that the spatial data of the p is Si. When only fp-l and fs-l are formed, the formed sRDFS is (s, p: Si1, Si2), indicating that the spatial data of the property is Si1 and the spatial data of s is Si2. If given an sRDFS model q (s, p: Si, o), an sRDFS graph for q is a labeled graph Q (V'', E'', F'', λ'', L') where:

- V" = s ∪ Range (fs-o ∪ fs-l) is the set of vertices.
- E" = {(r, r')} is the set of edges where ∀r, r' ∈ V''.
- F" (r, r') = {f | (r, f: Si, r') ∈ Q} is the mappings set of E'' where ∀r, r' ∈ V''.
- λ'' is the label given by vertices or edges.
- L' ∈ Range (fs-l ∪ fp-l).

In sRDFS graphs, there are two cases: the first one is those vertices contain spatial data, L' ∈ Range (fs-l) at this time, as shown in Figure 6(a); the second is that edges contain spatial data, as Figure 6(b) shows, L' ∈ Range (fp-l) at this time. Then the following examples verify this model.

Example 2. Mary has taken some pictures in many areas: area1 ([23.7°N, 24.0°N], [116.5°E, 116.8°E], 50m), area2 ([42.5°N, 43°N], [51.3°E, 51.4°E], 178m), area3 ([35.3°N, 35.8°N], [169.4°E, 169.8°E], 247m) and area4 ([43.4°N, 43.5°N], [74°W, 74.4°W], 12m). Described by sRDF model (s, p, o, l), the expression is: (picture, locate in, [area1, are2, area3, area4]), the resulting sRDF graph is shown in Figure 7. Before accessing spatial data through these nodes, we should search for the "area" node at first. Based on this, it will incur the unnecessary overhead of searching for spatial data. This problem can be solved with the help of sRDFS model, in which the information can be described as: (Mary, took1: area1, picture), (Mary, took2: area2, picture), (Mary, took3: area3, picture) and (Mary, took4: area4, picture). The sRDFS graph is shown in Figure 8. The sRDFS model uses both spatial data and the attribute "took" to form spatial attributes. Due to various spatial locations, the spatial attributes took1, took2, took3, and took4 are different. When querying spatial data, we can obtain the data directly by accessing the properties.

Example 3. Figure 1 shows the spatial data and temporal data of the mobile receiver through stRDF model. This example uses stRDFS model to describe the mobile receiver in the form of stRDFS graph which is shown in Figure 9.

3.2 Classes and Descriptions of stRDFs

In order to introduce the stRDFS description more clearly, this section introduces several main classes: strdfs: SpatialObject, strdfs: SpatialGeometry, strdfs: SpatialFeature, strdfs: TemporalObject, strdfs: TimeSlice, strdfs: TemporalFeature, strdfs: SpatiotemporalObject, strdfs: SpatiotemporalGeo and strdfs: SemiLinearPointSet. Their relations are shown in Figure 10.

1) Spatial classes and descriptions in spatiotemporal domain

This section defines several main stRDFS classes that describe spatial data in spatiotemporal domain. They are: strdfs: SpatialObject, strdfs: SpatialGeometry and strdfs: SpatialFeature.

Figure 9. The stRDFS graph of Example 3

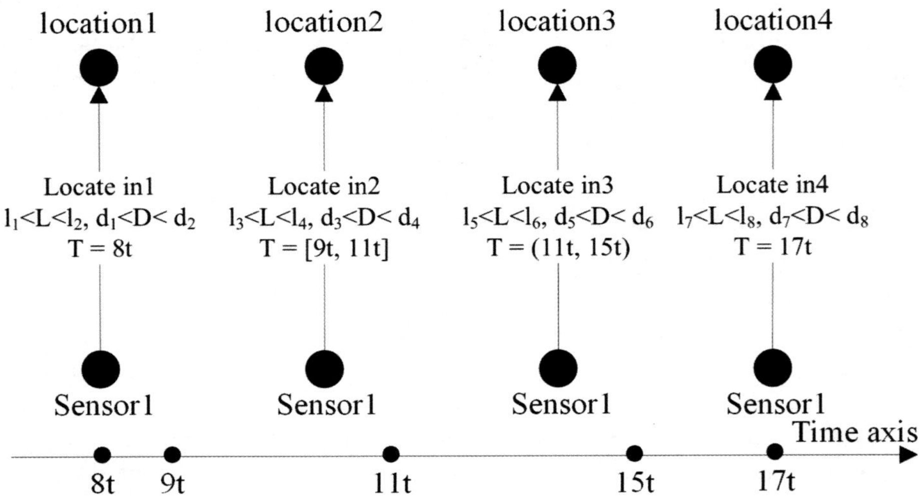

Figure 10. The relations of main stRDFS classes

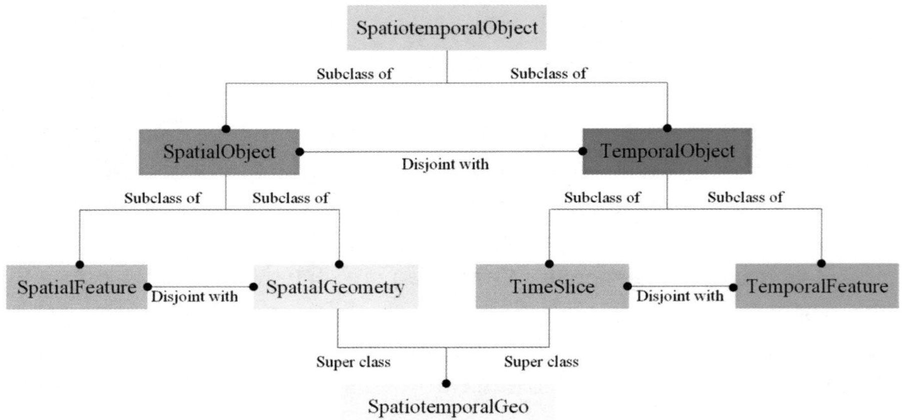

The class *strdfs: SpatialObject* is equivalent to the RDFS class *geo: SpatialObject*. The class set of RDFS contains *geo: SpatialObject* and the class set of stRDFS contains *strdfs: SpatialObject.*

The class *strdfs: SpatialObject* represents a set of all entities with only spatial information and its description is as follows:

Box 3.

strdfs: SpatialObject	a rdfs: Class, owl:Class;
rdfs: label	"Spatial Object" @en;
rdfs: comment	"The class SpatialObject represents everything that can have spatial information. It is super class of *SpatialFeature* and *SpatialGeometry*"@en

The class strdfs: SpatialGeometry is a subclass of strdfs: SpatialObject. It describes *Si* in stRDFS model (*s*, *p*: <*Ti*, *Si*>, o), including the data of latitude, longitude, and altitude.

The description of strdfs: SpatialGeometry is as follows:

Box 4.

strdfs: SpatialGeometry	a rdfs: Class, owl: Class;
rdfs: label	"SpatialGeometry" @ en;
rdfs:subClassOf	strdfs: SpatialObject;
owl:disjointWith	strdfs:SpatialGeometry;
rdfs:comment	"This class represents the spatial geometry characteristics of geographic locations. This class is equivalent to geo: Geometry for RDFS model, and it is superclass of all geometry types." @ en

The class *strdfs: SpatialFeature* is a subclass of strdfs: SpatialObject, which contains geographic information that is used for describing landforms, terrain, and so on. Besides, *strdfs: SpatialFeature* and *strdfs: SpatialGeometry* are exclusive mutually.

The description is as follows:

Box 5.

strdfs: SpatialFeature	a rdfs: Class, owl: Class;
rdfs: label	"Spatial Feature" @en;
rdfs: subClassOf	strdfs: SpatialObject;
owl: disjointWith	strdfs: SpatialGeometry;
rdfs: comment	"This class represents the spatial characteristics of geographic locations except geometric information. This class is equivalent to GFI_Feature defined in ISO 19156 and geo: Feature for RDFS model, and it is superclass of all feature types."@en

Let us illustrate spatial classes more clearly by Example 4. Since stRDF model can also describe spatial data, we compare stRDFS model with stRDF model by Example 4.

Example 4. There is a mobile large sound wave receiver whose several parts are placed in different places. By describing their spatial data, we compare stRDF model with stRDFS model.

The description of spatial data in stRDF model is as follows:

Box 6.

ex: receiver1	rdf: type	ex: SoundWaveReceiver
ex: receiver1	ssn: measures	ex: sound
ex: receiver1	ssn: hasLocation	ex: location
ex: location	strdf: hasGeometry	"(20.9°N < L < 21°N and 45.8°E < D <= 46°E) or (L = 21°N and D = 46°E) or (29°N < L < 30°N and 49°E < D <= 51°E)" ^^ strdf: SemiLinearPointSet

In the description of the above sound wave receiver, ssn is the namespace of CSIRO/SSN Ontology. The ex: location represents spatial location of sound wave receiver, and "($20.9°N < L < 21°N$ and $45.8°E < D <= 46°E$) or ($L = 21°N$ and $D = 46°E$) or ($29°N < L < 30°N$ and $49°E < D <= 51°E$)" is the attribute value of ex: location.

The description of the spatial data in stRDFS model is as follows:

Box 7.

ex: receiver1	rdf: type	ex: SoundWaveReceiver
ex: receiver1	ssn: measures	ex: sound
ex: receiver1	ssn: hasLocation1	ex: location1
ex: receiver1	ssn: hasLocation2	ex: location2
ex: receiver1	ssn: hasLocation3	ex: location3
ssn: hasLocation1	strdfs: SpatialGeometry	"(20.9°N < L < 21°N and 45.8°E < D <= 46°E)" ^^ strdfs: SemiLinearPointSet
ssn: hasLocation2	strdfs: SpatialGeometry	"(L = 21°N and D = 46°E)" ^^ strdfs: SemiLinearPointSet
ssn: hasLocation3	strdfs: SpatialGeometry	"(29°N < L < 30°N and 49°E < D <= 51°E)" ^^ strdfs: SemiLinearPointSet

By comparing the descriptions of stRDF and stRDFS, we can draw a conclusion: *strdf: hasGeometry* describes the spatial data of a spatial object; *strdfs: SpatialGeometry* describes the spatial data of any parts of spatial object or partial spatial data of the whole spatial object. On this basis, it can be concluded that stRDFS model supports fast search for spatial data and can represent changes of spatial data either overall or partial.

2) Temporal classes and descriptions in spatiotemporal domain

This section defines several main stRDFS classes that describe temporal data in spatiotemporal domain. They are: *strdfs: TemporalObject*, *strdfs: TimeSlice* and *strdfs: TemporalFeature*.

The class *strdfs: TemporalObject* is a set of all entities that contain temporal data. The description of *strdfs: TemporalObject* is as follows:

Box 8.

strdfs: TemporalObject	a rdfs: Class, owl: Class;
rdfs: label	"Temporal Object" @ en;
rdfs: comment	"The class TemporalObject represents everything that can have temporal information. It is superclass of TemporalFeature and TimeSlice"@en

The class *strdfs: TimeSlice* is a subclass of *strdfs: TemporalObject*. It is a set of valid time and reference time of entities, including time points and time intervals.

Box 9.

strdfs: TimeSlice	a rdfs: Class, owl: Class;
rdfs: label	"TimeSlice" @ en;
rdfs: subClassOf	strdfs: TemporalObject;
owl: disjointWith	strdfs: TemporalFeature;
rdfs:comment	"This class represents the time occupied by everything with temporal information. This class describes the time point or time interval" @ en

In stRDFS model, *strdfs: TimeSlice* describes parameter Ti. The description is as follows:

The class *strdfs: TemporalFeature* is a subclass of *strdfs: TemporalObject* and it is mutually exclusive in *strdfs: TimeSlice*. It includes other temporal data of temporal entities, such as time zone, tense, time dimension and the existence time.

The description of *strdfs: TemporalFeature* is as follows:

Box 10.

strdfs: TemporalFeature	a rdfs: Class, owl: Class;
rdfs: label	"Temporal Feature" @en;
rdfs: subClassOf	strdfs: TemporalObject;
owl: disjointWith	strdfs: TimeSlice;
rdfs:comment	"This class represents the temporal information of everything except the valid time and reference time." @ en

The temporal classes can be illustrated more clearly with Example 5. Since stRDF model can also describe temporal data, we compare stRDFS model with stRDF model by the description of Example 5.

Example 5. There is a Java program program1, which is called by the computer at 8t and 18t. There is a python program program2, which is called by the computer at [9t, 14t]. We set 0t as the reference time, and use this example to compare stRDF and stRDFS models.

stRDF model describes the above information as follows:

Box 11.

ex: program1	rdf: type	ex: JavaProgram
ex: program2	rdf: type	ex: PythonProgram
ex: program1	om: procedure	ex: CountProgram
ex: program2	om: procedure	ex: OutputProgram
ex: program1	om:hasPro1Call	ex: TimeSlice1
ex: program2	om: hasPro2Call	ex: TimeSlice2
ex: TimeSlice1	strdf: TimeSlice	"(t = 8t and t = 18t) and k = 0t." ^^ strdf: SemiLinearPointSet.
ex: TimeSlice2	strdf: TimeSlice	"9t ≤ t ≤ 14t and k = 0t." ^^ strdf: SemiLinearPointSet

In the description of the above program, om is the namespace of O&M-OWL ontology and ex represents an example ontology. The ex: TimeSlice1 represents the time slice when program1 was called and ex: TimeSlice2 represents the time slice when program2 was called.

The description of stRDFS model is as follows:

Box 12.

ex: program1	rdf: type	ex: JavaProgram
ex: program2	rdf: type	ex: PythonProgram
ex: program1	om: procedure	ex: CountProgram
ex: program2	om: procedure	ex: OutputProgram
ex: program1	om:hasPro1Call1	ex: TimeSlice1
ex: program1	om: hasPro1Call2	ex: TimeSlice2
ex: program2	om: hasPro2Call1	ex: TimeSlice2
om:hasPro1Call1	strdfs: TimeSlice	"t = 8t and k = 0t."^^ strdfs:SemiLinearPointSet.
om:hasPro1Call2	strdfs: TimeSlice	"t = 18t and k = 0t."^^ strdfs: SemiLinearPointSet.
om:hasPro2Call1	strdfs: TimeSlice	"9t ≤ t ≤ 14t and k = 0t."^^ strdfs: SemiLinearPointSet.

The class strdfs: TimeSlice represents the valid time and reference time of the program. When the valid time is the time point, stRDFS expresses temporal data by equation, such as $t = 8t$ and $t = 18t$. When the valid time is a time period, an inequation represents the time interval, such as $9t \leq t \leq 14t$. Compared with stRDF model, stRDFS makes temporal data link with the attributes: om: hasPro1Call1, om: hasPro1Call2 and om: hasPro2Call1, where om: hasPro1Call1 represents the first call of program1, om: hasPro1Call2 represents the second call of program1 and om: hasPro2Call1 represents the first call of program2. Based on this feature, the stRDFS model can represent temporal data of a temporal entity at any time and record changes of temporal attributes at any time.

3) Spatiotemporal classes and descriptions in spatiotemporal domain

In this section, we define several main stRDFS classes to describe spatiotemporal data in the spatiotemporal domain which are: strdfs: SpatiotemporalObject, strdfs: SpatiotemporalGeo and strdfs: SemiLinearPointSet.

Table 2. Spatiotemporal data of southwest 1524

Point	Time (CST)	Latitude	Longitude	Feet/m
P1	05:22:35 AM	33.9389	-118.3900	150
P2	05:24:37 AM	33.8877	-118.4981	4,150
P3	05:26:42 AM	33.8086	-118.6459	9,550
P4	05:28:48 AM	33.7913	-118.8754	14,375
P5	05:30:45 AM	33.8788	-119.0721	19,925
P6	05:32:35 AM	34.0390	-119.2378	24,675
P7	05:34:33 AM	34.2246	-119.4261	28,800
P8	05:36:33 AM	34.4233	-119.6296	32,050
P9	05:38:46 AM	34.6417	-119.8546	36,000
P10	05:40:24 AM	34.8029	-120.0215	36,000
P11	05:42:37 AM	35.0218	-120.2497	36,000
P12	05:44:37 AM	35.2173	-120.4552	36,000
P13	05:46:49 AM	35.4360	-120.6779	36,000
P14	05:48:49 AM	35.6380	-120.8695	36,000
P15	05:50:40 AM	35.8254	-121.0478	36,000
P16	05:52:32 AM	36.0149	-121.2312	34,775
P17	05:54:29 AM	36.2047	-121.4151	29,650
P18	05:56:31 AM	36.3925	-121.5987	25,125
P19	05:58:37 AM	36.5898	-121.7745	20,625
P20	06:00:26 AM	36.7608	-121.8987	16,700
P21	06:02:26 AM	36.9641	-121.9578	12,850
P22	06:04:26 AM	37.1471	-122.0294	10,000
P23	06:06:30 AM	37.3027	-122.0903	7,450
P24	06:08:39 AM	37.4542	-122.1459	4,950
P25	06:10:31 AM	37.5614	-122.1943	2,750
P26	06:12:30 AM	37.5886	-122.2975	1,075
P27	06:14:00 AM	37.6109	-122.3506	46

The class strdfs: SpatiotemporalObject is a set of all spatiotemporal entities, which is a superset of strdfs: TemporalObject and strdfs: SpatialObject.

The description is as follows:

Box 13.

strdfs: SpatiotemporalObject	a rdfs: Class, owl: Class;
rdfs: label	"Spatiotemporal Object" @ en;
rdfs: comment	"The class: SpatiotemporalObject represents everything that can have spatiotemporal information. It is super class of SpatialObject and TemporalObject" @ en

The class *strdfs: SpatiotemporalGeo* describes geometric data of spatiotemporal entities and it is a superset of *strdfs: SpatialGeometry* and *strdfs: TimeSlice*.

The description is as follows:

Box 14.

strdfs: SpatiotemporalGeo	a rdfs: Class, owl: Class;
rdfs: label	"Spatiotemporal Geometry" @ en;
rdfs: comment	"The class is based on strdf: hasTrajectory. It is super class of SpatialGeometry and TimeSlice " @ en

The class *strdfs: SemiLinearPointSet* is the set of rational numbers to represent time values, longitude values, latitude values and altitude values, etc.

The description is as follows:

Box 15.

strdfs: SemiLinearPointSet	a rdfs: Class, owl: Class;
rdfs: label	"SemiLinearPointSet" @ en;
rdfs: comment	"This class is the set of rational numbers" @ en

We illustrate the spatiotemporal classes through Example 6, and compare the descriptions of stRDF with stRDFS.

Example 6. There is a large sonic receiver which calls corresponding programs to analyze the sound waves after receiving them. We make a comparison between stRDF

model and stRDFS model in the description of spatiotemporal information.

stRDF model describes the above information as follows:

Box 16.

ex: program1	rdf: type	ex: JavaProgram
ex: program2	rdf: type	ex: PythonProgram
ex: program1	om: procedure	ex: CountProgram
ex: program2	om: procedure	ex: OutputProgram
ex: program1	om: hasPro1Call	ex: receiver2
ex: program2	om: hasPro2Call	ex: receiver2
ex: receiver2	rdf: type	ex: SoundWaveReceiver
ex: receiver2	ssn: measures	ex: sound
ex: receiver2	ssn: hasLocation	ex: location1
ex: location1	strdf: hasTrajectory	"(t = 6t and t = 16t or 7t ≤ t ≤ 14t) and k = 0t and ((21.8°N < L < 22.1°N and 45.9°E < D <= 46°E) or (L = 22.1°N and D = 46°E))" ^^ strdf: SemiLinearPointSet.

Table 3. Topological relations of spatiotemporal classes

Relation Name	Relation URI	Domain/Range
Equals	strdfs: geoEquals	strdfs: SpatialObject
Disjoint	strdfs: geoDisjoint	strdfs: SpatialObject
Meet	strdfs: geoMeet	strdfs: SpatialObject
Overlap	strdfs: geoOverlap	strdfs: SpatialObject
Covers	strdfs: geoCovers	strdfs: SpatialObject
CoveredBy	strdfs:geoCoveredBy	strdfs: SpatialObject
Inside	strdfs: geoInside	strdfs: SpatialObject
Contains	strdfs: geoContains	strdfs: SpatialObject
Before	strdfs: timBefore	strdfs:TemporalObject
Now	strdfs: timNow	strdfs:TemporalObject
After	strdfs: timAfter	strdfs:TemporalObject

In stRDF model, strdf: hasTrajectory is the attribute value of strdf: hasTrajectory of location1 which describes the spatiotemporal data. It is noted that only spatiotemporal data of the whole entities can be recorded in the spatiotemporal dimension instead of the spatiotemporal data of a certain part of the object. For instance, stRDF model cannot represent the spatial data at t = 6t and the temporal data when the object is at (L = 22.1°N and D = 46°E). Even worse, if there is an attribute value changing at a certain time or in a certain spatial position, stRDF is inaccurate in recording data for its weak capability in linking spatiotemporal data.

Table 4. Topological relations in example 7

Relation Name	Relation URI	Relation Name	Domain/Range
A	strdfs:geoEquals	*B*	strdfs:SpatiotemporalObject
A, B	strdfs:geoDisjoint	*C, D, E*	strdfs:SpatiotemporalObject
C	strdfs: geoMeet	*D*	strdfs:SpatiotemporalObject
C	strdfs:geoOverlap	*E*	strdfs:SpatiotemporalObject
F	strdfs:geoCovers	*D*	strdfs:SpatiotemporalObject
tabE	strdfs:geoCoveredBy	*A, B*	strdfs:SpatiotemporalObject
A, B	strdfs: geoInside	*F*	strdfs:SpatiotemporalObject
F	strdfs:geoContains	*A, B*	strdfs:SpatiotemporalObject
A, B, F	strdfs: timBefore	*C, D, E*	strdfs:SpatiotemporalObject
C	strdfs: timNow	*D*	strdfs:SpatiotemporalObject
C, D, E	strdfs: timAfter	*A, B, F*	strdfs:SpatiotemporalObject

The stRDFS model solves this problem and the results are as follows:

Box 17.

ex: program1	rdf: type	ex: JavaProgram
ex: program2	rdf: type	ex: PythonProgram
ex: program1	om: procedure	ex: AnalysisProgram
ex: program2	om: procedure	ex: AnalysisProgram
ex: program1	om:hasPro1Call	ex: receiver2
ex: program2	om: hasPro2Call	ex: receiver2
ex: receiver2	rdf: type	ex: SoundWaveReceiver
ex: receiver2	ssn: measures	ex: sound
ex: receiver2	ssn: hasLocation1	ex: location1
ex: receiver2	ssn: hasLocation2	ex: location2
om: hasPro1Call	strdfs: SpatiotemporalGeo	"t = 6t and t = 16t and k = 0t and (21.8°N < L < 22.1°N and 45.9°E < D <= 46°E)" ^^ strdfs: SemiLinearPointSet
om: hasPro2Call	strdfs: SpatiotemporalGeo	"7t ≤ t ≤ 14t and L = 22.1°N and D = 46°E and k = 0t" ^^ strdfs: SemiLinearPointSet
ssn: hasLocation1	strdfs: SpatialGeometry	"(21.8°N < L < 22.1°N and 45.9°E < D <= 46°E)" ^^ strdfs: SemiLinearPointSet
ssn: hasLocation2	strdfs: SpatialGeometry	"(L = 22.1°N and D = 46°E)" ^^ strdfs: SemiLinearPointSet

The receiver calls program1 to analyze the data at Location1 when t = 6t and t = 16t, and calls program2 to analyze the data at Location2 when t ∈ [7t, 14t]. In stRDFS model, spatiotemporal data describes om: hasPro1Call and om: hasPro2Call. Different from stRDF, stRDFS model can represent spatiotemporal data and record changes of spatiotemporal attributes at any time or in any location because that facilitates the modification of common attribute values, such as program names.

4) A case of spatiotemporal knowledge graph model

In order to verify the usability of the proposed model, it is applied in this subsection. We choose the flight of Southwest 1524, from Los Angeles to San Francisco, took off at 5:23 a.m. and landed at 6:14 a.m. on 9 August 2019. Picking the point in the flight path every two minutes and name it *Pi* (*i* = 1, 2, …), the flight information is shown in Table 2.

Taking *P2* as an example, as shown in Figure 11, we will apply the methodology above section proposed to aeronautics field.

According to *Ti* = *f* (*N*, *k*) (*i* = 1, 2 3 …) in Definition 6, and "*N* = 05:24:37 AM, *k* = 0t" in Table 2, whose temporal data can be represented by *T2* = (05:24:37 AM, 0t).

According to *Si* = *f* (*L*, *D*, *H*) (*i* = 1, 2 3 …) in Definition 7, and "*L* = 33.8877, *D* = -118.4981, *H* = 4150m", whose spatial data can be represented by *S2* = (33.8877, -118.4981, 4150m).

According to stRDFS expression *g* (*s*, *p*: <*t*, *l*>, *o*) in Definition 8, whose stRDFS model can be represented by (*P2*, *Locate in2*: <*T2*, *S2*>, *area2*).

According to Section 3.2, the description of Figure 11 is as follows:

Box 18.

ex: flight1	rdf: name	ex: Southwest 1524
ex: flight1	rdf: type	ex: B737
ex: flight1	om: hasPassedby1	ex: P1
ex: flight1	om: hasPassedby2	ex: P2
ex: flight1	om: hasPassedby3	ex: P3
…	…	…
ex: flight1	om: hasPassedby26	ex: P26
ex: flight1	om: hasPassedby27	ex: P27
ex: P1	ssn: hasLocation1	ex: area1
ex: P2	ssn: hasLocation2	ex: area2
ex: P3	ssn: hasLocation3	ex: area3
…	…	…
ex: P26	ssn: hasLocation26	ex: area26
ex: P27	ssn: hasLocation27	ex: area27
om: hasPassedby1	strdfs: SpatiotemporalGeo	"t = 05:24:37 AM t and k = 0t and (L = 33.9389, D = -118.3900 and H = 150m)" ^^ strdfs: SemiLinearPointSet
om: hasPassedby2	strdfs: SpatiotemporalGeo	"t = 05:24:37 AM and k = 0t and (L = 33.8877, D = -118.4981 and H = 4150m)" ^^ strdfs: SemiLinearPointSet
om: hasPassedby3	strdfs: SpatiotemporalGeo	"t = 05:26:42 AM and k = 0t and (L = 33.8086, D = -118.6459 and H = 9550m)" ^^ strdfs: SemiLinearPointSet
…	…	…

om: hasPassedby26	strdfs: SpatiotemporalGeo	"t = 06:12:30 AM and k = 0t and (L = 37.5886, D = -122.2975 and H = 1,075m)" ^^ strdfs: SemiLinearPointSet
om: hasPassedby27	strdfs: SpatiotemporalGeo	"t = 06:14:00 AM and k = 0t and (L = 37.6109, D = -122.3506 and H = 46m)" ^^ strdfs: SemiLinearPointSet
ssn: hasLocation1	strdfs: SpatialGeometry	"(L = 33.9389, D = -118.3900 and H = 150m)" ^^ strdfs: SemiLinearPointSet
ssn: hasLocation2	strdfs: SpatialGeometry	"(L = 33.8877, D = -118.4981 and H = 4150m)" ^^ strdfs: SemiLinearPointSet
ssn: hasLocation3	strdfs: SpatialGeometry	"(L = 33.8086, D = -118.6459 and H = 9550m)" ^^ strdfs: SemiLinearPointSet
...	...	...
ssn: hasLocation26	strdfs: SpatialGeometry	"(L = 37.5886, D = -122.2975 and H = 1,075m)" ^^ strdfs: SemiLinearPointSet
ssn: hasLocation27	strdfs: SpatialGeometry	"(L = 37.6109, D = -122.3506 and H = 46m)" ^^ strdfs: SemiLinearPointSet

4 TOPOLOGICAL RELATIONS OF ENTITIES

In order to describe the relations among spatiotemporal entities, this section defines eleven kinds of topological relations, which are: *Equal*, *Disjoint*, *Meet*, *Overlap*, *Cover*, *CoveredBy*, *Inside*, *Contain*, *Before*, *Now* and *After*. The spatial topological relations are *Equal*, *Disjoint*, *Meet*, *Overlap*, *Cover*, *CoveredBy*, *Inside* and *Contain*, so their domains are *strdfs: SpatialObject*. The temporal topological relations are *Before, Now and After*, so their domain is *strdfs: TemporalObject*. The relations among relation names, relation URI and domain are shown in Table 3.

Figure 11. The stRDFS graph of Southwest 1524

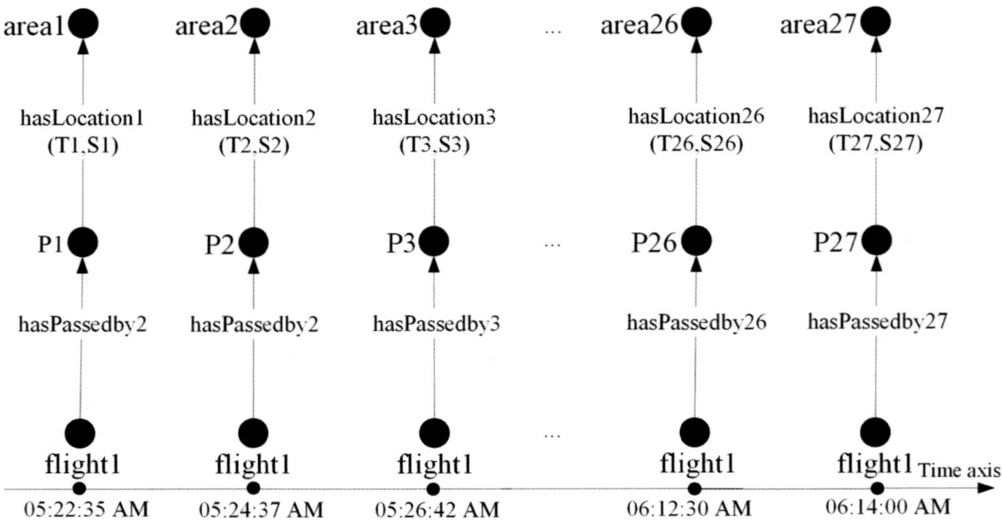

In the following, we define the following determination methods of topological relations among different spatiotemporal entities based on the stRDFS model:

Definition 9. Given two spatiotemporal entities A (s_A, p_A: <Ti_A, Si_A>, o_A) and B (s_B, p_B: <Ti_B, Si_B>, o_B), Equal (A, B) $\Leftrightarrow s_A = s_B \wedge o_A = o_B \wedge p_A = p_B \wedge Si_A = Si_B.(Ti_A = Ti_B?)$

Definition 10. Given two spatiotemporal entities A (s_A, p_A: <Ti_A, Si_A>, o_A) and B (s_B, p_B: <Ti_B, Si_B>, o_B), A is disjoint with B where:

- If o denotes spatial data, Disjoint (A, B) $\Leftrightarrow$ $Range\ (f_{sA\text{-}SisA} \cup f_{pA\text{-}SiA}) \cap Range\ (f_{sB\text{-}SisB} \cup f_{pB\text{-}SiB}) = \emptyset$.
- If o doesn't denote spatial data, Disjoint (A, B) $\Leftrightarrow$ $Range\ (f_{pA\text{-}SiA}) \cap Range\ (f_{pB\text{-}SiB}) = \emptyset$.

By Definition 10, if o represents spatial data, stRDF model can be expressed as (s_A, p_A: <Ti_A, Si_A>, Si_{SA}). As shown in Definition 3, Si_{SA} represents spatial data of s_A and Si_A represents spatial data of attributes p_A. The same is B. Therefore, both SiSA and SiA need to be considered, that is, Range $(f_{sA\text{-}SisA} \cup f_{pA\text{-}SiA}) \cap$ Range $(f_{sB\text{-}SisB} \cup f_{pB\text{-}SiB}) = \emptyset$. If o doesn't represent spatial data, stRDF model can be expressed as (s_A, p_A: <Ti_A, Si_A>, o_A) where oA is the object without spatial data. Therefore, only Si_A need to be considered.

Definition 12. Given two spatiotemporal entities A (s_A, p_A: <Ti_A, Si_A>, o_A) and B (s_B, p_B: <Ti_B, Si_B>, o_B), A overlaps B where:

- If o depicts spatial data, Overlap (A, B) $\Leftrightarrow$ Range° $(f_{sA\text{-}SisA} \cup f_{pA\text{-}SiA}) \cap$ Range° $(f_{sB\text{-}SisB} \cup f_{pB\text{-}SiB}) \neq \emptyset \wedge$ Range $(f_{sA\text{-}SisA} \cup f_{pA\text{-}SiA}) \cap$ Range $(f_{sB\text{-}SisB} \cup f_{pB\text{-}SiB}) \neq$ Range $(f_{sA\text{-}SisA} \cup f_{pA\text{-}SiA}) \wedge$ Range $(f_{sA\text{-}SisA} \cup f_{pA\text{-}SiA}) \cap$ Range $(f_{sB\text{-}SisB} \cup f_{pB\text{-}SiB}) \neq$ Range $(f_{sB\text{-}SisB} \cup f_{pB\text{-}SiB})$.
- If o doesn't depict spatial data, Overlap (A, B) $\Leftrightarrow$ Range° $(f_{pA\text{-}SiA}) \cap$ Range° $(f_{pB\text{-}SiB}) \neq \emptyset \wedge$ Range $(f_{pA\text{-}SiA}) \cap$ Range $(f_{pB\text{-}SiB}) \neq$ Range $(f_{pA\text{-}SiA}) \wedge$ Range $(f_{pA\text{-}SiA}) \cap$ Range $(f_{pB\text{-}SiB}) \neq$ Range $(f_{pB\text{-}SiB})$.

Definition 13. Given two spatiotemporal entities A (s_A, p_A: <Ti_A, Si_A>, o_A) and (s_B, p_B: <Ti_B, Si_B>, o_B), A covers B where:

- If o expresses spatial data, Cover (A, B) $\Leftrightarrow$ Range° $(f_{sA\text{-}SisA} \cup f_{pA\text{-}SiA}) \cap$ Range $(f_{sB\text{-}SisB} \cup f_{pB\text{-}SiB}) =$ Range $(f_{sB\text{-}SisB} \cup f_{pB\text{-}SiB})$
- If o doesn't express spatial data, Cover (A, B) $\Leftrightarrow$ Range° $(f_{pA\text{-}SiA}) \cap$ Range $(f_{pB\text{-}SiB}) =$ Range $(f_{pB\text{-}SiB})$

Definition 14. Given two spatiotemporal entities A (s_A, p_A: <Ti_A, Si_A>, o_A) and B (s_B, p_B: <Ti_B, Si_B>, o_B), A is covered by B where:

- If o represents spatial data, CoveredBy (A, B) $\Leftrightarrow$ $Range\ (f_{sA\text{-}SisA} \cup f_{pA\text{-}SiA}) \cap Range°\ (f_{sB\text{-}SisB} \cup f_{pB\text{-}SiB}) = Range\ (f_{sA\text{-}SisA} \cup f_{pA\text{-}SiA})$.
- If o doesn't represent spatial data, CoveredBy (A, B) $\Leftrightarrow$ $Range\ (f_{pA\text{-}SiA}) \cap Range°\ (f_{pB\text{-}SiB}) = Range\ (f_{pA\text{-}SiA})$

Definition 15. Given two spatiotemporal entities A (s_A, p_A: <Ti_A, Si_A>, o_A) and B (s_B, p_B: <Ti_B, Si_B>, o_B), A is inside B where:

- If o denotes spatial data, Inside (A, B) $\Leftrightarrow$ Range $(f_{sA\text{-}SisA} \cup f_{pA\text{-}SiB}) \cap$ Range $(f_{sB\text{-}SisB} \cup f_{pB\text{-}SiB}) =$ Range $(f_{sA\text{-}SisA} \cup f_{pA\text{-}SiB}) \wedge$ Range° $(f_{sA\text{-}SisA} \cup f_{pA\text{-}SiB}) \cap$ Range° $(f_{sB\text{-}SisB} \cup f_{pB\text{-}SiB}) \neq \emptyset$.
- If o doesn't denote spatial data, Inside (A, B) $\Leftrightarrow$ Range $(f_{pA\text{-}SiA}) \cap$ Range $(f_{pB\text{-}SiB}) =$ Range $(f_{pA\text{-}SiA})$ $\wedge$ Range° $(f_{pA\text{-}SiA}) \cap$ Range° $(f_{pB\text{-}SiB}) \neq \emptyset$.

Definition 16. Given two spatiotemporal entities A (s_A, p_A: <Ti_A, Si_A>, o_A) and B (s_B, p_B: <Ti_B, Si_B>, o_B), A contains B where:

- If o represents spatial data, Contain (A, B) $\Leftrightarrow$ Range ($f_{sA\text{-}SisA} \cup f_{pA\text{-}SiB}$) $\cap$ Range ($f_{sB\text{-}SisB} \cup f_{pB\text{-}SiB}$) = Range ($f_{sB\text{-}SisB} \cup f_{pB\text{-}SisB}$) $\wedge$ Range° ($f_{sA\text{-}SisA} \cup f_{pA\text{-}SiB}$) $\cap$ Range° ($f_{sB\text{-}SisB} \cup f_{pB\text{-}SiB}$) $\neq \emptyset$.
- If o doesn't represent spatial data, Contain (A, B) $\Leftrightarrow$ Range ($f_{pA\text{-}SiA}$) $\cap$ Range ($f_{pB\text{-}SiB}$) = Range ($f_{pB\text{-}SiB}$) $\wedge$ Range° ($f_{pA\text{-}SiA}$) $\cap$ Range° ($f_{pB\text{-}SiB}$) $\neq \emptyset$.

Definition 17. Given two spatiotemporal entities A (s_A, p_A: <Ti_A, Si_A>, o_A) and B (s_B, p_B: <Ti_B, Si_B>, o_B), A is earlier than B where:

- If o depicts temporal data, Before (A, B) $\Leftrightarrow \Pi_N$ $Range$ ($f_{sA\text{-}TisA}$) $< \Pi_N$ $Range$ ($f_{sB\text{-}TisB}$) $\wedge \Pi_N$ $Range$ ($f_{pA\text{-}TiA}$) $< \Pi_N$ $Range$ ($f_{pB\text{-}TiB}$).
- If o doesn't depict temporal data, Before (A, B) $\Leftrightarrow \Pi_N$ $Range$ ($f_{pA\text{-}TiA}$) $< \Pi_N$ $Range$ ($f_{pB\text{-}TiB}$).

Figure 12. The stRDFS graph of Example 7

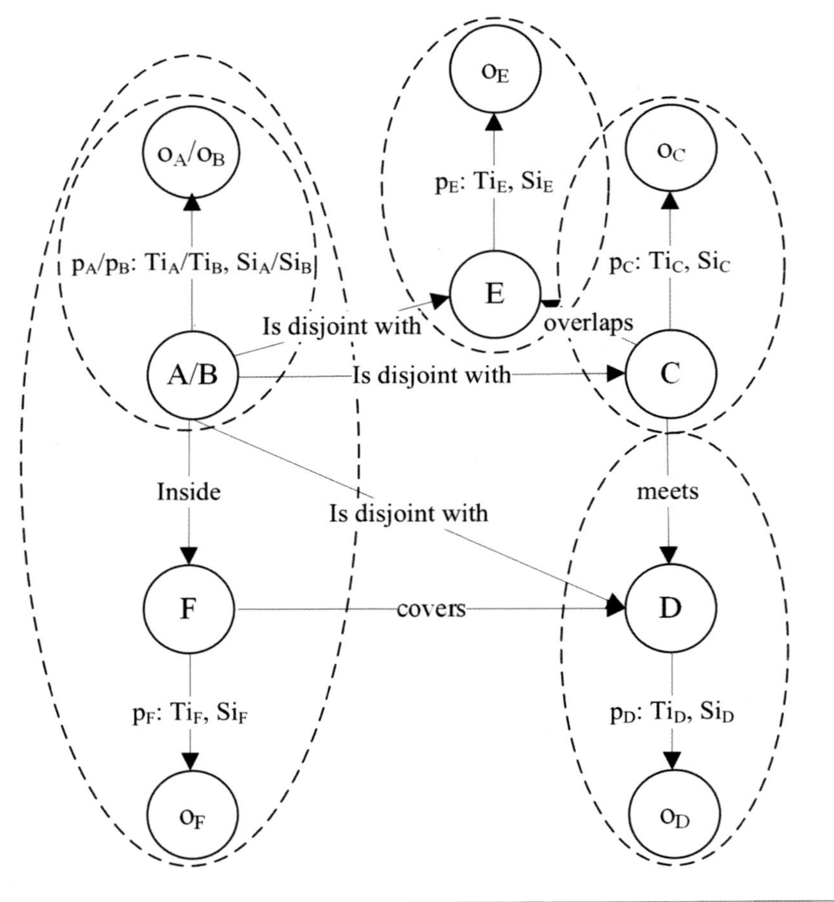

In Definition 17, $\Pi_N(x)$ represents the projection of x on N. For example, Π_N *Range* $(f_{sA\text{-}TisA})$ represents parameter N of the temporal data Ti_{sA}. If o represents temporal data, stRDF model can be expressed as $(s_A, p_A\text{: <}Ti_A, Si_A\text{>}, Ti_{SA})$. Ti_{SA} represents temporal data of s_A and Ti_A represents temporal data of attributes p_A. B is the same. If o doesn't represent temporal data, stRDF model can be expressed as $(s_A, p_A\text{: <}Ti_A, Si_A\text{>}, o_A)$ where o_A is the object without temporal data. Therefore, only Ti_A needs to be considered.

Figure 13. Data tables for some names and names of cities in which they are located

Nodes Edges | Configuration | Add node | Add edge | Search/Replace | Import Spreadsheet | Export table | More actions

Id	Label	City
0	David	A
1	Mary	A
2	James	B
3	Nix	A
4	Leland	B
5	Ackland	B
6	Hamm	C
7	Hans	D
8	Parr	D
9	Fitch	H
10	Nixon	H
11	Orval	B
12	Rock	B
13	Debbi	C
14	Tessie	H
15	Mac	C
16	Jen	C
17	Nelly	D
18	Fenton	H
19	Eric	B
20	Madison	A
21	Rodney	B
23	Lisa	M

Figure 14. The screen snapshot of running result in Gephi

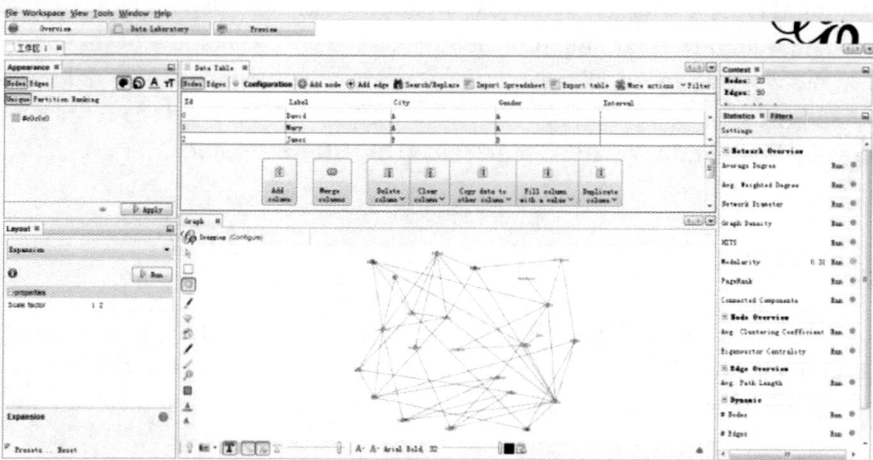

Definition 18. Given two spatiotemporal entities A (s_A, p_A: <Ti_A, Si_A>, o_A) and B (s_B, p_B: <Ti_B, Si_B>, o_B), A is later than B where:

- If o is temporal data, After $(A, B) \Leftrightarrow \Pi_N\ Range\ (f_{sA\text{-}TisA}) > \Pi_N\ Range\ (f_{sB\text{-}TisB})$ and $\Pi_N\ Range\ (f_{pA\text{-}TiA}) > \Pi_N\ Range\ (f_{pB\text{-}TiB})$.
- If o isn't temporal data, After $(A, B) \Leftrightarrow \Pi_N\ Range\ (f_{pA\text{-}TiA}) > \Pi_N\ Range\ (f_{pB\text{-}TiB})$.

Definition 19. Given two spatiotemporal entities A (s_A, p_A: <Ti_A, Si_A>, o_A) and B (s_B, p_B: <Ti_B, Si_B>, o_B), A and B are at the same time where:

- If o represents temporal data, Now $(A, B) \Leftrightarrow \Pi_N\ Range\ (f_{sA\text{-}TisA}) = \Pi_N\ Range\ (f_{sB\text{-}TisB})$ and $\Pi_N\ Range\ (f_{pA\text{-}TiA}) = \Pi_N\ Range\ (f_{pB\text{-}TiB})$.
- If o doesn't represent temporal data, Now $(A, B) \Leftrightarrow \Pi_N\ Range\ (f_{pA\text{-}TiA}) = \Pi_N\ Range\ (f_{pB\text{-}TiB})$.

In the following, we will describe the topological relations of spatiotemporal entities through Example 7.

Example 7. Given the six spatiotemporal entities in Example 4: *A*, *B*, *C*, *D*, *E* and *F*, their topological relations are shown in the Table 4.

Based on stRDFS model, topological relations are transformed into an stRDFS graph, as shown in Figure 12. The dotted elliptical portion indicates the spatial position range. In Figure 12, the position of *A* is equal to *B*, so subjects of *A* and *B* are expressed as an ellipse *A*/*B*, properties are P_A/P_B and objects are O_A/O_B. The position of *A*/*B* is disjoint with *C*, *D* and *E*, so the dotted ellipse of *A*/*B* is disjoint with the dotted ellipses of *C*, *D* and *E*. The dotted ellipse of *A*/*B* is contained in the dotted ellipse of *F* because that the position of *A*/*B* is inside of *F*. The temporal relation is $T_A = T_B = T_F < T_E < T_C = T_D$, and .The position of *A*/*B* and *F* changes into the position of *E* at Ti_E and *D* at Ti_D, respectively.

This chapter selects a part of David's circle of friends as experimental data. By recording their names, relationships, and locations, Gephi (a cross-platform complex network analysis software based on JVM and can display knowledge graphs with spatiotemporal information) can show the relationship between each person's spatial locations. The name of a person is the value of *S*, the relationship is the value of *P*, and the city is the value of *O*. Since the rest of the parameters have little effect on the spatial relationships determination of subjects, it is not necessary to introduce them into the data table. Figure 13 is a spatiotemporal data set that contains ids of people, names of people and cities in which people are located. The data in Figure 13 are input in Gephi, and the stRDFS model of these data is established and Figure 14 is the running result of the spatial position relationships among subjects. As shown in Figure 14, if person *A* meets person *B* (two persons are adjacent), they will be represented by the same color, and if they are disjoint, they will be represented by different colors.

5 INCONSISTENCY OF SPATIOTEMPORAL RDF DATA

On the basis of using RDF triple for RDF data with effective time and spatial location, according to the practical significance of effective time and spatial location in the real world, the inconsistencies of spatiotemporal RDF data are classified, and all kinds of inconsistencies are detected and repaired.

5.1 Classification of Inconsistency of Spatiotemporal RDF Data

Although semantic web has made great progress in information extraction technology, RDF database still faces a lot of redundancy and inconsistency with facts. It is necessary to add some additional consistency constraints to these inconsistent data. RDF data with time label has inconsistency in time information. The inconsistency of RDF data with time attribute is classified according to different situations.

In order to better explain the inconsistency of various spatiotemporal data, several basic definitions of time interval and spatial position are given below, which is convenient for subsequent analysis and research.

Definition 20. A time interval is expressed as [start, end], and the unit time is set to 1 where start $+ 1 \leq$ end;

In order to indicate the continuity in time, even if the number of seconds is used as the unit time, the time in reality is discontinuous. For the convenience and naturalness of the following use, the unit time is set to 1, and two moments t and t+1 indicate the continuity in time.

Definition 21. For two time intervals T_1 $[s_1, e_1]$ and T_2 $[s_2, e_2]$, analyze from the time axis:

(1) If $e_1+1=s_2$ or $e_2+1=s_1$, then T_1 and T_2 are continuous;
(2) If $s_1=s_2$ and $e_1=e_2$, T_1 and T_2 are equal, $T_1=T_2$;
(3) If $s_1 \leq s_2$ and $e_2 < e_1$ and $s_1 < s_2$ and $e_2 \leq e_1$ are both called T_1 containing T_2, and is expressed as $T_2 \subseteq T_1$;
(4) If $s_2 \leq s_1$ and $e_1 < e_2$ and $s_2 < s$ and $e_1 \leq e_2$, both of them are called T_2 including T_1 and are represented as $T_1 \subseteq T_2$;
(5) If $s_1 < s_2$, $s_2 < e_1$ and $e_1 < e_2$ hold true at the same time, it is said that T_1 and T_2 intersect $T_1 \cap T_2$ and $T_2 > T_1$, and the intersecting part is $[s_2, e_1]$;
(6) If $s_2 < s_1$, $s_1 < e_2$ and $e_2 < e_1$ hold at the same time, it is said that T_1 and T_2 intersect $T_1 \cap T_2$ and $T_1 > T_2$, and the overlapping part is $[s_2, e_1]$;
(7) If $e_1+1 < s_2$ or $e_2+1 < s_1$, T_1 and T_2 are said to be spaced.

The possible relationships of all time intervals are summarized above. These seven relationships are used directly below, and $t_1 < t_2 < t_3$ .... As shown in Figure 15, the relationship between T_1 and T_2 can be seen more clearly from the timeline.

Definition 22. Spatiotemporal RDF data is expressed as (s, p, o) [start, end] {x, y, z}. When transforming spatiotemporal RDF data into RDF graph, the subject is represented by node s, the object is represented by node o, the node is represented by n, and the arc connecting subject s and object o is called edge and attribute p. Put the time interval and spatial position on the side.

Definition 23. The lifespan of a node is the largest set of the union of the effective times of all the incoming and outgoing edges of the node.

Definition 24. In the spatial position {x, y, z}, the spatial unit is set to 1; In order to express the continuity in space and the use and nature below, in three-dimensional space coordinates, each data is simply regarded as a particle, and the unit of space length is set to 1, for example, {x, y, z} and {x+1, y, z} are adjacent in space.

The relationship between $\{x_1, y_1, z_1\}$ and $\{x_2, y_2, z_2\}$ can be expressed in the spatial coordinate system, so as to understand and analyze more clearly. As shown in Figure 2, the relationship between spatial positions can be seen intuitively.

Figure 15. Time interval diagram

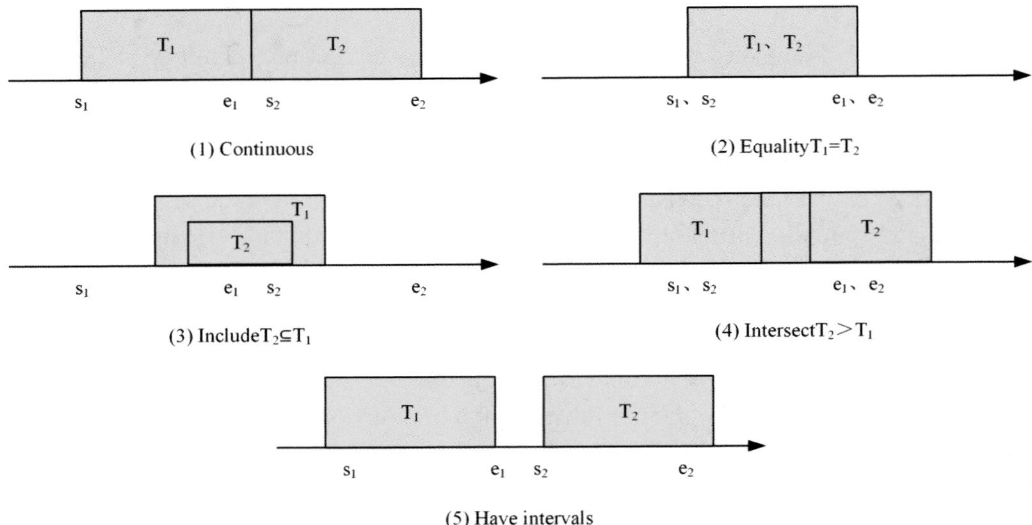

(1) Two spatial positions are completely coincident and equal $\{x_1, y_1, z_1\} = \{x_2, y_2, z_2\}$;
(2) Two spatial positions are adjacent, that is to say, at least one of the x coordinates, y coordinates and z coordinates of the two spatial positions differs by 1. If there are spatial positions $\{x_1, y_1, z_1\}$ and spatial positions $\{x_2, y_2, z_2\}$, where $x_2=x_1+1$, it means that these two spatial positions are adjacent;
(3) Two spatial positions are separated, that is to say, the difference between the values of x coordinates, y coordinates and z coordinates of the two spatial positions is greater than 1, that is to say, the two spatial positions are not adjacent in any plane, which means that the two spatial positions are separated.

It can be seen from Figure 16 that the spatial position relations represented by $\{x_1, y_1, z_1\}$ and $\{x_3, y_3, z_3\}$ are equal; The spatial positions $\{x_1, y_1, z_1\}$ and $\{x_2, y_2, z_2\}$ and $\{x_3, y_3, z_3\}$ and $\{x_2, y_2, z_2\}$ are separated; The spatial positions $\{x_2, y_2, z_2\}$ and $\{x_2, y_2+1, z_2\}$ are adjacent because of the difference of y coordinates by 1.

Definition 25. The active Area of a node represents the largest union of the effective areas of all outgoing and incoming edges of the node, that is, the spatial position of any edge should be within the active areas of its parent node and child node.

For example, it is necessary to count the information of residents who have not left a town in 2020. At this time, the activity area of permanent residents in all towns is within the boundary line of the town. If some residents are not within the area divided by the boundary line of the town for a certain period of time in 2020, it means that the resident has left the town, and the information of the resident cannot continue to be stored in the information database of permanent residents, otherwise it is not in line with the reality.

Spatiotemporal RDF data with time tags and spatial coordinates is added, and the inconsistency in time dimension of spatiotemporal RDF data is divided into the following situations:

Figure 16. Diagram of spatial position

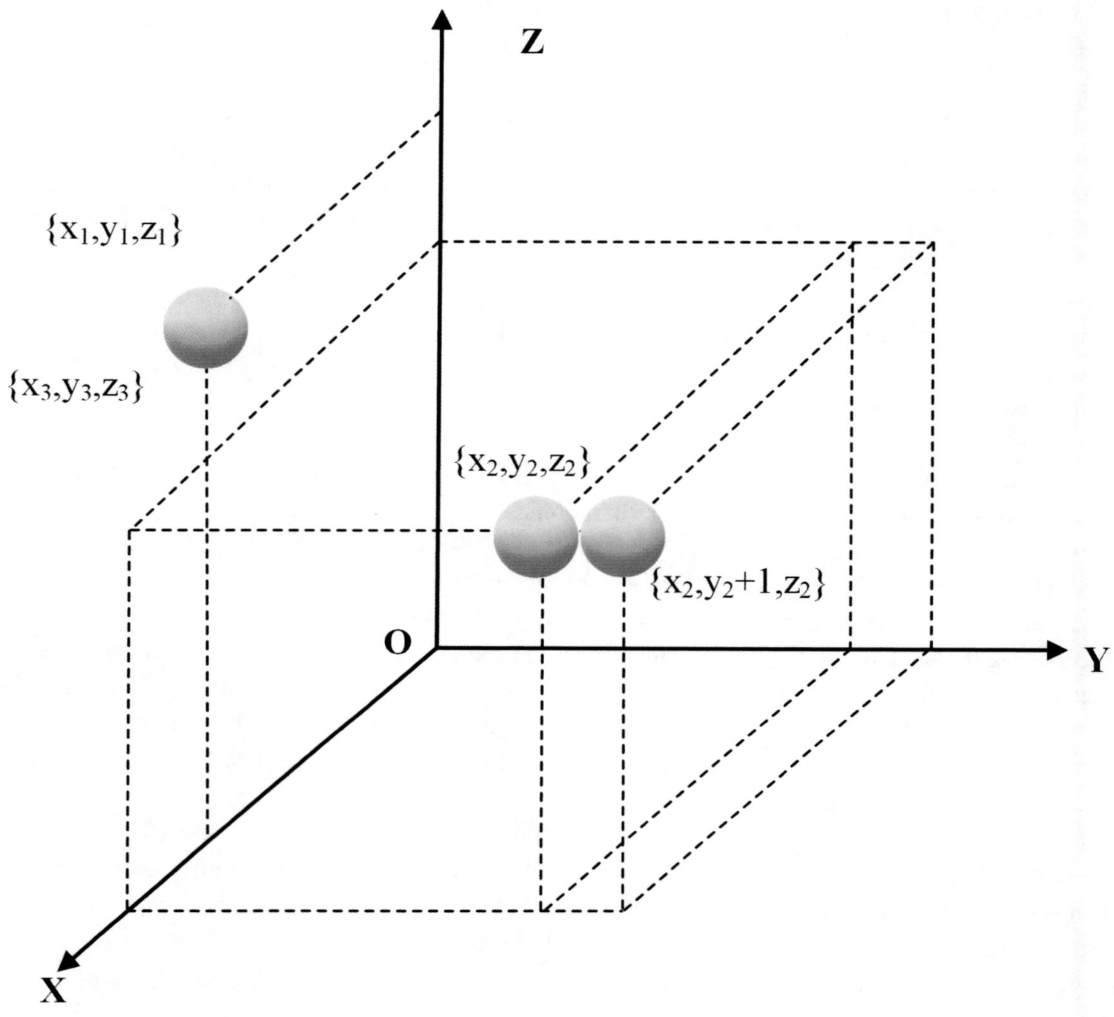

(1) The subject s, the attribute p, and the object o are all identical, i.e. the RDF triple is identical, expressed as (s, p, o) [T_1] {x_1, y_1, z_1} and (s, p, o) [T_2] {x_2, y_2, z_2} when the spatial coordinates {x_1, y_1, z_1} and {x_2, y_2, z_2} are at $x_1 \neq x_2$, $y_1 \neq y_2$ and $z_1 \neq z_2$, i.e. when the spatial positions are identical, and when the spatial coordinates {x_1, y_1, z_1} and {x_2, y_2, z_2} are at $x_1 = x_2$, $y_1 = y_2$ and $z_1 = z_2$, i.e. when the spatial positions are identical Relationship:

The first category: coincidence $T_1 = T_2$;
The second category: contains $T_2 \subseteq T_1$ or $T_1 \subseteq T_2$;
The third category: intersecting $T_1 \cap T_2$, $T_1 > T_2$ or $T_2 > T_1$;
The fourth category: continuous.

T_1 and T_2 do not belong to the above four relationships, which shows that T_1 and T_2 are discontinuous. It can be said that the information that the p attribute value of s is o is valid in T_1 and T_2 respectively, but it is invalid in the time between T_1 and T_2, so there is no inconsistency.

(2) If there is a piece of data expressed as (s, p, o) [T] {x, y, z} for the edge e connected by the parent node s and the child node o, If the effective time Te of this edge e exceeds the life interval If of the node, it will lead to the existence of p attribute but the existence of subject s and object o in a period of time interval, which is meaningless data in real life. That is to say, only Te=If and Te $\subseteq$ If are consistent, so inconsistencies can be divided into four types:

The first category: intersection, Te $\cap$ If, Te > If or If > Te;
The second category: there are intervals, and Te and If are discontinuous and do not intersect;
The third category: including, If $\subseteq$ Te;
The fourth category: continuous.

Only when both subject s and object o exist, in real life, the information that the p attribute value of subject s is o is meaningful, otherwise there is inconsistency.

For example, there is a building, which was built in 1999 and demolished in 2019, but there is a data that shows that the height of this building is 100 meters from 2020 to 2021. This building no longer exists after 2019, so this data is definitely inconsistent with the facts.

According to the spatial position information, if the spatial position {x, y, z} of this edge e is outside the active Area of the node, it leads to the existence of p attribute in a spatial Area, but the subject s and object o no longer exist in this Area, which is meaningless data in real life. That is to say, only {x, y, z}$\in$ Area is consistent, so the inconsistency means that the spatial position does not belong to the active Area, resulting in {x, y, z}$\notin$Area.

For example, during the butterfly census in Nanjing in 2006, researchers found 109 species of butterflies belonging to 9 families. There are about 80% butterflies in Yuhuatai Scenic Area. In 2016, China first observed the biodiversity of butterflies, which are internationally recognized as highly sensitive environmental change indicators. In the latest round of monitoring results, only 21 species of butterflies belonging to 5 families were found in Yuhuatai Scenic Area, and most of them disappeared due to the change of local plant varieties. If a piece of data shows that the spatial position of a butterfly is not in the observation area of Yuhuatai scenic spot, it means that the butterfly does not belong to the observation area, which is meaningless data and cannot be put in the monitoring result data.

(3) Subjects s and p have the same attribute, but different objects o1 and o2 have repeated effective times.

It is expressed as (s, p, o_1) [T_1] {x_1, y_1, z_1} and (s, p, o_2) [T_1] {x_2, y_2, z_2}. At this time, due to different objects, spatial position has no effect on inconsistency, so only the different relationship between time tags T_1 and T_2 is discussed, which can be divided into the following three types:
The first category: the effective time is equal T_1=T_2;
The second category: contains, $T_2 \subseteq T_1$ or $T_1 \subseteq T_2$;
The third category: intersection, $T_1 \cap T_2$, T_1>T_2 or T_2 > T_1.

(4) For different subjects s_1 and s_2, the attribute p is the same as the object o, where the valid time is repeated.

Represented as (s_1, p, o) [T_1] {x_1, y_1, z_1} and (s_2, p, o) [T_1] {x_2, y_2, z_2}. At this time, because the subjects are different, the spatial position has no effect on the inconsistency, so only the different relationship between time tags T_1 and T_2 is discussed, which can be divided into the following three types:

The first category: the effective time is equal, $T_1=T_2$;

The second category: contains, $T_2 \subseteq T_1$ or $T_1 \subseteq T_2$;

The third category: intersection, $T_1 \cap T_2$, $T_1>T_2$ or $T_2 > T_1$.

The inconsistency between the third and the fourth is due to the particularity of the attribute p.

After defining the relationship between life interval and spatial region, as well as the relationship between time interval and spatial position, the following analysis of specific spatiotemporal RDF based on temporal and spatial inconsistency is carried out.

5.2 Detection and Repair of Inconsistency of Triple Duplication

As shown in Figure 17, inconsistencies caused by triple repetition can be divided into four types of inconsistencies, namely equality, intersection, inclusion and continuity of effective time intervals.

At this time, because the attribute p and the object o are the same, the spatial position is also set to the same, focusing on the inconsistency of effective time. If the spatial position is different, it will be mentioned in the inconsistency analysis of divergent attributes later.

(1) The effective time of RDF triple (s, p, o) is [t_1, t_2], and the two data are in the same spatial position, saving two duplicate information, while only one of them is enough in spatiotemporal RDF database, and the redundant record is deleted directly.

(2) RDF triples (s, p, o) have effective times of [t_1, t_3] and [t_2, t_4]. The two data spaces are in the same position, and the effective times of the two records have overlapping parts. Therefore, it is necessary to merge time intervals and remove duplicate time intervals. As in Figure 3, modify the previous data (s, p, o), [t_1, t_3] {x_1, y_2, z_3} to have effective times of (s, p, o), [t_1, t_4] {x_1, y_2, z_3}, and then delete another data.

(3) The effective time of RDF triple (s, p, o) is from t_1 to t_6 and t_3 to t_4. The two data spaces are in the same position, and the repetition time is [t_3, t_4], so the contained record can be deleted directly.

(4) The effective time of RDF triple (s, p, o) is from t_1 to t_3 and t_3+1 to t_4. The two data spaces are in the same position, and the unit time is 1, so t_3 and t_3+1 are continuous, so the effective interval of connection is [t_1, t_5]. Modify an original record (s, p, o), [t_1, t_3] {x_1, y_2, z_3} to (s, p, o), [t_1, t_5] {x_1, y_2, z_3}, and delete another record.

These are four inconsistencies caused by repeated RDF triples.

5.3 Detection and Repair of Inconsistency Between Life Interval and Activity Area

As shown in Figure 18, the inconsistency of spatiotemporal RDF data can be divided into four types because the effective time of edges exceeds the life interval of parent nodes.

Figure 17. Four cases of inconsistency caused by repeated RDF triples

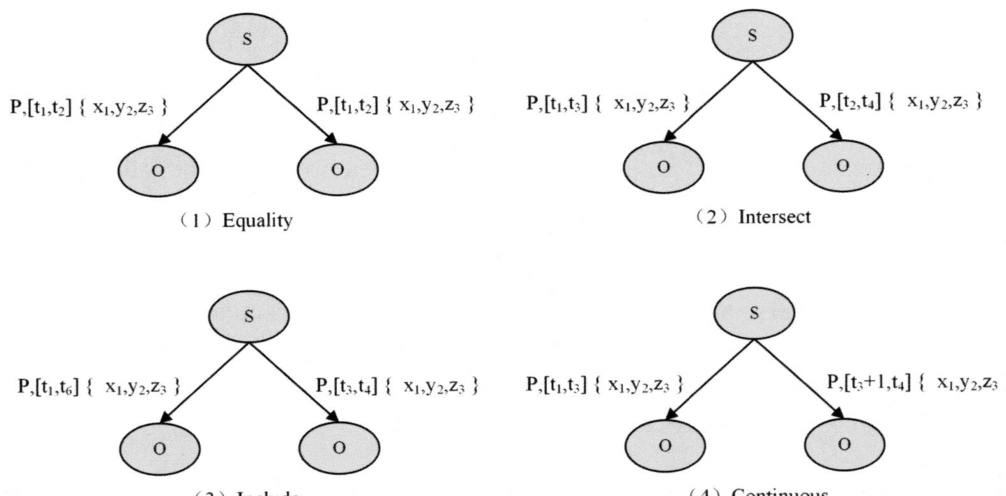

They are the intersection, interval, inclusion and continuity of two time intervals. The situation is the same for child nodes, so only the parent nodes are discussed.

If the effective area of the edge exceeds the active area of the parent node itself, it will also lead to the inconsistency of spatiotemporal RDF data, that is to say, the spatial position of the parent node falls outside the effective area of the edge, and this data does not exist in the real world at this time, resulting in the inconsistency of data.

In the first case, as shown in Figure 18, in two records of the same subject s_1, (s_1, p_1, o_1), [t_1, t_6] {x_1, y_2, z_3} and (s_1, p_2, o_2), [t_{15}, t_{43}] {x_4, y_5, z_6}, the effective time of attribute p_1 [t_1, t_6] and attribute p_2 are [t_{15}, t_{43}], which intersect the life intervals of nodes s_1, o_1 and o_2, and the two time periods [t_1, t_3-1] and [t_{20}+1, t_{43}] are beyond the life intervals of nodes s_1, o_1 and o_2. That is to say, during these two periods, nodes s_1, o_1 and o_2 do not exist in real life, and nodes are meaningful only between [t_3 and t_{20}]. It is necessary to delete the valid time interval of attribute p_1 and attribute p_2, and the time interval not included in the life interval. Therefore, the data (s_1, p_1, o_1), [t_1, t_6] {x_1, y_2, z_3} should be modified to (s_1, p_2, o_1), [t_3, t_6] {x_1, y_2, z_3}, and the data (s_1, p, o_2), [t_{15}, t_{20}] {x_4, y_5, z_6} should be modified.

By modifying the effective time of attribute p, the time interval is reduced to make it within the life interval of nodes, so as to ensure the consistency of data. Because the life interval of a node is calculated by the effective time of the entry and exit edges of the node, we use the time interval of reducing the effective time instead of expanding the life interval of the node.

At the same time, check the spatial positions {x_1, y_2, z_3} and {x_2, y_3, z_4} of edges, and do not exceed the active areas of parent nodes and child nodes. The data is reasonable and need not be processed in the next step.

In the second case, as shown in Figure 4, two records of the same subject s_2, (s_2, p_3, o_1), [t_1, t_2] {x_2, y_3, z_4} and (s_2, p_4, o_2), [t_{23}, t_{25}] {x_5, y_6, z_7}, the effective time of attribute p_3 is [t_1, t_2] and the effective time of attribute p_4 is [t_{15}, t_{43}], which are spaced from the life intervals of nodes s_2, node o_1 and node o_2, and do not coincide in any time interval.

Figure 18. Four Classifications of Inconsistency between life intervals and spatial regions

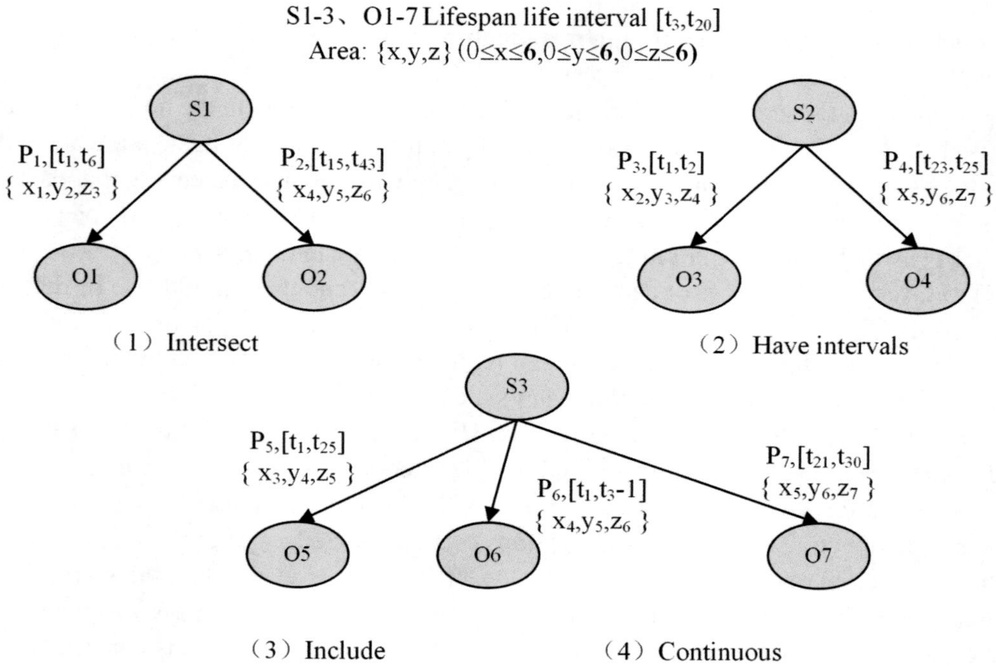

Node s_2 and Node o_3 in the graph are real in the life interval $[t_3, t_{20}]$, but there are no nodes s_2 and o_3 in the time interval $[t_1, t_2]$. After there are nodes s_2 and Node o_3 in the time interval $[t_3, t_{20}]$, the attribute p_3 does not exist, only two nodes exist. Therefore, this record cannot represent the meaning that the p_3 attribute value of s_2 is o_3. Similarly, before the existence of $[t_{23}, t_{25}]$ of attribute p_4, node s_2 and node o_4 have disappeared after t_{20}, which also does not mean that the value of p_4 attribute of s_2 is o_4.

That is to say, these two data are meaningless data, and these two records (s_2, p_3, o_1), $[t_1, t_2]$ $\{x_2, y_3, z_4\}$ and (s_2, p_4, o_2), $[t_{23}, t_{25}]$ $\{x_5, y_6, z_7\}$ should be deleted.

Then check the spatial positions $\{x_2, y_3, z_4\}$ and $\{x_5, y_6, z_7\}$ of the edges, and find that the p_4 attribute value of s_2 is o_4, which is not in the active area of nodes s_2 and o_4. Therefore, the information that there is no attribute p_4 in the spatial area where s_2 and o_4 exist should also be deleted.

In the third case, as shown in Figure 4, the main body is the record of s_3, (s_3, p_5, o_5), $[t_1, t_{25}]$ $\{x_3, y_4, z_5\}$, the effective time of attribute p_5 is $[t_1, t_{25}]$, while the life interval of node s_3 and node o_5 is $[t_3, t_{20}]$. Node s_3 and node o_5 only exist from t_3 to t_{20}, and the effective time interval contains the life interval of nodes, so the data is meaningful only in $[t_3, t_{20}]$, that is to say, the effective time interval of edges $[t_1, t_{25}]$ is reduced to the life interval of nodes $[t_3, t_{20}]$, so the spatiotemporal RDF triple (s_3, p_5, o_5), $[t_1, t_{25}]$, y_4, $z_5\}$ is modified to (s_3, p_5, o_5), $[t_3, t_{20}]$ $\{x_3, y_4, z_5\}$.

Finally, check the spatial position of the edge $\{x_3, y_4, z_5\}$, which does not exceed the active area of the parent node and the child node. The data is reasonable and need not be processed in the next step.

In the fourth case, two records of the same subject s_3, (s_2, p_6, o_6), $[t_1, t_3\text{-}1]$ $\{x_2, y_3, z_4\}$ and (s_2, p_7, o_7), $[t_{21}, t_{30}]$ $\{x_5, y_6, z_7\}$, where attribute p_6 has a valid time of $[t_1, t_3\text{-}1]$, attribute p_7 has a valid time of $[t_{21},$

t_{30}], and nodes s_3, o_6 and o_7 have a life interval of [t_3, t_{20}]. The two valid times [t_1, t_3-1] and [t_{21}, t_{30}] are continuous with the life interval of nodes [$t_{3,}$ t_{20}],

The effective time intervals of attribute p_1 and attribute p_2 coincide with the life intervals [t_3, t_{20}] of node s_3, node o_6 and node o_7 in no time interval.

Nodes s_3 and o_6 in the graph are real in the life interval [t_3, t_{20}], but there are no nodes s_2 and o_6 in the time interval [t_1, t_3-1]. After there are nodes s_2 and o_6 in the time interval [t_3, t_{20}], the attribute p_3 does not exist, only two nodes exist. Therefore, this record cannot represent the meaning that the p6 attribute value of s_2 is o_6. Similarly, before the existence of [t_{21}, t_{30}] of attribute p_7, node s_2 and node o_7 have disappeared after t_{20}, which also does not mean that the value of p_7 attribute of s_2 is o_7.

That is to say, these two pieces of data are meaningless data, and they should also be deleted directly (s_2, p_6, o_6), [t_1, t_3-1] {x_2, y_3, z_4} and (s_2, p_7, o_7), [t_{21}, t_{30}] {x_5, y_6, z_7}. Spatial positions {x_4, y_5, z_6} and {x_5, y_6, z_7} of edges, found that p_7 is not in the spatial region of nodes s_3 and o_7, so the information that attribute p_7 does not exist in the active region where s_3 and o_7 exist should be deleted.

The above are four kinds of inconsistencies caused by the different relationships between the effective time and space positions of attribute edges and the life interval and active area of nodes.

When detecting the inconsistency of spatiotemporal RDF data, it is necessary to detect each node, and compare the effective time and space positions of all access edges of each node, whether they are within the life interval and active area of the node. If it exists, it means that the stored RDF data is inconsistent due to the existence of life interval and active area, so it is necessary to modify the effective time or delete the inconsistent data. The stored spatiotemporal RDF data is consistent until all the detected nodes are not inconsistent.

5.4 Detection and Repair of Inconsistency of Divergent Attributes

There will be inconsistency of divergent attributes, which is aimed at special attributes, and not all attributes will have such requirements. The reason for the inconsistency of divergent attributes is that the effective time of different attribute values of the subject coincides, and it is required that the attribute values of the subject in the same time are unique.

As shown in Figure 19, the inconsistency of spatiotemporal RDF data caused by the overlap of effective times of different edges of p attribute of the same node can be divided into three cases: intersection, inclusion and equality of time intervals of two effective times. Where one valid time contains another valid time, it also belongs to the intersection relationship of two time intervals.

In the first case, as shown in Figure 5, the two pieces of data corresponding to the subject s_1 (s_1, p, o_2), [t_2, t_5] {x_2, y_2, z_2} and (s_1, p, o_3), [t_2, t_5] {x3, y3, z3} have valid times of [t_2, t_5], that is to say, in the time interval of [t_2, t_5], the p attribute value of s_1 has two o_2 and o_3, which is not in line with the actual situation. For example, if you count the attendance in class, it is impossible for you to have a classmate in two places during class.

That is to say, the requirement of the spatiotemporal RDF data model in this chapter is that at a certain time, there can only be one attribute value of a subject, so the stored data in the time interval [t_2, t_5] does not meet the requirements of the model. Therefore, there is an inconsistency of divergent attributes, and it is necessary to delete one of the data to repair its inconsistency. So that there is only one attribute value with p attribute in [t_2, t_5]. The data (s_1, p, o_3), [t_2, t_5] {x_3, y_3, z_3} needs to be deleted.

Figure 19. Three types of divergent attribute inconsistency

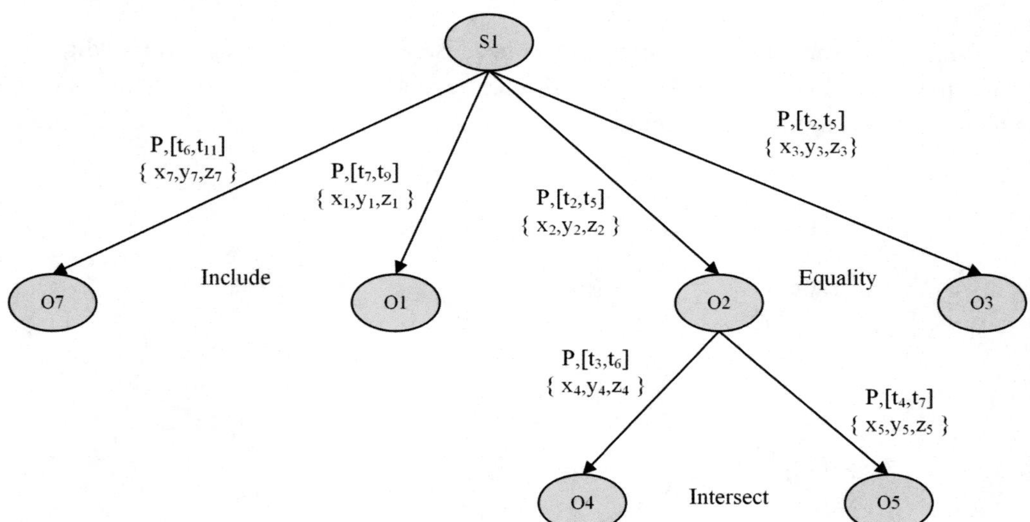

In the second case, as shown in Figure 19, the effective time and spatial positions of two attributes p corresponding to node o_2, which are o_4 and o_5, are $[t_3, t_6]$ $\{x_4, y_4, z_4\}$ and $[t_4, t_7]$ $\{x_3, y_3, z_3\}$, and the effective time $[t_3, t_6]$ intersects with the effective time $[t_4, t_7]$. Note that in $[t_3, t_4\text{-}1]$, the p attribute value of node o_2 is o_4. In $[t_6{+}1, t_7]$, the p attribute value of node o_2 is o_5. There is no inconsistency between these two time intervals. However, in the overlapping time interval $[t_4, t_6]$, the p attribute of node o_2 corresponds to two attribute values o_4 and o_5, which are inconsistent.

Therefore, it is necessary to delete the overlapping part $[t_4, t_6]$ within the effective time of an edge, and you can choose to reduce the effective time of the edge with the corresponding attribute value o_5 to $[t_6, t_7]$. In this way, the inconsistency of divergence attribute of this node can be eliminated.

In the third case, as shown in Figure 5, the two pieces of data corresponding to the subject s_1 (s_1, p, o_1), $[t_7, t_9]$ $\{x_1, y_1, z_1\}$ and (s_1, p, o_7), $[t_6, t_{11}]$ $\{x_7, y_7, z_7\}$ have valid times of $[t_7, t_9]$ and $[t_6, t_{11}]$ respectively, and these two valid time intervals have overlapping parts $[t_7, t_9]$. It shows that in the time interval $[t_6, t_7]$, the p attribute value of node s_1 is o_7, while in the time interval $[t_7, t_9]$, the p attribute of node s_1 corresponds to two attribute values o_1 and o_7, which are inconsistent.

At this time, it is necessary to delete one of the overlapping parts, so that node s_1 corresponds to only one attribute value in $[t_7, t_9]$. In these two pieces of data, you can choose to modify (s_1, p, o_7), $[t_6, t_{11}]$ $\{x_7, y_7, z_7\}$ to (s_1, p, o_7), $[t_6, t_7]$ $\{x_7, y_7, z_7\}$, so that node s1 corresponds to only one attribute value o_1 in $[t_7, t_9]$. In this way, the inconsistency of divergent attributes can be repaired.

In the detection of divergent attribute inconsistency, if there are overlapping parts in different effective times corresponding to the attribute values of a certain parent node, it means that there is divergent attribute inconsistency in spatiotemporal RDF. Only when all effective times of each outgoing edge with attribute p of each parent node are detected without any overlap, it can be determined that there is no divergent attribute inconsistency in the whole spatiotemporal RDF data.

5.5 Inconsistency Detection and Repair of Convergence Attributes

The inconsistency of convergence attribute exists because there is only one agent s whose p attribute value is o at the same time, and there can be different agents whose p attribute value is o at different times, which is similar to the inconsistency of divergence attribute.

Figure 20. Three cases of convergence attribute inconsistency

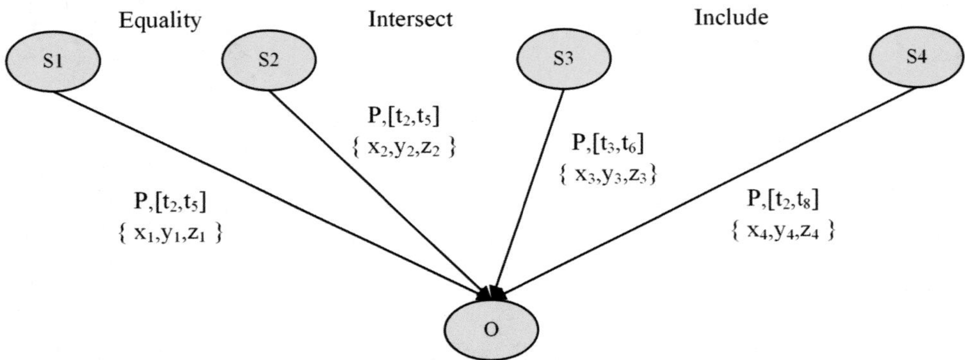

As shown in Figure 20, the inconsistency caused by the overlap of effective time of different entry edges of p attribute of the same node o can be divided into three categories, which are the equality, inclusion and intersection of two effective time intervals.

In the first case, as shown in Figure 6, the two pieces of data (s_1, p, o), [t_2, t_5] {x_1, y_1, z_1} and (s_2, p, o), [t_2, t_5] {x_2, y_2, z_2} corresponding to the main body s_1 have the same effective time and are all [t_2, t_5].

That is to say, the requirement of the spatiotemporal RDF data model in this chapter is that at a certain time, the attribute values of multiple subjects cannot be the same, so the stored data in the time interval [t_2, t_5] does not meet the requirements of the model.

Therefore, there is an inconsistency of convergence attributes, and it is necessary to delete one of the data to repair its inconsistency. So that there is only one principal in [t_2, t_5], and the attribute value with p attribute is o. At this point, the data (s_2, p, o), [t_2, t_5] {x_2, y_2, z_2} can be deleted to fix the inconsistency of convergence attributes.

In the second case, as shown in Figure 6, the p attribute of nodes s_2 and s_3 is o, and the corresponding two pieces of data are (s_2, p, o), [t_2, t_5] {x_2, y_2, z_2} and (s_3, p, o), [t_3, t_6] {x_3, y_3, z_3}, and the effective time [t_2, t_5] and the effective time [t_3, t_6] intersect. Note that in [t_2, t_3-1], the p attribute value of node s_2 is o. In [t_5+1, t_6], the p attribute value of node s_3 is o. In these two time intervals, there is no inconsistency of convergence attributes. However, in the overlapping time interval [t_3, t_5], there is inconsistency, because the corresponding attribute value of p attribute of nodes s_2 and s_3 is o.

Therefore, it is necessary to delete the overlapping part [t_3, t_5] within the effective time of an edge, and you can choose to reduce the effective time of the edge with the attribute value o corresponding to s_3 to [t_5+1, t_6]. In this way, the inconsistency of convergence attribute of this node can be eliminated.

In the third case, as shown in Figure 6, the two pieces of data corresponding to subjects s_3 and s_4 (s_3, p, o), [t_3, t_6] {x_3, y_3, z_3} and (s_4, p, o), [t_2, t_8] {x_4, y_4, z_4} have valid times of [t_3, t_6] and [t_2, t_8], respectively.

These two valid time intervals have overlapping parts $[t_3, t_6]$, that is, $[t_2, t_8]$ contains $[t_3, t_6]$. It shows that in time interval $[t_2, t_3]$ and $[t_6, t_8]$, the p attribute value of node s_3 is o, while in time interval $[t_3, t_6]$, the corresponding attribute values of nodes s_3 and s_4 are both o, so there is convergence attribute inconsistency.

At this time, it is necessary to delete one of the overlapping parts, so that there is only one node corresponding to the attribute value o in $[t_3, t_6]$. In these two pieces of data, you can choose to modify (s_4, p, o), $[t_2, t_8]$ $\{x_7, y_7, z_7\}$ to (s_4, p, o), $[t_2, t_3]$ $[t_6, t_8]$ $\{x_7, y_7, z_7\}$}, so that there is only one node s_3 corresponding to the attribute value o in $[t_3, t_6]$. In this way, the inconsistency of convergence attributes can be repaired.

The convergence attribute requires that only one subject s has a p attribute value of o at the same time, that is, the effective times for all p attributes of all objects with p attributes to enter edges cannot coincide.

Therefore, to detect whether there is convergence attribute inconsistency, we must first find all child nodes with attribute p, and then check whether there is coincidence in the effective time of all entry edges with attribute p of each child node. As long as there is coincidence, there is inconsistency. Only by detecting that there is no overlap in all effective time of each entry edge with attribute p of each child node, can we determine that there is no convergence attribute inconsistency in the whole spatiotemporal RDF data.

6 SUMMARY

Incorporation of spatiotemporal information in data model has been an important topic of database community because such information extensively exists in real-world applications, in which spatiotemporal data plays an important role in nature. Both classical RDF model and previous studies on RDF extension cannot satisfy the need for modeling and processing spatiotemporal data. Therefore, we explore the method to model Spatiotemporal Data based on RDF. In this chapter, we establish the stRDFS data model and introduce the classes and descriptions in spatiotemporal domain. This model can correlate temporal data with spatial data through properties and capture changes of spatiotemporal attribute value in time. Besides, in order to depict relations among different spatiotemporal entities, we define eleven kinds of topological relations and the determination methods, and then we describe them with stRDFS model.

REFERENCES

Ademaj, F., Schwarz, S., Berisha, T., & Rupp, M. (2019). A Spatial Consistency Model for Geometry-Based Stochastic Channels. *IEEE Access : Practical Innovations, Open Solutions*, *7*, 183414–183427. doi:10.1109/ACCESS.2019.2958154

Amjadi, J., & Soroudi, M. (2018). Twin signed total Roman domination numbers in digraphs. *Asian-European Journal of Mathematics*, *11*(3), 1850034. doi:10.1142/S1793557118500341

Arenas, H., Aussenac-Gilles, N., Comparot, C., & Trojahn, C. (2018). Ontologie pour l'intégration de données d'observation de la Terre et contextuelles basée sur les relations topologiques [Ontology for the integration of Earth observation and contextual data based on topological relations]. In *Proc. IC*, Nancy, France.

Bai, L., Liu, J., & Yu, C. (2016). *A spatiotemporal data model and marking dictionaries for sea surface meteorological data in XML*. In *Proc. ICNC-FSKD*, Huangshan, China. 10.1109/FSKD.2016.7603519

Batsakis, S., & Petrakis, E. G. M. (2010). SOWL: spatio-temporal representation, reasoning and querying over the semantic web. In *Proc. I-SEMANTICS*, Graz, Austria. 10.1145/1839707.1839726

Batsakis, S., & Petrakis, E. G. M. (2011). Representing Temporal Knowledge in the Semantic Web: The Extended 4D Fluents Approach. In Combinations of intelligent methods and applications (4th ed., Vol. 8, pp. 55-69). Springer.

Batsakis, S., & Petrakis, E. G. M. (2011). SOWL: a framework for handling spatio-temporal information in OWL 2.0. In *International Workshop on Rules and Rule Markup Languages for the Semantic Web* (6th ed., Vol. 6826, pp. 242-249). Springer. 10.1007/978-3-642-22546-8_19

Brodt, A., Nicklas, D., & Mitschang, B. (2010). Deep integration of spatial query processing into native RDF triple stores. In *Proc. ACM SIGSPATIAL*, San Jose, CA, USA. 10.1145/1869790.1869799

Chakkarwar, V. A., Professor, A., & Joshi, A. A. (2016). Semantic Web Mining using RDF Data. *International Journal of Computer Applications (0975 - 8887)*, 133FDLh (10), 14-19.

Chang, D. C., Dokos, S., & Lovell, N. H. (2011). Temporo-Spatial Model Construction Using the MML and Software Framework. *IEEE Transactions on Biomedical Engineering*, *58*(12), 3528–3531. doi:10.1109/TBME.2011.2168955 PMID:21947514

Cheng, H., & Ma, Z. (2017). f- ALL (D) - LTL: A Fuzzy Spatio-Temporal Description Logic. In *Proc. KSEM*, Melbourne, Australia.

Consoli, S. (2015). A Smart City Data Model based on Semantics Best Practice and Principles. In *Proc. WWW*, Florence, Italy, 1395-1400. 10.1145/2740908.2742133

Consortium, O. G. (2012). *OGC GeoSPARQL - A geographic query language for RDF data*. OGC Candidate Implementat. Stand.

Crouch, R., & Kalouli, A. L. (2018). Named Graphs for Semantic Representations. In Proc. *SEM@ NAACL-HLT, New Orleans, Louisiana, USA, 113-118. doi:10.18653/v1/S18-2013

Cui, Q., Wang, N. Z., & Haenggi, M. (2018). Vehicle distributions in large and small cities: Spatial models and applications. *IEEE Transactions on Vehicular Technology*, *67*(11), 10176–10189. doi:10.1109/TVT.2018.2865679

Dautov, R., & Distefano, S. (2018). *Semantic Web Languages for Policy Enforcement in the Internet of Things*. In *Proc. HCC*, Mérida, Mexico. 10.1007/978-3-319-74521-3_21

de Farias, T. M., Roxin, A., & Nicolle, C. (2016). SWRL rule-selection methodology for ontology interoperability. *Data & Knowledge Engineering*, *105*, 53–72. doi:10.1016/j.datak.2015.09.001

Debruyne, C., & O'Sullivan, D. (2017). *Client-side Processing of GeoSPARQL Functions with Triple Pattern Fragments*. Presented at the 26th WWW, Perth, Australia.

Di, X., Wang, J., Cheng, S., & Bai, L. (2019). Pattern Match Query for Spatiotemporal RDF Graph. In *The International Conference on Natural Computation, Fuzzy Systems and Knowledge Discovery* (pp. 532-539). Berlin, Germany: Springer.

Elzein, N. M., Majid, M. A., Fakherldin, M., & Hashem, I. A. T. (2018). Distributed Join Query Processing for Big RDF Data. *Advanced Science Letters*, *24*(10), 7758–7761. doi:10.1166/asl.2018.13013

Fossati, M., Dorigatti, E., & Giuliano, C. (2018). N-ary relation extraction for simultaneous T-Box and A-Box knowledge base augmentation. *Semantic Web*, *9*(4), 413–439. doi:10.3233/SW-170269

Gutierrez, C., Hurtado, C., & Vaisman, A. (2005). *Temporal RDF*. In *Proc. ESWC*, Heraklion, Greece.

Hernández, D., Hogan, A., & Krötzsch, M. (2015). Reifying RDF: What Works Well With Wikidata? In *Proc. ISWC*, Bethlehem, PA, USA, 32-47.

Ho, L. T., Arch-int, S., & Arch-int, N. (2017). Introducing Fuzzy Temporal Description Logic. In *Proc. ICIBE*, Sapporo, Japan.

Hoffart, J., Fabian, M. S., Berberich, K., & Weikum, G. (2013). YAGO2: A spatially and temporally enhanced knowledge base from Wikipedia. *Artificial Intelligence*, *194*, 28–61. doi:10.1016/j.artint.2012.06.001

Jiang, Z. (2020). Spatial Structured Prediction Models: Applications, Challenges, and Techniques. *IEEE Access : Practical Innovations, Open Solutions*, *8*, 38714–38727. doi:10.1109/ACCESS.2020.2975584

Kim, D. H., Ryu, K. H., & Kim, H. S. (2000). A spatiotemporal database model and query language. *Journal of Systems and Software*, *55*(2), 129–149. doi:10.1016/S0164-1212(00)00066-2

Koubarakis, M., & Kyzirakos, K. (2010). *Modeling and Querying Metadata in the Semantic Sensor Web: The Model stRDF and the Query Language stSPARQL*. In *Proc. ESWC*, Heraklion, Greece. 10.1007/978-3-642-13486-9_29

Li, C., Huang, J., Wang, B., Zhou, Y., Bai, Y., & Chen, Y. (2019). Spatial-Temporal Correlation Prediction Modeling of Origin-Destination Passenger Flow Under Urban Rail Transit Emergency Conditions. *IEEE Access : Practical Innovations, Open Solutions*, *7*, 162353–162365. doi:10.1109/ACCESS.2019.2951604

Lieberman, J., Singh, R., & Goad, C. (2007). W3c geospatial vocabulary. *Incubator group report*. W3C.

Lu, X., Hu, T., & Yin, F. (2019). A novel spatiotemporal fuzzy method for modeling of complex distributed parameter processes. *IEEE Transactions on Industrial Electronics*, *66*(10), 7882–7892. doi:10.1109/TIE.2018.2877118

Lutz, C., Wolter, F., & Zakharyashev, M. (2008). *Temporal Description Logics: A Survey*. In *Proc. TIME*, Montreal, Canada, 3-14.

Mandya, A., Bollegala, D., Coenen, F., & Atkinson, K. (2018). *Combining Long Short Term Memory and Convolutional Neural Network for Cross-Sentence n-ary Relation Extraction*. Department of Computer Science.

McBride, B. (2004). The resource description framework (RDF) and its vocabulary description language RDFS. In *Handbook on ontologies* (pp. 51–65). Springer Berlin Heidelberg. doi:10.1007/978-3-540-24750-0_3

Nikitopoulos, P., Vlachou, A., Doulkeridis, C., & Vouros, G. A. (2021). Parallel and scalable processing of spatio-temporal RDF queries using Spark. *GeoInformatica*, *25*(4), 623–653. doi:10.1007/s10707-019-00371-0

Peng, N., Poon, H., Quirk, C., Toutanova, K., & Yih, W. (2017). Cross-Sentence N-ary Relation Extraction with Graph LSTMs. *Transactions of the Association for Computational Linguistics*, *5*, 5. doi:10.1162/tacl_a_00049

Pfoser, D., & Tryfona, N. (2008). The Use of Ontologies in Location-based Services: The Space and Time Ontology in Protégé. *Research Academic Computer Technology Institute. Research Unit*, *3*, 15.

Pugliese, A., Udrea, O., & Subrahmanian, V. S. (2008). *Scaling RDF with Time*. In *Proc. WWW*, Beijing, China.

Qian, J., Li, X., Zhang, C., Chen, L., Jung, T., & Han, J. (2019). Social network de-anonymization and privacy inference with knowledge graph model. *IEEE Transactions on Dependable and Secure Computing*, *16*(4), 679–692. doi:10.1109/TDSC.2017.2697854

Song, Q., Wu, Y., Lin, P., Dong, L. X., & Sun, H. (2018). Mining Summaries for Knowledge Graph Search. *IEEE Transactions on Knowledge and Data Engineering*, *29*(10), 1887–1900. doi:10.1109/TKDE.2018.2807442

Takama, Y., & Hattori, S. (2007). Mining association rules for adaptive search engine based on RDF technology. *IEEE Transactions on Industrial Electronics*, *54*(2), 790–796. doi:10.1109/TIE.2007.891650

Tappolet, J., & Bernstein, A. (2009). Applied Temporal RDF: Efficient Temporal Querying of RDF Data with SPARQL. In *Proc. ESWC*, Heraklion, Greece. 10.1007/978-3-642-02121-3_25

Tong, Q. (2018). Mapping object-oriented database models into RDF (S). *IEEE Access : Practical Innovations, Open Solutions*, *6*, 47125–47130. doi:10.1109/ACCESS.2018.2867152

Tran, B. H., Plumejeaud-Perreau, C., & Bouju, A. (2018). A Web Interface for Exploiting Spatio-Temporal Heterogeneous Data. *Web and Wireless Geographical Information Systems*, 118-129.

Treur, J. (2018). Network Reification as a Unified Approach to Represent Network Adaptation Principles within a Network. In *International Conference on Theory and Practice of Natural Computing*. ACM. 10.1007/978-3-030-04070-3_27

Vaisman, A., & Chentout, K. (2019). Mapping Spatiotemporal Data to RDF: A SPARQL Endpoint for Brussels. *ISPRS International Journal of Geo-Information*, *8*(8), 353. doi:10.3390/ijgi8080353

Velayutham, V., Chandrasekaran, S., & Mohan, S. (2018). Web user interface based on OGC standards for sensor cloud using big data. *International Journal of Communication Networks and Distributed Systems*, *20*(4), 389. doi:10.1504/IJCNDS.2018.092143

Vlachou, A., Doulkeridis, C., Glenis, A., Santipantakis, G. M., & Vouros, G. A. (2019). *Efficient spatio-temporal RDF query processing in large dynamic knowledge bases*. In *Proc. SAC*, Limassol, Cyprus. 10.1145/3297280.3299732

Wang, D., Zou, L., & Zhao, D. (2014). gst-Store: An Engine for Large RDF Graph Integrating Spatio-temporal Information. Presented at the 17th EDBT, Athens, Greece, March 24-28.

Wang, J., Di, X., Liu, J., & Bai, L. (2019). *A Constraint Framework for Uncertain Spatiotemporal Data in RDF Graphs*. In *The International Conference on Natural Computation, Fuzzy Systems and Knowledge Discovery*, Berlin, Germany, 727-735.

Wangni, J. (2017). Stochastic Orthant-Wise Limited-Memory Quasi-Newton Method. *Clinical Orthopaedics and Related Research.*

Watkins, E. R., & Nicole, D. A. (2006). Named Graphs as a Mechanism for Reasoning About Provenance. In Proc. APWeb, Harbin, China, 943-948. doi:10.1007/11610113_99

Wlodarczyk, T. W., Rong, C., O'Connor, M., & Musen, M. (2011). SWRL-F: a fuzzy logic extension of the semantic web rule language. In *Proc. WIMS*, Sogndal, Norway. 10.1145/1988688.1988735

Xu, L., Wong, A., & Clausi, D. A. (2017). A Novel Bayesian Spatial–Temporal Random Field Model Applied to Cloud Detection From Remotely Sensed Imagery. *IEEE Transactions on Geoscience and Remote Sensing*, *55*(9), 4913–4924. doi:10.1109/TGRS.2017.2692264

Zhang, F., Wang, K., Li, Z., & Cheng, J. (2019). Temporal Data Representation and Querying Based on RDF. *IEEE Access : Practical Innovations, Open Solutions*, *7*, 85000–85023. doi:10.1109/ACCESS.2019.2924550

Zhang, X., Yang, Q., Ding, J., & Wang, Z. (2020). Entity Profiling in Knowledge Graphs. *IEEE Access : Practical Innovations, Open Solutions*, *8*, 27257–27266. doi:10.1109/ACCESS.2020.2971567

Zhu, L., Li, N., & Bai, L. (2020). Algebraic operations on spatiotemporal data based on RDF. *ISPRS International Journal of Geo-Information*, *9*(2), 80. doi:10.3390/ijgi9020080

Zhu, L., Li, N., Bai, L., Gong, Y., & Xing, Y. (2020). stRDFS: Spatiotemporal Knowledge Graph Modeling. *IEEE Access : Practical Innovations, Open Solutions*, *8*, 129043–129057. doi:10.1109/ACCESS.2020.3008688

Chapter 2
Algebraic Operations on Spatiotemporal RDF Data

ABSTRACT

The algebraic approach has been proven to be an effective way to process queries, and algebraic operations in RDF have been investigated extensively. However, the study of spatiotemporal RDF algebra has just started and still needs further attention. This chapter aims to explore an algebraic operational framework to represent the content of spatiotemporal data and support RDF graphs. The authors define a spatiotemporal data model based on RDF. On this basis, the spatiotemporal semantics and the spatiotemporal algebraic operations are investigated. The authors define five types of graph algebras. The filter operation can filter the spatiotemporal graphs using a graph pattern. Besides this, they put forward a spatiotemporal RDF syntax specification to help users browse, query, and reason with spatiotemporal RDF graphs. The syntax specification illustrates the filter rules, which contribute to capturing the spatiotemporal RDF semantics and provides a number of advanced functions for building data queries.

1 INTRODUCTION

The Resource Description Framework (RDF) (Brickley et al, 1998) was originally designed as a metadata model to publish or exchange data on the Semantic Web, and has since become the W3C standard. Recently, it has been used as a general method for conceptual description, and some researchers have started to focus on spatiotemporal data modeling and algebraic operations.

Towards spatiotemporal data modeling, there have been some achievements in representing spatiotemporal entities, such as a temporal data model (Crouch & Kalouli, 2018; Cheng et al., 2020; Batsakis & Petrakis, 2011; Artale & Franconi, 2005), a spatial data model (Reed et al., 2015), and a spatiotemporal data model (Kim et al., 2016). In previous studies on temporal data modeling, Tappolet et al. (Tappolet & Bernstein, 2009) present a syntax and storage format based on named graphs to express a temporal RDF. Due to the fact that all entities can be linked with relations through labels, Hernández et al. (Hernández et al., 2015) put forward an approach that adds temporal qualifiers and values to the RDF model representation in the form of labels. In this approach, the RDF triples are expanded into a

DOI: 10.4018/978-1-6684-9108-9.ch002

five-tuple (s, p, o, q, v), where (s, p, o) refers to the primary relation, q is the temporal qualifier property, and v is the temporal qualifier value. Besides this, there are some models that add temporal labels to RDF triples to form quads (Tappolet & Bernstein, 2009; Gutierrez et al., 2006). In addition to temporal models, there are some studies about spatial RDF modeling. For example, GeoRDF (Consoli et al., 2015) is an RDF-compatible profile for describing geometric information (points, lines, and polygons). In GeoRDF, GeoMetadataOverSvg is the geographic information notation, which plays a significant role in the spatial data connection of the Semantic Web. Benefiting from that, GeoRDF can be used to represent any point on the Earth. Regarding spatiotemporal data, the structured spatiotemporal RDF was first proposed by Koubarakis et al. (Koubarakis & Kyzirakos, 2010). It develops the stRDF data model based on RDF and puts forward the stSPARQL query language. The contribution of stRDF is regulating the representation principle of spatiotemporal data in RDF and standardizing the spatiotemporal data querying. It can also be applied to several spatiotemporal-related applications (Sheng, 2019; Zhao et al., 2019; Huang et al., 2019). However, the spatial information fails to associate with temporal information in the stRDF model, which means that it has a weak ability to record dynamically changing data. When the knowledge graph is updated, the changes in spatiotemporal attribute values cannot be captured in time and lead to inconsistencies in the data. Moreover, it will probably return multiple results or errors when we query it for spatial information at a given time.

With the prompt development of RDF graph querying (Tappolet & Bernstein, 2009; Nikitopoulos et al., 2019), graph algebra has received widespread attention. It is the key to applying standard database-style optimization to queries. In previous studies, several different RDF algebras have been proposed by research groups coming from academia. Due to the lack of an RDF algebra, such query languages use APIs to describe their semantics, and optimization issues have been mostly neglected. To solve this problem, Frasincar et al. (Frasincar et al., 2004) propose RAL (an RDF algebra) as a reference mathematical study for RDF query languages. Robertson (Robertson, 2004)proposes an algebraic operation of triadic relations for the RDF. An important aspect of this algebra is an encoding of triples, which implements a kind of reification. Chen et al. (Chen et al., 2005) incorporate semantics that infer into query answering and propose an RDF algebra based on a layered RDF graph model. The matrix algebra method MAGiQ was put forward by Jamour et al. (Jamour et al., 2018). MAGiQ represents an RDF graph as a sparse matrix, and translates SPARQL queries to matrix algebra programs, which takes advantage of the existing software infrastructure to process sparse matrices and is optimized for many architectures (e.g., central processing units (CPUs), graphical processing units (GPUs), and distributed architectures) effortlessly. On the basis of previous work, Thakkar et al. (Thakkar et al., 2017) consolidate existing graph algebra operators from the literature and propose two new traversal operators in an integrated graph algebra. Although researchers have proposed a lot of algebraic methods to assist with RDF queries, these methods or models cannot support spatiotemporal RDF queries. Therefore, it is necessary to develop a relatively complete spatiotemporal RDF graph algebra.

Motivated by such an observation, in this chapter, we study algebraic operations and a spatiotemporal syntax specification based on the RDF. We: (i) present a general algebraic operational framework for manipulating spatiotemporal data, which can represent the content of data more clearly and support spatiotemporal RDF graphs specifically; and (ii) propose a spatiotemporal RDF syntax specification. It will be of great benefit to query explicit spatiotemporal RDF data and capture spatiotemporal RDF semantics.

The remainder of this chapter is organized as follows. Section 2 presents related work. In Section 3, spatiotemporal algebraic operations based on the RDF are proposed. Section 4 explores the spatiotemporal RDF syntax specification, and Section 5 presents our conclusions and future work.

2 RELATED WORK

As it contributes a lot to optimizing queries, algebra has been identified as a core operation in querying. The research results that are presented in this section mainly include works about spatiotemporal algebra and the algebra of RDF graphs.

2.1 Algebra for Spatiotemporal Data

With the emergence of a large amount of spatiotemporal data, researchers began to devote themselves to the study of spatiotemporal algebra. To support spatial features, Córcoles et al. (Córcoles & González, 2001) present the Geography Markup Language (GML) based on XML. It inherits the interoperability of the XML and allows for the exchange of geographic information on the Web, and an extension to algebraic operations is provided on the basis of GML and a query language. Towards temporal data, Pan et al. (Pan & Hobbs, 2005) represent temporal aggregates in OWL-Time, and propose a systematic way of mapping iCalendar recurrence sets to OWL-Time temporal sequences. Baratis et al. (Baratis et al., 2009) propose a four-dimensional (4D)-Fluent representation that represents temporal information in OWL, where concepts varying in time are represented as 4D objects, and put forward the TOQL query language. Batsakis et al. (Batsakis & Petrakis, 2011) enhance this approach with qualitative temporal expressions allowing for the representation of temporal intervals with unknown starting and ending points by means of their relation (e.g., "before" and "after") to other time intervals. To handle qualitative temporal relationships and the extended 4D-Fluent representation, they also extend the TOQL query language. In (Moffitt & Stoyanovich, 2017), Moffitt et al. combine advances in graph databases and temporal relational databases. Then, they propose an algebra called TGA that adheres to point-based semantics. TGA includes principled temporal generalizations of conventional graph operators as well as novel operators that support exploratory analysis of evolving graphs at different levels of temporal and structural granularity. Aiming to perform operations over spatiotemporal data, Perry et al. (Perry et al., 2009) study geospatial and temporal semantic analytics and Hakimpour et al. (Hakimpour et al., 2009) present practical approaches to data processing in space, time, and theme dimensions using existing Semantic Web technologies. Perry et al. (Perry et al., 2011) devise SPARQL-ST to support spatiotemporal queries based on SPARQL. Bai et al. (Bai & Xu, 2015) develop an algebra based on Native XML to manipulate spatiotemporal XML data. In this work, the logical structure of a spatiotemporal database, data type systems, and querying operations were investigated. Bai et al. (Bai & Zhu, 2019) deal with fuzzy information and propose an algebra for fuzzy spatiotemporal data in XML.

2.2 Algebra of RDF Graphs

There is a rich set of studies on RDF graph algebra. For instance, an algebraic operation of triadic relations for RDF is introduced in (Robertson, 2004). Jamour et al. (Jamour et al., 2018) propose a matrix algebra method to answer RDF graph queries. Frasincar et al. (Frasincar et al., 2004) propose a prototype of an RDF algebra, including three types of operations: the first is the extraction operation, the second is the loop operation, and the third is the model construction operation. However, RAL does not support RDF graph structure queries. Chen et al. (Chen et al., 2005) introduce a set of operations for manipulating RDF graphs and an RDF query algebra (LAGAR) is proposed. LAGAR includes four operations: pattern-matching operations, construction operations, graphics set operations, and related functional operations, and this algebra optimizes RDF graph model matching operations. The use of a relational algebra for SPARQL query processing is investigated in (Cyganiak, 2005), in which the transformation from SPARQL into an abstract relational algebra is presented and the differences between the semantics of SPARQL and that of the relational model are discussed. GeoSPARQL (Perry & Herring, 2012) attempts to unify data access for the geospatial Semantic Web. Battle et al. (Battle & Kolas, 2011; Battle & Kolas, 2012) describe the motivation for GeoSPARQL and the implementation of GeoSPARQL. In order to better manage fuzzy data, Zuo et al. (Zuo et al., 2019) introduce a picture fuzzy graph based on a picture fuzzy relation, and describe the utility of the picture fuzzy graph. Ma et al. (Ma, 2018) put forward a fuzzy RDF model. In addition, a fuzzy RDF algebra is formally proposed and a set of algebraic operations is developed. To rewrite algebra expressions in a form that satisfies certain needs, they also present some algebraic equivalences based on a data graph isomorphism. Because the interval type 2 fuzzy set (IT2FS) increases the number of degrees of freedom to express uncertainty in the edge weight and has a greater capacity to describe fuzzy information in a logically correct manner, Dey et al. (Dey et al., 2019) propose the minimum spanning tree problem with an undirected connected weighted interval type 2 fuzzy graph (FMST-IT2FS), which can be used to optimize the query of fuzzy RDF graphs. Besides this, several RDF graph algebras are proposed to deal with specific domains, such as querying a large-scale distributed triple-store system (Nitta & Savnik, 2014) and optimizing RDF graph pattern matching in MapReduce (Ravindra et al., 2011).

In recent years, some query methods based on the spatiotemporal RDF have been developed, including stSPARQL (Koubarakis & Kyzirakos, 2010), SPARQL-ST (Perry et al., 2011), g^{st}-store (Wang et al., 2017), and ST-SPARQL (Lee et al., 2015). Koubarakis et al. (Koubarakis & Kyzirakos, 2010) propose the query language stSPARQL, which is an extension of SPARQL. Compared with SPARQL, it has the ability to query spatiotemporal attributes. The main statements are the *SELECT* statement, the *Filter* statement, and the *Having* statement. Since stRDF cannot dynamically connect spatiotemporal data, it is difficult to use stSPARQL to query large-scale dynamic spatiotemporal data. Perry et al. (Perry et al., 2011) describe a framework built over the RDF metadata model for analysis of thematic, spatial, and temporal relationships between named entities, and then present a formal syntax and semantics for SPARQL-ST based on the formalization of the SPARQL syntax given by (Perez et al., 2006). In addition, Perry et al. (Perry et al., 2015) also give an overview of GeoSPARQL's implementation in Oracle Spatial and Graph and show how to load, index, and query spatial RDF data. Wang et al. (Wang et al., 2017) present a spatiotemporal-information-integrated RDF data management system called g^{st}-Store and introduce a spatiotemporal query language that extends the SPARQL language with spatiotemporal assertions to query spatiotemporal-information-integrated RDF data. In (Lee et al., 2015), the authors put forward a spatiotemporal data type that adds spatial data on Geo-ontology to temporal data. They suggest that it should be applied in ST-OW because using the ST-ontology, which has been added to the temporal data in the semantic Web service, will make available new information for various inferences and queries.

However, the algebraic operations of the abovementioned RDF graph are mainly used for the traditional RDF dataset, which cannot handle a complex spatiotemporal RDF dataset. Therefore, this chapter aims to extend the traditional RDF graph operation and establish an RDF graph algebra for spatiotemporal data.

3 SPATIOTEMPORAL RDF SEMANTICS AND GRAPH ALGEBRA

In this section, we explore the spatiotemporal RDF semantics and graph algebra of spatiotemporal knowledge graphs.

3.1 Spatiotemporal RDF Semantics

In the following, we further study the semantics of the spatiotemporal RDF. Before that, we propose a spatiotemporal RDF model called stRDFS. stRDFS is defined as follows:

Definition 1. Given a URI set R, an empty vertex set B, a text description set K, a temporal data set I, and a spatial data set S, an stRDFS expression is g $(s, p: <t, l>, o)$, where:

- s is a resource name and $s \in R \cup B$.
- p is a property name and $p \in R$.
- is a value and $o \in R \cup B \cup K \cup I \cup S$.
- $t \in I$ is temporal data.
- $l \in S$ is spatial data.

In Definition 1, to solve the problem of data inconsistencies in stRDF, we add spatial labels and temporal labels to the predicate to associate spatial data with temporal data to form a spatiotemporal predicate p. When spatiotemporal data change, spatiotemporal attributes associated with them will change as well.

Definition 2. Given an stRDFS expression g $(s, p: <t, l>, o)$, $U = \{f_{s\text{-}o}, f_{s\text{-}t}, f_{s\text{-}l}, f_{p\text{-}t}, f_{p\text{-}l}\}$ is a mapping set of g, the value range of mapping $f_{x\text{-}y}$ is denoted as *Range* $(f_{x\text{-}y})$, *where Range* $(f_{x\text{-}y}) = y$, and an stRDFS graph for g is a labeled graph G (V, E, F, λ, T, L), where:

- $V = s \cup Range\ (U)$ is the set of vertexes.
- $E = \{(r, r')\}$ is the set of edges from r to r', where $\forall r, r' \in V$.
- $F\ (r, r') = \{f \mid (r, f: <t, l>, r') \in G\}$ is the set of mappings of E, where $\forall r, r' \in V^*$.
- is the set of labels given by vertexes or edges.
- $T \in Range\ (f_{s\text{-}t} \cup f_{p\text{-}t})$.
- $L \in Range\ (f_{s\text{-}l} \cup f_{p\text{-}l})$.

In Definition 2, f is a mapping relationship. $f_{s\text{-}o}$ represents the mapping, whose function is expressed as an attribute name, from s to o. The mapping $f_{s\text{-}t}$ indicates that s is linked with temporal data, and the formed triple is (s, p, t). In (s, p, t), the property represents "temporal information" and the attribute value t represents temporal data. The mapping $f_{s\text{-}l}$ indicates that s is linked with spatial data and the expression is (s, p, l). In the triple, the attribute represents "spatial information" and the attribute value l represents spatial data. The mapping $f_{p\text{-}t}$ indicates that p is linked with temporal data and combines with the other mappings to form an stRDFS tuple. When $f_{p\text{-}t}$ is combined with $f_{s\text{-}o}$, the formed tuple is $(s, p: t, o)$, indicating that the temporal data describe the valid time of (s, p, o). When $f_{p\text{-}t}$ is combined with $f_{s\text{-}t}$, the formed tuple is $(s, p: t_2, t_1)$, indicating that the valid time of s is t_1, and the valid time of the tuple (s, p, t_1) is t_2. When $f_{p\text{-}t}$ is combined with $f_{s\text{-}l}$, a tuple $(s, p: t, l)$ is formed, indicating that s is linked with spatial data l, and the valid time of tuple $(s, p: t, l)$ is t. The mapping $f_{p\text{-}l}$ represents that p is linked with spatial data and combines with other mappings to form an stRDFS tuple. When $f_{p\text{-}l}$ is combined with $f_{s\text{-}o}$, the formed tuple is (*s*, *p: l, o*), indicating that the spatial data *l* describes (*s, p, o*). When f_{p-l} is combined with f_{s-t}, the formed tuple is (*s, p: l, t*), indicating that the valid time of *s* is *t*, and the spatial data of (*s*, *p*, *t*) is *l*. When f_{p-l} is combined with f_{s-l}, a tuple (*s*, *p*: l_2, l_1) is formed, indicating that *s* is linked with the spatial data of l_1, and the spatial data of (*s*, *p*, l_1) is l_2. The mapping f_{p-o} is illegal. The f_{o-t} and f_{o-l} logically represent the temporal data and spatial data of *o*, respectively. In the stRDFS structure, f_{o-t} and f_{o-l} are converted into f_{s-t} and f_{s-l}, and they can appear as separate tuple mappings. For instance, (s_1, *p*, *o: t*) can be converted into two tuples (s_1, p_1, *o*) and (s_2, p_2, *t*), where $s_2 = o$ and p_2 represents "temporal information". Similarly, (s_1, *p*, *o: l*) can be converted into two tuples (s_1, p_1, *o*) and (s_2, p_2, *l*), where $s_2 = o$ and p_2 represents "spatial information".

According to Definition 2, there are two cases. The first one is that stRDFS graph vertexes contain spatiotemporal information, in this case, T ∈ Range (fs-t) and L ∈ Range (fs-l), as shown in Figure 1(a). The second case is that the stRDFS graph edges contain spatiotemporal information, in this case, T ∈ Range (fp-t) and L ∈ Range (fp-l), as shown in Figure 1(b).

Figure 1. Representation of spatiotemporal information in an stRDFS graph.

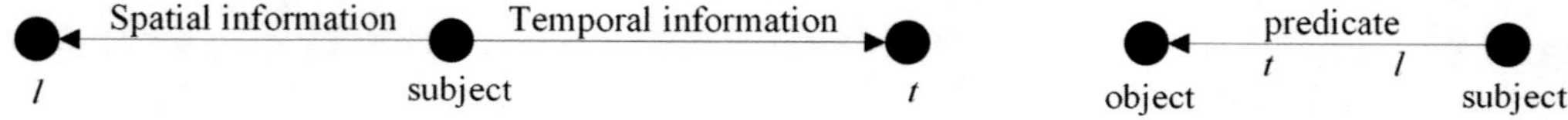

Definition 3. Given two stRDFS graphs G1 and G2, the implication relation of G1 and G2 is as follows:

- When G1, G2 are stRDFS basis graphs, G1 |= G2 only if G1 (Ti) |= G2 (Ti) and G1 (Si) |= G2 (Si).
- When G1, G2 are stRDFS graphs, G1 |= G2 only if μ1 (G1) for every base graph instance of G1, there exists a base graph instance μ2 (G2) of G2 and μ 1 (G1) |= μ2 (G2).

Here, |= denotes the implication relation and μ represents the mapping of entities to attribute values. The closure of figure G can be expressed as G'. ∪ (Si ∪ Ti) G (Si ∪ Ti) is the underlying stRDFS graph of the stRDFS graph G, the union of the graphs G (Si ∪ Ti), and the subgraphs of G.

Definition 4. Given an stRDFS graph G, the largest set and block closure are defined as follows.

- G' is the largest set on universe (G) that adds all RDF vocabularies, which can be expressed as tcl (G), where G ⊆ G' or G |=G'.
- The block closure of G is expressed as scl (G). It is a spatiotemporal RDF graph defined by ∪Si, Ti (cl(G (Si ∪ Ti)) Si, Ti, where cl(G (Si ∪ Ti) is an arbitrary closure of the RDF graph G(Si ∪ Ti).

Theorem 1. For two stRDFS graphs G1 and G2, a necessary and sufficient condition of G1 |= (Si ∪ Ti) G2 is that there is a mapping from G2 to scl (G1).

Proof of Theorem One

Sufficiency. Define μ as a mapping from G2 to scl(G1). μ1(G1) is an example of a base graph, such that μ2 = μ ○ μ1. We can obtain the conclusion that for any temporal function Ti and any spatial function Si, there is μ2G2 (Si ∪ Ti) ⊆ μ1(cl(G1)) (Si ∪ Ti) and ∀Si, ∀Ti, μ1(G1) (Si ∪ Ti) |= (Si ∪ Ti) μ2(G2) (Si ∪ Ti). Therefore, μ1(G1) |= (Si ∪ Ti) μ2(G2).

Necessity. Define μ1 as the mapping from any variable X in G1 to a different constant Cx. Make μ2(G2) an example of a basic graph, ∀Si, ∀Ti, μ1(G1) (Si ∪ Ti) |= (Si ∪ Ti) μ2(G2) (Si ∪ Ti). It is easy to see that ∀ Ti, ∀ Si, μ2G2 (Si ∪ Ti) ⊆ μ1(cl (G1)) (Si ∪ Ti). μ2G2 ⊆ ∪ (Si ∪ Ti) (cl (μ1 (G1) (Si ∪ Ti))) (Si ∪ Ti). Therefore, μ2 is a mapping from G2 to scl(G1).

Theorem 2. Given three stRDFS graphs A (VA, EA, FA, TA, LA), B (VB, EB, FB, TB, LB), and C (VC, EC, FC, TC, LC), an isomorphism from A to B is a bijective function h: VA → VB and it is an equivalence relation.

Proof of Theorem Two

Reflexivity. Consider the identity map h: V → V such that ∀s ∈ V, h(s) = s. h is a bijective mapping satisfying ∀s ∈ V, T(s) = T(h(s)), and L(s) = L(h(s)). Hence, h is an isomorphism of the spatiotemporal graph to itself. Therefore, it possesses reflexivity.

Symmetry. Consider the identity mapping h: VA → VB such that h (sA) = sB, sA ∈ VA satisfying TA (sA) = TB (h(sA)) and LA (sA) = LB (h(sA)). As h is bijective by h(sA) = sB, sA ∈ VA, then h-1(sB), ∀sB ∈ VB. Therefore, sA ∈ VA, TA (sA) = TB (h(sA)), then TA (h-1(sB)) = TB (sB) (∀sB ∈ VB). Additionally, sA ∈ VA, LA(sA) = LB(h(sA)), then LA (h-1(sB)) = LB(sB) (∀sB ∈ VB). Therefore, we obtain h-1: VB → VA, which is isomorphic from B to A.

Transitivity. Suppose that h1: VA → VB and h2: VB → VC are isomorphisms of A onto B and B onto C, respectively. As h1 is a bijective map h1 (sA) = sB, sA ∈ VA satisfies TA (sA) = TB (h(s A)), ∀ sA ∈ VA, and LA (sA) = LB (h(sA)). In the same way, h2 (sB) = sC, sB ∈ VB satisfies TB (sB) = TC (h(sB)), ∀sB ∈ VB, and LB (sB) = LC (h(sB)). From what has been discussed above, we draw the conclusion that TA (sA) = TB (sB) = TC (sC) and LA (sA) = LB (sB) = LC (sC).

Hence, h2 ○ h1 is an isomorphism between A and C. It satisfies transitivity.

In conclusion, the isomorphism between spatiotemporal RDF graphs is an equivalence relation.

3.2 Spatiotemporal Classes and Descriptions in the Spatiotemporal Domain

In order to introduce the stRDFS description more clearly, we introduce several main classes: strdfs: SpatialObject, strdfs: SpatialGeometry, strdfs: SpatialFeature, strdfs: TemporalObject, strdfs: TimeSlice, strdfs: TemporalFeature, strdfs: SpatiotemporalObject, strdfs: SpatiotemporalGeo, and strdfs: SemiLinearPointSet. Their relations are shown in Figure 2.

The class *strdfs: SpatialObject* represents a set of all entities with only spatial information. Its subclass *strdfs: SpatialGeometry* describes parameter *Si* in the stRDFS model (*s*, *p*: <*Ti*, *Si*>, *o*), including the data on latitude, longitude, and altitude, and the other subclass *strdfs: SpatialFeature* describes landform, terrain, and so on. The class *strdfs: TemporalObject* is a set of all entities that contain temporal data. Its subclass *strdfs: TimeSlice* describes parameter *Ti* in the stRDFS model (*s*, *p*: <*Ti*, *Si*>, *o*), and the other subclass *strdfs: TemporalFeature* includes other temporal data on temporal entities, such as a time zone,

Figure 2. The relations among the main stRDFS classes.

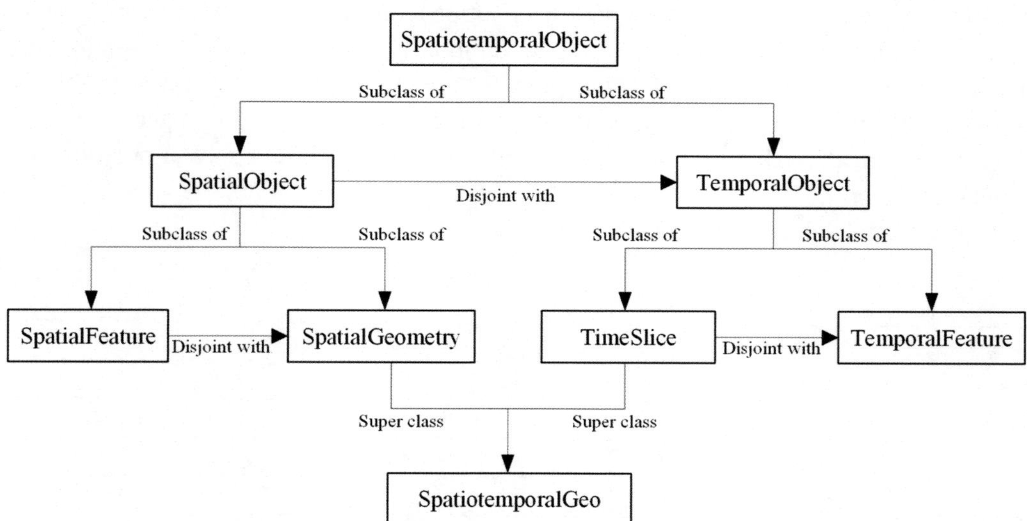

a tense, a time dimension, or the time of existence. The class *strdfs: SpatiotemporalObject* is a set of all spatiotemporal entities, which is a superset of *strdfs: TemporalObject* and *strdfs: SpatialObject.* The class *strdfs: SpatiotemporalGeo* describes geometric data of spatiotemporal entities and it is a superset of *strdfs: SpatialGeometry* and *strdfs: TimeSlice*. The class *strdfs: SemiLinearPointSet* is the set of rational numbers that represent time values, longitude values, latitude values, altitude values, etc.

For example, there is a large sonic receiver that calls corresponding programs to analyze sound waves after receiving them. The software class has the instances Program1 and Program2, whose types are JavaProgram and PythonProgram, respectively. The receiver class has the instances Receiver1 and Receiver2, and Receiver2's type is SoundWaveReceiver. We compare the stRDF model and the stRDFS model by describing the spatiotemporal information.

The stRDF model is as follows:

ex: program1	rdf: type	ex: JavaProgram
ex: program2	rdf: type	ex: PythonProgram
ex: program1	om: procedure	ex: CountProgram
ex: program2	om: procedure	ex: OutputProgram
ex: program1	om: hasPro1Call	ex: receiver2
ex: program2	om: hasPro2Call	ex: receiver2
ex: receiver2	rdf: type	ex: SoundWaveReceiver
ex: receiver2	ssn: measures	ex: sound
ex: receiver2	ssn: hasLocation	ex: location1
ex: location1	strdf: hasTrajectory	"(t = 8t and t = 18t or 9t ≤ t ≤ 14t) and k = 0t and ((20.9°N < L < 21°N and 45.8°E < D <= 46°E) or (L = 21°N and D = 46°E))" ^^ strdf: SemiLinearPointSet.

In the stRDF model, strdf: hasTrajectory describes the spatiotemporal data, which is considered to be the attribute value of strdf: hasTrajectory for Location1. In the stRDF model, only spatiotemporal data on whole entities can be recorded in the spatiotemporal dimension, while the spatiotemporal data on a certain part of the object cannot. For example, the stRDF model cannot represent the spatial data at t = 8t and record the temporal data when the object is in position (L = 21°N and D = 46°E). At the same time, if an attribute value changes at a certain time or in a certain spatial position, stRDF will record inaccurate data.

The stRDFS model solves this problem as follows:

ex: program1	rdf: type	ex: JavaProgram
ex: program2	rdf: type	ex: PythonProgram
ex: program1	om: procedure	ex: AnalysisProgram
ex: program2	om: procedure	ex: AnalysisProgram
ex: program1	om:hasPro1Call	ex: receiver2
ex: program2	om: hasPro2Call	ex: receiver2
ex: receiver2	rdf: type	ex: SoundWaveReceiver
ex: receiver2	ssn: measures	ex: sound
ex: receiver2	ssn: hasLocation1	ex: location1
ex: receiver2	ssn: hasLocation2	ex: location2
om: hasPro1Call	strdfs: SpatiotemporalGeo	"t = 8 t and t = 18t and k = 0t and (20.9°N < L < 21°N and 45.8°E < D <= 46°E)" ^^ strdfs: SemiLinearPointSet
om: hasPro2Call	strdfs: SpatiotemporalGeo	"9t ≤ t ≤ 14t and L = 21°N and D = 46°E and k = 0t" ^^ strdfs: SemiLinearPointSet
ssn: hasLocation1	strdfs: SpatialGeometry	"(20.9°N < L < 21°N and 45.8°E < D <= 46°E)" ^^ strdfs: SemiLinearPointSet
ssn: hasLocation2	strdfs: SpatialGeometry	"(L = 21°N and D = 46°E)" ^^ strdfs: SemiLinearPointSet

Table 1. Topological relations among spatiotemporal classes

Relation Name	Relation URI	Domain/Range
Equals	strdfs: geoEquals	strdfs: SpatialObject
Disjoint	strdfs: geoDisjoint	strdfs: SpatialObject
Meet	strdfs: geoMeet	strdfs: SpatialObject
Overlap	strdfs: geoOverlap	strdfs: SpatialObject
Covers	strdfs: geoCovers	strdfs: SpatialObject
CoveredBy	strdfs: geoCoveredBy	strdfs: SpatialObject
Inside	strdfs: geoInside	strdfs: SpatialObject
Contains	strdfs: geoContains	strdfs: SpatialObject
Before	strdfs: timBefore	strdfs: TemporalObject
Now	strdfs: timNow	strdfs: TemporalObject
After	strdfs: timAfter	strdfs: TemporalObject

At Location1, when t = 8t and t = 18t, the receiver calls Program1 to analyze the data. At Location2, when t ∈ [9t, 14t], the receiver calls Program2 to analyze the data. In the stRDFS model, spatiotemporal data are used to describe om: hasPro1Call and om: hasPro2Call, which facilitates the modification of common attribute values, such as program names. Based on this feature, the stRDFS model can represent spatiotemporal data and record changes in spatiotemporal attributes at any time or in any location.

We define 11 kinds of topological relations to describe the relations among spatiotemporal entities: *Equal*, *Disjoint*, *Meet*, *Overlap*, *Cover*, *CoveredBy*, *Inside*, *Contain*, *Before*, *Now*, and *After*. The corresponding domains are shown in Table 1.

3.3 Spatiotemporal RDF Graph Algebra

This subsection introduces five types of stRDFS graph algebras: union, intersection, difference, Cartesian product, and filter. In order to make these operations suitable for the model proposed in this chapter, we improve the union, intersection, difference, and Cartesian product operations to provide solutions when the relationship between two points does not necessarily exist and add a filter operation to meet the specified requirements. These stRDFS graph algebras are sufficient and can satisfy the known operations. We provide an example in Figure 3 to show the algebraic process for stRDFS graphs by the method proposed in this chapter.

Definition 5. Given two stRDFS graphs A (VA, EA, FA, TA, LA) and B (VB, EB, FB, TB, LB), the union of A and B is defined as A ∪ B = (V, E, F, T, L), where:

- V = VA ∪ VB
- E = EA ∪ EB
- F = FA ∪ FB
- ΠNT = ΠN TA ∪ ΠN TB
- ΠkT = min(ΠN TA, ΠN TB)
- L = LA ∪ LB.

In Definition 5, ΠN/k (x) represents the projection of x on N/k, where N = [ts(f), te(f)] is the valid time and k = tr(f) is the reference time recorded at present. In N= [ts(f), te(f)], ts(f) represents the start time of mapping fvi-vj, and te(f) represents the terminal time of mapping fvi-vj. min represents the minimum reference time. The stRDFS graph requires that the reference time in the temporal data for each edge and each node must be consistent. When the union operation is performed over two stRDFS graphs, the reference time of the two graphs must be consistent. For convenience of description, we uniformly selected the minimum reference time as the reference time of the resulting graph.

As shown in Figure 3, there are two stRDFS graphs (a) and (b), and we performed the union operation in Definition 5 to obtain the graph (c). The solid line indicates that the relationship between two points must exist, and the dotted line indicates that the relationship between the two points does not necessarily exist.

Definition 6. Given two stRDFS graphs A (VA, EA, FA, TA, LA) and B (VB, EB, FB, TB, LB), the intersection of A and B is defined as A ∩ B = (V, E, F, T, L), where:

- V= VA ∩ VB
- E = EA ∩ EB

- $F = FA \cap FB$
- $\Pi NT = \Pi N\ TA \cap \Pi N\ TB$
- $\Pi kT = \min (\Pi N\ TA, \Pi N\ TB)$
- $L = LA \cap LB$.

As shown in Figure 3, there are two stRDFS graphs (c) and (d), and we performed the intersection operation in Definition 6 to obtain the graph (e).

Definition 7. Given two stRDFS graphs A (VA, EA, FA, TA, LA) and B (VB, EB, FB, TB, LB), the difference of A and B is defined as A − B = (V, E, F, T, L), where:

- $E = EA - EB$
- V is the set of vertexes of E.
- F is the set of mappings of E.
- T is the temporal dataset of F.
- L is the spatial dataset of F.

However, the algebraic operations of the abovementioned RDF graph are mainly used for the traditional RDF dataset, which cannot handle a complex spatiotemporal RDF dataset. Therefore, this chapter aims to extend the traditional RDF graph operation and establish an RDF graph algebra for spatiotemporal data.

As shown in Figure 3, we can obtain graph (f) using Definition 7 with the difference of the two stRDFS graphs (d) and (a).

Figure 3. Algebraic operations of stRDFS graphs

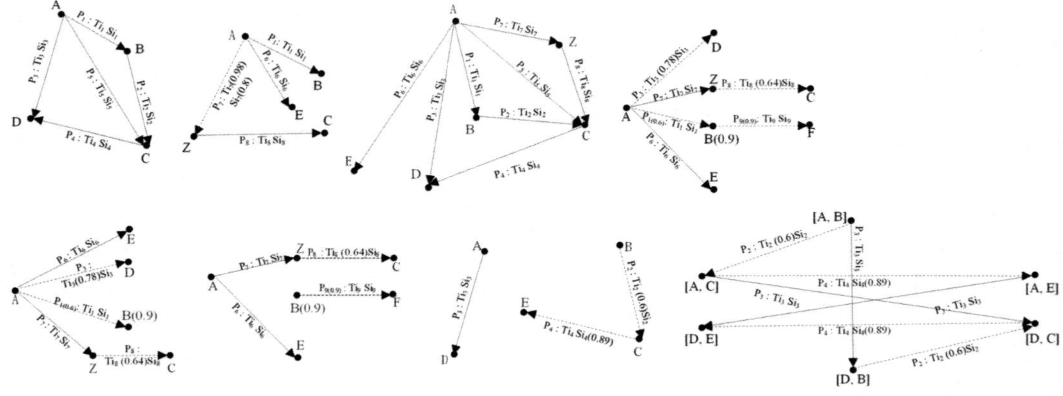

Definition 8. Given two stRDFS graphs A (VA, EA, FA, TA, LA) and B (VB, EB, FB, TB, LB), the Cartesian product of A and B is defined as A × B = (V, E, F, T, L), where:

- $V = VA \times VB$
- $E = \{(u, u2)(u, v2) \mid u \in VA, u2\ v2 \in EB\} \cup \{(u1, \omega)(v1, \omega) \mid \omega \in VB, u1\ v1 \in EA\}$

- F is the set of mappings of E.
- T is the temporal dataset of F.
- L is the spatial dataset of F.

There are two stRDFS graphs (g) and (h) in Figure 3. We can obtain graph (i) with their Cartesian product using Definition 8.

Theorem 3. Given two stRDFS graphs A (VA, EA, FA, TA, LA) and B (VB, EB, FB, TB, LB), we have the following.

- A ∪ B is an stRDFS graph.
- A ∩ B is an stRDFS graph.
- A − B is an stRDFS graph.
- A × B is an stRDFS graph.

Definition 9. (stRDFS graph pattern). An stRDFS graph pattern is defined as P = (VP, EP, FP, TP, LP, Re), where:

- VP is a finite set of vertexes.
- EP is a finite set of directed edges.
- Fp is the set of mappings of Ep.
- TP is a temporal dataset.
- LP is a spatial dataset.
- Re = {R1R2, R1|R2, R+, ε} is a set of filter rules describing Ep, where R represents a filter rule.

In practice, the stRDFS graph needs to be filtered according to certain rules so that the resulting graph meets the specified requirements. The stRDFS graph pattern described in Definition 9 represents the filter rules. In the program, the input is often filter rules and the stRDFS graph that needs to be processed, and the output is the resulting graph that satisfies specified requirements. According to the stRDFS graph filter rules, we can obtain the following conclusions: V_p is a vertex pattern abstracted from the rules and each vertex pattern corresponds to a set of vertexes in the filtered stRDFS graph. E_p is an abstraction of the attributes in the filter rules and each edge represents a type of edge of the stRDFS graph being filtered. F_p is an abstract collection of attribute names in the rule. T_p is the temporal dataset in the filter rules. Similarly, L_p is the spatial dataset in the filter rules. *Re* is regular expression and can have four forms: R_1R_2, $R_1|R_2$, R^+, and ε. R_1R_2 is a concatenation of expressions that represents that two rules are next to each other. $R_1|R_2$ is an alternative of expressions that represents that filtering can be done by meeting one of the two rules. R^+ denotes one or more occurrences of *R*. *ε* represents that there are no filter rules to filter stRDF graphs.

For example, consider an stRDFS graph pattern *P*, which models information concerning a writer (? *w*) who is born in *A* city, the fee for a book (? book) that the writer had written from 2016 to 2018 in *A* city, which is more than $10 (? *f* > $ 10), and the book's genre, which is comedy. *P* can be expressed in the form of Figure 4.

Using the stRDFS graph *G* shown in Figure 5, we performed the filter operation in Definition 9. The result of spatiotemporal filtering of *P* and *G* is shown in Figure 6.

Figure 4. The stRDFS graph pattern P

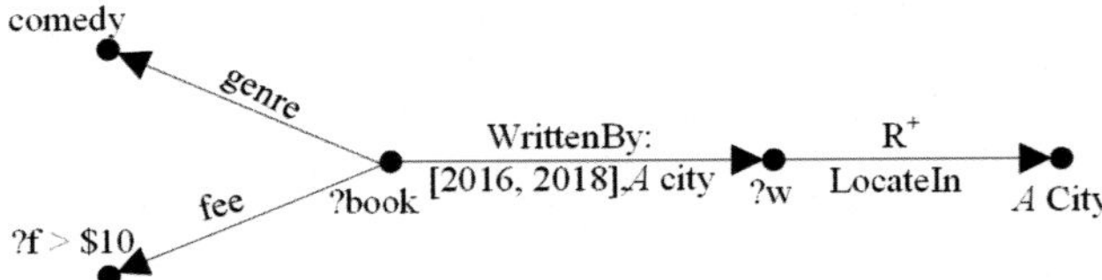

Figure 5. The stRDFS graph pattern G

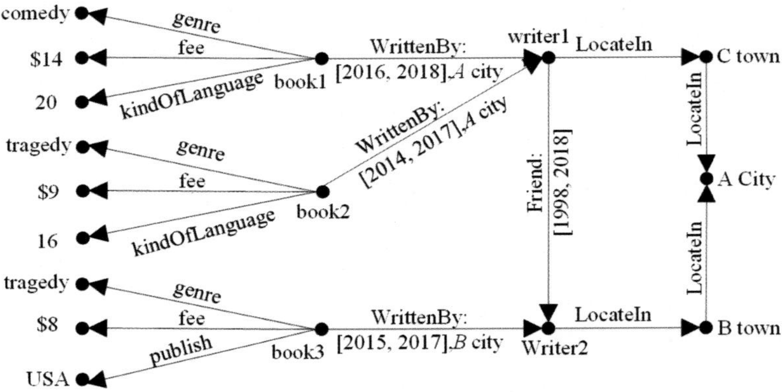

Figure 6. The result of performing the filter operation over P and G

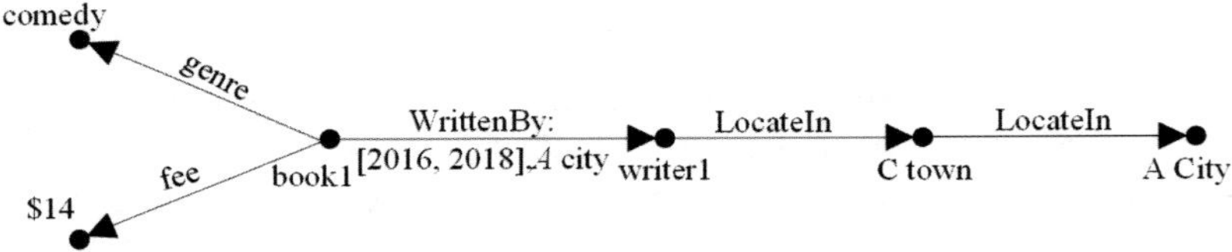

4 SPATIOTEMPORAL RDF SYNTAX SPECIFICATION

In the stRDFS model, we define several topological relations to describe the relations among spatiotemporal entities and introduce five types of stRDFS graph algebras. However, stSPASQL does not define corresponding functions to deal with spatiotemporal data queries. While the queries contain the operations we proposed, stSPASQL cannot meet the requirements of the queries and needs to be improved. To solve this problem, we specify a spatiotemporal RDF syntax on the basis of stSPASQL (Koubarakis & Kyzirakos, 2010). The syntax proposed in this subsection is similar to the SQL syntax, and it is designed so that stRDFS format datasets can be easily accessed. It also provides a number of advanced functions for building more expressive queries that illustrate other filter conditions and then format the final output. The overall structure of the syntax is similar to that of SQL, which has three main parts represented by the uppercase keywords SELECT, FROM, and WHERE.

- The keyword SELECT determines the specification of the query result. It is followed by the rest of the query: the list of identifiers of the query result.
- The keyword FROM specifies the query's scope, which is normally a spatiotemporal dataset or several stRDFS graphs.
- The keyword WHERE represents the actual query and is followed by the query criteria, which are given by a pattern that corresponds to some stRDFS graphs replaced by variables. More complicated patterns are also allowed to be formed with some algebraic operators. This mode can be used not only to query a single spatiotemporal dataset but also multiple spatiotemporal datasets.

Table 2. Spatiotemporal functions

Function	Type	Syntax format	Meaning
strdfs: distance	Spatial Function	FILTER (strdfs: distance(A, B))	Returns the shortest distance between A and B
strdfs: intersection		FILTER (strdfs: intersection (A, B))	Returns a geometric object that represents all points in the intersection of A and B
strdfs: union		FILTER (strdfs: union (A, B))	Returns a geometric object that represents all points in the union of A and B
strdfs: difference		FILTER (strdfs: difference (A, B))	Returns a geometric object that represents all points in the difference set of A and B
strdfs: spCartesian		FILTER (strdfs: spCartesian (A, B))	Returns a geometric object that represents all points in the Cartesian product set of A and B
strdfs: spfilter		FILTER (strdfs: spfilter (A, B))	Returns a geometric object that represents all points in the subgraph of A after filtering according to the pattern B
strdfs: spEquals		FILTER (strdfs: spEquals (?A, ?B))	The query result satisfies A = B
strdfs: spDisjoint		FILTER (strdfs: spDisjoint (?A, ?B))	The query result satisfies that A is disjoint with B
strdfs: spMeet		FILTER (strdfs: spMeet (?A, ?B))	The query result satisfies that A meets B
strdfs: spOverlap		FILTER (strdfs: spOverlap (?A, ?B))	The query result satisfies that A overlaps B
strdfs: spCovers		FILTER (strdfs: spCovers (?A, ?B))	The query result satisfies that A covers B
strdfs: spCoveredBy		FILTER (strdfs: spCoveredBy (?A, ?B))	The query result satisfies that A is covered by B
strdfs: spInside		FILTER (strdfs: spInside (?A, ?B))	The query result satisfies that A is inside B
strdfs: spContains		FILTER (strdfs: spContains (?A, ?B))	The query result satisfies that A contains B
strdfs:spEnvelope		FILTER (strdfs: spEnvelope (A))	Returns the minimum bounding box of A
strdfs: spBefore	Temporal Function	FILTER (strdfs: spBefore (?A, ?B))	The query result satisfies that A is earlier than B
strdfs: spNow		FILTER (strdfs: spNow (?A, ?B))	The query result satisfies that A and B are at the same time
strdfs: spAfter		FILTER (strdfs: spAfter (?A, ?B))	The query result satisfies that A is later than B

The function indicates the relations between the variables expressed by the FILTER statement, which is a part of the WHERE statement. In order to browse the spatiotemporal syntax, we define the spatial functions and temporal functions shown in Table 2.

In order to demonstrate the application of the proposed functions, we provide some examples. Examples 1, 2, and 3 represent queries of spatial data, temporal data, and spatiotemporal data, respectively.

Example 1. When we query the name and spatial data of a destroyed forest less than 0.1 km from a city, the syntax is as follows:

```
SELECT ?NAME ?FGEO
WHERE {
?R rdf: type noa: Region
?R strdfs: SpatialGeometry ?RGEO
?R noa: hasCorineLandCoverUse ?S
?S rdfs: subclassof clc: Forests
?C rdf: type dbpedia: City
?C strdfs: SpatialGeometry ?CGEO
?NAME rdf: type noa: DestroyedArea
?NAME strdfs: SpatialGeometry ?FGEO
FILTER(strdfs: spInside (?RGEO, ?FGEO) && strdfs: distance (?FGEO, ?CGEO) <
0.1))
}
```

The SELECT statement is followed by a list of the names of the results, namely: the region name and the spatial data on the region. The WHERE statement states the relations of the triples that need to be satisfied between the following variables: ?R indicates the area containing the forest ?F, ?C indicates the mentioned city, and ?NAME represents the mentioned destroyed forest. The FILTER statement represents the spatial function of spatial variables: strdfs: spInside (?RGEO, ?FGEO) represents that ?R is inside ?F and strdfs: distance (?FGEO, ?CGEO) < 0.1 represents that the shortest distance between ?F and ?C is less than 0.1 kilometers.

Example 2. When we query the temporal data in a program that is called simultaneously with a certain other program, the syntax is as follows:

```
SELECT ?P ?PTS
WHERE {
?P rdf: type ex: Program
?P om: hasProCallP ex: TimeSlice1
om: hasProCallP strdfs: TimeSlice ?PTS
?Q rdf:type ex: Program
?Q om: hasProCallQ ex: TimeSlice2
om: hasProCallQ strdfs: TimeSlice ?QTS
FILTER (strdfs: spNow (?PTS, ?QTS))
}
```

Since the program's name and the temporal data of the program are sought, the SELECT statement is followed by ?P and ?PTS, that is, the temporal information of ?P is ?PTS. FILTER (strdfs: spNow (?PTS, ?QTS)) represents that ?P and ?Q have the same temporal information.

Example 3. On the basis of the example in Section 3.2, when we query the name of the programs that are called by the sound wave receiver in the adjacent area and its spatiotemporal data, the syntax is as follows:

```
SELECT ?P ?PGT
WHERE {
?P rdf: type ex: Program
?P om: hasCallPBy ex: SoundWaveReceiver
om: hasCallPBy strdfs: SpatiotemporalGeo
?PGT (?PGEO, ?PTS)
?Q rdf:type ex: Program
?Q om: hasCallQBy ex: SoundWaveReceiver
om: hasCallQBy strdfs: SpatiotemporalGeo
?QGT (?QGEO, ?QTS)
FILTER (strdfs: spMeet (?PGEO, ?QGEO) && strdfs:spNow (?PTS, ?QTS))
}
```

Since the program's name and the spatiotemporal data of the program are sought, the SELECT statement is followed by ?P and ?PTS, that is, the spatiotemporal information of ?P is ?PGT. FILTER (strdfs: spMeet (?PGEO, ?QGEO) && strdfs: spNow (?PTS, ?QTS)} means that ?P meets ?Q and they have the same temporal information.

This chapter has a proposed spatiotemporal data model and the corresponding algebraic operations. A lot of missing or insufficient operations that do not exist in conventional models have also been put forward. Little related work on spatiotemporal RDF algebras has involved experimental results, so we consider only the theoretical feasibility of the proposed method in this chapter. However, there are several intermediate algebras for optimizing RDF graph pattern matching, and they were proposed from a matching or querying viewpoint, not the algebra viewpoint. As a result, we will continue to study the corresponding querying method in our future work.

5 SUMMARY

In this chapter, we explored a spatiotemporal RDF semantics and defined a spatiotemporal data model based on the RDF. Based on this model, we proposed algebraic operations for manipulating spatiotemporal RDF data. In our method, in contrast to previous works, filtering rules are contained in the algebraic operations so that the resulting graph meets the specified requirements. This algebra consists of a series of operations that make it possible to express the content of data and the structure of a spatiotemporal RDF graph. Furthermore, we also introduced a syntax specification for the spatiotemporal RDF, which may contribute to the study of spatiotemporal RDF querying in the future.

REFERENCES

Artale, A., & Franconi, E. (2005). Temporal Description Logics. Handbook of Temporal Reasoning in Artificial Intelligence, 1, 375-388.

Bai, L., & Xu, C. (2015). Spatiotemporal query algebra based on native XML. In L. Liu & M. T. Özsu (Eds.), *Handbook of Research on Innovative Database Query Processing Techniques* (pp. 275–293). IGI Global.

Bai, L., & Zhu, L. (2019). An Algebra for Fuzzy Spatiotemporal Data in XML. *IEEE Access : Practical Innovations, Open Solutions*, *7*, 22914–22926. doi:10.1109/ACCESS.2019.2898228

Baratis, E., Petrakis, E. G. M., Batsakis, S., Maris, N., & Papadakis, N. (2009). TOQL: Temporal ontology querying language. In *Proceedings of the International Symposium on Spatial and Temporal Databases* (pp. 338-354). Springer. 10.1007/978-3-642-02982-0_22

Batsakis, S., & Petrakis, E. G. M. (2011). Representing temporal knowledge in the semantic web: The extended 4d fluents approach. In H. S. Nguyen, A. M. Tjoa, E. Weippl, & E. J. Neuhold (Eds.), *Combinations of Intelligent Methods and Applications* (pp. 55–69). Springer. doi:10.1007/978-3-642-19618-8_4

Battle, R., & Kolas, D. (2011). Geosparql: Enabling a geospatial semantic web. *Semantic Web Journal*, *3*, 355–370. doi:10.3233/SW-2012-0065

Battle, R., & Kolas, D. (2012). Enabling the geospatial semantic web with parliament and geosparql. *Semantic Web*, *3*(4), 355–370. doi:10.3233/SW-2012-0065

Brickley, D., Guha, R. V., & Layman, A. (1998). *Resource description framework (RDF) schema specification*. W3C. http://www. w3. org/TR/PR-rdf-schema

Chen, L., Gupta, A., & Kurul, M. E. (2005). *A semantic-aware RDF query algebra*. In *Proceedings of the International Conference on Management of Data (COMAD)* (pp. 1-12). Hyderabad, India.

Cheng, H., Ma, Z., & Li, P. (2020). A fuzzy spatial description logic for the semantic web. *Journal of Ambient Intelligence and Humanized Computing*.

Consoli, S., Mongiovì, M., & Nuzzolese, A. G. (2015). *A smart city data model based on semantics best practice and principles*. In *Proceedings of the 24th International Conference on World Wide Web* (pp. 1395-1400). Italy. 10.1145/2740908.2742133

Córcoles, J. E., & González, P. (2001). A specification of a spatial query language over GML. In *Proceedings of the 9th ACM International Symposium on Advances in Geographic Information Systems*. Atlanta, GA, USA. 10.1145/512161.512186

Crouch, R., & Kalouli, A. L. (2018). *Named Graphs for Semantic Representations*. In *Proceedings of the 2nd Joint Workshop on Semantic Parsing and Semantic Analysis* (pp. 113-118). New Orleans, Louisiana, USA.

Cyganiak, R. (2005). *A relational algebra for SPARQL*. Digital Media Systems Laboratory HP Laboratories Bristol.

Dey, A., Pal, A., & Long, H. V. (2019). Fuzzy minimum spanning tree with interval type 2 fuzzy arc length: Formulation and a new genetic algorithm. *Soft Computing*, *23*, 1–12.

Frasincar, F., Houben, G. J., Vdovjak, R., & Barna, P. (2004). RAL: An algebra for querying RDF. *World Wide Web (Bussum)*, *7*(1), 83–109. doi:10.1023/B:WWWJ.0000015866.43076.06

Gutierrez, C., Hurtado, C. A., & Vaisman, A. (2006). Introducing time into RDF. *IEEE Transactions on Knowledge and Data Engineering*, *19*(2), 207–218. doi:10.1109/TKDE.2007.34

Hakimpour, F., Aleman-Meza, B., Perry, M., & Sheth, A. (2009). Spatiotemporal-thematic data processing for the semantic web. In A. G. Cohn, D. M. Mark, & A. R. Frank (Eds.), *The Geospatial Web* (pp. 79–89). Springer.

Hernández, D., Hogan, A., & Krötzsch, M. (2015). Reifying RDF: What Works Well With Wikidata? In *Proceedings of the 11th International Workshop on Scalable Semantic Web Knowledge Base Systems* (pp. 23-31). Bethlehem, PA, USA.

Huang, L., Hu, Y., Li, Y., Kishore Kumar, P. K., Koley, D., & Dey, A. (2019). A study of regular and irregular neutrosophic graphs with real-life applications. *Mathematics*, *7*(6), 551. doi:10.3390/math7060551

Jamour, F., Abdelaziz, I., & Kalnisk, P. (2018). A demonstration of magiq: matrix algebra approach for solving RDF graph queries. In *Proceedings of the VLDB Endowment* (pp. 1978-1981). Rio de Janeiro, Brazil. 10.14778/3229863.3236239

Kim, J. J., Shin, I. S., Lee, Y. S., & Moon, J.-Y. (2016). Spatio-Temporal Ontology Management Systems for Semantic Web. *Information (Basel)*, *19*, 4237–4254.

Koubarakis, M., & Kyzirakos, K. (2010). *Modeling and querying metadata in the semantic sensor web: The model stRDF and the query language stSPARQL.* In *Proceedings of the Extended Semantic Web Conference* (pp. 425-439). Crete, Greece. 10.1007/978-3-642-13486-9_29

Lee, K. S., Lee, K. Y., Kim, Y. H., Choi, J. J., & Jang, G. S. (2015). Spatio-Temporal Ontology for the Semantic Web. *International Information Institute (Tokyo). Information (Basel)*, *18*, 329–334.

Ma, Z., Li, G., & Yan, L. (2018). Fuzzy data modeling and algebraic operations in RDF. *Fuzzy Sets and Systems*, *351*, 41–63. doi:10.1016/j.fss.2017.11.013

Moffitt, V. Z., & Stoyanovich, J. (2017). *Temporal graph algebra.* In *Proceedings of the 16th International Symposium on Database Programming Languages* (pp. 10). Munich, Germany.

Nikitopoulos, P., Vlachou, A., Doulkeridis, C., & Vouros, G. A. (2019). Parallel and scalable processing of spatio-temporal RDF queries using Spark. *GeoInformatica*, *23*, 797–826.

Nitta, K., & Savnik, I. (2014). A Distributed Query Execution Method for RDF Storage Managers. In *Proceedings of the 10th International Workshop on Scalable Semantic Web Knowledge Base Systems* (pp. 7-18). Riva del Garda, Trentino, Italy.

Pan, F., & Hobbs, J. R. (2005). *Temporal Aggregates in OWL-Time.* In *Proceedings of the FLAIRS conference* (pp. 560-565). Clearwater Beach, Florida, USA.

Perez, J., Arenas, M., & Gutierrez, C. (2006). Semantics and complexity of SPARQL. In *Proceedings of the 5th International Semantic Web Conference* (pp. 30-43). Athens, GA, USA.

Perry, M., Estrada, A., Das, S., & Banerjee, J. (2015). *Developing GeoSPARQL Applications with Oracle Spatial and Graph*. In *Proceedings of the ISWC* (pp. 57-61). Bethlehem, Pennsylvania, USA.

Perry, M., Herring, J. (2012). OGC GeoSPARQL-A geographic query language for RDF data. *OGC Implement. Standard*, 40.

Perry, M., Jain, P., & Sheth, A. P. (2011). SPARQL-ST: Extending SPARQL to Support Spatiotemporal Queries. *Geospatial Semantics and the Semantic Web*, *12*, 61–86. doi:10.1007/978-1-4419-9446-2_3

Perry, M., Sheth, A., Arpinar, I. B., & Hakimpour, F. (2009). Geospatial and temporal semantic analytics. In *Handbook of Research on Geoinformatics* (pp. 161–170). IGI Global. doi:10.4018/978-1-59140-995-3.ch021

Ravindra, P., Kim, H. S., & Anyanwu, K. (2011). *An intermediate algebra for optimizing RDF graph pattern matching on MapReduce*. In *Proceedings of the Extended Semantic Web Conference* (pp. 46-61). Berlin, Germany. 10.1007/978-3-642-21064-8_4

Reed, T. W., Reitsma, F., & McMeekin, D. A. (2015). Browsing spatial knowledge with linked ontologies. In *2015 11th International Conference on Innovations in Information Technology (IIT)* (pp. 196-200). IEEE. 10.1109/INNOVATIONS.2015.7381539

Robertson, E. L. (2004). *Triadic relations: An algebra for the semantic web*. In *Proceedings of the International Workshop on Semantic Web and Databases* (pp. 63-77). Toronto, Canada.

Sheng, G. L., Su, Y. L., & Wang, W. D. (2019). A new fractal approach for describing induced-fracture porosity/permeability/compressibility in stimulated unconventional reservoirs. *Journal of Petroleum Science Engineering*, *179*, 855–866. doi:10.1016/j.petrol.2019.04.104

Tappolet, J., & Bernstein, A. (2009). *Applied temporal RDF: Efficient temporal querying of RDF data with SPARQL*. In *Proceedings of the European Semantic Web Conference* (pp. 308-322). Crete, Greece. 10.1007/978-3-642-02121-3_25

Thakkar, H., Punjani, D., Auer, S., & Vidal, M. E. (2017). Towards an integrated graph algebra for graph pattern matching with Gremlin. In *Proceedings of the International Conference on Database and Expert Systems Applications* (pp. 81-91). Lyon, France. 10.1007/978-3-319-64468-4_6

Wang, D., Zou, L., & Zhao, D. (2017). gst-store: Querying Large Spatiotemporal RDF Graphs. *Data and Information Management*, *1*(2), 84–103. doi:10.1515/dim-2017-0008

Zhao, H., Xu, L., Guo, Z., Liu, W., Zhang, Q., Ning, X., Li, G., & Shi, L. (2019). A new and fast waterflooding optimization workflow based on INSIM-derived injection efficiency with a field application. *Journal of Petroleum Science Engineering*, *179*, 1186–1200. doi:10.1016/j.petrol.2019.04.025

Zuo, C., Pal, A., & Dey, A. (2019). New Concepts of Picture Fuzzy Graphs with Application. *Mathematics*, *7*(5), 470. doi:10.3390/math7050470

Chapter 3
Pattern Match Query for Spatiotemporal RDF Data

ABSTRACT

RDF is designed to provide a common way of describing resources so that it can be read and understood by computer applications. In RDF model, the statement in the resource description may correspond to a natural language statement, the resource corresponds to the subject in the natural language, the attribute type corresponds to the predicate, and the attribute value corresponds to the object. Meanwhile, RDF information has temporal attribute and spatial attribute. But classical RDF model can't show the spatial and temporal properties of resources. So, combining spatiotemporal information with RDF is necessary. However, SPARQL, the W3C-recommended query language of RDF, only meets the classic RDF queries. This chapter presents a spatiotemporal RDF representation model. Based on this model, a find isomorphic graphs of the query graph algorithm is introduced to obtain some candidate isomorphic graph of the query graph. Finally, the authors define the process of pattern matching.

1 INTRODUCTION

RDF(Broekstra et al, 2002) refers to the Resource Description Framework, which is recommended as the W3C standard in February 2004 (Klyne & Carroll, 2006). RDF is designed to provide a common way of describing information. In RDF model, a statement is a triple (Yan et al., 2008), which consists of resources, attribute types, and attribute values, indicating an attribute of the resource.

At present, spatiotemporal data has been widely used in all aspects of human life, such as traffic monitoring (Zhang et al., 2003), GIS (Mennis & Fountain, 2001), climate change monitoring (Antonić et al., 2001) and so on. Nowadays, data forms and dimensions are increasingly diverse. Data is no longer confined to one-dimensional and two-dimensional space, and more and more data not only show temporal attributes, but also show spatial attributes.

Therefore, introducing spatiotemporal attributes to RDF is the general trend(Tan & Yan, 2017; Kuper et al., 2016; Vatsavai et al., 2012; Venkateswara, 2012). Some related works were discussed. Koubarakis et al. (Koubarakis & Kyzirakos, 2010) develop the data model stRDF and the query language stSPARQL.

DOI: 10.4018/978-1-6684-9108-9.ch003

Perry et al. (Perry et al., 2007) describe a framework built around the RDF metadata model for analysis of thematic, spatial and temporal relationships between named entities and present a set of semantic query operators. Perry et al. (Perry et al., 2011) present a SPARQL-ST query language, which is an extension of SPARQL for complex spatiotemporal queries, and describe an implementation of SPARQL-ST.

RDF graphs are composed of RDF triples. The growing popularity of RDF graph databases has generated some interesting algorithms for RDF graph queries(Tappolet & Bernstein, 2009; Nikitopoulos et al., 2019), such as: sub-graph matching, and pattern match. For example: Zou et al. (Zou et al., 2011) propose a graph-based approach to store and query RDF data, transform an RDF graph into a data signature graph, and develop a filtering rule for sub-graph query over the data signature graph. Li et al. (Li et al., 2019) develop an algorithm by extending graph homomorphism for efficiently evaluating sub-graph patterns over such fuzzy RDF graph. Zou et al. (Zou et al., 2009) transform the vertices into points in a vector space, and convert a pattern match query into a distance-based multi-way join problem over the converted vector space.

Among these, a pattern match query is more flexible compared to a sub-graph matching (Zou et al., 2009). But we have not yet found pattern matching and sub-graph matching related to spatiotemporal RDF.

In this chapter, according to the advantages of (Zhu et al., 2022) and (Li et al., 2019) mentioned above, we propose pattern matching query based on spatiotemporal RDF. The main research contents are divided into the following aspects:

- a representation model of spatiotemporal RDF.
- an algorithm to obtain some candidate isomorphic graph of the query graph.
- a pattern matching process of spatiotemporal RDF graph.

The reminder of the chapter is organized as follows: Section 2 introduces a modeling process of spatiotemporal RDF. Section 3 describes three steps for querying spatiotemporal RDF graph. Section 4 discusses the correctness and validity of our algorithm. And Section 5 gives conclusions and directions for future work.

2 MODELING SPATIOTEMPORAL RDF

2.1 RDF

We draw on the form of the RDF triple given in (Perry et al., 2011), as shown in Definition 1:

Definition 1 (RDF Triple). Let U, L and B be three pair-wise disjoint sets of URIs, literals and blank nodes, respectively. The RDF statement can be represented by a triple: $(s, p, o) \in (U \cup B) \times U \times (U \cup L \cup B)$, where s, p, and o represent subject, predicate, and object, respectively.

The RDF graph is a labeled directed graph composed of RDF triples. The subject points to the object through the predicate. The number of triples is usually used to represent the size of the RDF graph.

According to the requirements of this chapter, we modify the definition of RDF data graph given by (Zou & Özsu, 2017), as shown in Definition 2:

Definition 2 (RDF Graph). RDF triples consist of an RDF graph, which is denoted as $G = (V, E, L_E)$, where

(1) V denotes all RDF vertices.
(2) E is a collection of the edges between vertices, $E = \{(v_i, v_j) \mid i \neq j, v_i, v_j \in V\}$.
(3) L_E is the collection of edge labels, i.e., all possible predicates.

In Definition 2, a vertex $v_i \in V$ of graph G. Moreover, $(v_i, v_j) \in E$ is a directed edge from vertex v_i to vertex v_j, with a label.

2.2 Spatiotemporal RDF

As mentioned above, RDF triples are valid in a period of time. If valid period is up, the RDF information will be invalid or modified.

Meanwhile, RDF data has spatial attributes, that is, longitude and latitude, but the classical RDF model does not show the spatial properties of the resource, which causes certain limitations when users need to query related information, so some proposes was discussed to introduce the spatial attributes into the classical RDF model. Most of the forms of spatial RDF mentioned in Sect.1 are (s, p, o, L), where L represent location, that is spatial attributes. But in an RDF triple, both the subject and the object may have spatial properties and their spatial properties may be different. For example, (West Lake, locatedIn, Hangzhou), the spatial attributes of the West Lake are (30° 13' N, 120° 07' E) and the spatial attributes of Hangzhou are (30° 16' N, 120° 10' E). If we write this RDF triple as either (West Lake, locatedIn, Hangzhou, (30° 13' N, 120° 07' E)) or (West Lake, locatedIn, Hangzhou, (30° 16' N, 120° 10' E)), we do not distinguish whether the spatial attribute is subject-related or object-related, so it is improper.

In view of this, we introduce spatial attributes into the subject and object as their labels and add a temporal label to the spatial triple. We represent a spatiotemporal RDF model based on the above-mentioned spatial RDF. As follows:

On the basis of definition of (Analyti & Pachoulakis, 2008), we add spatial attributes and give Definition 3:

Definition 3 (Spatiotemporal RDF Triple). A spatiotemporal triple is a spatial RDF triple (s/Ss, p, o/So) with a time label t. We will use the notion (s/Ss, p, o/So)[t]. The expression (s/Ss, p, o/So)[t1, t2] is a notion for {(s/Ss, p, o/So)[t] | t1 ≦ t ≦ t2}, where s is spatial subject, Ss denotes the coordinate position of s, p is predicate, o is spatial object, So expresses the coordinate position of o, t is the valid period of spatiotemporal RDF, t1 is the start time, and t2 is the end time.

Definition 4 (Spatiotemporal RDF Graph). A set of spatiotemporal RDF triples consist of a spatiotemporal RDF graph, which is represented as GST = (VST, EST, $\sum$, FV, LE, T, FE), here

(1) VST denotes all vertices.
(2) EST is a set of the edges between vertices, EST = {(vi, vj) | i ≠ j, vi, vj ∈ VST}.
(3) $\sum$ is a set of spatial labels of vertices.
(4) FV shows a function assigning spatial label to specific vertex.
(5) LE is the collection of edge labels, i.e., all possible predicates.
(6) T stands for a set of valid period of RDF triples.
(7) FE shows a function assigning temporal label to specific triple.

In Definition 4, a vertex vi ∈ VST of graph GST has one spatial label, FV(vi), corresponding to either subjects or objects in spatiotemporal RDF triples datasets. Moreover, (vi, vj) ∈ EST is a directed edge from vertex vi to vertex vj, with a label. And a RDF triple has temporal label (t1, t2) ∈ T, FE(t1, t2), corresponding to the triple. A simple spatiotemporal RDF graph is shown in Figure 1.

Figure 1. Spatiotemporal RDF graph G_{ST}

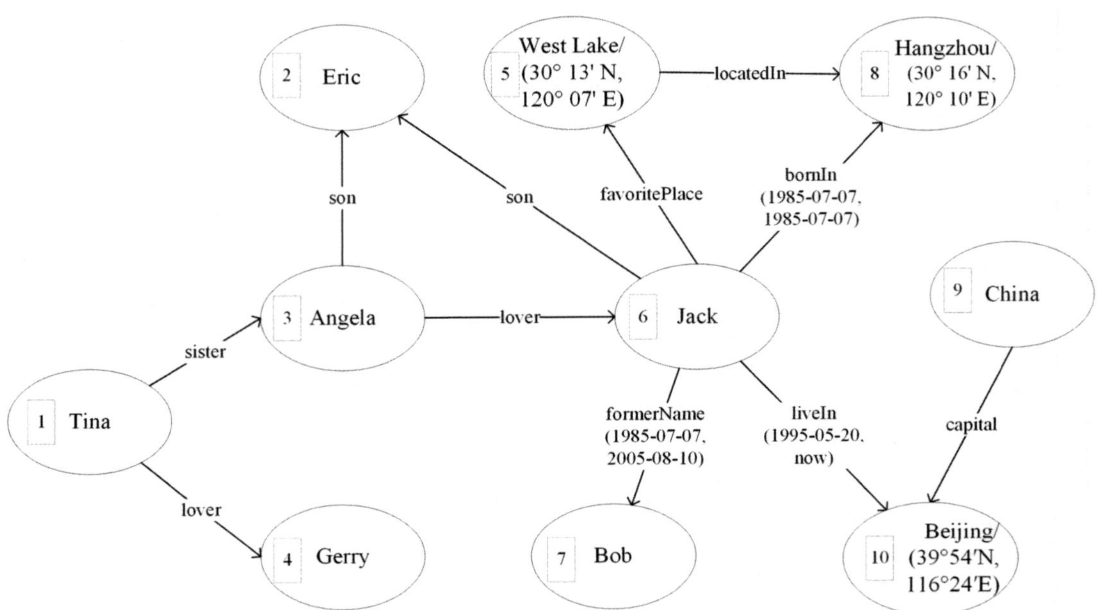

3 QUERYING SPATIOTEMPORAL RDF GRAPH

In the section, we propose two steps for querying spatiotemporal RDF graph: constructing a query graph Q_{ST}, and matching the query graph Q_{ST} with the graph G_{ST}.

3.1 Constructing Query Graph

In order to do pattern matching more efficiently, we need to construct an appropriate query graph based on the search criteria. Take an example. We want to find out "what is the former name of Tina's sister's lover in 2000, and where is his favorite place?" in the graph G_{ST}. Based on the form of the RDF triple, we can split the query conditions into "Tina's sister is *?1*", "*?1*'s lover is *?2*", "*?2*'s name is *?3* in 2000", "*?2* favorite place is *?4*" According to this query condition, we construct the query graph Q_{ST} as shown in Figure 2.

Figure 2. Query graph Q_{ST}.

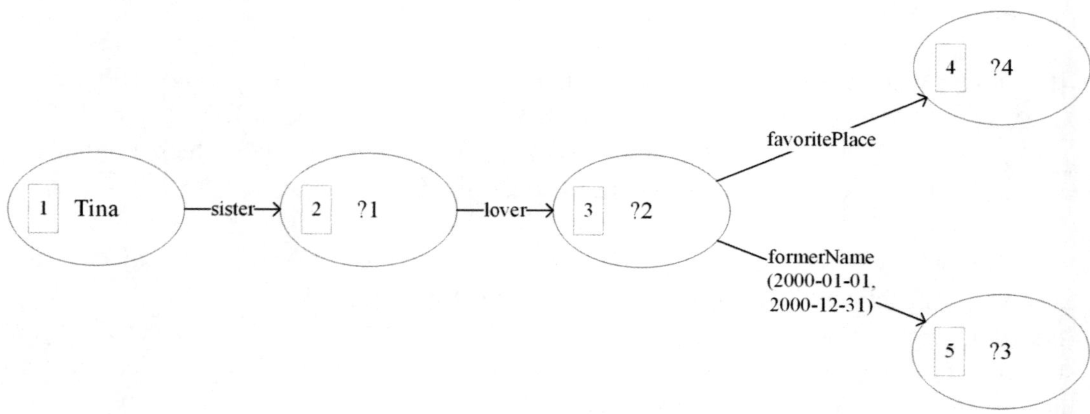

3.2 Pattern Match Query

Since RDF data has a natural representation in the form of a graph, this problem has been often addressed in terms of graph matching between a small graph representing the query and a very large graph representing the database (Li et al., 2019).

We reference the forms of (Zhu et al., 2022), and give some definitions:

Definition 5 (Spatiotemporal RDF Sub-Graph). A spatiotemporal RDF graph GST' = (VST', EST', ∑', FV', LE', T', FE') is called a spatiotemporal RDF sub-graph of GST = (VST, EST, ∑, FV, LE, T, FE), if

(1) VST' ⊆ VST, EST' ⊆ EST, ∑' ⊆ ∑, LE' ⊆ LE, T' ⊆ T, and FE' ⊆ FE.
(2) ∀ u ∈ VST', FV'(u) = FV(u).
(3) ∀ (t1, t2) ∈ T', FE'(t1, t2) = FE(t1, t2).

A spatiotemporal RDF graph GST' is called a spatiotemporal RDF sub-graph of GST, written as GST' ⊆ GST'.

Definition 6 (Spatiotemporal RDF Graph Isomorphism). Given spatiotemporal RDF graphs GST1 = (VST1, EST1, ∑1, FV1, LE1, T1, FE1) and GST2 = (VST2, EST2, ∑2, FV2, LE2, T2, FE2), an isomorphism from GST1 to GST2 is a mutual function f: VST1 → VST2 such that:

(1) ∀ u ∈ VST1, f(u) ∈ VST2, FV1(u) = FV2(f(u)).
(2) ∀ (t1, t2) ∈ T1, (f(t1), f(t2)) ∈ T2, FE1(t1, t2) = FE2(f(t1), f(t2)).

If f exists, then GST1 is isomorphic to GST2, denoted it as GST1 ≅ GST2.

Definition 7 (Spatiotemporal RDF Graph Pattern). A spatiotemporal RDF graph pattern is represented as GSTP = (VSTP, ESTP, FVP, LEP, FEP), here

(1) VSTP denotes all vertices.
(2) ESTP is a set of the edges between vertices, ESTP = {(vi, vj) | i ≠ j, vi, vj ∈ VSTP}.
(3) FVP shows a function assigning spatial label to specific vertex.

(4) LEP is the collection of edge labels, i.e., all possible predicates.
(5) FEP shows a function assigning temporal label to specific triple.

Definition 8 (Spatiotemporal RDF Graph Pattern Matching). A spatiotemporal RDF graph pattern GSTP = (VSTP, ESTP, FVP, LEP, FEP) is matching with a spatiotemporal RDF graph GST = (VST, EST, $\sum$, FV, LE, T, FE), if there exists an injective mapping Φ: GSTP → GST which is a total mapping from vertexes and edges of GSTP to vertexes and edges of GST such that:

(1) (matching vertex) Every vertex on VSTP has an image vertex on VST by the injective function. Formally, for each vertex u ∈ VSTP matches a vertex Φ(u) ∈ VST.
(2) (matching edge) For each edge (ui, uj) ∈ ESTP, there exist two vertices Φ(ui) and Φ(uj) of VST such that Φ(ui) and Φ(uj) match vertices ui and uj respectively, and there is an edge from vertex Φ(ui) to Φ(uj) in GST.
(3) (checking spatial label of vertex) The spatial labels of all vertex of GSTP is matched with GST. Formally, FV(Φ(u)) satisfies the function FVP for u ∈ VSTP. If the condition is met, go to the next step; otherwise the match fails.
(4) (checking predicate of edge) The predicate of all edge of GSTP is matched with GST. Formally, LE(Φ(u), Φ(v)) satisfies the function LEP for all (u, v) ∈ ESTP. If the condition is met, go to the next step; otherwise the match fails.
(5) (checking temporal label of triple) The temporal labels of all triple of GSTP is matched with GST. Formally, FE(Φ(triple)) satisfies the function FEP for all triple ⊆ GSTP. If the condition is met, go to the next step; otherwise the match fails. That is, GSTP does not match GST.

As we can see from the above definition, the process of the query graph QST matching the graph GST is actually to find sub-graph GSTQ in the graph GST which is isomorphic with the query graph QST.

The following is the detailed process of finding isomorphic graph given in Algorithm 1.

Algorithm 1 Find Isomorphic Graphs of the Query Graph

Input: Q_{ST}
Output: some candidate isomorphic graphs of Q_{ST}

```
find(v); //v ∈ G_ST,
initial point = u; //u ∈ Q_ST
if(u.out_degree ≤ v.out_degree && u.in_degree ≤ v.in_degree)
departure_edge(u, v)
if(exist(u. neighbor) && exist(v. neighbor) && flag(u, v) != 1)
match(u, v);
flag(u, v) = 1;
u = u. neighbor; v = v. neighbor;
goto 03;
else
match(u, v);
flag(u, v) = 1;
u = u.precursor; v = v.precursor;
goto 03;
else
find(v1); //v1 ∈ G_ST
v = v1;
goto 02;
```

At first, find the first vertex v in the graph G_{ST} (line 01). Select any vertex u in the query graph Q_{ST} as the initial point of pattern matching (line 02).If $u.out\_degree \leq v.out\_degree$ and $u.in\_degree \leq v.in\_degree$ are established, v may be a match of u (line 03). Second, we search for nodes according to the departure edges of u and v respectively. If both u and v have neighboring nodes, we match u with v, and search for their neighbor nodes; else, we match u with v and search for their precursor nodes; After each match we mark the pair of nodes to prevent duplicate matches and repeat the steps above (line 04~14). Finally, if $u.out\_degree > v.out\_degree$ or $u.in\_degree > v.in\_degree$ are established, v isn't a match of u. We need to find next vertex $v1$, and repeat the steps above (line 15~18). Therefore, we can get some candidate isomorphic graphs.

Based on Definition 4, we can compare information of Q_{ST} with G_{STQ}'s by using Definition 8. At this point, we have finished the query on the graph G_{ST}.

4 DISCUSSION

In this section, we show the correctness and the effectiveness of Algorithm 1 through presenting the query process of the query graph Q_{ST} in the graph G_{ST} and analyzing the space and time complexity.

Choose a node 1 in the query graph Q_{ST}. Choose the node 6 in the graph G_{ST}, and determine whether the *out_degree* and *in_degree* of node 1 in the query graph Q_{ST} are smaller than node 6's in the graph G_{ST} and whether they have neighbor nodes. If right, do match (1, 6). Repeat above steps, do match (2, 5), do match(3, 8), and node 3 have neighbor nodes but node 8 haven't neighbor nodes, so this match is a failure. Choose the node 3 in the graph G_{ST}, do match(1, 3), do match(2, 6), do match(3, 5), do match(4, 8), do match(5, none), so this match process is a error. Choose the node 1 in the graph G_{ST}, do match(1, 1), do match(2, 3), do match(3, 6), do match(4, 5), do match(5, 8), or match(4, 5) and match(5, 7), or match(4, 5) and match(5, 10), or match(4, 8) and match(5, 5), etc. Similarly, we can see that the rest nodes don't match. We find 12 isomorphic graphs of the query graph Q_{ST}.

We analyze the space and time complexity of the Algorithm 1 and show the results of comparison with other algorithms. As follows:

Table 1. The results by comparing our algorithm with other's.

	(Li et al., 2019)	**Our's**	
Complexity	Average	Best	Worst
Time	$O(\|G\|^2*N')$	$O(N*N')$	$O(N*N'!)$
Spatial	$O(N+E+N'+E')$	$O(N+N')$	$O(N+N')$

Here, G is the target graph, N and N' are the number of nodes in the target graph and the query graph, respectively, E and E' are the number of edges in the target graph and the query graph, respectively. From above Table 1, we can see that our algorithm saves space. But for runtime, our algorithm has an advantage on the large graph. So, the algorithm's validity is undoubted.

5 SUMMARY

This work introduced a novel representation model of spatiotemporal RDF to express RDF information more precisely. In order to find some candidate isomorphic graphs of the query graph Q_{ST} in graph G_{ST} more quickly, we proposed the *Find Isomorphic Graphs of the Query Graph* algorithm. And we defined a pattern matching process of spatiotemporal RDF graph to find the final query results. In the end, we illustrated the correctness and validity of algorithms.

REFERENCES

Analyti, A., & Pachoulakis, I. (2008). A survey on models and query languages for temporally annotated RDF. *International Journal of Advanced Computer Science and Applications*, *1*(3), 28–35.

Antonić, O., Križanb, J., & Marki, A. (2001). Spatio-temporal interpolation of climatic variables over large region of complex terrain using neural networks. *Ecological Modelling*, *138*(1-3), 255–263. doi:10.1016/S0304-3800(00)00406-3

Broekstra, J., Kampman, A., & Van Harmelen, F. (2002). Sesame: A generic architecture for storing and querying rdf and rdf schema. In *International semantic web conference* (pp. 54-68). Berlin, Heidelberg: Springer Berlin Heidelberg.

Klyne, G., Carroll, J. J. (2006). *Resource description framework (RDF): Concepts and abstract syntax.*

Koubarakis, M., & Kyzirakos, K. (2010). Modeling and querying metadata in the semantic sensor web: The model stRDF and the query language stSPARQL. *Extended Semantic Web Conference*, (pp. 425-439). Springer, Berlin, Heidelberg. 10.1007/978-3-642-13486-9_29

Kuper, P. V., Breunig, M., & Al-Doori, M. (2016). Application of 3d spatiotemporal data modeling, management, and analysis in db4geo. *ISPRS Annals of the Photogrammetry, Remote Sensing and Spatial Information Sciences*, *4*, 63–170.

Mennis, J. L., & Fountain, A. G. (2001). A spatio-temporal GIS database for monitoring alpine glacier change. *Photogrammetric Engineering and Remote Sensing*, *67*(8), 967–974.

Nikitopoulos, P., Vlachou, A., Doulkeridis, C., & Vouros, G. A. (2019). Parallel and scalable processing of spatio-temporal RDF queries using Spark. *GeoInformatica*.

Perry, M., Jain, P., & Sheth, A. P. (2011). Sparql-st: Extending sparql to support spatiotemporal queries. In *Geospatial semantics and the semantic web* (pp. 61–86). Springer. doi:10.1007/978-1-4419-9446-2_3

Perry, M., Sheth, A. P., & Hakimpour, F. (2007). Supporting complex thematic, spatial and temporal queries over semantic web data. *International Conference on GeoSpatial Sematics*, (pp. 228-246). Springer, Berlin, Heidelberg. 10.1007/978-3-540-76876-0_15

Tan, C., & Yan, S. (2017). Spatiotemporal data organization and application research. *The International Archives of the Photogrammetry, Remote Sensing and Spatial Information Sciences*, *42*(W7), 1363–1366. doi:10.5194/isprs-archives-XLII-2-W7-1363-2017

Tappolet, J., & Bernstein, A. (2009). Applied temporal RDF: Efficient temporal querying of RDF data with SPARQL. In *Proceedings of the European Semantic Web Conference* (pp. 308–322). Springer, Berlin/Heidelberg, Germany. 10.1007/978-3-642-02121-3_25

Vatsavai, R. R., Ganguly, A., & Chandola, V. (2012). Spatiotemporal data mining in the era of big spatial data: Algorithms and applications. In *Proceedings of the 1st ACM SIGSPATIAL International Workshop on Analytics for Big Geospatial Data* (pp. 1–10). ACM. 10.1145/2447481.2447482

Venkateswara, R.K. (2012). Spatiotemporal data mining: Issues, tasks and applications. *Int. J. Comput. Sci. Eng. Surv.*

Yan, Y., Wang, C., & Zhou, A. (2008). Efficiently querying rdf data in triple stores. In *Proceedings of the 17th international conference on World Wide Web* (pp. 1053-1054). ACM. 10.1145/1367497.1367652

Zhang, C., Chen, S. C., Shyu, M. L., & Peeta, S. (2003). Adaptive background learning for vehicle detection and spatio-temporal tracking. In *Fourth International Conference on Information, Communications and Signal Processing, 2003 and the Fourth Pacific Rim Conference on Multimedia. Proceedings of the 2003 Joint* (Vol. 2, pp. 797-801). IEEE. 10.1109/ICICS.2003.1292566

Zhu, L., Meng, X., & Mi, Z. (2022). Fuzzy Spatiotemporal Data Modeling and Operations in RDF. *Information (Basel)*, *13*(10), 503. doi:10.3390/info13100503

Zou, L., Chen, L., & Özsu, M. T. (2009). Distance-join: Pattern match query in a large graph database. *Proceedings of the VLDB Endowment International Conference on Very Large Data Bases*, *2*(1), 886–897. doi:10.14778/1687627.1687727

Zou, L., Mo, J. H., Chen, L., Özsu, M. T., & Zhao, D. (2011). gStore: Answering SPARQL queries via subgraph matching. *Proceedings of the VLDB Endowment International Conference on Very Large Data Bases*, *4*(8), 482–493. doi:10.14778/2002974.2002976

Zou, L., & Özsu, M. T. (2017). Graph-based RDF data management. *Data Science and Engineering*, *2*(1), 56–70. doi:10.1007/s41019-016-0029-6

Chapter 4
Ranking Properties of Spatiotemporal RDF Data

ABSTRACT

Based on the sorting algorithm, the authors discuss the ranking of spatiotemporal RDF data properties and attempt to improve the query efficiency of large RDF datasets. The chapter introduces three sorting algorithms in machine learning: LR (logistic regression) algorithm, GBDT (gradient boosting decision tree) and FM (factorization machines) model algorithm. After the data sorting system is completed, the authors use A/B test method to test the system. It is self-evident that the recommendation algorithm based on FM ranking is more efficient than linear regression ranking. Using the model performance evaluation index-AUC and target detection evaluation index-MAP, the effect of FM model algorithm is significantly better than the other two algorithms. Finally, based on the Hadoop open-source big data framework, the scalability and high performance of the ranking recommendation system are guaranteed. The result of the research shows the page hits increased by 98.0% in a week.

1 INTRODUCTION

In recent years, the Internet is transforming from a document web that includes only hyperlinks between web pages into a data web that contains a large number of complex relationships between entities. Among them, the Semantic World Wide Web is used to solve the problem that information explosion on the current web makes it difficult for people to obtain target information (He et al., 2016). Endowing the information with a clear structure and semantics, the machine can understand and integrate them while displaying the information. Semantic search requires analysis and processing of structured semantic data with finer granularity. Therefore, the original storage and indexing techniques for unstructured web documents are no longer applicable to RDF data. Furthermore, the current ranking algorithms cannot be directly applied to the related semantic search between entities.

At present, scholars have evaluated the user experience of some prevalent English search engines. By evaluating the response speed and the relevance, diversity, and ranking quality of search results, they have found that the ranking quality of search results is the key factor in affecting the quality of search engines (Christina et al., 2016; Carlo & Alexandros, 2015).

DOI: 10.4018/978-1-6684-9108-9.ch004

Traditional sorting learning algorithms in real scenes with large RDF data sets is often unsatisfactory (Wen & Amir, 2017; Psychas et al., 2017; Khaled & Afnan, 2013; Sardar & Abdul, 2009). In the context of massive data sets, exploring a sorting model is meaningful to efficiently and quickly provide users with search-related recommendation results(Ali, 2017). Based on the open-source big data framework, this study incorporated two user behaviors into the ranking features, including the clicking behaviors on results pages of search engines and the browsing behaviors of landing pages, aiming to design a new set of sorting model system. Finally, we use A/B test and the common metrics of the ranking model such as AUC and MAP to compare various algorithms.

2 METHODS

2.1 RDF Data Model

RDF(Powers, 2003) is a framework for metadata that provides interoperability between applications by machine-understandable web data (Kim et al., 2017). The RDF definition can be expressed as:

$$(\text{Subject, Predicate, Object}) \in (U \cup B) \times (U \cup B \cup L) \quad (1)$$

Where U represents the collection of URI, B is a collection of anonymous resources, and L is a collection of literal property values.

In addition to the storage of triples, scholars have proposed to store RDF data as property tables which are shown in Table 1. In the table 1, the first column is the subject in the RDF triple, the remaining columns are the properties of the subject, and each row corresponds to the subject and its corresponding property value in turn (Tathiane et al., 2018). The storage method of the property table can effectively reduce the number of connections and improve the query speed when processing the query requests.

Table 1. RDF property table storage method

subject	predicate1	predicate2	predicate3	predicate5	predicate6	predicate7	...
subjec1	Object1		Object2			Object7	
subjec2	Object2	Object2	Object4				
subjec3	Object2			Object6	Object9	Object10	
...							

2.2 Construction of the Sorting Model for Spatiotemporal Properties of Search Engine RDF Data

The objects of spatiotemporal rdf(Kyzirakos et al, 2010) property analysis are rdf data with time, absolute position and relative position in three-dimensional space. The space correlations (global and local correlations) are common in space data, coupled with the randomness and complexity of the time dimension; the spatiotemporal data(Pan & Hobbs, 2005) presents features such as multi-dimensional, semantic, and spatiotemporal dynamic correlation (Mashechkin et al., 2019). The basic framework of the ranking algorithm is shown in Figure 1. The key point of sorting learning is how to design an efficient and accurate sorting model, which is also the point of this study.

Figure 1. A basic framework for ranking learning

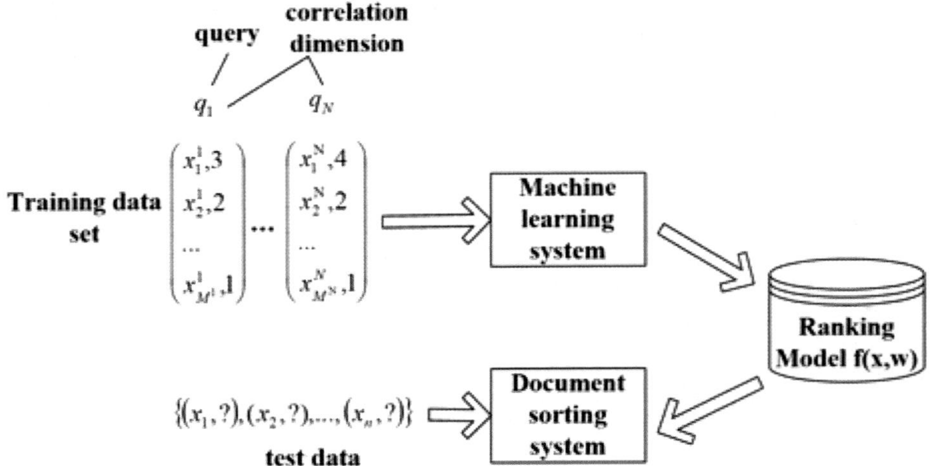

For online users of search engine, the retrieval process can be described as that the system cuts the query words of the users into individual single words; then, according to the inverted index of each single word, the table selects multiple web page linked lists and merges them to obtain several web pages that match all the single words. The weight of every single word is calculated by the positive index of these web pages, and the web pages with the highest weight are merged and transmitted to the advanced ranking module, providing information to users after advanced sorting (Bartosz et al., 2018). The main requirements of search engines for sorting are rapid strategy iteration and accurate user feature extraction. However, the weights of each feature in the traditional sorting algorithm are manually formulated by experience and statistical data; therefore, it takes a lot of time and seriously affects the iteration speed of the sorting strategy. The currently proposed machine learning ranking algorithm can calculate the optimal weight of each ranking feature on the sample through machine training, and improve the accuracy and efficiency of the ranking.

2.3 Comparative Analysis of RDF Data Sorting Algorithm Based on Machine Learning

The main sorting algorithm in this study included logistic regression algorithm (LR), gradient boosting decision tree (GBDT), and factorization machines (FM) model algorithm.

LR algorithm. It is applied to deal with regression problems where the dependent variable is categorical. It is necessary to find a prediction function h (Jeroen et al., 2018). Using the logistic function, the function form is:

$$g(z)=\frac{1}{1+e^{-z}} \tag{2}$$

The selected binomial logistic regression model could be represented by a conditional probability distribution P (z|y). Where z ∈ R, y ∈ {0,1}; its conditional probability distribution can be expressed as:

$$P(Y=1|z)=\frac{\exp(wz+b)}{1+\exp(wz+b)} \tag{3}$$

$$P(Y=0|z)=\frac{1}{1+\exp(wz+b)} \tag{4}$$

Where z ∈ R^n (R indicates real number set, R^n indicates the n-dimension real number vector space), Y ∈ {0,1}; w is weight vector, b is bias vector; w ∈ R^n, b ∈ R ; w · z is the internal volume of w and z.

GBDT model algorithm. GBDT passes multiple rounds of iteration. Each round of iteration generates a weak classifier, and each classifier is trained based on the residual of the previous classifier. The training process of GBDT is shown in Figure 2.

Figure 2. Training process of GBDT

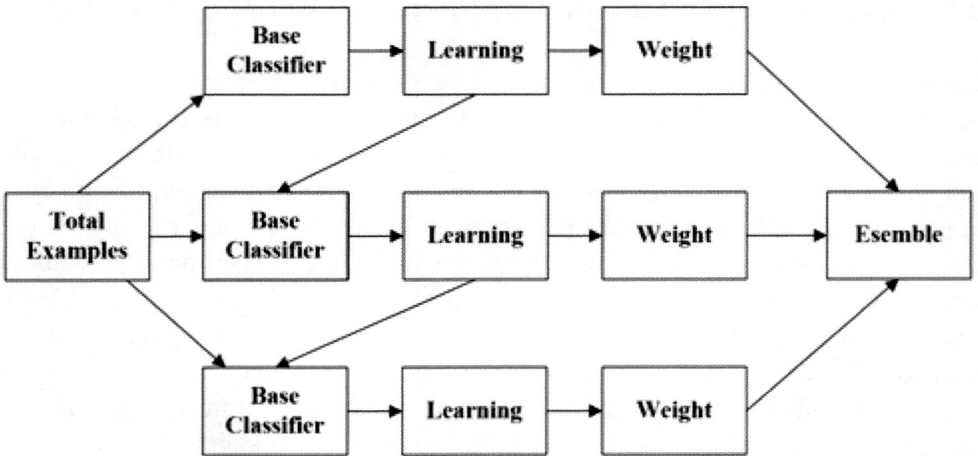

Weak classifiers are generally chosen as a CART TREE. The final total classifier is obtained by weighting and summing the weak classifiers acquired from each round of training.

$$\mathrm{F}_m(x)=\sum_{m=1}^{M}T(x;\theta_m) \tag{5}$$

The model trains a total of M rounds, and each round generates a weak classifier $T(x,\theta m_j)$. GBDT determines the parameters of the next weak classifier through empirical risk minimization.

FM model algorithm. FM algorithm aims to solve the problem of feature combination under sparse data (Mark et al., 2019). Polynomial models are the most intuitive models that include feature combinations, which can be expressed as:

$$y(x) = w_0 + \sum_{i=1}^{n} w_i x_i + \sum_{i=1}^{n} \sum_{j=i+1}^{n} w_{ij} x_i y_j \tag{6}$$

In the above equation, n represents the number of samples, xi is the value of the i-th feature, and w_0, w_i, and w_{ij} are the model parameters. Using matrix factorization to solve the training problem of quadratic parameters improves the performance of the model while solving sparse data problems. The quadratic term coefficients w_{ij} can be combined to form a square matrix W. The model equation of FM can be expressed as:

$$y(x) = w_0 + \sum_{i=1}^{n} w_i x_i + \sum_{i=1}^{n} \sum_{j=i+1}^{n} v_i, v_j x_i x_j \tag{7}$$

3 RESULTS AND DISCUSSION

3.1 Test Results of System Function Based on FM Ranking Algorithm

This study uses A/B testing to count the number of users visiting the page, thereby verifying the effectiveness of the new recommendation algorithm. In this study, users are divided into two different groups based on user IDs, i.e. A and B. The different recommendation algorithms are applied, i.e. the recommendation algorithms based on FM ranking and based on linear regression ranking. Linear regression is a common model in industrial applications and is mainly used to predict probability. Taking personalized recommendation as an example, regression mainly analyzes the possible factors when users choose to consume content based on the history of a large number of users and recommend the content that users are most interested in. Therefore, the ranking algorithm based on linear regression is chosen as the control group and compared with the performance of the FM algorithm. Selecting the data from February 17th, 2020 to February 23rd, 2020, and the statistical results were shown in Figure 3.

The two sorting algorithms has no significant fluctuations in the number of users visited during the respective test time. However, when the user traffic ratio was 1:1, the recommendation quality based on the FM ranking algorithm was higher; therefore, the user hits increase significantly, and the number of visiting users is more than the number of visiting users based on the linear regression ranking algorithm. This suggests that the FM ranking algorithm has gained better recommendation results in actual search engine recommendations and received more page views.

3.2 Comparison of the Three Sorting Algorithms

According to the common metrics of recommendation systems and ranking algorithms, this study compares the effects of the three times feedback functions and the ranking algorithms. Detection indicators included accuracy, model performance evaluation index-AUC, and target detection evaluation index-MAP.

Figure 3. Comparison of user visits

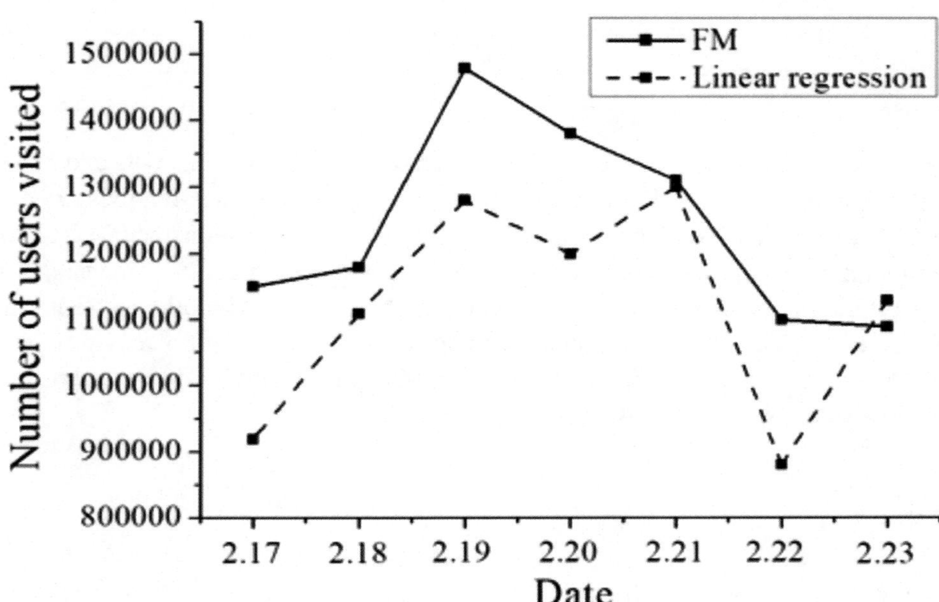

In this study, three forms of the linear function, convex function, and concave function are used as time feedback functions. During the experiment, the three function forms are applied in the ranking algorithm, and the accuracy is used to compare the three function forms. The results are shown in Table 2:

As shown in the table, the LR linear model used the linear function as a time feedback function, which had a better effect in terms of accuracy. The comparison of the performance of the three functions in each model found that the accuracy of the concave function was significantly higher than that of the linear function and the convex function. Therefore, the concave function was used as a time feedback function in the comparison of the models.

Table 2. Comparison of the accuracy of time feedback functions among the three algorithms

Sorting algorithm	Linear function	Convex function	Concave function
LR	0.768	0.749	0.771
GBDT	0.803	0.815	0.820
FM	0.812	0.830	0.825

After determining the functional form of the time feedback factor, this study chose an algorithm that was more in line with the current engineering environment and applied it. The results obtained were shown in Table 3:

Table 3. Comparison of AUC and MAP indicators among three sorting algorithms

Sorting algorithm	AUC	MAP
LR	0.665	0.455
GBDT	0.751	0.472
FM	0.780	0.497

As shown in the table, the two indexes of the FM ranking algorithm, i.e., AUC and MAP, were significantly better than those of the LR and GBDT ranking algorithms, indicating that a nonlinear model was more suitable for systems based on the FM ranking algorithm. In addition, the FM ranking algorithm had linear computational complexity, and it had advantages in processing high-dimensional sparse data. Then, all the traffic was transferred into the new version of the recommendation system. The FM ranking algorithm system achieved excellent recommendation results in the online environment. Since the launch of the new recommendation system in February 2020, page views had increased from 32,083,245 to 63,524,823 in a week, which increased by 98.0%.

4 SUMMARY

This study analyzed and processed the users' clicking behavior characteristics in search engines and completed the design of the data ranking system according to user needs. The functional testing of the system found that the recommendation quality based on the FM ranking algorithm was higher; therefore, the user hits had increased significantly, and the number of visiting users was higher than that based on the linear regression ranking algorithm. Meanwhile, comparing AUC and MAP to LR, GBDT and FM three sorting algorithm, the results illustrate that FM is significantly better than LR and GBDT. Besides, using the page sorting algorithm of FM, the page hits in a week increased from 32,083,245 to 63,524,823, which increased by 98.0%. In summary, the data sorting system based on the FM sorting algorithm in machine learning can address the issue of ranking properties in large-scale spatiotemporal RDF data, and ensure the reliability and effectiveness of sorting, thereby the index volume is greatly improved.

REFERENCES

Ali, K. (2017). A comparative study of well-known sorting algorithms. *International Journal of Advanced Research in Computer Science*, *8*(1).

Bartosz, C., Jakub, N., & Katarzyna, J. (2018). Machine learning modeling of plant phenology based on coupling satellite and gridded meteorological dataset. *International Journal of Biometeorology*, *62*(7), 1297–1309. doi:10.1007/s00484-018-1534-2 PMID:29644431

Carlo, A., & Alexandros, G. A. (2015). Preliminary Investigation of Reversing RML: From an RDF dataset to its Column-Based data source. *Biodiversity Data Journal*, *3*(3), e5464. PMID:26312054

Christina, L., Panagiotis, P., & Anastasia, A. (2016). Radius-aware Approximate Blank Node Matching using Signatures. *Knowledge and Information Systems*, *50*(2), 1–38.

He, J., Liu, L. Y., Yu, F., & Han, Y. (2016). A Method of RDF Fuzzy Query Based on No Query Language Service with Permutated Breadth First Search Algorithm. *Procedia Computer Science*, *100*, 321–328. doi:10.1016/j.procs.2016.09.163

Jeroen, A., Gilad, M., & Anjali, D. Z. (2018). A machine learning model to determine the accuracy of variant calls in capture-based next-generation sequencing. *BMC Genomics*, *19*(1), 263. doi:10.1186/s12864-018-4659-0 PMID:29665779

Khaled, T., & Afnan, B. (2013). A novel approach to the selection sort algorithm with parallel computing and dynamic programming concepts. *JKAU: Comp. IT*, *2*, 27-44.

Kim, R. G., Doppa, J. R., Pande, P. P., Marculescu, D., & Marculescu, R. (2017). Machine Learning and Manycore Systems Design: A Serendipitous Symbiosis. *Computer*, *51*(7), 66–77. doi:10.1109/MC.2018.3011040

Kyzirakos, K., Karpathiotakis, M., & Koubarakis, M. (2010). Developing registries for the semantic sensor Web using stRDF and stSPARQL. In *International Workshop on Semantic Sensor Networks*. ACM.

Mark, A. F., Stephen, L., & Gourab, K. S. (2019). Can Machine Learning Algorithms Predict Which Patients Will Achieve Minimally Clinically Important Differences From Total Joint Arthroplasty? *Clinical Orthopaedics and Related Research*, *477*(6), 1267–1279. doi:10.1097/CORR.0000000000000687 PMID:31094833

Mashechkin, I. V., Petrovskiy, M. I., Tsarev, D. V., & Chikunov, M. N. (2019). Machine Learning Methods for Detecting and Monitoring Extremist Information on the Internet. *Programming and Computer Software*, *45*(3), 99–115. doi:10.1134/S0361768819030058

Pan, F., & Hobbs, J. R. (2005). *Temporal Aggregates in OWL-Time*. In *Proceedings of the FLAIRS conference*, Clearwater Beach, Florida, USA.

Powers, S. (2003). *Practical RDF: solving problems with the resource description framework*.

Psychas, I. D., Marinaki, M., Marinakis, Y., & Migdalas, A. (2017). Non-dominated sorting differential evolution algorithm for the minimization of route-based fuel consumption multi-objective vehicle routing problems. *Energy Systems*, *8*(4), 785–814. doi:10.1007/s12667-016-0209-5

Sardar, Z., & Abdul, W. (2009). A new friends sort algorithm. In *2009 2nd IEEE International Conference on Computer Science and Information Technology*. IEEE. 10.1109/ICCSIT.2009.5234550

Tathiane, M., Artem, S., & Andrew, J. G. (2018). Machine Learning Identifies Stemness Features Associated with Oncogenic Dedifferentiation. *Cell*, *173*(2), 338–354. doi:10.1016/j.cell.2018.03.034 PMID:29625051

Wen, F., & Amir, A. (2017). Two-dimensional sorting algorithm for high-throughput K-best MIMO detection. *IET Communications*, *11*(6), 817–822. doi:10.1049/iet-com.2016.0790

Chapter 5
Path-Based Approximate Matching of Spatiotemporal RDF Data

ABSTRACT

Due to an ever-increasing number of RDF data with time features and space features, it is an important task to query efficiently spatiotemporal RDF data over RDF datasets. In this chapter, the spatiotemporal RDF data contains time features, space features and text features, which are processed separately to facilitate query. Meanwhile, the authors propose an algorithm for path-based approximate matching of spatiotemporal RDF data, which includes the decomposition graph algorithm and the combination query path algorithm. The query graph with spatiotemporal features is split into multiple paths, and then every path in the query graph is used to search for the best matching path in the path sets contained in the data graph. Due to the existence of inaccurate matchings, approximate matchings are performed according to the evaluation function to find the best matching path. Finally, all the best paths are combined to generate a matching result graph.

1 INTRODUCTION

Resource Description Framework (RDF) (Manola et al., 2004) is a metadata model and language recommended by W3C. As Web resources are put into use, a framework (Hurtado & Vaisman, 2006) for adding temporal inference to RDF is designed and contains an inference process and a corresponding query language. However, there has been no in-depth study on query indexes of temporal RDF. Pugliese et al. (Pugliese et al., 2008) construct an index structure-tGRIN, which is the specialized index for temporal RDF, and design scalable algorithms for temporal RDF database to handle complex queries. In order to perfect the indexing technique of temporal RDF, Yan et al. (Yan et al., 2019) propose a new index method that can insert and delete temporal triples in the graph of temporal RDF. The index efficiency is improved by using frequent elements.

DOI: 10.4018/978-1-6684-9108-9.ch005

On semantic web data, users need to query spatial RDF data to extend the technical study of querying RDF data with temporal properties (Chakkarwar et al., 2016; Elzein et al., 2018). Wang et al. (Wang et al., 2013) introduce a spatial query method for querying RDF data with spatial properties. The spatial query method uses spatial predicates and introduces a new index SS-Tree, and includes a pruning rule and search algorithm based on SS tree. This method reduces the unnecessary spatial search range and has higher query efficiency, but it needs further study in the storage and management of RDF data with spatial information. Liagouris et al. (Liagouris et al., 2014) propose a technique of RDF storage extension to manage spatial RDF data, which can effectively encode entities with spatial positions, and meanwhile define spatial connection algorithms. This method can reduce the cost of spatial components and realize the application of spatial RDF data management. It further promotes the deep research of spatial RDF data queries.

The spatial and temporal characteristics of RDF data are related to each other to a certain degree (Smeros & Koubarakis, 2016; Zêzere et al., 2014; Jeon et al, 2009). For RDF data information of time and space, Wang et al. (Wang et al., 2017) define the RDF data information integration of time and space, design a kind of flexible spatiotemporal and semantic constraints of the spatiotemporal query language, and establish a tree-like index of ST-tree based on cost model and a new kind query processing algorithm of S-T to provide spatiotemporal RDF data query with the technical support. Further optimization is needed for spatiotemporal RDF data storage. A technical method (Nikitopoulos et al., 2018) of storing and accessing encoded RDF data is proposed and implemented. The one-dimensional encoding scheme is used to perform efficient spatiotemporal RDF queries, which can effectively process simple RDF spatiotemporal queries in a few seconds. Nevertheless, due to the dynamic and large-scale nature of spatiotemporal RDF data, this approach requires an optimized query technique. Vlachou et al. (Vlachou et al., 2019) devise an encoding scheme for dynamic spatiotemporal RDF data, which compresses the spatiotemporal information of each RDF entity into a unique integer value. It improves the performance of query spatiotemporal RDF. In terms of the technology of querying RDF data does not support scalability, a graph-based search method is designed to store and query RDF data (Zou et al., 2011). It first stores RDF data as large graphs (Tong et al., 2007) and then converts the RDF graphs into data signature graphs, enabling precise queries in a uniform manner. In order to extend the query function to realize the inexact query of RDF data (Virgilio et al., 2013), an approximate matching algorithm is used for large graph data in (Tian & Patel, 2008). The algorithm differentiates nodes by their importance in the graph structure, and then extends node matching to generate larger graph matching. In order to construct more efficient approximate graph matching approach, a new structure-aware and attribute-aware index (Zhu et al., 2011) are built for processing approximate graph matching. According to the structure similarity and attribute similarity, the approach divides the search space into subgraphs, then constructs the indexes according to the attribute similarity, and calculates the best results through the index and greedy algorithm comparison. The query processing in the approach using the index is an order of magnitude faster than the previous work. Since the path is more indexable than the graph (Li et al., 2019), it can carry out further experimental research on the path index.

Li et al. (Li et al., 2019) establish an index based on path RDF data, define the selection and combination path algorithm, split the graph into paths, and transform the query problem of the graph into the matching problem of the paths. Aiming to better serve the path search algorithm with query technology, the processing of approximate queries needs to be further studied and refined. Virgilio et al. (Virgilio et al., 2015) demonstrate a new method of approximately querying RDF data by path, which combines the query result matching strategy and the evaluation correlation sorting method to query accurate and inaccurate RDF data and the generated query results are accurate and approximate respectively. This method reduces the complexity of the query process and has a flexible way to query. But this method is insufficient in querying RDF data with temporal and spatial characteristics, which needs to be created and optimized.

In view of the high indexing and efficiency of path matching and the fact that there is now a large amount of spatiotemporal RDF data that needs to be processed efficiently, we put forward a new path-based solution for approximately querying RDF data sets with temporal and spatial information in order to effectively answer the spatiotemporal RDF data graph of an approximately matched query. In this chapter, the path matching operations are carried out to find the paths with the highest approximation with the target path. Simultaneously, a decomposition graph algorithm and a combination query path algorithm are designed to find the indexes with the best matching paths according to the score values of the evaluation function. The paths with the indexes are combined to produce a result graph with the best matching, ultimately. Specifically, our contribution can be summarized as follows:

(1) The algorithm to decompose the graph into paths and the algorithm to combine the paths into graphs are proposed.
(2) A method to calculate path similarity is designed in the process of path matching.

The rest of this chapter is organized as follows. Some definitions and concepts are introduced in section 2. In section 3, the path matching algorithm is proposed. Firstly, the spatiotemporal RDF graph is split into paths, and the optimal path sets are found by the calculation of path similarity, which then combines with each other. In section 4, the effectiveness and efficiency of our algorithm are demonstrated through lots of experiments. Finally, in section 5, conclusions are drawn and future works are described.

2 SPATIOTEMPORAL RDF DATA RELATED CONCEPTS

2.1 Spatiotemporal RDF Graph

The formalized descriptions of spatiotemporal RDF graph are introduced.

Definition 1: A spatiotemporal RDF data graph is represented as a 6-tuple $G= (V,E,C,F,T,L)$, where $V=V_{st} \cup V_{-st}$ is a set of vertices, V_{st} represents vertexes with temporal or spatial information, and V_{-st} represents vertexes with no temporal or spatial information, $E \in V \times V$ is a set of directed edges, C is a set of textual information labels. F: $V \cup E \rightarrow C\ (T/L)$ is a function, used to assign corresponding textual information labels to vertices and edges (temporal information labels or spatial information labels), T represents the effective time, and L represents geographical location information.

In definition 1, the vertex $V_i \in V$ in spatiotemporal RDF data graph G has a label F_{vi}, and F_{vi} may contain a temporal information T, where the temporal information T is measured in days, and the temporal information T contains the starting time point T_s and the ending time point T_e.

Example 1: The spatiotemporal RDF graph G described in Figure 1 represents a character's experience relationships. The temporal information and spatial information in each vertex label represent the valid time of the vertex and its geographical location in the real world, respectively, in graph G. The temporal information and spatial information in each edge label respectively represent the effective time and the geographical location in the world of the triple (s, p, o) where the edge is contained. For example, the triple (Stan, Born [1879-03-14], Ulm {48.23, 9.59}) indicates that Stan was born in Ulm on March 14, 1879, and Ulm is located at 48.23 longitudes and 9.59 latitude.

Define a variable vertex V_a whose label is denoted by a prefix "?" (Virgilio et al., 2015). Similarly, a variable edge E_a whose label is denoted by a prefix "?".

Definition 2: A spatiotemporal RDF query graph is expressed= (V,E,C,F,T,L), where $V = V_{st} \cup V_{-st} \cup V_a$ is a set of vertices, V_{st} and V_{-st} are just like definition 1, V_a represents variable vertices, $E \in V \times V$ is a set of directed edges, C is a set of labels that contains the variable labels and textual information labels, $F : V \cup E \rightarrow C/T/L$ is a function used to assign corresponding labels to vertices and edges. T and L are defined as definition 1.

In definition 2, the vertex $V_i \in V$ in graph G can be a vertex with temporal information, spatial information, textual information, or a variable vertex. Similarly, the label representation of edge e is similar to the vertex.

Example 2: The spatiotemporal RDF query graph Q is described in Figure 2, where vertices represent specific resources, specific classes, temporal information, spatial information, or variables, and edges represent some relationship between two adjacent vertices. For example, the triple (?b, become, Lecturer 2) presents that there is a person who becomes a Lecturer 2, and that person is uncertain.

Definition 3: An approximate query q^* for graph Q contains a sub-graph of graph G, where there is add operation function $\odot$, delete operation function Θ, modify operation function $\bigcirc$, operation time relation function ξ, and operation position relation function £, represented as: $q^*=f(Q)\bullet ¾(Q)\bullet\circ(Q)\bullet\tilde{}(Q)\bullet\odot(Q)$.

Figure 1. The spatiotemporal RDF data graph

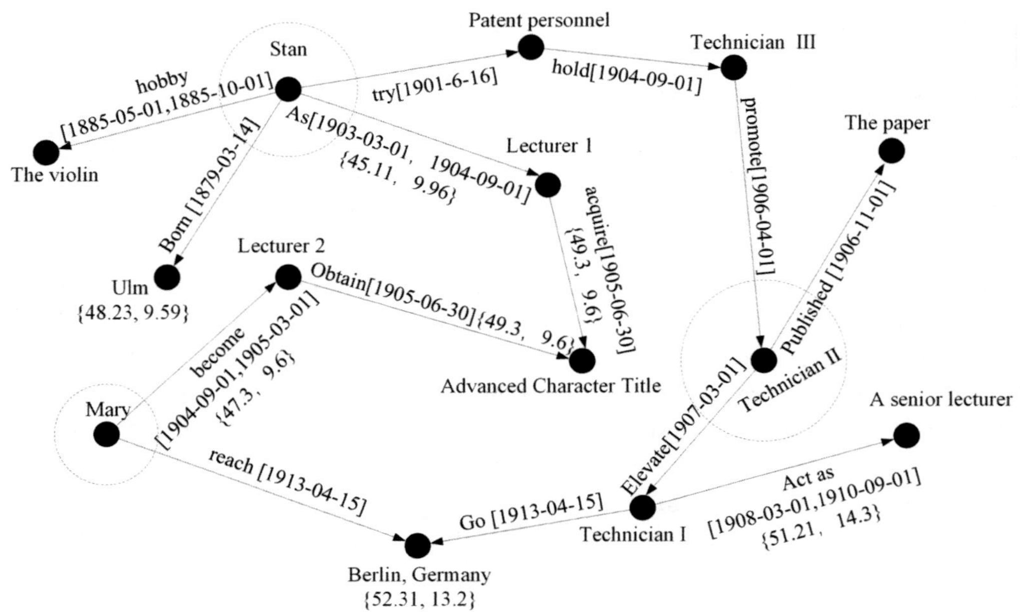

Figure 2. The spatiotemporal RDF query graph

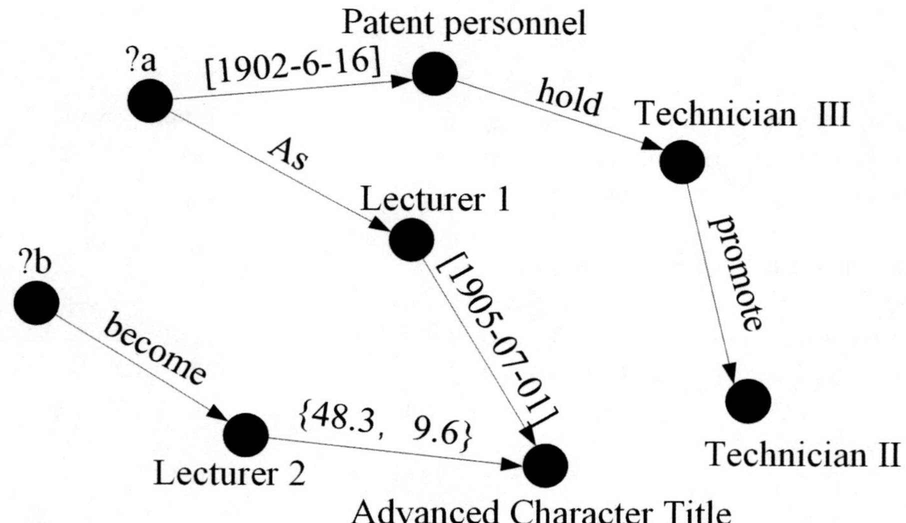

The cost of operation function is denoted by ω. For example, there are two approximate query results: the first result is

$$q_1{*}=\underline{f}_1(Q)\ \bullet ¾_1(Q)\ \bullet\ \circ_1(Q)\ \bullet\tilde{}_1(Q)\ \bullet\odot_1(Q),$$

the second result is

$$q_2{*}=\underline{f}_2(Q)\ \bullet\ ¾_2(Q)\ \bullet\circ_2(Q)\ \bullet\ \tilde{}_2(Q)\ \bullet\odot_2(Q).$$

The two functions are

$$É(q_1{*})=É(\underline{f}_1(Q)\ \bullet\ ¾_1(Q)\bullet\circ_1(Q)\bullet\tilde{}_1(Q)\bullet\odot_1(Q))$$

and

$$É(q_2{*})=É(\underline{f}_2(Q)\ \bullet\ ¾_2(Q)\bullet\circ_2(Q)\bullet\tilde{}_2(Q)\bullet\odot_2(Q)).$$

If there is $\omega(q1_*)<\omega(q2*)$ then Q *and* q1* *are* more similar than Q *and* q2*.
Definition 4: If there is $\omega(q1*)<\omega(q2*)$, Q and

$$q_1{*}=\underline{f}_1(Q)\ \bullet\ ¾_1(Q)\ \bullet\circ_1(Q)\ \bullet\ \tilde{}_1(Q)\ \bullet\odot_1(Q)$$

are much closer than Q and

$$q_2{}^*=\underline{f}_2(Q) \bullet ¾_2(Q) \bullet \circ_2(Q) \bullet \tilde{}_2(Q) \bullet \odot_2(Q).$$

Definition 4.1: For data g_1 and g_2 in data graph G, if data q in query graph Q is more similar to data g_1 than to data g_2 in three aspects of textual information, temporal information, and spatial information, then the better matching data of data q is data g_1.

2.2 Paths and Matching Results

The vertex with the number of incoming edges is zero is taken as the starting vertex (Li et al., 2019).

Definition 5: Suppose $G=(V,E,C,F,T,L)$ is a spatiotemporal RDF data graph G, a directed path is defined as

$$g= F(v_1) \rightarrow F(e_1) \rightarrow F(v_2) \rightarrow F(e_2) \rightarrow F(v_{n-1}) \rightarrow F(e_{n-1}) \rightarrow F(v_n),$$

where $F(v_i)$ represents the label of v_i, $F(e_i)$ represents the label of e_i, $e_i=(v_i, v_{i+1})$, and i belongs to $[1, n\text{-}1]$. At the same time, v_1 is the starting vertex and v_n is the end vertex of path G.

The length of path is the sum of the number of vertices and edges in the path.

Example 3: In data graph G, there are two starting vertices marked by red dotted circle as shown in Figure 1, and they are "Mary" and "Stan" respectively. The path is obtained as follows:

g_i = Mary→ become[1904-09-01, 1905-03-01]{47.3, 9.6}→ Lecturer 2 → Obtain[1905-06-30]{49.3, 9.6}→ Advanced Character Title

The path shows that Mary became a Lecturer 2 at the latitude and longitude of 47.3 and 9.6 respectively between September 1, 1904 and March 1, 1905, and then obtained the Advanced Character Title at the latitude and longitude of 49.3 and 9.6 respectively on June 30, 1905. The length of the path is 5, where the position of the time label [1904-09-01, 1905-03-01] in the path is 2.

Definition 6: For a graph G and a graph Q, there is a path

$$g_i=\underline{f}_i(q_i) \bullet ¾_i(q_i) \bullet \circ_i(q_i) \bullet \tilde{}_i(q_i) \bullet \odot_i(q_i)$$

contained in graph G in graph Q.

The graph Q is split into three paths as follows:

q_1 = ?a→[1902-6-16]→ Patent personnel → hold → Technician III → promote → Technician II

q_2 = ?a→ As → Lecturer 1→[1905-07-01]→ Advanced Character Title

q_3 = ?b→ become → Lecturer 2→{48.3, 9.6}→ Advanced Character Title

Three paths q1, q2 and q3 in graph Q are converted into three paths in graph G, and these paths are:

g_1 = Stan → try [1901-6-16] → Patent personnel → hold [1904-09-01] → Technician III→ promote [1906-04-01] → Technician II

g_2 = Stan → As [1903-03-01, 1904-09-01] {45.11, 9.96} → Lecturer 1 → acquire [1905-06-30] {49.3, 9.6} → Advanced Character Title

g_3 = Mary → become [1904-09-01, 1905-03-01] {47.3, 9.6} → Lecturer 2 → Obtain [1905-06-30] {49.3, 9.6} → Advanced Character Title

Definition 7: In a spatiotemporal RDF data graph $G= (V,E,C,F,T,L)$, there are path

$g_1 = Fv_i\ Fe_i\ Fv_{i+1} \ldots\ Fe_{n-1}\ Fv_n$ and path $g_2 = Fv_i\ Fe_i\ Fv_{i+1} \ldots\ Fe_{m-1}\ Fv_m$.

(1) containment. If any label in path g_1 is included in path g_2, then path g_1 is contained in path g_2. (2) intersection. If there is a vertex label Fv_s in the path g_1 and the same label Fv_r in the path g_2, where s belongs to $[i, n]$, r belongs to $[j, m]$ and $Fv_s = Fv_r$, path g_1 is called to intersect path g_2. (3) no correlation. Path g_1 and path g_2 don't satisfy the above two conditions.

2.3 Evaluation Function

The evaluation function is a function that evaluates the matching degree of the resulting path by considering the two aspects of validity and similarity.

In terms of validity, the paper defines εt (p, q) function to represent the consistency of text contents between path p and path q, as follows:

$$\mu t(p, q) = \frac{|F_p \cup F_q| - |F_p \cap F_q|}{|F_p \cup F_q|} \tag{1}$$

Where $|F_p \cup F_q|$ represents the total number of labels in path p and path q, $|F_p \cap F_q|$ represents the number of the same labels between path p and path q. This paper defines the εs (p, q) function to represent the distance between path p and path q in terms of time and space. As follows:

$$\varepsilon s\ (p, q) = \|p, q\|\ F_{pi}, F_{qi} \in \text{Space} \tag{2}$$

$$p - qF_{pj}, F_{qj} \in \text{Time}$$

When F_{pi} and F_{qi} are space information, Euclidean distance formula is used to obtain the distance between corresponding vertices. When F_{pj} and F_{qj} are time information, if two time periods are compared, the middle distances of the time periods are calculated and the differences between the corresponding intermediate time periods are compared. If two points of time are being compared, the differences are directly compared. ε(p, q) is defined to evaluate the comprehension of the two elements, as follows:

$$\varepsilon(\mathrm{p},q) = \mathrm{e}\cdot\varepsilon\mathrm{t}(\mathrm{p},q) + \mathrm{f}\cdot\varepsilon\mathrm{s}(\mathrm{p},q) \tag{3}$$

The parameters e and f are used to weigh the weight of the two elements. D(p, q) is defined as the operation function that converts path p to path q, as follows:

$$\mathrm{D}(p, q) = a \cdot n\circ \ + b \cdot n^{\sim} \ + c \cdot n\odot \tag{4}$$

Where, n○ represents the number of modification operations, which is the modification of text information; Similarly, $n\Theta$ represents the number of deletion operations, and $n\odot$ represents the number of increase operations. Parameters a, b, and c are used to weigh the weight of the three operations. The validity function is expressed as follows:

$$\lambda(p, q) = \sum_{q \in Q} (\mathrm{D}(p, q) + \mu(p, q)) \tag{5}$$

In terms of similarity, the degree of relation similarity between the retrieved path and the path in the query graph is calculated as follows:

$$\hbar(p, q) = \sum_{q_i, q_j \in Q} k \cdot (\varnothing(p_i, p_j)\ \varnothing(q_i, q_j)) \tag{6}$$

In the equation, qi and qj are two paths in the query graph Q, while pi and pj are two paths in the data graph G, where

$$p_i = f_1(q_i) \bullet \tfrac{3}{4}(q_i) \bullet \ \circ_1(q_i) \bullet^{\sim}{}_1(q_i) \bullet \odot_1(q_i),$$

and

$$p_j = f_1(q_j) \bullet \tfrac{3}{4}(q_j) \bullet \ \circ_1(q_j) \bullet^{\sim}{}_1(q_j) \bullet \odot_1(q_j).$$

$\varnothing(p_i, p_j)$ is used to calculate the number of overlapping labels in the relationship between path pi and pj. $\varnothing(p_i, p_j)\ \varnothing(q_i, q_j)$ is to calculate whether the relationship between path pi and pj is consistent with the relationship between path qi and qj. If so, the value is 0, otherwise, the value is 1. k is the parameter that is used to consider the weight of similarity. The calculation form of the evaluation function evl(p, q) is:

$$\mathrm{evl}(p, q) = \lambda(p, q) + \hbar(p_i, p_j) \tag{7}$$

By selecting appropriate parameters in the evaluation function, a score calculated by the evaluation function can correspond to the degree of the matching result of the query, accurately. For example, when p_1 and q are more similar than p_2 and q, there is evl(p_1, q)<evl(p_2, q).

Theorem 1: Given a query graph Q and a data graph G, there are two corresponding paths p_i and p_j in G for a path q in Q. If p_i and q are more similar than p_j and q, there is evl(p_i, q)<evl(p_j, q).

Proof: In the graph G, there are two paths $g1$ and $g2$. In terms of textual information, temporal information and spatial information, path $g1$ is more similar to path q. According to definition 4.1, path $g1$ has a more similar match with path q, so

$$\varepsilon(g1,q) < \varepsilon(g2,q) \tag{8}$$

If the cost ω_1 of the operation on the path $g1$ is less than that ω_2 of the operation on the path $g2$, according to definition 4, the path $g1$ is more similar to the path q than the path $g2$ is to the path q, so

$$D(g1,q) < D(g2,q) \tag{9}$$

Formula (8) and (9) are combined to get the (10):

$$\lambda\!\!\!^{-} (g1, q) < \lambda\!\!\!^{-} (g2, q) \tag{10}$$

When considering the relationship between path $q1$ and path $q2$ in the query graph, the relationship between path $g1_1$ and path $g1_2$ in the data graph and the relationship between path $g2_1$ and path $g2_2$ are compared. It can be expressed as:

$$\sum_{q_1, q_2 \in Q} k \cdot (\varnothing(g1_1, g1_2)\, \varnothing(q_1, q_2)) < \sum_{q_1, q_2 \in Q} k \cdot (\varnothing(g2_1, g2_2)\, \varnothing(q_1, q_2)) \tag{11}$$

Obviously, there are:

$$\hbar\, (g1, q) < \hbar\, (g2, q) \tag{12}$$

Combining (10) and (12), the relation of evaluation function is obtained: evl($g1$, q)< evl($g2$, q).

2.4 Matching Calculation

In order to measure the matching degree of approximate paths, query graph Q is decomposed into a set of paths. According to definition 5, query graph Q in Figure 2 is decomposed into the following three paths:

q_1: ?a→[1902-6-16]→Patent personnel→ hold→ Technician III→ promote→ Technician II

q_2: ?a→ As→ Lecturer 1→[1905-07-01]→ Advanced Character Title

q_3: ?b→ become→ Lecturer 2→{48.3, 9.6}→Advanced Character Title

Assume that the path set p consists of the three paths from data graph G:

p_1:Stan→ try [1901-6-16] → Patent personnel→ hold [1904-09-01] → Technician III→ promote [1906-04-01] → Technician II

p_2:Stan→ As [1903-03-01, 1904-09-01] {45.11, 9.96} → Lecturer 1→ acquire [1905-06-30] {49.3, 9.6} → Advanced Character Title

p_3:Mary→ become [1904-09-01, 1905-03-01] {47.3, 9.6} → Lecturer 2→ Obtain [1905-06-30] {49.3, 9.6} → Advanced Character Title

Path set p is the approximate query result with the highest matching of query graph Q. The first edge label [1902-6-16] of path q_1 in path set p is the time tag, so the first temporal tag in edge of path p_1 is found [1901-6-16]. Because these labels are inconsistent, the time label [1901-6-16] needs to be modified, while ignoring the text information label "try", and the next tag is compared in turn to realize the consistency. For example, path p_2 in data graph G is matched to path q_2 and path q_3 in query graph Q. Path p_2 is as follows:

p_2:Stan→ As [1903-03-01, 1904-09-01] {45.11, 9.96} → Lecturer 1→ acquire [1905-06-30] {49.3, 9.6} → Advanced Character Title

Path q_2 and path q_3 are as follows:

q_2: ?a → As→ Lecturer 1→[1905-07-01]→ Advanced Character Title

$£_1(q_2)●ξ_1(q_2)●O_1(q_2)●Θ_1(q_2)●⊙_1(q_2)$:

Stan→ As [1903-03-01, 1904-09-01]{45.11, 9.96}→Lecturer 1→acquire[1905-06-30] {49.3, 9.6}→ Advanced Character Title

q_3: ?b→ become→ Lecturer 2→{48.3, 9.6}→Advanced Character Title

$£_3(q_3)●ξ_3(q_3)●O_3(q_3)●Θ_3(q_3)●⊙_3(q_3)$:

Stan→ As[1903-03-01, 1904-09-01]{45.11, 9.96}→Lecturer 1→acquire[1905-06-30] {49.3, 9.6}→ Advanced Character Title

In this example, the path q_2 matched the path p_2 is evaluated, and the degree of consistency of the content measured is $εt(p_2,q_2)=(5–3)/5=0.4$. The time information label is inconsistent, so the time distance is measured as $εs(p_2,q_2)=1905/07/01–1905/06/30=1$, and the formula is $ε(p_2,q_2)=0.4e+f$. Due to the inconsistency of the text information, the modification operation needs to be carried out and the formula is $D(p_2, q_2) = a \cdot n∘ = 2a$. Therefore, the validity function value is $ƛ(p_2, q_2) = 0.4e+f + 2a$. Similarly, the path q_3 is evaluated, and the content consistency degree is obtained $εt(p_2,q_3)=0.8$. Due to inconsistent labels of spatial information, the Euclidean distance measured is $εs(p_2,q_3)=[(49.3,9.6),(48.3,9.6)]=1$, so the formula is $εs(p_2,q_3)=0.8e+f$. Existing the inconsistency in the text message, the modification operation needs to be carried out, and the formula is $D(p_2, q_2) =a \cdot n∘ = 4a$.

Therefore, the validity function value is $\lambda\ (p_2, q_3) = 0.8e+f\ + 4a$. If a=0.5, e=10 and f=0.01 are set, $\lambda\ (p_2, q_2) = 5.01$ and $\lambda(p_2, q_3) = 10.01$ are acquired. As a result, path p_2 matches path q_2 better than path p_2 matches path q_3. The problem of approximate matching of query graph is solved, and the optimal matching graph of query graph is obtained.

3 MATCHING ALGORITHM

The general idea of the algorithm is introduced in section A. Then the matching process of this algorithm is further introduced in section B.

3.1 Overview of the Method

In the process of approximate query, there are mainly two stages. The first stage is to split query graph Q into paths, and the second stage is to combine approximate matching paths.

(1) Decomposition processing. The decomposition graph algorithm splits the query graph Q into a group of paths. In the process of path generation, the path length is calculated, which is marked at the last position of the path including the first column in the list. In order to save the structure information of query graph Q, the positions of vertices and edges in the path are numbered to determine the positions of intersection points, which are saved in the second column of the list containing the last position of the corresponding path, as shown below.

q_1: ?b→ become→ Lecturer 2→{48.3, 9.6}→Advanced Character Title <5, < q_2:5>>

q_2: ?a→ As→ Lecturer 1→[1905-07-01]→Advanced Character Title <5, < q_1:5, q_3:1>>

q_3: ?a→[1902-06-16]→Patent personnel→ hold→ Technician III→ promote→ Technician II<7, < q_2:1>>

(2) Paths combination. According to the length of path q in the graph Q, the path p is found in the data graph G. For example, when u=2 is set, the approximate matching path length of path q_3 is in the range of [5, 9]. Meanwhile, the lengths of paths p_4, p_5 and p_6 are in this range. Then, the validity function is used to calculate the validity evaluation values of paths q_3 and p_4, p_5 and p_6, which are 14.58, 19.96 and 8.05, respectively. Then, according to the validity evaluation values, the order of paths p_4, p_5 and p_6 is p_6, p_4 and p_5. Finally, according to the structure information in the query graph Q, the path p_6 with the best validity evaluation value is connected. The paths contained in the data graph G are shown below.

p_1:Stan→ hobby [1885-05-01, 1885-10-01] →The violin <3>

p_2:Stan → Born [1879-03-14] → Ulm { 48.23, 9.59} <3>

p_3:Mary→ reach [1913-04-15] → Berlin Germany {52.31, 13.2} <3>

p_4:Stan→ As [1903-03-01, 1904-09-01] {45.11, 9.96} → Lecturer 1→ acquire [1905-06-30] {49.3, 9.6} → Advanced Character Title <5>

p_5:Mary→ become [1904-09-01, 1905-03-01] {47.3, 9.6} → Lecturer 2→ Obtain [1905-06-30] {49.3, 9.6} → Advanced Character Title <5>

p_6:Stan→ try [1901-6-16] → Patent personnel→ hold [1904-09-01] →Technician III→ promote [1906-04-01] → Technician II→Published [1906-11-01] → The paper <9>

3.2 Matching Methods of Graph

(1) The process of splitting a graph into paths. The query graph Q is split into different paths. In algorithm 1, the path set, a queue, and a variable are first initialized, and the function seekStartVertex(Q) is called to infer the starting vertex (lines 1-4). Select a vertex from start vertex to traverse, and judge whether the edge label adjacent to the start vertex exists. If the edge label exists and has not been visited, it is marked as visited and enqueued for operation. The number of labels i increases by 1, then judge whether the vertex label exists adjacent to the edge. If there is the vertex label and it is not accessed, the vertex label is marked as visited and enqueued for operation. In the same way, until the next label is null (lines 5-10). Add the generated path to the path set and save the number of labels in the path (line 11). When a path has been traversed, the queue is left empty and the next path is traversed (line 12). Next, initialize a set, and traverse two different paths (lines 13-15) to determine whether there is an intersection label.

If it exists, the label is the intersecting label of two paths (lines 16-18). Finally, A set is made empty, and all paths are traversed and the resulting set of paths (lines 19-20) is output.

(2) Approximate paths combination. After the query graph Q is divided into paths, the approximate paths are searched in the data graph G. In algorithm 2, an approximate path set and multi-queues are initialized. The length of each path is calculated (lines 1-4). According to the path length m, the path with its length in the range $[m - u, m + u]$ is found in the data graph G (line 5). The path p found and q_r are evaluated (line 6), and the evaluation results, path p and the serial number of the path q are stored in the queue (line 7). The paths are sorted from low to high in queue according to the evaluation results. Next, the number of paths is calculated in the path set, the top-1 path in queue is output and then saved to the approximate path set (lines 8-12). Finally, the generated approximate path set is traversed. According to the relationship between the paths in the query graph, the corresponding two paths are connected according to the serial number of the join points (lines 13-17). After the traversal is completed, the best approximate result (line 18) is returned.

4 EXPERIMENTAL STUDY

In this section, the theoretical methods proposed in this chapter are analyzed and verified through experiments. Section A describes the setting parameters in the experiment. Section B and C respectively introduce the effectiveness and efficiency of theoretical methods.

Algorithm 1. Decomposition graph

Input:The query graph Q
Output:The path set
pathSet ← { };
Queue ← { };
i← 1;
S ← seekStartVertex(Q);
foreach s ∈S **do**
EnQueue(Queue, s);
foreach ((n ← getUnVisitNeighbor (Q, s))! =null) **do**
n.visit ← true;
EnQueue (Queue, n);
i ← i+ 1;
pathSet← pathSet U Queue U i;
Queue←Φ;
union ← { };
foreach q ∈pathSet **do**
foreach q' ∈ pathSet-q **do**
if (q' n q !=null) **then**
union ← q' n q;
q ∪ union and q' ∪ union;
union ← { };
return pathSet;

Algorithm 2. Combination query paths

Input:The path set, the data graph G
Output:The best approximate result graph
ApproximatePathSet ←{ };
mp ← Φ;
foreach q_r ∈pathSet **do**
m ←CountNum(q_r);
foreach p ← seekPath(G, m, u) **do**
d ←evl(p, q_r);
mp_r.enqueue(p, d, $q_{r.id}$);
i ←0; n ← 0;
j←CountPath(pathSet);
foreach n < j and mp_n != Φ **do**
p_o←mp_n.dequeue();
ApproximatePathSet ←ApproximatePathSet U {p_o, i, q_{id} };
foreach q_y ∈ApproximatePathSet **do**
foreach q_x ∈ApproximatePathSet **do**
if q_x.union == q_y.union **then**
ApproximatePathSet← connectPath($q_x.p_x$, $q_y.p_y$).$union_{id}$
Best_result←ApproximatePathSet;
return Best_result;

4.1 Experimental Settings

Data set. The data set used for the experiment is a subset of YAGO, which contains information from Wikipedia, WordNet and GeoNames. The entity relation diagrams about time and place are extracted to construct the spatiotemporal data diagram with the experience of people.

Query patterns. Query graphs with four different patterns are constructed. The four patterns are linear query pattern, star query pattern, tree query pattern (Tong et al., 2007) and loop query pattern, as shown in Figure 3. Figure 3(a) can be used as a path to query in the path set. Figure 3(b) can be decomposed into four paths, which can be queried in the path set respectively. These four paths have a common vertex A. Figure 3(c) can be decomposed into four paths, meanwhile path A→B→C and path A→B→D has common vertexes A and B, and a common edge. Figure 3(d) can be decomposed into four paths, including path A→B→C, path A→C, path A→D→C and path A→D→B→C. According to definition 7, path A→D→B→C contains the other three paths. The query patterns including the linear query pattern, star query pattern, tree query pattern and loop query pattern are abbreviated to LN, ST, TR and LP, respectively

Figure 3. Query patterns

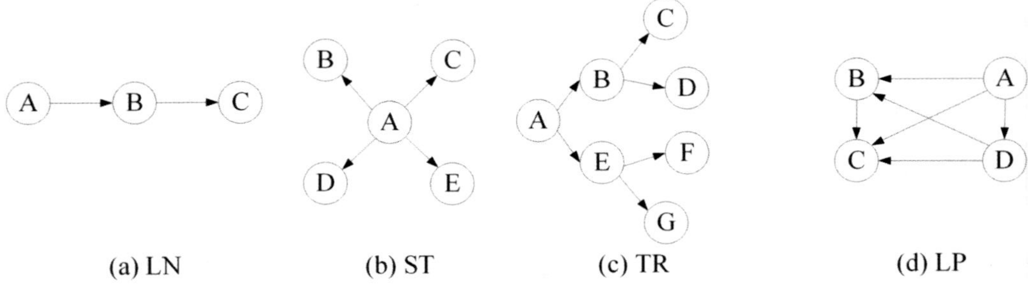

Figure 4. Approximate quality ratio

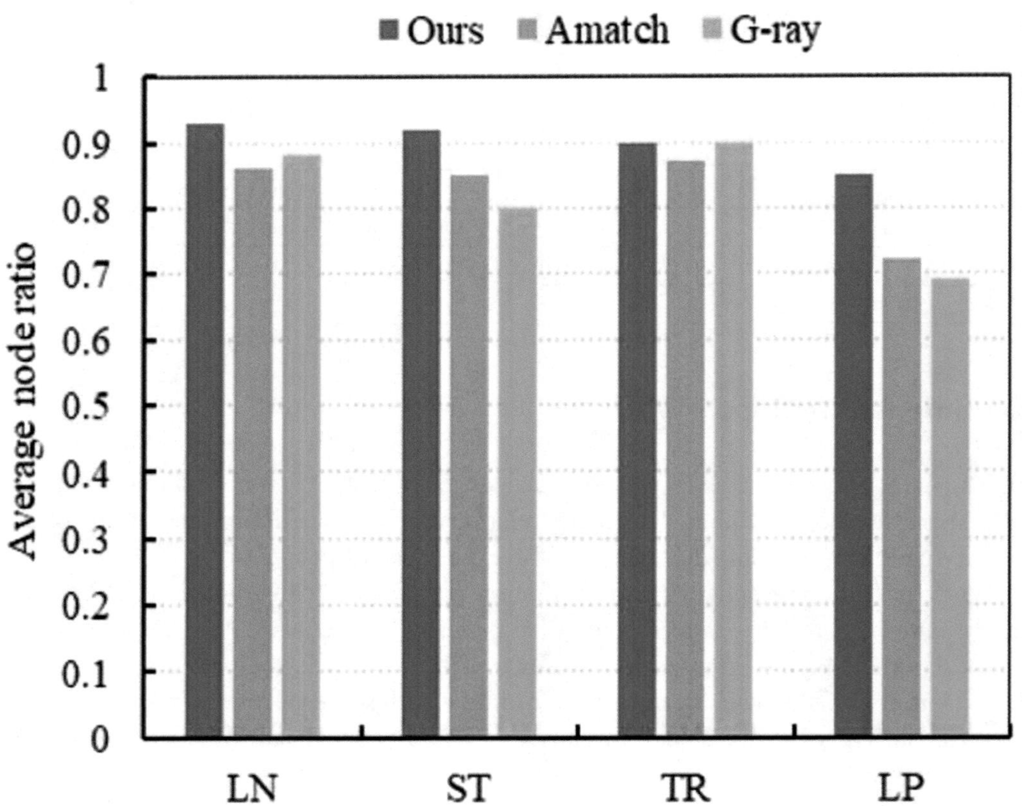

Figure 5. Approximate node ratio

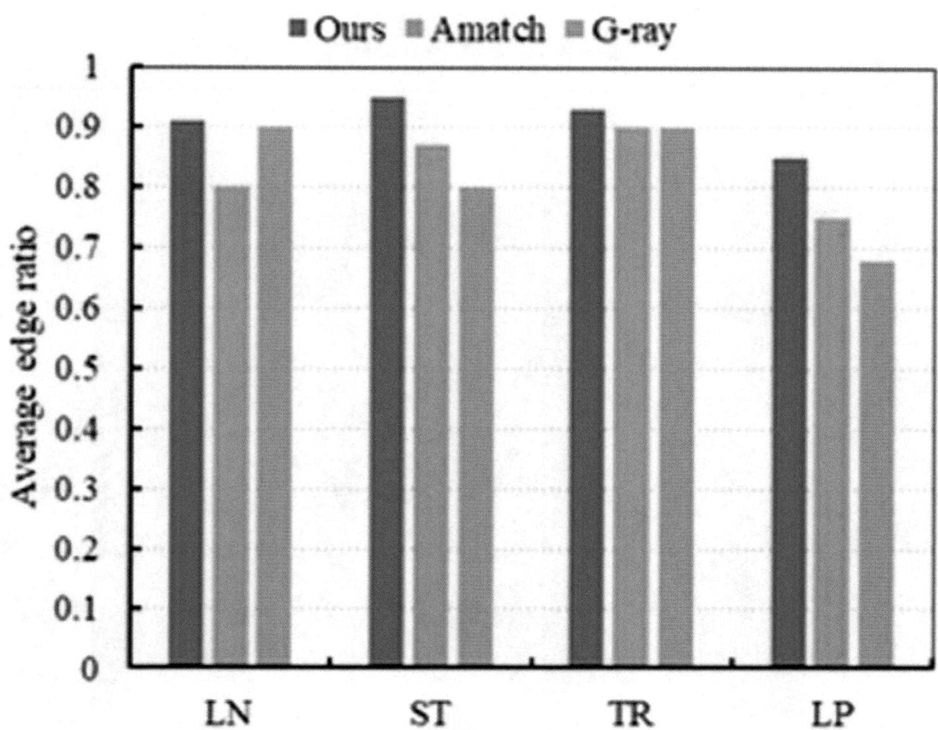

All algorithms are run on a Win10 system with 2.2 GHz Intel (R) Core (TM) i5 processor and 12GB memory. Our algorithm is compared with two other matching algorithms: Amatch (Li et al., 2019) and G-ray (Tong et al., 2007).

4.2 Effectiveness Evaluation

In order to verify the effectiveness of our method, the effectiveness evaluation experiments with Amatch algorithm and G-ray algorithm are conducted out from three aspects: the average approximate result ratio, the average approximate vertex ratio and the average edge similarity ratio. We only consider top-1 matching results to evaluate the approximation of the results with a query threshold of 0.1.

Figure 4 shows an experimental analysis of the average approximation result ratios for all algorithms in four patterns. The average approximation result ratio is the average similarity ratio between the approximate path found by the algorithm and the corresponding path in the data graph. Under the patterns LN, ST, TR and LP, the average approximation result ratios measured by our algorithm are 0.92, 0.86, 0.87 and 0.73, respectively. Our algorithm has a higher average approximation ratio, and its approximation degree is slightly higher than that of Amatch algorithm. The key reason is that our algorithm can make better use of structure information and vertex information, although its accuracy is lower than other algorithms.

Figure 6. Approximate edge ratio

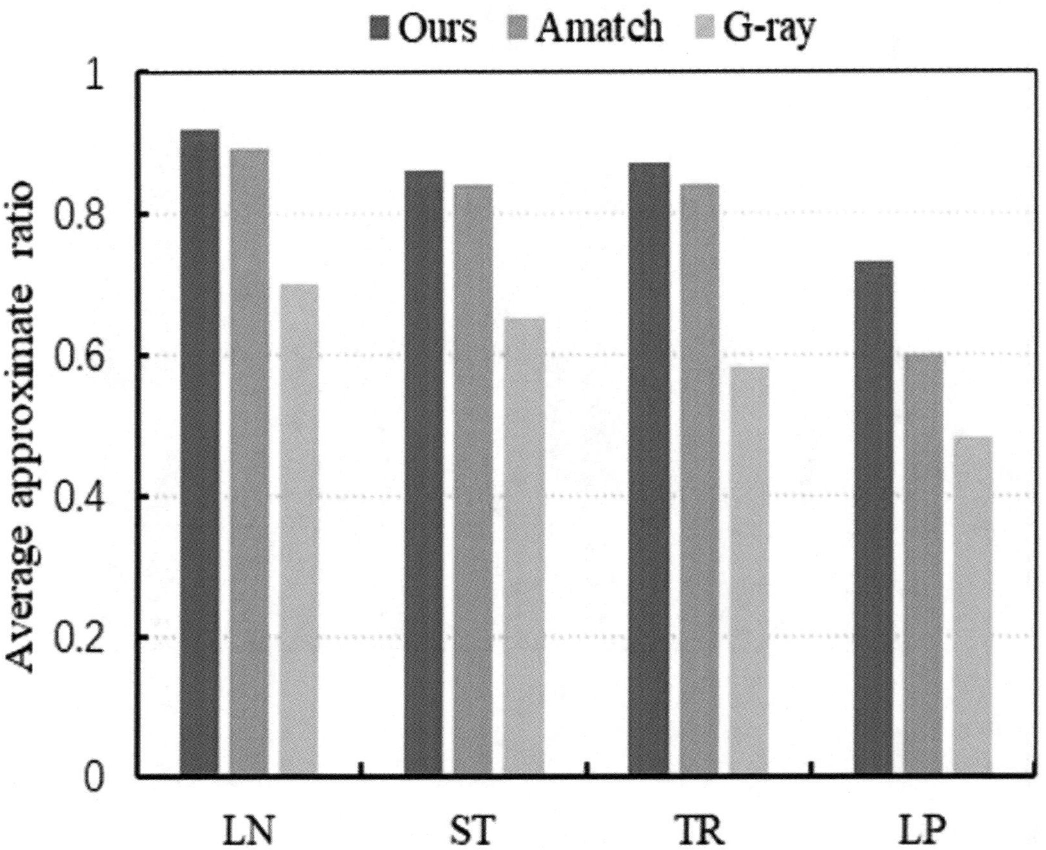

Figure 5 shows an experimental analysis of the average approximate vertex ratios of all algorithms in the four patterns. The average approximate vertex ratio is the average ratio of the vertices on the query path to the vertices on the corresponding path in the data graph. Under the patterns LN, ST, TR and LP, the average approximate vertex ratios measured by our algorithm are 0.93, 0.92, 0.90 and 0.85 respectively. Our algorithm has better average vertex similarity than Amatch algorithm and G-ray algorithm. Since our algorithm uses the length information of path, the search range does not increase with the increasing length of the path.

Figure 6 shows the experimental analysis of average edge similarity ratio of all algorithms under four patterns. Average edge similarity ratio refers to the average similarity ratio between the edges of the path found by the algorithm and the edges of the corresponding path in the data graph. Under the patterns LN, ST, TR and LP, the average edge similarity ratio measured by our algorithm are 0.91, 0.95, 0.93 and 0.85, respectively. In the four patterns, the average vertex similarity of our algorithm is high, while the Amatch and G-ray algorithms are unstable. This is because the Amatch and G-ray algorithms are more accurate than ours, and their queries in approximate paths take more time to find matching results.

4.3 Efficiency Evaluation

After verifying the effectiveness of our algorithm, experimental studies with datasets of different sizes are conducted on efficiency evaluation. Figure 7 shows how query times change as the number of vertices in the data graph changes. When the total number of vertices in the data graph is 2M, the total query time of our algorithm and the Amatch algorithm reaches a peak. When the total number of vertices in the data graph is more than 2M, the total query time required by our algorithm tends to be stable, between 300s and 600s.

The number of edges is changed in the query path to verify our algorithm performance in Figure 8. The number of edges in the query path is set to 5, 10, 15, 20, 25, and 30. As the number of edges in the path increases, the running time of G-ray algorithm increases greatly, and Amatch and our algorithm have stable time cost. In Figure 9, time consumption analyses are conducted for three algorithms in four different patterns, and our algorithm and Amatch algorithm have good stability. In LN pattern, the three algorithms show high performance. The performance of G-ray algorithm is unstable, and it takes the most time in LP pattern than in the other two patterns.

Figure 7. Effect of nodes size

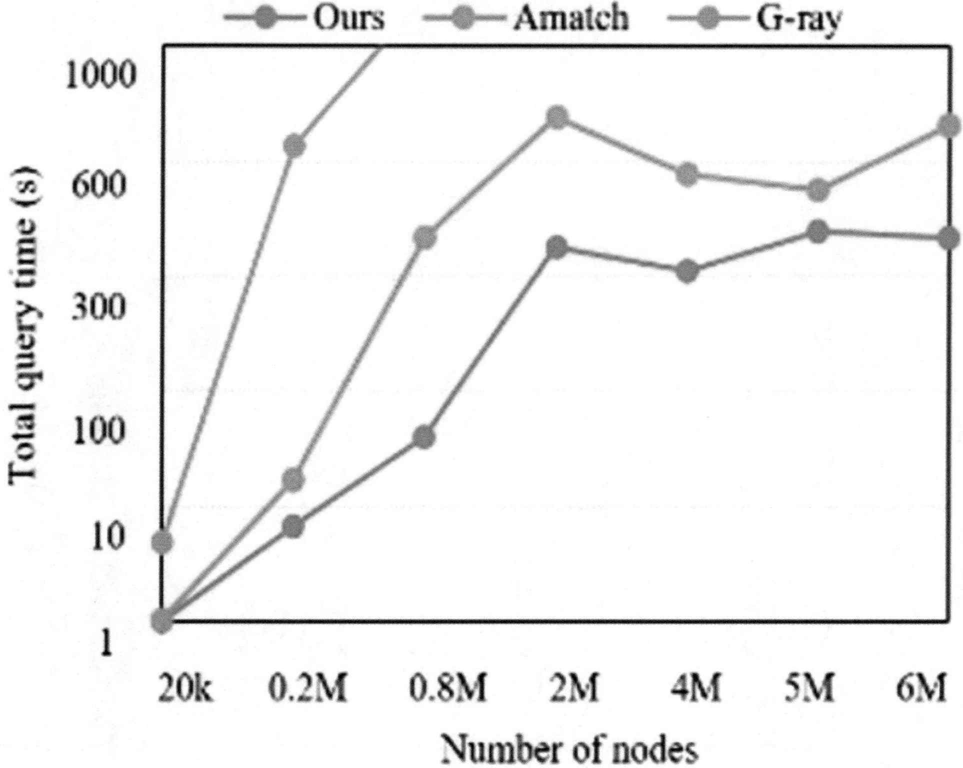

Figure 8. Effect of edges size

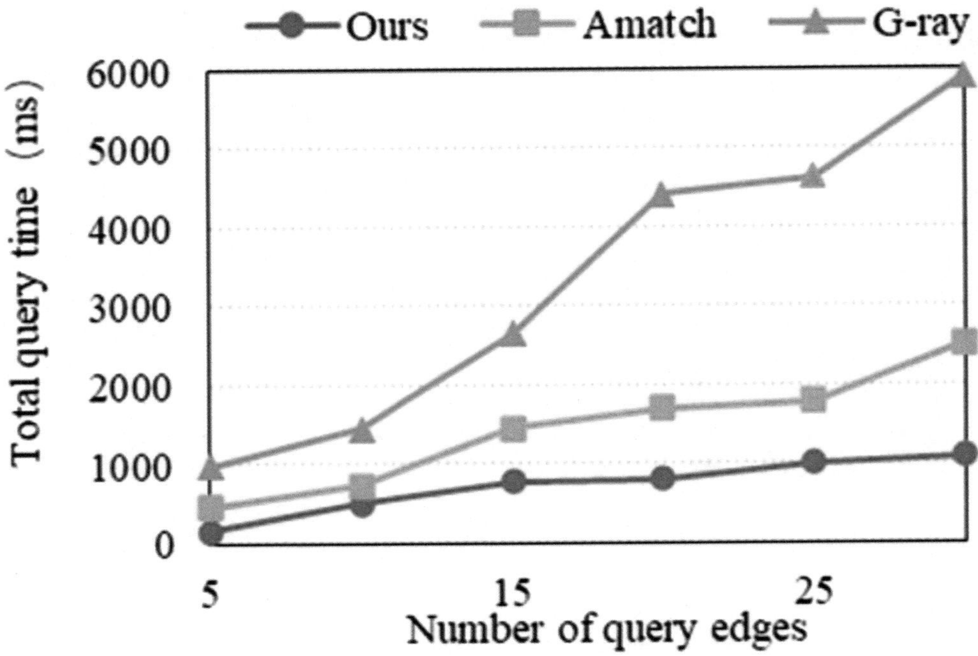

Figure 9. Average time cost

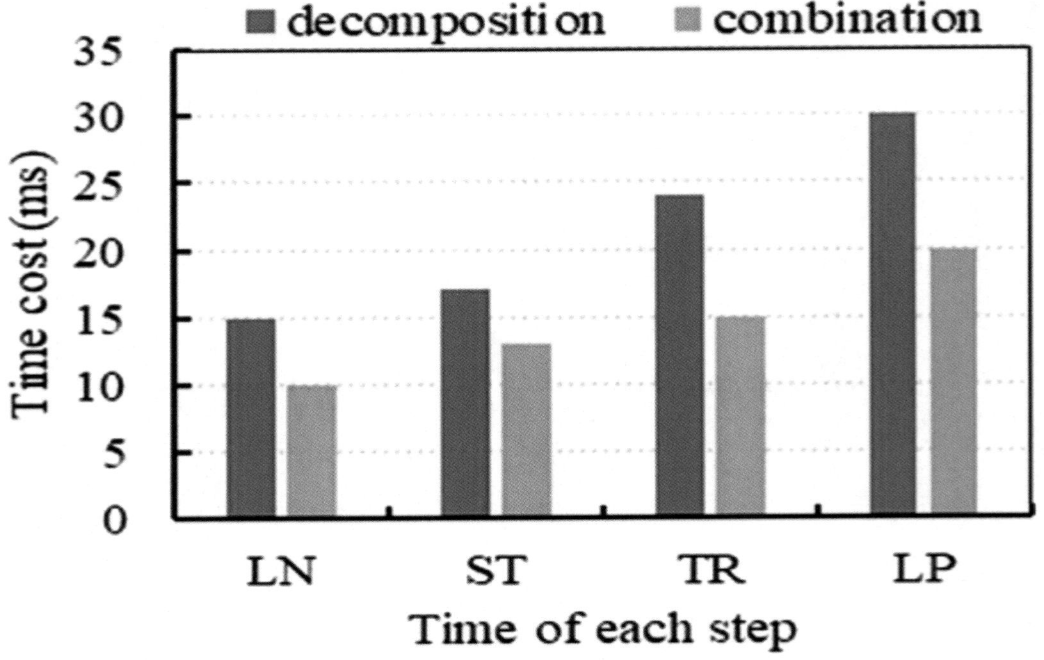

Figure 10. Average response time

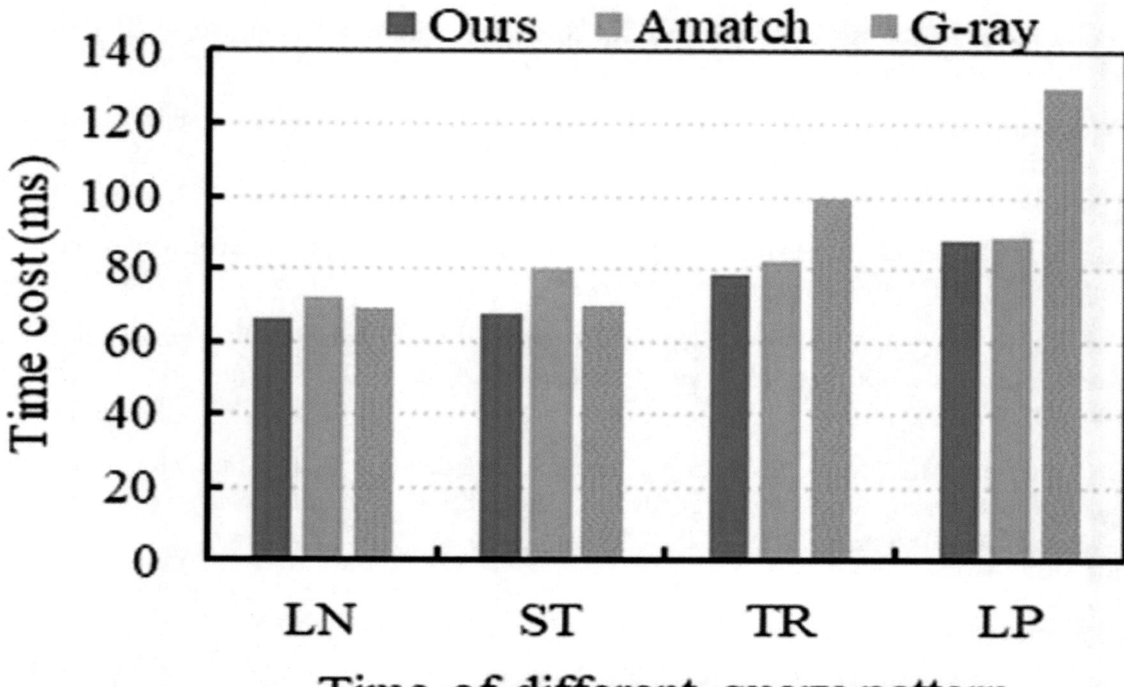

In Figure 10, our algorithm is divided into two parts for experiment: decomposition graph algorithm and combination query paths algorithm. As can be seen from the graph, under the four patterns, the decomposition graph algorithm takes more time than the combination query paths algorithm. In the LN pattern, the performance of the decomposition graph algorithm and the combination query paths algorithm is higher than that of the other three patterns. In LP pattern, the performance of decomposition graph algorithm and combination query paths algorithm is the worst.

5 SUMMARY

Because RDF data with temporal and spatial characteristics is ubiquitous in our lives, processing this data in an efficient way will provide us with a lot of valuable information and help us better analyze and research problems. In this chapter, we propose a path-based approximate matching algorithm for spatiotemporal RDF data. The algorithm decomposes the spatiotemporal RDF data graph into a set of highly indexed paths that match the target path, and retrieves the most similar paths based on the evaluation function defined in this chapter. Subsequently, the optimized approximate paths are combined according to the relationships among the target paths. Experimental results demonstrate that our method outperforms other approaches in terms of effectiveness and efficiency.

REFERENCES

Chakkarwar, V. A., Professor, A., & Joshi, A. A. (2016). Semantic Web Mining using RDF Data. *International Journal of Computer Applications*, *133FDLh*(10), 14-19.

De Virgilio, R., Maccioni, A., & Torlone, R. (2013). A similarity measure for approximate querying over RDF data. In *Proceedings of the Joint EDBT/ICDT 2013 Workshops* (pp. 205-213). ACM. 10.1145/2457317.2457352

Elzein, N. M., Majid, M. A., Fakherldin, M., & Hashem, I. A. T. (2018). Distributed Join Query Processing for Big RDF Data. *Advanced Science Letters*, *24*(10), 7758–7761. doi:10.1166/asl.2018.13013

Hurtado, C., & Vaisman, A. (2006). Reasoning with temporal constraints in RDF. In *International Workshop on Principles and Practice of Semantic Web Reasoning* (pp. 164-178). Springer Berlin Heidelberg. 10.1007/11853107_12

Jeon, G., Anisetti, M., Kim, D., Bellandi, V., Damiani, E., & Jeong, J. (2009). Fuzzy rough sets hybrid scheme for motion and scene complexity adaptive deinterlacing. *Image and Vision Computing*, *27*(4), 425–436. doi:10.1016/j.imavis.2008.06.001

Li, G., Yan, L., & Ma, Z. (2019). An approach for approximate subgraph matching in fuzzy RDF graph. *Fuzzy Sets and Systems*, *376*, 106–126. doi:10.1016/j.fss.2019.02.021

Liagouris, J., Mamoulis, N., Bouros, P., & Terrovitis, M. (2014). An effective encoding scheme for spatial RDF data. *Proceedings of the VLDB Endowment International Conference on Very Large Data Bases*, *7*(12), 1271–1282. doi:10.14778/2732977.2733000

Manola, F., Miller, E., & McBride, B. (2004). RDF primer. *W3C recommendation*, *10*(1-107), 6.

Nikitopoulos, P., Vlachou, A., Doulkeridis, C., & Vouros, G. A. (2018). DiStRDF: Distributed Spatio-temporal RDF Queries on Spark. In EDBT/ICDT Workshops (pp. 125-132). ACM.

Pugliese, A., Udrea, O., & Subrahmanian, V. S. (2008). Scaling RDF with time. In *Proceedings of the 17th international conference on World Wide Web* (pp. 605-614). ACM. 10.1145/1367497.1367579

Smeros, P., & Koubarakis, M. (2016). Discovering Spatial and Temporal Links among RDF Data. In LDOW@WWW.

Tian, Y., & Patel, J. M. (2008). Tale: A tool for approximate large graph matching. In *2008 IEEE 24th International Conference on Data Engineering* (pp. 963-972). IEEE. 10.1109/ICDE.2008.4497505

Tong, H., Faloutsos, C., Gallagher, B., & Eliassi-Rad, T. (2007). Fast best-effort pattern matching in large attributed graphs. In *Proceedings of the 13th ACM SIGKDD international conference on Knowledge discovery and data mining* (pp. 737-746). ACM. 10.1145/1281192.1281271

Virgilio, R., & De. (2015). Approximate querying of RDF graphs via path alignment. *Distributed and Parallel Databases*, *33*(4), 555–581. doi:10.1007/s10619-014-7142-1

Vlachou, A., Doulkeridis, C., Glenis, A., Santipantakis, G. M., & Vouros, G. A. (2019). Efficient spatio-temporal RDF query processing in large dynamic knowledge bases. In *Proceedings of the 34th ACM/SIGAPP Symposium on Applied Computing* (pp. 439-447). ACM. 10.1145/3297280.3299732

Wang, D., Zou, L., Feng, Y., Shen, X., Tian, J., & Zhao, D. (2013). S-store: An engine for large rdf graph integrating spatial information. In *International Conference on Database Systems for Advanced Applications* (pp. 31-47). ACM. 10.1007/978-3-642-37450-0_3

Wang, D., Zou, L., & Zhao, D. (2017). gst-store: Querying large spatiotemporal RDF graphs. *Data and Information Management*, *1*(2), 84–103. doi:10.1515/dim-2017-0008

Yan, L., Zhao, P., & Ma, Z. (2019). Indexing temporal RDF graph. *Computing*, *101*(10), 1457–1488. doi:10.1007/s00607-019-00703-w

Zêzere, J. L., Pereira, S., Tavares, A. O., Bateira, C., Trigo, R. M., Quaresma, I., Santos, P. P., Santos, M., & Verde, J. (2014). DISASTER: A GIS database on hydro-geomorphologic disasters in Portugal. *Natural Hazards*, *72*(2), 503–532. doi:10.1007/s11069-013-1018-y

Zhu, L., Ng, W. K., & Cheng, J. (2011). Structure and attribute index for approximate graph matching in large graphs. *Information Systems*, *36*(6), 958–972. doi:10.1016/j.is.2011.03.009

Zou, L., Mo, J., Chen, L., Özsu, M. T., & Zhao, D. (2011). gStore: Answering SPARQL queries via subgraph matching. *Proceedings of the VLDB Endowment International Conference on Very Large Data Bases*, *4*(8), 482–493. doi:10.14778/2002974.2002976

Chapter 6
Subgraph Matching of Spatiotemporal RDF Data

ABSTRACT

With the growing importance of RDF data in web data management, there is an increasing need for modeling and querying RDF data. In this chapter, firstly, the authors formally define spatiotemporal RDF data and construct a spatiotemporal RDF model st-RDF that is used to represent and manipulate spatiotemporal RDF data. Secondly, they propose the stQuery algorithm for subgraph matching of spatiotemporal RDF data. This algorithm can quickly determine whether the query result is empty for queries whose temporal or spatial range exceeds a specific range by adopting a preliminary query filtering mechanism in the query process. Thirdly, they propose a sorting strategy that calculates the matching order of query nodes to speed up the subgraph matching. Finally, they conduct experiments in terms of effect and query efficiency. The experimental results show the performance advantages of this approach.

1 INTRODUCTION

Resource Description Framework (RDF), as a standard metadata description framework proposed by the World Wide Web Consortium (W3C) (Manola et al, 2004), can be used in various fields such as intelligent software agents, privacy preferences, and privacy policies. Based on the advantages of RDF in data and knowledge representation, many researchers have proposed to use RDF in the management of temporal data in recent years. In the representation of temporal data, some researchers have tried to introduce the time dimension into standard RDF or add time stamp information after the predicate or the entire triplet (Perry, 2008), to achieve RDF-based temporal data modeling. Gutierrez et al. (Gutierrez et al., 2005) propose a framework that incorporates temporal reasoning into RDF to generate temporal RDF graphs, and at the same time provides a semantic for these graphs, including a grammar that uses RDF vocabulary and time labels to integrate the grammatical framework into standard RDF graphs. Since then, in response to the query requirements of temporal RDF data, Pugliese et al. (Pugliese et al., 2008) propose the tGRIN index structure, which establishes a special index for the temporal RDF physically stored in the RDBMS. Motik (Motik, 2011) raises a logic-based method to represent the effective time

DOI: 10.4018/978-1-6684-9108-9.ch006

in RDF and OWL and devises a query evaluation algorithm. Recently, Zhang et al. (Zhang et al., 2019) put forward a new RDF-based temporal data representation model, RDFt, and its query method. This model is suitable for querying temporal data in practical applications.

There are information and datasets in the real world have spatial attributes such as geographic location (Hayes, 2004). Kolas et al. (Kolas et al., 2006) come up with ontology types that can support geographic spatial semantics systems in order to realize the analysis and query operations of spatial data and expound the motivation of each ontology type and the potential areas of geospatial community standardization. Smart et al. (Smart et al., 2007) use qualitative spatial reasoning to support geographic ontology management system development tools and introduce the realization of the spatial reasoning engine, where the Web ontology language (OWL) and its associated reasoning tools are applied, and the space rules engine extension of the OWL associated reasoning tool is used to represent spatial reasoning and integrity rules. Subsequently, Batsakis and Petrakis (Batsakis & Petrakis, 2011) propose SOWL, demonstrating how spatial and spatiotemporal information and spatiotemporal evolution can be effectively represented in OWL. Recently, Ademaj et al. (Ademaj et al. 2019) introduce a novel spatial consistency model that applies to all geometrically based popular stochastic channel models. Cui et al. (Cui et al., 2018) focus on modeling the spatial point process of random vehicle positions in large and small cities, and experimentally verify the real location data of moving taxi tracks recorded by the global positioning system (GPS), thus forming a spatial RDF model.

With the development of temporal data models (Artale et al., 2007) and spatial data models (Goodhue et al., 2015), some researchers have begun to consider integrating temporal attributes and spatial attributes, and are committed to constructing spatiotemporal RDF data models that can simultaneously represent temporal and spatial information. Some relevant departments provide real RDF data sets integrating time information and spatial information. These data sets include YAGO2, OpenStreetMap, and GovTrack, where YAGO2 is an RDF dataset based on Wikipedia and WordNet (Semantic Web) Hoffart et al., 2013; Hoffart et al., 2011). At the same time, Koubarakis and Kyzirakos (Koubarakis & Kyzirakos, 2010) developed a constrained data model stRDF, which has the ability to represent spatial and temporal data. Wang et al. (Wang et al., 2014) designed a spatiotemporal data model of spatiotemporal RDF quintuples, and spatiotemporal RDF data can be organized in the form of graphs containing spatiotemporal features based on the model. Lu et al. (Lu et al., 2018) take the fuzziness of the data into account and conceived a novel fuzzy spatiotemporal data model DPS. Xu et al. (Xu et al., 2017) constituted a Bayesian spatiotemporal stochastic model to fully explain the spatiotemporal correlation in RSI. Sun et al. (Sun et al., 2019) proposed a framework for unifying geospatial data, which can effectively organize geospatial data. Kyzirakos et al. (Kyzirakos et al., 2012) proposed a new RDF store that supports the state of the art semantic geospatial query languages stSPARQL and GeoSPARQL.

The work of querying spatiotemporal RDF data has also received widespread attention, apart from constructing a spatiotemporal RDF data model to realize the representation function of spatiotemporal data. Vlachou et al. (Vlachou et al., 2019) compressed the spatiotemporal information of each RDF entity into a unique integer value and use this code in the filtering and optimization framework to effectively query spatiotemporal RDF data. Wu et al. (Wu et al., 2020) proposed a keyword-based spatiotemporal RDF data query method kSPT, which does not rely on the use of a structured query language. Eom et al. (Eom et al., 2015) used the method of constructing an index to query the spatiotemporal data. However, since the spatiotemporal RDF data model is modeled based on the RDF data model, it can also be represented and stored in the form of graphs. With the rapid development of graph query algorithms based on subgraph matching, it is necessary to clarify the concepts of RDF graph mapping,

RDF graph equivalence, and graph isomorphism (Hayes, 2004). The representative subgraph matching algorithms include VF2 (Cordella et al., 2004), Quicks I (Shang et al., 2008), GraphQL (He & Singh, 2008), GADDI (Zhang et al., 2009), SPATH (Zhao & Han, 2010), and TurbOiso (Han et al., 2013). In order to improve query performance, Lee et al. (Lee et al., 2012) constructed a general framework of a subgraph matching algorithm.

Although current efforts have advantages of querying RDF data, they mainly focus on temporal RDF or spatial RDF. In order to model and query spatiotemporal RDF data, not only do their respective temporal and spatial features need to be considered, but the overall spatiotemporal features over time also need to be considered, which is not a straightforward task. Consequently, a range of research for spatiotemporal RDF data management is investigated. However, they mainly focus on spatiotemporal RDF data representations formally, or they are not well compatible with efficient querying. The existing spatiotemporal models or standard vocabularies dedicated to spatiotemporal data will generate redundant information when querying spatiotemporal RDF data based on subgraph matching. In this chapter, we propose st-RDF model first. We introduce a temporal component to RDF datasets and after a spatial component to RDF datasets, which are finally mixed in a spatiotemporal component. An illustrative example is shown after the corresponding definitions and figures. The temporal component is defined as an interval and the spatial component is defined as a pair of coordinates (rectangles). After, a spatiotemporal query graph is defined and illustrated with an example. Two operations are defined for intervals and coordinates: intersection and merging. Intersection for intervals is defined as usual, and merging of intervals is defined as the smallest interval containing the merged internals. The same can be said for coordinates. The intersection of rectangles and the smallest rectangle containing the merged rectangles. On the basis of the proposed model, we propose a subgraph matching of spatiotemporal RDF data approach. Experimental results verify that our approach has performance advantages and application discussions give general steps on how to use our approach in spatiotemporal applications. The main contributions of this chapter are described as follows:

- We construct a spatiotemporal RDF model st-RDF. On the basis of the data model, it can represent and operate data with temporal and spatial attributes.
- We propose a preliminary query filtering mechanism. For queries whose spatiotemporal range exceeds the data graph, this mechanism can quickly determine that the query result is empty and we feed it back to the user.
- We propose a spatiotemporal RDF query algorithm stQuery based on subgraph matching. At the same time, we sort nodes according to the degree of association between query nodes and candidate nodes.
- We use the control variable method to compare stQuery with the other three query algorithms to test the query efficiency.

The rest of this chapter is organized as follows. We propose definitions and concepts about the spatiotemporal RDF model st-RDF in Section 2. In Section 3, a spatiotemporal RDF query algorithm stQuery based on subgraph matching is proposed. We show the performance of our algorithm through experimental design and result analysis in Section 4. Section 5 gives application discussions and Section 6 draws conclusions and explains future research work.

2 SPATIOTEMPORAL DATA MODEL BASED ON RDF

This section introduces the temporal and spatial features of spatiotemporal data and proposes a spatiotemporal RDF data model. The representative features of spatiotemporal data are spatial feature and temporal features, and the most representative feature of spatial feature is coordinate feature. For simplicity, we only consider latitude and longitude as spatial features. Of course, there are several other spatial features such as area and other geometries, but such features can be easily extended by our representation. On the other hand, our subgraph matching on spatiotemporal RDF data mainly relates to locations. As a result, in this chapter, we mainly consider latitude and longitude to space.

2.1 The Temporal Feature of Spatiotemporal Data

Time is closely related to our lives, and there are a lot of instances with temporal features around us at the same time. Instances with temporal attributes include temporal entities and temporal facts. We focus on the following four types of temporal entities: persons, groups, artifacts, and events.

i. Person: uses the temporal predicates "wasBornOnDate" and "diedOnDate" to identify the temporal attributes.
ii. Groups: (bands, football clubs, companies, etc.). Use the temporal predicates "wasCreatedOnDate" and "wasDestroyedOnDate" to identify the temporal attributes.
iii. Artifact: (buildings, songs, cities, etc.). Use the temporal predicates "wasCreatedOnDate" and "wasDestroyedOnDate" to identify the temporal attributes.
iv. Events: (sports events, wars, etc.). Use the temporal predicates "startedOnDate" and "endedOnDate" to identify the temporal attribute.

We combine the temporal predicates "wasBornOnDate", "wasCreateOnDate" and "startedOnDate" into the temporal predicate "startsExistingOnDate". The temporal predicates "DiedOnDate", "WasdestroyOnDate" and "EndEndOnDate" are united into the temporal predicate "EndSExistingOnDate". Furthermore, the temporal predicate "beginning existence" and the temporal predicate "ending existence" can be merged to obtain the valid existence temporal predicate "hasExistingTemporal" of the temporal entity, and the corresponding object is usually a valid temporal period. The above process is described in detail in Figure 1.

Temporal entities can be represented by a special RDF triplet et-RDF. Definition 1 introduces the temporal entity model et-RDF.

Definition 1 (et-RDF) The et-RDF triple is denoted as $(s, p^T, o^T) \in (E \cup B) \times U \times (T \cup B)$, where:

- s stands for subject, p^T stands for temporal predicate, and o^T stands for temporal object;
- E is the entity set and $E \subset U$, B stands for the blank node set, and T stands for the temporal label set.

Figure 1. Representation model of temporal entities

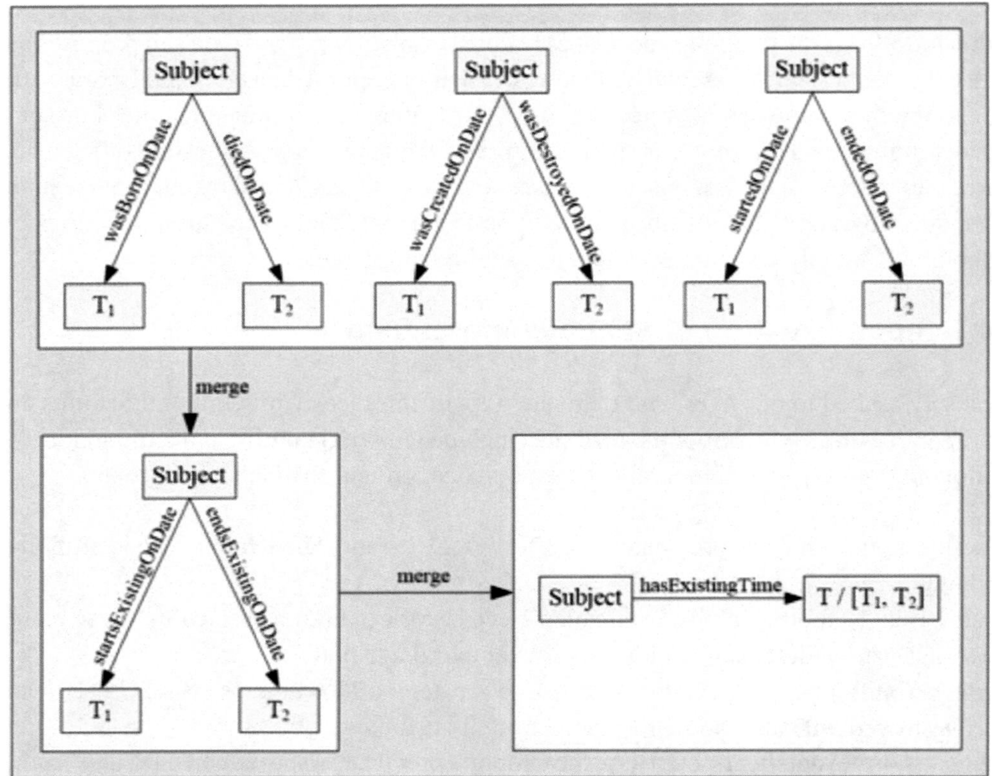

In Definition 1, T can be further expressed as temporal interval $[T_S, T_E]$, where T_S represents the starting existence time, T_E represents the ending existence time, and $T_S \leq T_E$, $T \subset L$. The et-RDF triple can be represented as a directed graph with two nodes and an edge. An et-RDF triple instance is represented in the purple elliptical dashed line as shown in Figure 2. The yellow node ([1936-05-17,2013-02-02]) represents the temporal entity and the information inside the node stands for the entity information. The blue node (Juan_B_Tudela) stands for the temporal object, the information inside the node stands for the temporal label, and the temporal predicate is represented by a directed arc from the temporal entity to the temporal object, including the temporal attribute marked on the directed arc. For example, the location information of Saipan is 15.21233 longitude and 145.7545 latitudes; Juan_B._Tudela's lifetime is from 1936-05-17 to 2013-02-02; Juan_B._Tudela has a name from 1936-05-17 to 2013-02-02.

A fact can be represented in the form of an RDF triple. Similarly, the temporal fact can be represented in the form of the corresponding RDF triple with temporal information. We define the concept of temporal fact model ft-RDF.

Definition 2 (ft-RDF) The ft-RDF triplet with a temporal label is denoted as (s, p, o) $[T]$, where:

- s stands for subject, p stands for predicate, o stands for object, and $(s, p, o) \in (U \cup B) \times U \times (U \cup B \cup L)$ stands for a fact;
- T represents the temporal label.

Figure 2. Spatiotemporal RDF data graph

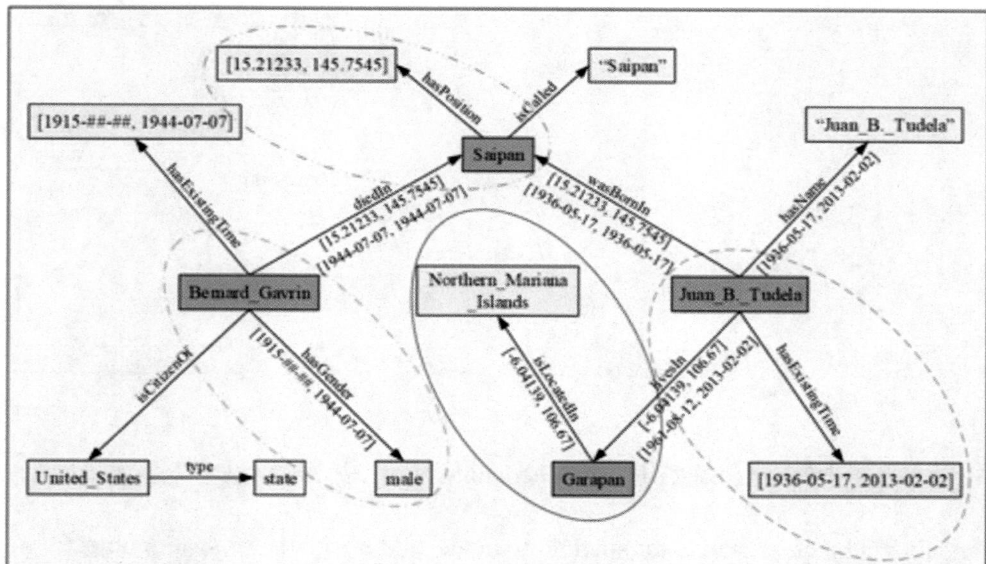

According to Definition 2, T is represented by the temporal interval [TS, TE], where TS represents the starting time, TE represents the ending time, and TS ≤ TE. In particular, [TS, TE] represents a moment when TS = TE. The ft-RDF triples can be converted into graphs. As shown in Figure 2, there is an instance of a ft-RDF triple in the green elliptical dotted line. The yellow node (male) represents the subject of the statement, and the information within the node is the label of the subject. The blue node (Bernard_Gavrin) represents the object of the statement, and the information within the node is the label of the object. The predicate in this statement is represented by a directed arc from the subject to the object, and the predicate label is marked on the directed arc. The temporal attribute is the attribute of the whole statement. In the ft-RDF graph, the corresponding temporal label is marked on the directed arc together with the predicate label.

2.2 Spatial Features of Spatiotemporal Data

Each physical object has a position on the earth, and we represent their spatial attributes with the position information. The same as temporal attributes, instances with spatial attributes also include spatial entities and spatial facts. The latitude and longitude coordinates of the physical objects on the earth are used to identify the spatial features.

In terms of spatial entities, spatial predicates "hasLatitude" (to identify the latitude coordinates) and "hasLongitude" (to identify the longitude coordinates) are used to identify the spatial attributes. The spatial predicates "hasLatitude" and "hasLongitude" are merged to obtain the geographic spatial predicate "hasPosition" of the spatial entity in order to represent the spatial information of the spatial entity more effectively. The corresponding object is a geographic coordinate represented by longitude and latitude. This process is described in detail in Figure 3. Definition 3 describes the spatial entity model es-RDF.

Figure 3. Representation model of spatial entities

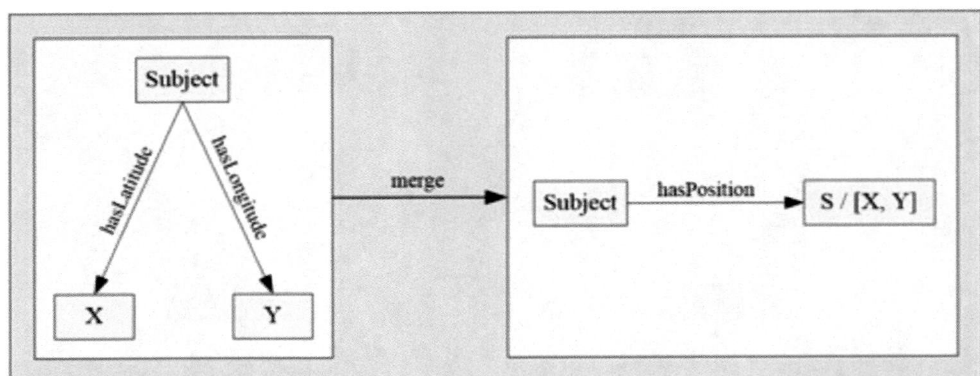

Definition 3 (es-RDF) An es-RDF triplet is denoted as $(s, p^S, o^S) \in (E \cup B) \times U \times (S \cup B)$, where:

- s stands for subject, p^S stands for spatial predicate, and o^S stands for spatial object;
- E stands for the set of entities and $E \subset U$, B stands for the set of blank nodes, S stands for the set of spatial labels.

As for Definition 3, an es-RDF triple can be represented as a directed graph with two nodes and one edge, as shown in Figure 2. An instance of an es-RDF triple is shown in the red elliptical double-dotted line. The yellow node ([15.21233,145.7545]) represents the spatial entity, and the information inside the node is the entity information. The blue node (Saipan) represents the spatial object, and the information inside the node is the spatial label. The spatial predicate is represented by a directed arc from the spatial entity to the spatial object, and the spatial attribute is marked on the directed arc.

Spatial facts can be represented as a statement with spatial attributes. Similarly, a spatial fact can be represented by an RDF triple with spatial attributes to represent the geo-location information.

Definition 4 (fs-RDF) A fs-RDF triple with a spatial label is denoted as (s, p, o) $[S]$, where:

- s stands for subject, p stands for predicate, and o stands for object, where $(s, p, o) \in (U \cup B) \times U \times (U \cup B \cup L)$;
- S represents the spatial label.

According to Definition 4, S is represented by the longitude and latitude coordinates $[X, Y]$, where X represents the longitude value and Y represents the latitude value. The fs-RDF triples can also be converted into graphs. An fs-RDF triple is represented by a directed graph with two nodes, where spatial attributes are attached to a directed arc between the two nodes. As shown in Figure 2, there is an instance of a fs-RDF triple in the black elliptical solid line. The blue node (Garapan) represents the subject of the statement, and the information within the node is the label of the subject. The yellow node (Northern_Mariana_Islands) represents the object of the statement, and the information within the node is the label of the object. The predicate in this statement is represented by a directed arc from the subject to the object, and the predicate label is marked on the directed arc. The spatial attribute is the attribute of the entire statement. In the fs-RDF graph, the corresponding spatial label is labeled along with the predicate label on the directed arc.

2.3 The Spatiotemporal RDF Data Model

In this subsection, we merge et-RDF, ft-RDF, es-RDF, and fs-RDF models to form a spatiotemporal RDF data model st-RDF, which can represent temporal and spatial attributes simultaneously.

Definition 5 (st-RDF) A spatiotemporal RDF triple with a temporal label and a spatial label is denoted as (s, p, o) $[S]$ $[T]$, where:

- s stands for subject, p stands for predicate, and o stands for object, where $(s, p, o) \in (U \cup B) \times U \times (U \cup B \cup L)$;
- S represents the spatial label;
- T represents the temporal label.

In Definition 5, p contains temporal predicates, spatial and ordinary predicates. o contains temporal objects, spatial and ordinary objects. S is represented by the longitude and latitude coordinates $[X, Y]$, where X represents the longitude value and Y represents the latitude value. T is represented by the temporal interval $[T_S, T_E]$, where T_S represents the starting time, T_E represents the ending time, and $T_S \leq T_E$. Therefore, the spatiotemporal RDF triplet can also be denoted as (s, p, o) $[X, Y]$ $[T_S, T_E]$. In st-RDF, the information in "["and"]" can be omitted according to whether the triple (i.e., the corresponding statement) has spatiotemporal attributes. If the triple does not have a temporal attribute, then $[T]$ is null. Similarly, if the triple does not have a spatial attribute, then we have $[S]$ is null.

A spatiotemporal RDF graph is a directed graph composed of multiple spatiotemporal RDF triples, in which the subject s and object o are presented in the form of nodes, and the predicate p is represented as a directed arc that s points to o. When the triples have spatiotemporal attributes, the spatiotemporal attributes of the triples are attached to the directed arc. When the entity has a spatiotemporal attribute, it is represented by a new triple, in which the subject is the entity, the predicate is the spatiotemporal predicate, and the object is the spatiotemporal information. For the query of spatiotemporal RDF data, we further divide the spatiotemporal RDF graph into a spatiotemporal RDF data graph and spatiotemporal RDF query graph. Definition 6 and Definition 7 define the concepts of spatiotemporal RDF data graph and spatiotemporal RDF query graph.

Definition 6 (spatiotemporal RDF data graph) An RDF data graph is denoted as $stG = (V, E, L, F_{st})$, where:

- $V = V_L \cup V_E \cup V_C \cup V_B \cup V_S \cup V_T$ represents a set of vertices;
- E represents the set of edges between two nodes;
- $L = L_V \cup L_E$ is the label set of all vertices and edges;
- F_{st}: $V \cup E \rightarrow L$ is the mapping function from vertices and edges to the label set L.

In Definition 6, V_L, V_E, V_C and V_B represent text vertex, entity vertex, class vertex and blank vertex, respectively. V_S represents space node and V_T represents temporal node. $L_V = \{\text{URI}\} \cup \{\text{Literal Value}\} \cup L_T \cup L_S$ is as the set of all vertex labels, and $L_E = L_R \cup L_T \cup L_S$ is as the label set of all edge labels, where L_R is as the label set of ordinary relational predicate, L_T is as the temporal label set, and L_S is as the spatial label set. $F_{st}(V)$: $V \rightarrow L_V$ is the mapping function from vertices to vertex labels, and $F_{st}(E)$: $E \rightarrow L_E$ is the mapping function from edges to edge labels. For different types of vertices, the mapping relationship is as follows:

i. $v \in V_L \Leftrightarrow F_{st}(v) \in$ {Literal Value};
ii. $v \in V_E \cup V_C \Leftrightarrow F_{st}(v) \in$ {URI};
iii. $v \in V_B \Leftrightarrow F_{st}(v) =$ NULL;
iv. $v \in V_S \Leftrightarrow F_{st}(v) \in$ {Spatial Label};
v. $v \in V_T \Leftrightarrow F_{st}(v) \in$ {Temporal Label}.

Table 1 shows 12 spatiotemporal RDF triples, containing Id, subject, predicate, object, position, and time. The corresponding spatiotemporal RDF data graph is shown in Figure 2.

Table 1. Spatiotemporal RDF data

Id	Subject	Predicate	Object	Position	Time
1	Bernard_Gavrin	hasExistingTime	[1915-##-##, 1944-07-07]		
2	Bernard_Gavrin	hasGender	male		[1915-##-##, 1944-07-07]
3	Bernard_Gavrin	diedIn	Saipan	[15.21233, 145.7545]	[1944-07-07, 1944-07-07]
4	Bernard_Gavrin	isCitizenOf	United_States		
5	United_States	type	state		
6	Saipan	hasPosition	[15.21233, 145.7545]		
7	Saipan	isCalled	"Saipan"		
8	Juan_B._Tudela	hasExistingTime	[1936-05-17, 2013-02-02]		
9	Juan_B._Tudela	wasBornIn	Saipan	[15.21233, 145.7545]	[1936-05-17, 1936-05-17]
10	Juan_B._Tudela	hasName	"Juan_B._Tudela"		[1936-05-17, 2013-02-02]
11	Juan_B._Tudela	livesIn	Garapan	[−6.04139, 106.67]	[1961-08-12, 2013-02-02]
12	Garapan	isLocatedIn	Northern_Mariana _Islands	[−6.04139, 106.67]	

Definition 7 (spatiotemporal RDF query graph) The spatiotemporal RDF query graph is denoted by $stQ = (V^q, E^q, L^q, F_{st}^{\ q})$, where:

- $V^q = V_L \cup V_E \cup V_C \cup V_B \cup V_S \cup V_T \cup V_P$ represents a set of vertices;
- E^q represents the set of edges between two nodes;
- $L^q = L_V \cup L_E$;

- F_{st}^{q}: $V^q \cup E^q \rightarrow L^q$ is a mapping function from vertices and edges to a set of labels L^q.

According to Definition 7, the meanings of V_L, V_E, V_C, V_B, V_S, V_T and L^q are the same as those in definition 6, and V_P represents the parameter vertices in the RDF query graph. $F_{st}^{q}(V^q)$: $V^q \rightarrow L_V$ is a mapping function from vertices to vertex labels, and $F_{st}^{q}(E^q)$: $E^q \rightarrow L_E$ is the mapping function from edges to edge labels. For different types of vertices, the mapping relationship is the same as the spatiotemporal RDF query graph, except $v \in V_P \Leftrightarrow F_{st}^{q}(v) = \text{NULL}$.

It is noted that the variable "V" can appear at any position in the query graph but cannot appear in the relevant temporal period or coordinates.

Figure 4 shows an example of a spatiotemporal RDF query graph that contains a total of seven vertices, three of which are parametric vertices. "*?x*" died in Saipan at a position of 15.21233 longitude and 145.7545 latitude; Saipan has a position "*?z*" and is called "Saipan".

Figure 4. Spatiotemporal RDF query graph

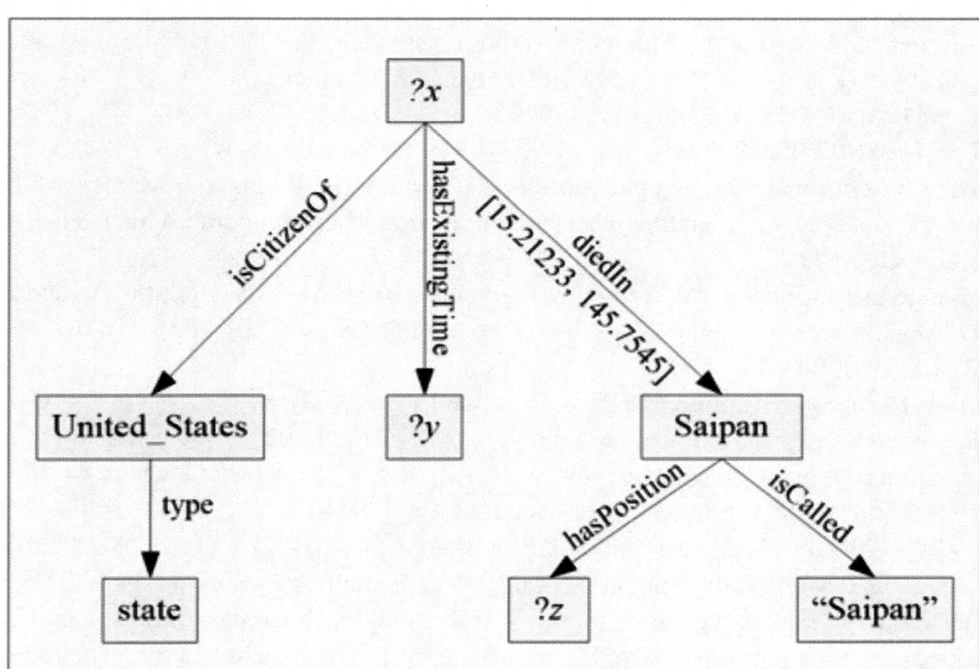

3 SPATIOTEMPORAL RDF DATA QUERY BASED ON SUBGRAPH MATCHING

Based on the spatiotemporal RDF data model proposed in the previous section, this section proposes a spatiotemporal RDF data query approach based on subgraph matching.

3.1 Preliminary Spatiotemporal Determination

The matching degree of related spatiotemporal intervals is determined firstly when performing subgraph matching, i.e., the degree of spatiotemporal matching between the query graph and the data graph is determined. The temporal interval matching and spatial interval matching are introduced below.

3.1.1 Temporal Interval Matching

In terms of temporal interval matching, τ is the temporal interval function, and $\tau(stG)$ is the temporal span of *stG* in the spatiotemporal RDF graph. Accordingly, $\tau(e)$ is the temporal span of the spatiotemporal RDF triples, where $e \in \{e \mid e \in E \text{ in } stG\}$. Each $e \in E$ has $\tau(e) \subset \tau(stG)$. For the temporal relationships between the spatiotemporal RDF data graph and the spatiotemporal RDF query graph, the concepts of temporal intersection operation, temporal merger operation, and temporal span are given.

Definition 8 (temporal intersection operation $\wedge_t$) Let $t_s = \text{Max}(t_{s1}, t_{s2})$ and $t_e = \text{Min}(t_{e1}, t_{e2})$ be temporal segments $[t_{s1}, t_{e1}]$ and $[t_{s2}, t_{e2}]$. If and only if $t_s \leq t_e$, the intersecting operation of the temporal segments is $[t_{s1}, t_{e1}] \wedge_t [t_{s2}, t_{e2}] = [t_s, t_e]$. Otherwise, the intersecting operation is $[t_{s1}, t_{e1}] \wedge_t [t_{s2}, t_{e2}] = \varnothing$, when $t_s > t_e$.

In Definition 8, if there is the following temporal segment T_1 = [1961-02-05, 1982-06-10], T_2 = [1970-07-05, 1992-06-15], and T_3 = [1989-10-03, 1992-06-15], then

$T_1 \wedge_t T_2$ = [1961-02-05, 1982-06-10] $\wedge_t$ [1970-07-05, 1992-06-15] = [1970-07-05, 1982-06-10];

$T_1 \wedge_t T_3$ = [1961-02-05, 1982-06-10] $\wedge_t$ [1989-10-03, 1992-06-15] = $\varnothing$.

Definition 9 (temporal merger operation $\vee_t$) Let $t_s = \text{Min}(t_{s1}, t_{s2})$ and $t_e = \text{Max}(t_{e1}, t_{e2})$ be temporal segments $[t_{s1}, t_{e1}]$ and $[t_{s2}, t_{e2}]$, then the intersecting operation of the temporal segments is $[t_{s1}, t_{e1}] \vee_t [t_{s2}, t_{e2}] = [t_s, t_e]$, where $t_s \leq t_e$.

According to Definition 9, for the temporal segments T_1 = [1961-02-5, 1982-06-10] and T_2 = [1970-07-05, 1992-06-15], there is a union $T_1 \vee_t T_2$ = [1961-02-05, 1982-06-10] $\vee_t$ [1970-07-05, 1992-06-15] = [1961-02-05, 1992-06-15].

Definition 10 (temporal span τ) There is a temporal span $\tau(stG) = \{ [t_{si}, t_{ei}] \mid 1 \leq i \leq |E|, t_{si} \leq t_{ei} \}$ for the spatiotemporal RDF graph *stG*. Let $t_s = \text{Min}_{1 \leq i \leq |E|}(t_{si})$ and $t_e = \text{Max}_{1 \leq i \leq |E|}(t_{ei})$, then the temporal span of spatiotemporal RDF graph *stG* is $[t_{s1}, t_{e1}] \vee_t [t_{s2}, t_{e2}] \vee_t \dots \vee_t [t_{sn}, t_{en}] = [t_s, t_e]$, where $n = |E|$, and $t_s \leq t_e$.

As for Definition 10, there is temporal span $\tau(stG)$ = [1944-07-07, 1944-07-07] $\vee_t$ [1936-05-17, 1936-05-17] $\vee_t$ [1936-05-17, 2013-02-02] $\vee_t$ [1915-##-##, 1944-07-07] $\vee_t$ [1961-08-12, 2013-02-02] = [1915-##-##, 2013-02-02] for the spatiotemporal RDF data graph *stG* given in Figure 2. For the spatiotemporal RDF query graph *stQ* given in Figure 4, if the temporal attributes of all spatiotemporal RDF triples are empty, the temporal span $\tau(stQ)$ is an infinite set *T*. The span indicates the merging operation and from the set of intervals and rectangles of data or query graph.

For a spatiotemporal RDF data graph *stG* and a spatiotemporal RDF query graph *stQ*, it is possible for the *stQ* to have a matching subgraph in *stG* when $\tau(stG) \wedge_t \tau(stQ)$ is not null. Otherwise, *stQ* must have no matching subgraph in *stG*. Considering the spatiotemporal RDF data graph *stG* in Figure 2 and the spatiotemporal RDF query graph *stQ* in Figure 4, there is $\tau(stG) \wedge_t \tau(stQ)$ = [1915-##-##, 2013-02-02] $\wedge_t$ *T* = [1915-##-##, 2013-02-02]. If the result is not empty, it is preliminarily determined that the spatiotemporal RDF query graph *stQ* is likely to find a matching subgraph in the spatiotemporal RDF data graph *stG*.

3.1.2 Spatial Interval Matching

For spatial interval matching, ρ is the spatial interval function, and $\rho(stG)$ is the spatial span of the spatiotemporal RDF data graph. Accordingly, $\rho(e)$ represents the spatial span of spatiotemporal RDF triples, where $e \in \{e \mid e \in E \text{ in } stG\}$, and each $e \in E$ has $\rho(e) \subset \rho(stG)$. In terms of the spatial relationship between the spatiotemporal RDF data graph and the spatiotemporal RDF query graph, the concepts of the spatial intersection operation, spatial merger operation, and spatial span are defined.

As shown in Figure 5a, the spatial coordinates are denoted as $A(P_{xA}, P_{yA})$ and $B(P_{xB}, P_{yB})$, where P_{x1} = Min(P_{xA}, P_{xB}), P_{x2} = Max(P_{xA}, P_{xB}), P_{y1} = Min(P_{yA}, P_{yB}), and P_{y2} = Max(P_{yA}, P_{yB}). When latitude interval $P_{xAB} = [P_{x1}, P_{x2}]$ and longitude interval $P_{yAB} = [P_{y1}, P_{y2}]$, the region consisting of points A and B is P_{AB} $(P_{xAB}$ & $P_{yAB})$. For Figure 5b, the other spatial coordinates are denoted as $C(P_{xC}, P_{yC})$ and $D(P_{xD}, P_{yD})$, where P_{x3} = Min(P_{xC}, P_{xD}), P_{x4} = Max(P_{xC}, P_{xD}), P_{y3}= Min(P_{yC}, P_{yD}), and P_{y4} = Max(P_{yC}, P_{yD}). If the longitude interval $P_{xCD} = [P_{x3}, P_{x4}]$ and latitude interval $P_{yCD} = [P_{y3}, P_{y4}]$, the region composed of points C and D is $P_{CD}(P_{xCD}$ & $P_{yCD})$.

Definition 11 (spatial intersection operation $\wedge_s$) Let P_{xi} = Max(P_{x1}, P_{x3}), P_{xj} = Min(P_{x2}, P_{x4}), P_{yi} = Max(P_{y1}, P_{y3}), and P_{yj} = Min(P_{y2}, P_{y4}), then the intersecting operation of spatial regions P_{AB} and P_{CD} is $P_{AB} \wedge_s P_{CD} = (P_{xAB}$ & $P_{yAB}) \wedge_s (P_{xCD}$ & $P_{yCD}) = (P_x$ & $P_y)$, where the longitude interval $P_x = [P_{xi}, P_{xj}]$ and latitude interval $P_y = [P_{yi}, P_{yj}]$.

The spatial intersection operation can be represented as shown in Figure 6.

Definition 12 (spatial merger operation $\vee_s$) Let P_{xi} = Min(P_{x1}, P_{x3}), P_{xj} = Max(P_{x2}, P_{x4}), P_{yi} = Min(P_{y1}, P_{y3}), and P_{yj} = Max(P_{y2}, P_{y4}), then the intersection of spatial regions P_{AB} and P_{CD} is $P_{AB} \vee_s P_{CD}$ = $(P_{xAB}$ & $P_{yAB}) \vee_s (P_{xCD}$ & $P_{yCD}) = (P_x$ & $P_y)$, where the longitude interval $P_x = [P_{xi}, P_{xj}]$ and latitude interval $P_y = [P_{yi}, P_{yj}]$.

The spatial merger operation is shown in Figure 7.

Definition 13 (spatial span ρ) The spatial span $\rho(stG) = \{ [P_{xi}, P_{xj}]$ & $[P_{yi}, P_{yj}] \mid 1 \leq i, j \leq |E|, P_{xi} \leq P_{xj}, P_{yi} \leq P_{yj} \}$ for the spatiotemporal RDF graph stG. Let $P_{xmin} = \text{Min}_{1 \leq i \leq |E|} (P_{xi})$, $P_{xmax} = \text{Max}_{1 \leq i \leq |E|} (P_{xi})$, $P_{ymin} = \text{Min}_{1 \leq i \leq |E|} (P_{yi})$, and $P_{ymax} = \text{Max}_{1 \leq i \leq |E|} (P_{yi})$, then the spatial span of the graph stG is $(P_{x12}$ & $P_{y12}) \vee_s (P_{x23}$ & $P_{y23}) \vee_s \ldots \vee_s (P_{x(n-1)n}$ & $P_{y(n-1)n}) = ([P_{xmin}, P_{xmax}]$ & $[P_{ymin}, P_{ymax}])$, where $n = |E|$, and $P_{xmin} \leq P_{xmax}$, $P_{ymin} \leq P_{ymax}$.

Figure 5. Spatial region graph: (a) The spatial region consisting of points A and B; (b) The spatial region consisting of points C and D

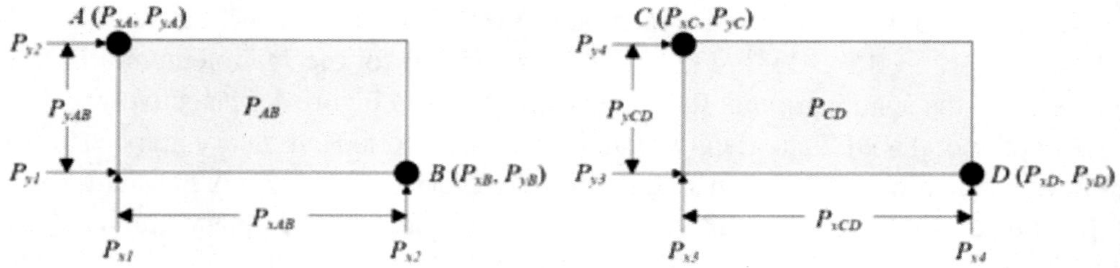

Figure 6. Spatial intersection operation

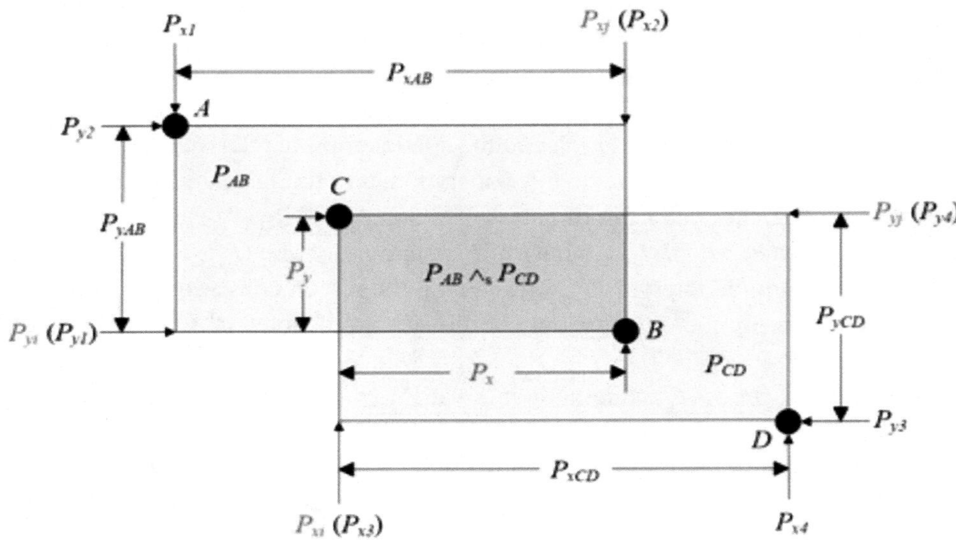

Figure 7. Spatial merger operation

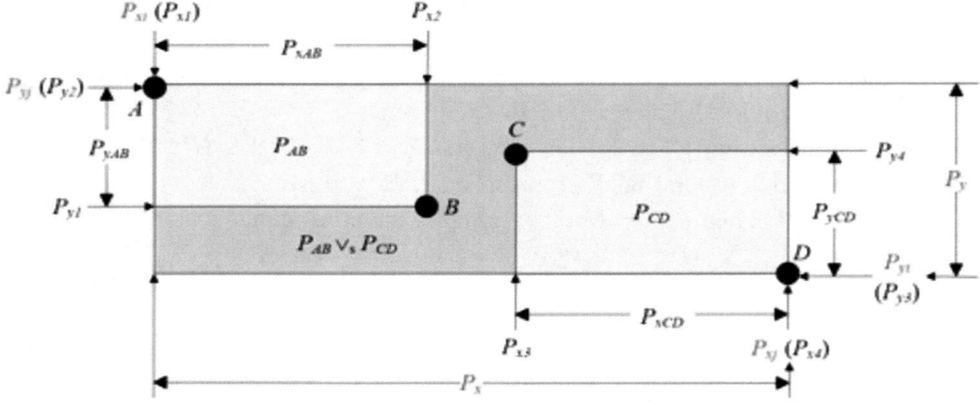

As for Definition 13, there is a spatial span $\rho(stG)$ = ([-6.04139, 15.21233] & [106.67, 145.7545]) and $\rho(stQ)$ = ([15.21233, 15.21233] & [145.7545, 145.7545]) for the spatiotemporal RDF data graph *stG* in Figure 2 and the spatiotemporal RDF query graph *stQ* in Figure 4, respectively.

For a spatiotemporal RDF data graph *stG* and a spatiotemporal RDF query graph *stQ*, it is possible for *stQ* to have a matching subgraph in *stG*, if and only if $\rho(stG) \wedge_s \rho(stQ)$ is non-null. For the spatiotemporal RDF data graph *stG* in Figure 2 and the spatiotemporal RDF query graph *stQ* in Figure 4, there is $\rho(stG) \wedge_s \rho(stQ)$ = ([-6.04139, 15.21233] & [106.67, 145.7545]) $\wedge_s$ ([15.21233, 15.21233] & [145.7545, 145.7545]) = ([15.21233, 15.21233] & [145.7545, 145.7545]). When the result is non-null, it is preliminarily determined that the spatiotemporal RDF query graph *stQ* is likely to find a matching subgraph in the spatiotemporal RDF data graph *stG*.

3.2 Calculation of the Matching Order

The query process based on subgraph matching can be carried out if $\tau(stG) \wedge_t \tau(stQ)$ and $\rho(stG) \wedge_s \rho(stQ)$ are non-null. Only considering the spatiotemporal RDF query graph, the matching orders of query nodes are calculated in the process of subgraph matching. In order to clarify the matching order of query nodes, the node query candidate regions are given in the following.

For the matching order, $D(u)$ is the query candidate region of node u in the spatiotemporal RDF data graph, where $D(u)$ contains all data nodes that may match u. Node u and any node v in $D(u)$ should meet the following conditions:

i. $\deg(u) \leq \deg(v)$;
ii. $\text{deg-in}(u) \leq \text{deg-in}(v)$;
iii. $\text{deg-out}(u) \leq \text{deg-out}(v)$.

The deg function $\deg(u)$ represents the degree of node u, where indegree function deg-in(u) represents the indegree of node u, and outdegree function deg-out(u) represents the outdegree of node u. Outdegree and indegree are numbers of outcoming and incoming edges from a node. If deg-in(u) $\leq$ deg-in(v) and deg-out(u) $\leq$ deg-out(v) are satisfied for nodes u and v, then $\deg(u) \leq \deg(v)$. In addition, if there is an edge connecting the query nodes u_1 and u_2 in two spatiotemporal RDF query graphs, a node v_1 in the query candidate region $D(u_1)$ of u_1 must be adjacent to a node v_2 in the query candidate region $D(u_2)$ of u_2, i.e., there is an edge between v_1 and v_2. The rule is called as the principle of AC (Arc Consistency). This means that if a node in the spatiotemporal RDF data graph exists in the query candidate region of a node u in the spatiotemporal RDF query graph, but not meeting the AC principle, then it should be removed from $D(u)$.

The first query node should be determined to query spatiotemporal RDF data by a subgraph matching algorithm and the first query node is selected according to the following rules:

i. Select the node in the smallest query candidate region (i.e., the least number of nodes in the query candidate region) as the first query node. When the query candidate region with two or more nodes is the smallest, the approach in (ii) is adopted to select these nodes.
ii. Select the node with the largest degree as the first node. When there are two or more query nodes with the same degree, the approach in (iii) is adopted to select these nodes.
iii. Select the node with the maximum outdegree. When there are two or more nodes with the same outdegree, any node is selected as the first query node.

It is assumed that there are n query nodes in the spatiotemporal RDF query graph, and the order of the remaining n-1 query nodes is determined by the degree of association with the nodes that have been sorted. The query node with the largest degree of association that already exist in the partial matching order is ranked earlier. An approach similar to an RI algorithm is adopted to sort subsequent query nodes (Bonnici & Giugno, 2016). $\zeta_i = \{ u_1, u_2, \ldots, u_i \}$ represents a partial query order consisting of i nodes, where $i < n$. ξ_I is the collection of nodes that do not participate in sorting. Three sets about the candidate query node u are defined to select the next node in the sort:

i. $V_{u, vis}$: The set of adjacency nodes belonging to u in i query nodes of ζ_I;
ii. $V_{u, neig}$: The set of query nodes in ζ_i that are adjacent to at least one node in ξ_i and connected to u;
iii. $V_{u, unv}$: The set of adjacent nodes of u that are not in ζ_i and are not adjacent to any node in ζ_i.

Select the next node in the sort as follows:

i. Firstly, choose the node whose value of $V_{u, vis}$ | is the maximum;
ii. If the values of | $V_{u, vis}$ | are the same, then choose the node whose value of | $V_{u, neig}$ | is the maximum;
iii. If the values of | $V_{u, neig}$ | are the same, then choose the node whose value of | $V_{u, unv}$ |is the maximum;
iv. If the values of | $V_{u, unv}$ | are the same, then select any of the nodes.

Taking Figure 8a as an example, if the first query node u_I has been selected, $\zeta_I = \{ u_I \}$ and $\xi_6 = \{ u_2, u_3, u_4, u_5, u_6, u_7 \}$. When selecting the next query node, consider that $V_{u2, vis} = \{ u_I \}$, $V_{u3, vis} = \{ u_I \}$, and $V_{u7, vis} = \{ u_I \}$. If $V_{u4, vis}$, $V_{u5, vis}$ and $V_{u6, vis}$ are all $\varnothing$, so $| V_{u2, vis} | = | V_{u3, vis} | = | V_{u7, vis} | > | V_{u4, vis} | > | V_{u5, vis} | > | V_{u6, vis} |$, then the next query node can be considered in u_2, u_3, and u_7. Consider $V_{u2, neig} = \{ u_I \}$, $V_{u3, neig} = \{ u_I \}$, $V_{u7, neig} = \{ u_I \}$, and $| V_{u2, neig} | = | V_{u2, neig} | = | V_{u7, neig} | = 1$, but the next query node is still not determined. Then continue to determine $| V_{u,unv} |$ value, including $V_{u2, unv} = \{ u_4, u_5, u_6 \}$, $V_{u3, unv} = \{ u_6 \}$, and $V_{u7, unv} = \{ u_6 \}$. Because $| V_{u2, unv} | = 3$, and $| V_{u3, unv} | = | V_{u7, unv} | = 1$, then $| V_{u2, unv} | > | V_{u3, unv} | = | V_{u7, unv} |$, which can determine the next query node for u_2. After updating the sets ζ_i and ξ_i, there is $\zeta_2 = \{ u_I, u_2 \}$and $\xi_5 = \{ u_3, u_4, u_5, u_6, u_7 \}$, then the next query node can be selected, and the final query sequence is $\zeta_7 = \{ u_I, u_2, u_3, u_6, u_7, u_5, u_4 \}$.

Figure 8. Query node selection order

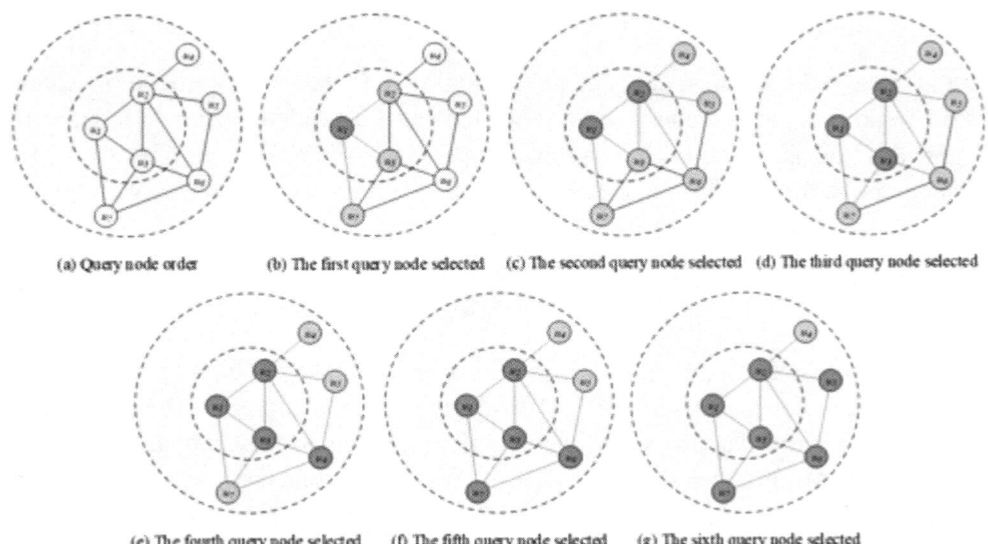

(a) Query node order
(b) The first query node selected
(c) The second query node selected
(d) The third query node selected
(e) The fourth query node selected
(f) The fifth query node selected
(g) The sixth query node selected

Figure 8b–g shows the node state at each sorting step, where the blue node has participated in sorting, and the remaining nodes have not participated in sorting. The purple node is the adjacent node of the node that has participated in sorting. The specific sorting process is explained as follows:

i. When $\zeta_1 = \{ u_1 \}$ and $\xi_6 = \{ u_2, u_3, u_4, u_5, u_6, u_7 \}$, the node status is shown in Figure 8b. When $V_{u2, vis} = \{ u_1 \}$, $V_{u3, vis} = \{ u_1 \}$, $V_{u7, vis} = \{ u_1 \}$, and $V_{u4, vis}$, $V_{u5, vis}$, $V_{u6, vis} = \varnothing$, the node is selected in u_2, u_3, and u_7; When $V_{u2, neig} = \{ u_1 \}$, $V_{u3, neig} = \{ u_1 \}$, and $V_{u7, neig} = \{ u_1 \}$, the node is selected in u_2, u_3, and u_7; When $V_{u2, unv} = \{ u_4, u_5, u_6 \}$, $V_{u3, unv} = \{ u_6 \}$, and $V_{u7, unv} = \{ u_6 \}$, u_2 is removed from the unordered set and added to the partial query order set.
ii. When $\zeta_2 = \{ u_1, u_2 \}$ and $\xi_5 = \{ u_3, u_4, u_5, u_6, u_7 \}$, the node state is shown in Figure 8c. When $V_{u3, vis} = \{ u_1, u_2 \}$, $V_{u4, vis} = \{ u_2 \}$, $V_{u5, vis} = \{ u_2 \}$, $V_{u6, vis} = \{ u_2 \}$, and $V_{u7, vis} = \{ u_1 \}$, u_3 *is* removed from the unordered set and added to the partial query order set.
iii. When $\zeta_3 = \{ u_1, u_2, u_3 \}$and $\xi_4 = \{ u_4, u_5, u_6, u_7 \}$, the node status is shown in Figure 8d. When $V_{u4, vis} = \{ u_2 \}$, $V_{u5, vis} = \{ u_2 \}$, $V_{u6, vis} = \{ u_2, u_3 \}$, and $V_{u7, vis} = \{ u_1, u_3 \}$, the node is selected between u_6 and u_7; When $V_{u6, neig} = \{ u_1, u_2, u_3 \}$ and $V_{u7, neig} = \{ u_1, u_2, u_3 \}$, the node is selected between u_6 and u_7; When $V_{u6, unv} = \varnothing$ and $V_{u7, unv} = \varnothing$, the node is selected between u_6 and u_7; One of the nodes u_6 is selected and deleted from the unsorted set, and it is added to the partial query order set.
iv. When $\zeta_4 = \{ u_1, u_2, u_3, u_6 \}$ and $\xi_3 = \{ u_4, u_5, u_7 \}$, the node state is shown in Figure 8e. When $V_{u4, vis} = \{ u_2 \}$, $V_{u5, vis} = \{ u_2, u_6 \}$and $V_{u7, vis} = \{ u_1, u_3, u_6 \}$, u_7 is removed from the unordered set and added to the partial query order set.
v. When $\zeta_5 = \{ u_1, u_2, u_3, u_6, u_7 \}$and $\xi_2 = \{ u_4, u_5 \}$, the node status is shown in Figure 8f. When $V_{u4, vis} = \{ u_2 \}$ and $V_{u5, vis} = \{ u_2, u_6 \}$, u_5 is removed from the unsorted set and added to the partial query order set.
vi. $\zeta_6 = \{ u_1, u_2, u_3, u_6, u_7, u_5 \}$ and $\xi_1 = \{ u_4 \}$. As shown in Figure 8b, only u_4 is the node that does not participate in sorting at this time, so the next selected query node is u_4. Thus, the final query sequence $\zeta_7 = \{ u_1, u_2, u_3, u_6, u_7, u_5, u_4 \}$. In this case, ξ set is empty.

The node with the largest out-degree in the smallest query candidate domain is selected as the first query vertex. The purpose is to find the most favorable result with the greatest probability and reduce the useless traversal. After determining the first query node, the order of the remaining *n*-1 query nodes are determined according to the degree of association with the sorted node. The significance of this sorting is to comprehensively consider the closeness of the relationship between the nodes, so as to facilitate the generation of the best query results.

For example, considering the variable "*?x*" in the query in spatiotemporal RDF query graph, we set u_1 = *"Antonio"*, u_2 = *"Miguel"*, u_3 = *"Benito"*, u_4 = *"Mateo"*, u_5 = *"Federico"*, u_6 = *"Luis"*, and u_7 = *"Lope"*. The node u_1 = " *Antonio*" is selected as the first query node, so there are ζ_1 = { *Antonio* }and ξ_6 = { *Miguel, Benito, Mateo, Federico, Luis, Lope* }. When selecting the next query node, we consider $V_{u2, vis}$ = { *Antonio* }, $V_{u3, vis}$ = { *Antonio* }, and $V_{u7, vis}$ = { *Antonio* }. When $V_{u4, vis}$,$V_{u5, vis}$,$V_{u6, vis}$ are all empty, there is $| V_{u2, vis} | = | V_{u3, vis} | = | V_{u7, vis} | > | V_{u4, vis} | > | V_{u5, vis} | > | V_{u6, vis} |$. The next query node is generated in *"Miguel"*, *"Benito"* and *"Lope"*. Considering $V_{u2, neig}$ = { *Antonio* }, $V_{u3, neig}$ = { *Antonio* }, $V_{u7, neig}$ = { *Antonio* }, and $| V_{u2, neig} | = | V_{u2, neig} | = | V_{u7, neig} | = 1$, we cannot sure the next query node. We continue to judge the value of $| V_{u,unv} |$, where $V_{u2, unv}$ = { *Mateo, Federico, Luis* }, $V_{u3, unv}$ = { *Luis* }, and $V_{u7, unv}$ = { *Luis* }. Because of $| V_{u2, unv} | = 3$ and $| V_{u3, unv} | = | V_{u7, unv} | = 1$, we have $| V_{u2, unv} | > | V_{u3, unv} | = | V_{u7, unv} |$. After updating the collections ζ_i and ξ_i, we have ζ_2 = { *Antonio, Miguel* } and ξ_5 = { *Benito,*

Mateo, Federico, Luis, Lope }, and then we can continue to select the next query node. The final query sequence is ζ_7 = { *Antonio, Miguel, Benito, Luis, Lope, Federico, Mateo* }.

When querying vertices, we define the chain query pattern, star query pattern and loop query pattern (Section 4.2). For example, Tom goes to school, then visits the library, and finally goes home. The query is about where Tom goes from school. This kind of query belongs to a chain query pattern. Tom's hobbies are running, playing basketball, and playing football. The query is about what Tom's hobbies are. This kind of query belongs to a star query pattern. Tom visits his teacher Traka while going to the library, and Traka goes to the English corner. The English corner is in the library. The query is about inquiring where Tom is. This kind of query belongs to a loop query pattern. Therefore, the proposed approach is interesting and the three kinds of queries are of value for spatiotemporal real applications.

The whole process of selecting the query node matching order is given by Algorithm 1, in which the ChooseFirstVertex function is used to select the first query node. Details on Algorithm 1 are described as follows:

Algorithm 1 Calculating the Matching Order Algorithm OrderMatchNodes

Input: Spatiotemporal RDF query graph *stQ*
Output: matching order *Ord*
ChooseFirstVertex(stQ)
if $num(V_Q) > 1$
if $Max(degree(V_Q)) > 1$
$Ord \leftarrow Max(Outdegree(V_Q))$
end if
end if
$\xi \leftarrow V_Q$
while $|Ord| < |V_Q|$ do
for each u in ξ
$V_{u,vis}, V_{u,neig}, V_{u,unv} \leftarrow \varnothing$
for each u' in V_Q
if u' in Ord
if u' in $N(u)$
$V_{u,vis} = V_{u,vis} \cup \{ u' \}$
else if u' in $N(\xi \cap N(u))$
$V_{u,neig} = V_{u,neig} \cup \{ u' \}$
else if u' in $N(u)$ && u' not in $N(Ord)$
$V_{u,unv} = V_{u,unv} \cup \{ u' \}$
end for
end for
$M_{vis} = \max_{u \in Ord} | V_{u,vis} |$
$M_{neig} = \max_{u \in Mvis} | V_{u,neig} |$
$u_{max} = \text{random}(\max_{u \in Mneig} | V_{u,unv} |)$
append(Ord, u_{max})
$\xi = \xi \setminus \{ u_{max} \}$
end while

3.3 Spatiotemporal RDF Subgraph Matching

The querying of spatiotemporal RDF data is the process of finding the isomorphic subgraph to the spatiotemporal RDF query graph in the spatiotemporal RDF data graph. The concept of spatiotemporal RDF subgraph isomorphism is defined as follows.

Definition 14 (spatiotemporal RDF subgraph isomorphism) The spatiotemporal RDF subgraph isomorphism means that there exists the injective function $f: V \rightarrow V^q$, which satisfies:

- For any vertex $u \in V^q$, there is $F_{st}^{\,q}(u) \subseteq F_{st}(f(u))$;
- For any edge $(u_1, u_2) \in E^q$, there are $(f(u_1), f(u_2)) \in E$, and $F_{st}^{\,q}(u_1, u_2) = F_{st}(f(u_1), f(u_2))$.

In Definition 14, the injective function $f: V \rightarrow V^q$ is used for the spatiotemporal RDF data graph $stG(V, E, L, F_{st})$ and the spatiotemporal RDF query graph $stQ(V^q, E^q, L^q, F_{st}^{\,q})$. In order to find the matching subgraphs (isomorphic subgraphs) corresponding to the spatiotemporal RDF query graph *stQ* embedded in the spatiotemporal RDF data graph *stG* and complete the query of spatiotemporal RDF data, a spatiotemporal RDF query algorithm stQuery based on the general framework of subgraph matching algorithms is proposed. Algorithm 2 outlines the overall process of spatiotemporal RDF data query algorithm stQuery based on subgraph matching.

Algorithm 2 Spatiotemporal RDF Query Algorithm stQuery

```
Input: Spatiotemporal RDF data graph stG, spatiotemporal RDF query graph stQ
Output: All subgraphs in stG that match stQ
1: M ← ∅
2: ST_G = GetSTSpan(stG)
3: ST_Q = GetSTSpan(stQ)
4: if ST_G ∧ ST_Q is not null
5: u = ChooseFirstVertex(stQ)
6: D(u) ← GetCanddidate(stG, u)
7: if D(u) is not null
8: Ord ← OrderMatchNodes(stQ)
9: for each v ∈ D(u)
10: UpdateState(u, v, M)
11: SubgraphSearch(stG, stQ, Ord, u, v)
12: report M
13: RestoreState(u, v, M)
14: end for
15: end if
16: end if
17: OrderMatchNodes(stQ)
18: for each v ∈ stQ
19: if num(Max(| V_u, vis |)) > 1
20: for each v ∈ Max(| V_u, neig |)
21: U ← add(v)
22: end for
23: end if
24: end for
25: Ord ← U
```

In the process of query, the set M of matched subgraphs is initially assigned to null (line 1). Then, the spatiotemporal spans of *stG* and *stQ* are obtained by the *GetSTSpan* function. If the spatiotemporal span intersection between *stG* and *stQ* is empty, it means that there is no subgraph matching with *stQ* in *stG*. On the other hand, the next step of the query process is continued (lines 2–4). Next, the first query node in *stQ* is selected by the *ChooseFirstVertex* function, and the candidate regions of this node are obtained by the *GetCanddidate* function (lines 5–6). If the candidate region is not empty, the nodes other than the initial query node in *stQ* are sorted. Each node of the candidate region in turn performs a *SubgraphSearch* algorithm (in Algorithm 3). When a query node *u* and a matching of the data node *v* are found, (*u*, *v*) is added to *M*, ending up with an updated matching subgraph set *M* (lines 9–13). Finally, *M* contains all the matched subgraphs of *stQ* in *stG*.

The core of the subgraph matching process of spatiotemporal RDF query is the recursive process based on a backtracking strategy. Algorithm 3 gives the spatiotemporal RDF subgraph matching algorithm SubgraphSearch.

Algorithm 3 Subgraph Matching Algorithm SubgraphSearch

Input: Spatiotemporal RDF data graph *stG*, spatiotemporal RDF query graph *stQ*, matching order set *Ord*, data node *v*, query node *u*
Output: The subgraph M matched with *stQ* in *stG*

1: if $|V| = |V_Q|$&& $|E| = |E_Q|$
2: return *M*
3: else
4: $u' \leftarrow$ *NextQueryVertex*()
5: $D(u') \leftarrow$ *Neighbor*(*f*(*u*)) ∩ *Canddidate*(*stG*, *u'*)
6: if $D(u')$ is not null
7: for each $v' \in D(u')$
8: if $(u, u') \in E_Q$ && $(v, v') \notin E_G$
9: $D(u') \leftarrow D(u') \setminus \{ v' \}$
10: for each $v' \in D(u')$ such that v' is not matched do
11: *CheckFeasibility*(*u'*, *v'*)
12: *UpdateState*(*u'*, *v'*, *M*)
13: *SubgraphSearch*(*stG*, *stQ*, *u'*, *v'*)
14: *RestoreState*(*u'*, *v'*, *M*)
15: end for
16: end if
17: end if

When the number of matched nodes and edges is equal to the number of nodes and edges in the query graph, a matching subgraph *M* (lines 1–2) that matches *stQ* in *stG* can be returned. Otherwise, the next node is denoted as u', and the candidate region of u' is found. If the node *u* is located before node u' in the sorting ζ, then the candidate node set $C(u')$ matching node u' is obtained from *Neighbor*(*f*(*u*)) ∩ $D(u')$ (line 5). Next, the *CheckFeasibility* function is needed to verify whether the query nodes and data nodes meet the feasibility conditions. When all the query nodes are matched, a match for the query graph *stQ* is found in the data graph *stG* and added to the set of matching results. Traceback means deleting the last matching pair of query nodes and target nodes from *M* and deleting the mappings between such nodes. This algorithm returns all the matches found.

4 EXPERIMENTS

In this section, we evaluate the spatiotemporal RDF data query approach. The experiments are all carried out under the windows 10_64 bit operating system. The processor is Intel(R) Core(TM) i5-8265U CPU @ 1.60GHz 1.80GHz, and RAM is 16.0GB.

4.1 Experimental Dataset

The dataset in the experiment is extracted from yago (version 3.1), which is from the real world, and its accuracy has been manually evaluated. Many facts and entities are endowed with temporal and spatial attributes to form spatiotemporal data. In this subsection, four sub-datasets are selected to extract spatiotemporal datasets, and they are yagoFacts dataset, yagoMetaFacts dataset, yagoDateFacts dataset and yagoGeonamesOnlyData dataset, which are introduced as follows:

i. yagoFacts dataset: The dataset is 972 MB in size, involving a total of 12,430,700 pieces of data and including all the instance data in the yago dataset (no spatiotemporal information);
ii. yagoMetaFacts dataset (395 MB): This dataset is 395 MB in size and contains 3,824,875 pieces of data, including all the temporal and spatial metadata in the yago dataset;
iii. yagoDateFacts dataset: The data set is 412 MB in size, involving a total of 4,190,241 pieces of data and including data only with time attribute in the yago dataset, in which the temporal information is presented in the form of date (year, month, day);
iv. yagoGeonamesOnlyData dataset: The dataset is 4.11 GB in size, involving a total of 61,605,695 pieces of data and including all the data with spatial attributes in the yago dataset, as well as a large number of relevant information data, in which the spatial information is presented in the form of geographic coordinates (longitude and latitude).

Table 2 introduces the original datasets and indicates the specific information contained in each dataset.

Table 2. Statistics of the four real datasets

Datasets	Number of Data	Temporal Information	Spatial Information
yagoFacts	12430700	N	N
yagoMetaFacts	3824875	Y	Y
yagoDateFacts	4190241	Y	N
yagoGeonamesOnlyData	61605695	N	Y

After taking a series of extraction and integration operations, a synthetic dataset is obtained. The subsequent experiments in this chapter are conducted on this Dataset. The Dataset is 481.65MB in size and contains temporal data (involving only temporal information), spatial data (involving only spatial information), spatiotemporal data (involving both temporal and spatial information), and non-spatiotemporal data (involving neither temporal nor spatial information). This dataset is described in Table 3.

4.2 The Experimental Setup

This subsection divides experiments into two parts and conducts the corresponding experiments on the effect and efficiency of the query approach.

Table 3. Statistics of the synthetic datasets

Data Type	Number
temporal data	417963
spatial data	3965854
spatiotemporal data	7901
non-spatiotemporal data	442607

The first part is the experiment to test the effects of stQuery through the query about different types of data. Four groups of queries with different types of data are set. Each group of queries includes three similar samples (the same number of query vertices and similar query contents) and twelve query samples to reduce the contingency of experimental results. The specific contents of queries in these four groups are as follows:

i. Temporal queries (test sample 1, test sample 2, test sample 3): Queries containing only temporal data, involve temporal entities or facts;
ii. Spatial queries (test sample 4, test sample 5, test sample 6): Queries containing only spatial data, involve spatial entities and facts;
iii. Spatiotemporal queries (test sample 7, test sample 8, test sample 9): Queries containing temporal data and spatial data at the same time, include temporal data and spatial information;
iv. Non-spatiotemporal queries (test sample 10, test sample 11, test sample 12): Queries involve neither temporal nor spatial information.

The second part is the experiment to test the query performance. Through the comparative experiments based on the control variable method, stQuery is compared with the current more advanced query algorithms st-SDS (Eom et al., 2015), $\text{Turbo}_{\text{HOM++}}$ (Kim et al., 2015) and f-ASM (Li et al., 2019). The control variable method refers to the method of turning the problem of multiple factors into a problem of multiple single factors, and changing only one of them so as to study the influence of this factor during the experiments. A control variable is any factor that is controlled or held constant during an experiment. The query efficiency is tested by comparing the query response time for different query graph patterns. Three query graph patterns are the chain query pattern, star query pattern, and loop query pattern. Figure 9 shows simple examples of these three query graph patterns. Figure 9a is a sample of chain query pattern with a double-hop path. Figure 9b is a sample of star query pattern with six nodes. Figure 9c is a sample of loop query pattern with four nodes. We divide this part of the experiment into three groups. Each group contains three different sizes of test sample queries, and each test sample use stQuery, st-SDS, $\text{Turbo}_{\text{HOM++}}$ and f-ASM to query.

4.3 Experimental Results

This subsection presents the experimental results into two parts: the effect and performance analysis of the algorithm.

Figure 9. Query pattern graph

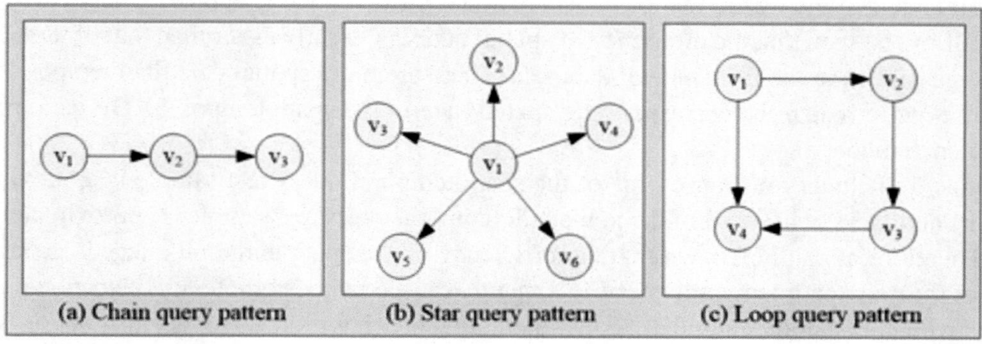

4.3.1 The Effect of the Algorithms

Twelve test samples are of similar size in order to ensure the uniqueness of variables, which contain seven query nodes. The experimental results are shown in Tables 4–6. Table 4 describes the experimental effects of temporal and spatial queries. Table 5 describes the experimental effects of spatiotemporal and non-spatiotemporal queries. Taking the above query results into comprehensive consideration, Table 6 describes the average experimental effects about queries of each group.

Table 4. stQuery implementation effect of temporal and spatial queries

Temporal Query	Response Time (s)	Spatial Query	Response Time (s)
test sample 1	105.0624387	test sample 4	108.7450422
test sample 2	100.1976586	test sample 5	108.8466299
test sample 3	102.9692515	test sample 6	109.6339075

Table 5. stQuery implementation effect of spatiotemporal and non-spatiotemporal queries

Spatiotemporal Query	Response Time (s)	Non-Spatiotemporal Query	Response Time (s)
test sample 7	114.3038049	test sample 10	97.1463715
test sample 8	111.7024177	test sample 11	96.9176396
test sample 9	111.7339461	test sample 12	98.7803164

Table 6. Average response time

Query Category	Temporal Query	Spatial Query	Spatiotemporal Query	Non-Spatiotemporal Query
Response Time (s)	102.6697829	109.0751932	112.5800562	97.6147758

As shown in Table 4, the query response time of the temporal query test sample is approximately between 100 s and 106 s, while that of the spatial query test sample is approximately between 108 0s and 110 s. It can be seen that the efficiency of spatial query is slightly faster than that of temporal query. The main reason lies in the influence of data sets. There are more spatial data than temporal data, so it takes more time to match the corresponding spatial data in the spatiotemporal RDF data graph in the process of spatial query.

For Table 5, the query response time of the spatiotemporal query test sample is approximately between 111 s and 115 s, while that of the non-spatiotemporal query test sample is approximately between 96–99s. Therefore, it can be known that the efficiency of the spatiotemporal query is generally faster than that of the non-spatiotemporal query. It is mainly caused by the complexity of spatiotemporal data. Compared with non-spatiotemporal data, spatiotemporal data has more attribute information, which also requires more complex matching in the process of query.

The average query response time is shown in Table 6. The average query time is represented roughly: spatiotemporal query > spatial query > temporal query > non-spatiotemporal query. This is mainly caused by the complexity of the query information and the composition of the dataset. Therefore, the more complex the query information is, the lower the query efficiency is. In the case of similar complexity of query information, the more relevant the data, the lower the query efficiency.

In the experiment of spatiotemporal query, besides the above query tests, the query whose spatiotemporal range exceeds the spatiotemporal RDF data graph is also tested to verify the effectiveness of the "preliminary spatiotemporal determination" method. Experiments show that for the general spatiotemporal RDF query graph, when the spatiotemporal range exceeds the spatiotemporal RDF data graph, the feedback that the query result is empty can always be obtained within 90 s, which avoids a large amount of time consumption in the subgraph matching process.

4.3.2 The Performance Analysis of the Algorithms

In the performance analysis part, stQuery is compared with st-SDS, $\text{Turbo}_{\text{HOM++}}$ and f-ASM in three aspects: chain query pattern, star query pattern and loop query pattern.

(a) chain query pattern

As shown in Figure 10, when the query graph is a chain query pattern, five groups of experiments are carried out on the query graphs with nodes 3, 4, 5, 6, and 7. The $\text{turbo}_{\text{HOM++}}$ algorithm has the shortest query response time and the highest query efficiency when the query node is 3. With the increase of query nodes, the query response time of this algorithm grows faster, surpassing the other three algorithms. The query response time of the stQuery algorithm almost does not change significantly in each group of experiments, and the query efficiency is relatively high, which indicates that the algorithm has a good performance to the query graph of chained query pattern.

(b) star query pattern

In Figure 11, when the query graph is a star query pattern, five groups of experiments are carried out for the query graphs with nodes of 4, 5, 6, 7, and 8. The experimental results show that the stQuery has a lower time cost than st-SDS and TurboHOM++, and has slightly better query efficiency than f-ASM.

Figure 10. Experimental comparison of the chain query pattern

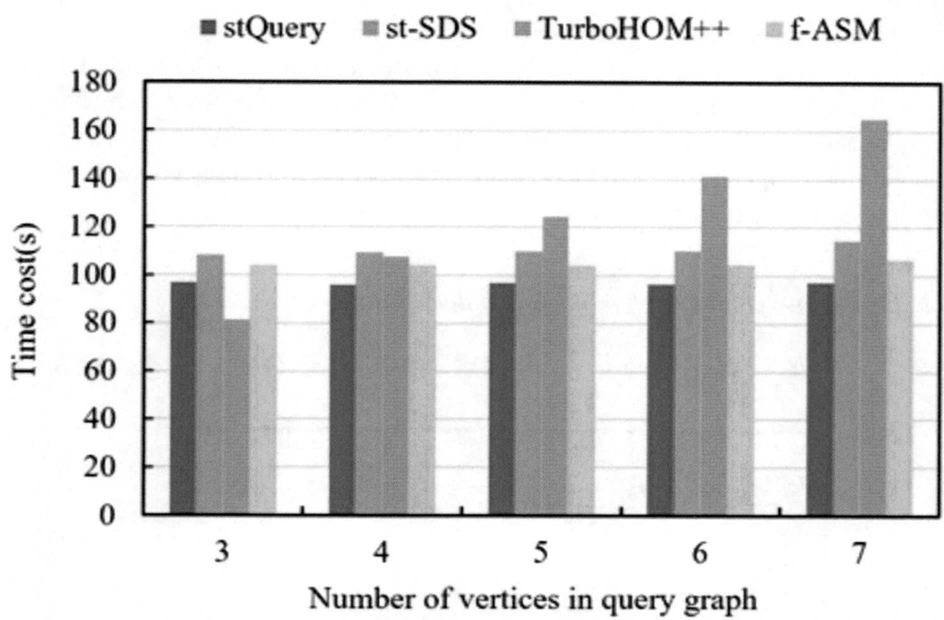

Figure 11. Experimental comparison of the star query pattern

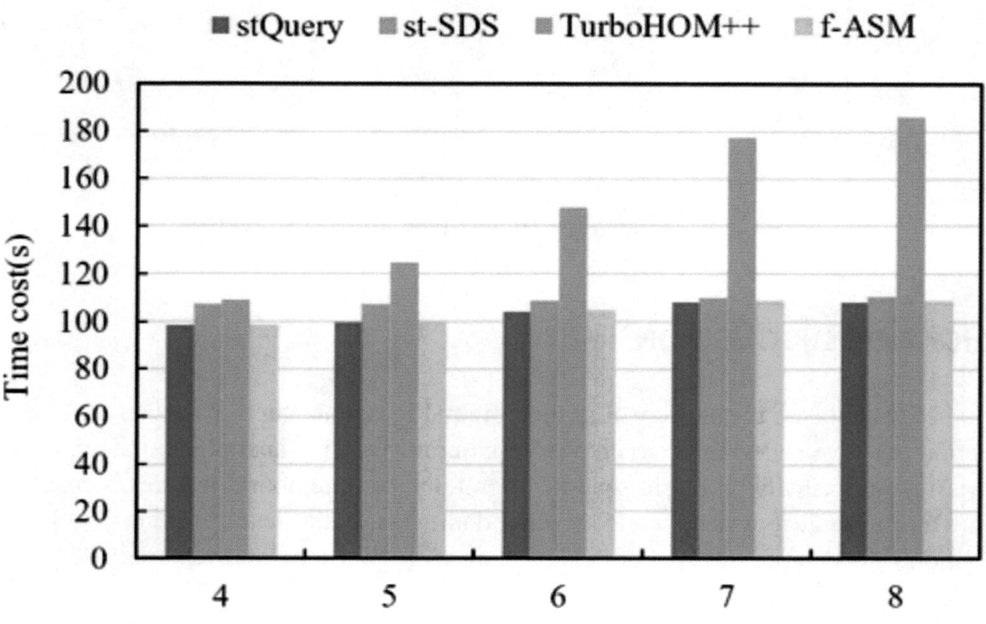

(c) loop query pattern

According to Figure 12, when the query graph is the loop query pattern, five groups of experiments are carried out on the query graphs with nodes 3, 4, 5, 6, and 7. Experimental results show that $\text{Turbo}_{\text{HOM++}}$ algorithm has the best query efficiency when the query node is 3. When the query nodes are increased to 4, 5, and 6, stQuery has the greatest advantage in query efficiency, which is generally better than $\text{Turbo}_{\text{HOM++}}$ and slightly better than f-ASM. The overall query efficiency of stQuery is relatively stable. The query performance of the stQuery algorithm has slight advantages over f-ASM in loop query patterns, but it is generally better than st-SDS and TurboHOM++.

Figure 12. Experimental comparison of the loop query pattern

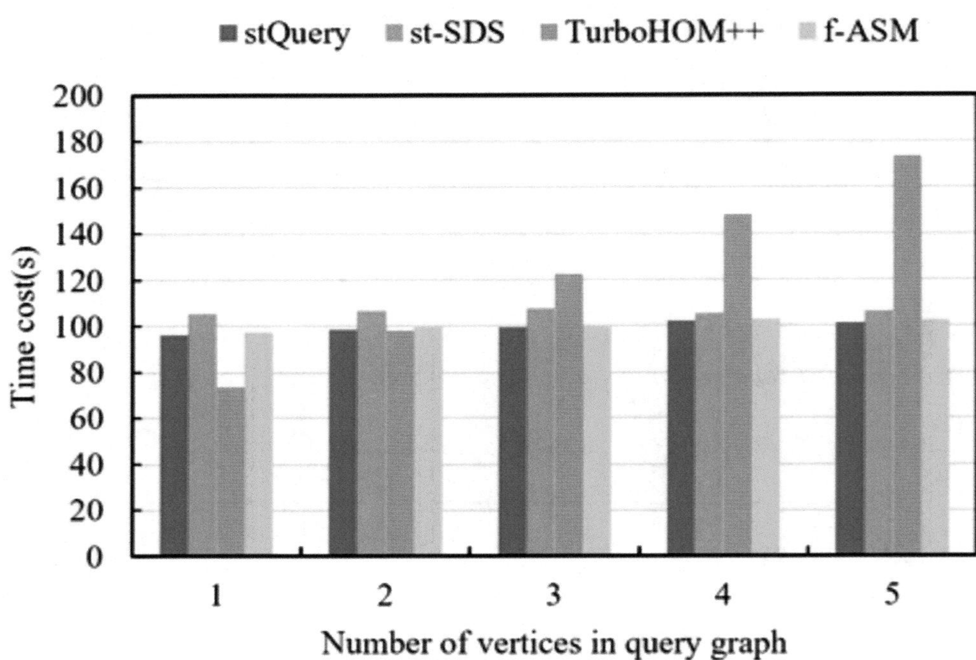

5 APPLICATION DISCUSSION

In order to better apply the technology of spatiotemporal RDF data query based on subgraph matching, in this section, we give general steps on how to use our approach in spatiotemporal applications.

Step 1: We can formally represent spatiotemporal data with temporal features according to Definition 1 and Definition 2, represent spatiotemporal data with spatial features according to Definition 3 and Definition 4, and represent spatiotemporal data with both temporal features and spatial features according to Definition 5.

Step 2: According to Algorithm 1, we can calculate the matching order. In this process, we can perform temporal interval matching according to Definition 8 to Definition 10, and perform spatial interval matching according to Definition 11 to Definition 13.

Step 3: On the basis of Step 1 and Step 2, for a specific query in spatiotemporal applications, we can obtain the desired query results according to Algorithm 2 and Algorithm 3.

6 SUMMARY

In this chapter, a spatiotemporal RDF model st-RDF is proposed. Based on this data model, spatiotemporal data with temporal and spatial attributes can be represented and operated. This chapter then proposes the stQuery algorithm for subgraph matching of spatiotemporal RDF data, and mainly uses the sorting method of RI algorithm to sort the query node according to the correlation degree between the query node and the candidate node, which promotes the further improvement of the query efficiency. Experiments show that the proposed spatiotemporal RDF model and the corresponding query approach have relatively good performances.

REFERENCES

Ademaj, F., Schwarz, S., Berisha, T., & Rupp, M. (2019). A Spatial Consistency Model for Geometry-based Stochastic Channels. *IEEE Access : Practical Innovations, Open Solutions*, *7*, 183414–183427. doi:10.1109/ACCESS.2019.2958154

Artale, A., Kontchakov, R., Lutz, C., Wolter, F., & Zakharyaschev, M. (2007). Temporalising tractable description logics. In *14th International Symposium on Temporal Representation and Reasoning (TIME'07)* (pp. 11-22). IEEE. 10.1109/TIME.2007.62

Batsakis, S., & Petrakis, E. G. (2011). SOWL: A framework for handling spatio-temporal information in OWL 2.0. In *International Workshop on Rules and Rule Markup Languages for the Semantic Web. Proceedings of the 5th International Symposium, RuleML 2011–Europe, Barcelona, Spain, 19–21 July 2011* (pp. 183-194). Springer. 10.1007/978-3-642-22546-8_19

Bonnici, V., & Giugno, R. (2016). On the Variable Ordering in Subgraph Isomorphism Algorithms. *IEEE/ACM Transactions on Computational Biology and Bioinformatics*, *14*(1), 193–203. doi:10.1109/TCBB.2016.2515595 PMID:26761859

Cordella, L. P., Foggia, P., Sansone, C., & Vento, M. (2004). A (Sub) Graph Isomorphism Algorithm for Matching Large Graphs. *IEEE Transactions on Pattern Analysis and Machine Intelligence*, *26*(10), 1367–1372. doi:10.1109/TPAMI.2004.75 PMID:15641723

Cui, Q., Wang, N., & Haenggi, M. (2018). Vehicle Distributions in Large and Small Cities: Spatial Models and Applications. *IEEE Transactions on Vehicular Technology*, *67*(12), 10176–10189. doi:10.1109/TVT.2018.2865679

Eom, S., Shin, S., & Lee, K. H. (2015). Spatiotemporal query processing for semantic data stream. In *Proceedings of the 9th International Conference on Semantic Computing,* (pp. 7–9). IEEE. 10.1109/ICOSC.2015.7050822

Goodhue, P., McNair, H., & Reitsma, F. (2015). Trusting crowdsourced geospatial semantics. *The International Archives of the Photogrammetry, Remote Sensing and Spatial Information Sciences*, *40*(W3), 25–28. doi:10.5194/isprsarchives-XL-3-W3-25-2015

Gutierrez, C., Hurtado, C., & Vaisman, A. (2005). *Temporal RDF*. In *Proceedings of the European Semantic Web Conference*, Crete, Greece.

Han, W. S., Lee, J., & Lee, J. H. (2013). Turboiso: Towards ultrafast and robust subgraph isomorphism search in large graph databases. In *Proceedings of the 2013 ACM SIGMOD International Conference on Management of Data*. ACM. 10.1145/2463676.2465300

Hayes, J. (2004). *A graph model for RDF. Darmstadt University of Technology: Darmstadt, Germany*. University of Chile.

He, H., & Singh, A. K. (2008). Graphs-at-a-time: Query language and access methods for graph databases. In *Proceedings of the 2008 ACM SIGMOD International Conference on Management of Data* (pp. 405-418). ACM. 10.1145/1376616.1376660

Hoffart, J., Berberich, K., & Weikum, G. (2013). YAGO2: A spatially and temporally enhanced knowledge base from Wikipedia. *Artificial Intelligence*, *194*, 28–61. doi:10.1016/j.artint.2012.06.001

Hoffart, J., Suchanek, F. M., Berberich, K., Lewis-Kelham, E., De Melo, G., & Weikum, G. (2011). Yago2: Exploring and querying world knowledge in time, space, context, and many languages. In *Proceedings of the 20th International Conference Companion on World Wide Web* (pp. 229-232). ACM. 10.1145/1963192.1963296

Kim, J., Shin, H., Han, W. S., Hong, S., & Chafi, H. (2015). Taming subgraph isomorphism for RDF query processing. *Proceedings of the VLDB Endowment International Conference on Very Large Data Bases*, *8*(11), 1238–1249. doi:10.14778/2809974.2809985

Kolas, D., Dean, M., & Hebeler, J. (2006). Geospatial Semantic Web: Architecture of Ontologies. In *Proceedings of the 2006 IEEE Aerospace Conference* (pp. 183–194). IEEE.

Koubarakis, M., & Kyzirakos, K. (2010). Modeling and querying metadata in the semantic sensor web: The model stRDF and the query language stSPARQL. In *Extended Semantic Web Conference. Proceedings of the 7th Extended Semantic Web Conference, ESWC 2010* (pp. 431-445). Springer: Berlin/Heidelberg. 10.1007/978-3-642-13486-9_29

Kyzirakos, K., Karpathiotakis, M., & Koubarakis, M. (2012). Strabon. A semantic geospatial DBMS. In *Proceedings of ISWC* (pp. 362-376). IEEE.

Lee, J., Han, W. S., Kasperovics, R., & Lee, J. H. (2012). An in-depth comparison of subgraph isomorphism algorithms in graph databases. *Proceedings of the VLDB Endowment International Conference on Very Large Data Bases*, *5*(7), 594–605. doi:10.14778/2535568.2448946

Li, G., Yan, L., & Ma, Z. (2019). A method for fuzzy quantified querying over fuzzy resource description framework graph. *International Journal of Intelligent Systems*, *34*(6), 1086–1107. doi:10.1002/int.22087

Lu, X., Hu, T., & Yin, F. (2018). A novel spatiotemporal fuzzy method for modeling of complex distributed parameter processes. *IEEE Transactions on Industrial Electronics*, *66*(10), 7882–7892. doi:10.1109/TIE.2018.2877118

Manola, F., Miller, E., & McBride, B. (2004). RDF primer. *W3C recommendation, 10*(1-107), 6.

Motik, B. (2012). Representing and querying validity time in RDF and OWL: A logic-based approach. *Journal of Web Semantics*, *12*, 3–21. doi:10.1016/j.websem.2011.11.004

Perry, M. S. (2008). A framework to support spatial, temporal and thematic analytics over semantic web data.

Pugliese, A., Udrea, O., & Subrahmanian, V. S. (2008). Scaling RDF with time. In *Proceedings of the 17th International Conference on World Wide Web* (pp. 1365-1366). IEEE.

Shang, H., Zhang, Y., Lin, X., & Yu, J. X. (2008). Taming verification hardness: An efficient algorithm for testing subgraph isomorphism. *Proceedings of the VLDB Endowment International Conference on Very Large Data Bases*, *1*(1), 730–741. doi:10.14778/1453856.1453899

Smart, P. D., Abdelmoty, A. I., El-Geresy, B. A., & Jones, C. B. (2007). A framework for combining rules and geo-ontologies. In *International Conference on Web Reasoning and Rule Systems* (pp. 111-125). Springer. 10.1007/978-3-540-72982-2_10

Sun, K., Zhu, Y., Pan, P., Hou, Z., Wang, D., Li, W., & Song, J. (2019). Geospatial data ontology: The semantic foundation of geospatial data integration and sharing. *Big Earth Data*, *3*(3), 269–296. doi:10.1080/20964471.2019.1661662

Vlachou, A., Doulkeridis, C., Glenis, A., Santipantakis, G. M., & Vouros, G. A. (2019). Efficient spatio-temporal RDF query processing in large dynamic knowledge bases. In *Proceedings of the 34th ACM/SIGAPP Symposium on Applied Computing* (pp. 303-310). ACM. 10.1145/3297280.3299732

Wang, D., Zou, L., & Zhao, D. (2014). gst-Store: An Engine for Large RDF Graph Integrating Spatiotemporal Information. In *Proceedings of the 17th International Conference on Extending Database Technology* (pp. 79-90). ACM.

Wu, D., Zhou, H., Shi, J., & Mamoulis, N. (2020). Top-k relevant semantic place retrieval on spatiotemporal RDF data. *The VLDB Journal*, *29*(6), 893–917. doi:10.1007/s00778-019-00591-8

Xu, L., Wong, A., & Clausi, D. A. (2017). A novel Bayesian spatial-temporal random field model applied to cloud detection from remotely sensed imagery. *IEEE Transactions on Geoscience and Remote Sensing*, *55*(9), 4913–4924. doi:10.1109/TGRS.2017.2692264

Zhang, F., Wang, K., Li, Z., & Cheng, J. (2019). Temporal Data Representation and Querying Based on RDF. *IEEE Access : Practical Innovations, Open Solutions*, *7*, 85000–85023. doi:10.1109/ACCESS.2019.2924550

Zhang, S., Li, S., & Yang, J. (2009). GADDI: Distance index based subgraph matching in biological networks. In *Proceedings of the 12th International Conference on Extending Database Technology* (pp. 1062-1065). ACM. 10.1145/1516360.1516384

Zhao, P., & Han, J. (2010). On graph query optimization in large networks. *Proceedings of the VLDB Endowment International Conference on Very Large Data Bases, 3*(1-2), 340–351. doi:10.14778/1920841.1920887

Chapter 7
Spatiotemporal Data Modeling Based on XML

ABSTRACT

In this chapter, the authors propose a framework for representing spatiotemporal data in XML, specifically addressing the spatiotemporal changes of multiple objects. By utilizing this model, spatiotemporal data can be naturally represented in XML documents. Additionally, we leverage the nesting representation in XML to overcome the issues of generating new tuples and excessive redundancy found in traditional databases. This framework establishes a robust foundation for representing dynamic spatiotemporal changes. Additionally, the authors introduce spatiotemporal functions within XML, encompassing both spatiotemporal topological functions and spatiotemporal geometric functions. They explore spatiotemporal operations using XQuery, presenting the architecture of the querying process for spatiotemporal data. They illustrate how to query spatiotemporal data using XQuery and provide query cases that demonstrate the application of our proposed spatiotemporal functions. These findings demonstrate that complex queries can be expanded based on the primary query cases using these spatiotemporal functions.

1 INTRODUCTION

In the past, spatial database and temporal database are two mutually independent research fields. From the 1990s, researchers gradually realize that there are relations between these two fields and begin to study the combined knowledge: spatiotemporal database (Pelekis et al., 2004; Vazirgiannis & Wolfson, 2001). As establishment of spatiotemporal data model is the core issue of spatiotemporal database, researchers have proposed many spatiotemporal data models (Akhter et al., 2012; Camossi et al., 2003; Jonathan et al., 2001; Pelekis et al., 2004). However, the topics of representing and querying spatiotemporal data have received little attention in XML, which has emerged as the lingua franca for data exchange, and even possibly for heterogeneous data representation. This leads us to the question of spatiotemporal data model based on XML.

DOI: 10.4018/978-1-6684-9108-9.ch007

Being one of the most important branches of database, spatiotemporal database has extensive applications (Baazizi et al., 2011; Chen & Revesz., 2003) and receives increasing attention (Cobb & Petry, 1998). As the purpose of spatiotemporal database is managing spatiotemporal data, researchers have made a great amount of effort in dealing with spatiotemporal data. To this end, how to accurately and effectively operate spatiotemporal data is the core issue of managing spatiotemporal data. Unfortunately, those proposed efforts are based on traditional database, which will generate new tuples and produce a great deal of redundancy (Chen & Revesz., 2003; Deng et al., 2009). Furthermore, the traditional database imposes strict restrictions on structure (Du et al., 2012) and data types (Chen & Revesz., 2003) of spatiotemporal data.

As the next generation language of the Internet, XML is rapidly emerging and playing an increasingly important role. In addition, XML has good expansibility and has great influence on data management (Franceschet et al., 2007) since it can remain tree structure of XML and can consider node or subtree as metadata. Furthermore, XML can augment each node with time labels to represent validation so that can coalesce meeting or overlapping time intervals into one time interval and then group them (Baazizi et al., 2011; Franceschet et al., 2007; Hadjieleftheriou et al., 2002). In that case, the advent of XML seems to provide a good way to solve the problem of operating spatiotemporal data.

Table 1 describes changing history of a spatiotemporal object using traditional database mode, which will generate a new tuple when any attribute value changes. Thus it will produce a great deal of redundancy. For example, the owner of o_1 is Jerry from 2000-01-01 to 2002-05-31. However, two tuples store it. What's more, frequently coalescing tuples will occur when query deals with time and those coalesce is also complex in database.

Representation of spatiotemporal information using XML will solve the problems. We augment time labels to represent the validity of the element node or attribute node. Any meeting or overlapping time interval will coalesce into one time interval, and then they will be grouped as shown in Table 2. This nesting representation is hard to present in plane table, while XML just has the advantages of representing nesting objects. As shown below:

Table 1. The snapshot history of land

OID	owner	position	motion	Ts	T_e
o_1	Jerry	location1	constant	2000-01-01	2000-12-31
o_1	Jerry	location2	constant	2001-01-01	2002-05-31
o_1	Ken	location2	larger	2002-06-01	2006-09-30
o_1	Sandy	location3	smaller	2006-10-01	2009-10-31

```
<objects Ts=" 2000-01-01" Te="2000-12-31">
<object Ts=" 2000-01-01" Te="2000-12-31">
<OID Ts=" 2000-01-01" Te="2000-12-31"> o1</OID>
<owner Ts=" 2000-01-01" Te=" 2002-05-31">Jerry</owner>
<owner Ts=" 2002-06-01" Te=" 2006-09-30">Ken</owner>
<owner Ts="2006-10-01" Te=" 2009-10-31">Sandy</owner>
<position Ts=" 2000-01-01" Te=" 2000-12-31">location1</position>
```

```
<position Ts=" 2001-01-01" Te=" 2006-09-30">location2</position>
<position Ts=" 2006-10-01" Te=" 2009-10-31">location3</position>
<motion Ts=" 2000-01-01" Te=" 2002-05-31">constant</motion>
<motion Ts=" 2002-06-01" Te=" 2006-09-30">larger</motion>
<motion Ts=" 2006-10-01" Te=" 2009-10-31">smaller</motion>
</object>
<objects>
```

Table 2. Temporally grouped history of land

OID	owner	position	motion
2000-01-01 OID 2009-10-31	2000-01-01 Jerry 2002-05-31	2000-01-01 location1 2000-12-31	2000-01-01 constant 2002-05-31
	2002-06-01 Ken 2006-09-30	2001-01-01 location2 2006-09-30	2002-06-01 larger 2006-09-30
	2006-10-01 Sandy 2009-10-31	2006-10-01 location3 2009-10-31	2006-10-01 smaller 2009-10-31

With the traditional approach, any change of attribute value will lead to a new tuple so that causes a lot of redundancy information between tuples. However, in XML, because attributes have been grouped, coalescing times decrease. Thus representation based on XML has great expressing power (Chen & Revesz., 2003; Huang et al., 2004).

Although XML has been applied to model and handle spatiotemporal data (Chen & Revesz., 2003; Du et al., 2012; Franceschet et al., 2007; Hadjieleftheriou et al., 2002), their efforts have not concentrated on spatiotemporal changes of more than one spatiotemporal object and operations of spatiotemporal data integrated with functions. Accordingly, the motivation of this chapter is to propose a framework for spatiotemporal data representation in XML, specifically addressing the spatiotemporal changes of multiple objects. In addition, we aim to introduce spatiotemporal functions for operating spatiotemporal data in XML.

In this chapter, we first present the structure of the spatiotemporal data model in XML. Next, we introduce spatiotemporal functions, including spatiotemporal topological functions and spatiotemporal geometric functions. Finally, we provide query cases to illustrate how to apply our proposed spatiotemporal functions in queries.

The rest of the chapter is organized as follows. After a discussion of the prerequisites in Section 2, we propose a framework for representing spatiotemporal data in XML in Section 3. In Section 4, we introduce spatiotemporal functions in XML. In Section 5, we provide an overview of the architecture for querying spatiotemporal data and how to use XQuery for querying.

Query cases are presented in Section 6. Section 7 discusses related work, and Section 8 concludes the chapter.

2 PRELIMINARIES

2.1 Temporal Characteristics

Time contains valid time, transaction time, and user defined time. In this chapter, we will work with the valid time. Transaction time and user defined time could be addressed in an analogous way. On the other hand, time contains time points and time intervals. The former one is interpreted as a representation of a set of time points and the latter one is interpreted as a representation of a set of time intervals. For simplicity, we assume time is isomorphic to a natural number in this chapter as a result that time is linearly ordered.

2.2 Spatiotemporal Changes

From the perspective of object-oriented view, spatiotemporal objects in the real world are determined by Object ID (OID), whereas states of spatiotemporal objects are determined by internal attributes. Internal attributes of spatiotemporal objects contain spatial attributes and thematic attributes. Changes in spatiotemporal objects over time are divided into two types according to the internal structure of spatiotemporal objects: changes in internal attributes of spatiotemporal objects over time, and changes in Object ID of spatiotemporal objects over time.

Since changes in internal attributes of spatiotemporal objects over time can be divided into changes in spatial attributes and changes in thematic attributes, spatiotemporal changing process can be represented by such three types above. On the other hand, spatiotemporal changes can also be divided into two kinds according to changing characteristics: continuous spatiotemporal changes, and discrete spatiotemporal changes. Accordingly, spatiotemporal changes of a spatiotemporal object can be divided into six types shown in Table. 1.

Table 3. Types of spatiotemporal changes

	OID changes	**Thematic attribute changes**	**Spatial attribute changes**
Continuous spatiotemporal changes	Continuous OID changes	Continuous attribute changes	Continuous spatial changes
Discrete spatiotemporal changes	Discrete OID changes	Discrete attribute changes	Discrete spatial changes

In the above types of spatiotemporal changes, continuous Object ID changes don't exist in the real world because changes in Object ID occur abruptly. In addition, continuous attribute changes don't exist either because changes in thematic attributes also occur abruptly such as changes in the name of a land. Consequently, we only focus on the following four types of spatiotemporal changes:

- Discrete Object OID changes: One or more spatial objects change to another one or more spatial objects, or disappear. For example, division and emergence of land.
- Discrete attribute changes: thematic attribute of a spatial object changes abruptly. For example, changes of land owner.

- Continuous spatial changes: spatial attributes of spatial objects change continuously over time. For example, spread of fire (spatial area change over time), and moving cars (spatial position changes continuously).
- Discrete spatial changes: spatial attributes of spatial objects change abruptly. For example, changes in land bounds. Discrete spatial changes always occur at a certain time.

Changes in OID describe ID of spatiotemporal objects changing over time. As changes in OID must be discrete, we only focus on discrete OID changes. Discrete OID changes describe evolving history of objects. Accordingly, discrete OID changes can inform us of history relationship between objects.

Changes in one or more objects lead to changes in another one or more objects. It is called changes of spatiotemporal OID. In the real world, spatiotemporal objects exist in different forms and their changes are also various. In order to record them, we divide discrete OID changes into four types:

Creation of spatial objects: the creation of spatial objects represents they come into being from that moment.

- Split of spatial objects: when one object splits into many objects, its information splits correspondingly and forms many objects. The successor of original object is the set of new objects while the predecessor of spitted objects is the original object.
- Mergence of spatial objects: when many objects merge into a new object, all information of these objects merge into new information and form a new object. The successor of original object is the new object while the predecessor of the new object is the set of original objects.
- Elimination of spatial objects: elimination of an object represents its vanished in the real world.

In that case, it can not only represent changing types of objects (i.e. creation, split, emergence, and elimination) but also can represent objects coming from which objects (i.e. predecessor) and changing into which objects (i.e. successor). In other words, it can represent evolving history of objects.

2.3 Changes of ATTR

For simplicity, we use ATTR to describe intrinsic attributes. Changes of ATTR depicts intrinsic changes of spatiotemporal objects, containing thematic attribute changes and spatial attribute changes, where thematic attribute changes can be one or more and spatial attribute changes can be unique.

Thematic attributes are usually static attributes. For example, land owner, land address, etc. do not or seldom change over time, and occur at a certain time. To this end, these changes are discrete changes. An object could have one or more thematic attributes, while thematic attribute could contain one or more attributes because different situations have different operations. We can treat thematic attributes as a whole one, and we can also classify them to describe different characters of the spatiotemporal object. Take land for example. The address of a land contains city, district, and street. From practical point of view, we can take many attributes as thematic attributes to describe spatial object and form thematic attribute change descriptions with other thematic attributes.

Spatial attributes can be static attributes or dynamic attribute changes. For example, land boundary changes are static attribute changes, and happen at a certain time point; fire spread and motion of cars are dynamic attribute changes. Fire spread belongs to spatial boundary change, and motion of cars belongs to spatial position change. Both of them are continuous changes. Static attribute value changes at a certain time point and dynamic attribute value changes over time, which are functions of time. Spatial attribute of an object must be one because any object in the real world has no reason to represent two values at a certain time point.

3 REPRESENTATION OF SPATIOTEMPORAL DATA IN XML

3.1 Classifications of XML Nodes

Since XML documents are labeled ordered rooted trees, we introduce several types of nodes:

Root node: r is the distinguished and unique *root* node of the document, which has no parent node and all other nodes are its child. Consequently, *r* has no incoming edges, and every node in the graph is reachable from *r*.

- *Element nodes*: nodes labeled with the name of an element, which has attribute child, value child, or other element child.
- *Attribute nodes*: nodes labeled with the name of an attribute, and they are associated with their parent element node.
- *Value nodes*: nodes representing values, which are text or numeric. They have exactly one incoming edge from attribute or element or even root node and have no outgoing edges.

Each node is uniquely identified by an integer called *node number* and is described by a string called *node label*. Edges in the document graph are augmented with a temporal interval that describes the starting time point and ending time point of the interval respectively.

3.2 Attribute XML Nodes

For our purpose, we treat attributes as special kinds of elements so that we make no difference between an attribute node and an element node except that attribute nodes cannot contain other elements. In that case, we define a special element denoted <ATTRIBUTE> to show that the followings are attributes. For example, an element <land> represents land, with an attribute called area. The value for this attribute may change over time, assuming it changes at time *t*. In the beginning, the element <land> looks like

```
<land>
  <ATTR>
<area Ts="0" Te="Now">
  100
</area>
  </ATTR>
</land>
```

At time *t*, the element will look like

```
<land>
  <ATTR>
<area T_s="0" T_e="t-1">
  100
</area>
<area T_s="t" T_e="Now">
  200
</area>
</ATTR>
</land>
```

Here we extend T_s and T_e to express the starting point and ending point of the valid time.

3.3 Evolving History of Spatiotemporal Objects in XML

Evolving history is changes of spatiotemporal objects, which are actually changes of OID. It can not only represent changing types of spatiotemporal objects but also can represent their predecessor and successor. In this subsection, we propose it based on XML and give the corresponding tips. We will first give the definition of evolving history.

Definition 1 (Evolving history) The evolving history of a spatiotemporal object can be represented as EH(o) = (P, S,∇, T) where

1. P is the predecessor of the spatiotemporal object.
2. S is the successor of the spatiotemporal object.
3. ∇ is the changing type value of the spatiotemporal object where 1: create; 2: split; 3: merge; 4: eliminate.
4. T is the time when change occurs.

Figure 1. The evolving history of a land

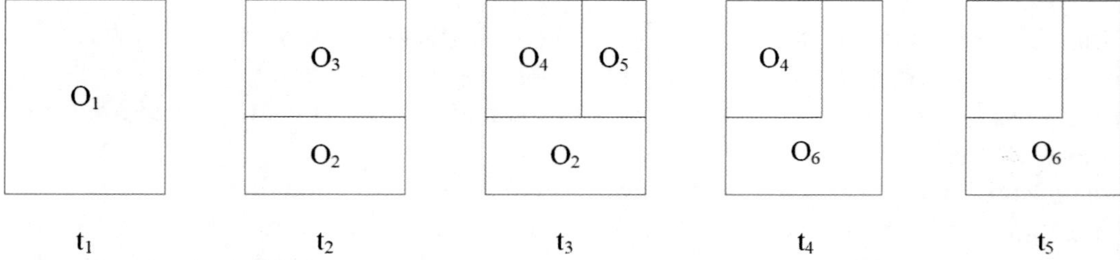

In Figure 1, it describes the evolving history of a land. In the real world, as shape of a land is complex and irregular, we choose MBR (Cobb & Petry, 1998) of the land to represent shape of land for simplicity. The advantages of that option are: a) computation of projecting to axis is simple; b) it is convenient to compute changes and properties of spatial attributes. In Figure 1, O_1 creates at the time t_1, and splits into

O_2 and O_3 at the time t_2. O_3 splits into O_4 and O_5 at the time t_3. O_2 and O_5 merge into O_6 at the time t_4. At the time t_5, O_4 eliminates. The evolving history of O_1 represented by XML is shown in the following:

```
<land>
<OID ID="O1" Ts="t1" Te="t2-1">
    <type Ts="t1" Te="t2 -1 ">
  1
</type>
<predecessor Ts=" t1" Te="t2-1">
  Ø
</predecessor>
<successor Ts=" t1" Te="t2-1">
  Ø
</successor>
<type Ts="t2">
  2
</type>
<predecessor Ts="t2">
  Ø
</predecessor>
<successor Ts="t2">
  O2
</successor>
<successor Ts="t2">
  O3
</successor>
  </OID>
</land>
```

For the above representation, there are several points:

(i) From the representation above, we can get EH (O_1) = (Ø, Ø, 1, t_1), (Ø, {O_2, O_3}, 2, t_2). Others can also get from corresponding evolving history of the spatiotemporal object.

(ii) We choose single intervals instead of temporal elements, and we treat time as attribute of element instead of subelement.

(iii) We append T_s and T_e to represent starting and ending points of valid time.

(iv) For simplicity, we define type value of OID as 1: create; 2: split; 3: merge; 4: eliminate.

(v) A spatiotemporal object has at most one "create" state change, and such change must be the first state change. Because only after the spatiotemporal object is created, it comes into being in the real world. In that case, creation once more is not reasonable, and other state changes must happen after creation of the object.

(vi) A spatiotemporal object has at most one "eliminate" state change, and such change must be the last state change. Because after elimination, it vanishes in the real world. So there are not any other state changes.

(vii) Each spatiotemporal object has at most two state changes, and each state change represents the change of OID. The first state change represents the object coming into being, and the second state change represents it vanishing.

(viii) The life span of a spatiotemporal object in XML document is actually the time attributes of OID.

(ix) If there is no T_e in the element, we cannot say that the element is invariable. Because discrete OID changes occur abruptly, the state of the object after T_s is another spatiotemporal object. Accordingly, we do not care about the state of this element after T_s.

3.4 Position of Spatiotemporal Objects in XML

Position of spatiotemporal objects are represented by projection to *x* and *y* axis, and the shape of the spatiotemporal object is presented by MBR. Actually, we can use two points to represent MBR.

Definition 2 (MBR) At a certain time instant, set of *x* coordinate and *y* coordinate in object is $\{x_1, x_2, \ldots, x_n\}$, $\{y_1, y_2, \ldots, y_n\}$, we can get $xstart = \min\{x_1, x_2, \ldots, x_n\}$, $ystart = \min\{y_1, y_2, \ldots, y_n\}$, $xend = \max\{x_1, x_2, \ldots, x_n\}$, and $yend = \max\{y_1, y_2, \ldots, y_n\}$ to represent MBR.

For example, shape of a spatiotemporal object is shown in Figure 2a. We can get the two points to represent MBR shown in Figure 2b.

Figure 2. a) Shape of an object; b) MBR of the object

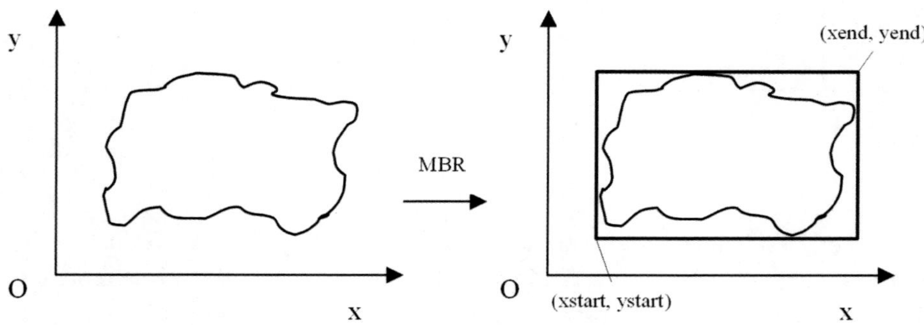

We can represent it in XML:

```
<position>
<xstart>xstart</xstart>
<ystart>ystart</ystart>
<xend>xend</xend>
<yend>yend</yend>
</position>
```

3.5 Motion of Spatiotemporal Objects in XML

Spatiotemporal motion describes changing tread and changing value, which are actually velocity. As we only discuss 2-dimension spatiotemporal objects, we only consider changing tread and changing value of x coordinate and y coordinate.

Definition 3 (motion trend) A spatiotemporal object is presented as $\{(xstart, ystart), (xend, yend)\}$ at time t, $\{(xstart', ystart')\ (xend', yend')\}$ at time t', $t' > t$. If $1/2\ (xstart' + xend') - 1/2\ (xstart + xend) > 0$, it is defined as →; if $1/2\ (xstart' + xend') - 1/2(xstart + xend) < 0$, it is defined as ←; if $1/2\ (xstart' + xend') - 1/2\ (xstart + xend) = 0$, it is defined as ↔; if $1/2\ (ystart' + yend') - 1/2\ (ystart + yend) > 0$, it is defined as ↑; if $1/2\ (ystart' + yend') - 1/2\ (ystart + yend) < 0$, it is defined as ↓; if $1/2\ (ystart' + yend') - 1/2\ (ystart + yend) = 0$, it is defined as ↨.

Definition 4 (motion change value) A apatiotemporal object is presented as $\{(xstart, ystart), (xend, yend)\}$ at time t, $\{(xstart', ystart'), (xend', yend')\}$ at time t', $t' > t$. $xval = (xend' - xstart')\ /\ (xend - xstart)$, $yval = (yend' - ystart')\ /\ (yend - ystart)$, $xcp = (1/2\ (xstart' + xend'))\ /\ (1/2\ (xstart + xend))$, $ycp = (1/2\ (ystart' + yend'))\ /\ (1/2\ (ystart + yend))$.

Figure 3. Motion of a spatiotemporal object

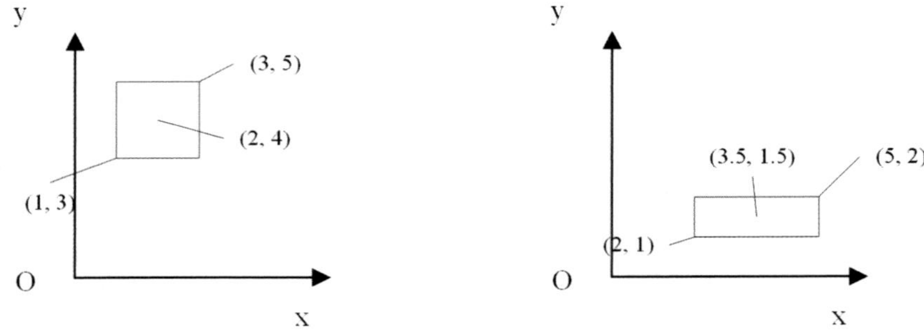

For example, motion of a spatiotemporal object is shown in Figure 3. According to Definition 4 and Definition 5, we can get: $1/2\ (2 + 5) - 1/2\ (1 + 3) = 3.5 - 2 = 1.5 > 0$, so it is represented as →; $1/2\ (1 + 2) - 1/2\ (3 + 5) = 1.5 - 4 = -2.5 < 0$, so it is represented as ↓; $xval = (5 - 2)\ /\ (3 - 1) = 3/2 = 1.5$; $yval = (2 - 1)\ /\ (5 - 3) = 1/2 = 0.5$; $xcp = (1/2\ (2 + 5))\ /\ (1/2\ (1 + 3)) = 1.75$; $ycp = (1/2\ (1 + 2))\ /\ (1/2\ (3 + 5)) = 0.375$.

We can represent the *motion* part of the spatiotemporal object in XML:

```
<motion>
  < κ >
<xaxis>
  →
</xaxis>
<yaxis>
  ↓
```

```
</yaxis>
  </κ >
  <value>
<xval>
  1.5
</xval>
<yval>
  0.5
</yval>
<xcp>
  1.75
</xcp>
<ycp>
  0.375
</ycp>
  </value>
</motion>
```

From this example, we can get that the spatiotemporal object move along the positive direction of *x-axis* and the negative direction of *y-axis*. The motion changing value along *x-axis* (*xval*) is 1.5 (the spatiotemporal object becomes 1.5 times larger than the original one along *x-axis*); the motion changing value along *y-axis* (*yval*) is 0.5 (the spatiotemporal object becomes half the value of the original one along *y-axis*). The function of *xcp* and *ycp* are to help us find the location of spatiotemporal object at the next time point when given the original position.

3.6 Structure of Spatiotemporal Data Model in XML

The spatiotemporal data model is augmented with temporal labels and spatial attributes, and the structure of it is shown in Figure 4. In Figure 4, κ represents changing tread of a spatiotemporal object; x*axis* and y*axis* represent changing tread in x coordinate and y coordinate; → represents spatiotemporal object moving along positive direction of x-*axis;* ← represents spatiotemporal object moving along negative direction of x-*axis;* ↔ represents spatiotemporal object staying static along x-*axis;* ↑ represents spatiotemporal object moving along positive direction of y-*axis;* ↓ represents spatiotemporal object moving along negative direction of y-*axis;* ↕ represents spatiotemporal object staying static along y-*axis;* x*val* represents motion change value of x-*axis;* y*val* represents motion change value of y-*axis;* x*cp* represents motion change value of the center point along x-*axis;* y*cp* represents motion change value of the center point along y-*axis.* In the following, we give some illustrations about the model.

- The *lifespan* of a node *n* is the union of temporal elements of all containment edges incoming to this node.
- All temporal labels outgoing from a node is contained in the *lifespan* of the node.
- Given two nodes n_i and n_j that n_j is the child node of n_i, if the edge between n_i and n_j has no time label, then the *lifespan* of n_i is the same as *lifespan* of n_j.

- For a time instant t, there must be an order of the model, denoted $<_t$. In general, for any two nodes n_1 and n_2, we may have $n_1 <_t n_2$ and $n_2 <_t n_1$ in two different instant t_1 and t_2. However, these two nodes have definitely one order $n_1 <_t n_2$ or $n_2 <_t n_1$ in a given time point, and also have definitely one order $n_1 <_t n_2$ or $n_2 <_t n_1$ in time interval $T = T_1 \cap T_2$, which T_1 is the time interval of node n_1, and T_2 is the time interval of node n_2, respectively.
- Given two times intervals T_1 and T_2, we will say T_1 succeeds T_2 if $T_{1^{\cdot}end} > T_{2^{\cdot}end}$, denoted by $T_1 \ni T_2$, and T_1 precedes T_2 if $T_{1^{\cdot}end} < T_{2^{\cdot}end}$, denoted by $T_1 \in T_2$, respectively.

Figure 4. The whole structure of the model

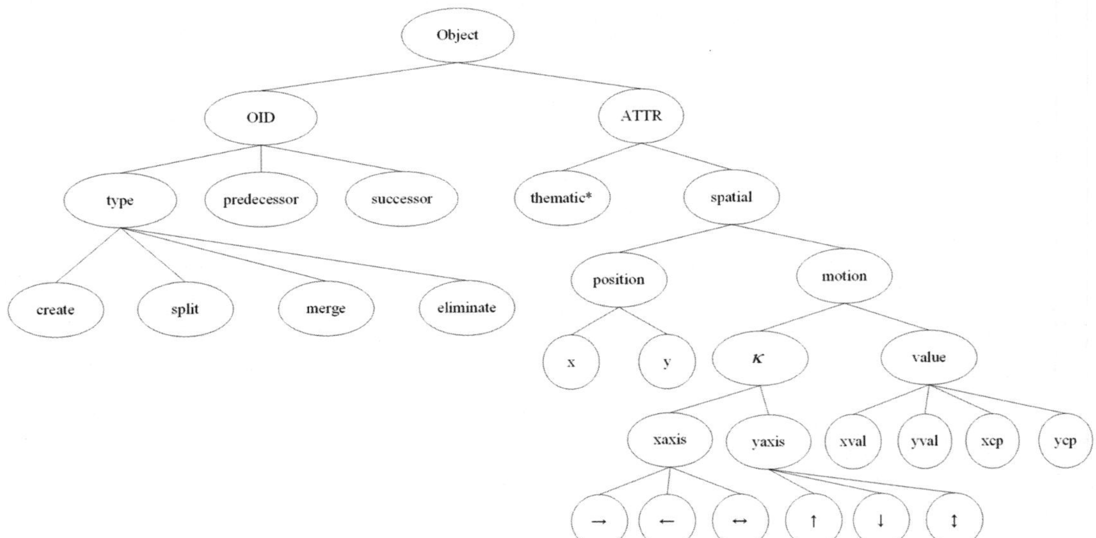

3.7 Example

Here, we will give a specific example of a spatiotemporal XML document for a portion of spatiotemporal database, which is shown in Figure 5. We use the example to explain how to represent spatiotemporal data in XML.

The spatiotemporal database is composed of spatiotemporal objects that contain spatiotemporal object ID and internal attributes. The former one describes one or more spatiotemporal objects changing into other spatiotemporal objects whereas the latter one describes internal attributes containing thematic attributes and spatial attributes. The database also records position and motion for each spatiotemporal object. It is noted that some of the dynamics in this example models (owner of a spatiotemporal object) may change. For instance, in this database, node 19 represents Williams and node 20 represents John. The dashed line between nodes10 and 20, labeled [0, 33], indicates that the owner of spatiotemporal object o_1 is John between time points '0' and '33'. After that, the owner of spatiotemporal object o_1 is changed to Williams. This is represented by the solid line joining nodes 10 and 19, labeled [34, Now]. In spite of the change of owner, there is only one node for each owner. Thus, regardless of the owner of spatiotemporal object o_1, the graph shows that the address of o_1 is *Jing Kong district* throughout its *lifespan*. As another example, node 17 represents spatial attribute of spatiotemporal object o_2 between time points '0' and '15', whose position is {(2, 5), (3, 9)}, and becomes 2 times larger than the original one along positive direction of *x-axis*, and becomes half the value of the original one along positive direction of *y-axis*; node 16 represents spatial attribute of spatiotemporal object o_2 since then, whose position is {(3, 6), (4, 10)}, and becomes 5 times larger than the original one along positive direction of *x-axis*, and becomes 3 times larger than the original one along positive direction of *y-axis*.

Figure 5. Spatiotemporal XML database

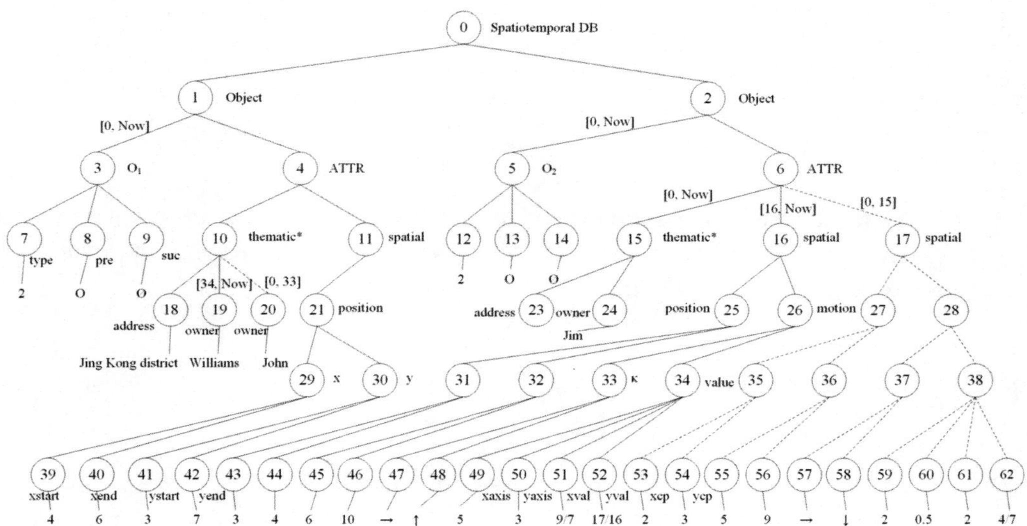

4 SPATIOTEMPORAL FUNCTIONS

Since spatiotemporal data is different from spatial data and temporal data, operations between spatiotemporal objects are different as well. For this reason, it is necessary to define new functions to operate spatiotemporal data (all the functions should support the special "now" timestamp).

Spatiotemporal operations contain spatiotemporal topological operations and spatiotemporal geometric operations. Spatiotemporal topological operations return TRUE or FALSE to determine topological relations between spatiotemporal objects, while spatiotemporal geometric operations return spatial or spatiotemporal data. Spatiotemporal topological operations contain *stDisjoint*, *stMeet*, *stIntersects*, *stContain*, *stOverlap*, and *stEqual*. Spatiotemporal geometric operations mainly contain *stWhen* and *stHistory*. In this section, we define those spatiotemporal functions in XML, and give each spatiotemporal function a simple corresponding example.

4.1 Spatiotemporal Topological Operations

Spatiotemporal topological relation is defined as *stDisjoint* if there are no intersections between the two spatiotemporal objects. It can not only represent the topological relationship of two spatiotemporal objects at a certain time point but also two time points of each spatiotemporal object. Element *a* and element *b* are defined from four directions in the plane as we mainly talk about 2-dimensional spatiotemporal objects in this chapter.

```
Function stDisjoint ($a, $b)
{
for $a/@T ∩ $b/@T
if ($a/../xend < $b/../xstart or
$a/../yend < $b/../ystart or
$a/../xstart > $b/../xend or
$a/../ystart>$b/../yend
then true ()
else false ()
}
```

For a portion of the structure of spatiotemporal data in XML, the *position* part is presented in Figure 6, while *xstart, xend, ystart, yend* of O_1 is 1, 2, 2, 4, and 4, 6, 5, 8 for O_2. Representations of O_1 and O_2 can be described in XML shown in Figure 7.

Figure 6. The position part of Figure 1

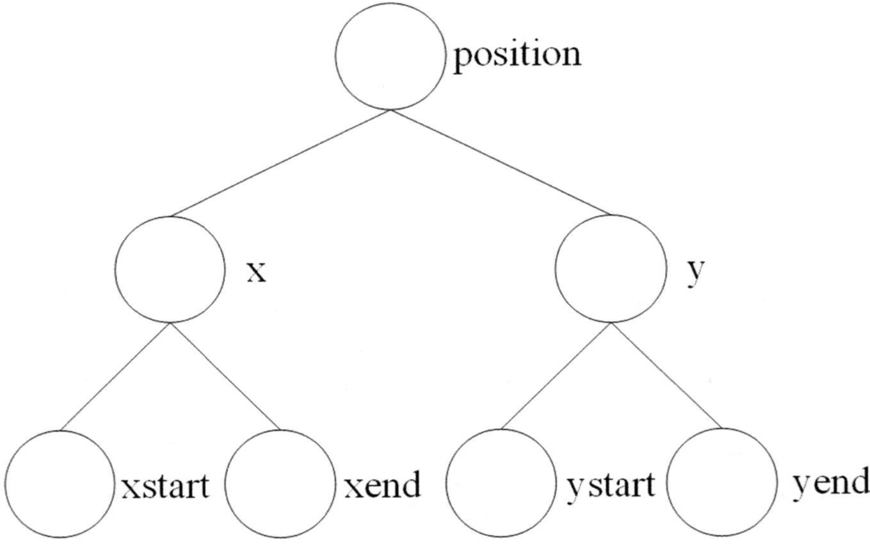

For this example, we can easily get the topological relationship of O_1 and O_2 being *stDisjoint* according to *function stDisjoint ($a, $b)* since $a/../xend < $b/../xstart. This example gives the topological relationship at a certain time point. If we want to get the topological relationship at two time points of each spatiotemporal object, we retrieve the state of *position* part of each spatiotemporal object at each time point. Actually, this is one of the cases of *stDisjoint*.

Figure 7. Example presented in XML

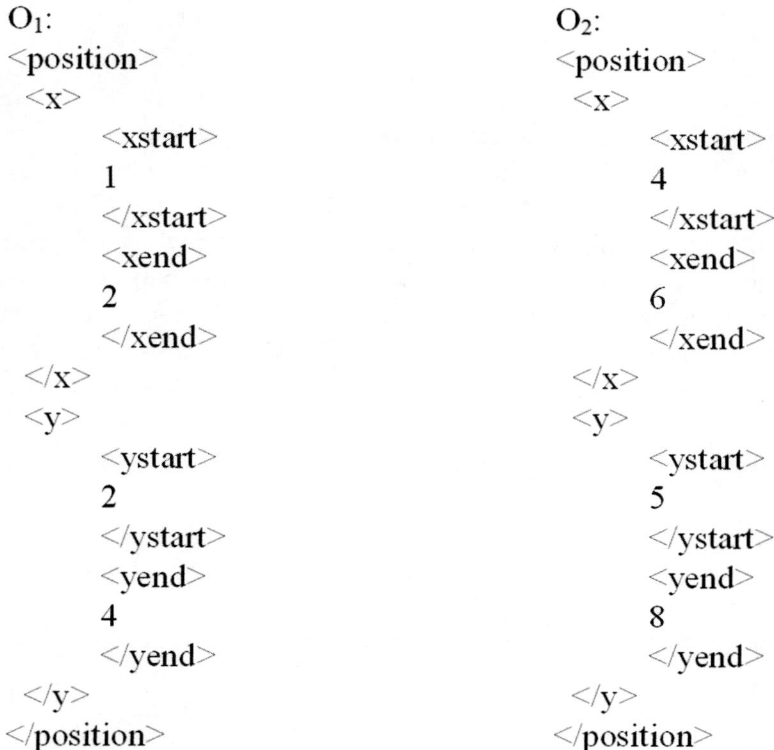

Spatiotemporal topological relation is defined as *stMeet* if there are intersections between boundaries of two spatiotemporal objects. As an important spatiotemporal topological relationship, *stMeet* can not only represent the topological relationship of two spatiotemporal objects at a certain time point but also two time points of each spatiotemporal object. Element *a* and element *b* are defined as *stMeet* if there are intersections between boundaries of elements *a* and *b*.

```
Function stMeet ($a, $b)
{
for $a/@T ∩ $b/@T
if ((($a/../xend = $b/../xstart and ($a/../ystart <= $b/../ystart <= $a/../
yend or $a/../ystart <= $b/../yend <= $a/../yend)) or
($a/../yend = $b/../ystart and ($a/../xstart <= $b/../xstart <= $a/../xend or
$a/../xstart <= $b/../xend <= $a/../xend)) or
($a/../xstart = $b/../xend and ($a/../ystart <= $b/../ystart <= $a/../yend or
$a/../ystart <= $b/../yend <= $a/../yend)) or
($a/../ystart = $b/../yend and ($a/../xstart <= $b/../xend <= $a/../xend or
$a/../xstart <= $b/../xstart <= $a/../xend)))
then true ()
```

```
else false ()
}
```

For example, the *position* part is presented in Figure. 2, while *xstart*, *xend*, *ystart*, *yend* of O_1 is 2, 5, 2, 6, and 4, 7, 6, 8 for O_2. Representations of O_1 and O_2 can be described in XML shown in Figure. 3 except values. We can take Figure. 3 as this example only displacing values given. From the example, we can easily get the topological relationship of O_1 and O_2 being *stMeet* according to *function stMeet ($a, $b)* since $a/../yend = $b/../ystart and $a/../xstart <= $b/../xstart <= $a/../xend.

Spatiotemporal topological relation is defined as *stOverlap* if there are overlapped areas between two spatiotemporal objects. As discussed above, *stOverlap* can also not only represent the topological relationship of two spatiotemporal objects at a certain time point but also two time points of each spatiotemporal object. Element *a* and element *b* are defined as *stOverlap* if one of the angle point of element *a* stays within the element *b* and the opposite angle point of element *a* stays outside the element *b*.

```
Function stOverlap ($a, $b)
{
for $a/@T ∩ $b/@T
if ((($a/../xstart <= $b/../xend and $a/../ystart <= $b/../yend) and $a/../
xstart > $b/../xstart) or
(($a/../xend >= $b/../xstart and $a/../ystart <= $b/..yend) and $a/../xstart >
$b/../xstart) or
(($a/../xend >= $b/../xstart and $a/../ystart <= $b/../yend) $a/../xend <
$b/../xend) or
(($a/../xend >= $b/../start and $a/..yend >= $b/../ystart) and $a/../xend <
$b/../xend))
then true ()
else false ()
}
```

For example, the *position* part is presented in Figure. 2, while *xstart*, *xend*, *ystart*, *yend* of O_1 is 3, 7, 4, 7, and 5, 9, 5, 8 for O_2. Representations of O_1 and O_2 can be described in XML shown in Figure. 3 except values. We can take Figure. 3 as this example only displacing values given. From the example, we can easily get the topological relationship of O_1 and O_2 being *stOverlap* according to *function stOverlap ($a, $b)* since ($a/../xstart < $b/../xend and $a/../ystart < $b/../yend) and $a/../xstart > $b/../xstart.

As is known, *stOverlap* deals with two 2-dimensional spatiotemporal objects while *stIntersect* deals with a 1-dimensional spatiotemporal object with another 2-dimensional spatiotemporal object. What's more, we take two ending point {(xstart, ystart), (xend, yend)} to represent 1-dimensional spatiotemporal objects, and MBR (Cobb & Petry, 1998) to represent 2-dimensional spatiotemporal objects. Consequently, *stIntersect* is a special case of *stOverlap* to some extent. So the definition of *function stIntersect* ($a, $b) is the same as the definition of *stOverlap*. *stOverlap* can represent topological relationship of two spatiotemporal objects at a certain time point, and two time points of each spatiotemporal object.

Spatiotemporal topological relation is defined as *stContain* if one spatiotemporal object contains another spatiotemporal object. *stContain* can represent the topological relationship of two spatiotemporal objects at a certain time point, and two time points of each spatiotemporal object. Element *a* and element *b* are defined as *stContain* if the boundary of element *a* stays within the boundary of element *b*.

```
Function stContain ($a, $b)
{
for $a/@T ∩ $b/@T
if ($a/../xstart < $b/../xstart and $a/../ystart < $b/../ystart) and
($a/../xend > $b/../xend and $a/../yend > $b/../yend)
then true ()
else false ()
}
```

For example, the *position* part is presented in Figure. 2, while *xstart*, *xend*, *ystart*, *yend* of O_1 is 1, 6, 2, 7, and 3, 5, 4, 5 for O_2. Representations of O_1 and O_2 can be described in XML shown in Figure. 3 except values. We can take Figure. 3 as this example only displacing values given. From the example, we can easily get the topological relationship of O_1 and O_2 being *stOverlap* according to *function stContain ($a, $b)* since ($a/../xstart < $b/../xstart and $a/../ystart < $b/../ystart) and ($a/../xend > $b/../xend and $a/../yend > $b/../yend).

Spatiotemporal topological relation is defined as *stEqual* if boundaries and areas of two spatiotemporal objects are equal. *stEqual* can also not only represent the topological relationship of two spatiotemporal objects at a certain time point but also two time points of each spatiotemporal object. Element *a* and element *b* are defined as *stEqual* if the four angle points of element *a* are equal to the corresponding angle points of element *b*.

```
Function stEqual ($a, $b)
{
for $a/@T ∩ $b/@T
if ($a/../xstart = $b/../xstart and $a/../ystart = $b/../ystart) and
($a/../xend = $b/../xend and $a/../yend = $b/../yend)
then true ()
else false ()
}
```

For example, the *position* part is presented in Figure. 2, while *xstart*, *xend*, *ystart*, *yend* of O_1 and O_2 is 2, 6, 3, and 7 respectively. Representations of O_1 and O_2 can be described in XML shown in Figure. 3 except values. We can take Figure. 3 as this example only displacing values given. From the example, we can easily get the topological relationship of O_1 and O_2 being *stEqual* according to *function stEqual ($a, $b)* since ($a/../xstart = $b/../xstart and $a/../ystart = $b/../ystart) and ($a/../xend = $b/../xend and $a/../yend = $b/../yend).

4.2 Spatiotemporal Geometric Operations

In succession, we will define spatiotemporal geometric functions, which contain *stWhen* and *stHistory*. To some extent, *stWhen* is similar to snapshot.

Given a time point *t*, *stWhen* returns spatial state of the spatiotemporal data at the time point *t*.

```
Function stWhen ($a, t)
{
if element n is static element and t_s < t < t_e,
if n is OID
return n, n/type, n/predecessor, and n/successor
end if
return n
end if
if element n is dynamic element
return n
end if
}
```

For the above spatiotemporal geometric function *stWhen*, there are several points:

1. In this chapter, spatiotemporal attribute is viewed as a special element in XML, so we generally use element.
2. We introduce the notion of *lifespan* of a node. In this example, we denote *lifespan(n)* = $[t_s, t_e]$.
3. Value node is regarded as dynamic element in this example.

Take Figure. 1 for example, *stWhen* (O_1) at the time point 3 is type = 2, predecessor = *O*, and successor = Ø; *stWhen (owner)* of spatiotemporal object O_1 at the time point 15 is John; *stWhen (position)* of spatiotemporal object O_2 at the time point 20 is xstart = 3, xend = 4, ystart = 6, and yend = 10.

Given a time interval, *stHistory* returns changing history of the spatiotemporal data during the time interval.

```
Function stHistory ($a, t_s, t_e)
{
if element n is static element
compute lifespan(n)and t_s < t < t_e
if t_s < t < t_e
if n is OID
return n, n/type, n/predecessor, and n/successor
end if
return n
end if
end if
group the results and return
if element n is dynamic element
return the grouped results n
}
```

In *function stHistory ($a, t_s, t_e)*, we use a significant function denoted by *group*, which returns all distinct results.

Take Figure. 1 for example, *stHistory (owner)* of spatiotemporal object O_1 is John at time interval [0, 33] and Williams at time interval [34, Now]; *stHistory (κ)* of spatiotemporal object O_2 is xaxis = →, yaxis = ↓ at time interval [0, 15] and xaxis = →, yaxis = ↑ at time interval [16, Now].

4.3 Discussion

Actually, examples given are just one of the cases of that spatiotemporal topological relationship. In Figure 8, we give all possible cases of *stDisjoint*, *stMeet*, *stOverlap*, *stIntersect*, *stContain*, and *stEqual*. Take object *B* as reference object, object *A* possibly appears at area denoted dashed line, which can ensure spatiotemporal object *A* and *B* maintain the spatiotemporal topological relationship at a certain time point. We can also get the topological relationship of O_1 and O_2 at two different time points according to the corresponding spatiotemporal functions.

All spatiotemporal topological functions are just dealing with one of two situations. Since element *a* and element *b* are symmetric, we can easily extend it to another situation.

Figure 8. Possible cases of the spatiotemporal topological relations

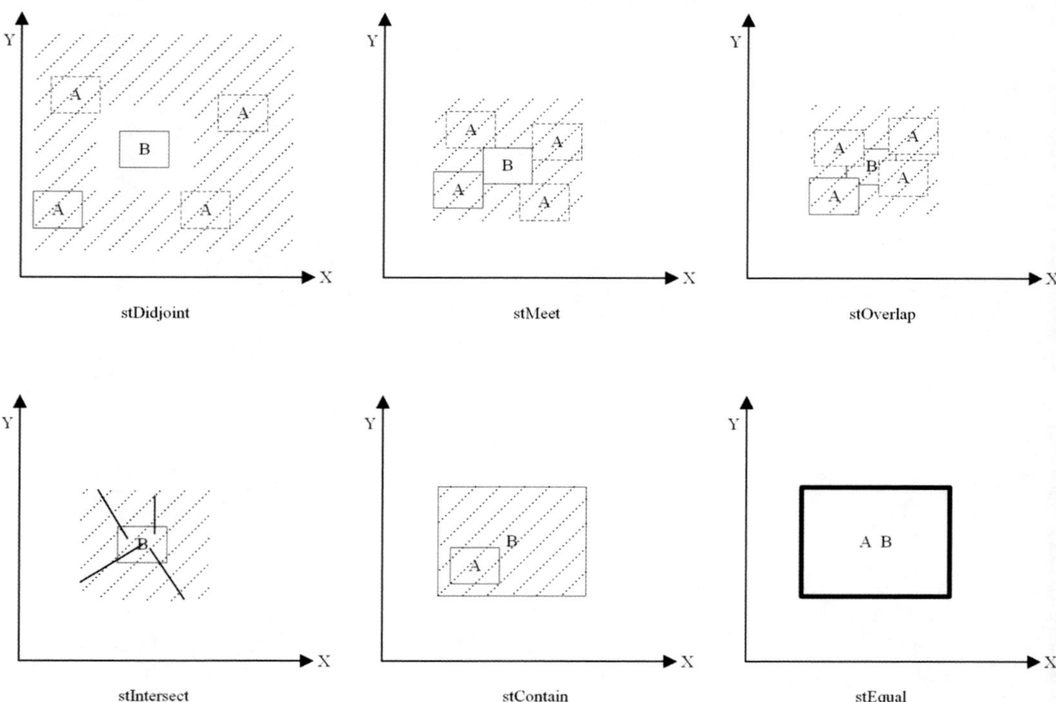

5 ARCHITECTURE OF QUERYING PROCESS AND XQUERY QUERY

5.1 Architecture of Querying Process

XQuery is a query language of XML data. The key advantage of our approach is that powerful spatiotemporal queries can be expressed using XQuery without requiring the introduction of new query language. The architecture of querying process is shown in Figure 9.

When there is a query request, we operate the query request based on the spatiotemporal data model (Bai et al., 2015) and spatiotemporal functions (Bai et al., 2014). After result processing, we finally obtain wanted result. The reason why we process the result is that the result operated based on the model may be implicit. For example, when there is a query request for velocity, the returned result are *xaxix, yaxis, xval, yval, xcp, ycp* according the model. Although the returned result expresses the velocity information, the information is implicit. Accordingly, the result should be processed. Take velocity information for example, we can determine velocity value by $v = \sqrt{xval^2 + yval^2}$, and can determine velocity direction by direction of *xaxis* and *yaxis*. Another request example is area of spatiotemporal objects. The returned result is *xstart*, *ystart*, *xend*, and *yend*. Because the result is also implicit, we could process it by $area = (xend - xstart) \times (yend - ystart)$ to determine the area of the spatiotemporal object.

Figure 9. Architecture of querying process

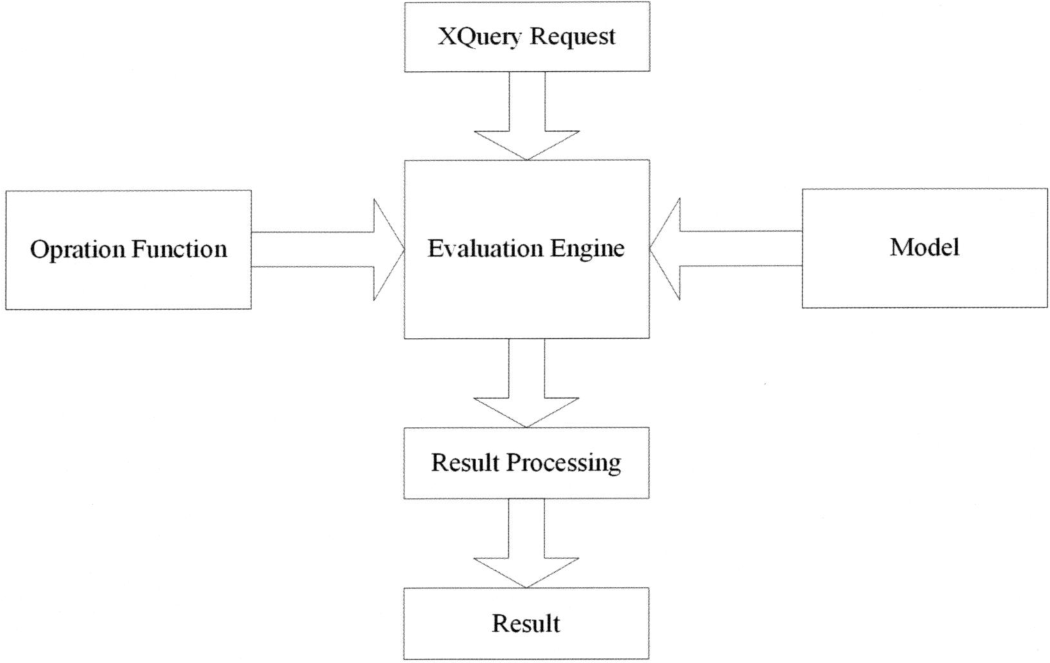

5.2 Queries Using XQuery

In this section, we illustrate how to query spatiotemporal data using XQuery.

XQuery is a query language of XML, which is based on XML document structure. The key advantage of our approach is that powerful spatiotemporal queries can be expressed in XQuery without requiring the introduction of new query language as we just introduce some new functions. FLWOR, which is the most effective and most commonly used expression, can be directly used, and its expressions remain unchanged. As we introduce eight spatiotemporal operations (Bai et al., 2014), query results are results by calling those operations. Accordingly, we could bind spatiotemporal operations after *return*. It can be represented as:

return Funtion.

Funtion indicates spatiotemporal functions, which contain *stDisjoint* (*$a, $b*), *stMeet* (*$a, $b*), *stOverlap* (*$a, $b*), *stIntersects* (*$a, $b*), *stContain* (*$a, $b*), *stEqual* (*$a, $b*), *stWhen* (*$n, $t*), and *stHistory* (*$n*, $\$T_s$, $\$T_e$). As a result, when query using XQuery, the former part FLWOR remain unchanged, and bind spatiotemporal functions after *return*.

When we want query spatiotemporal data using XQuery, we should firstly query attributes of the spatiotemporal object based on the model and then return the corresponding attributes using FLWOR expressions. For example, if we want to query position of the spatiotemporal object, we should firstly return *xstart*, *ystart*, *xend*, *yend* Then we could call functions and finally get the result.

For example, if we want to know whether the topological relationship of the two spatiotemporal objects is *stContain*, we could firstly use FLWOR expressions to return MBR of these two spatiotemporal objects, and then call *stContain($a, $b)*. The topological relationship is *stContain* if the return result is true and is not *stContain* if the return result is false.

6 QUERY CASES

In this section, we give three query cases using the proposed spatiotemporal functions. Complex queries can be expressed on the basis of our query cases.

QUERY 1: Topological relationship queries. Find the topological relationship of spatiotemporal object O_1 and O_2 after object O splits into object O_1 and O_2:

```
for $a in Object [OID="O1"] and
$b in Object [OID="O2"]
let $a:= O1/predecessor [.="O" ] and O1/ts > 0
let $b:= O2/predecessor [.="O" ] and O2/ts > 0
return stDisjoint ($a, $b)
return stMeet ($a, $b)
return stIntersect ($a, $b)
return stContain ($a, $b)
return stOverlap ($a, $b)
return stEqual ($a, $b)
```

Here, *stDisjoint*, *stMeet*, *stIntersect*, *stContain*, *stOverlap*, and *stEqual* are user-defined functions, which are used to check the topological relationships of two spatiotemporal objects. The first let clause ruturns O_1, whose predecessor is O after the time point 0. The second let clause returns O_2, whose predecessor is also O after the time point 0. These two let clauses indicate object O split into O_1 and O_2 after the time point 0. Actually, the spatiotemporal object O split into O_1 and O_2 at the time point 3. As we mentioned above, there are six spatiotemporal topological relationships between two spatiotemporal objects, so we use these six operations to return the topological relationship since there must be a unique spatiotemporal topological relationship at a certain time point.

Take Figure 10 for example, from the *position* part of spatiotemporal object O_1, we can easily get MBR of O_1 after the time point 0 since the spatiotemporal object O_1 is static. As regards to the spatiotemporal object O_2, it is dynamic and there is a change of ATTR at the time point 16. For simplicity, we just talk about the state at time 0, 1, 16, 17. Others can get in an analogical way.

According to Figure. 1, we get MBR of spatiotemporal object O_1 and O_2 at time instant 0, 1, 16, and 17 as shown in Figure. 6. Actually, the positions of spatiotemporal object O_2 at the time point 1 and 17 are computed by the *motion* part of spatiotemporal object O_2 at the time point 0 and 16, respectively. Thus, according to the corresponding spatiotemporal topological functions we can easily get the topological relationship of spatiotemporal object O_1 and O_2 at the time point 0, 1, 16, and 17, which are *stDisjoint*, *stOverlap*, *stMeet*, and *stContain* respectively. For simplicity, we only talk about the topological relationship of O_1 and O_2 at the time point 0, 1, 16, and 17 in this example. Others can be got in an analogously way.

Figure 10. MBR of spatiotemporal object O_1 and O_2 at time point 0, 1, 16, and 17

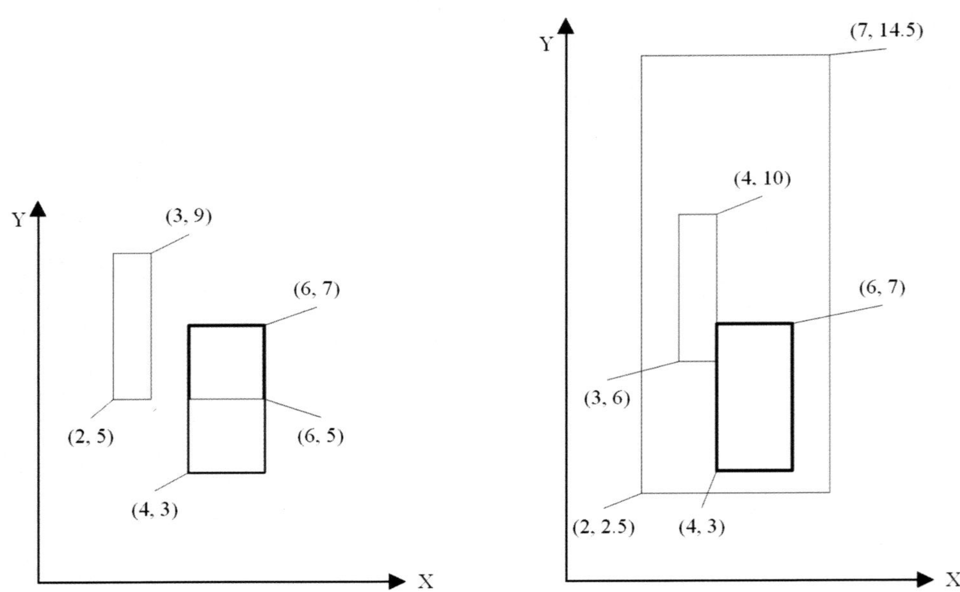

QUERY 2: Snapshot queries. Find velocity of spatiotemporal object O_2 at the time point 16.

```
for $e in Object [OID=" O2"]
return stWhen ($e/../κ, "16")
return stWhen ($e/../value, "16")
```

The two "return" return *motion* part of the spatiotemporal object O_2, which is actually the velocity of O_2. "16" is the time point, which is actually T_s = "16" = T_e.

Take Figure. 1 for example, we can just observe the *motion* part of spatiotemporal object O_2 at the time point 16. Accordingly, we can get xaxis being →, yaxis being ↑, xval being 5, yval being 3, xcp being 9/7, and ycp being 17/16 from this query.

QUERY 3: Evolutionary queries. Find changing history of spatiotemporal object *O_2's motion* part at time interval T_e = *[3, 30]* since O_1 comes into being.

```
for $e in Object [ OID="O1"]
let Ts:=max{0, O2/type[.="1"]}
return stHistory ($e, Ts, Te)
```

The let clause returns T_e = [3, 30] because the time point when O_1 comes into being is earlier than 3. Type value "1" represents this spatiotemporal object being created. Accordingly, *stHistory* could return the desired result.

Take Figure. 1 for example, we can actually observe the state of *motion* part at the time point 0 and 16. Others from the time point 1 to 15 and from the time point 17 to Now is the same as those at time point 0 and 16. Above, at time interval T_e = [3, 15], we can get xaxis being →, yaxis being ↓, xval being 2, yval being 0.5, xcp being 2, ycp being 4/7; at time interval T_e = [16, 30], we can get xaxis being →, yaxis being ↑, xval being 5, yval being 3, xcp being 9/7, ycp being 17/16.

The above query cases illustrate that the eight spatiotemporal operations can be retrieved using the proposed spatiotemporal functions. Other complex queries can be extended based on the above basic queries in an analogously way.

7 RELATED WORK

Regarding the representation of spatiotemporal data, several categories of approaches are related to our work according to their focuses, including spatiotemporal models in traditional database, representation of spatiotemporal data in traditional database, representation of spatiotemporal data in XML.

The first category focuses on spatiotemporal models in traditional database. A considerable amount of efforts concerning on spatiotemporal models are made, including Sequent Snapshot Model (Gilberto et al., 2005), Base State with Amendment Model (Song et al., 2011), Space-Time Composite Model (Langran, 1988), Space-Time Cube Model (Kristensson et al., 2009), Event-Based Spatio-Temporal Data Model (Peuquet & Duan, 1995), Data Model based on Simple Time-Stamping (Hunter & Williamson, 1990), Three-Domain Model (Parrott et al., 2008), History Graph Model (Renolen, 1996), Spatio-Temporal Entity-Relationship Model (Tryfona & Jensen, 2000), Object-Relationship Model (Parent et al., 1999), Spatio-Temporal Object-Oriented Data Model (Montgomery, 1995), Moving Object Data Model (Erwig et al., 1999). For a comprehensive review of spatiotemporal models, ones can refer to (Pelekis et al.,

2004). All those above spatiotemporal data models are proposed based on tradition database, which will generate new tuples and produce a great deal of redundancy.

The second category focuses on spatiotemporal data in traditional database. In modeling spatiotemporal data, two common approaches have been widely used, which are field based modeling and object oriented modeling (Senellart & Abiteboul, 2007). For a comprehensive review of spatiotemporal models, ones can refer to (Mendelzon et al., 2004). In operating and querying spatiotemporal data, Kim et al. (Kim et al., 2000) design a spatiotemporal database query language supporting a bitemporal concept for spatio-temporal objects; Hadjieleftheriou et al. (Hadjieleftheriou et al., 2002) address the problem of indexing large volumes of spatiotemporal data, and propose approaches for splitting a given spatiotemporal object.

The third category focuses on spatiotemporal data in XML. There are efforts to analyze spatiotemporal data in XML. In (Liu & Wan, 2010), Liu and Wan propose a feature-based spatiotemporal data model and use the Native XML Database to store the spatiotemporal data. Huang et al. (Huang et al., 2004) propose an approach to represent and query spatiotemporal data in XML. In (Bai et al., 2013), Bai et al. propose approaches of XML twig pattern for determining topological relationship of two fuzzy spatiotemporal data. Unfortunately, although spatiotemporal data in XML have been studied, relatively little work has been carried out in spatiotemporal operations integrated with functions in XML.

Compared to their work, our proposed approaches for spatiotemporal functions in XML are well-defined and robust enough to handle various query cases. These functions are generic in nature, as they can be applied to both spatiotemporal topological operations and spatiotemporal geometric operations. Furthermore, our model for representing spatiotemporal data in XML is highly useful and efficient. It supports dynamic changes and minimizes redundancy compared to traditional databases.

8 SUMMARY

In this chapter, we propose a comprehensive data model for representing spatiotemporal data using XML. We thoroughly analyze and discuss complex spatiotemporal data by breaking it down into individual components. Additionally, our focus is on the spatiotemporal operations. The proposed framework and functions provide a well-defined and powerful approach to handle spatiotemporal data, capturing its unique characteristics and supporting a wide range of query cases.

REFERENCES

Akhter, I., Simon, T., Khan, S., Matthews, I., & Sheikh, Y. (2012). Bilinear Spatiotemporal Basis Models. *ACM Transactions on Graphics*, *31*(2), 17–29. doi:10.1145/2159516.2159523

Baazizi, M. A., Bidoit, N., & Colazzo, D. (2011). Efficient Encoding of Temporal XML Documents. In *Proceedings of the 18th International Symposium on Temporal Representation and Reasoning* (pp. 15-22). IEEE.

Bai, L. Y., Xu, C. M., & Liu, X. L. (2015). A Framework for Spatiotemporal Data Representation in XML. *Journal of Computer Information Systems*, *11*(14), 5091–5098.

Bai, L. Y., Yan, L., & Ma, Z. M. (2013). Determining Topological Relationship of Fuzzy Spatiotemporal Data Integrated with XML Twig Pattern. *Applied Intelligence*, *39*(1), 75–100. doi:10.1007/s10489-012-0395-3

Bai, L. Y., Yan, L., & Ma, Z. M. (2014). Spatiotemporal Operations Integrated with Functions in XML. *Journal of Computer Information Systems*, *10*(21), 9079–9086.

Camossi, E., Bertolotto, M., & Bertino, E. (2003). A Multigranular Spatiotemporal Data Model. In *Proceedings of the 11th ACM International Symposium on Advances in Geographic Information Systems* (pp. 94-101). ACM.

Chen, Y., & Revesz, P. (2003). Querying Spatiotemporal XML Using DataFox. In Proceedings of Web Intelligence (pp. 301-309). doi:10.1109/WI.2003.1241208

Cobb, M. A., & Petry, F. E. (1998). Modeling Spatial Relationships within a Fuzzy Framework. *Journal of the American Society for Information Science*, *49*(3), 253–266. doi:10.1002/(SICI)1097-4571(199803)49:3<253::AID-ASI6>3.0.CO;2-F

Deng, S. S., Xia, L. H., & Wang, F. (2009). Analysis of Spatio-Temporal Characteristics of Urban Land Cover and its Landscape Pattern: a Case Study in NanHai District of Foshan City. In Proceedings of Joint Urban Remote Sensing Event (pp. 1-9).

Du, Z., Jeong, Y. S., Jeong, M. K., & Kong, S. G. (2012). Multidimensional Local Spatial Autocorrelation Measure for Integrating Spatial and Spectral Information in Hyperspectral Image Band Selection. *Applied Intelligence*, *36*(2), 542–552. doi:10.1007/s10489-010-0274-8

Erwig, M., Guting, R. H., Schneider, M., & Vazirgiannis, M. (1999). Spatio-temporal data types: An approach to modeling and querying moving objects in databases. *GeoInformatica*, *3*(3), 265–291. doi:10.1023/A:1009805532638

Franceschet, M., Montanari, A., & Gubiani, D. (2007). Modeling and Validating Spatio-Temporal Conceptual Schemas in XML Schema. In *Proceedings of the 18th International Conference on DEXA* (pp. 25-29). ACM. 10.1109/DEXA.2007.106

Gilberto, A. G., Gonzalo, N., & Andrea, R. (2005). A spatiotemporal access method based on snapshots and events. In *Proceedings of the 13th Annual ACM International Workshop on Geographic Information Systems* (pp. 115-124). ACM.

Hadjieleftheriou, M., Kollios, G., Tsotras, V. J., & Gunopulos, D. (2002). Efficient Indexing of Spatiotemporal Objects. *Lecture Notes in Computer Science*, *2287*, 251–268. doi:10.1007/3-540-45876-X_17

Huang, B., Yi, S. Z., & Chan, W. T. (2004). Spatio-Temporal Information Integration in XML. *Future Generation Computer Systems*, *20*(7), 1157–1170. doi:10.1016/j.future.2003.11.005

Jonathan, R. S., Peter, M., & Bruno, S. (2001). Dynamic Models for Spatiotemporal Data. *Journal of the Royal Statistical Society. Series A, (Statistics in Society)*, *63*(4), 673–689.

Kim, D. H., Ryu, K. H., & Kim, H. S. (2000). A Spatiotemporal Database Model and Query Language. *Journal of Systems and Software*, *55*(2), 129–149. doi:10.1016/S0164-1212(00)00066-2

Kristensson, P. O., Dahlback, N., Anundi, D., Bjornstad, M., Gillberg, H., Haraldsson, J., Martensson, I., Nordvall, M., & Stahl, J. (2009). An evaluation of space time cube representation of spatiotemporal patterns. *IEEE Transactions on Visualization and Computer Graphics, 15*(4), 696–702. doi:10.1109/TVCG.2008.194 PMID:19423892

Langran, G., & Chrisman, N. R. (1988). A framework for temporal geographic information systems. *Cartographica, 25*(3), 1–14. doi:10.3138/K877-7273-2238-5Q6V

Liu, X. H., & Wan, Y. C. (2010). Storing Spatio-Temporal Data in XML Native Database. In *Proceedings of the 2nd International Workshop on Database Technology and Applications* (pp. 1-4). IEEE. 10.1109/DBTA.2010.5659107

Mamoulis, N., Cao, H., & Kollios, G. (2004). Mining, Indexing, and Querying Historical Spatiotemporal data. In *Proceedings of the 10th ACM SIGKDD international conference on Knowledge Discovery and Data Mining* (pp. 236-245). ACM. 10.1145/1014052.1014080

Mehrotra, R., & Sharma, A. (2009). Evaluating Spatio-Temporal Representations in Daily Rainfall Sequences from Three Stochastic Multi-Site Weather Generation Approaches. *Advances in Water Resources, 32*(6), 948–962. doi:10.1016/j.advwatres.2009.03.005

Mendelzon, A. O., Rizzolo, F., & Vaisman, A. (2004). Indexing Temporal XML Documents. In *Proceedings of the 30th International Conference on VLDB* (pp. 216-227). ACM.

Montgomery, L. D. (1995). *Temporal geographic information systems technology and requirements: where we are today.* [PhD thesis, Department of Geography, Ohio State University].

Noh, S. Y., & Gadia, S. K. (2005). An XML-Based Framework for Temporal Database Implementation. In *Proceedings of the 12th International Symposium on Temporal Representation & Reasoning* (pp. 180-182). IEEE.

Parent, C. S., Spaccapietra, S., & Zimanyi, E. (1999). Spatio-temporal conceptual models: data structures + space + time. In *Proceedings of the 7th ACM Symposium on Advances in Geographic Information Systems* (pp. 26-33). ACM. 10.1145/320134.320142

Parrott, L., Proulx, R., & Plante, X. T. (2008). Three-dimensional metrics for analysis of spatiotemporal data in ecology. *Ecological Informatics, 3*(6), 343–353. doi:10.1016/j.ecoinf.2008.07.001

Pelekis, N., Theodoulidis, B., Kopanakis, I., & Theodoridis, Y. (2004). Literature Review of Spatio-Temporal Database Models. *The Knowledge Engineering Review, 19*(3), 235–274. doi:10.1017/S026988890400013X

Peuquet, D. J., & Duan, N. (1995). An event-based spatio-temporal data model (ESTDM) for temporal analysis of geographical data. *International Journal of Geographical Information Systems, 9*(1), 7–24. doi:10.1080/02693799508902022

Renolen, A. (1996). *History graphs: conceptual modeling of spatio-temporal data.* [PhD thesis, in GIS Frontiers in Business and Science, International Cartographic Association].

Rizzolo, F., & Vaisman, A. A. (2008). Temporal XML: Modeling, Indexing, and Query Processing. *The VLDB Journal, 17*(5), 1179–1212. doi:10.1007/s00778-007-0058-x

Senellart, P., & Abiteboul, S. (2007). On the Complexity of Managing Probabilistic XML Data. In *Proceedings of the 26th ACM SIGACT-SIGMOD-SIGART Symposium on Principles of Database Systems* (pp. 283-292). ACM. 10.1145/1265530.1265570

Song, X. Y., Wang, Y. H., Wu, G., & Wang, S. J. (2011). Base state amendments spatio-temporal data model with dynamic selection of base state. In *Proceedings of the 4th International Congress on Image and Signal Processing* (pp. 15-17). IEEE. 10.1109/CISP.2011.6100782

Tao, Y., & Papadias, D. (2001). MV3R-tree: a Spatio-Temporal Access Method for Time-Stamp and Interval Queries. In *Proceedings of VLDB* (pp. 431-440). IEEE.

Tryfona, N., & Jensen, C. S. (2000). Using abstractions for spatio-temporal conceptual modeling. In *Proceedings of the 2000 ACM Symposium on Applied Computing* (pp. 313-322). ACM. 10.1145/335603.335775

Vazirgiannis, M., & Wolfson, O. (2001). A Spatiotemporal Model and Language for Moving Objects on Road Networks. *Lecture Notes in Computer Science*, *2121*, 20–35. doi:10.1007/3-540-47724-1_2

Wang, X. Y., Zhou, X. F., & Lu, S. Lu. (2000). Spatiotemporal Data Modeling and Management: A Survey. In *Proceedings of the 36th International Conference on Technology of Object-Oriented Languages and Systems* (pp. 202-211). ACM.

Xiong, X., Mokbel, M. F., & Aref, W. G. (2008). Spatio-Temporal Database. Encyclopedia of GIS, 1114-1115.

Chapter 8
Transformation of Spatiotemporal Data Between Object-Oriented Database and XML

ABSTRACT

Extensible markup language (XML) is increasingly accepted as a medium for integrating and exchanging data, gradually becoming de facto standard for information exchange. At the same time, object-oriented databases possess powerful data storage capabilities, especially with the widespread adoption of object-oriented database management systems. Consequently, the exchange of data from object-oriented databases to XML becomes crucial, and vice versa, transforming data from XML to object-oriented databases is equally important. In this chapter, the authors propose a comprehensive approach to achieve the transformation of spatiotemporal data between object-oriented databases and XML. We focus on exploring a set of mapping functions and rules to identify the most suitable XML schema that describes the existing object-oriented database. By leveraging the characteristics of XML and object-oriented databases, we successfully accomplish the transformation of spatiotemporal data. This research holds significant importance in achieving seamless data exchange between object-oriented databases and XML.

1 INTRODUCTION

In the current computer science field, the need for interoperability of autonomous databases results in the multi-database system, which contains heterogeneous or homogenous database. Therefore, transformation between operations of databases with different data models is critical in any heterogeneous multi-database system (Wu et al., 2005). A mount of previous research has focused on the problem of data exchange in different databases, for example, Fong (Fong, 1995; Fong, 2002), Soutou (Soutou, 2001) and Zhang and Fong (Zhang & Fong, 2000). Recently, the web-based applications are more and more popular, XML which is the lingua franca for data exchange on the Internet, has become the de-

DOI: 10.4018/978-1-6684-9108-9.ch008

facto standard of information exchange and coding format (Liu et al., 2006; Lo et al., 2010; Nierrman & Jagadish, 2002; Bai et al, 2015). Especially, the development of XML Schema descriptions such as DTD(Document Type Declaration) (Turowski & Weng, 2002) and XML Schema (Oliboni & Pozzani, 2008) opens new opportunities for effective data representation and handling XML data. But these advantages also bring limitations to presenting its structure using semantics to store data (Fong & Cheung, 2005). Object-oriented databases are considered better than other databases, due to demand for new approaches to deal with complex data and complex relationships. At the same time, object-oriented databases own a strong ability to store data (Ma et al., 2001; Sicilia & Barriocana, 2006). Consequently, the research of data exchange between object-oriented database and XML is critical. There are a lot of efforts in the area, for example, the both-way transformation approach introduced by (Naser et al., 2009), the formal transformation from fuzzy objected-oriented databases to fuzzy XML (Liu & Ma, 2013), and formal approach for reengineering data between XML and object-oriented database in (Liu et al., 2013).

In recent years, spatial (Condotta, 2004) and temporal (Nandal, 2013) information plays an important role in many applications such as the monitoring of environmental changes and the tracking of moving vehicles (Pereira et al, 2016; Mehrotra & Sharma, 2009; Tao et al, 2004). The advent of XML can provide an opportunity for effective representation and the advantages of object-oriented database can cope with complex spatiotemporal data(Huang et al, 2004). Establishing the bridge of spatiotemporal data between object-oriented database and XML is an important research project(Bai & Xu, 2015). However the existing methods are solved the common and static data, they are not suitable to copy with the multidimensional and dynamic spatiotemporal data.

In this chapter, we have investigated the transformation of spatiotemporal data between object-oriented databases and XML. The main contributions of this chapter can be summarized as follows:

- Establishing the relationship between spatiotemporal data in XML and object-oriented database.
- We recognize the significance of transforming spatiotemporal data between object-oriented database and XML, and have developed a set of functions and rules to accomplish the transformation process.

The remaining parts of this chapter are organized as follows. Section 2 begins by introducing the object-oriented spatiotemporal data model. Then, in Section 3, we discuss the transformation of spatiotemporal data from an object-oriented database to XML. Section 4 covers the transformation of spatiotemporal data from XML to an object-oriented database. Finally, in Section 5, we provide a summary of this chapter.

2 OBJECT-ORIENTED SPATIOTEMPORAL DATA MODEL

In this section, the object-oriented spatiotemporal data model (OOSDM) is introduced. Object-oriented spatiotemporal data have a set of characteristics that make them different from the more familiar lists and tables of alphanumeric data used in traditional business applications.

According to the nature of spatiotemporal data, we give the definition of object-oriented spatiotemporal data.

Definition 1. Object-oriented spatiotemporal data. Object-oriented spatiotemporal data is 4-tuple, STDM = (*OID*, *AT*, *SP*, *TM*), where

- *OID* provides a means to refer to different spatiotemporal objects.
- *AT* describes the non-spatiotemporal properties of spatiotemporal objects.
- *SP* describes the spatial properties of spatiotemporal objects.
- *TM* describes the temporal properties of spatiotemporal objects.

According to the definition above, we talk about all of the *OID*, *AT*, *SP*, *TM* in the following.

OID is the unique identity of spatiotemporal objects. Changes in OID depict spatiotemporal objects changing into other spatiotemporal objects. It can not only represent changing type of objects (i.e., creation, split, emergence, and elimination) but also can represent objects that come from objects(i.e., predecessor) and change into objects(i.e., successor).

AT is the static attributes (i.e., textual and numerical) of spatiotemporal objects, rather than dynamic attributes. There may be one or more attributes in the spatiotemporal data.

SP is the spatial attribute of spatiotemporal objects. Spatial attributes include spatial position and spatial motion. There are three conditions in spatial position, and they are point, line, and region. In addition, spatial motion contains motion direction and motion value. Spatial position contains point, line, and region. For simplicity, we talk about only two-dimensional regions without holes. As to point, we can use coordinate point (x, y) to represent the point. Figure 1(a) shows the spatial point. Figure 1(b) shows the line, which is represented by two coordinate points, (x_1, y_1) and (x_2, y_2), obviously, we consider the straight line or approximate straight line. For spatial region, we use a series of anticlockwise points to represent it. At first, some special points are labeled, for example, (x_1, y_1), (x_2, y_2),..., (x_n, y_n). Then we choose a starting point, if $x \leq \min\{x_1, x_2, ..., x_n\} \cap y \leq \min\{y_1, y_2, ..., y_n\}$, the point(x, y) is assumed the starting point. Last, all of the labeled points are recorded in anticlockwise order, just as Figure 1(c) shows the region, (x_1, y_1), (x_2, y_2),..., (x_5, y_5). Spatial motion contains the direction of movement and value of movement, certainly, we only consider the two-dimensional area.

Figure 1. (a) Point, (b) Line, (c) Region

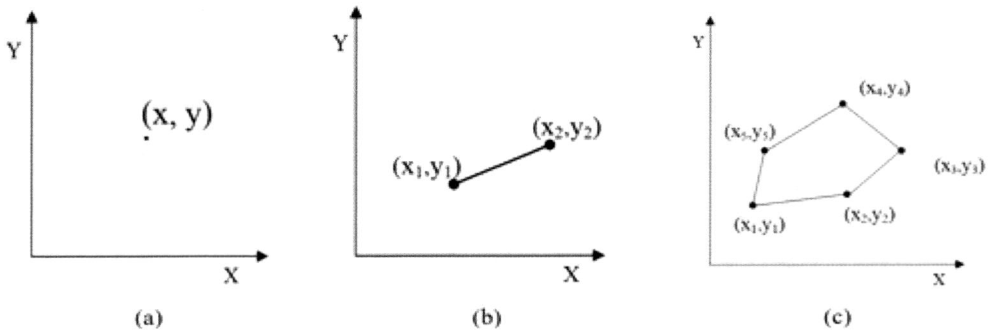

TM is the temporal attribute of spatiotemporal objects. It includes time points and time intervals. Firstly, a suitable chronon should be created. Then, time point is a chronon, and time interval is some continuous chronons. Figure 2(a) shows the crisp time point I_1, and Figure 2(b) shows the time interval H_1, from I_1 to I_3, which is consisted of some chronons.

Figure 2. (a) Time point, (b) Time interval

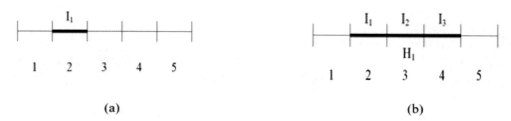

3 TRANSFORMING SPATIOTEMPORAL DATA FROM OBJECT-ORIENTED DATABASE TO XML

OOSDM schema is often represented as a class definition and XML Schema is represented as a tree definition. The schema of transforming spatiotemporal data from OOSDM to XML maps a class-based definition to a tree-base schema definition. We assume an OOSDM schema *F*, which includes class, object identifier(*OID*), reference attribute, temporal attributes, spatial attributes, common attributes(non-*OID* and non-spatiotemporal attributes) and method. The basic mapping functions are depicted as follows.

Function 1: F_1 (SchemaF) = Rname;

SchemaF is an OOSDM schema *F*. *Rname* is a root element and *Rname* is created in the corresponding XML Schema as follows:

```
<?xml version ="1.0"?>
<xsd: schema xmlns:xsd
            =https://www.w3.org/2001/XMLSchema
            targetNamespace="targetNamespaceURI"
            xmlns="targetNamespaceURI"
            elementFormDefault="qualified">
<xsd: element name="Rname">
 <xsd: complexType>
  <xsd: sequence>
   <!--transformed fuzzy XML Schema of S -->
  </xsd: sequence>
 </xsd: complexType>
</xsd: element >
</xsd: schema>
```

Function 2: F_2 *(Cname) = Celement;*

Cname is a class *C* in OOSDM schema *F*. *Celement* which is the corresponding element with the same name as *C* is created and then put under the root element.

```
<xsd: element name=C minOccurs ="0" maxOccurs="unbounded">
 <xsd: complexType>
  <!--sub-elements of C -->
```

```
 </xsd: complexType>
</xsd: element>
```

Function 3: F_3 (*Oidentifier*) = *Oattribute*;

Oidentifier is an Object identifier (*OID*) in class *C* of OOSDM schema *F*. *Oattribute* is the corresponding attribute in XML and *Oattribute* is the required attribute.

```
<xsd: element name= "C" minOccurs = "0" maxOccurs =" unbounded">
 <xsd: complexType>
  <xsd: attribute name ="Oattribute" type ="xsd:ID" use ="required"/>
 </xsd: complexType>
</xsd: element>
```

Function 4: F_4 (*Ridentifier*) = *Rattribute*;

Ridentifier is an reference attribute in class *C* of OOSDM schema *F*. *Rattribute* which is the corresponding attribute in XML is created and the xsd:IDREF type is also required. Then *Rattribute* is placed as a child element of *C*.

```
<xsd: element name= "C" minOccurs = "0" maxOccurs =" unbounded">
 <xsd: complexType>
  <xsd: attribute name ="Rattribute" type ="xsd:IDREF" use ="required"/>
 </xsd: complexType>
</xsd: element>
```

Function 5: F_5 (*COattribute*) = *COelement*;

COattribute is a common attribute (non-*OID* and non-spatiotemporal attribute) or method, an element with the name *COelement* and data type is created and then placed as a child element of *C*.

```
<xsd: element name="C" minOccurs ="0" maxOccurs ="unbounded">
 <xsd: complexType>
  <xsd: element name ="COelement" type ="original-definition"/>
 </xsd: complexType>
</xsd: element>
```

Functions 1-5 can accomplish the transformation of the non-spatiotemporal attributes and method from OOSDM schema to XML Schema. As to spatiotemporal data, which exists spatial and temporal attributes, thus we will produce the transformation functions applied to spatial and temporal attributes.

Spatial attribute concludes spatial point, spatial line and spatial region. The point can be represented by coordinate point (x,y), for simplicity, we assume that x and y are integers. Spatial line is represented by two coordinate points, thus we use "minOccurs="2" maxOccurs="2"" to define two points. In addition, we use "minOccurs="3" maxOccurs="unbounded"" to define greater than or equal to three points. In the following, they are transformation function of spatial attributes.

Function 6: F_6 (*SPattribute*) = *SPelement*;

SPattribute is spatial point attribute in class *C* of OOSDM Schema *F*, *SPelement* is the corresponding element in XML. *SPelement* is created and placed as a child element of *C*.

```
<xsd: element name="C" minOccurs="0" maxOccurs="unbounded">
 <xsd: complexType>
  <xsd: element name="SPattribute">
   <xsd: complexType>
    <xsd: sequence>
         <xsd: element name="Xaxis" type="integer"/>
         <xsd: element name="Yaxis" type="integer"/>
    </xsd: sequence>
   </xsd: complexType>
  </xsd: element>
 </xsd: complexType>
</xsd: element>
```

Function 7: F_7 (*SLattribute*) = *SLelement*;

SLattribute is spatial line attribute in class *C* of OOSDM Schema *F*, corresponding element named *SLelement* is created in XML and placed as a child element of *C*.

```
<xsd: element name="C" minOccurs="0" maxOccurs="unbounded">
 <xsd: complexType>
  <xsd: element name="SLelement"/>
   <xsd: complexType>
    <xsd: sequence>
         <xsd: element ref="SPelement"/>
    </xsd: sequence>
   </xsd: complexType>
  </xsd: element>
  <xsd: element name="SPelement" minOccurs="2" maxOccurs="2"/>
   <xsd: complexType>
    <xsd: sequence>
         <xsd: element name="Xaxis" type="integer"/>
         <xsd: element name="Yaxis" type="integer"/>
    </xsd: sequence>
   </xsd: complexType>
  </xsd: element>
 </xsd: complexType>
</xsd: element>
```

Function 8: F_8 (*SRattribute*) = *SRelement*;

SRattribute is spatial region attribute in class *C* of OOSDM Schema *F*, *SRelement* which is the corresponding is created in XML and placed as a child element of *C*.

```
<xsd: element name="C" minOccurs="0" maxOccurs="unbounded">
 <xsd: complexType>
  <xsd: element name="SRelement"/>
   <xsd: complexType>
    <xsd: sequence>
         <xsd: element ref="SPelement"/>
    </xsd: sequence>
   </xsd: complexType>
  </xsd: element>
  <xsd: element name="SPelement" minOccurs="0" maxOccurs="unbounded"/>
   <xsd: complexType>
    <xsd: sequence>
         <xsd: element name="Xaxis" type="integer"/>
         <xsd: element name="Yaxis" type="integer"/>
    </xsd: sequence>
   </xsd: complexType>
  </xsd: element>
 </xsd: complexType>
</xsd: element>
```

Apart from spatial attributes, there are temporal attributes in spatiotemporal data. Temporal attribute includes time point and time interval. We use *DateTime* Data Type (dataTime) to present the time type in XML. For time intervals, *timeStart* and *timeEnd* are used to represent starting time and ending time respectively. Consequently, we have the following rules.

Function 9: F_9 (*TPattribute*) = *TPelement*;

TPattribute is time point attribute in class *C* of OOSDM schema *F*. *TPelement* which is the corresponding element is created and then placed as a child element of *C*.

```
<xsd: element name="C" minOccurs ="0" maxOccurs ="unbounded">
 <xsd: complexType>
  <xsd: element name ="TPelement" type ="dataTime"/>
 </xsd: complexType>
</xsd: element>
```

Function 10: F_{10} (*TIattribute*) = *TIelement*;

TIattribute is time point attribute in class C of OOSDM schema F. An corresponding element named *TIelement* is created and then placed as a child element of C.

```
<xsd: element name= "C" minOccurs="0" maxOccurs="unbounded">
 <xsd: complexType>
  <xsd: element name="TIelement">
   <xsd: simpleType>
    <xsd: restriction base="dataTime">
         <xsd: minInclusive value="timeStart">
```

```
    <xsd: minInclusive value="timeEnd">
       </xsd: restriction>
   </xsd: simpleType>
  </xsd: element>
 </xsd: complexType>
</xsd: element>
```

Based on the transforming functions above, the algorithm which transforms spatiotemporal data from object-oriented database to XML is proposed. The pseudo-code is depicted in Algorithm 1.

Algorithm 1 Transforming object-oriented database

Input: OOSDM schema *F*
Output: corresponding XML Schema *T*
01 create root element *Rname* for *F* by applying Function 1.
02 get OOSDM class *C*, return generated XML element by applying Function 2.
03 map the *OID* by applying Function 3.
04 map the *RID* by applying Function 4.
05 transform the common attribute (or method) by Function 5.
06 if there exists spatial attribute, Function 6, Function 7 and Function 8 can be used to transform the spatial attribute from OOSDM schema to XML Schema.
07 if there exists temporal attribute, Function 9 and Function 10 can be applied to map time points and time intervals respectively.

To understand the steps of Algorithm 1, a supporting example will be taken in the following. Figure 3 shows a class named LAND, in which there are a time point attribute, object identifier(*OID*), reference attribute *RID*, common attribute Name, method named Operator, and spatial point attribute named *PPosition* with a time interval attribute. For the class LAND, we first use Function 2 to map class. In addition, we can use Function 3 and Function 4 to map OID and RID. Moreover, attribute Name and method Operator can be transformed by applying Function 5. Next step, TIME is time point attribute, PPosition is a spatial point attribute, and Function 9 and Function 6 are adopted to transform them respectively. Finally, we use Function 10 to map the time interval attribute WITH *TimeStart* and *TimeEnd*.

According to the analysis above, the final transformation result is as follows.

```
<xsd: element name="LAND" minOccurs ="0" maxOccurs="unbounded">
 <xsd: complexType>
  <xsd: attribute name ="OID" type ="xsd:ID" use ="required"/>
  <xsd: attribute name ="RID" type ="xsd:IDREF" use ="required"/>
  <xsd: element name ="Name" type ="original-definition"/>
  <xsd: element name ="Operator" type ="original-definition"/>
  <xsd: element name ="TIME" type ="dataTime"/>
  <xsd: element name="SPattribute">
          <xsd: complexType>
           <xsd: sequence>
            <xsd: element name="Xaxis" type="integer"/>
            <xsd: element name="Yaxis" type="integer"/>
```

```
          </xsd: sequence>
          <xsd: element name="TIelement">
           <xsd: simpleType>
            <xsd: restriction base="dataTime">
             <xsd: minInclusive value="timeStart">
             <xsd: minInclusive value="timeEnd">
            </xsd: restriction>
           <xsd: simpleType>
          </xsd: element>
         </xsd: complexType>
  </xsd: element>
 </xsd: complexType>
</xsd: element>
```

Figure 3. A class in OOSDM

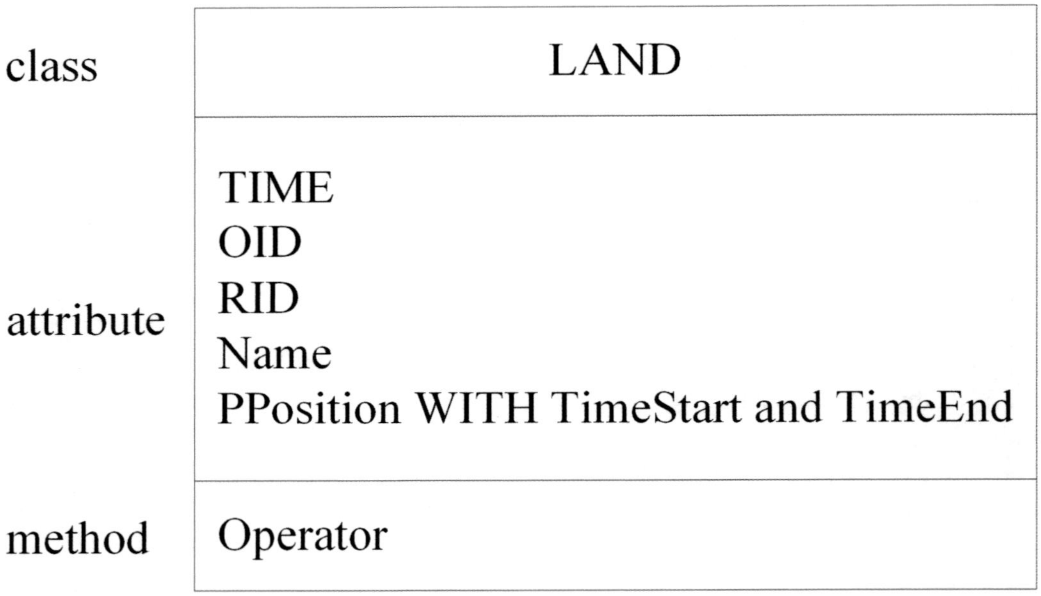

class	LAND
attribute	TIME OID RID Name PPosition WITH TimeStart and TimeEnd
method	Operator

4 TRANSFORMING SPATIOTEMPORAL DATA FROM XML TO OBJECT-ORIENTED DATABASE

In this section, we first introduce the modified spatiotemporal data model which is based on the five dimensions of fuzzy spatiotemporal data model in (Bai et al., 2015). In (Bai et al., 2015), the data model includes the fuzzy spatiotemporal attributes, however, in this chapter, the spatiotemporal attributes are deterministic, and thus we propose a modified spatiotemporal data model. There are four dimensions in the modified spatiotemporal data model, which include ID, AT, SP, and TM. ID provides a means to refer to different spatiotemporal objects. It can not only represent changing type of objects (i.e., creation, split, emergence, and elimination), but also can represent objects that come from objects (i.e., predecessor) and change into objects (i.e., successor). AT describes the non-spatiotemporal properties of spatiotemporal objects. It is the static attributes (i.e., textual and numerical), rather than dynamic attributes. SP describes the spatial properties of spatiotemporal objects. Spatial attributes include spatial position and spatial motion. There are three conditions in spatial position, which are point, line, and region. In addition, spatial motion contains motion direction and motion value. TM describes the temporal properties of spatiotemporal objects. It includes time points and time intervals. In the following, we will accomplish transforming spatiotemporal data from XML to object-oriented database, which is based on the modified spatiotemporal data model.

4.1 Transformation of Spatiotemporal Data From Flat XML to Object-Oriented Database

The template is used to format your paper and style the text. All margins, column widths, line spaces, and text fonts are prescribed; please do not alter them. You may note peculiarities. For example, the head margin in this template measures proportionately more than is customary. This measurement and others are deliberate, using specifications that anticipate your paper as one part of the entire proceedings, and not as an independent document. Please do not revise any of the current designations.

The flat XML document is a very simple XML format that only has simple leaf element as subelements of non-leaf element. In this subsection, we propose an approach that transforms the spatiotemporal data from flat XML to object-oriented databases.

We assume a flat XML *T* with spatiotemporal data, which includes key attributes, reference attributes, temporal attributes, root element, and leaf elements. The basic mapping functions are depicted as follows.

Function 11: F_1 (*Rname*) = *Cname*;

Rname is the root of *T*, *Cname* is a class name, and *Cname* with the same name as T and corresponding method is created.

Function 12: F_2 (*Kattribute*) = *Oname*;

Katrribute is the key attribute with the name *K* in the flat XML *T*, *Oname* is the *OID* (object identifier) in the class *T*, and *Oname* with the same name as *K* is created.

Function 13: F_3 (*Rattribute*) = *Rname*;

Rattribute is the reference attribute with the name *R* in the XML *T*, *Rname* is an attribute in the class *T*, and *Rname* with the same name as *R* is created.

Function 14: F_4 (*Lelement*) = *Lname*;

Lelement is a normal leaf element with the name *L* in the XML *T*, *Lname* is an attribute in the class *T*, and *Lname* with the same name as *L* is created and then put inside class *T*.

Function 15: F_5 (*LSelement*) = *LSname*;

For spatiotemporal data in the XML, it has a required attribute Type, and its value must be one of creation, split, mergence, and elimination. So we consider Type as a selective leaf element.

LSelement is a selective leaf element with the name *LS* in the XML T, *LSname* is an attribute in the class *T*, and *LSname* with the same name as *LS* followed by a keyword Selective is created and then put inside class *T*.

Because of the temporal attribute in the spatiotemporal data, we propose some rules to transform the spatiotemporal data from XML to OO database in consideration of the temporal attribute.

Rule 1: For the root of *T*, if it has the attribute of time point, we consider time point as a normal attribute of the class *T*, and *TIME* is created and then put inside class *T*. If it has the attribute of time interval, we also consider time interval as a normal attribute on the class *T*, and a pair of words *TimeStart* and *TimeEnd* is created and then put inside class *T*.

Rule 2: For the non-root of *T*, if it has the attribute of time point, a pair of words *WITH Time* follows the corresponding attribute name in class *T*. If it has the attribute of time interval, a pair of words *WITH TimeStart* and *TimeEnd* follows the corresponding attribute name in class *T*.

Based on the transforming functions and rules above, we present the algorithm for transforming spatiotemporal data from flat XML to object-oriented databases. The pseudo-code is depicted in Algorithm 3.

Algorithm 3 Transforming Flat XML

Input: Flat spatiotemporal XML DTD *T*
Output: Corresponding OO database schema *O*
01 Create a class in *O* by applying Function 1
02 Map the temporal attribute of the root in *T* to the attribute within the generated class by applying Rule 1
03 Define the *OID* for each class identified in step1 by applying Function 2
04 Map the reference attribute *R* in *T* to the attribute within the generated class by applying Function 3 and Rule 2
05 Transform the normal leaf element *L* in *T* into attributes within the generated class by applying Function 4 and Rule 2
06 Transform the selective leaf element *LS* in *T* into attributes within the generated class by applying Function 4 and Rule 2

To understand the steps of Algorithm 3, we illustrate more details with the following supporting examples. Figure 4 shows a flat spatiotemporal XML DTD, in which the root element *LAND* has a key attribute *OID*, a reference attribute *RID*, a time attribute Time, and three leaf elements Name Type and position. According to Algorithm 3, the class *LAND* is first created, then the time attribute of *LAND* Time is created, in addition, OID and RID are translated into the created class. Finally, we can apply the Function 14 to transform Name, apply Function 15 to transform Type and apply the Function 14 and Rule 2 to transform Position. Figure 5 shows the final transforming result according to Algorithm 3.

4.2 Transformation From Nested XML to Object-Oriented Database

In this subsection, we will give the transforming rules of spatiotemporal data which include the relationships such as generalization, association, and aggregation in an OO database.

Generalization in OO database defines a subclass/ superclass relationship between classes: one class, which is called a superclass, is a more general description of a set of other classes, which are called subclasses.

Given any element *e* in XML, a child element clue, denoted as $CE(e)=\{c_1,c_2,...,c_n\}$, $n=1,2,...,i$, is all different child elements of *e*. Given two elements e_i and e_j belonging to a common class in XML, a common child element clue, denoted as $CCE\ (e_i,e_j)$, is all common child elements between e_i and e_j.

Function 6: F_6 (NLelement1, NLelement2) = {GErelationship, SPclass, SBclass}

Figure 4. Flat spatiotemporal XML DTD

```
<!ELEMENT LAND(Name,Type,Position)>
<!ATTLIST LAND OID ID #REQUIRED>
<!ATTLIST LAND RID IDREF #REQUIRED>
<!ATTLIST LAND Time CDATA #IMPLIED>
<!ELEMENT Name (#PCDATA)>
<!ELEMENT Type(creation|split|mergence|elimination)>
<!ATTLIST Type Time CDATA #IMPLIED>
<!ELEMENT creation(#PCDTTA)>
<!ELEMENT split(#PCDTTA)>
<!ELEMENT mergence(#PCDTTA)>
<!ELEMENT elimination(#PCDTTA)>
<!ELEMENT Position(#PCDATA)>
<!ATTLIST Position Time CDATA #IMPLIED>
```

NLelement1 and NLelement2 are two non-leaf element e_i and e_j in XML, $CE(e_i) = \{c_1,c_2,...,c_i\}$, $i = 1, 2,...,i$, $CE(e_j) =\{c_1,c_2,...,c_j\}$, $j = 1, 2,...,j$. GErelationship is the generalization relationship, if $CCE(e_i,e_j)$ is not null, assume that $CCE(e_i,e_j) = \{c_1,c_2,...,c_k\}$, $k<=i$, and $k<=j$, then a generalization relationship is created when transforming from nested XML to OO database. SPclass which is superclass with attributions with the same names as $c_1,c_2,...,c_k$ is created, and then SBclass which are two subclasses with attributes with the same name as $c_{k+1},c_{k+2},...,c_i$ and $c_{k+1},c_{k+2},...,c_j$ are created respectively.

Figure 5. Transformation of flat spatiotemporal XML DTD

class name	LAND
attribute name	TIME OID RID Name selective Type Position WITH TimeStart and TimeEnd
method	Operator create

Figure 6. Nested spatiotemporal XML DTD

```
<!ELEMENT Land(Farm, Garden)>
<!ELEMENT Farm(Name, Animal, Position)>
<!ATTLIST Farm Time CDATA #IMPLIED>
<!ELEMENT Name(#PCDATA)>
<!ELEMENT Animal(#PCDATA)>
<!ELEMENT Position(#PCDATA)>
<!ELEMENT Garden(Name, Flower, Position)>
<!ATTLIST Garden Time CDATA #IMPLIED>
<!ELEMENT Name(#PCDATA)>
<!ELEMENT Flower(#PCDATA)>
<!ELEMENT Position(#PCDATA)>
<!ELEMENT Owner(Address, Salary, Own)>
<!ELEMENT Address(#PCDATA)>
<!ELEMENT Salary(#PCDATA)>
<!ELEMENT Own(Garden, Building)>
<!ELEMENT Building(OfficeSpace, FitnessCenter, Position)>
<!ATTLIST Building Time CDATA #IMPLIED>
<!ELEMENT OfficeSpace(Capcity)>
<!ELEMENT Capcity(#PCDATA)>
<!ELEMENT FitnessCenter(Name, Equipment)>
<!ATTLIST FitnessCenter Time CDATA #IMPLIED>
<!ELEMENT Name(#PCDATA)>
<!ELEMENT Equipment(#PCDATA)>
<!ELEMENT Position(#PCDATA)>
<!ATTLIST Position Time CDATA #IMPLIED>
```

In XML, associations among XML trees are represented by using links. Link is a physical conceptual connection between object instances. Associations in XML describe a group of links with common structure and semantics and pointer as an attribute in an object that combines an explicit reference to another object.

Function 17: F_7 *(NLelement1, NLelement2)* = {*ASrelationship, class1, class2, degree*}

NLelement1 and *NLelement2* are two non-leaf element e_i and e_j in XML, and assume that e_i exists as an explicit reference to e_j, *ASrelationship* which is an association relationship is created when transforming these two non-leaf elements of XML to the OO database, *class1* and *class2* are two classes with the same names as e_i and e_j are created, then degree is the association on an *n:m* basis with its corresponding multiplicity of links and pointers is then created.

Aggregations are relationships that describe combinations among class instances. In an OO database, aggregations permit the combination of class that is related into a higher level of a composite class.

Function 18: F_8 *(NLelement1, NLelement2, NLelement3)* = {*AGrelationship, Cclass, class1, class2*}

NLelement1, *NLelement2* and *NLelement3* are three non-leaf elements e_i, e_j and e_k in XML respectively, and we assume that e_i is the composite element of e_j and e_k. *AGrelationship* which is a aggregation relationship is created when transforming these three non-leaf elements of XML to the OO database. Then *Cclass*, *class1* and *class2* are three classes with the same names as e_i, e_j and e_k are created.

Based on the transforming functions above, we now propose the algorithm for transforming spatiotemporal data from nested XML to OO database. The pseudo-code is depicted in Algorithm 4.

Figure 7. Transformation of nested spatiotemporal XML DTD

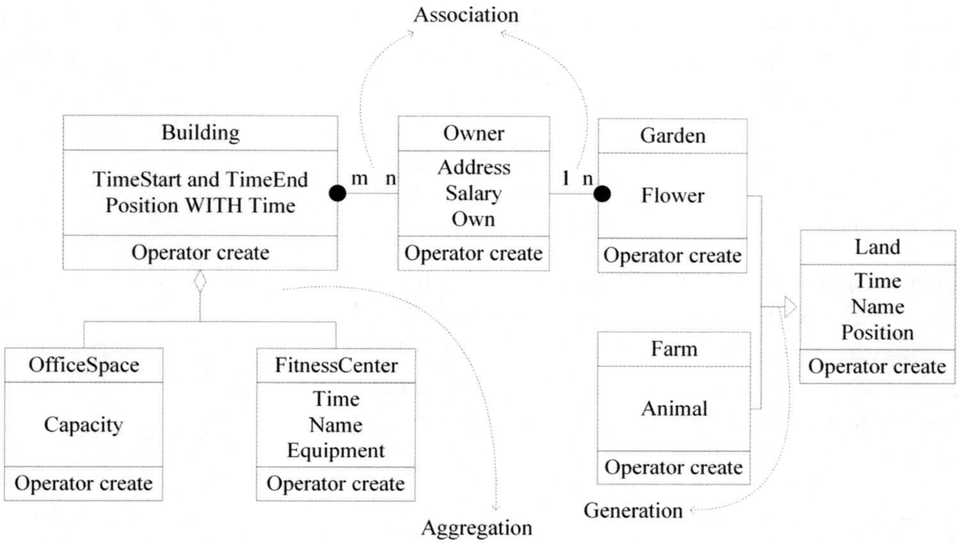

Algorithm 4 Transforming Nested XML

Input: Nested spatiotemporal XML DTD *T*
Output: Corresponding OO database schema *O*
for each non-leaf element in *T*
create a class whose attributes are created in *O* by Algorithm 1
end for
for each non-leaf element in *T*
if non-leaf element with generalization
transform generalizations applying Function 6
end if
if non-leaf element with association
transform associations applying Function 7
end if
if non-leaf element with aggregation
transform associations applying Function 8
end if
end for

To understand the steps of Algorithm 4, we present more details with the following supporting example. Figure 6 shows a nested spatiotemporal XML DTD, in which there are non-leaf elements Land, Farm, Garden, Owner, Building, OfficeSpace, FitnessCenter, thus they are firstly transformed to corresponding class. Since the relationships among Land, Farm, and Garden are generation, then we can apply the Function 16 to transform them. Moreover, the relationships among Owner, Garden, and Building are association, and then they can be transformed based on Function 17 in an OO database. The relationships among Building, OfficeSpace, and FitnessCenter are aggregation, and then we can apply the Function 18 to accomplish the transformation. Finally, Figure 7 shows the transforming result according to the Algorithm 4.

5 SUMMARY

In this chapter, we present a methodology for transforming spatiotemporal data between object-oriented databases and XML. Firstly, we introduce a spatiotemporal data model based on object-oriented databases. Then, we design a set of functions and algorithms to accomplish the transformation process and handle the exchange of spatiotemporal data between object-oriented databases and XML. Finally, we illustrate the application of our methodology through an example.

REFERENCES

Bai, L., & Xu, C. (2015). *Spatiotemporal Query Algebra Based on Native XML. Handbook of Research on Innovative Database Query Processing Techniques*. IGI Global.

Bai, L. Y., Yan, L., & Ma, Z. M. (2015) Fuzzy Spatiotemporal Data Modeling and Operations in XML. Applied Artificial Intelligence, 29, pp,259-282. doi:10.1080/08839514.2015.1004615

Condotta, J. F. (2004). A general qualitative framework for temporal and spatial reasoning. *Constraints*, *9*(2), 99–121. doi:10.1023/B:CONS.0000024047.02149.64

Fong, J. (1995). Mapping Extended Entity Relationship Model to Object Modeling Technique. *SIGMOD Record*, *24*(3), 18–22. doi:10.1145/211990.212007

Fong, J. (2002). Translating Object-oriented Database Transactions into Relational Transactions. *Information and Software Technology*, *44*(1), 41–51. doi:10.1016/S0950-5849(01)00211-7

Fong, J., & Cheung, S. K. (2005). Translating Relational Schema into XML Schema Definition with Data Semantic Preservation and XSD Graph. *Information and Software Technology*, *47*(7), 437–462. doi:10.1016/j.infsof.2004.09.010

Huang, B., Yi, S., & Chan, W. T. (2004). Spatio-Temporal Information Integration in XML. *Future Generation Computer Systems*, *20*(7), 1157–1170. doi:10.1016/j.future.2003.11.005

Liu, C., Vincent, M. W., & Liu, J. (2006). Constraint Preserving Transformation from Relational Schema to XML Schema. *World Wide Web (Bussum)*, *9*(1), 93–110. doi:10.1007/s11280-005-4263-5

Liu, J., & Ma, Z. M. (2013). Formal Transformation from Fuzzy Object-oriented Databases toFuzzy XML. *Applied Intelligence*, *39*(3), 630–641. doi:10.1007/s10489-013-0438-4

Liu, J., Ma, Z. M., & Feng, X. (2013). Formal Approach for Reengineering Fuzzy XML in Fuzzy Object-oriented Databases. *Applied Intelligence*, *38*(4), 541–552. doi:10.1007/s10489-012-0386-4

Lo, A., Ozyer, T., Kianmehr, K., & Alhajj, R. (2010). VIREX and VRXQuery: Interactive Approach for Visual Querying of Relational Databases to Produce XML. *Journal of Intelligent Information Systems*, *35*(1), 21–49. doi:10.1007/s10844-009-0087-6

Ma, Z. M., Zhang, W. J., Ma, W. Y., & Chen, G. Q. (2001). Conceptual Design of Fuzzy Object–Oriented Databases Utilizing Extended Entity-Relationship Model. *International Journal of Intelligent Systems*, *16*(6), 697–711. doi:10.1002/int.1031

Mehrotra, R., & Sharma, A. (2009). Evaluating Spatio-temporal Representations in Daily Rainfall Sequences from Three Stochastic Multisite Weather Generation Approaches. *Advances in Water Resources*, *32*(6), 948–962. doi:10.1016/j.advwatres.2009.03.005

Nandal, R. (2013). Spatio-temporal database and its models: A review. *IOSR Journal of Computer Engineering*, *11*(2), 91–100. doi:10.9790/0661-11291100

Naser, T., Alhajj, R., & Ridley, M. J. (2009). Two-way Mapping Between Object-oriented Databases and XML. *Informatica (Vilnius)*, *33*(3), 297–308.

Nierrman, A., & Jagadish, H. V. (2002). ProTDB: Probabilistic Data in XML. In: Proceedings of Very Large Data Bases, Pages 646–657.

Oliboni, B., & Pozzani, G. (2008). Representing Fuzzy Information by Using XML Schema. *In: Proceedings of the 19th International Conference on Database and Expert Systems Application*, (pp. 683–687). IEEE. 10.1109/DEXA.2008.44

Pereira, S., Zêzere, J. L., Quaresma, I., Santos, P. P., & Santos, M. (2016). Mortality patterns of hydro-geomorphologic disasters. *Risk Analysis*, *36*(6), 1188–1210. doi:10.1111/risa.12516 PMID:26616470

Sicilia, M., & Barriocana, E. G. (2006). Extending Object Database Interfaces with Fuzziness Through Aspect-Oriented Design. *SIGMOD Record*, *35*(2), 4–9. doi:10.1145/1147376.1147377

Soutou, C. (2001). Modeling Relationships in Object-relational Databases. *Data & Knowledge Engineering*, *36*(1), 79–107. doi:10.1016/S0169-023X(00)00035-5

Tao, Y. F., Kollios, G., Considine, J., & Li, F. (2004) Papadias, D. Spatio-temporal aggregation using sketches. *Proc. 20th International Conference on Data Engineering*. IEEE.

Turowski, K., & Weng, U. (2002). Representing and Processing Fuzzy Information—An XML-based Approach. *Knowledge-Based Systems*, *15*(1-2), 67–75. doi:10.1016/S0950-7051(01)00122-8

Wu, X., Zhang, C., & Zhang, S. (2005). Database Classification for Multidatabase Mining. *Information Systems*, *30*(1), 71–88. doi:10.1016/j.is.2003.10.001

Zhang, X., & Fong, J. (2000). Translating Update Operations From Relational to Object-oriented Databases. *Information and Software Technology*, *42*(3), 197–210. doi:10.1016/S0950-5849(99)00058-0

Chapter 9
Querying Spatiotemporal Data Based on XML Twig Pattern

ABSTRACT

With the increasing applications based on location, research on spatiotemporal data, especially queries of spatiotemporal data have attracted a lot of attention. XML, as a standard language of information exchange over the Web, has the ability to query spatiotemporal data. In this chapter, the authors propose an algorithm, TwigStackSP, for matching a spatiotemporal XML query twig pattern. They represent spatiotemporal data by adding spatial and temporal attributes in general data and extending region coding scheme to filter the nodes in P-C relationship. This technique uses a chain of linked stacks to compactly represent partial results to root-to-leaf query paths, which are then composed to obtain matches for the twig pattern. It can be proved that TwigStackSP is I/O and CPU optimal when there are no text nodes in P-C relationship of twig pattern.

1 INTRODUCTION

With the prompt development of positioning system, a considerable amount of spatiotemporal applications merged (Stefanakis, 2001; Parent et al, 1999; Sammatat et al, 2016; Guan et al., 2011; Wikle, 2001; Kwan, 2004), e.g. environment management and geographic information system. Spatiotemporal data is characterized by both spatial (Balbiani & Condotta, 2002) and temporal (Obeid, 2000) semantics. With the development of spatiotemporal data, some operations based on spatiotemporal data are researched (Peuquet, 2001; Yuan et al, 2011; Sellis, 1999), such as spatiotemporal data query (Ďuračiová & Faixová Chalachanová, 2018) and spatiotemporal data indexing (Emrich et al., 2012).

Currently, a large number of theories have been proposed for XML queries (Bruno et al., 2002; Che et al., 2011), such as global matching theory, two element structure connection theory, and approximate query processing theory. Most of the research in this field are based on XML twig pattern (Bruno et al., 2002; Lu et al., 2005; Lu et al., 2005). proposed an algorithm called TwigStack that uses a chain of linked stacks to compactly represent partial results of individual query root-to-leaf paths, the approach is I/O and CPU optimal with only ancestor-descendant edges, but for queries with parent-child edges,

DOI: 10.4018/978-1-6684-9108-9.ch009

TwigStack can't control the size of intermediate results. In (Lu et al., 2005), Lu et al. proposed a new holistic twig join algorithm, called TwigStackList, which is significantly more efficient than TwigStack for queries with the presence of parent-child edges. while TwigStackList needs to read more elements from all non-leaf node streams. So, an algorithm, called TJFast, is proposed by (Lu et al., 2005) based on extended Dewey labeling scheme which only scans query leaf nodes.

As the development of querying general data becomes mature gradually, more and more researchers have found the potential of querying spatiotemporal data in XML (Chen & Revesz, 2003; Bai et al., 2014). In (Chen & Revesz, 2003), Chen and Revesz introduced Layer Algebra, which is a novel extension of relational algebra for XML and provides the basis of query evaluation and optimization for XML queries. They present a rule-based XML query language, DataFox (Datalog For XML), which combines the simplicity of Datalog with the support for spatiotemporal data in constraint databases. In (Bai et al., 2014), Bai et al. make fuzzy-set-based extensions to XQuery including truth degrees, fuzzy spatiotemporal linguistic terms, and FLOWR expressions after proposing the architecture of querying fuzzy spatiotemporal data using XQuery. These researches provide a reference for further research in the field of spatiotemporal XML data querying.

In this chapter, we simplify the data model proposed by (Bai et al., 2013) to represent spatiotemporal data with minimum bounding rectangle by adding spatial and temporal attributes in general data. We also extend the region coding by adding childrenClue information which can remove the nodes with P-C relationship that are not in the final results definitely in the first phase of our algorithm TwigStackSP, and we improve the function of getting solutions to make it suitable for processing spatiotemporal XML data.

The rest of chapter is organized as follows. Section 2 discusses preliminaries. Section 3 focuses on spatiotemporal XML twig pattern matching algorithm called TwigStackSP and then presents the analysis of the correctness and complexity of the algorithm. Section 4 concludes this chapter.

2 PRELIMINARIES

2.1 Twig Pattern Matching

Definition 1 (twig query matching) Given a twig query Q=(V_Q,E_Q) and a XML database D=(V_D,E_D), the process of matching Q in D is a mapping from query node Q to element node D, the mapping h: $\{u:u \in Q\} \rightarrow \{x:x \in D\}$ must satisfy the following condition:

- Query node predicates are satisfied by the corresponding database nodes, and they have the same tag name.
- The structure relationships between query nodes are satisfied by the corresponding database nodes.

2.2 Solution

Definition 2 (solution) For any two nodes p,c in subtree rooted q, the node q has a solution when the structure of p and c (Edge(p,c)) is the same as the structure of nodes corresponding to their current elements c_p and c_c ($Edge(c_p,c_c)$). For specifically, node q has a solution when node q is a leaf node and c_q is not null.

2.3 Extended Region Code

The intermediate results can be reduced for improving query efficiency in processing twig query with P-C relationship by removing some data elements that are not involved in the final results definitely, if there is enough information, especially the information of sub-element, in XML data encoding. The schema information of XML document will be used when adding sub-element information in XML data elements encoding.

Children's information of elements is presented with some binary bits named childrenClue. Representing all the different sub-label of label t in XML schema information with DCT(t)={t_0,t_1,…,t_n}, representing all different tag names corresponding to sub-element of XML document data element e with $DCE(\mathrm{e})=\{\mathrm{t}_{\mathrm{e1}},\mathrm{t}_{\mathrm{e2}},\ldots,\mathrm{t}_{\mathrm{e(m\text{-}1)}}\}$, representing all different tag names corresponding to sub-node in P-C relationship of node n in a twig query with $\mathrm{DCQ}(\mathrm{n})=\{\mathrm{t}_{\mathrm{n0}},\mathrm{t}_{\mathrm{n1}},\ldots,\mathrm{t}_{\mathrm{n(l\text{-}1)}}\}$. Tag names {$t_0$,$t_1$,…,$t_n$} in DCT(t) are sorted by alphabet. Data elements in XML document and childrenClue information of nodes in twig query are represented with n+1 binary bits (b_0,b_1,b_2,…,b_n), childrenClue information is computed as follows:

(1) There is no childrenClue information of leaf elements and string elements in XML documents, and there is also no childrenClue information of leaf nodes and string nodes in twig query.

(2) The first binary bit in childrenClue represent whether elements(nodes) contain text, the first bit in childrenClue of e will be 1, if there are text elements in sub-elements of a data element e, otherwise, it's 0; the first bit in childrenClue of q is 1, if there are text nodes in sub-nodes of a query node q's P-C relationship.

(3) childrenClue (b_0,b_1,b_2,…,b_n) of element e in XML document whose tag name is t, if t_i∈DCT(t) and $\mathrm{t_i} \in \mathrm{DCE}(\mathrm{e}), \mathrm{b_{i+1}}=1$, otherwise, $\mathrm{b_{i+1}}=0$.

(4) childrenClue (b_0,b_1,b_2,…,b_n) of node q in twig query whose tag name is t, if t_i∈DCT(t) and $\mathrm{t_i} \in DCQ(\mathrm{n}), \mathrm{b_{i+1}}=1$, otherwise, $\mathrm{b_{i+1}}=0$.

In extended region code, if data element is leaf node or text node, its code is represented by a 3-tuple (start, end, level), other data elements code are represented by a 4-tuple (start, end, level, childrenClue), start, end and level have the same meaning with them in region code respectively, childrenClue is depicted as above.

Supposing that there is the same tag name of data element e in XML document and node n in twig query, then we can determine whether data element e is not belong to the final result of twig query according to the result of label(e).childrenClue AND label(n).childrenClue. If the result doesn't equal to label (n).childrenClue, it can be seen that element e mustn't be in the final result. Because there must be a t belongs to DCQ(n), but don't belong to DCE(e), it's also to say, there is a P-C relationship isn't satisfied.

3 TWIG JOIN ALGORITHMS

3.1 Notation

Let q (with or without subscripts) denotes twig patterns, as well as (interchangeably) the root node of the twig pattern. In our algorithms, we make use of the following twig node operations: isLeaf: Node→Bool, isRoot: Node→Bool, isSP: Node→Bool, parent: Node→Node, children: Node→{Node}, PCchildren: Node→{Node}, PCNodes: q→{Node}, childrenClue: Node→childrenClue, and subtree-Nodes: Node→{Node}. Children (n) returns all the children nodes of node n in twig query. PCchildren (n) returns the children nodes of node n that have P-C relationship with n in twig query. The result of PCNodes (q) is subnodes that have P-C relationship in sub tree rooted q. childrenClue(n) returns the children clue information childrenClue of node n, and subtreeNodes(n) returns nodes contained in the query tree rooted node n.

In the process of querying, associated with each node q in a query twig pattern there is a stream T_q. What is stored in the stream T_q is ordered list of extended region codes corresponding to all data elements of query node q in XML document. The nodes in the stream are sorted by their (start) values. The operations over streams are: current(T_q), advance(T_q), eof(T_q), and remove (T_q,e). current (T_q) returns elements of T_n in processing; advance (T_q) moves the current element of T_n back; eof(T_q) judges whether the current element is the last one; remove (T_q,e) remove e from T_q. Current (T_q).*start*, current (T_q).*end*, current (T_q).*level* and current (T_q).childrenClue represents the attribute of the current element in T_q respectively.

In our stack-based algorithms, we also associate each query node q with a stack S_q. Each data node in the stack consists of a pair: (extended region code of element in T_q, pointer to a node in $S_{parent(q)}$). The operations over stack S_q are: empty, pop, push, topstart, topEnd. The last two operations return start and end information of elements at the top of the stack. At every point during the computation, (i) the nodes in stack S_q (from bottom to top) are guaranteed to lie on a root-to-leaf path in the XML database and sorted by start values, (ii) the set of stacks contain partial and total answers to the query twig pattern.

3.2 TwigStackSP

Before processing twig pattern matching, we should do some changes on the extended region code mentioned in section 2 to be suitable for processing general data firstly, when the data has spatial and temporal attributes. We need to identify whether the data is spatiotemporal because the process between spatiotemporal and general data is different. So we add a bit in childrenClue $(b_0, b_1, b_2, \ldots, b_n, b_{n+1})$ to identify whether the data is spatiotemporal as follows: childrenClue $(b_0, b_1, b_2, \ldots, b_n, b_{n+1})$ of element e in XML document whose tag name is t, if there are sub-elements with spatiotemporal information, $b_{n+1} = 1$, otherwise, $b_{n+1} = 0$.

Algorithm TwigStackSP, which computes answers to a query path pattern on spatiotemporal data, is presented in Fig 3. It improved the algorithm TwigStackBE to query spatiotemporal data on the basis of not changing the tree structure of XML.

Algorithm TwigStackSP operates in three phases. In the first phase remove some data elements that are not sure to be involved in the final results in processing twig query with P-C relationship (line 1). In the second phase, some (but not all) solutions to individual query root-to-leaf paths are computed (lines 2-13). In the third phase, these solutions are merge-joined to compute the answers to the query twig pattern (line 14).

Algorithm

Algorithm *TwigstackSP(q)*

```
// Phase 1
cleanStreamSP(q)
// Phase 2
While (¬end (q))
n_act = getNext (root)
If(isRoot(n_act))
cleanStack(parent(n_act), C_{n_act} → start)
if(isRoot(n_act)∨¬empty( S_{parent(n_act)} ))
cleanStack( n_act , C_{n_act} → end)
moveStreamToStack( T_{n_act} , S_{n_act} , pointertotop(S_parent(n_act)))
if(isLeaf(n_act))
showSolutions( S_{n_act} , 1)
pop( S_{n_act} )
else
advance( T_{n_act} )
// Phase 3
mergeAllPathSolutions()
FUNCTION cleanStreamSP(q)
for each n_i in PCNodes(q)
if(n_i.childrenClue is NULL)
for each e_j in T_{n_i}
if((e_j.childrenClue is NULL) OR
(e_j.childrenClue & n_i.childrenClue≠n_i.childrenClue))
remove( T_{n_i} , e_j );
FUNCTION cleanStackSP(S_n, actValue)
while(¬empty(S_n)∧topEnd(S_n)<actValue)
pop(S_n)
end while
```

In the processing of TwigStackSP query, the function getNext(q) is also very important. The correctness of getNext(q) directly determines whether all occurrences of a twig pattern can be found.

getNext accesses leftmost node through recursive call from root, and check bottom-to-top to search high level query node with solution. Give a node q, if its children nodes all have solutions, we need to guarantee that q also has solution for returning node q. If there is no element that can be the common ancestor of all elements C_{qni} in the stream T_q, then return the node with minimum start value.

The key difference between TwigStackSP and TwigStack (Balbiani & Condotta, 2002) is that the algorithm TwigStackSP processes querying on spatiotemporal data on the basis of not changing the structure of XML. In this chapter, we first extended region code to identify the data with spatiotemporal attributes using a binary bit. In the process of querying, we improve the function getNext to confirm whether the node with spatiotemporal attribute has solution. If a node with spatiotemporal attribute is query node, it needs to satisfy the condition as follows:

$$(i)\, q.x_0 \le C_q.x_0 \le C_q.x_1 \le \mathrm{q.x}_1 \quad (ii)\, q.y_0 \le C_q.y_0 \le C_q.y_1 \le \mathrm{q.y}_1 \quad (iii)\, C_q.t_0 \le q.t_0 \le q.t_1 \le C_q.t_1$$

Function

```
FUNCTION getNext(q)
If(isLeaf(q))
If(q.childrenClue.last = 0)
return q;
else if((C_q.position ⊆ q.position)∧(C_q.time⊆q.time))
return q;
for(each n_i in children(q))
g_i= getNext(n_i);
If(g_i≠n_i) return g_i;
n_max = getNmax(q);
n_min = getNmin(q);
While(C_q → end < C_{n_max} → start)
advance(T_q);
if(C_q → start < C_{n_i} → start)
return q;
else
return n_min;
FUNCTION getNmax(q)
startAtt = max{ C_{n_i} → start | n_i ∈ children(q)}
for each n_i in children(q)
if( C_{n_i} → start = startAtt)
return n_i;
FUNCTION getNmin(q)
startAtt = min{ C_{n_i} → start n_i ∈ children(q)}
for each n_i in children(q)
if( C_{n_i} → start = startAtt)
return n_i;
```

3.3 Analysis of TwigStackSP

In this section we discuss algorithm TwigStackSP for processing twig query, and then we analyze its correctness and complexity.

Lemma 3.1 The data element e removed from stream T_q in the process of cleanStreams in first phase of algorithm TwigStackSP is not in the final result definitely.

Proof: Suppose that data element e removed in the process of cleanStreams is in the final result of twig query, the element e and query node q have the same tag name t, at the same time, e.childrenClue & q.childrenClue ≠ q.childrenClue and they are not null because element e is removed. We can know there must be a tag name $t_i \in DCQ(q)$, but $t_i \notin DCE(e)$. It is to say that the query node q has a sub node q_{t_i} labeled t_i and there are P-C relationship between q and q_{t_i}. But element e has no sub node labeled t_i leading to not satisfy the relationship between q and q_{t_i}. It's contradictory with what we supposed, so, the lemma is proved.

Theorem 3.1 Given a query twig pattern q, and an XML database D, Algorithm TwigStackSP correctly returns all answers for q on D.

Proof: In Algorithm TwigStackSP, we first call function cleanStream to remove the nodes in P-C relationship that are not in final results definitely. It can be proved that there are not nodes removed in the final results. Then we repeatedly find getNext (q) for query q. Assume that getNext(q) = q_N. Let A_{qN} be the set of nodes in the query that are ancestors of q_N. getNext returns all elements from the stream of spatiotemporal nodes in A_{qN} that are part of a solution that uses h_{q_N} (the first element in T_{q_N} that participates in a solution for the sub-query rooted at q_N). If $q \neq q_N$, in line 5 we pop from parent(q_N)'s stack all elements that are guaranteed not to participate in any new solution. After that, in line 6 we test whether h_{q_N} participate in a solution. We know that has a descendant extension (Balbiani & Condotta, 2002). If $q \neq q_N$ and parent(q_N)'s stack is empty, nodes q_N does not have an ancestor extension. Therefor it is guaranteed not to participate in any solution, so we advance q_N in line 13 and continue with the next iteration. Otherwise, node q_N has both ancestor and descendant extensions and therefor it participates in at least one solution. We then cleanq_N's stack and after that we push h_{q_N} to it (lines 7-8). The pointer to the top of parent (q_N)'s stack correctly identifies all solutions using h_{q_N}. Finally, if h_{q_N} is a leaf node, we decompress the stored solutions from the stacks (lines 9-11).

We use a binary bit to identify whether the node has spatiotemporal attribute depicted with minimum bounding rectangle. We can remove some intermediate result by judging whether there are same bit mark in q and nodes in T_q. Also, in the process of getting solutions, we need to do some special treatment when we process spatiotemporal node. The function cleanStream (q) removed the results that are not sure in the final result except text node in P-C relationship. Then the matching path in the latter process will not be useless result caused by not satisfying P-C relationship. We can conclude that there is only A-D relationship in the latter query process if there is no text node in P-C relationship. The P-C relationship without text node is translated into A-D relationship by the first phase process. That's to say that the CPU and I/O cost is optimal in algorithm TwigStackSP when it processes the twig query without text nodes.

4 SUMMARY

In this chapter we represent spatiotemporal data with minimum bounding rectangle by adding spatial and temporal attributes in general data. On this platform, an effective algorithm to match the desired twigs is proposed after extending the region codding scheme. The extended coding scheme adds childrenClue information to determine whether a node has spatiotemporal attributes. In addition, we can remove the nodes that are not in final results definitely. In addition, the proposed algorithm TwigStackSP is I/O and CPU optimal for a large class of querying spatiotemporal data since we remove the nodes that do not satisfy P-C relationship and get suitable solutions with spatiotemporal attributes by inclusion relationship of spatiotemporal range in getNext(q).

REFERENCES

Bai, L. Y., Yan, L., & Ma, Z. M. (2013). Determining topological relationship of fuzzy spatiotemporal data integrated with XML twig pattern. *Applied Intelligence*, *39*(1), 75–100. doi:10.1007/s10489-012-0395-3

Bai, L. Y., Yan, L., & Ma, Z. M. (2014). Querying fuzzy spatiotemporal data using XQuery. *Integrated Computer-Aided Engineering*, *21*(2), 147–162. doi:10.3233/ICA-130454

Balbiani, P., & Condotta, J. F. (2002). Spatial reasoning about points in a multidimensional setting. *Applied Intelligence, 17*(3), 221–238. doi:10.1023/A:1020079114666

Bruno, N., Koudas, N., & Srivastava, D. (2002). Holistic twig joins: optimal XML pattern matching. *Proceedings of the 2002 ACM SIGMOD International Conference on Management of Data* (pp. 310-321). ACM. 10.1145/564691.564727

Che, D., Ling, T. W., & Hou, W. C. (2011). Holistic boolean-twig pattern matching for efficient XML query processing. *IEEE Transactions on Knowledge and Data Engineering, 24*(11), 2008–2024. doi:10.1109/TKDE.2011.128

Chen, Y., & Revesz, P. (2003). Query spatiotemporal XML using DataFox. *Proceedings of ACM Internal Conference on Web Intelligence* (pp. 301-309). ACM.

Ďuračiová, R., & Faixová Chalachanová, J. (2018). Fuzzy spatio-temporal querying the PostgreSQL/PostGIS database for multiple criteria decision making. In *Dynamics in GIscience 4* (pp. 81–97). Springer International Publishing. doi:10.1007/978-3-319-61297-3_7

Emrich, T., Kriegel, H. P., & Mamoulis, N. (2012). Indexing uncertain spatio-temporal data. *Proceedings of the 21st ACM International Conference on Information and Knowledge Management* (pp. 395-404). ACM.

Guan, D., Li, H., Inohae, T., Su, W., Nagaie, T., & Hokao, K. (2011). Modeling urban land use change by the integration of cellular automaton and Markov model. *Ecological Modelling, 222*(20-22), 3761–3772. doi:10.1016/j.ecolmodel.2011.09.009

Kwan, M. P. (2004). GIS methods in time-geographic research: Geocomputation and geovisualization of human activity patterns. *Geografiska Annaler. Series B, Human Geography, 86*(4), 267–280. doi:10.1111/j.0435-3684.2004.00167.x

Lu, J. H., Chen, T., & Ling, T. W. (2005). Efficient processing of XML twig patterns with parent child edges: A look-ahead approach. *Proceedings of the 13th internal conference on very Large Data Bases* (pp. 193-204). ACM.

Lu, J. H., Chen, T., & Ling, T. W. (2005). From region encoding to extended dewey: on efficient processing of XML twig pattern matching. *Proceeding of the 31st ACM Internal Conference on very Large Data Bases* (pp. 533-542). ACM.

Obeid, N. (2000). Towards a model of learning through communication. *Knowledge and Information Systems, 2*(4), 498–508. doi:10.1007/PL00011655

Parent, C., Spaccapietra, S., & Zimanyi, E. (1999). Spatio-temporal conceptual models: data structures+ space+ time. In *Proceedings of the 7th ACM international symposium on Advances in geographic information systems* (pp. 26-33). ACM. 10.1145/320134.320142

Peuquet, D. J. (2001). Making space for time: Issues in space-time data representation. *GeoInformatica, 5*(1), 11–32. doi:10.1023/A:1011455820644

Sammatat, S., Boonsith, N., & Lekdee, K. (2016). *Generalized linear mixed models for spatio-temporal data with an application to leptospirosis in thailand.*

Sellis, T. (1999). Research issues in spatio-temporal database systems. In *International Symposium on Spatial Databases* (pp. 5-11). Springer Berlin Heidelberg.

Stefanakis, E. (2001). A unified framework for fuzzy spatio-temporal representation and reasoning. In *Proceedings of the 20th international cartographic conference* (pp. 2678-2687). ACM.

Wikle, C. K. (2001). A kernel-based spectral approach for spatio-temporal dynamic models. In *Proceedings of the 1st Spanish Workshop on Spatio-Temporal Modelling of Environmental Processes (METMA)* (pp. 167-180). ACM.

Yuan, L., Yu, Z., Luo, W., Zhou, L., & Lü, G. (2011). A 3D GIS spatial data model based on conformal geometric algebra. *Science China. Earth Sciences*, *54*(1), 101–112. doi:10.1007/s11430-010-4130-9

Chapter 10
Fast Leaf-to-Root Holistic Twig Query on Spatiotemporal XML Data

ABSTRACT

With the increasing applications based on location, the research on spatiotemporal data, especially queries of spatiotemporal data, has attracted a lot of attention. XML, as a standard language of information exchange over the web, should have the ability to query spatiotemporal data. In this chapter, they propose a fast leaf-to-root holistic twig query algorithm on spatiotemporal XML data, TwigSPFast. The authors represent spatiotemporal data by adding spatial and temporal attributes in common data and extending Dewey code to mark spatiotemporal data for special processes and determine the structure relationship of spatiotemporal nodes. This technique uses streams to store leaf nodes in XML corresponding to leaf query node and filters the streams to delete unmatched nodes, after filtering, they build output list for every matched leaf node that matches the query path from leaf node to root. It can be proved that TwigSPFast is optimal in time complexity and space complexity.

1 INTRODUCTION

With the prompt development of positioning system, a considerable amount of spatiotemporal applications (Mehrotra & Sharma, 2009; Tryfona & Hadzilacos, 1998; Sammatat et al, 2020; Al-sharif & Pradhan, 2014; Cheng, 2016; Xu et al., 2005; Shaw & Yu, 2009) merged, e.g. environment management, land management, and geographic information system. Spatiotemporal data is characterized by both spatial (Balbiani et al, 2002) and temporal (Augusto, 2003) semantics. Development and research in this area started decades ago, when management and manipulation of data, relating to both spatial and temporal changes, was recognized as an indispensable assignment. In the development of spatiotemporal data, several spatiotemporal data models have been proposed(Langran & Chrisman, 1988; Rathee & Yadav, 2013; Frank et al., 1999; Yuan et al., 2012), e.g. the snapshot model, the space-time composite data model, object-relationship model, and spatiotemporal object-oriented data model. With the development

DOI: 10.4018/978-1-6684-9108-9.ch010

of spatiotemporal data, people begin to study the management of spatiotemporal XML data, whose query operation is a key part.

Currently, a large number of theories have been proposed for XML queries(Bruno et al., 2002; Babu et al., 2012), such as global matching theory, two element structure connection theory, and approximate query processing theory. The process of querying is based on a good data model that can present spatial and temporal attributes of spatiotemporal data. Bai et al. (Bai et al., 2013) proposed a data model which uses a 5-tuple to represent spatiotemporal data. It added information on position, motion, and time in the traditional XML data to describe the spatiotemporal attributes. An important work for querying is to determine the structure of nodes in XML. To solve this problem, most researchers take region code(Bruno et al., 2002; Chen et al., 2006). The algorithms proposed by (Bruno et al., 2002; Chen et al., 2006)need to read and filter lots of data and push data down to stack continually which wastes lots of time and space. Extended Dewey code (Babu et al., 2012) is a kind of prefix code that not only can determine structure relationship of nodes in XML but also can get ancestor nodes according to the Dewey code of node. The work of querying spatiotemporal data in XML is very arduous and it leaves lots of interspace for us to research.

In this chapter, we use a 3-tuple(ATTR, PS, TM) to represent spatiotemporal data without changing tree structure of XML document. We use minimum bounding rectangle to depict the position attribute, which can represent point, line, region in space well. The time attribute is represented by a time period consisting of two points. We also extended Dewey coding by adding an integer at the start of code to mark spatiotemporal node for special processes. We propose the fast leaf-to-root holistic twig query on spatiotemporal XML data algorithm. In the process of querying, we associate every leaf query node with a stream to store matched leaf nodes in XML and filter the leaf nodes in stream to delete nodes unmatched, after that, we sort the leaf query nodes to determine the sequence of processing. In the phase of getting desired results, we call the algorithm buildList to build output list from leaf node to root that matches query path.

The rest of the chapter is organized as follows. Section 2 discusses preliminaries and related work. Section 3 focuses on spatiotemporal XML twig pattern matching algorithm called TwigSPFast and then presents the analysis of the correctness and complexity of time and space. Section 4 concludes this chapter.

2 PRELIMINARIES

2.1 Twig Pattern Matching

Definition 1 (twig query matching)

Given a twig query $Q = (V_Q,E_Q)$ and a XML database $D = (V_D,E_D)$, the process of matching Q in D is a mapping from query node Q to element node D, the mapping h: $\{u: u \in Q\} \rightarrow \{x: x \in D\}$ must satisfy the following condition:

(i) Query node predicates are satisfied by the corresponding database nodes, and they have the same tag name.
(ii) The structure relationships between query nodes are satisfied by the corresponding database nodes.

2.2 Semantic Foundations of Spatiotemporal Data

Spatiotemporal data have a set of characteristics that make them distinctly different from the more familiar lists and tables of alphanumeric data used in traditional business applications, the data model is restricted to tree structure in XML documents especially. In (Bai et al., 2013), Bai et al. measures fuzzy spatiotemporal XML data by five dimensions: OID, ATTR, FP, FT and FM. In the case of spatiotemporal data, we measure it by three dimensions according to characteristics of spatiotemporal data on the basis of those five dimensions. The dimensions of spatiotemporal data are shown as follows:

ATTR: It is used to describe static properties of spatiotemporal data (e.g., land owner's name, area, population, etc.). There may be one or more attributes in a spatiotemporal data whose dimension heavily depends on the application domain.

PT: It describes the spatial attributes of spatiotemporal data, which contains point, line and region.

TM: It describes the temporal attribute of spatiotemporal data, which contains time point and time interval.

2.3 Extended Dewey Code

Dewey code is a kind of prefix encoding, it can only determine the structural relationship between nodes, when it comes to getting node's name from root to a certain node, the Dewey code needs extending that is proposed in (Balbiani et al, 2002).

There is a label t in XML, $CT(t) = \{t_0, t_1, \ldots, t_{n-1}\}$ is used to express all child nodes of t got from DTD structure information of XML document. For every element e_i tagged t_i, it can be given a integer x_i satisfied $x_i \bmod n = i$. Extended Dewey code can be computed by depth first traversal and code of every XML node is expressed by integer vector. We use label (u) to express the code of node u, if label (u) = label (s).x, then s is the parent node of u, the value of x can be computed as follows:

If u is a text node, then x = -1
Else, suppose u is the kth(k = 0,1,2,…,n-1) tag of node t_s, then
(2.1) if u is the leftmost child, then x = k;
(2.2) else, suppose the code of u's left child node is label(s).y, if (y mod n) < k, then $x = \lfloor (y/n) \rfloor \times n + k$; else $x = \lceil (y/n) \times n + k$. n is number of t_s's child nodes.

We can translate the code into sequence of element's names from root to a certain node by a finite state transducer (FST) after giving extended Dewey code of one node. FST is expressed by a 5-tuple (I, S, i, ,τ): (i) I=Z∪{-1}, Z is nonnegative integer set; (ii) S=Σ∪{PCDATA}, PCDATA expresses the state of text; (iii) initial state of i is element's name of root in XML document; (iv) the function of state translating is defined as follows: for $\forall$ t∈Σ, if x=-1, then (t,x) = PCDATA; else (t,x)= t_k, k=x mod n; (v) τ depicts name of current state. The example of extended Dewey code and FST is showed in Fig.1.

Figure 1. Examples of extended Dewey code

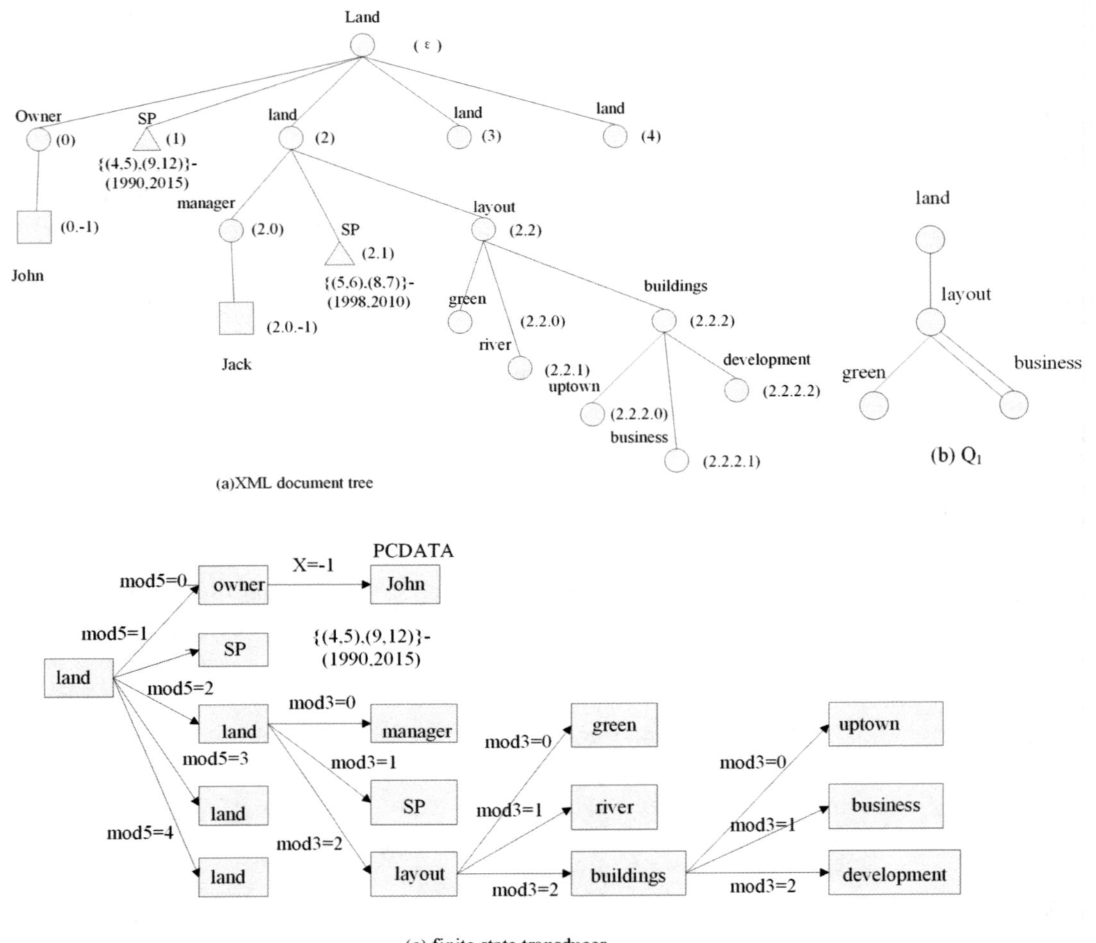

3 HOLISTIC TWIG QUERY ON SPATIOTEMPORAL DATA

The process of querying is based on a good data model, to depict spatiotemporal attributes well, we simplify the data model proposed by (Bai et al., 2013) to represent spatiotemporal data with minimum bounding rectangle by adding spatial and temporal attributes in general data.

3.1 Process Spatiotemporal Node in XML Tree

The spatial and temporal attribute of spatiotemporal data makes it distinctly different from common data, the same process of common node is not available when it comes to spatiotemporal node. As for spatiotemporal node, we need to mark and process it specially. The extended Dewey introduced in section 2 is not available for spatiotemporal data, we need to do some improvement: we add an integer that values 0

node n with a variable nodeCount to count the amount of XML nodes matching n. If n is a leaf node, nodeCount is the amount of element in T_f, else, nodeCount values the minimum nodeCount of all query nodes in DBL(n). The detail of DBL sort is shown as follows:

Algorithm DBLSort(n)

```
/* At the beginning, the value nodeCount(n) for each query node n is zero */
01: if (isLeafNode(n))
02: locateMatchedLabel(n)
03: nodeCount[n] = T_n.length
04: s = L_DBL(n)
05: for each node a in list s
06: DBLSort(a)
07: if (nodeCount[n] < nodeCount[a])
08: nodeCount[n] = nodeCount[a]
09: sort(s, nodeCount[a]) // ascendantly
```

In the algorithm TwigSPFast, line 8 calls buildList algorithm to establish list of each query node. Algorithm buildList is the core part of the whole algorithm, lines 1-10 establish the list of leaf query node, line 11 establishes list of internal query node by calling algorithm buildInternalList.

Algorithm buildList(f, e, p)

```
01: if (f == SortNodeArray[0])
02: if (tuple(e, null) ∉ L_f)
03: addtoList(L_f, e, null)
04: else
// assume the index of f in SortNodeArray[] is i
05: a = closestCommonAncestor (SortNodeArray[i],SortNodeArray[i-1])
06: if (tuple(e, null) ∈ L_a ∧ Pa matches P_f)
07: if (tuple(e, null) ∉ L_f)
08: addtoList(L_f, e, null)
09: else
10: return
11: buildInternalList(f, e, p, pointer to the tuple(e, null))
```

In the algorithm TwigSPFast, if f is the first node of SortNodeArray and there is not 2-tuple (e, null) in list L_f, add 2-tuple (e, null) to L_f (line 1-3); if f is not the first node of SortNodeArray (line 4), the list L_a of closet common ancestor of f and previous query node of f in SortNodeArray that has contained the 2-tuple(element e_2, pointers) and the tuple and its ancestors match the path query P_f correspond to e (lines 5-6), if there is no tuple(e, null), then add tuple (e, null) to L_f (lines 7-8).

In the algorithm buildInternalList, s is the set of element b that is an ancestor of e such that b can be match node p in the path solution of e to path pattern P_f; for each element b in set s(line 2) if there is tuple_p(b, pointers array_p), the tuple and its ancestors match the path query P_f correspond to e(line 3), then add a pointer that points to tuple_f to the pointer array of tuple_p; else add a new tuple(b, pointer to tuple_f) to list L_p, after that, recursive call buildInternalList.

Algorithm BUILDINTERNALLIST(F, E, P, TUPLE_F(E, POINTERS))

```
/* let s be a set of element b that is an ancestor of e such that b can be match node p in the path solution of e to path pattern P_f*/
if (p != null)
for each b ∈ s
if (tuple_p(b, pointers array_p) ∈ L_p ∧ P_p matches P_f)
addPointer(L_p, tuple_p, pointer to tuple_f)
else
addtoList(L_p, b, pointer to tuple_f)
buildInternalList (p, b, parent(p), tuple_new)
```

3.4 Analysis of Query Algorithm

3.4.1 Analysis of Correctness

Theorem 1: Given a twig query Q and a XML document D, TwigSPFast can return all matching results in D correctly.

Proof: Suppose twig query Q is (A_1, A_2,..., A_n) rooted A_1, {A_k, A_{k+1}, ..., A_n| $1 \leq k \leq n$} are leaf nodes, A_j ($1 \leq j \leq n$) is topBranchingNode. When (a_1, a_2, ..., a_n) matches (A_1, A_2,..., A_n) a_i (i=k, k+1, ..., n) must be in T_{A_i} after filtering of T_f in lines 1-2 of TwigSPFast, then in lines 5-10, the algorithm gets next leaf query node f according to results of DBL sort and call buildList to build lists for all elements of T_f, so, {a_1, a_2, ..., a_n} is all in L_{A_i} according to the process of build list. At last, the algorithm call function outputSolutions to output query result (a_1, a_2, ..., a_n) matching (A_1, A_2,..., A_n). When algorithm TwigSPFast output (a_1, a_2, ..., a_n), it indicates a_i (i=1, 2, ..., n) is in the list L_{A_i} , we can know that a_j is must in the path from A_1 to A_j according to the process of build list. So, (a_1, a_2, ..., a_n) matches (A_1, A_2,..., A_n).

3.4.2 Analysis of Time Complexity

Theorem 2: Given a twig query Q and a XML document D, the temporal complexity in the worst case is O (n_1*d). n_1 is the sum of leaf nodes in T_f, n_2 is the sum of leaf nodes in T_f after filtering of locateMatchedLabel, d is the maximum between depth of Q and depth of D.

Proof: In algorithm TwigSPFast, lines 1-2 filter all leaf query nodes in T_f time complexity is O (n_1*d), lines 5-10 build list by calling buildList for all leaf query nodes in T_f, time complexity is O (n_2*d), n_1 > n_2, so, the time complexity of the whole algorithm is (n_1*d).□

Above all, we can know that the algorithm TwigSPFast is optimal in time complexity.

3.4.3 Analysis of space complexity

Theorem 3: Given a twig query Q and a XML document D, the temporal complexity in the worst case is O (n_1+n_2*d). n_1 is the sum of leaf nodes in T_f, n_2 is the sum of leaf nodes in T_f after filtering of locateMatchedLabel, d is the depth of D.

Proof: In algorithm TwigSPFast, cost of space is mainly consist of stream and list. The space complexity of all leaf nodes of twig query Q in T_f is O (n_1). Lines 5-10 build list by calling buildList for all leaf query nodes in T_f, the algorithm establish a new tuple for elements matched for every query node in the worst case, the space complexity of list is $O(n_2*d)$. So, the space complexity of the whole algorithm is $O(n_1+n_2*d)$.

Above all, we can know that the algorithm TwigSPFast is optimal in space complexity.

4 SUMMARY

In this chapter we developed a 3-tuple(ATTR, PS, TM) to represent spatiotemporal data in XML as a triangle, which can represent spatiotemporal attributes well without changing the tree structure of XML. Based on this data model, we propose an fast leaf-to-root holistic twig query algorithm on spatiotemporal XML data, TwigSPFast. The algorithm TwigSPFast reduces cost of time and space by sorting leaf query nodes and filtering leaf nodes that don't match query path in XML, so, algorithm TwigSPFast is optimal in time complexity and space complexity.

REFERENCES

Al-sharif, A. A., & Pradhan, B. (2014). Monitoring and predicting land use change in Tripoli Metropolitan City using an integrated Markov chain and cellular automata models in GIS. *Arabian Journal of Geosciences*, *7*(10), 4291–4301. doi:10.1007/s12517-013-1119-7

Augusto, J. C. (2003). A general framework for reasoning about change. *New Generation Computing*, *21*(3), 209–246. doi:10.1007/BF03037474

Babu, D. B., Prasad, R. S. R., & Santhosh, M. (2012). XML twig pattern matching algorithms and query processing [J] [IJERT]. *International Journal of Engineering Research & Technology (Ahmedabad)*, *1*(3), 1–6.

Bai, L. Y., Yan, L., & Ma, Z. M. (2013). Determining topological relationship of fuzzy spatiotemporal data integrated with XML twig pattern. *Applied Intelligence*, *39*(1), 75–100. doi:10.1007/s10489-012-0395-3

Balbiani, P., Condotta, J. F., & Del Cerro, L. F. (2002). Tractability results in the block algebra. *Journal of Logic and Computation*, *12*(5), 885–909. doi:10.1093/logcom/12.5.885

Bruno, N., Koudas, N., & Srivastava, D. (2002). Holistic twig joins: optimal XML pattern matching. *Proceedings of the 2002 ACM SIGMOD International Conference on Management of Data* (pp. 310-321). ACM. 10.1145/564691.564727

Chen, S., Li, H. G., & Tatemura, J. (2006). Twig2Stack: bottom-up processing of generalized-treepattern queries over XML documents. *Proceedings of the 32nd International Conference on Very Large Data Bases* (pp. 283-294). ACM.

Cheng, H. (2016). Modeling and querying fuzzy spatiotemporal objects. *Journal of Intelligent & Fuzzy Systems*, *31*(6), 2851–2858. doi:10.3233/JIFS-169167

Claramunt, C., Parent, C., & Spaccapietra, S. (1999). Database modelling for environmental and land use changes. Proceedings of Geographical Information and Planning Springer Berlin Heidelberg (pp. 181-202). doi:10.1007/978-3-662-03954-0_10

Frank, A., Grumbach, S., Güting, R. H., Jensen, C. S., Koubarakis, M., Lorentzos, N., Manolopoulos, Y., Nardelli, E., Pernici, B., Schek, H.-J., Scholl, M., Sellis, T., Theodoulidis, B., & Widmayer, P. (1999). Chorochronos: A research network for spatiotemporal database systems. *SIGMOD Record*, *28*(3), 12–21. doi:10.1145/333607.333609

Langran, G., & Chrisman, N. (1988). A framework for temporal geographic information. *Cartographica*, *40*(1), 1–14. doi:10.3138/K877-7273-2238-5Q6V

Liu, J., Ma, Z. M., & Qv, Q. L. (2014). Dynamic querying possibilistic XML data. *Information Sciences*, *261*(4), 70–88.

Liu, J., Ma, Z. M., & Yan, L. (2013). Efficient labeling scheme for dynamic XML trees. *Information Sciences*, *221*(2), 338–354. doi:10.1016/j.ins.2012.09.036

Liu, J., Ma, Z. M., & Yan, L. (2013). Querying and ranking incomplete twigs in probabilistic XML. *World Wide Web (Bussum)*, *16*(3), 325–353. doi:10.1007/s11280-011-0149-x

Mehrotra, R., & Sharma, A. (2009). Evaluating spatio-temporal representations in daily rainfall sequences from three stochastic multi-site weather generation approaches. *Advances in Water Resources*, *32*(6), 948–962. doi:10.1016/j.advwatres.2009.03.005

Nørvåg, K. (2002). Temporal query operators in XML database. *Proceedings of the 2002 ACM Symposium on Applied Computing* (pp. 402-406). ACM. 10.1145/508791.508868

Rathee, S., & Yadav, A. (2013). Survey on spatio-temporal database and data models with relevant features. *International Journal of Scientific and Research Publications*, *3*(1), 152–156.

Sammatat, S., Boonsith, N., & Lekdee, K. (2020). *Estimation and detection of rice yields in Thailand using spatial and longitudinal data analysis*.

Shaw, S. L., & Yu, H. (2009). A GIS-based time-geographic approach of studying individual activities and interactions in a hybrid physical–virtual space. *Journal of Transport Geography*, *17*(2), 141–149. doi:10.1016/j.jtrangeo.2008.11.012

Theodoridis, Y., Papadias, D., Stefanakis, E., & Sellis, T. (1998). Direction relations and two-dimensional range queries: Optimization techniques. *Data & Knowledge Engineering*, *27*(97), 313–336. doi:10.1016/S0169-023X(97)00060-8

Tryfona, N., & Hadzilacos, T. (1998). Logical data modeling of spatiotemporal applications: Definitions and a model. In *Proceedings. IDEAS'98. International Database Engineering and Applications Symposium (Cat. No. 98EX156)* (pp. 14-23). IEEE.

Xu, K., Wikle, C. K., & Fox, N. I. (2005). A kernel-based spatio-temporal dynamical model for nowcasting weather radar reflectivities. *Journal of the American Statistical Association*, *100*(472), 1133–1144. doi:10.1198/016214505000000682

Yuan, L., Lü, G., Luo, W., Yu, Z., Yi, L., & Sheng, Y. (2012). Geometric algebra method for multidimensionally-unified GIS computation. *Chinese Science Bulletin*, *57*(7), 802–811. doi:10.1007/s11434-011-4891-3

Chapter 11
Interpolation and Prediction of Spatiotemporal XML Data Integrated With Grey Dynamic Model

ABSTRACT

Interpolation and prediction of spatiotemporal data are integral components of many real-world applications. Thus, approaches to interpolating and predicting spatiotemporal data have been extensively investigated. Currently, the grey dynamic model has been used to enhance the performance of interpolating and predicting spatiotemporal data. Meanwhile, the extensible markup language (XML) has unique characteristics of information representation and exchange. In this chapter, the authors first couple the grey dynamic model with the spatiotemporal XML model. Based on a definition of the position part of the spatiotemporal XML model, they extract the corresponding position information of each time interval and propose an algorithm for constructing an AVL tree to store them. Then, the authors present the architecture of an interpolating and predicting process and investigate change operations in positions. On this basis, the chapter presents an algorithm for interpolation and prediction of spatiotemporal data based on XML integrated with the grey dynamic model.

1 INTRODUCTION

The management of spatiotemporal data has been intensively studied in recent years on account of the global spatiotemporal data increase (Blekas et al., 2008; Jadidi et al., 2014; Hallot & Billen, 2016). Among various applications (e.g., flight control, land management, blood forecasting, traffic supervision), the objects whose positions change over time, such as airplanes, ships, clouds, and so on, significantly contribute to the study of spatiotemporal data (Nalica, 2010; Aburas et al., 2017; Yu, 2006).

DOI: 10.4018/978-1-6684-9108-9.ch011

Researchers have addressed a variety of approaches in modeling and querying the location of the moving spatiotemporal data both in relational databases (Dobra et al., 2004; Güting et al., 2010; Alamri et al., 2014; Wu et al., 2001) and spatiotemporal databases (Choi & Chung, 2002; Hadjieleftheriou et al., 2003; Tao et al., 2004). Early studies on the positions of spatiotemporal data assumed that the spatiotemporal data remain static at each time interval (Langran, 1989; Seqev & Shoshani, 1987). In addition, representing and querying the locations of moving spatiotemporal data as a linear function of time, which assigns a set of possible values rather than a unique value, was introduced (Sistla et al., 1997). With respect to continuously moving regions, Tøssebro and Güting (Tøssebro & Güting, 2001) provided algorithms to interpolate between two snapshots, transitioning from simple convex polygons to arbitrary polygons. Güting et al. (Güting et al., 2010) identified the *k* nearest neighbors of a set of moving object trajectories for any instant of time within the lifetime. However, the fixed value model and linear model generate too many errors on account of the limited sampling rate and indeterminacy of the snapshot when increasing indeterminacy is concerned (Bao & Qin, 2005). Furthermore, the linear prediction models have limits (Sun et al., 2004). For example, the movement is not always linear; if it is linear, it is not usually known. If it is linear and known, it changes so fast that prediction using the movement parameter information is meaningless. Moreover, many spatiotemporal applications not only query the historical spatiotemporal data, but also strive to retrieve the near-future evolution of spatiotemporal data. Although the fixed value model and moving objects spatiotemporal (MOST) model (Wolfson, 1998) can provide the near-future evolution of spatiotemporal data, they assume the movement functions are already known. Additionally, when information is limited, the originally sampled data will generate errors. Therefore, a new modeling technology of interpolation and prediction of spatiotemporal data is required to overcome these problems.

In recent years, the grey system theory (Kayacan et al., 2010) has developed rapidly, and its applications have extended to the spatiotemporal data field. The grey prediction model, GM (1, 1), is used to enhance the estimation performance because it can reduce the randomness inside the history query results sequence and it generates a holistic measure. The grey system theory is fairly appropriate for predicting spatiotemporal information because the accumulated generating operation is the most important characteristic of the grey system theory. Its purpose is to reduce the randomness of data.

However, for grey generation in snapshots, the model reduces the randomness in the snapshot data sequence. Moreover, the model can more precisely predict the near-future evolution of spatiotemporal data. In (Bao & Qin, 2005), the grey modeling approach was used to generate the discrete spatiotemporal model for two-dimensional indeterminate moving point objects. In (Bao et al., 2006), Bao introduced a histogram-based grey estimator for spatiotemporal selectivity estimation according to the continuity of movement. However, their study was based on the traditional database. Thus, interpolation and prediction of spatiotemporal data are relatively complex primarily because of the imposing of strict restrictions on structure (Tryfona & Jensen, 1999) and data types (Claramunt & Theriault, 1995) of spatiotemporal data. In such a case, interpolation and prediction of spatiotemporal data require a new efficient medium.

The next-generation language of the Internet, the Extensible Markup Language (XML) is playing an increasingly important role as a medium for integrating and exchanging data from different sources. Furthermore, XML significantly influences data management (Algergawy et al., 2011; Guo, 2013) (e.g., interpolation and prediction of spatiotemporal data) because the data can remain in a tree structure and a node or subtree can be considered metadata. Thus, interpolation and prediction of spatiotemporal data based on XML seem to have greater performance advantages than a traditional database. This can be explained by two factors. Firstly, the basic data structure in XML is the labeled ordered rooted tree

(Ma et al., 2010), which can facilitate extraction of the corresponding position nodes for interpolating and predicting spatiotemporal data. Secondly, XML can handle time by adding labeled edges with time intervals as the time dimension (Mendelzon et al, 2004), as opposed to the complex extensions of traditional models (Claramunt & Theriault, 1995; Peuquet & Duan, 1995). This handling of time can facilitate extraction of the corresponding temporal information. In that case, it makes interpolation and prediction of spatiotemporal data much easier because the desired interpolating or predicting of spatiotemporal data can be achieved by directly extracting the corresponding position nodes and corresponding temporal information. Accordingly, it is significant to lead XML into interpolation and prediction of spatiotemporal data.

To the best of our knowledge, there are no reports on interpolation and prediction of spatiotemporal data based on XML integrated with the grey dynamic model. In this chapter, we present a novel approach to interpolating and predicting the positions of moving spatiotemporal data, as well as the first use of GM (1, 1) on the spatiotemporal XML model. According to the structure of the spatiotemporal XML model, we add development Functions along the x- and y-axis into the position part. Then, we extract the position information of each time interval and construct an AVL tree to store them. After discussing the architecture of the interpolating and predicting processes based on GM (1, 1), we investigate the change operations in the position containing the update, delete, and insert functions. Then, we provide an algorithm for interpolation and prediction based on XML integrated with GM (1, 1). Our experimental results validate our analysis and show a substantial performance improvement.

The remainder of this chapter is organized as follows. In Section 2, we discuss basic information on types of interpolation and prediction models, the grey system theory, and GM (1, 1). We then couple GM (1, 1) with the spatiotemporal XML model in Section 3. Section 4 presents the architecture of interpolating and predicting processes, and Section 5 investigates the change operations in the position. In Section 6, we propose an algorithm for interpolation and prediction. Section 7 presents the experimental results, and Section 8 concludes the chapter.

2 BASIC KNOWLEDGE

2.1 Types of Interpolation and Prediction Model

In many areas of spatiotemporal databases, positions of spatiotemporal data are usually interpolated or predicted for both continuous and discrete changes because only finite position data are recorded in the database. Accordingly, some desired position information of spatiotemporal data should be interpolated or predicted. Continuous changes mean that changes occur throughout their entire lifespans, while discrete changes indicate that changes occur at specific time instants. For several phenomena (e.g., blood forecasting, forest fires, cloud waves, typhoon movements, etc.), we must track and monitor the respective spatiotemporal data to analyze or predict near-future movements.

We first introduce interpolation and prediction models of spatiotemporal data, which are mainly comprised of a fixed value model, linear model, and grey model. The fixed value model (Seqev & Shoshani, 1987) assumes values of spatiotemporal data between snapshots to be constant, and it changes when a new snapshot is generated. Figure 1a shows the actual tracking of a moving point; Figure 1b represents it using the fixed value model. In Figure 1b, there are only five values in each time interval, and the values change when a new snapshot is generated. For instance, an individual waiting in a queue for tickets is found at a certain position, but the individual may change position from time to time (a new snapshot is generated).

The linear model (Sistla et al., 1997) assumes that the development of spatiotemporal data during a time interval is a linear function. In each time interval, the beginning spatiotemporal data are stored as well as its development function. They are both used for interpolation or prediction when the spatiotemporal data are required at an arbitrary time point. In Figure 1c, there are four lines to record the spatiotemporal data tracking (the trends of the first two lines are the same). The grey model (Kayacan et al., 2010) generates movement functions from a sequence of spatiotemporal data. Figure 1d simulates tracking of the moving point in Figure 1a. It can be observed that the approximation in Figure 1d is the closest one to the actual track.

Figure 1. Types of interpolation and prediction models

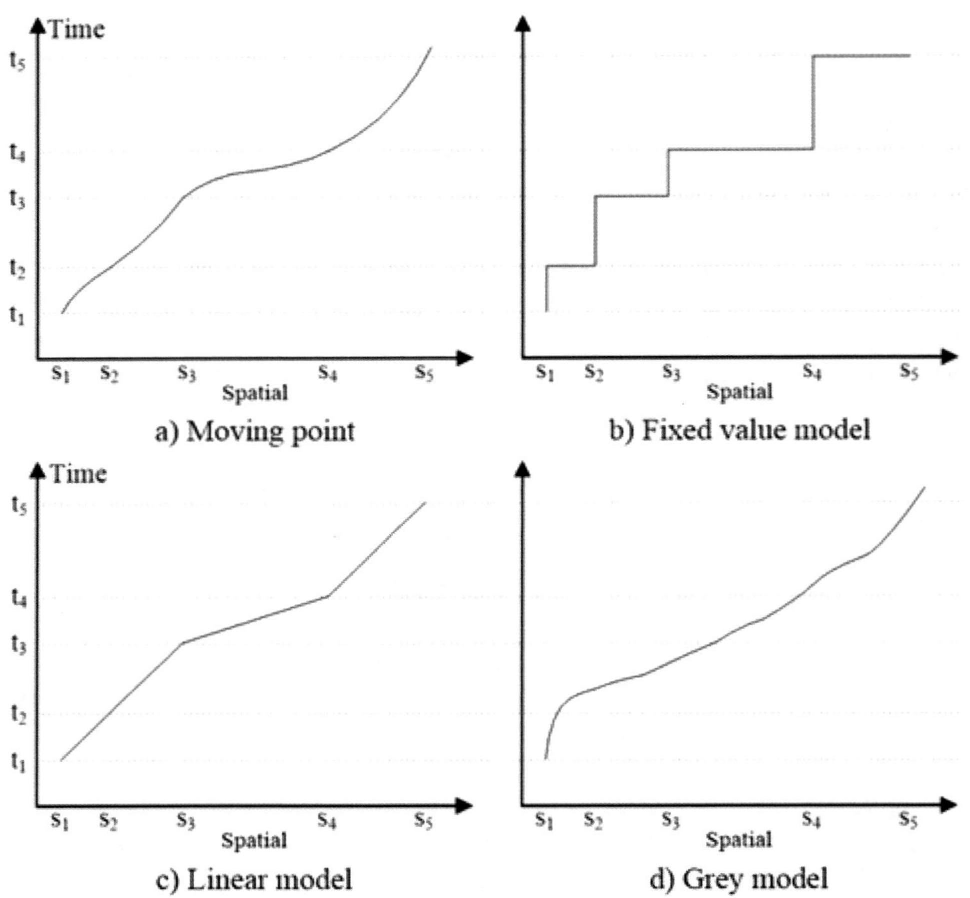

2.2 Grey System Theory and GM (1, 1)

The grey system theory (Kayacan et al., 2010) was first presented in the late 1970s. Its main task is to seek the mathematic relations and movement rule among factors from the behavioral data of a system. The core of this theory is the dynamic grey model, whose characteristic is the generating function and the grey differential equation. The dynamic grey model uses differential fitting as a modeling method based on the concept of the grey generating function. Assuming the system's internal behavioral data is unknown, the single series first-order linear dynamic model GM (1, 1) of the grey system theory uses grey generations on the random external behavioral data to reduce randomness. It then establishes the grey difference equation for calculation and prediction. The arithmetic to generate GM (1, 1) from behavior data sequence X can be described as follows:

Let X be a non-negative behavioral data sequence:

$$X^{(0)} = \{x^{(0)}(1), x^{(0)}(2), x^{(0)}(3), x^{(0)}(4), ..., x^{(0)}(n)\}, n > 3$$

Step 1: Use the accumulated generation operation on $x^{(0)}$,

$$X^{(1)}(k) = \sum_{m=1}^{k} x^{(0)}(m), k = 2, 3, ..., n$$

Step 2: Use the mean operation on $x^{(1)}$,

$$Z^{(1)}(k) = 1/2[x^{(1)}(k-1) + x^{(1)}(k)], k = 2, 3, ..., n$$

Step 3: Use the least squares difference approach to obtain coefficients a and b:

$$P = \begin{bmatrix} a \\ b \end{bmatrix} = \left[B^T B\right]^{-1} B^T y_n,\ B = \begin{bmatrix} -z^{(1)}(2) & -z^{(1)}(3) & ... - z^{(1)}(n) \\ 1 & 1 \ ... & 1 \end{bmatrix}^T$$

and $y_n = [x^{(0)}(2), x^{(0)}(3), \ldots, x^{(0)}(n)]^T$.

The grey difference equation, $x^{(0)}(k) + az^{(1)}(k) = b$, is called the GM (1, 1) of sequence X. It can be used in near-future evolution prediction, even when the behavioral data sequence has a relatively high error rate or randomness (Liu & Lin, 1998). In addition, it can predict data not recorded in database.

3 COUPLING GM (1, 1) WITH SPATIOTEMPORAL XML MODEL

To interpolate and predict the positions of spatiotemporal data more accurately and efficiently, GM (1, 1) is integrated into the spatiotemporal XML model. In this section, we first illustrate the utilized spatiotemporal XML model. We then demonstrate how the spatiotemporal XML model is integrated with GM (1, 1) to interpolate and predict the positions of the spatiotemporal data.

An XML document is a labeled ordered rooted tree. We thus regard spatiotemporal data as a structured tree for metadata. As a result, operations between spatiotemporal data are actually operations between trees. According to the nature of spatiotemporal data, the definition of the spatiotemporal XML model is defined as follows.

Definition 1 Spatiotemporal XML model *XSP* is a five-tuple, *XSP* = (*OID*, *ATTR*, *P*, *M*, *T*), where

- *OID* is the changing history of the spatiotemporal data.
- *ATTR* denotes the attributes of the spatiotemporal data.
- *P* is the position of the spatiotemporal data.
- *M* is motion of the spatiotemporal data.
- *T* is time of the spatiotemporal data.

Because GM (1, 1) uses grey generations to seek the mathematic relations and movement rule, the corresponding part of the spatiotemporal XML model only involves the position part. Accordingly, we mainly investigate how to use GM (1, 1) on the position part of the spatiotemporal XML model.

We consider the position part of the spatiotemporal XML model as a sub-data tree and provide its definition as follows.

Definition 2 (Position part of the spatiotemporal XML model.) The position part of the spatiotemporal XML model *XP* is a five-tuple, $XP = (x, y, f_x, f_y, T)$, where

- x and y are abscissa and vertical coordinates.
- f_x and f_y are development functions along the x- and y-axis, respectively.
- T is the time of the position.

Following the GM (1, 1) model, the position part of the spatiotemporal XML model can be expressed as a five-tuple. The development functions f_x and $_{\mathrm{fy}}$ can be generated from the GM (1, 1) model according to x and y in history records at each time T. Note that the position part of the spatiotemporal XML model defined above is used for zero-dimensional spatiotemporal data because it is the most common case. Furthermore, some one-dimensional or even two-dimensional spatiotemporal data can be considered zero-dimensional spatiotemporal data when the shape of the spatiotemporal data is irrelevant in terms of the whole situation.

The approach can be applied to one-dimensional or even two-dimensional spatiotemporal data as the development of functions. For instance, when we study an airplane route, we can consider the airplane as a point, even though it is actually two-dimensional spatiotemporal data. Another case is a typhoon. We are primarily concerned about the central part of the typhoon called the typhoon eye when its track is studied.

The position part fragment of the spatiotemporal XML model is shown in Figure 2. Node *p* is an abbreviation connoting that it is the position part of the spatiotemporal data node. For the case of x and y nodes, we not only add their value nodes, but we also add their development function nodes. Firstly, we use two child nodes of node *p*, denoted x and y, to identify the x node and y node, respectively. Then, for each child node of node *p*, the two child nodes are added to store the value and development functions. For the value nodes *xval* or *yval*, they are usually obtained by observation or even interpolation and prediction; for the development function nodes f_x and f_y, they are computed by GM (1, 1) using original values of x nodes and y nodes. Accordingly, the position node can store the position information (*xval* and *yval*) as well as the development functions (f_x and f_y). In that case, we can interpolate and predict the position of spatiotemporal data by reading the corresponding position values and the development functions. Although it may generate a great amount of redundancy since the development functions of *x* and *y* should be generated and stored at each transaction time interval, it saves the query time because we need only read the corresponding node values; it is not necessary to compute the development functions when querying. On the other hand, the so-called redundancy is actually useful and may be used when interpolating position nodes at a distant-past times.

Figure 2. Structure of the position fragment

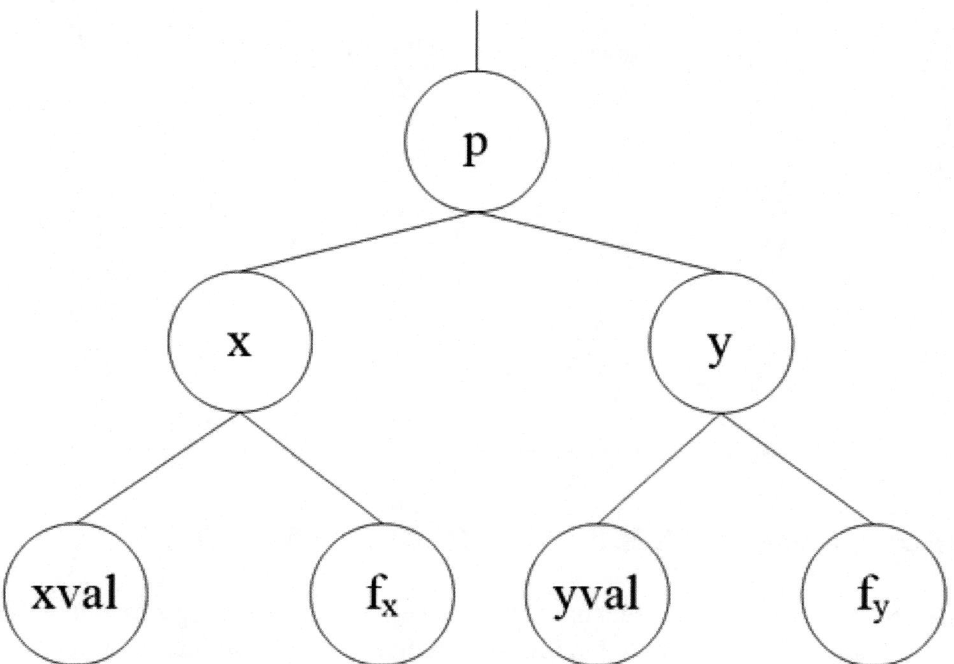

Since the structure of the spatiotemporal XML model is not a regular tree, and the attribute nodes may be multiple, searching for the corresponding position information becomes complicated. To overcome this difficulty, we extract the position information in the spatiotemporal XML model and construct an AVL tree to store them. The advantage is mainly comprised of the following: (a) useful position information is extracted; (b) the data used in the experiment in the later section are relatively small and are suitable for using an AVL tree to store the extracted information; and (c) both the AVL tree and B− tree are similar in that they are data structures that cause the heights of their respective trees to be minimized according to their requirements. This "shortness" allows searching to be performed in *O (log n)* time because the largest possible number of reads corresponds to the height of the tree.

An AVL tree is a self-balancing binary search tree that is balanced to maintain *O (log n)* height. A B− tree is a balanced tree, but it is not a binary tree. Nodes have more children. This increases the per-node search time, but it decreases the number of nodes the search must visit. We choose the AVL tree because its overall performance is better than that of the B− tree and B+ tree. In addition, inserting, deleting, updating, and querying nodes in the AVL tree is faster than those in the B− (Belbaraka & Stojmenović, 1994) tree and B+ (Mendelzon et al, 2004) tree. Moreover, (d) techniques of creating, deleting, inserting, and searching nodes in the AVL tree have been studied and are applicable. Accordingly, we introduce an AVL tree to store the extracted position information.

In the algorithm *Construct_AVL_Tree*, we construct an AVL tree from the spatiotemporal XML model, extract the position information used, and store them in the constructed tree. Function *Grey_Estimate* calculates the GM (1, 1) model from the given subsequence. Its algorithm is given in Section 7.

Algorithm

Algorithm Construct_AVL_Tree (x, y, f_x, f_y)

```
let t = null
for (m = i; m <= i; m−−)
let a_i = $o/../position/x/xval_i [@T_s = T_i]
let b_i = $o/../position/y/yval_i [@T_s = T_i]
let c_i = $o/../position/x/f_xi [@T_s = T_i]
let d_i = $o/../position/y/f_yi [@T_s = T_i]
Sequence (s_i) = add (a_i, b_i, c_i, d_i)
Sequence_B () = add (s_i)
end for
for each s_i in Sequence_B () do
let x = Grey_Estimate (a_i.x)
let y = Grey_Estimate (b_i.y)
insert the current node (x, y, c_i, d_i) to result tree t
end for
return t
```

4 INTERPOLATION AND PREDICTION PROCESS ARCHITECTURE

The architecture of the interpolating and predicting process is based on the spatiotemporal XML model integrated with GM (1, 1), as illustrated in Figure 3. When there is an XQuery request, we should first normalize the corresponding data. Take the typhoon eye route as an example. The data recorded are the longitude and latitude coordinates for predicting the typhoon's eye position. We should normalize the position data into coordinates along the x- and y-axis. Then, the GM (1, 1) generator is set up according to the GM (1, 1) model using a certain number of the most recent history data in the constructed AVL tree as the initial sequence for interpolating and predicting the query result at a given time.

Furthermore, we should also process the result into readable data since the corresponding generating process data are based on the spatiotemporal XML model and coordinate system. In that case, we should process the computed data into the exact position (longitude and latitude) so that they are readable. Finally, the query result can be returned. In the case of the interpolation or prediction of position of the spatiotemporal data, GM (1, 1) is actually used twice to generate *x*- and *y-axis* values, respectively.

The interpolating and predicting process architecture, as shown in Figure 3, mainly contains two parts: a user-related part and a machine-related part. The former provides two user interfaces, including the readable input and output data; the latter deals with the data and gives it the capability of satisfying user needs based on the spatiotemporal XML model integrated with GM (1, 1). The latter can be further divided into two parts: data processing and data computing. Data processing contains data normalization, which transforms the user-readable data into machine-readable data. The result processing reverses the normalized data. Data computation interpolates and predicts the desired result according to the GM (1, 1) model using a certain number of the most recent history data items in the constructed AVL tree as the initial sequence.

Figure 3. Interpolating and predicting process architecture

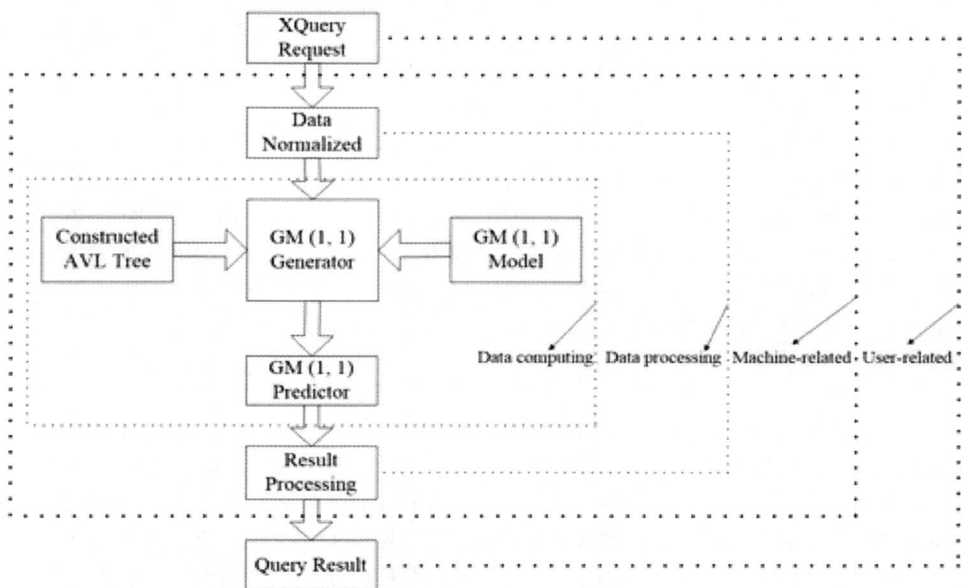

5 POSITION CHANGE OPERATIONS

Spatiotemporal XML documents are subject to continuously changing operations, namely update, delete, and insert. These continuously changing operations may lead to different effects on elements and attributes in the position part of the spatiotemporal XML model. These change operations are related to interpolation or prediction of spatiotemporal data. Because the integrated grey dynamic model only deals with the position part of the spatiotemporal XML model, in this section we demonstrate how their effect on elements and attributes can be represented in the position part of the spatiotemporal XML model. The following is the effect of performing each operation on position elements and attributes.

Update. Updating the value of a position can be seen as replacement of the corresponding elements and attributes with other ones that have the same name but different content. Actually, not only the content of the position (x and y) but also the temporal interval of the position and development functions (f_x and f_y) should be updated. We discuss the transaction time and data recorded in the database. When position element p is updated at time t:

A new element with the same name p and all its descendants (x, y, f_x, f_y) are appended after the original ones.

Compute f_x and f_y according to the original corresponding elements using GM (1, 1).

The attributes T_s and T_e of position element p and all its descendants are set to [t, Now].

Delete. Deleting the value of a position involves only deleting the position node and all its descendants and corresponding attributes. However, the deletion of the positioning node affects the development functions of later position nodes because the development functions are generated by later position nodes.

When position element p is deleted at time t:

- For $t \in [T_1, T_2] \wedge T_1 = \max(T_s) \wedge T_2 = \min(T_e)$, delete position element p and all its descendants at time intervals $[T_1, T_2]$.
- For position element p where // p [@T$_s$ > @T$_2$], again compute f_x and f_y of the position element nodes after position element node p according to fresh original corresponding elements using GM (1, 1), respectively.

Insert. Inserting the value of a position can be considered insertion of the corresponding elements and attributes. The position element whose attribute time is involved in the insertion should also be updated. In addition, the insertion of the positioning node affects the development functions of later position nodes because the development functions are generated by later position nodes. In that case, these development functions should be updated.

When position element p is inserted at time t:

- For the position element p whose time interval contains t ($t \in [T_s, T_e]$), the inserted element with the same name p and all its descendants (x, y, f_x, f_y) are appended after this position p.
- The time attributes of the inserted element and all its descendants are set to $[t, T_e]$.
- The time attributes of position element p and all its descendants are set to $[T_s, t-1]$.
- For the position elements after this position element p, again compute f_x and f_y according to the fresh original corresponding elements using GM (1, 1), respectively.

6 INTERPOLATIONS AND PREDICTIONS

In this section, we propose an approach to interpolating and predicting the positions of spatiotemporal data. Following the definition of the position part of the spatiotemporal XML model, the position of spatiotemporal data can be expressed as (x1, y1, fx1, fy1, T1), (x2, y2, fx2, fy2, T2), …, (xi, yi, fxi, fyi, Ti), …, (xn, yn, fxn, fyn, Tn), where xi and yi are coordinates along the x- and y-axis, and Ti is the time of the position as (xi, yi). The development functions, fxi and fyi, are the GM (1, 1) model generated from xi and yi, respectively.

Because the position contains two variables, it can be resolved into (x_1, f_{x1}, T_1), (x_2, f_{x2}, T_2), …, (x_i, f_{xi}, T_i), …, (x_n, f_{xn}, T_n) and (y_1, f_{y1}, T_1), (y_2, f_{y2}, T_2), …, (y_i, f_{yi}, T_i),…, (y_n, f_{yn}, T_n). When the position information at time t is needed, simply find i, which makes $t \in [T_{i-1}, T_i]$. Then, the interpolation is obtained as initial value $(x_{i-1}) + f_x(t)$ and initial value $(y_{i-1}) + f_y(t)$. The formula can also be used for the near-future prediction of the positions of spatiotemporal data. However, the prediction time length should be limited in $[T_m, T_m + r]$, where $r \leq \min(T_i - T_{i-1})$. The algorithm for interpolation and prediction in the spatiotemporal XML model using GM (1, 1) is described below.

Algorithm

Algorithm Grey_Estimate (o)

```
for (m = i; m <= i; m--)
let a_i = $o/../position/x/xval_i [@T_s = T_i]
let b_i = $o/../position/y/yval_i [@T_s = T_i]
Sequence_x () = add (a_i)
Sequence_y () = add(b_i)
end for
if Length (Sequence_x > 3) and Length (Sequence_y > 3)
Coefficient_x = Calculate_GM_Coeffcient (Sequence_x)
Coefficient_y = Calculate_GM_Coeffcient (Sequence_y)
Result_x = Estimate_at (Coefficient_x, Sequence_x, T_i)
Result_y = Estimate_at (Coefficient_y, Sequence_y, T_i)
end if
return Result_x
return Result_y
```

According to the algorithm *Grey_Estimate*, we can interpolate or predict the position of spatiotemporal data. The difference between interpolation and prediction is whether the time queried is between the time interval of recorded spatiotemporal data or after the maximum time point of recorded spatiotemporal data. In the process of interpolation or prediction, we should obtain the latest data on the position information. To employ the GM (1, 1) model, the latest data of the position should be more than three. The functions *Calculate_GM_Coeffcient* and *Estimate_at* generate the GM (1, 1) model from the sequence data and interpolate or predict the required value. Their algorithms can be designed from the arithmetic presented in Section 2; they are not addressed here on account of space constraints.

When we use the GM (1, 1) model, the latest data of the position information are required. According to definition 2, the latest data of *Sequence* () are obtained in reverse order (from recent time to distant-past time). In addition, the number of data in *Sequence* () is random according to actual needs and must be more than three. In other words, it is difficult to acquire the latest required data since the latest data are computed in reverse order. Consequently, we use two stacks to process the latest data so they are easily obtained, as shown in Figure 4.

Firstly, the required latest data produce a data stream $(x_1, \ldots, x_{i-1}, x_i)$. Stack processes the data stream. Hence, the recent data are located at the bottom of stack *a*, and the distant-past data are located at the top of stack *a*. Then, these data are extracted so that the data stream is transformed into $(x_i, x_{i-1}, \ldots, x_1)$. Finally, stack *b* processes the extracted data stream so that the distant-past data are located at the bottom of the stack, and the recent data are located at the top of the stack. After processing the two stacks, the latest data can be easily added to *Sequence* (), and it can guarantee that the latest data in *Sequence* () are ordered from the most recent time to the distant-past time.

Figure 4. Stacks for processing the most current data

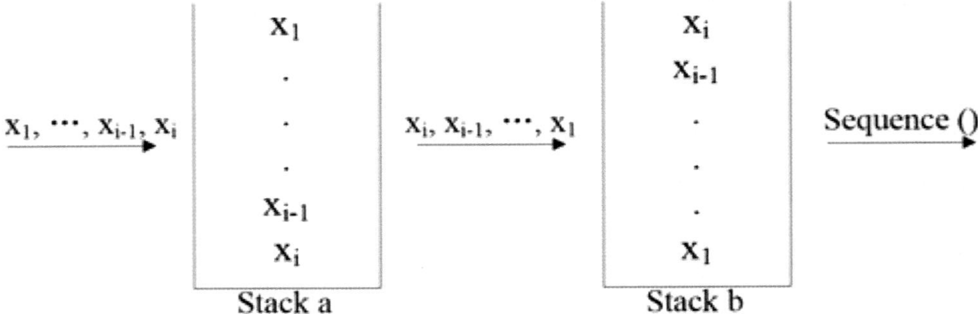

7 EXPERIMENTS

To evaluate the effectiveness of interpolation and prediction of spatiotemporal data based on XML integrated with the grey dynamic model, we evaluated the feasibility and accuracy using GM (1, 1). We compared its performance with that of GM (1, 1) based on MATLAB. The experiments were implemented in MATLAB 7.0.1 and Microsoft Visual C++ 6.0, and they were performed on a system with a 1.8-GHz Pentium IV processor, 1 GB RAM, and the Windows XP operating system.

7.1 Experimental Setup

Data set: The data set, shown in Figure 5, was from tropical storm data (Mufia, 2012). The left part of Figure 5 shows the track of the Muifa storm; the right part of Figure 5 displays data information on the Muifa storm containing the name, date, time (UT), latitude (degrees), longitude (degrees), course (true), speed (knots), pressure (mb), and wind (knots). Because interpolation and prediction of spatiotemporal data only address the position part, we extracted the latitude and longitude information of each time from the data set, which consisted of 60 data items. In the case of the generated AVL tree, there were 60 nodes, and the depth of the AVL tree was six. In other words, the generated AVL tree had six levels.

Experimental environment: The experimental environment was comprised of MATLAB 7.0.1 and Microsoft Visual C++ 6.0. In the MATLAB environment, we evaluated the effectiveness of the interpolation and prediction of storm tracking based on XML integrated with a grey dynamic model with the actual track. We considered the 60 time instants of the actual time as isomorphic to a natural number in the experiment. For a performance comparison, both experimental environments were used. Searching for the corresponding node in the AVL tree and reading its contents were evaluated in Microsoft Visual C++ 6.0, while generating the development function and computing the values of x and y were evaluated in MATLAB.

Figure 5. Data of Muifa storm tracking

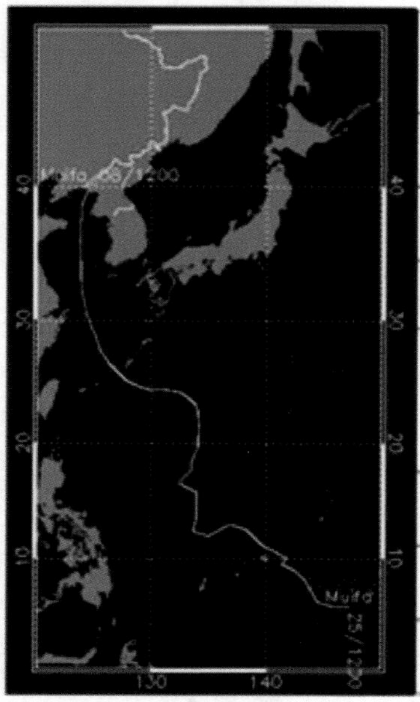

Name	Date	Time (UT)	Lat (degrees)	Lon (degrees)
Muifa	2011-07-25	12:00	5.6N	147.2E
Muifa	2011-07-25	18:00	5.7N	145.6E
Muifa	2011-07-26	00:00	6.1N	144.4E
⋮	⋮	⋮	⋮	⋮
Muifa	2011-08-09	00:00	43.2N	126.8E
Muifa	2011-08-09	12:00	45.4N	130.1E
Muifa	2011-08-10	00:00	47.0N	133.9E

7.2 Experimental Results

We compared the interpolation and prediction of spatiotemporal data based on XML integrated with the grey dynamic model to the interpolation and prediction in a normal environment over the above data set. To analyze the effectiveness of our proposed approach, we performed three groups of experiments. The first two experiments were performed to demonstrate the feasibility and accuracy of the proposed approach using GM (1, 1), and the last experiment was performed to demonstrate the performance advantages of our approach.

In the first group of experiments, we performed interpolation and prediction of Muifa storm tracking based on the spatiotemporal XML model integrated with GM (1, 1). Figure 6 shows the comparison between the actual track of the Muifa storm and the fitting storm tracked by the GM (1, 1) model. The solid curve represents the actual track of the Mufia storm; the dashed curve represents the fitting storm tracked by the GM (1, 1) model. As shown in Figure 6, a considerable deviation of the fitting storm track from the actual Mufia storm track is apparent. The deviation increases because all 60 data items are fitted in one time; thus, the deviation of the fitting track increases when the track tendency varies. However, the fitting track by GM (1, 1) still holds the holistic moving tendency and remains stable.

In the second group of experiments, we improved the fitting track by the GM (1, 1) model to reduce the deviation, as Figure 7 shows. As depicted in the figure, the solid curve represents the actual track of the storm; the dashed curve represents the fitting storm tracked by the GM (1, 1) model. The approach we used in this experiment involved dividing the 60 data items into 12 groups and generating the corresponding storm track, respectively. The improvement enabled the storm tracking to flexibly adjust to the actual storm track. In that case, Figure 6 shows the storm track with high indeterminacy; Figure 7 shows the storm track with low indeterminacy. It is observed that the latter performs better than the former.

Figure 6. Storm track with a high indeterminacy

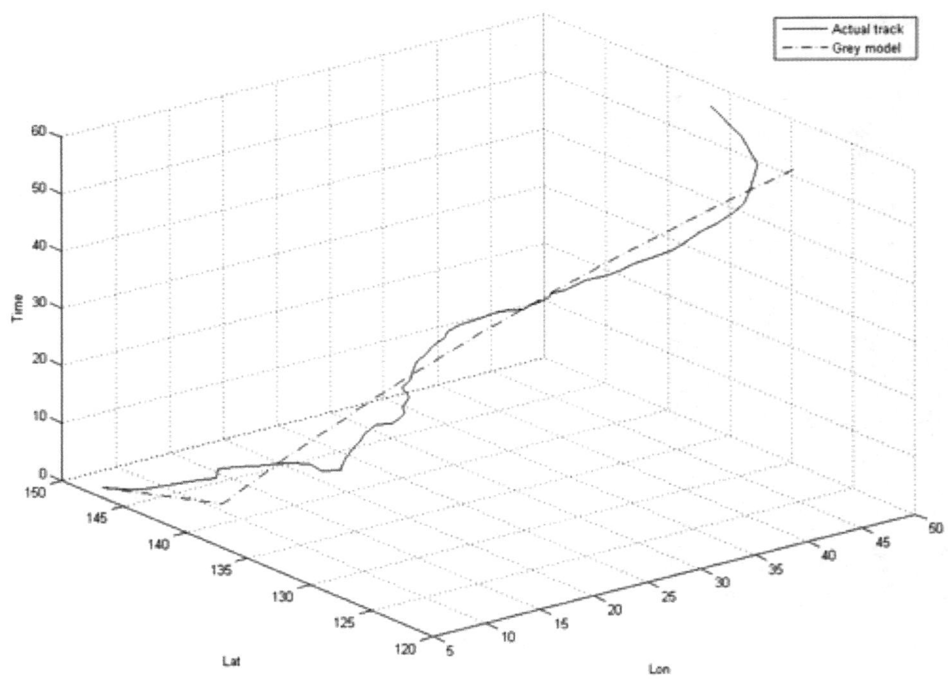

Figure 7. Storm track with low indeterminacy

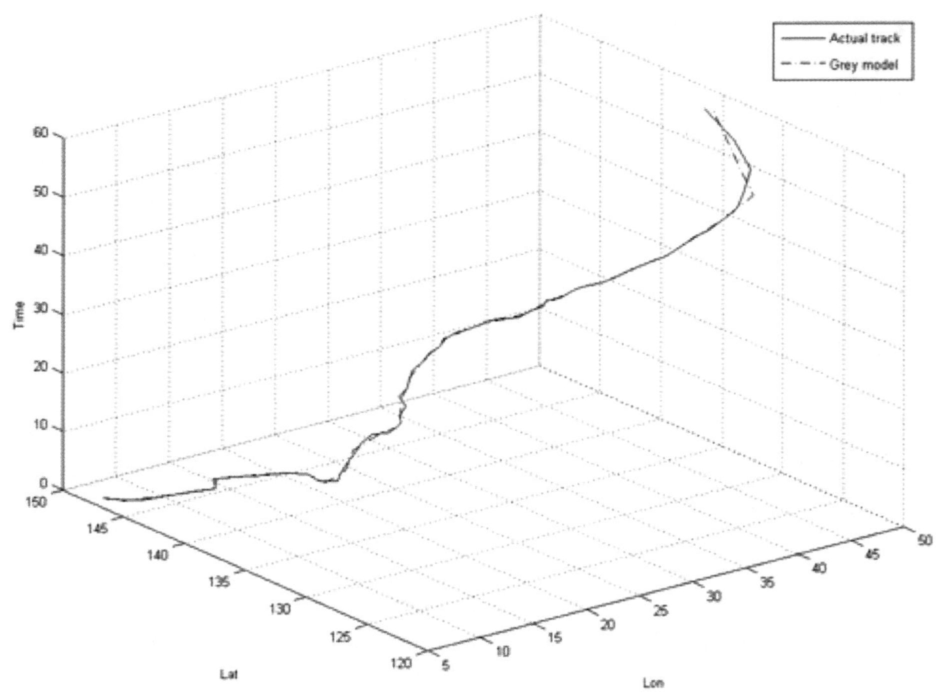

Finally, in the third group of experiments, we compared the performances. To this end, we evaluated the execution time and memory cost of interpolating and predicting the Muifa storm tracking based on XML integrated with the grey dynamic model (noted as GXML for simplicity), as well as the execution time of that in the relational databases (here we used MATLAB for the evaluation), as shown in Figures 8 and 9. Figure 8 shows the performance comparison between the execution times computed with GXML and MATLAB. We observe that the execution time of GXML increases slightly more than that in MATLAB in accordance with the increasing number of data items. The execution time of GXML is longer than that of MATLAB when the number of data items is small (less than approximately five data items), and the GXML execution time is less than that of MATLAB with an obvious increase in the difference over time. This can be explained by the fact that GXML first needs structural transforming; then, the position information can be directly extracted.

Figure 9 shows a memory cost comparison between GXML and MATLAB. It is observed that the memory cost of GXML is smaller than that of MATLAB. This can be explained by the fact that the memory costs not only depend on the cost size of the dataset, but also depend on the complexity of the approach. In our approach, after structural transformation, only the position nodes of the structural model should be considered.

Figure 8. Execution time comparison

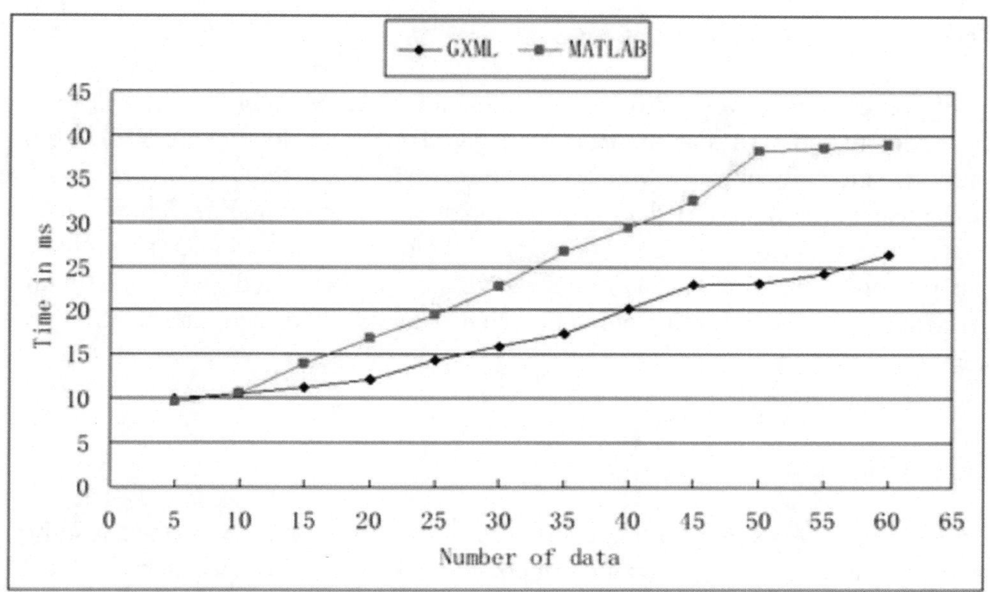

Figure 9. Memory cost comparison

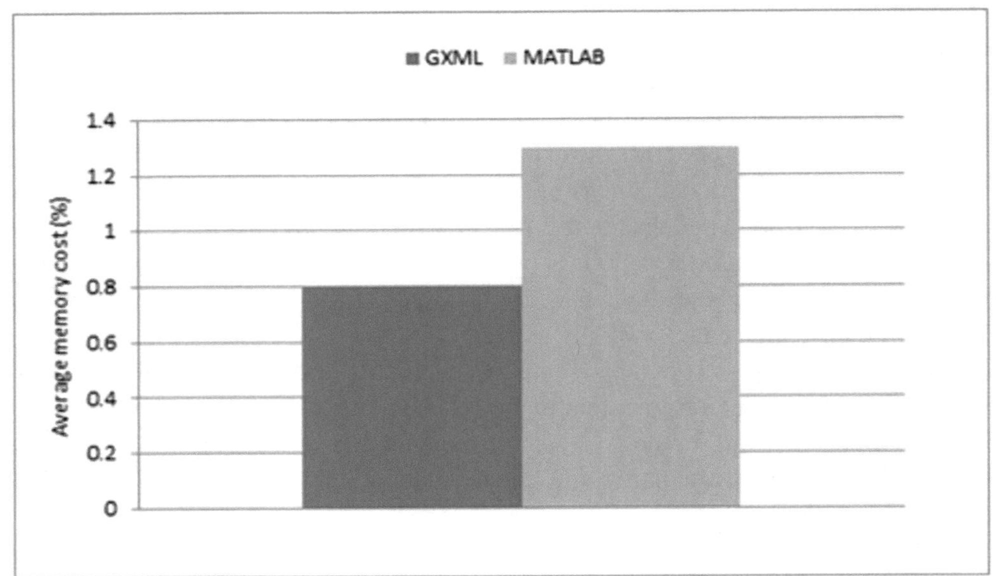

8 SUMMARY

To effectively process the interpolation and prediction of spatiotemporal data, a novel approach for interpolation and prediction of spatiotemporal data based on the spatiotemporal XML model integrated with the grey dynamic model was introduced in this chapter. We extracted the corresponding position information of each time interval from the position part of the proposed model. We then constructed an AVL tree to store them. After discussing change operations, we additionally presented an algorithm for interpolation and prediction based on the spatiotemporal XML model integrated with GM (1, 1). The experimental results showed that our approach efficiently performed interpolation and prediction of spatiotemporal data.

REFERENCES

Aburas, M. M., Ho, Y. M., Ramli, M. F., & Ash'aari, Z. H. (2017). Improving the capability of an integrated CA-Markov model to simulate spatio-temporal urban growth trends using an Analytical Hierarchy Process and Frequency Ratio. *International Journal of Applied Earth Observation and Geoinformation*, *59*, 65–78. doi:10.1016/j.jag.2017.03.006

Alamri, S., Taniar, D., & Safar, M. (2014). A taxonomy for moving object queries in spatial databases. *Future Generation Computer Systems*, *37*, 232–242. doi:10.1016/j.future.2014.02.007

Algergawy, A., Mesiti, M., Nayak, R., & Saake, G. (2011). XML data clustering: An overview. *ACM Computing Surveys*, *43*(1), 1–41. doi:10.1145/1978802.1978804

Bao, L., & Qin, X. (2005). The discrete representation of continuously moving indeterminate objects. *Chinese Journal of Aeronautics*, *18*(1), 59–64. doi:10.1016/S1000-9361(11)60283-5

Bao, L., Zhou, M., & Li, Q. (2006). A histogram-based grey estimator for spatiotemporal selective queries. In *Proceedings of the 5th International Conference on Machine Learning and Cybernetics* (pp. 325-329). IEEE. 10.1109/ICMLC.2006.259127

Belbaraka, M., & Stojmenović, I. (1994). On generating B-trees with constant average delay and in lexicographic order. *Information Processing Letters*, *49*(1), 27–32. doi:10.1016/0020-0190(94)90050-7

Blekas, K., Nikou, C., Galatsanos, N., & Tsekos, N. V. (2008). A regression mixture model with spatial constraints for clustering spatiotemporal data. *International Journal of Artificial Intelligence Tools*, *17*(06), 1023–1041. doi:10.1142/S0218213008004278

Choi, Y., & Chung, C. (2002). Selectivity estimation for spatio-temporal queries to moving objects. In *Proceedings of the ACM SIGMOD International Conference on Management of Data* (pp. 276-287). ACM. 10.1145/564691.564742

Claramunt, C., & Theriault, M. (1995). Managing time in GIS: an event-oriented approach. In *Proceedings of the International Workshop on Temporal Databases* (pp. 32-45). ACM. 10.1007/978-1-4471-3033-8_2

Dobra, A., Garofalakis, M., Gehrke, J., & Rastogi, R. (2004). Sketch-based multi-query processing over data streams. *Lecture Notes in Computer Science*, *2992*, 621–622. doi:10.1007/978-3-540-24741-8_32

Guo, L. (2013). Pioneering GML deployment for NSDI—Case study of USTIGER/GML. *ISPRS International Journal of Geo-Information*, *2*(2), 82–93. doi:10.3390/ijgi2010082

Güting, R. H., Behr, T., & Xu, J. (2010). Efficient k-nearest neighbor search on moving object trajectories. *The VLDB Journal*, *19*(6), 687–714. doi:10.100700778-010-0185-7

Hadjieleftheriou, M., Kollios, G., & Tsotras, V. (2003). Performance evaluation of spatio-temporal selectivity estimation techniques. In *Proceedings of the 15th International Conference on Scientific and Statistical Database Management* (pp. 207-216). IEEE. 10.1109/SSDM.2003.1214981

Hallot, P., & Billen, R. (2016). Enhancing spatio-temporal identity: States of existence and presence. *ISPRS International Journal of Geo-Information*, *5*(5), 62. doi:10.3390/ijgi5050062

Jadidi, A., Mostafavi, M. A., Bédard, Y., & Shahriari, K. (2014). Spatial representation of coastal risk: A fuzzy approach to deal with uncertainty. *ISPRS International Journal of Geo-Information*, *3*(3), 1077–1100. doi:10.3390/ijgi3031077

Kayacan, E., Ulutas, B., & Kaynak, O. (2010). Grey system theory-based models in time series prediction. *Expert Systems with Applications*, *37*(2), 1784–1789. doi:10.1016/j.eswa.2009.07.064

Langran, G. (1989). A review of temporal database research and its use in GIS applications. *International Journal of Geographical Information Systems*, *3*(1), 215–232. doi:10.1080/02693798908941509

Liu, S., & Lin, Y. (1998). *An Introduction to Grey Systems: Foundations, Methodology and Applications*. Emerald Publishing Limited.

Ma, Z. M., Liu, J., & Li, Y. (2010). Fuzzy data modeling and algebraic operations in XML. *International Journal of Intelligent Systems*, *25*(9), 925–947. doi:10.1002/int.20424

Mendelzon, A. O., Rizzolo, F., & Vaisman, A. (2004). Indexing temporal XML documents. In *Proceedings of the Thirtieth international conference on Very large data bases-Volume 30* (pp. 216-227). IEEE.

Nalica, A. D. (2010). Spatial-Temporal Modeling of Growth in Rice Production in the Philippines. *The Philippine Statistician*, *59*, 15–25.

Peuquet, D., & Duan, N. (1995). An event-based spatiotemporal data model for temporal analysis of geographical data. *International Journal of Geographical Information Systems*, *9*(1), 7–24. doi:10.1080/02693799508902022

Seqev, A., & Shoshani, A. (1987). Logical modeling of temporal data. In *Proceedings of the ACM SIGMOD International Conference on Management of Data* (pp. 114-121). IEEE.

Sistla, A. P., Wolfson, O., Chamberlain, S., & Dao, S. (1997). Modeling and querying moving objects. In *Proceedings of the 13th International Conference on Data Engineering* (pp. 422-431). IEEE. 10.1109/ICDE.1997.581973

Sun, J., Papadias, D., Tao, Y., & Liu, B. (2004). Querying about the past, the present, and the future in spatio-temporal databases. In *Proceedings of the 20th International Conference on Data Engineering* (pp. 433-444). IEEE. 10.1109/ICDE.2004.1319997

Tao, Y., Kollios, G., Considine, J., Li, F., & Papadias, D. (2004). Spatio-temporal aggregation using sketches. In *Proceedings of the 20th International Conference on Data Engineering* (pp. 632-643). IEEE.

Tøssebro, E., & Güting, R. H. (2001). Creating representations for continuously moving regions from observations. In *Proceedings of the 7th International Symposium on Spatial and Temporal Databases* (pp. 158-175). ACM. 10.1007/3-540-47724-1_17

Tryfona, N., & Jensen, C. S. (1999). Conceptual data modeling for spatiotemporal applications. *GeoInformatica*, *3*(3), 245–268. doi:10.1023/A:1009801415799

Wolfson, O. (1998). Querying the uncertain position of moving objects. *Lecture Notes in Computer Science*, *1399*, 310–337. doi:10.1007/BFb0053708

Wu, Y., Agrawal, D., & Abbadi, A. (2001). Applying the golden rule of sampling for query estimation. In *Proceedings of the ACM SIGMOD International Conference on Management of Data* (pp. 325-336). ACM. 10.1145/375663.375724

Yu, H. (2006). Spatio-temporal GIS design for exploring interactions of human activities. *Cartography and Geographic Information Science*, *33*(1), 3–19. doi:10.1559/152304006777323136

Chapter 12
Keyword Coupling Query of Spatiotemporal XML Data

ABSTRACT

With the increasing popularity of XML for data representations, there is a lot of interest in keyword query on XML. Many algorithms have been proposed for XML keyword queries. But the existing approaches fall short in their abilities to analyze the logical relationship between keywords of spatiotemporal data. To overcome this limitation, in this chapter, the authors first propose the concept of query time series (QTS) according to the data revision degree. For the logical relationship of keywords in QTS, the authors study the intra-coupling logic relationship and the inter-coupling logic relationship separately. Then a calculation method of keyword similarity is proposed and the best parameter in the method is found through experiment. Finally, the authors compare this method with others. Experimental results show that this method is superior to previous approaches.

1 INTRODUCTION

The Extensible Markup Language (XML) has evolved to be a paradigm for data exchange over the network since its foundation in 1998 (An et al., 2005). XML is perceived as an adaptable hierarchical model that is appropriate to communicate a large amount of data without a rigid structure (Ahuja & Gadicha, 2014). Hence, the ability to acquire knowledge from XML documents for decision support is certainly optimistic and it has been dominant format used on the web (Ahuja & Gadicha, 2014). Besides, XML's self-describing property enables XML to represent data without losing its semantics information (Chang & Chen, 2012).

Keyword query on XML document has received wide attention. The query semantics and algorithms of keyword queries on XML documents have been extensively studied in the literature (Bhalotia et al., 2002; Chang & Chen, 2012; Cost & Salzberg, 1993; Deerwester et al., 1990; Guo et al., 2003; Hristidis et al., 2006; Hristidis & Papakonstantinou, 2002; Hu & Hammad, 2005; Kong et al., 2009; Li et al., 2007; Li et al., 2009; Li et al., 2012; Li et al., 2004; Wang & Aggarwal, 2010; Chen et al., 2009; Tian et al., 2011). The keyword search semantics on XML documents are mainly focused on the Lowest com-

DOI: 10.4018/978-1-6684-9108-9.ch012

mon ancestor (LCA) based semantics, including the LCA semantics and its variants (Cost & Salzberg, 1993; Hristidis et al., 2006; Hristidis & Papakonstantinou, 2002; Li et al., 2009; Li et al., 2012; Li et al., 2004) to improve the search quality. In (Xu & Papakonstantinou, 2005), Xu and Papakonstantinou propose the SLCA semantics for keyword query processing on XML documents, and therefore two algorithms are presented. Guo et al. (Guo et al., 2003) introduce an ELCA (Exclusive lowest common ancestor) semantics to the keyword queries on XML documents, and an efficient algorithm named Indexed Stack for keyword queries on XML documents with the ELCA semantics is presented in (Xu & Papakonstantinou, 2008). The Valuable Lowest Common Ancestor (VLCA) semantics is proposed by (Li et al., 2007) to answer keyword queries effectively, which not only improves the accuracy of LCAs by eliminating redundant LCAs that should not contribute to the answer but also retrieves the false negatives filtered out wrongly by SLCA. Sun et al. (Sun et al., 2007) propose a Multiway SLCA (MSLCA) semantics to support the keyword search both in AND and OR Boolean operators, and two algorithms named basic multiway-SLCA (BMS) and incremental multiway-SLCA (IMS) are presented. Literature (Li & M, 2018) proposes a structure-based approach to keyword querying for XML data, which combines the structure query language into the keyword query over XML to get more meaningful and comprehensive results. Literature (Hu & Hammad, 2005) uses indexes to improve the performance of the query engines for XML data.

There have been many achievements in terms of capturing the keyword relationship based on XML documents. The Generalized Vector Space Model (GVSM) (Wong et al., 1985) and the Context Vector Model (CVM-VSM) (Billhardt et al., 2002) use the co-occurrence information between the terms in the document to capture each other mutual relations. Latent semantic indexing (LSI) proposed by (Deerwester et al., 1990) uses the projection feature step to estimate the similarity between documents, which captures the semantic information of the keywords in the original document. Compared with traditional bag-of-words (BOW), these models have made some improvements. However, these models only consider the co-occurrence frequency of words, ignoring the implicit relationship between words. Hristidis V (Hristidis & Papakonstantinou, 2002) proves that the coupling relationship is very effective for capturing implicit relationships in machine learning and data mining tasks (such as clustering and document analysis). Cost and Salzberg (Cost & Salzberg, 1993) propose MVDM based on labels, while Wilson and Martinez (Wilson & Martinez, 1997) study heterogeneous distances for instance-based learning. The measures in their study are only designed for supervised approaches. Wang and Tao (Wang et al., 2011) have proposed a novel coupled object similarity metric called Coupled Object Similarity (COS), which involves both attribute value frequency distribution (intra-coupling) and feature dependency aggregation(inter-coupling) in measuring attribute value similarity for unsupervised learning of nominal data. Wang and Dong(Wang et al., 2015) propose a coupled attribute similarity for objects (CASO) measure based on the coupled attribute similarity for values (CASV), by considering both the intra-coupled and inter-coupled attribute value similarities (IaASV and IeASV), which globally capture the attribute value frequency distribution and feature dependency aggregation.

The contributions of this chapter are the following:

- We propose the concept of QTS and data revision degree. QTS segmentation algorithm is proposed based on the data revision degree to analyze the coupling relationship of keywords.
- We propose a calculation method for keyword coupled similarity, combining intra-coupling and inter-coupling relationships.

The rest of the chapter is organized as follows. Section 2 devises a spatiotemporal data model based on XML. The framework is presented in Section 3. Section 4 proposes the QTS segmentation algorithm. The keyword coupled similarity is proposed based on time series in Section 5. Experimental evaluation is given in Section 6 and Section 7 concludes the chapter.

2 SPATIOTEMPORAL DATA MODEL BASED ON XML

According to the characteristics of spatiotemporal data, the concept of spatiotemporal data model based on XML is introduced in this section. The Model is based on literature (Cheng, 2016).

Definition 1(spatiotemporal data model) The spatiotemporal data model is represented by a 5-tuple SP= (OID, ATTR, P, T, M) where

- *OID* is the changing history of a spatiotemporal object;
- *ATTR* is the attributes of a spatiotemporal object;
- *P* is the position of a spatiotemporal object;
- *T* is the time of a spatiotemporal object;
- *M* is the motion of a spatiotemporal object.

Definition 2(changing history) The changing history of a spatiotemporal object is represented by a 4-tuple OID= (type, pre, suc, t_{change}) where

- *type* is the type of change in spatiotemporal objects;
- *pre* is the predecessor in a changing process;
- *suc* is the successor in a changing process;
- t_{change} is the time of a changing process.

Definition 3(attribute) The attributes of a spatiotemporal object is represented by a 3-tuple ATTR= (genAt, spAt, t_{valid}) where

- *genAt* is the general attribute of a spatiotemporal object;
- *spaAt* is the spatial attribute of a spatiotemporal object;
- t_{valid} is the valid time for *spaAt* of a spatiotemporal object.

Example 1: In Figure 1, it describes cloud *A* moves to *B* and then splits into *C* and *D*.

ATTR= ({name,color}, {size}, t_1–t_0) denotes some attributes of the cloud *A* within the time t_1–t_0, where name and color are general attributes, size is the spatial attribute. OID= (split, {B}, {C,D}, t_2–t_1) reflects the changing history of the cloud *A* where *B* is the *predecessor*, *C* and *D* are the *successors* and the change happened in time interval t_2–t_1. For cloud *A*, the position information *P* is represented as [(90°E,120°W),30m] and *T* records the time at position *P*. *M* records the *direction* and *value* when cloud *A* changes.

3 FRAMEWORK

In order to analyze the relationship between keywords and return accurate query results, this section proposes a two-step processing approach to address this problem. The framework of keyword query and result sort of spatiotemporal data is shown in Figure 2.

The first step is to calculate the coupling relationship between different keywords during the offline time. Firstly, an XML document tree is constructed using keywords extracted from query history. Then use the correlation analysis method to obtain the coupling relationship between different keywords. Finally, select typical queries from the query history based on the coupling relationship to form a query set.

The second step is to process the user's query and return results during the online time. The spatiotemporal data in traditional databases is represented by XML document tree in advance to facilitate the processing of queries. A query sentence is divided into many keywords. Then the semantic similarity between the user query and the typical query is calculated according to the keyword coupling relationship. Finally, the first *k* relevant results are presented to the user.

Figure 1. Schematic diagram of space-time objects

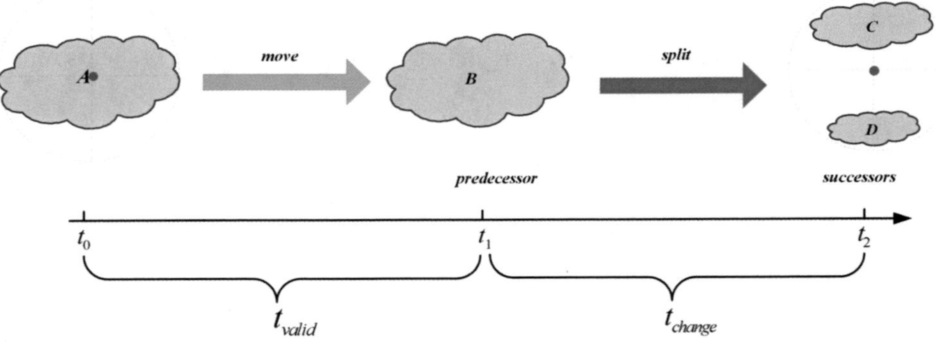

Figure 2. The framework of keyword query and result sort of spatiotemporal data

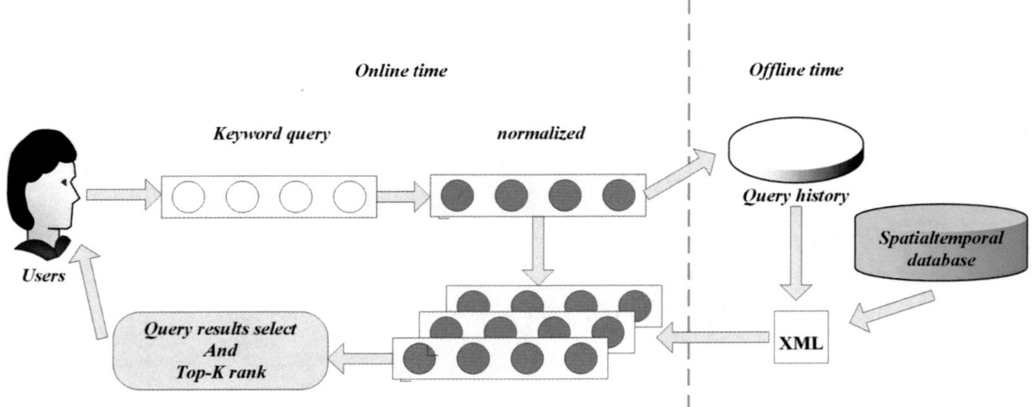

4 KEYWORD TIME SERIES OF SPATIOTEMPORAL QUERY

In this section, we first propose the QTS to describe a series of query requests by the user. Then we put forward the concept of data revision degree. Finally, a time series segmentation algorithm is proposed based on data revision degree. The work in this section provides a theoretical foundation for analyzing the coupling relationship of keywords.

4.1 Query Time Series (QTS)

A query process includes many query operations (named subqueries). For explaining the changes of subqueries intuitively, we propose the following definitions.

Definition 4(time series) $T=[t_0,t_1,\&,t_{n-1}]$ denotes a time series containing *n* observations in chronological order, where *t* denotes observations at equal time interval points.

Definition 5(keyword QTS) $Q^T=\left[q^{t_0},q^{t_1},\&,q^{t_{n-1}}\right]$ denotes the keyword QTS containing *n* queries. $q=(k_0,k_1,\&,k_{n-1})$ where k_i denotes the ith keyword in the query.

Example 2: Firefighters request regular updates of temperature maps within a mile radius to keep alert for surrounding fires. The firefighters make the following three queries at t_1, t_2 and t_3 respectively.

q_1: (temperature, 10:28, 200m^2)
q_2: (temperature, 10:31, 160m^2)
q_3: (temperature, 10:35, 120m^2)

In this example, the time series is $T=[t_1,t_2,t_3]$. q_1, q_2, and q_3 have the same query object temperature, and the query range is more and more accurate (from 200m^2 to 120m^2). The keyword QTS of this query process is expressed as follows:

$$Q^T=\begin{bmatrix}(\text{temperature, 10:28,200m}^2),\\(\text{temperature, 10:31,160m}^2),\\(\text{temperature, 10:35,120m}^2)\end{bmatrix}$$

4.2 Data Revision Degree

During the query process, the spatiotemporal data will change with time, which affects the query results. In order to measure the change in spatiotemporal data, we define the revision of data updates.

Definition 6(data revision degree)

$=(1-\rho)\times\varphi+\rho\times\phi$ denotes the data revision degree, where φ represents the variation in the attributes, ϕ indicates the variation in the entity movement and ρ is a weight between 0 and 1.

The process of data revision degree calculation is shown in Figure 3. For time interval $\left[t_{n-2}, t_n\right]$, the current state of the object changes with the update of the position, and the latest state of the object is defined as the state at the end of the last time interval. Based on this theory, time changes in space points and regions $t \rightarrow \left[t_{n-2}, t_n\right]$ is replaced with $t \rightarrow t_n$. For spatial changes, we use minimum covering circle (MCC) in Figure 3 to explain. There are two types of spatial changes: entity movement and attribute changes. For the first type, the position change is the position change of the MCC center approximately, which is measured by Euclidean distance $\phi=\left|\overrightarrow{O_{pre}O'_{suc}}\right|$. O_{pre} is the center of the state before the change, O'_{suc} represents the center of the state after the change. The second type, attribute changes, it divided into two aspects *genAt* and *spaAt*. *genAt* is an ignorable static variable. For *spaAt*, it includes the types of changes on an entity, including creation, elimination, splitting, merging, expansion, contraction, retention, and conversion. The change in the MCC area indicates the change in attributes which denotes as $\varphi=\frac{S_{suc}}{S_{pre}}$, where S_{pre} and S_{suc} are the MCC area before and after change respectively.

Combining the two aspects, the data revision degree is defined as

$$_{t_1\rightarrow[t_{n-2},t_n]}=(1-\rho)\times\varphi_{t_1\rightarrow t_n}+\rho\times\phi_{t_1\rightarrow t_n}$$

where $t_1 \rightarrow [t_{n-2}, t_n]$ denotes that the data revision process is from time point t_1 to time interval $[t_{n-2}, t_n]$. For time intervals, the target object is always the latest state at ending instant of the interval and the process can be replaced by $t_1 \rightarrow t_n$.

Algorithm

ALGORITHM 1 QTS SEGMENTATION

Input: QTS Q^T, weight ρ, threshold ℓ.

Output: $Q_1^T, Q_2^T, \cdots, Q_m^T (m \geq 1)$

```
k ← 1
t_start ← 1
t_end ← n
for i from t_start to t_end do
j ← i+1
w_[i-1][j-1] ← 0
t_i→t_j ← (1-ρ)×φ_{t_i→t_j} + ρ×ϕ_{t_i→t_j}
w_[i][j] ← w_[i-1][j-1] + t_i→t_j
if w_[i][j] ≤ ℓ then
i ← i+1
else
Q_k^T ← Q_k^T − {q_j, q_{j+1}, ···, q_n}
Q_{k+1}^T ← {q_j, q_{j+1}, ···, q_n}
segment (Q_{k+1}^T, ℓ, j, n)
end for
return Q_1^T, Q_2^T, ···, Q_m^T (m ≥ 1)
```

Figure 3. Data revision degree calculation

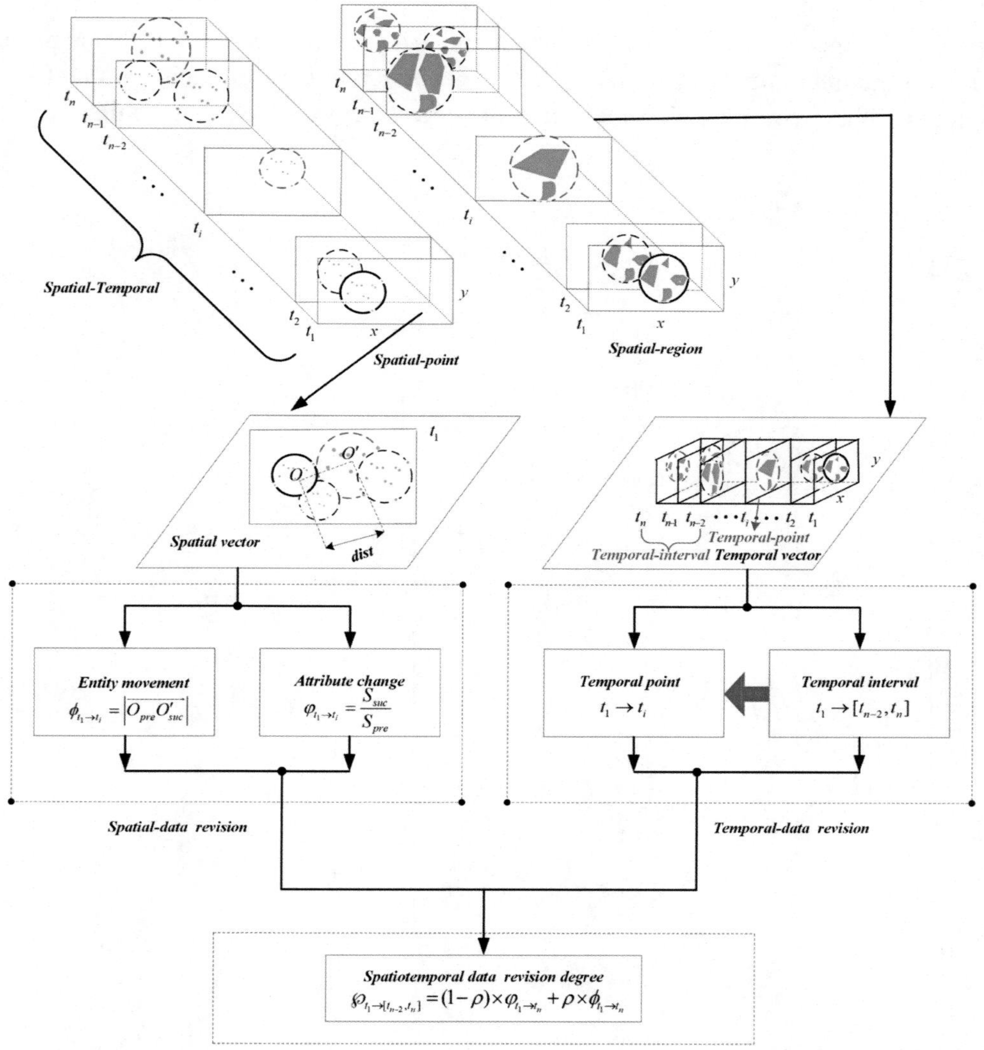

4.3 QTS Segmentation Algorithm

In actual query process, the query series is updated dynamically, which is measured by the degree of data revision. The algorithm is proposed to segment the updated QTS. The pseudo code of the algorithm is described as follows

For each query Q, initialize the parameters first (line 1-3). Then a mark w indicates the degree of data revision between Q and the previous query (line 4-8). The QTS are segmented when w exceed the revision threshold ℓ (line 12-15). Figure 4 shows the process of the segmentation algorithm. For the different revisions of the query history, the QTS is re-segmentation, which affects the coupling relationship between keywords in the QTS. The coupling relationship between keywords is discussed in the next section.

5 COUPLING ANALYSIS OF KEYWORDS IN TIME SERIES

In this section, we first propose the intra coupling similarity for the keywords in the same query. Then we put forward the inter coupling similarity for the keywords in different queries. Finally, combining intra coupling and inter coupling, the calculation method of keyword coupling similarity is proposed.

Figure 4. The process of the segmentation algorithm

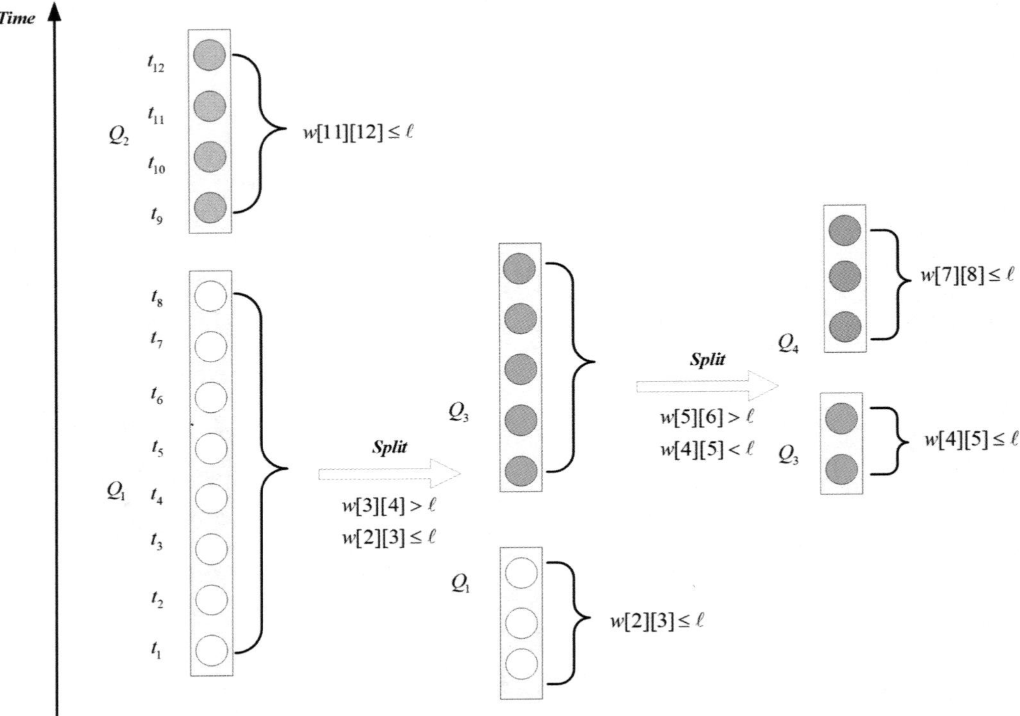

5.1 Intra-Coupling of Spatiotemporal Keywords Within a Query

The user's query activity is recorded in the time series, and the user's query intent can be clarified by analyzing the similarity between keywords in the time series. We use the *Jac* coefficient to evaluate the co-occurrence frequency of two keywords in the same time series. The formula is described as follows

$$\mathrm{Jac}(p,q)\begin{cases} 0 & |W(p)\cap W(q)| < \beta \\ \dfrac{|W(p)\cap W(q)|}{|W(p)\cup W(q)|} & |W(p)\cap W(q)| \ge \beta \end{cases}$$

where *w(p)* represents the query set where the keyword *p* is located, *w(q)* represents the query set where the keyword *q* is located, and β is a threshold given by the user.

Keywords *p* and *q* are intra-related if they are *Sibling relationship (SR)* in query history XML document V_j. The *intra-similarity* (*IaS*) between *p* and *q* is quantified as follows

$$\delta_{IaS}(p,q|Q) = Jac(p,q)$$

where *Q* denotes the common parent of them. As is shown in Figure 6, $keyword_1$ and $keyword_3$ have the common parent $Query_1^{t0}$, so the $keyword_1$ and $keyword_3$ have intra-coupling similarity. The intra-coupling relationship of keywords is represented by the solid blue line in the Figure 5(a).

5.2 Inter-Coupling of Spatiotemporal Keywords Across Queries

Intra-coupling relationships can only reflect the similarity of keywords in the same query, for the similarity of keywords in different queries, we propose the concept of inter-coupling. Some keywords are co-related with each other even though they are not in the same query. As shown in Figure 7, $keyword_1$ and $keyword_4$ belong to $Query_1^{t0}$ and $Query_2^{t0}$ respectively and $keyword_3$ belongs to both $Query_1^{t0}$ and $Query_2^{t0}$. $keyword_1$ and $keyword_4$ are connected $keyword_3$. This connection is defined as inter-coupling. The strength of the connection(*inter-similarity*) is calculated by the following formula

$$\delta^{j}_{IeS}(k_1,k_2|k_3)=\min\{\delta^{J}_{IaS}(k_1,k_3),\delta^{j}_{IaS}(k_2,k_3)\}$$

where $\delta^{J}_{IaS}(k_1,k_3)$ is the *intra-similarity* between $keyword_1$ and $keyword_3$, $\delta^{j}_{IaS}(k_2,k_3)$ is the *intra-similarity* between $keyword_2$ and $keyword_3$. The inter-coupling relationship of keywords is represented by the red dotted line in the Figure 5(b).

Figure 5. Intra-coupling and inter-coupling

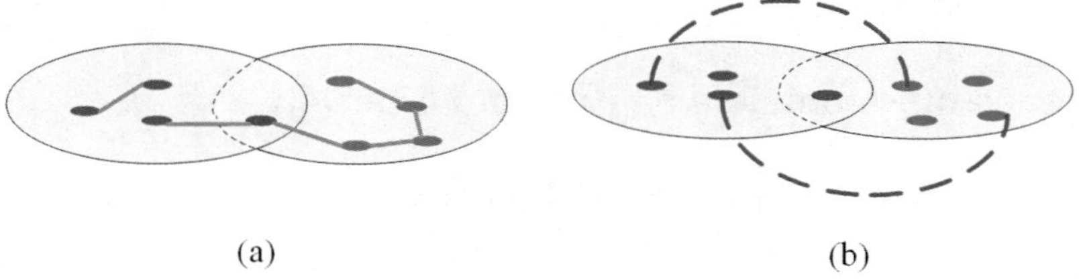

5.3 Keyword Coupled Similarity

The coupling relationship between keywords needs to consider intra coupling and inter coupling comprehensively. The keyword coupling similarity is defined as following

$$\delta_{KCS}^{j}(p,q)=\begin{cases} 1 & p=q \\ \alpha \cdot \delta_{IaS}^{j}(p,q)+(1-\alpha)\cdot \delta_{IeS}^{j}(p,q) & p \neq q \end{cases}$$

where $\delta_{IaS}^{j}(p,q)$ and $\delta_{IeS}^{j}(p,q)$ denote the intra and inter coupling between keyword *p* and *q* respectively. α is a weight between 0 and 1. $\delta_{KCS}^{j}(p,q)=0$ indicates that the keywords *p* and *q* are completely different, $\delta_{KCS}^{j}(p,q)=1$ indicates the keywords *p* and *q* are same. The relevance of the two keywords is positively correlated with $\delta_{KCS}^{j}(p,q)$.

6 EXPERIMENT

6.1 Experimental Setup

The experiments are carried out on a computer running Windows10 with Intel Core i5-1.9 GHz CPU, 8 GB RAM. We implement all the algorithms in (Python 3.7).

The experiments use two different datasets. The first dataset NHDB is a large database of hotel information in the United States, which includes the location, business hours, reviews, and nature of the hotel. We use these attributes to simulate spatiotemporal datasets. The 3000 records are generated as historical queries. The second dataset is DBLP, which is a data set designed in XML format. We selected attributes such as author, paper name, writing, and publisher to construct an XML document tree, and 2568 records are generated.

To present evaluations of our approach, we performed two groups of experiments. In the first group of experiments, the impact of the value of α on keyword coupled similarity is tested. In the second group of experiments, we compare KQ algorithm with V-COS algorithm and random approach in terms of accuracy rate and recall rate to evaluate the effectiveness.

6.2 Experimental Results

6.2.1 The Influence of Parameters on Keyword Similarity

This group of experiment aims at testing the impact of the weight α on the similarity of keywords in terms of *Precision* (formula 1) and *Recall* (formula 2). We first randomly select 10 keywords from NHDB and DBLP. For each keyword, set the weight α from 0 to 1 in increments of 0.1. Under each weight, the keyword coupling algorithm gets top-10 related keywords. Then mix these keywords to form a set containing 110 keywords. Next, we calculate the frequency of each different keyword in the set.

Finally, sort the results in descending order and select top-10 as the relevant keywords.

$$\text{Precision} = \frac{\text{relevant keywords}}{\text{retrieved keywords}} \tag{1}$$

$$\text{Recall} = \frac{\text{relevant keywords}}{\text{keywords marked as relevant}} \tag{2}$$

Figure 10 shows the results under NHDB and DBLP datasets. In order to simplify the research process, we set the number of retrieved keywords and keywords marked as relevant to be 10, so that the precision rate and the recall rate are equal. For the NHDB and DBLP databases, the precision and recall are 0.87 and 0.82 when α=0.4 and α=0.5 respectively, which represents the highest performance of our algorithm. In addition, the max precision and recall of NHDB are higher than DBLP, indicating that we can get better performance when we treat time and space keywords as the spatiotemporal attributes of the query XML tree instead of ordinary attributes.

Figure 6. Intra-coupling XML tree

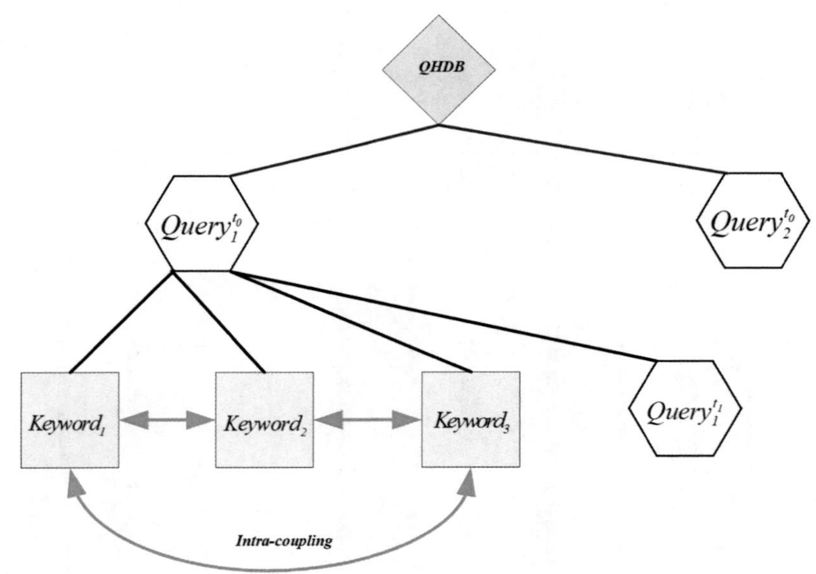

Figure 7. Inter-coupling XML tree

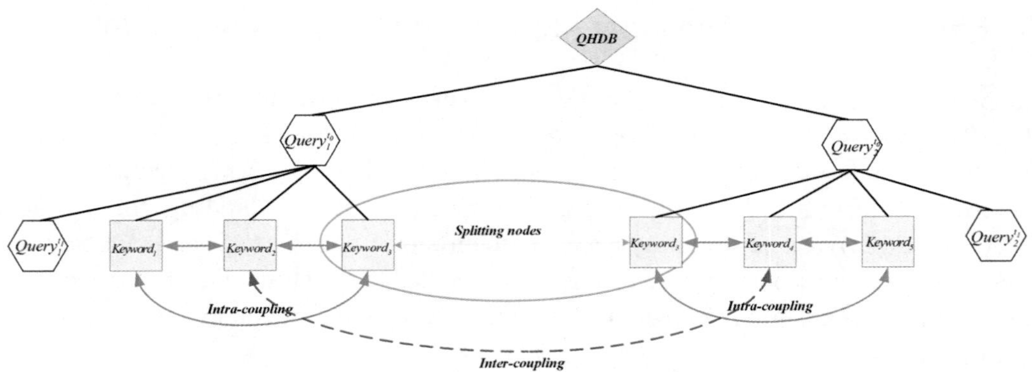

Figure 8. The precision of three algorithms

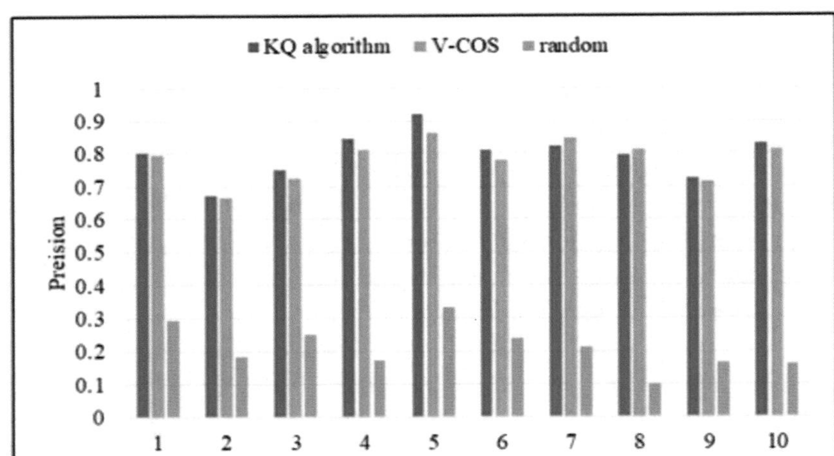

Figure 9. The recall of three algorithms

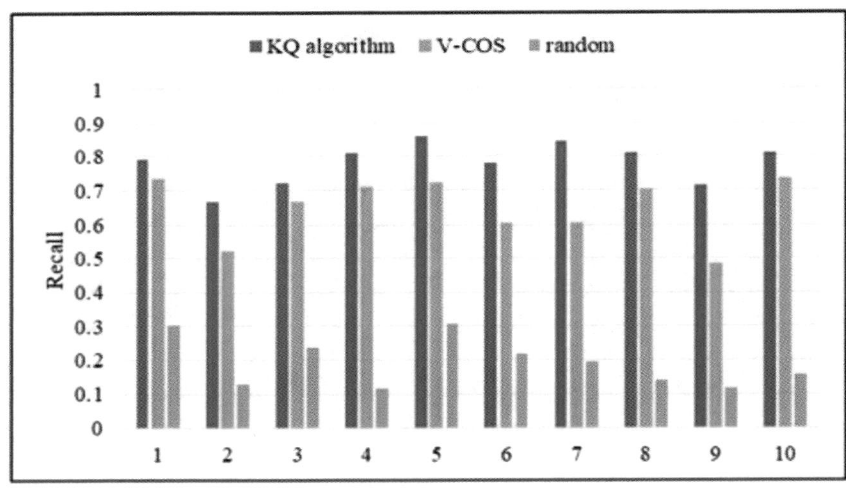

6.3 The Effectiveness of Similarity Algorithm of Spatiotemporal Data

This group of experiment aims to evaluate the effectiveness of the similarity algorithm of spatiotemporal data. The precision and are recall used to evaluate the effectiveness. Firstly, 10 users randomly select query Q_i from the NHDB query history. For each selected query, a set K_i containing 30 queries is generated from the query history. The queries in the set are generated by three algorithms: data revision degree (KQ algorithm), cosine similarity based on traditional VSM (V-COS) and random (as a benchmark experiment). Then each user marks the top 10 queries that they think are semantically relevant in K_i. Finally, the matching degree between the query marked by the user and the query returned by each algorithm is calculated.

Figure 10. Recall and precision under different weights

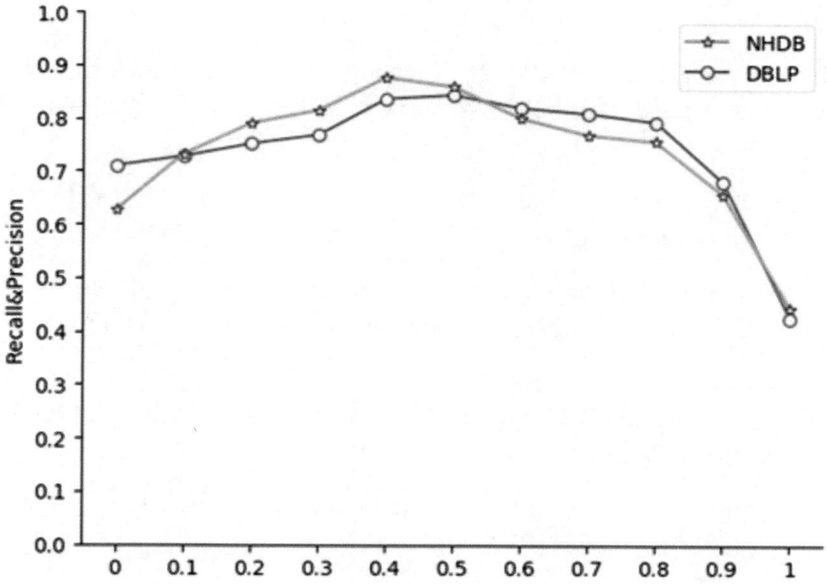

The experimental results are shown in Figure 8 and Figure 9. For algorithm in this chapter, the average precision and recall are 0.798 and 0.782 respectively. For the V-COS algorithm, the precision and recall averages are 0.609 and 0.652 respectively. For random queries, the rates are 0.211 and 0.191 respectively. Our algorithm is higher than the V-COS algorithm and the benchmark algorithm in terms of precision and recall. V-COS algorithm takes the local overlapping information between queries into account, which makes its recall rate relatively high. Our algorithm can adapt to the changes of time attribute and space attribute, and divide the time series in time through the segmentation algorithm when querying.

7 SUMMARY

In this chapter, we study the problem of keyword querying on XML data. We firstly introduce the spatiotemporal data model based on XML to support our research. Then we propose a QTS segmentation algorithm based on data revision degree. For analyzing the relationship between keywords in the QTS, we propose the keyword coupled similarity. Experimental results confirm the efficiency of our approach.

REFERENCES

Ahuja, A. G., & Gadicha, A. B. (2014). Answering XML query using tree based association rule. *International Journal of Applied Innovation in Engineering & Management*, *3*(3), 143–146.

An, Y., Borgida, A., & Mylopoulos, J. (2005). Constructing complex semantic mappings between XML data and ontologies. In *Proceedings of the International Semantic Web Conference* (pp. 6-20). ACM. 10.1007/11574620_4

Bhalotia, G., Nakhe, C., & Hulgeri, A. (2002). Keyword searching and browsing in databases using BANKS. In *Proceedings of the 18th Conference on Data Engineering* (pp. 431–440). IEEE. 10.1109/ICDE.2002.994756

Billhardt, H., Borrajo, D., & Maojo, V. (2002). A context vector model for information retrieval. *Journal of the Association for Information Science and Technology*, *53*(3), 236–249.

Chang, T. P., & Chen, S. Y. (2012). An efficient algorithm of frequent XML query pattern mining for ebXML applications in E-commerce. *Expert Systems with Applications*, *39*(2), 2183–2193. doi:10.1016/j.eswa.2011.07.011

Chen, Y., Wang, W., Liu, Z., & Lin, X. (2009). Keyword search on structured and semi-structured data. In SIGMOD. doi:10.1145/1559845.1559966

Cheng, H. (2016). Modeling and querying fuzzy spatiotemporal objects. *Journal of Intelligent & Fuzzy Systems*, *31*(6), 2851–2858. doi:10.3233/JIFS-169167

Cohen, S., Mamou, J., Kanza, Y., & Sagiv, Y. (2003). XSEarch: a semantic search engine for XML. In *Proceedings of the 29th International Conference on Very Large Data Bases* (pp. 45-46). ACM.

Cost, S., & Salzberg, S. (1993). A weighted nearest neighbor algorithm for learning with symbolic features. *Machine Learning*, *10*(1), 57–78. doi:10.1007/BF00993481

Deerwester, S., Dumais, S., Furnas, G., Landauer, T. K., & Harshman, R. (1990). Indexing by latent semantic analysis. *Journal of the American Society for Information Science*, *41*(6), 391–407. doi:10.1002/(SICI)1097-4571(199009)41:6<391::AID-ASI1>3.0.CO;2-9

Guo, L., Shao, F., Botev, C., & Shanmugasundaram, J. (2003). XRANK: ranked keyword search over XML documents. In *Proceedings of the ACM SIGMOD International Conference on Management of Data* (pp. 28-39). ACM. 10.1145/872757.872762

Hristidis, V., Koudas, N., Papakonstantinou, Y., & Srivastava, D. (2006). Keyword proximity search in XML trees. *IEEE Transactions on Knowledge and Data Engineering*, *18*(4), 525–539. doi:10.1109/TKDE.2006.1599390

Hristidis, V., & Papakonstantinou, Y. (2002). Keyword Search in Relational Databases. In *Proceedings of the 28th International Conference on Very Large Data Bases* (pp. 670-681). ACM.

Hu, G. Z., & Hammad, R. (2005). Querying and indexing XML documents. *Journal of Computer and System Sciences*, *71*(4), 219–233.

Kong, L. B., Gilleron, R., & Lemay, A. (2009). Retrieving meaningful relaxed tightest fragments for XML keyword search. In *Proceedings of the 12th International Conference on Extending Database Technology* (pp. 815-826). ACM. 10.1145/1516360.1516454

Li, G. L., Feng, J. H., Wang, J. Y., & Zhou, L. Z. (2007). Efficient keyword search for valuable LCAs over XML documents. In *Proceedings of the 16th ACM Conference on Information and Knowledge Management* (pp. 31–40). ACM.

Li, J., Liu, C., Rui, Z., & Bo, N. (2009). Processing XML keyword search by constructing effective structured queries. In *Proceedings of the Joint International Conferences on Advances in Data and Web Management* (pp. 88–99). ACM. 10.1007/978-3-642-00672-2_10

Li, T., & M, Z. M. (2018). A structure-based approach of keyword querying for fuzzy XML data. *International Journal of Intelligent Systems*, *22*(2), 125–140.

Li, T., Xin, L., & Meng, X. F. (2012). Rtop-k: a keyword proximity search method based on semantic and structural relaxation. In *Proceedings of the IEEE International Conference on Systems, Man, and Cybernetics* (pp. 2079–2084). IEEE. 10.1109/ICSMC.2012.6378046

Li, Y. Y., Yu, C., & Jagadish, H. V. (2004). Schema-free XQuery. In *Proceedings of the VLDB Conference* (pp. 72–83). ACM.

Mazuran, M., Quintarelli, E., & Tanca, L. (2012). Data mining for XML query answering support. *IEEE Transactions on Knowledge and Data Engineering*, *24*(8), 1393–1407. doi:10.1109/TKDE.2011.80

Sun, C., Chan, C. Y., & Goenka, A. K. (2007). Multiway SLCA-based keyword search in XML data. In *Proceedings of the World Wide Web Conference* (pp. 1043-1052). ACM. 10.1145/1242572.1242713

Tian, Z., Lu, J., & Li, D. (2011). A survey on XML keyword search. In APWeb. doi:10.1007/978-3-642-20291-9_52

Wang, C., Dong, X. J., Zhou, F., Cao, L., & Chi, C.-H. (2015). Coupled Attribute Similarity Learning on Categorical Data. *IEEE Transactions on Neural Networks and Learning Systems*, *26*(4), 781–797. doi:10.1109/TNNLS.2014.2325872 PMID:25794382

Wang, C., Tao, L. B., & Wang, M. C. (2011). Coupled nominal similarity in unsupervised learning. In *Proceedings of the 20th ACM Conference on Information and Knowledge Management* (pp. 973-978). ACM. 10.1145/2063576.2063715

Wang, H., & Aggarwal, C. C. (2010). A survey of algorithms for keyword search on graph data. In Managing and Mining Graph Data. doi:10.1007/978-1-4419-6045-0_8

Wilson, D., & Martinez, T. (1997). Improved heterogeneous distance functions. *Journal of Artificial Intelligence Research*, *6*(1), 1–34. doi:10.1613/jair.346

Wong, S., Ziarko, W., & Wong, P. (1985). Generalized vector spaces model in information retrieval. In *Proceedings of the 8th Annual International ACM SIGIR Conference on Research and Development in Information Retrieval* (pp. 18–25). ACM. 10.1145/253495.253506

Xu, Y., & Papakonstantinou, Y. (2005). Efficient keyword Search for Smallest LCAs in XML Databases. In *Proceedings of the ACM SIGMOD International Conference on Management of Data* (pp. 527–538). ACM. 10.1145/1066157.1066217

Xu, Y., & Papakonstantinou, Y. (2008). Efficient LCA based keyword search in XML data. In *Proceedings of the ACM Conference on Conference on Information and Knowledge Management* (pp. 535–546). ACM. 10.1145/1353343.1353408

Chapter 13
Uncertain Spatiotemporal Data Modeling Based on XML

ABSTRACT

Information is often imprecise and imperfect. In addition, traditional data models suffer from some inadequacy of necessary semantics such as inability to handle imprecise and uncertain information. In this chapter, the authors establish an uncertain spatiotemporal data model based on XML. Then, on the basis of the model, the authors provide a set of algebraic operations for capturing and handling uncertain spatiotemporal data. By employing algebraic operations, they demonstrate how to translate queries expressed in XQuery to this algebra. A translation example shows that these algebraic operations are full of expressive power and illustrates that this algebra can be applied to general data. Apart from this, the authors also propose a set of equivalence rules to optimize the process of query and give an example to show how the optimization approach works.

1 INTRODUCTION

With the spatiotemporal applications increasing such as applications of agriculture (Sammatat et al, 2020), land use change (Mishra & Rai, 2016), meteorological information systems (Ribaric & Hrkac, 2012) and geographic information systems (Yu & Shaw, 2004), spatiotemporal data has received a great deal of interest and spatiotemporal management has shown urgent requirements. In the context of spatiotemporal data, how to establish a spatiotemporal data model and effectively operate it by algebra is a key issue.

A number of research efforts have been undertaken to address the issue of modeling and operating the spatiotemporal data (Pelekis et al., 2004; Wang et al., 2000; Luo et al., 2010). Wang et al. (Wanget al., 2000) present two spatiotemporal data models which are abstract model and conceptual model. Abstract model is simple and its semantics can be defined easily. But obviously, the abstract model is not realistic and it is not easy to store and manipulate spatiotemporal data in it. Conceptual model which extends previous work on spatial and temporal data modeling can capture spatiotemporal information. In the comprehensive survey of spatiotemporal data modeling (Pelekis et al., 2004), numerous existing spatiotemporal data models have been outlined and compared such as the snapshot model, the space-time

DOI: 10.4018/978-1-6684-9108-9.ch013

composite data model, data model based simple time-stamping and so on. The contribution of Pelekis et al. (Pelekis et al., 2004) can be divided into two aspects. One is comparing the different spatiotemporal data models and another is identifying the possible research direction in the field of spatiotemporal data modeling. In (Viqueira, 2000), a general spatiotemporal model is presented, and an algebra extended from relational algebra is proposed based on it.

In the real world, to the reason of limitation of knowledge or capturing method, most information is uncertain and imprecise, which is one of the inherent features of spatiotemporal data. Uncertainty is either measurement error or imprecision due to incomplete knowledge (Duckham et al., 2001). The researches on uncertain spatiotemporal data focus on how to model uncertain spatiotemporal data and most of the research are studied in the context of traditional databases. Aiming to provide a framework for establishing a model which can support spatial or spatiotemporal data with uncertainty, a type constructor which can create spatiotemporal types from spatial ones is proposed, and several operations which can be used on new data types when data is uncertain are also developed (Tøssebro & Nygård, 2002). In (Tøssebro & Nygård, 2002), an abstract model is established by modeling positional uncertainty with spatial data, and relevant operations are defined based on uncertain points, uncertain lines and uncertain regions and so on. On the basis of these works, uncertain spatiotemporal data models based on traditional databases (Kuijpers & Othman, 2010), object-oriented databases (OODB) (Tøssebro, 2002) and moving objects databases (Trajcevski et al., 2004) are addressed. But the models of uncertain spatiotemporal data based on traditional databases or object-oriented databases (OODB) fall short of representing uncertain information and extension of data types which allow one to define complex data types. Consequently, there is a demand to overcome these problems.

With the requirement of managing information based on the Web increasing, XML, as the next generation language of the Internet, has received much attention in the fields of managing information on the Web. Furthermore, data from different sources can be stored, integrated and exchanged in the format of XML and XML contains a rich set of data types and has extension of data types. Due to these advantages, XML gradually becomes a medium for information storing, integrating and exchanging. Consequently, the advent of XML seems to provide an opportunity for modeling uncertain spatiotemporal data and operating it by algebra (Bai et al., 2015).

The emergence of XML has attracted a number of researchers to move their focus to this point. Some relevant researches are foundation for uncertain spatiotemporal data modeling and operating based on XML. For example, modeling general data in XML (Li & Xu, 2010), modeling uncertain data in XML (Abiteboul et al., 2009; Nierman & Jagadish, 2002), and modeling spatiotemporal data in XML (Huang et al., 2004). Modeling uncertain spatiotemporal data based on XML is the basis of querying uncertain spatiotemporal data, and the algebra is then used to support query optimization. Therefore, formal algebra is essential for applying standard database querying. In the context of algebra based on XML, a number of researches have been studied. For general data, Jagadish et al. (Jagadish et al., 2001) propose a simple algebra called *Tree Algebra for XML* (TAX). TAX specifies nodes and attributes by *pattern tree*. Frasincar et al. (Frasincar et al., 2002) propose XAL, which is an XML algebra. Simplicity of data model and well-defined logical operators make it suitable for composability, optimizability, and semantics definition of a query language for XML data. The study of spatiotemporal data is based on both temporal data and spatial data. In (Bai & Xu, 2015), Bai et al. propose a spatiotemporal XML data model and develop an algebra based on Native XML to manipulate spatiotemporal XML data. Córcoles et al. (Córcoles et al., 2000) show a query language for a spatiotemporal model based on XML, called STQ.

However, a large proportion of the existing research assume that the data is known, accurate and complete and addressed in the context of traditional database which suffers from some inadequacy of necessary semantics such as inability to handle imprecise and uncertain information. In order to store and handle uncertain spatiotemporal data, we propose an uncertain spatiotemporal data model based on XML. Apart from this model, we also provide relevant algebra operations to capture and handle uncertain spatiotemporal data.

The main contribution of this chapter is to model uncertain spatiotemporal data in XML and investigate algebraic operations to capture uncertain spatiotemporal information. The main contributions of this chapter are summarized as follows:

- We propose an uncertain spatiotemporal data model based on XML.
- On the basis of the uncertain spatiotemporal data model, we provide our algebraic operations for capturing the uncertain spatiotemporal information and show the expressive power of our algebra.
- We propose the general steps of query optimization approach by applying our algebra based on equivalence rules and an example is given to illustrate how to use the optimization approach in the query process.

The remainder of the chapter is organized as follows. Related work is presented in Section 2. In Section 3, we provide our uncertain spatiotemporal XML data model followed by a real-life example. Section 4 investigates algebraic operations which are applied to the uncertain spatiotemporal XML data query. The expressive power of algebraic operations by translating XQuery to our algebra is shown in Section 5. In Section 6, we study the equivalence rules and propose generic steps of the optimization approach based on those rules. Section 7 concludes the chapter.

2 RELATED WORK

The importance of managing spatiotemporal data has prompted the development of modeling spatiotemporal data, which includes spatial data, temporal data, spatiotemporal data and uncertain spatiotemporal data. According to their focuses, there are several categories that are associated with our research work.

Uncertain spatiotemporal data modeling. For uncertain spatiotemporal data, most of the research are carried out in the area of moving object and the uncertain information are considered in modeling the trajectories of moving objects (Kuijpers & Othman, 2010; Mokhtar & Su, 2004; Trajcevski et al., 2004). Mokhtar and Su (Mokhtar & Su, 2004) consider a data model for uncertain trajectories of moving objects. In their model, the trajectory is vector of uniform random process. In order to capture uncertainty, Trajcevski et al. (Trajcevski et al., 2004) propose a model of uncertain trajectories of moving objects, which is modeling the trajectory as a cylindrical volume in 3D. Unlike the approach of Trajcevski et al. (Trajcevski et al., 2004), Kuijpers and Othman (Kuijpers & Othman, 2010) present a more efficient approach to managing uncertainty than other approaches based on cylinders. They describe a data model for trajectories and trajectory samples and present an efficient way to model uncertainty via beads for trajectory samples. Cheng et al. (Cheng et al., 2014) present a comprehensive overview of models, algorithms, solutions and techniques in the field of managing uncertain spatiotemporal data, hoping to teach the background necessary for uncertain data management.

Spatial data modeling based on XML. As the next generation language of the Internet, XML has attracted much attention both from academia and industry. The problem of whether XML can be used to express spatial information and associate it with XML elements and attributes has been solved (Mitakos & Almaliotis, 2009). Mane et al. (Mane et al., 2004) also show great interest in the representation of spatial data in the format of XML and they have implemented the spatial data model in XML. This model stores information about geographical regions like region name, location of regions, landmarks in the region, related information and buildings. In (Lehto & Kilpeläinen, 2001), Lehto and Kilpeläinen use XML techniques in data transformations. Their focus in the research lies in the XSLT process as a means to generalize XML-encoded spatial data in real-time.

Temporal data modeling based on XML. Amagasa et al. (Amagasa et al., 2000) propose a logical data model for representing histories of XML documents. The proposed model extends the XPath data model and can be employed to represent change histories of XML documents. In (Baazizi et al., 2011), Baazizi et al. studies how to generate or maintain temporal XML documents, and formally define a notion of compactness, which allows for comparing documents. On the basis of this work, they develop two techniques for generating and maintaining encoding of abstract temporal documents. The techniques are applicable to two cases. One is that no information is available on the abstract temporal document and another is designed to manipulate document history. Grandi et al. (Grandi et al., 2003) present the result of an on-going research activity concerning the temporal management of normative texts in XML format. Furthermore, four temporal dimensions (publication, validity, efficacy and transaction times) are used to correctly represent the evolution of norms in time and their resulting versioning. Wang and Zaniolo (Wang & Zaniolo, 2003) present efficient techniques to query temporal data in XML format.

Spatiotemporal data modeling based on XML. To combine spatial and temporal properties into one framework, and analyze spatiotemporal data in XML, a number of research efforts have been carried out (Franceschet et al., 2007; Huang et al., 2004; Liu & Wan, 2010). Franceschet et al. (Franceschet et al., 2007) demonstrate a translation algorithm that maps spatiotemporal conceptual schemas. Huang et al. (Huang et al., 2004) propose an ODMG-based object model to represent and query spatiotemporal data in the format of XML. Liu and Wan (Liu & Wan, 2010) suggest a feature-based spatiotemporal data model and employ the Native XML Database to store the spatiotemporal data. Existing models for spatial data, temporal data and spatiotemporal data are various, but they assume that the data is deterministic. In the real world, handling uncertain spatiotemporal data is still in requirement.

Uncertain spatiotemporal data modeling based on XML. In order to represent uncertainty, some recent efforts have been devoted to the probabilistic XML (Abiteboul et al., 2009; Kimelfeld et al., 2008; Nierman & Jagadish, 2002). In (Abiteboul et al., 2009), Abiteboul et al. provides algorithms to do aggregate queries for discrete and continuous probabilistic XML data. Kimelfeld et al. (Kimelfeld et al., 2008) propose an abstract framework for representing probabilistic XML as *p-documents* that have two kinds of nodes. On the basis of this framework, query efficiency in probabilistic XML models is studied. Nierman and Jagadish (Nierman & Jagadish, 2002) also present a probabilistic tree database to manage probabilistic data represented in the format of XML. As they mentioned in their paper, sources of data uncertainty and data imprecision are numerous.

Other approaches to model uncertain spatiotemporal data. XML is one way to develop the data models, and there are other approaches such as semantic modeling, ontology development (Budak Arpinar et al., 2006; Ding et al., 2006; Yazici et al., 2001). Yazici et al. (Yazici et al., 2001) present a semantic data modeling approach for spatiotemporal database applications and specifically focuses on various aspects of spatial and temporal database issues and uncertainty and fuzziness in various abstract levels. The semantic data model proposed in it utilizes unified modeling language (UML) for handling spatiotemporal information, uncertainty, and fuzziness, especially at the conceptual level of database design. Budak Arpinar et al. (Budak Arpinar et al., 2006) present the summary of their geospatial ontology development efforts and some new semantic analytics methods on their ontology such as STTP. Ding et al. (Ding et al., 2006) propose a framework that is based on Bayesian networks (BN) to enhance and supply the semantic web ontology language OWL for representing and reasoning with uncertainty.

We have discussed a variety of spatiotemporal data models which include spatial data models, temporal data model, spatiotemporal data models and uncertain spatiotemporal data models. The significance of algebraic operation is equal to modeling spatiotemporal data. Algebraic operations can be introduced from four perspectives which consist of algebraic operations on general data, spatial data, temporal data and spatiotemporal data.

Algebraic operations. Formal algebra is essential for applying optimization of the query process. Fernandez et al. (Fernandez et al., 2000) early propose an algebra whose novelty feature is the use of regular-expression type. The algebra has been submitted to the W3CXML Query Working Group. Most of the algebras which can cope with data in the format of XML are based on relational algebra (Frasincar et al., 2002; Jagadish et al., 2001). In (Frasincar et al., 2002), Frasincar et al. propose an XML algebra (XAL) based on relational algebra. XAL provides operators similar to the relational algebra ones which are familiar to the relational database world. Simplicity of data model and well-defined logical operators make it suitable for composability, optimizability, and semantics definition of a query language for XML data. Jagadish et al. (Jagadish et al., 2001) develop an algebra, called TAX (Tree Algebra for XML), for manipulating XML data. TAX, as a natural extension of relational algebra, with a small set of operators, is complete for relational algebra extended with aggregation. TAX specifies nodes and attributes by *pattern tree*. Moreover, algebraic operations on spatial data and temporal data in the format of XML are important. To support spatial features, Córcoles and González (Córcoles & González, 2001) present the Geography Markup Language (GML) which is based on XML and inherits the interoperability from the XML, allowing the exchange of geographic information on the Web. On the basis of GML and query language, an extension to algebraic operations is provided. Considering temporal data, Nørvåg (Nørvåg, 2002) provides a set of algebraic operations that are based on traditional operators to support temporal XML queries. Chen and Revesz (Chen & Revesz, 2003) present a rule-based XML query language, called *Datalog For XML* (DataFoX), which is a novelty query language for spatiotemporal data in the format of XML and extends Datalog with support for trees as the domain of the variables. They also develop Layer Algebra, which is a novel extension of relational algebra for XML. Algebraic operations mentioned above only care about spatial data or temporal data in the format of XML. In reality, however, there are requirements for doing algebraic operations on spatiotemporal data. Therefore, it is necessary to study how to do algebraic operations on spatiotemporal data. Aiming to operate spatiotemporal data, Bai et al. (Bai & Xu, 2015) propose a spatiotemporal XML data model and develop an algebra based on Native XML to manipulate spatiotemporal XML data. Logical structure of spatiotemporal database, data type system and querying operations are investigated. The model and algebra establish a foundation for managing spatiotemporal XML data. To retrieve and analyze spatiotemporal information in the format of XML, Córcoles et al. (Córcoles et al., 2000) show a query language for a spatiotemporal model based on XML, called STQ, which relies on relational algebra query. STQ includes a set of spatial operators and set of temporal operators. In addition, STQ includes traditional operators for non-spatial information.

To summarize, uncertain spatiotemporal data has only recently started and still merits further attention. Although uncertain spatiotemporal data modeling and algebraic operations based on XML cannot be extended by the researchers mentioned above directly, their efforts play a fundamental role in our study. The motivation of the paper is to propose an uncertain spatiotemporal data model based on XML and provide relevant algebraic operations. Aiming to observe intuitively, we give a comparative study in terms of uncertain features, spatial features, temporal features, spatiotemporal features, and algebraic operations shown in Table 1.

Table 1. Comparative study in terms of different features

	Reference	Uncertain Feature	Spatial Feature	Temporal Feature	Spatiotemporal Feature	Algebraic Operation
Uncertain spatiotemporal data modeling	(Kuijpers & Othman, 2010)	√	√	√	√	
	(Mokhtar & Su, 2004)	√	√	√	√	
	(Trajcevski et al., 2004)	√	√	√	√	
Spatial data modeling based on XML	(Mitakos & Almaliotis, 2009)		√			
	(Mane et al., 2004)		√			
	(Lehto & Kilpeläinen, 2001)		√			
Temporal data modeling based on XML	(Amagasa et al., 2000)			√		
	(Baazizi et al., 2011)			√		
	(Grandi et al., 2003)			√		
	(Wang & Zaniolo, 2003)			√		
Spatiotemporal data modeling based on XML	(Franceschet et al., 2007)		√	√	√	
	(Huang et al., 2004)		√	√	√	
	(Liu & Wan, 2010)		√	√	√	
Uncertain spatiotemporal data modeling based on XML	(Abiteboul et al., 2009)	√				
	(Kimelfeld et al., 2008)	√				
	(Nierman & Jagadish, 2002)	√				
Other approaches to model uncertain spatiotemporal data	(Budak Arpinar et al., 2006)		√	√	√	
	(Ding et al., 2006)	√				
	(Yazici et al., 2001)	√	√	√	√	

Table 1. Continued

	Reference	Uncertain Feature	Spatial Feature	Temporal Feature	Spatiotemporal Feature	Algebraic Operation
Algebraic operations	(Fernandez et al., 2000)					√
	(Frasincar et al., 2002)					√
	(Jagadish et al., 2001)					√
	(Córcoles & González, 2001)		√			√
	(Nørvåg, 2002)			√		√
	(Chen & Revesz, 2003)			√		√
	(Bai & Xu, 2015)		√	√	√	√
	(Córcoles et al., 2000)		√	√	√	√
Uncertain spatiotemporal data modeling based on XML	Our work	√	√	√	√	√

3 UNCERTAIN SPATIOTEMPORAL DATA MODEL

In this section, we propose basics of representation of uncertain spatiotemporal data in XML. There are two kinds of uncertainty in XML: the first is the uncertainty in elements and the second is the uncertainty of in attribute values of elements and we use possibility distribution to represent such values.

The basic data structure of uncertain spatiotemporal XML data model is the data tree. First, we introduce some simple concepts as follows:

Definition 1. Let V be a finite set of vertices, E be a set of edges, L is a set of strings called labels and $\alpha: E \rightarrow L$ be a mapping from edges to labels. The triple $G = (V, E, \alpha)$ is an edge-directed graph.

Definition 1 presents the simple concept of edge-directed graph but not including the ordering and temporal features of uncertain spatiotemporal data that we are interested in, thus we propose the definition of time interval and the partial order firstly.

Definition 2. Let t_s represent the start of time interval, t_e represents the end of time interval. (t_s, t_e) represents the time interval. when t_s is equal to t_e, (t_s, t_e) represents a time point.

Definition 3. A relation "$\prec$" is a partial order on a set S if it has

- Inreflexivity: $a \nprec a$ for all $a \in S$.
- Antisymmetry: $a \prec b$ implies $b \nprec a$ for all $a, b \in S$.
- Transitivity: $a \prec b$ and $b \prec c$ implies $a \prec c$ for all $a, b, c \in S$.

Based on the definitions above, we propose the data model of uncertain spatiotemporal XML data as follows:

Definition 4. Uncertain spatiotemporal XML data tree U is a 9-tuple, $U=(V, E, \alpha, T, \tau, \prec, \kappa, \rho, \partial)$, where

- $V=V_g \cup V_s$ is a finite set of vertices. Here V_g is a finite set of general vertices, V_s is a finite set of special vertices with spatiotemporal features.
- $e = \{(v_i, v_j) \mid v_i, v_j \in V\}$, E is a finite set of e. (V, E) is a directed tree.
- α: $V \rightarrow (L \cup \{\text{null}\})$, here L is a set of labels. For each node $v \in V$ and each label $l \in L$, $\alpha(v, l)$ specifies node v exists with label l.
- T is a finite set of time intervals.
- τ: $T \rightarrow V$ is a mapping from T to V, specifies time of $v \in V$.
- $\prec$ is a possibly empty partial order on V. It preserves the order information between nodes in the uncertain spatiotemporal XML data tree.
- κ is a mapping that constrains the number of children with a given label. κ associates with each node $v \in V$ and each label $l \in L$, an integer-valued interval function. $\kappa(v, l) = [min, max]$, where $min \geq 0$, $max \geq min$. We use κ to represent the lower and upper bounds.
- ρ is a integer-valued function. $\rho(v)$ represents the possibility that the element node v exists. $\rho(v)$ is equal to 1, as default.
- ∂ is a integer-valued function. $\partial(v)$ represents the possibility that the attribute node v exists. $\partial(v)$ is equal to 1, as default.

Example 1. We take a real life event as an example to explain the definition in detail. Oil spill is a frequent accident of Marine pollution, we take oil spill as an example as follows: in uncertain spatiotemporal XML data tree, the vertices represent the element or attribute of specific event; edges connecting those nodes are directed trees; each element nodes and attribute nodes exists with specific labels; time is considered as an attribute of element nodes; there exists partial order between nodes, possibly not all nodes. A pair of nodes has a relationship of ancestor-descendant or parent-child. For example, nodes a, b and c have partial order as follows: a $\prec$ b, b $\prec$ c. a $\prec$ b represents that node a and node b have parent-child relationship. In like manner, node b and node c have the same relationship. The partial order a $\prec$ b, b $\prec$ c implies a $\prec$ c, i.e. node a and node c have ancestor-descendant relationship; elements contain data or other elements in an XML document, similarly, element nodes possibly have child element nodes in an uncertain spatiotemporal XML data tree; elements of specific event possibly are uncertain, similarly attributes of oil spill also possibly are uncertain.

We give a fragment of XML document with uncertain spatiotemporal data in Figure 1. It describes specific information about marine pollution which includes the information of oil spills such as OID, predecessor, successor and position and the information on species such as name and number which represents the change number of species by positive number describing increase and negative number describing reduction. For example, the negative number "-5000" in Line 53 represents the number of sea birds declining 5000. Consider Val Poss in Figure 1, it represents the possibility of the specific element with uncertainty such as an element in Line 10 denoted area, <Val Poss="0.6"> in Line 9, where it is stated that the possibility of the size of area being 6000m2 in time [t2, t3] is equal to 0.6. Position information is described through MBR (Minimum Bounding Rectangle). From Lines 16-23, we can see the position of oil spill described by the two represented points of MBR (10, 20) and (15, 23). We use conjunctive or disjunctive to represent the type of uncertain attribute possibility distributions, because sometimes uncertainty of event can be several situations. For example, <Dist type="disjunctive"> in

Line 8 indicates the size of area is unique in time [t2, t3], because the area can only be a determined value at the same time. Instead, conjunctive represents several situations that can exist at the same time.

Figure 1. A fragment of an XML document with uncertain spatiotemporal data

```
1.  <Marine pollution>
2.   <Oil spill OName="Mexico oil spill">
3.    <Val Poss="0.9">
4.     <oil spill OID="O2" Ts="t2" Te="t6-1">
5.      <type Ts="t2" Te="t6-1">splite</type>
6.      <pre Ts="t2" Te="t6-1">O1</pre>
7.      <suc Ts="t2" Te="t6-1">O3</suc>
8.      <Dist type="disjunctive">
9.       <Val Poss="0.6">
10.       <area Ts="t2" Te="t3">6000</area>
11.      </Val>
12.      <Val Poss="0.2">
13.       <area Ts="t2" Te="t3">7000</area>
14.      </Val>
15.     </Dist>
16.     <position Ts="t4" Te="t6">
17.      <Val Poss="0.7">
18.       <x1>10</x1>
19.       <y1>20</y2>
20.       <x2>15</x2>
21.       <y2>23</y2>
22.      </Val>
23.     </position>
24.     <position Ts="t7" Te="t8">
25.      <Val Poss="0.6">
26.       <x1>32</x1>
27.       <y1>25</y2>
28.       <x2>45</x2>
29.       <y2>36</y2>
30.      </Val>
31.     </position>
32.    </oil spill>
33.   </Val>
34.  </Oil spill>
35.  <Species>
36.   <species SID="1101">
37.    <sname>sea bird</sname>
38.    <Val Poss="0.6">
39.     <number>-10000</number>
40.    </Val>
41.    <position Ts="t4" Te="t6">
42.     <Val Poss="0.6">
43.      <x1>10</x1>
44.      <y1>20</y2>
45.      <x2>15</x2>
46.      <y2>23</y2>
47.     </Val>
48.    </position>
49.   </species>
50.   <species SID="1102">
51.    <sname>sea otter</sname>
52.    <Val Poss="0.5">
53.     <number>-5000</number>
54.    </Val>
55.    <position Ts="t4" Te="t6">
56.     <Val Poss="0.6">
57.      <x1>10</x1>
58.      <y1>20</y2>
59.      <x2>15</x2>
60.      <y2>23</y2>
61.     </Val>
62.    </position>
63.   </species>
64.  </Species>
65.   ...
66. </Marine pollution>
```

The basic data structure of an uncertain spatiotemporal XML document is the data tree. The relationship of uncertain spatiotemporal data trees and forest is investigated as follows:

Definition 5. An uncertain spatiotemporal XML data forest is a set in which contains uncertain spatiotemporal XML data trees.

On the basis of uncertain spatiotemporal XML data tree as defined, characteristics of two uncertain spatiotemporal data trees are discussed in the following.

Definition 6. Suppose $U = (V, E, \alpha, T, \tau, \prec, \kappa, \rho, \partial)$ and $u' = (V', E', \alpha', T', \tau', \prec', \kappa', \rho', \partial')$ are two uncertain spatiotemporal XML data trees. u' is a sub-tree of U, recorded $u' \propto U$, when

- $V' \subseteq V$, $E' = E \cap (V' \times V')$.
- if $v_i \in V'$ and $(v_i, v_j) \in E$, then $v_j \in V'$.
- α' and τ' indicate the restriction of α and τ to the nodes in V', respectively.
- $T' \in T$. For $\forall(t_s', t_e') \in T'$, $\exists(t_s, t_e) \in T$ and $t_s' \geq t_s$, $t_e' \leq t_e$.
- $\prec' \in \prec$, $\kappa' \in \kappa$.

Definition 7. Let uncertain spatiotemporal XML data tree $u_1 = (V_1, E_1, \alpha_1, T_1, \tau_1, \prec_1, \kappa_1, \rho_1, \partial_1)$ and $u_2 = (V_2, E_2, \alpha_2, T_2, \tau_2, \prec_2, \kappa_2, \rho_2, \partial_2)$ be the sub-trees of $U = (V, E, \alpha, T, \tau, \prec, \kappa, \rho, \partial)$. u_1 and u_2 are isomorphic (recorded $u_1 \cong u_2$),when

- $V_1 \cup V_2 \subseteq V$, $E_1 \cup E_2 \subseteq E$, $\tau_1 \cup \tau_2 \subseteq \tau$, $T_1 \cup T_2 \subseteq T$.
- ς_α: $\alpha_1 \to \alpha_2$ is a one-to-one mapping from α_1 to α_2, which makes $\forall \varsigma_\alpha(\alpha_1) = \alpha_2$.
- Suppose $e_1 = (v_{1i}, v_{1j}) \in E_1$, $e_2 = (v_{2i}, v_{2j}) \in E_2$, There is a one-to-one mapping, $\varphi_\prec : \prec_1 \to \prec_2$,which makes $\forall \varphi_\prec (e_1) = e_2$, i.e. $v_{1i} = v_{2i}, v_{1j} = v_{2j}$.

Theorem 1. Uncertain spatiotemporal XML data tree U and its sub-tree u' are isomorphic.

The proof of this theorem follows analysis of uncertain spatiotemporal data model and the corresponding definitions. In this chapter, we consider the attribute nodes as a special kind of element nodes. Our model considers a number of XML features such as the ordering, the parent-child and the ancestor-descendant relationships of nodes in the XML document.

4 THE ALGEBRAIC OPERATORS

This section presents the issues on the how to conceptually design XML algebra of uncertain spatiotemporal data. All operators in our model take collections of data trees as input and produce a collection of data trees as output.

4.1 Set Operations

In this subsection, we propose several common operations of uncertain spatiotemporal data trees: union operation(∪), intersection operation(∩), difference operation(——). $\rho(v)$ represents the possibility that element node v exists. Similarly, $\partial(v)$ represents the possibility that attribute node v exists.

The union operation takes two uncertain spatiotemporal trees u_1 and u_2 as input and these trees are isomorphic. The union operation produces an uncertain spatiotemporal data tree as output.

Definition 8 (Union operation). Suppose $u_1 = (V_1, E_1, \alpha_1, T_1, \tau_1, \prec_1, \kappa_1, \rho_1, \partial_1)$ and $u_2 = (V_2, E_2, \alpha_2, T_2, \tau_2, \prec_2, \kappa_2, \rho_2, \partial_2)$ are isomorphic uncertain spatiotemporal data trees. The output of union operation is uncertain spatiotemporal data tree $u = (V, E, \alpha, T, \tau, \prec, \kappa, \rho, \partial)$. The union operation is defined as follows:

- $V = V_1 \cup V_2$, $E = E_1 \cup E_2$, $\alpha = \alpha_1 \cup \alpha_2$, $\tau = \tau_1 \cup \tau_2$, $\prec = \prec_1 \cup \prec_2$, $\kappa = \kappa_1 \cup \kappa_2$.
- $T = T_1 \cup T_2$.
- $\rho(v_i) = \text{Max}(\rho_1(v_i), \rho_2(v_i))$.
- $\partial(v_i) = \text{Max}(\partial_1(v_i), \partial_2(v_i))$.

The intersection operation takes two uncertain spatiotemporal trees u_1 and u_2 as input and these trees are isomorphic. The intersection operation produces an uncertain spatiotemporal data tree $u = (V, E, \alpha, T, \tau, \prec, \kappa, \rho, \partial)$ as output.

Definition 9 (Intersection operation). Suppose $u_1 = (V_1, E_1, \alpha_1, T_1, \tau_1, \prec_1, \kappa_1, \rho_1, \partial_1)$ and $u_2 = (V_2, E_2, \alpha_2, T_2, \tau_2, \prec_2, \kappa_2, \rho_2, \partial_2)$ are isomorphic uncertain spatiotemporal data trees. The intersection operation is defined as follows:

- $V = V_1 \cap V_2$, $E = E_1 \cap E_2$, $\alpha = \alpha_1 \cap \alpha_2$, $\tau = \tau_1 \cap \tau_2$, $\prec = \prec_1 \cap \prec_2$, $\kappa = \kappa_1 \cap \kappa_2$.
- $T = T_1 \cap T_2$.
- $\rho(v_i) = \text{Min}(\rho_1(v_i), \rho_2(v_i))$.
- $\partial(v_i) = \text{Min}(\partial_1(v_i), \partial_2(v_i))$.

The difference operation takes two uncertain spatiotemporal trees u_1 and u_2 as input and these trees are isomorphic. The difference operation produces an uncertain spatiotemporal data tree $u = (V, E, \alpha, T, \tau, \prec, \kappa, \rho, \partial)$ as output.

Definition 10 (Difference operation). Suppose $u_1 = (V_1, E_1, \alpha_1, T_1, \tau_1, \prec_1, \kappa_1, \rho_1, \partial_1)$ and $u_2 = (V_2, E_2, \alpha_2, T_2, \tau_2, \prec_2, \kappa_2, \rho_2, \partial_2)$ are isomorphic uncertain spatiotemporal data trees. The difference operation is defined as follows:

- $V = V_1 - V_2$, $E = E_1 - E_2$, $\alpha = \alpha_1 - \alpha_2$, $\tau = \tau_1 - \tau_2$, $\prec = \prec_1 - \prec_2$, $\kappa = \kappa_1 - \kappa_2$.
- $T = T_1 - T_2$.
- $\rho(v_i) = \text{Min}(\rho_1(v_i), 1 - \rho_2(v_i))$.
- $\partial(v_i) = \text{Min}(\partial_1(v_i), 1 - \partial_2(v_i))$.

Example 2. Suppose there are two uncertain spatiotemporal XML trees shown in Figure 2. According to Definition 7, these two uncertain spatiotemporal trees are isomorphic. Hence we can operate them on union operation, intersection operation and difference operation, respectively. Figure 3 shows the results of union operation, intersection operation and difference operation of u_1 and u_2 in Figure 2, respectively. Figure 3a shows the result of union operation. In the union operation, the time interval $[t_2, t_6]$ in the result of the union operation above comes from the union of time interval $[t_2, t_4]$ and $[t_3, t_6]$. In the result of union operation, all the possibilities in the original two trees have appeared. Figure 3b shows the result of intersection operation. In the intersection operation, the time interval $[t_3, t_4]$ is the result of intersection operation on the time intervals $[t_2, t_4]$ and $[t_3, t_6]$. The possibilities only appeared the same part and the value of possibility is the lower values according to Definition 9. Figure 3c shows the result of difference operation. In the difference operation, we removed the same parts of u_1 and u_2 from u_1. The time interval $[t_2, t_3]$ is the result of difference operation on the time intervals $[t_2, t_4]$ and $[t_3, t_6]$. The values of possibilities are equal to subtract the values of possibilities in u_2 from u_1, respectively.

Figure 2. Two uncertain spatiotemporal XML trees

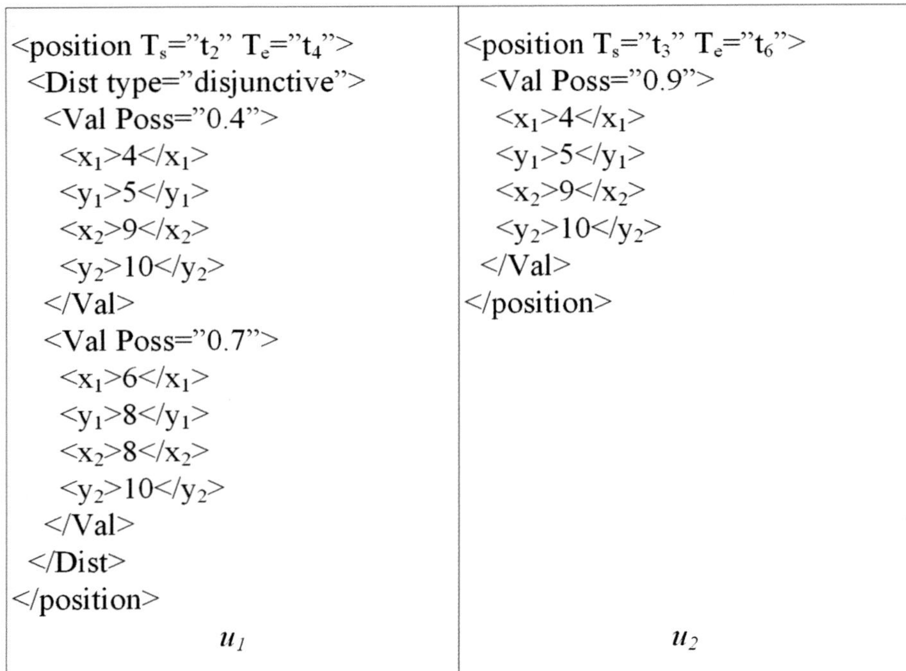

```
<position Ts=”t2” Te=”t4”>
  <Dist type=”disjunctive”>
    <Val Poss=”0.4”>
      <x1>4</x1>
      <y1>5</y1>
      <x2>9</x2>
      <y2>10</y2>
    </Val>
    <Val Poss=”0.7”>
      <x1>6</x1>
      <y1>8</y1>
      <x2>8</x2>
      <y2>10</y2>
    </Val>
  </Dist>
</position>
```

u_1

```
<position Ts=”t3” Te=”t6”>
  <Val Poss=”0.9”>
    <x1>4</x1>
    <y1>5</y1>
    <x2>9</x2>
    <y2>10</y2>
  </Val>
</position>
```

u_2

Figure 3. The results of union, intersection, difference operation

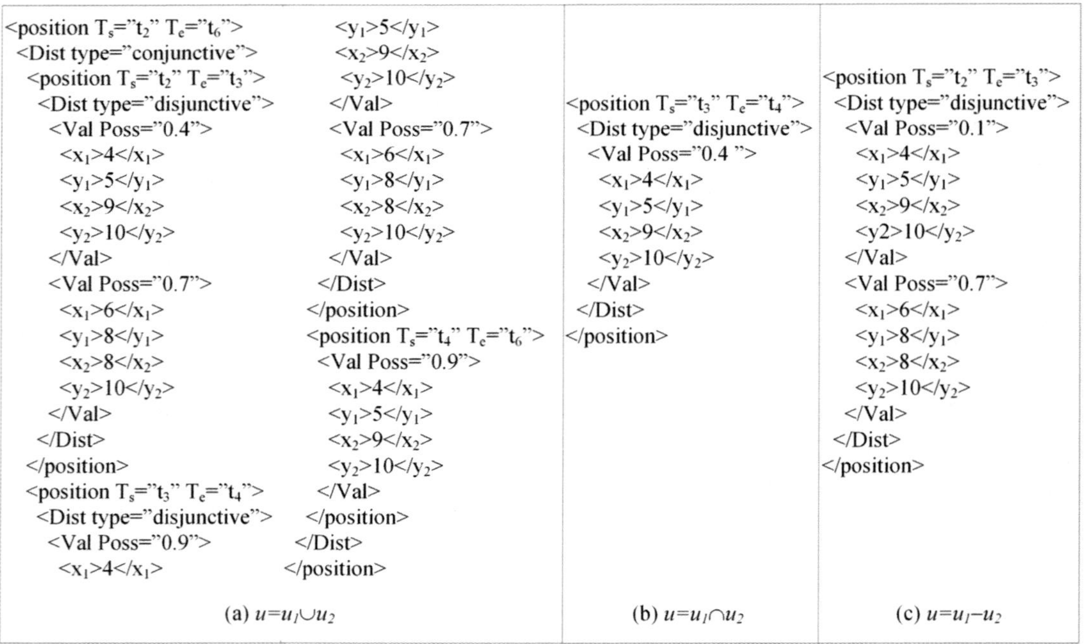

```
<position Ts=”t2” Te=”t6”>
  <Dist type=”conjunctive”>
    <position Ts=”t2” Te=”t3”>
      <Dist type=”disjunctive”>
        <Val Poss=”0.4”>
          <x1>4</x1>
          <y1>5</y1>
          <x2>9</x2>
          <y2>10</y2>
        </Val>
        <Val Poss=”0.7”>
          <x1>6</x1>
          <y1>8</y1>
          <x2>8</x2>
          <y2>10</y2>
        </Val>
      </Dist>
    </position>
    <position Ts=”t3” Te=”t4”>
      <Dist type=”disjunctive”>
        <Val Poss=”0.9”>
          <x1>4</x1>
          <y1>5</y1>
          <x2>9</x2>
          <y2>10</y2>
        </Val>
        <Val Poss=”0.7”>
          <x1>6</x1>
          <y1>8</y1>
          <x2>8</x2>
          <y2>10</y2>
        </Val>
      </Dist>
    </position>
    <position Ts=”t4” Te=”t6”>
      <Val Poss=”0.9”>
        <x1>4</x1>
        <y1>5</y1>
        <x2>9</x2>
        <y2>10</y2>
      </Val>
    </position>
  </Dist>
</position>
```

(a) $u=u_1 \cup u_2$

```
<position Ts=”t3” Te=”t4”>
  <Dist type=”disjunctive”>
    <Val Poss=”0.4 ”>
      <x1>4</x1>
      <y1>5</y1>
      <x2>9</x2>
      <y2>10</y2>
    </Val>
  </Dist>
</position>
```

(b) $u=u_1 \cap u_2$

```
<position Ts=”t2” Te=”t3”>
  <Dist type=”disjunctive”>
    <Val Poss=”0.1”>
      <x1>4</x1>
      <y1>5</y1>
      <x2>9</x2>
      <y2>10</y2>
    </Val>
    <Val Poss=”0.7”>
      <x1>6</x1>
      <y1>8</y1>
      <x2>8</x2>
      <y2>10</y2>
    </Val>
  </Dist>
</position>
```

(c) $u=u_1-u_2$

4.2 Other Operations

The algebraic operations also include Cartesian product operation($\times$), selection operation(σ), projection operation(π) and join operation($\bowtie$) except union operation, intersection operation and difference operation. In this section, we will investigate how these operations process uncertain spatiotemporal data. $f_i(e)$ is a restriction function which is to match with each node t of the input u where e is a logical expression. Standard comparison operators (such as $>$, $<$, $\geq$, $\leq$, $=$, $\neq$) and Boolean operators ($\wedge$, $\vee$, $\neg$) can be used to construct complex expressions.

4.2.1 Cartesian Product

The Cartesian product operation takes two uncertain spatiotemporal trees u_1 and u_2 as input and produces output uncertain spatiotemporal trees corresponding to the "juxtaposition" of every pair of trees from u_1 and u_2.

Definition 11 (Cartesian product). Suppose $u_1 = (V_1, E_1, \alpha_1, T_1, \tau_1, \prec_1, \kappa_1, \rho_1, \partial_1)$ and $u_2 = (V_2, E_2, \alpha_2, T_2, \tau_2, \prec_2, \kappa_2, \rho_2, \partial_2)$ are isomorphic uncertain spatiotemporal data trees. The output $u = u_1 \times u_2 = (V, E, \alpha, T, \tau, \prec, \kappa, \rho, \partial)$ of Cartesian product operator is defined as follows:

- $V = V_1 \times V_2$, $E=E_1 \times E_2$, $\alpha=\alpha_1 \times \alpha_2$, $\tau = \tau_1 \times \tau_2$, $\prec=\prec_1 \times \prec_2$, $\kappa=\kappa_1 \times \kappa_2$.
- $T= T_1 \cap T_2$.
- $\rho(v_i) = \rho(v_j) = \rho_1(v_i) * \rho_2(v_j)$.
- $\partial(v_i) = \partial(v_j) = \partial_1(v_i) * \partial_2(v_j)$.

According to Definition 11, the possibilities in Figure 5 are equal to the product of the possibilities of nodes with the same pedigree. *Dist* is disjunctive in the result because the area and moving direction is unique in the same period of time.

Figure 4. The inputs of Cartesian product operation

```
<Dist type="disjunctive">
 <Val Poss="0.5">
  <area>3000</area>
 </Val>
 <Val Poss="0.7">
  <area>5000</area>
 </Val>
</Dist>
```

u_1

```
<Dist type="disjunctive">
 <Val Poss="0.3">
  <direction>southeast</dreaction>
 </Val>
 <Val Poss="0.5">
  <direction>northeast</direaction>
 </Val>
</Dist>
```

u_2

Figure 5. The result of Cartesian product operation

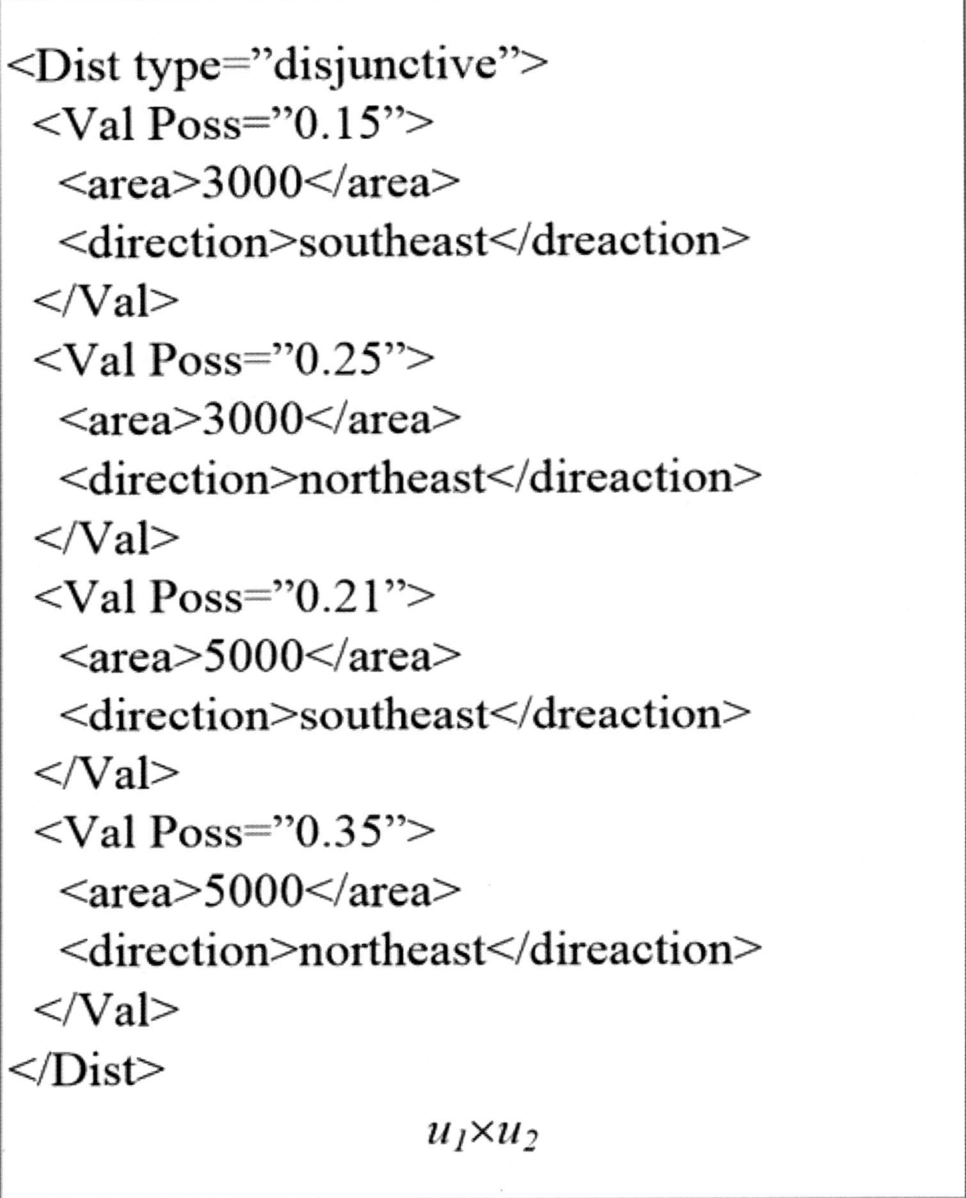
<Dist type="disjunctive">
<Val Poss="0.15">
<area>3000</area>
<direction>southeast</dreaction>
</Val>
<Val Poss="0.25">
<area>3000</area>
<direction>northeast</direaction>
</Val>
<Val Poss="0.21">
<area>5000</area>
<direction>southeast</dreaction>
</Val>
<Val Poss="0.35">
<area>5000</area>
<direction>northeast</direaction>
</Val>
</Dist>
$u_1 \times u_2$

4.2.2 Selection Operation

The selection operation takes one uncertain spatiotemporal trees u_1 as input and produces an uncertain spatiotemporal data tree u_2 as output.

Definition 12 (Selection operation). Suppose $u_1 = (V_1, E_1, \alpha_1, T_1, \tau_1, \prec_1, \kappa_1, \rho_1, \partial_1)$ is an uncertain spatiotemporal data tree, $u_2 = (V_2, E_2, \alpha_2, T_2, \tau_2, \prec_2, \kappa_2, \rho_2, \partial_2)$ is operational outcome. The selection operation can be defined in the following way:

$$\sigma[e](u_1) = \{t \mid t \in u_1 \wedge f_t(e) = true\}$$

In the definition, $f_t(e)$ evaluates *true* the corresponding *t* and its descendant are added to the outcome i.e. u_2. If it evaluates false, *t* is not added to the outcome i.e. u_2.

Figure 6. The input u_1 and the output u_2 of selection operation

```
<oil spill>
  <position Ts="t2" Te="t6">
    <Dist type ="disjunctive">
      <Val Poss="0.7">
        <x1>10</x1>
        <y1>20</y2>
        <x2>15</x2>
        <y2>23</y2>
      </Val>
      <Val Poss="0.4">
        <x1>22</x1>
        <y1>15</y2>
        <x2>25</x2>
        <y2>20</y2>
      </Val>
    </Dist>
  </position>
  <position Ts="t7" Te="t8">
    <Val Poss="0.6">
      <x1>32</x1>
      <y1>25</y2>
      <x2>45</x2>
      <y2>36</y2>
    </Val>
  </position>
</oil spill>
```

u_1

```
<oil spill>
  <position Ts="t4" Te="t6">
    <Dist type ="disjunctive">
      <Val Poss="0.7">
        <x1>10</x1>
        <y1>20</y2>
        <x2>15</x2>
        <y2>23</y2>
      </Val>
    </Dist>
  </position>
</oil spill>
```

$u_2 = \sigma[e](u_1)$

e ="T=[t4, t6] $\wedge$ Val Poss >0.5"

In Figure 6, the condition of selection operation is that the value of *Val Poss* lager than 0.5 and in time interval $[t_4, t_6]$. The result shows the all uncertain spatiotemporal information that satisfied the selection expression.

4.2.3 Projection Operation

The projection operation takes one uncertain spatiotemporal trees u_1 as input and produces an uncertain spatiotemporal data tree u_2 as output.

Definition 13 (Projection operation). Suppose $u_1 = (V_1, E_1, \alpha_1, T_1, \tau_1, \prec_1, \kappa_1, \rho_1, \partial_1)$ is an uncertain spatiotemporal data tree, $u_2 = (V_2, E_2, \alpha_2, T_2, \tau_2, \prec_2, \kappa_2, \rho_2, \partial_2)$ is operational outcome. The projection operation can be defined in the following way:

$$\pi[A](u_1) = \{t[A] \mid t \in u_1\}$$

The projection operation is performed from the point of view of the labels. In Definition 13, *A* is the restrictive condition of projection operation i.e. the labels that we need to extract from the input u_1. The projection operation extract the all uncertain spatiotemporal information that label satisfied the restrictive condition *A*.

Figure 7. The result of projection operation

<oil spill OID="O_2" T_s="t_2" T_e="t_6-1">
<pre T_s="t_2" T_e="t_6-1">O_1</pre>
<suc T_s="t_2" T_e="t_6-1">O_3</suc>
</oil spill>

$$u_2 = \pi[A](u_1)$$
$$A = \text{"pre, suc"}$$

The example of projection operation in Figure 7 used the data tree of Figure 1 as input. According to the condition of projection in Figure 7, we capture the uncertain spatiotemporal information of predecessor and successor because the collection A is equal to labels of *pre* and *suc*. Thus we extract the uncertain spatiotemporal information of predecessor "O_1" and successor "O_3".

4.2.4 Join Operation

The join operation takes two uncertain spatiotemporal trees u_1, u_2 as input and produces an uncertain spatiotemporal data tree u as output. Actually join operation is the combination of Cartesian product operation and selection operation.

Definition 14 (Join operation). Suppose $u_1 = (V_1, E_1, \alpha_1, T_1, \tau_1, \prec_1, \kappa_1, \rho_1, \partial_1)$ and $u_2 = (V_2, E_2, \alpha_2, T_2, \tau_2, \prec_2, \kappa_2, \rho_2, \partial_2)$ are uncertain spatiotemporal data trees. The output $u = u_1 \bowtie [e] u_2$ of join operator is defined as follows:

$$u = u_1 \bowtie [e] u_2 = \{ t \mid t \in u_1 \times u_2 \wedge f_t(e) = true \}$$

In Definition 14, $f_t(e)$ is selection function to select the result of Cartesian product on inputs.

In Figure 8, the results come from the combination of the result of Cartesian product operation in Figure 5 and selection operation that the condition is "*Val Poss≥0.25*". We do the Cartesian product operation on the two inputs in Figure 4 firstly. Then we do the selection operation on the result of the Cartesian product operation to select the information of possibility larger than or equal to 0.25.

4.2.5 Grouping and Ordering Operation

The objective of grouping is to split a collection into subsets of data trees and we can represent each subset as an ordered tree in any desired way.

Figure 8. The result of join operation

```
<Dist type=”disjunctive”>
  <Val Poss=”0.25”>
    <area>3000</area>
    <direction>northeast</direaction>
  </Val>
  <Val poss=”0.35”>
    <area>5000</area>
    <direction>northeast</direaction>
  </Val>
</Dist>
```

$$u = u_1 \bowtie [e] u_2$$

$$e = \text{"}Val\ Poss \geq 0.25\text{"}$$

Definition 15 (Grouping operation). Suppose the uncertain spatiotemporal data trees $u_1 = (V_1, E_1, \alpha_1, T_1, \tau_1, \prec_1, \kappa_1, \rho_1, \partial_1)$ is an input of grouping operation. Then the grouping operation ξ can be defined as follows:

$$\xi[e](u_1) = \{\Gamma(t) \mid t \in u_1 \wedge f_t(e) = true\}$$

According to Definition 15, the nodes satisfied the same condition *e* will be divided into the same group by the grouping operation. $\Gamma(t)$ represents a collection of *t* which is satisfied for the condition.

Definition 16 (Ordering operation). Suppose the uncertain spatiotemporal data tree $u_1 = (V_1, E_1, \alpha_1, T_1, \tau_1, \prec_1, \kappa_1, \rho_1, \partial_1)$ and an ordering rule $\lambda: a \rightarrow b$ as inputs. Then the ordering operation λ can be defined as follows:

$$O(u_1) = \{t \mid t \in u_1 \wedge \lambda(t, \prec_{1,} a) \Rightarrow \lambda(t, \prec_{1,} b)\}$$

4.2.6 Bind and Tree Operation

The feature of XML data is to arbitrarily nest, thus we propose the Bind and Tree operation to capture the relevant information from the nested XML documents. By the Bind operation we can extract the relevant uncertain spatiotemporal information and produce a structure, which explicitly shows the uncertain spatiotemporal information we need and hides the uncertain spatiotemporal information we don't need i.e. the Bind operation can bind the uncertain spatiotemporal information that we need. Bind and Tree operations are a pair of opposite operations. The purpose of Tree operation is to generate a new nested XML structure. In general, the two operations appear at the same time.

Definition 17 (Bind operation). Suppose $u_l = (V_l, E_l, \alpha_l, T_l, \tau_l, \prec_1, \kappa_l, \rho_l, \partial_l)$ is an uncertain spatiotemporal data tree, function $B_t(e)$ is to extract uncertain spatiotemporal information from u_l under the condition e. If there is a rule $\lambda: a \rightarrow b$, then the definition of Bind operation is as follows:

$$\text{Bind}(u_l) = \{B_t(e) \mid t \in u_l \wedge \lambda(t, a) \Rightarrow \lambda(t, b)\}$$

Bind operation extracts uncertain spatiotemporal information from an input under a given restriction. It embodies the bound variables that satisfied the condition.

Definition 18 (Tree operation). Tree operation processes the result of Bind operation i.e. Tree operation show the uncertain spatiotemporal information that is hidden in Bind operation.

Figure 9. A bind operation

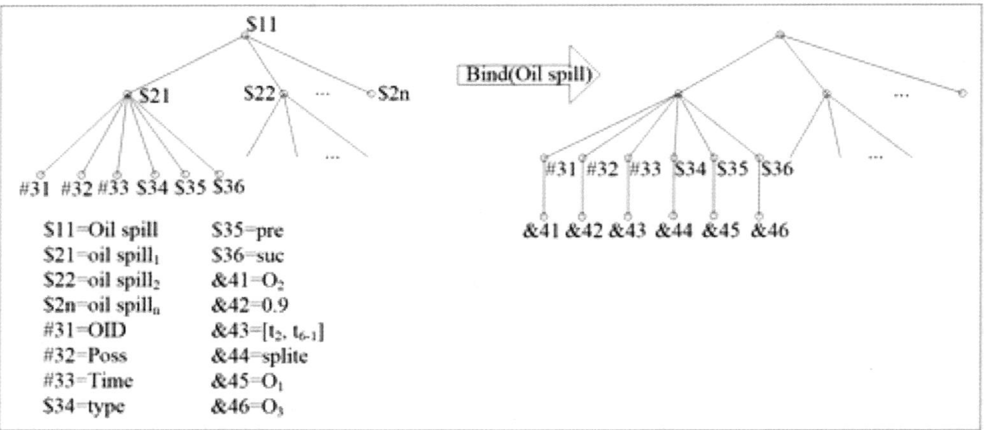

In XML data trees, we use "$" to represent element nodes, "#" to express attribute nodes, and "&" to represent value nodes. Thus we can easily specify the types of nodes. Figure 9 is a Bind operation. For the XML data tree of *Oil spill*, element node "*oil spill*" contains *OID*, *Poss*, *Time*, *type*, *pre* (i.e. predecessor) and *suc* (i.e. successor) where *OID*, *Poss* and *Time* are attribute nodes and the rest are element nodes. We extract uncertain spatiotemporal information by Bind operation under the filter conditions. Figure 10 is a Tree operation.

Figure 10. Tree operation

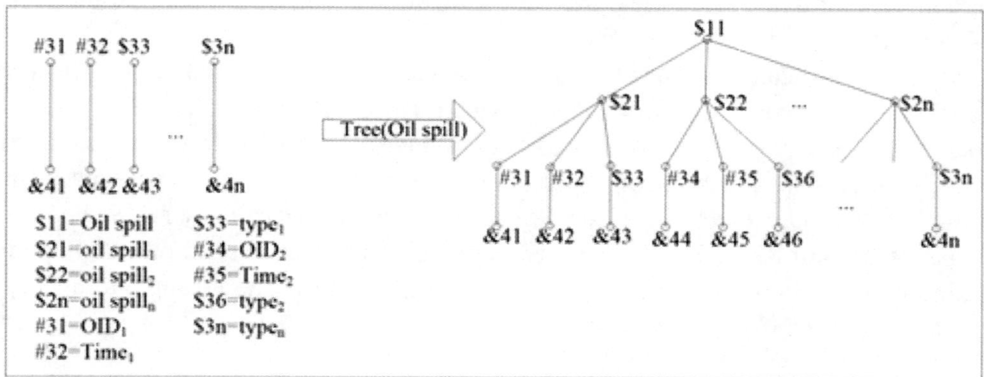

5 EXPRESSIVE POWER

In this section, we show the expressive power of our algebraic operations. We will discuss the translation of XQuery into our algebraic operations. XQuery is a standard query language of XML. As the powerful expression of XQuery, FLWOR expression is the most popular expression that supports iteration and binding of variables to intermediate results. FLWOR expression is acronym for clauses of "for", "let", "where", "order by" and "return". Thus we mainly carry on the translation of FLWOR expression. After translating from FLWOR expression to our algebraic expressions, the new FLWOR expression can query the uncertain spatiotemporal data.

5.1 Complete Syntax of FLWOR Expression

```
for clause | let clause
[where  <where_condition> ]
[order by  <order_expression>]
return return_expression
```

In FLWOR expression, the "for" and "let" clauses generate an ordered sequence of tuples of bound variables. The "where" clause is used to filter the outcome processed by the "for" and "let" clauses. The "order by" clause sorts the result of a FLWOR expression. The condition of "where_condition" and "order_condition" both contain two types, the one is ordinary condition of ordinary variables and the other is special condition of special variables with uncertain, temporal and spatial features. The "return" clause returns the result of the FLWOR expression in the specified form.

5.2 The "for" and "let" Clauses

The "for" clause is used to bind one or more iterator variables to the input sequences. If it binds multiple variables, then each variable is bound to a sequence and the clause iterates each variable over its binding sequence. Each tuple of the "for" clause result corresponds to a bound sequence. In the new "for" clause, variables can be divided into two types, one is ordinary variables, and another is special variables with uncertain, temporal and spatial features. The variables of two types also bind the corresponding sequences, respectively.

The "let" clause also can embodies multiple variables, each with an associated expression. Unlike a "for" clause, the "let" clause bind all variables to a sequence without iteration. The result of the "let" clause is one tuple containing all the bound variables. Similarly the variables are divided into two types, the one is ordinary variables and the other is special variables with uncertain, temporal and spatial features.

Definition 19. Suppose there is a clause '*$i* in doc("*Sname*")$\psi_i[r_i]$', where "*Sname*" is the input uncertain spatiotemporal XML data tree, ψ_i is a path expression and r_i is an ordinary condition r_{1i} or a special condition r_{2j} with uncertain, temporal and spatial features. Then using our algebra, the "for" clause and "let" clause can be transformed as follows:

for: $\sigma/[r_{1i} \mid r_{2j}](\pi/\psi_i(\ldots(\sigma[r_{11} \mid r_{21}]($Bind("*Sname*"$)))))$

let: Tree rootname$(\sigma/[r_{1i} \mid r_{2j}](\pi/\psi_i(\ldots(\sigma[r_{11} \mid r_{21}]($Bind("*Sname*"$))))))$

5.3 The "Where" Clause

The "where" clause is optional and serves as a filter for the tuples of variable bindings generated by the "for" and "let" clauses. The two kinds of "where_condition" restrict two kinds of variables, respectively. If the return value of "where_condition" is true, then the corresponding item exists in the result. Otherwise, it is not in the result.

Definition 20. Suppose there is a clause 'where *$i* $\psi[r]$', *u* is the input uncertain spatiotemporal XML data tree and ψ' is a path expression that locates the object bound to the variable *$i*. Then the "where" clause can be transformed as follows:

where: $\sigma\psi'\ \psi[\ r_{1i} \mid r_{2j}\ ](u)$

5.4 The "Order by" and "Return" Clauses

An "order by" clause contains one or more ordering specifications. It is easy for the "order by" clause to sort the result of a FLWOR expression. Each sort expression generates a single sequence for each item. The translation of "order by" clause is quite straightforward.

The "return" clause constructs the result of the FLWOR expression. The content of the "return" clause maybe is the result of another FLWOR expression. Thus the "return" clause can be nested.

Definition 21. Suppose there is a "return" clause, *Re* is a function that can represent the result of our algebraic operation translated from another FLWOR expression. If it is nested, the "return" clause can be transformed as follows:

return: Tree rootname(*Rname*)($\sum / \psi i$.value)(*Re*(*e*_FLWOR)$^+$)

when there is no nested structure in the "return" clause, we have

return: Tree rootname(*Rname*)($\sum / \psi i$.value)($\pi / \psi i$(Bind("*Sname*")))

Here, the "+" represents the nested clause can be one or multiple. The "*Rname*" represents the name of the root of result tree.

5.5 XQuery Examples

In this subsection, we will give a specific description of the uncertain spatiotemporal XML query processing according to the definitions of uncertain spatiotemporal XML algebraic operations presented before. Key to uncertain spatiotemporal XML query is the matching between the multipath expression pattern and the instance mode of the uncertain spatiotemporal XML data trees.

We use the XML document in Figure 12 to give examples to illustrate how to query by using our algebraic operations.

Query Q. Return the name and declining number of species which belong to the same position as the oil spill whose area is more than "5000" and the "*Poss*" is more than 0.5 during $[t_4, t_6]$.

For convenience of understanding and expressing the query expression, we use capital letter I to represent the intermediate results. According to the definition above, we have

Tree result ((*sname*, number) ((π/[species](π/[*sname*](I_2)))∪ π/[species](π/[number](I_2)))

Here,

I_1 = (σ/[oil spill/position/$\$x_1$=species/position/$\$x_1$∧oil spill/position/$\$x_2$=species/position/$\$x_2$
∧oil spill/position/$\$y_1$=species/position/$\$y_1$∧ oil spill/position/$\$y_2$=species/position/$\$y_2$]
((σ/[#t_e=t_6∧#t_s=t_4] (π/[oil spill] (Bind(Oil spill))))
×σ/[#t_e=t_6∧#t_s=t_4] (π/[species] (Bind(Species)))))

I_2= (σ/oil spill/area/[$\$a$>5000∧#$p$>0.5] ($I_1$)∪$\sigma$/species/number/[$\$n$<0] ($I_1$)))

From query optimization point of view the query expression is not optimum. Thus in next section, we will introduce the equivalences and optimization of our algebraic query and take this query as an example to optimize.

6 EQUIVALENCES AND OPTIMIZATION

6.1 Equivalences

The proposed optimization rules aims at reducing the cost of the query of uncertain spatiotemporal data. The proposed of the optimization rules based on equivalent rules and data tree isomorphism we proposed before. Thus, we introduce the equivalent rules of our algebra in this subsection.

Let u_1, u_2 and u_i be uncertain spatiotemporal XML data trees, e is expression of condition and A is collection of labels, then we have several rules as follows:

Rule 1.(Commutativity of ∪, ∩,×, ⋈)

$u_1 \theta u_2 \equiv u_2 \theta u_1$

Here, θ is one of the operators: ∪, ∩, × and ⋈.

Rule 2.(Associativity of ×, ⋈)

$(u_1 \theta u_2) \theta u_3 \equiv u_1 \theta (u_2 \theta u_3)$

Here, θ is one of the operators: × and ⋈.

Rule 3.(Commutativity of σ with ∪, −, ⋈)

$\sigma[e](\text{Bind}(u_1\ \theta\ u_2)) \equiv \sigma[e](\text{Bind}(u_1))\ \theta\ \sigma[e](\text{Bind}(u_2))$

Here, θ is one of the operators: ∪, − and ⋈.

Rule 4.(Commutativity of π with ∪)

$\pi[A](\text{Bind}(u_1 \cup u_2)) \equiv \pi[A](\text{Bind}(u_1)) \cup \pi[A](\text{Bind}(u_2))$

Here, A is the collection of labels and u_1 and u_2 both involves the all of labels in the collection A.

Rule 5.(Cascading of σ)

$\sigma[e_1 \wedge e_2 \wedge \ldots \wedge e_n](\text{Bind}(u_1)) \equiv \sigma[e_1](\sigma[e_2](\ldots(\sigma[e_n](\text{Bind}(u_1)))\ldots))$

Rule 6.(Cascading of π)

$\pi[A_1](\pi[A_2](\text{Bind}(u_1))) \equiv \pi[A_1](\text{Bind}(u_1))$

Here, A_1 is the subset of A_2.

Rule 7.(Decomposition of ⋈)

$\text{Bind}(u_1) \bowtie [e] \text{Bind}(u_2) \equiv \sigma[e](\text{Bind}(u_1) \times \text{Bind}(u_2))$

Rule 8.(Commutativity of σ with π)

$\sigma[e](\pi[A](\text{Bind}(u_1))) \equiv \pi[A](\sigma[e](\text{Bind}(u_1)))$

Rule 9.(Commutativity of σ with ×)

If the expression e involves solely nodes from u_1, then

$\sigma[e](\text{Bind}(u_1 \times u_2)) \equiv \sigma[e](\text{Bind}(u_1)) \times u_2$

If $e = e_1 \wedge e_2$, and the expression e_1 involves solely nodes from u_1, the expression e_2 embodies solely nodes from u_2, then

$\sigma[e](\text{Bind}(u_1 \times u_2)) \equiv \sigma[e_1](\text{Bind}(u_1)) \times \sigma[e_2](\text{Bind}(u_2))$

If $e = e_1 \wedge e_2$, and the expression e_1 involves solely nodes from u_1, the expression e_2 embodies nodes from u_1 and u_2, then

$\sigma[e](\text{Bind}(u_1 \times u_2)) \equiv \sigma[e_2](\sigma[e_1](\text{Bind}(u_1)) \times u_2)$

Rule10. (Decomposition of π with ∪)

$\pi[A_1](\text{Bind}(u_1)) \cup \pi[A_2](\text{Bind}(u_1)) \equiv \pi[A_1 \cup A_2](\text{Bind}(u_1))$

Here, $A = A_1 \cup A_2$, A_1 involves solely labels from u_1 and A_2 involves solely labels from u_2.

Rule 11.(Commutativity of π with ×)

$\pi[A](\text{Bind}(u_1 \times u_2)) \equiv \pi[A_1](\text{Bind}(u_1)) \times \pi[A_2](\text{Bind}(u_2))$

Here, $A = A_1 \cup A_2$, A_1 involves solely labels from u_1 and A_2 involves solely labels from u_2.

The proposed of the above equivalence rules makes it possible to optimize the query of uncertain spatiotemporal data tree. Thus we can reduce the cost of the query as much as possible.

6.2 Optimization

In this subsection, we propose the heuristic approach of optimization that applies the above equivalence rules to transform a query tree of uncertain spatiotemporal data into an optimized tree of uncertain spatiotemporal data. The optimized tree is more efficient to query than the initial tree.

The principle of optimization is to adjust the order of operations of query expression to minimize the size of the sequence to be traversed in order to reduce the cost of the query.

We follow several heuristic thoughts in the application of the above equivalence rules. The heuristic thoughts are as follows:

1. Selection operation and projection operation should be done as soon as possible.
2. Decompose complex operation into simple operation.

3. Minimize the size of the intermediate results as much as possible.

According to the equivalence rules and heuristic thoughts, we can outline the optimization approach of uncertain spatiotemporal data query in Figure 11. Each step of optimization process of uncertain spatiotemporal data is described in detail as follows:

Figure 11. The optimization process of uncertain spatiotemporal data query

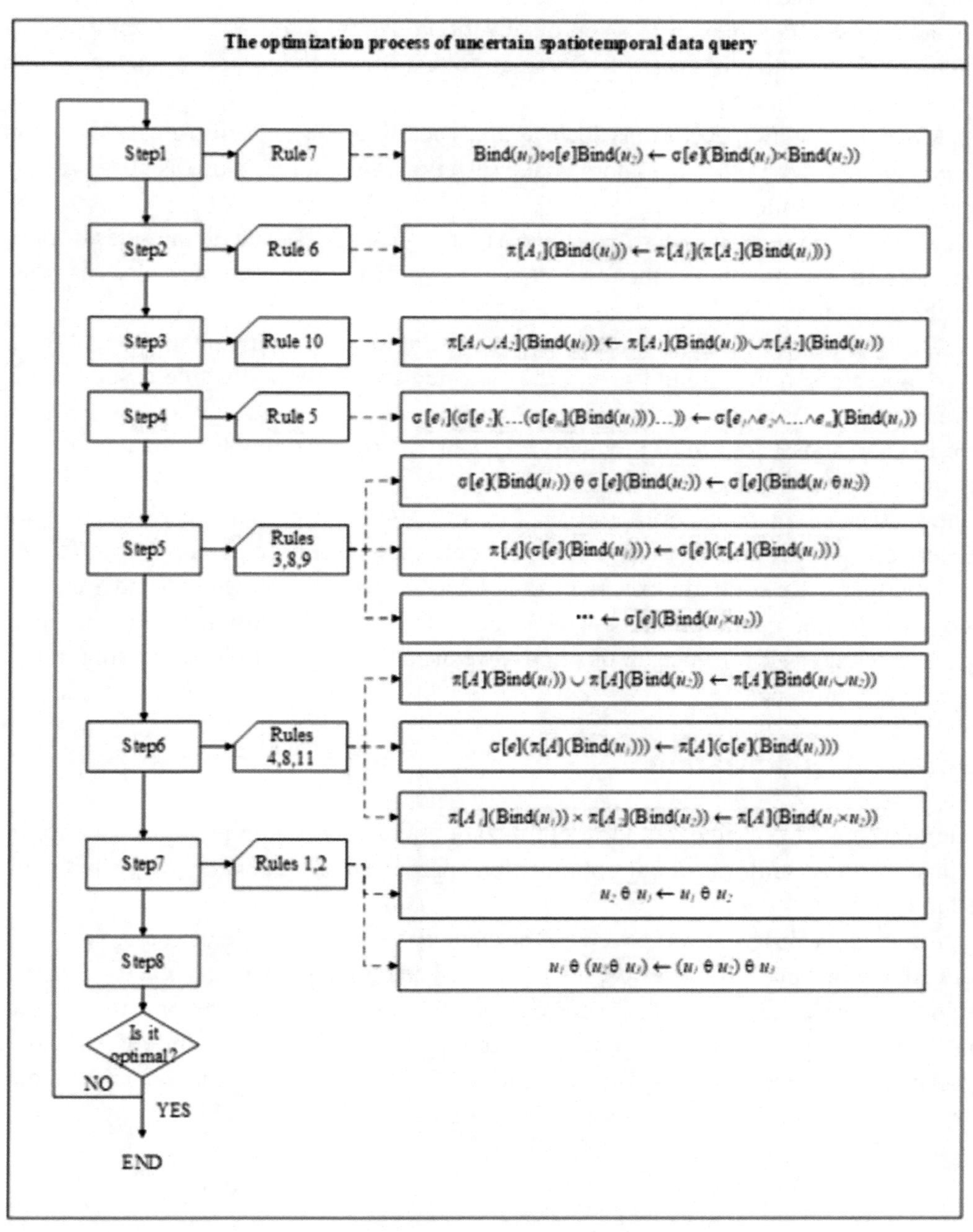

Step 1. Combine selection operation with Cartesian product operation into join operation. Based on the decomposition of join operation, eliminate Cartesian product operation from the query tree so that the query can be more effective. (use Rule 7)

Step 2. Remove redundant projection operation. Based on the cascading of projection operation, decompose the cascade of several projection operations into a single projection operation so that eliminate unnecessary projection operation and reduce the cost of the query. (use Rule 6)

Step 3. Combine several collections of labels of projection operations into a collection so that we can minimize traversal times of the same sequence. Hence the time cost of the query can be minimized as much as possible. (use Rule 10)

Step 4. Decompose complex expression of selection operation into several sample expressions i.e. break down selections into a cascade of selections so that the selection operation can be moved down as far as possible. (use Rule 5)

Step 5. Move the selection operations down as far as possible. Based on the rules of the commutativity of selection operation with other operators, make selection operation as close as possible to the bottom of the query tree. (use Rules 3, 8, 9)

Step 6. Move the projection operations down as far as possible. Based on the rules of the commutativity of projection operation with other operators, make projection operation as close as possible to the bottom of the query tree. (use Rules 4, 8, 11)

Step 7. Reduce the size of the intermediate results. Based on the commutativity and the associativity of binary operators, minimize the size of the intermediate results so that the cost can be lower. (use Rules 1, 2)

Step 8. Repeat steps 1 to 7 until the query tree can't be optimized, then finish the optimization of the query tree.

The above steps are just a generic process of optimization approach and each step is not necessary in the process of optimization. In Steps above, an identical rule maybe has several different treatment schemes, actually it is not contradictory. For example, Rule 8 is applied in Step 5 and Step 6. As a result, in practice, the selection operation first maybe is the better choice, but also maybe the projection operation first is the better choice. Hence, at this point, we usually apply flexible processing rules according to the specific circumstance.

6.3 Example of Optimization

We outline the steps of our algebra query optimization approach in the previous section. In this section, we illustrate the usefulness of our optimization approach using an example which is described and expressed in Query Q.

In order to identify different vertexes with the same name in query tree of Query Q, we prefix them by the name of the original parent vertex, respectively. The initial query tree of Query Q is in Figure 12.

The initial query tree directly includes the combination of selection operation and Cartesian product operation. Thus we can optimize the initial query tree by applying Step 1 according to the optimization approach. The initial query tree also fits in with Step 2 as the result of "*sname*" and "number" being subsets of "species". Thus firstly applying Rule 7 in Step 1 and Rule 6 in Step 2 one can get the query tree in Figure 13.

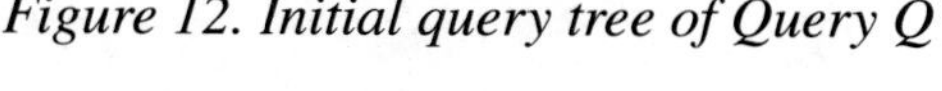

Figure 12. Initial query tree of Query Q

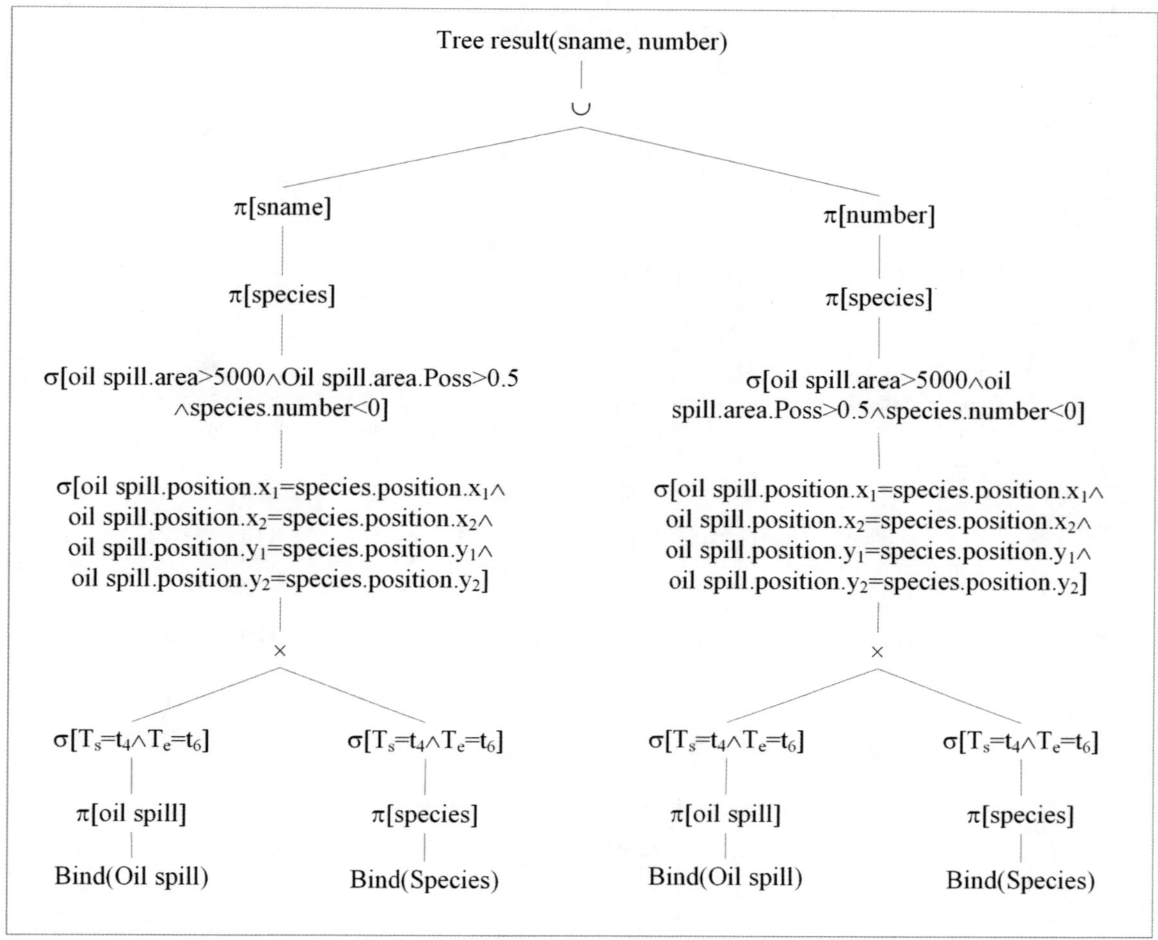

In Figure 13, the projection operation extracts the information of labels being "*sname*" and "number" by traversing the same sequence, respectively. It is obvious that the query tree justifies Rule 10 in Step 3. Combining labels of "*sname*" and "number" into a collection can reduce the traversal times of the same sequence, thus we make second optimization by applying Rule 10. We get the query tree in Figure 14 by making the second optimization.

The query tree directly includes many complex restrictive expression of selection operation, thus by applying Rule 5 in Step 4 from the optimization approach to decompose the complex expression of selection operation. A further improvement can be realized by making selection operation as close as possible to the bottom of the query tree so that we apply Rule 3 in Step 5 of the optimization approach to reduce the size of the intermediate results. It is worth noting that the different execution order of selection operations has different influence of the query cost. Hence the specific execution order should be determined according to the actual situation. The query tree after further optimization is given in Figure 15.

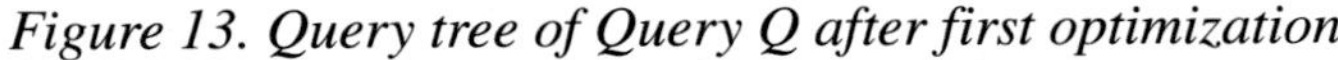

Figure 13. Query tree of Query Q after first optimization

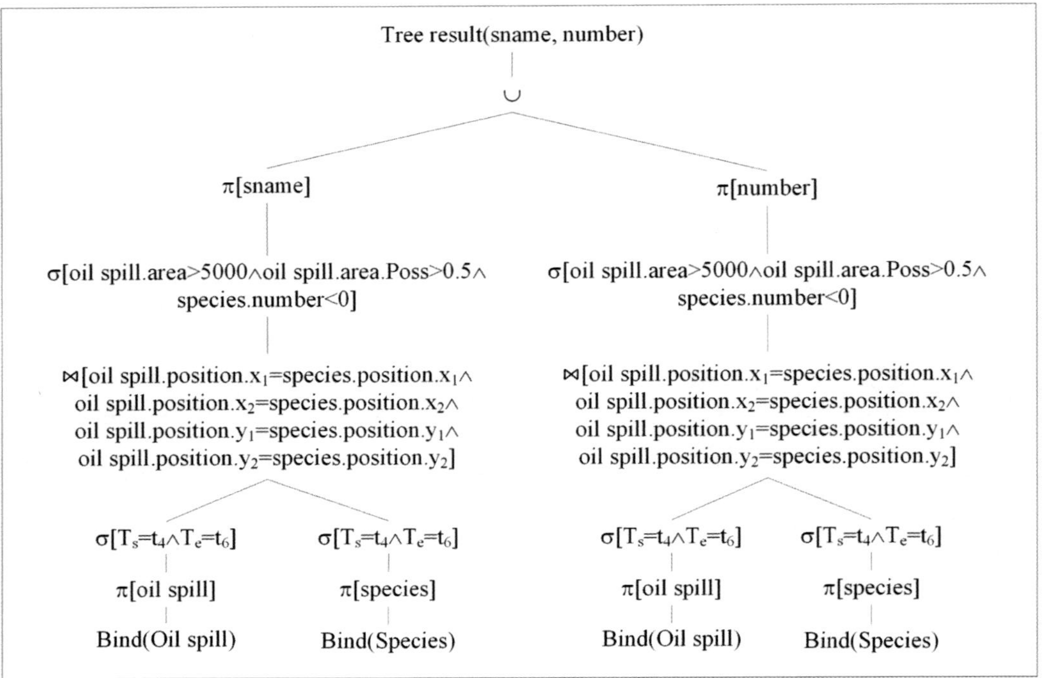

Figure 14. Query tree of Query Q after second optimization

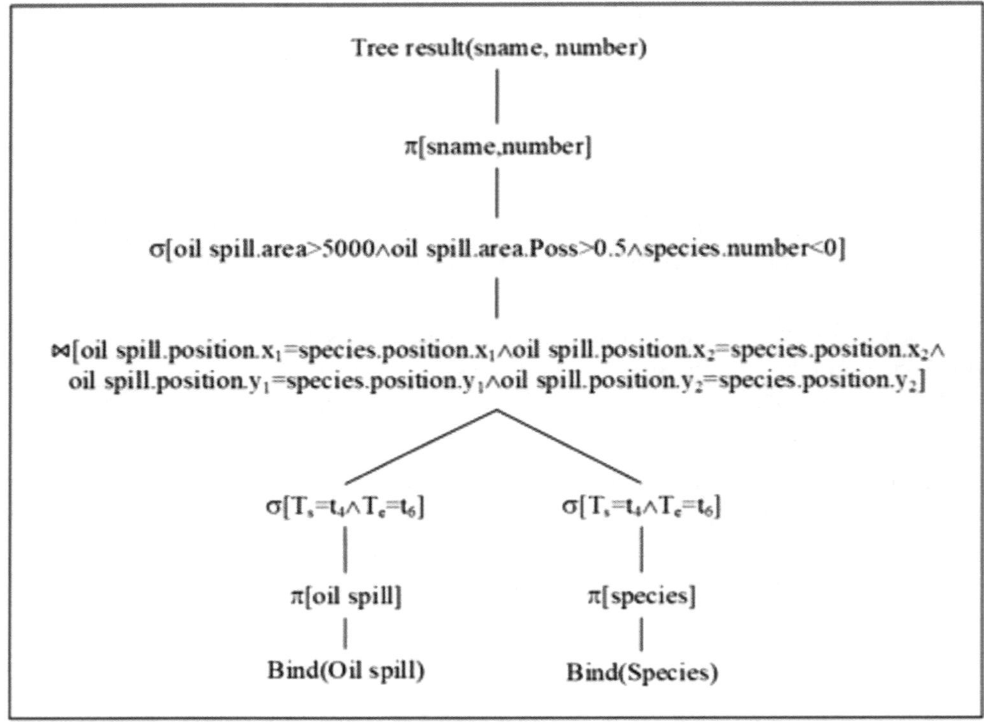

Figure 15. The final query tree of Query Q after third optimization

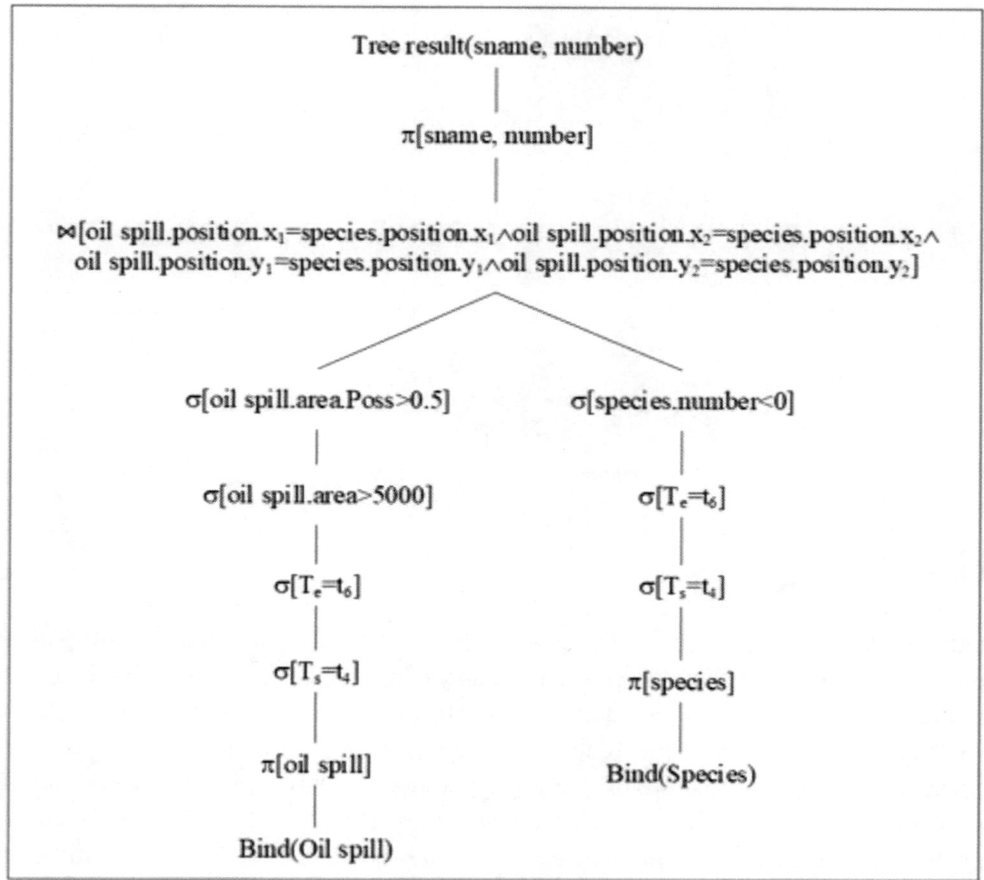

According to the actual circumstance of our query, Step 6 and Step 7 are unnecessary in the optimization process of Query Q. Then the query tree in Figure 15 cannot apply any rules of optimization approach to optimize, hence the query tree is the final outcome of Query Q.

All the query trees in the above are equivalent because of the optimization based on the equivalence rules. In fact, the core principle is reducing the size of the intermediate results and making the query simpler than initial query in the process of the optimization. That is the reason why executing the final query tree is more efficient than the others.

In the architecture of querying uncertain spatiotemporal data, the core part is the translation query request into algebraic operations and query optimization which are contained in the dashed line in Figure 16. The core part plays a key role in the query process because it relates to whether the query is efficient and fast.

Figure 16. The architecture of querying uncertain spatiotemporal data

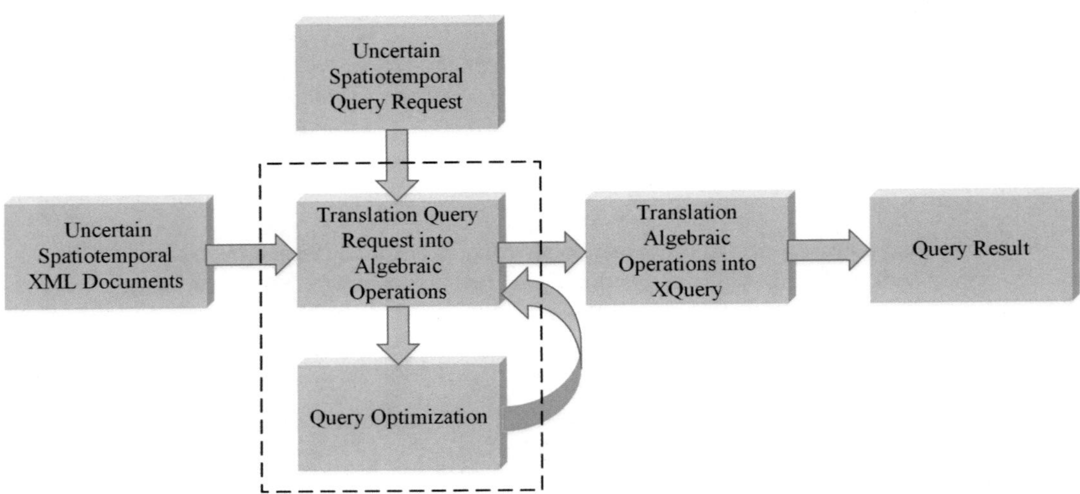

7 SUMMARY

In this study, we focus on modeling the uncertain spatiotemporal data and algebraic operations on it. A number of researches have been undertaken to address modeling spatiotemporal data, but uncertain spatiotemporal data has not been adequately addressed and this is the focus of our work. In this chapter, we propose the uncertain spatiotemporal data model based on XML. In addition, for processing uncertain spatiotemporal data, we present a series of algebraic operations based on the model we proposed to capture uncertain spatiotemporal information. The advantage of this algebra is that it is flexible and powerful to translate XQuery into our algebra. Finally, we propose the equivalence rules and optimization approach to optimize our algebraic query and an example to illustrate how to apply the optimization approach.

REFERENCES

Abiteboul, S., Kimelfeld, B., Sagiv, Y., & Senellart, P. (2009). On the Expressiveness of Probabilistic XML Models. *The VLDB Journal, 18*(5), 1041–1064. doi:10.100700778-009-0146-1

Amagasa, T., Yoshikawa, M., & Uemura, S. (2000). A Data Model for Temporal XML Documents. In *Proceedings of DEXA*, (pp. 334-344). ACM. 10.1007/3-540-44469-6_31

Baazizi, M. A., Bidoit, N., & Colazzo, D. (2011). Efficient Encoding of Temporal XML Documents. In *Proceedings of the 18th IEEE International Symposium on Temporal Representation and Reasoning*, (pp. 15-22). IEEE.

Bai, L., & Xu, C. (2015). Spatiotemporal Query Algebra Based on Native XML. In B. Sheng & X. Li (Eds.), *Handbook of Research on Innovative Database Query Processing Techniques* (pp. 275–293). IGI Global.

Bai, L. Y., Yan, L., & Ma, Z. M. (2015). Fuzzy Spatiotemporal Data Modeling and Operations in XML. *Applied Artificial Intelligence*, *29*(3), 259–282. doi:10.1080/08839514.2015.1004615

Budak Arpinar, I., Sheth, A., Ramakrishnan, C., Lynn Usery, E., Azami, M., & Kwan, M. P. (2006). Geospatial ontology development and semantic analytics. *Transactions in GIS*, *10*(4), 551–575. doi:10.1111/j.1467-9671.2006.01012.x

Chen, Y., & Revesz, P. Z. (2003). Querying Spatiotemporal XML Using DataFoX. In *Proceedings of WI*, pp. 301-309.

Cheng, R., Emrich, T., & Kriegel, H. P. (2014). Managing Uncertainty in Spatial and Spatio-Temporal Data. In *Proceedings of ICDE*, (pp. 1302-1305). IEEE. 10.1109/ICDE.2014.6816766

Córcoles, J. E., Garcia-Consuegra, J., & Peralta, J. (2000). *A Spatio-Temporal Query Language for a Data Model based on XML.* In *Proceedings of the 6th ECGI & GIS Workshop*, Lyon, France.

Córcoles, J. E., & González, P. (2001). A Specification of a Spatial Query Language over GML. In *Proceedings of the 9th ACM International Symposium on Advances in Geographic Information Systems*, (pp. 112-117). ACM. 10.1145/512161.512186

Ding, Z., Peng, Y., & Pan, R. (2006). BayesOWL: Uncertainty modeling in semantic web ontologies. *Soft computing in ontologies and semantic web*, 3-29.

Duckham, M., Mason, K., Stell, J., & Worboys, M. (2001). A Formal Approach to Imperfection in Geographic Information. *Computers, Environment and Urban Systems*, *25*(1), 89–103. doi:10.1016/S0198-9715(00)00040-5

Fernandez, M., Simeon, J., & Wadler, P. (2000). An Algebra for XML Query. In *Proceedings of the 2000 International Conference on Foundations of Software Technology and Theoretical Computer Science*, (pp. 11-45). IEEE.

Franceschet, M., Montanari, A., & Gubiani, D. (2007). Modeling and Validating Spatio-Temporal Conceptual Schemas in XML Schema. In *Proceedings of DEXA*, (pp. 25-29). IEEE. 10.1109/DEXA.2007.106

Frasincar, F., Houben, G. J., & Pau, C. (2002). XAL: An Algebra for XML Query Optimization. *Australian Computer Science Communications*, *24*(2), 49–56.

Grandi, F., Mandreoli, F., & Tiberio, P. (2003). A Temporal Data Model and Management System for Normative Texts in XML Format. In *Proceedings of the 5th ACM International Workshop on Web Information and Data Management*, (pp. 29-36). ACM. 10.1145/956699.956706

Huang, B., Yi, S., & Chan, W. T. (2004). Spatio-Temporal Information Integration in XML. *Future Generation Computer Systems*, *20*(7), 1157–1170. doi:10.1016/j.future.2003.11.005

Jagadish, H. V., Lakshmanan, L. V., & Srivastava, D. (2001). TAX: a Tree Algebra for XML. In *Proceedings of the 8th International Workshop on Database Programming Languages*, (pp. 149-164). IEEE.

Kimelfeld, B., Kosharovsky, Y., & Sagiv, Y. (2008). Query Efficiency in Probabilistic XML Models. In *Proceedings of the 2008 ACM SIGMOD International Conference on Management of Data*, (pp. 701-714). ACM. 10.1145/1376616.1376687

Kuijpers, B., & Othman, W. (2010). Trajectory Databases: Data models, Uncertainty and Complete Query Languages. *Journal of Computer and System Sciences*, *76*(7), 538–560. doi:10.1016/j.jcss.2009.10.002

Lehto, L., & Kilpeläinen, T. (2001). Generalizing XML-Encoded Spatial Data on the Web. In *Proceedings of the 20th International Cartographic Conference*, (pp. 2390-2396). IEEE.

Li, S., & Xu, M. (2010). A Novel Approach of Computing XML Similarity based on Weighted XML Data Model. In *Proceedings of the 8th IEEE International Conference on Control and Automation*, (pp. 1157-1162). IEEE. 10.1109/ICCA.2010.5524091

Liu, X., & Wan, Y. (2010). Storing Spatio-Temporal Data in XML Native Database. In *Proceedings of the 2nd International Workshop on Database Technology and Applications*, (pp. 1-4). IEEE. 10.1109/DBTA.2010.5659107

Luo, W., Yuan, L., Wu, M., & Yu, Z. (2010). Spatial-temporal data analysis with spacetime algebra: A case study with satellite altimetry data. In *2010 18th International Conference on Geoinformatics* (pp. 1-5). IEEE. 10.1109/GEOINFORMATICS.2010.5567880

Mane, A., Babu, D. R., & Anand, M. C. (2004). XML Representation of Spatial Data. In *Proceedings of the 2004 IEEE India Annual Conference*, (pp. 490-493). IEEE.

Mishra, V. N., & Rai, P. K. (2016). A remote sensing aided multi-layer perceptron-Markov chain analysis for land use and land cover change prediction in Patna district (Bihar), India. *Arabian Journal of Geosciences*, *9*(4), 1–18. doi:10.100712517-015-2138-3

Mitakos, T., & Almaliotis, I. (2009). Representing Geographic Information in Multidimensional XML: Applying Dimensions in Spatial Databases. In *Proceedings of the 16th IEEE International Conference on Systems, Signals and Image Processing*, (pp. 1-4). IEEE. 10.1109/IWSSIP.2009.5367760

Mokhtar, H. M., & Su, J. (2004). Universal Trajectory Queries for Moving Object Databases. In *Proceedings of the 2004 IEEE International Conference on Mobile Data Management*, (pp. 133-144). IEEE. 10.1109/MDM.2004.1263051

Nierman, A., & Jagadish, H. V. (2002). ProTDB: Probabilistic Data in XML. In *Proceedings of VLDB*, (pp. 646-657). IEEE.

Nørvåg, K. (2002). Algorithms for Temporal Query Operators in XML Databases. In *Proceedings of the 2002 International Conference on Extending Database Technology*, (pp. 169-183). IEEE.

Pelekis, N., Theodoulidis, B., Kopanakis, I., & Theodoridis, Y. (2004). Literature Review of Spatio-Temporal Database Models. *The Knowledge Engineering Review*, *19*(3), 235–274. doi:10.1017/S026988890400013X

Ribaric, S., & Hrkac, T. (2012). A model of fuzzy spatio-temporal knowledge representation and reasoning based on high-level Petri nets. *Information Systems*, *37*(3), 238–256. doi:10.1016/j.is.2011.09.010

Tøssebro, E. (2002). *Representing Uncertainty in Spatial and Spatiotemporal Databases*. [Doctoral Thesis, Norwegian University of Science and Technology].

Tøssebro, E., & Nygård, M. (2002). Abstract and Discrete Models for Uncertain Spatiotemporal Data. In *Proceedings of the 14th IEEE International Conference on Scientific and Statistical Database Management*, (pp. 240-240). IEEE. 10.1109/SSDM.2002.1029727

Tøssebro, E., & Nygård, M. (2002). Uncertainty in Spatiotemporal Databases. *Advanced Information Systems*, 43–53.

Trajcevski, G., Wolfson, O., Hinrichs, K., & Chamberlain, S. (2004). Managing Uncertainty in Moving Objects Databases. *ACM Transactions on Database Systems*, *29*(3), 463–507. doi:10.1145/1016028.1016030

Viqueira, J. R. R. (2000). Relational Algebra for Spatio-Temporal Data Management. In *Proceedings of the EDBT 2000 PhD Workshop*, (pp. 43-46). ACM.

Wang, F., & Zaniolo, C. (2003). Temporal Queries in XML Document Archives and Web Warehouses. In *Proceedings of the 10th International Symposium on Temporal Representation and Reasoning and the 4th IEEE International Conference on Temporal Logic*, (pp. 47-55). ACM.

Wang, X., Zhou, X., & Lu, S. (2000). Spatiotemporal Data Modelling and Management: a Survey. In *Proceedings of the 36th IEEE International Conference on Technology of Object-Oriented Languages and Systems*, (pp. 202-211). IEEE.

Yazici, A., Zhu, Q., & Sun, N. (2001). Semantic data modeling of spatiotemporal database applications. *International Journal of Intelligent Systems*, *16*(7), 881–904. doi:10.1002/int.1040

Yu, H., & Shaw, S. L. (2004, August). Representing and visualizing travel diary data: A spatio-temporal gis approach. In *2004 ESRI International User Conference* (pp. 1-13). IEEE.

Chapter 14
Schema of Uncertain Spatiotemporal XML Data

ABSTRACT

In this chapter, the authors first construct an uncertain spatiotemporal data model based on XML, and then use probabilistic attributes to represent the uncertainty of spatiotemporal data, and write XML documents of uncertain spatiotemporal data according to the model. Secondly, the definition of XML Schema normalization based on the proposed model is used to obtain generalized XML Schema constraint documents for uncertain spatiotemporal data. Finally, a practical example is used to validate the correctness of the method in this chapter by applying the uncertain spatiotemporal data model based on XML and the XML Schema constraint document.

1 INTRODUCTION

At present, with the development of temporal database and spatial database, scholars have further created spatiotemporal database which is more conducive to spatiotemporal data management(Ye et al., 2007). Compared with the traditional relational database, the biggest advantage of spatiotemporal database is that it supports spatiotemporal data effectively and avoids a large amount of data redundancy caused by the change of the relationship between temporal and spatial attributes in the traditional relational database. Much research has been done to address the modeling and manipulation of spatiotemporal data (Pelekis et al. 2004; Wang et al. 2000; Yuan et al. 2010). (Wang et al., 2000) proposed two spatiotemporal data models: abstract model and conceptual model. In the comprehensive research of spatiotemporal data modeling (Pelekis et al., 2004), many existing spatiotemporal data models are summarized and compared, such as snapshot model, spatiotemporal composite data model, data model based on simple timestamp and so on. In the aspect of spatiotemporal data modeling, Chen et al.(Chen et al 2016) proposed a spatiotemporal data model based on compressed linear reference. (Cheng et al., 2021) proposed a dynamic spatiotemporal logic to represent and reason dynamic spatiotemporal knowledge. Because of the fuzziness and uncertainty of information in the real world, Bai et al.(Bai et al., 2015) put forward the research of fuzzy spatiotemporal XML data Schema.

DOI: 10.4018/978-1-6684-9108-9.ch014

The temporal data model based on XML can process the temporal data well and manage the temporal data effectively(Ye et al., 2007). In the literature (Ye et al., 2007; Zhang et al., 2009; Rizzolo et al., 2008), the research results of XML-based temporal data model by domestic and foreign researchers in recent years are fully displayed. Reference (Chen et al., 2006) focuses on the research of temporal XML indexing. All the above studies take advantage of XML's convenience in expressing tenses. However, objects in the real world have spatial attributes as well as temporal attributes, so the study of spatiotemporal data becomes an indispensable part. Spatiotemporal database, as an important research direction of emerging database, has more important and extensive application fields and practical significance, which has aroused strong concern of scholars at home and abroad. Temporal database and spatial database are mature in their respective fields. On this basis, it is more natural for the fusion of the two to form a spatiotemporal data field. Nowadays, the research on spatiotemporal data at home and abroad is still in the primary stage, and the development is not mature enough, and there are still a lot of contents waiting for scholars to study in depth. The research of spatiotemporal data mainly focuses on the related aspects of data model, query and index, which can be reflected in references(Liu et al., 2013; Yu et al., 2012; Cao, 2011; Chen et al., 2009; Bai, 2010). At the same time, the unavoidable uncertainty of spatiotemporal data caused by data distortion, network delay or uncertainty of spatiotemporal data in the real world is also one of the research directions, such as literature(Gao, 2015; Bao, 2006). Literature (Guo et al., 2011; Ma et al., 2006; Hao et al., 2006) is about XML Schema specification research literature, related to XML Schema specification document design, indexing research direction.

The above research contents are all selected a single direction of research, in the XML and uncertain spatiotemporal data combination of this research direction, the current research is not deep enough. This chapter combines XML with uncertain spatiotemporal data, and makes use of the advantages of XML, such as extensibility, customization and clear structure, to express spatiotemporal data more clearly. At the same time, it introduces probability attribute elements to express uncertainty, and express uncertain spatiotemporal data clearly. Then, based on the XML-based uncertain spatiotemporal data model, a correct and effective XML Schema specification definition document is written to ensure the correctness and validity of spatiotemporal data. It is convenient for the management of spatiotemporal data.

The rest of the article is as follows: Section 2 is the construction of XML-based uncertain spatiotemporal data model. Combining with XML, an XML-based uncertain spatiotemporal data model is created. Section 3 is the XML Schema specification for uncertain spatiotemporal data models based on XML. Section 4 is an application example, and a typhoon named "Cyclone Matthew" is selected as an example. Finally, the XML document is used to verify the correctness and validity of the XML Schema document.

2 UNCERTAIN SPATIOTEMPORAL DATA MODEL BASED ON XML

In this section, according to the characteristics of uncertain spatiotemporal data, tuples are used to define spatiotemporal data models. Then, the model will be refined in parts, and each part of the model will be illustrated with an example, and each part will be represented in XML documents. Finally, a complete spatiotemporal data model is formed.

2.1 Uncertain Spatiotemporal Data

Definition 1. Uncertain spatiotemporal data (USD) is represented as a quintuple:

$USD = \{OID, ATTR, UP, UM, UT\}$

where:

(1) OID describes the changing process of uncertain spatiotemporal data, which can not only describe the types of changes experienced by objects, such as splitting and migration, but also point out what objects will change from the future and what objects will change into;
(2) ATTR represents the attributes of uncertain spatiotemporal data. In this model, attributes can be divided into general attributes and spatial attributes. Attributes have no fixed requirements in quantity and certainty;
(3) UP represents the location of uncertain spatiotemporal data. We use coordinate system to represent the position, and use this to describe the position relationship between two or more spatiotemporal data;
(4) UM is used to represent the change trend of uncertain spatiotemporal data, which is specifically expressed as the direction and value of spatiotemporal data movement;
(5) UT represents the time of uncertain spatiotemporal data change, which can be expressed as a time node or a time period.

The following will use the above tuple definition to represent a real spatiotemporal data.

Cold current is a typical spatiotemporal data, and each cold current can refer to OID to express its change process. For example, if cold current A and B meet somewhere and interact to form cold current C, this type of spatiotemporal data change is called fusion. At the same time, it can be known that cold current C changes from cold current A and B in the process of spatiotemporal data change, that is, cold current A and B are ancestors of cold current C. In terms of attributes, it can be determined that each cold current has its general attributes, such as the name of the cold current, the intensity of the cold current, etc., and also has uncertain attributes, such as the possibility of the cold current occurring in F land, etc. Similarly, the cold current also has its position information. Because the coverage area of the cold current cannot be regarded as a particle, this chapter uses the smallest outer rectangle to represent its position. For example, the coordinate point set {(30 E, 50 N), (40 E, 70 N)} is used to indicate that its position is a rectangular range with these two points as the leftmost lower point and the leftmost upper point. At the same time, in order to express the motion information of cold current, this chapter introduces the element of motion trend. For example, when the cold current at {(30E, 50N), (40E, 70N)} moves to {(60E, 60N), (70E, 80N)}, it can be judged that the motion direction of cold current is northeast. Its time attribute can be expressed as (t-start: t_1, t-end: t_2), or as a point in time t_1.

2.2 Classification of Model Node

In order to express the uncertain spatiotemporal data model more clearly and make readers understand it more clearly, this chapter will classify and explain the nodes with different characteristics that may be involved in the model. Nodes in the model can be divided into the following types as shown below:

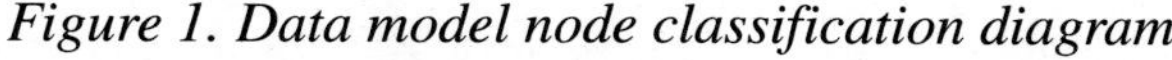

Figure 1. Data model node classification diagram

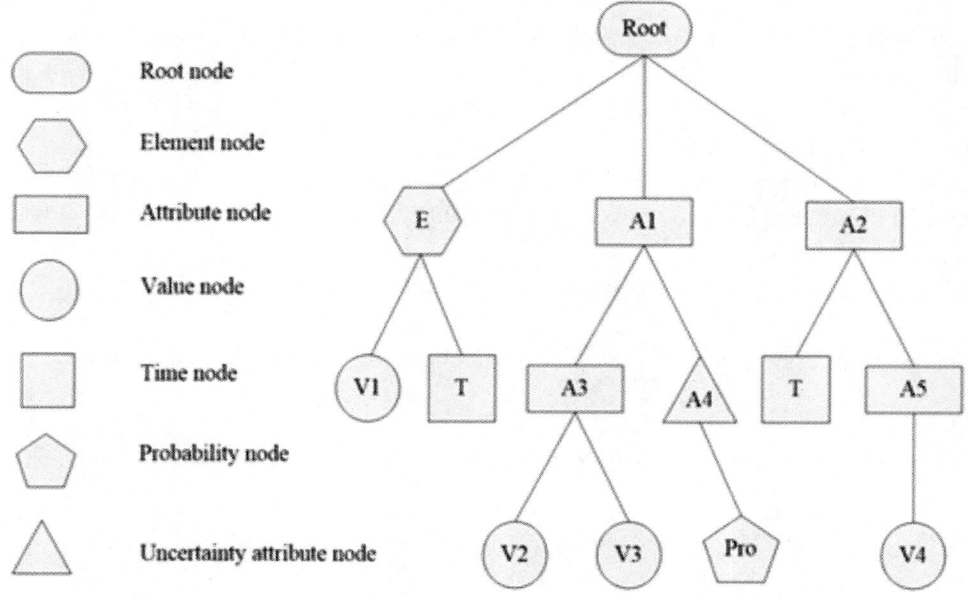

1. Root node: The XML document with uncertain spatiotemporal data is a tree structure, so it can be known that the model has only one root node, which is represented by a round-edged rectangle.
2. Element Node: The parent of an element node can only be a root node or an element node. Represented as a hexagon.
3. Attribute nodes: Attribute nodes may be root nodes, element nodes, or attribute nodes. Represented as a rectangle in the model.
4. Value node: As a leaf node, it is the same as an attribute node, and its father can be a root node, an element node or an attribute node, which is represented by a circle.
5. Special nodes: Because the research object of this chapter is uncertain spatiotemporal data, this chapter will specify two special nodes here, one is time node, which is one of the attributes of spatiotemporal data and is represented by a special rectangle, that is, square. Another special node is the probability node representing uncertain attributes, which is represented by pentagons, and its leaf nodes have a value range of [0, 1].
6. Uncertain nodes: In the definition of uncertain spatiotemporal data, it can be known that the attributes of data are not required in quantity and certainty, so the attributes with uncertainty are represented by triangles.

2.3 XML Representation of Uncertain Spatiotemporal Data

Definition 2. (OID-the evolution of uncertain spatiotemporal data) is a quintuple, *OID = {ID, pre, suc, type, time}*, where:

(1) As an attribute of spatiotemporal data object, "*ID*" is the unique identification of spatiotemporal data object.
(2) "*pre*" indicates the original object of spatiotemporal data change, that is, what changes come from the current spatiotemporal data.
(3) "*suc*" indicates the final object of spatiotemporal data change, that is, what the current spatiotemporal data changes into.
(4) "*type*" indicates the type of spatiotemporal data change, which can be divided into create, split, merge and eliminate. For the convenience of expression, this chapter simplifies these four types into c, s, m and e.
(5) "*time*" indicates the time that the spatiotemporal data changes.

The data model of uncertain spatiotemporal data change course (OID) is as follows:

Figure 2. Evolution of Uncertainty spatiotemporal data

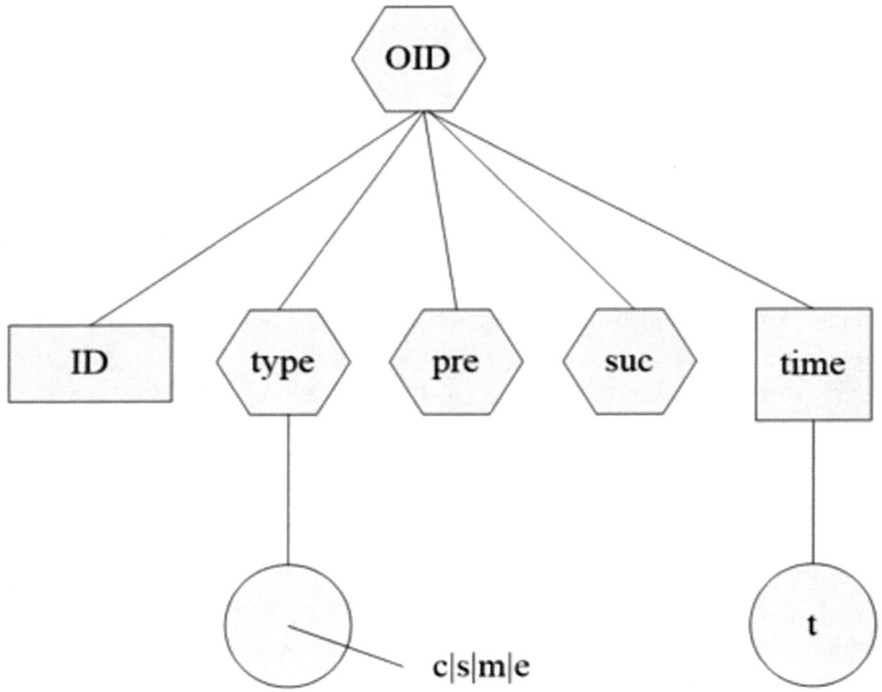

Apply the cold snap example mentioned in 2.1 to this model and represent it as an XML document.

In 2.1, it is mentioned that cold current A and B meet somewhere and interact to form cold current C, so the type of spatiotemporal data change is fusion, which is expressed by m, and *suc* = C. The *OID* of Cold Current A is represented in an XML document as follows:

OID

XML Document(.xml)
<?xml version="1.0" encoding="UTF-8"?> <OID ID="A"> <pre>Ø</pre> <suc>C</suc> <type>m</type> <time/> <t-start>t_1</t-start> <t-end>t_2</t-end> </OID>

According to Definition 1, the attributes of uncertain spatiotemporal data can be divided into General attributes and spatial attributes, and there is no fixed requirement for the number and certainty of the two attributes. Two attributes are described below:

Definition 3. (General-General attribute of uncertain spatiotemporal data) General is a binary group, *General= {time, uncertain attribute}*. Because the time attribute has been defined as a special attribute to represent it separately in the node definition in this chapter, in the General attribute of uncertain spatiotemporal data, *time* is used to represent the duration of the uncertain spatiotemporal data object owning this attribute. An *uncertain attribute* represents an indeterminate attribute.

Definition 4. (Uncertain attribute) Uncertain attribute is a binary group, *Uncertain attribute = {patt, per}*, where: *patt* represents the value category of Uncertain attribute, which is divided into conjunctive and disjunctive. *per* represents one or more elements that can be selected. In order to express the uncertainty of spatiotemporal data, probability nodes are added at the same time. Conjunctive means taking the union of all pers, and disjunctive means that only one of pers can be selected.

The data model of General of uncertain spatiotemporal data is as follows:

Apply the cold snap example mentioned in 2.1 to this model and represent it as the following XML document:

Definition 5. (Spatial-Spatial attributes of uncertain spatiotemporal data) Spatial is a binary group, *Spatial = {position, Motion}*, where *position* represents the position of the uncertain spatiotemporal data and *Motion* represents the Motion of the uncertain spatiotemporal data.

Definition 6. (Position-Position of uncertain spatiotemporal data) Position is a binary group, *position= {time, val}*, where *time* represents the time when the uncertain spatiotemporal data is at a certain position, and *val* represents the spatial position of the uncertain spatiotemporal data.

Definition7. (Val-Spatial Position of Uncertain Spatiotemporal Data) In this model, in order to describe the location of uncertain spatiotemporal objects conveniently, this chapter refers to the minimum enclosing rectangle *(MBR)* to describe the location of data. *Val= {xstart, ystart, xend, yend}*, where:

(1) *xstart* represents the minimum value of the location of uncertain spatiotemporal data in the X-axis direction, that is, *xstart = min {x1, x2, … xn}*
(2) *ystart* represents the minimum value of the position of the uncertain spatiotemporal data in the Y-axis direction, that is, *ystart = min {y1, y2, … yn}*
(3) *xend* denotes the maximum value of the location of uncertain spatiotemporal data in the X-axis direction, that is, *xend = max {x1, x2, … xn}*
(4) *yend* denotes the maximum value of the position of uncertain spatiotemporal data in the Y-axis direction, that is, *ystart = max {y1, y2, … yn}*

Figure 3. General attributes of Uncertainty spatiotemporal data

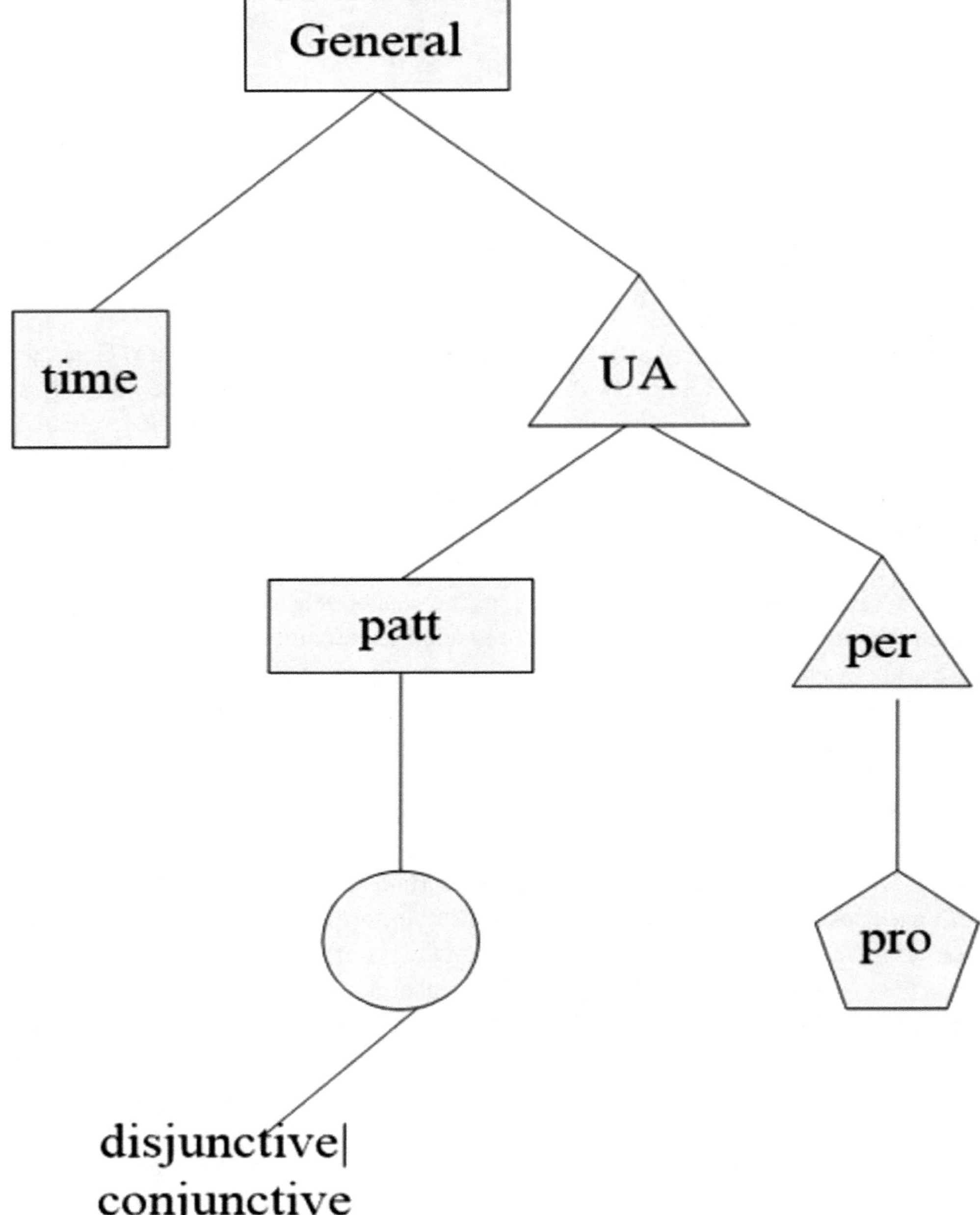

XML

XML Document(.xml)

```xml
<?xml version="1.0" encoding="UTF-8"?>
<General ID="C">
 <time>
   <t-start>t1</t-start>
   <t-end>t2</t-end>
 </time>
 <UA>
   <patt>conjunctive</patt>
   <per pro="0.5">A</per>
   <per pro="0.8">B</per>
 </UA>
</General>
```

According to Definition 7, we can create the following spatiotemporal data model to represent the location information of uncertain spatiotemporal data:

Figure 4. Position of Uncertainty spatiotemporal data

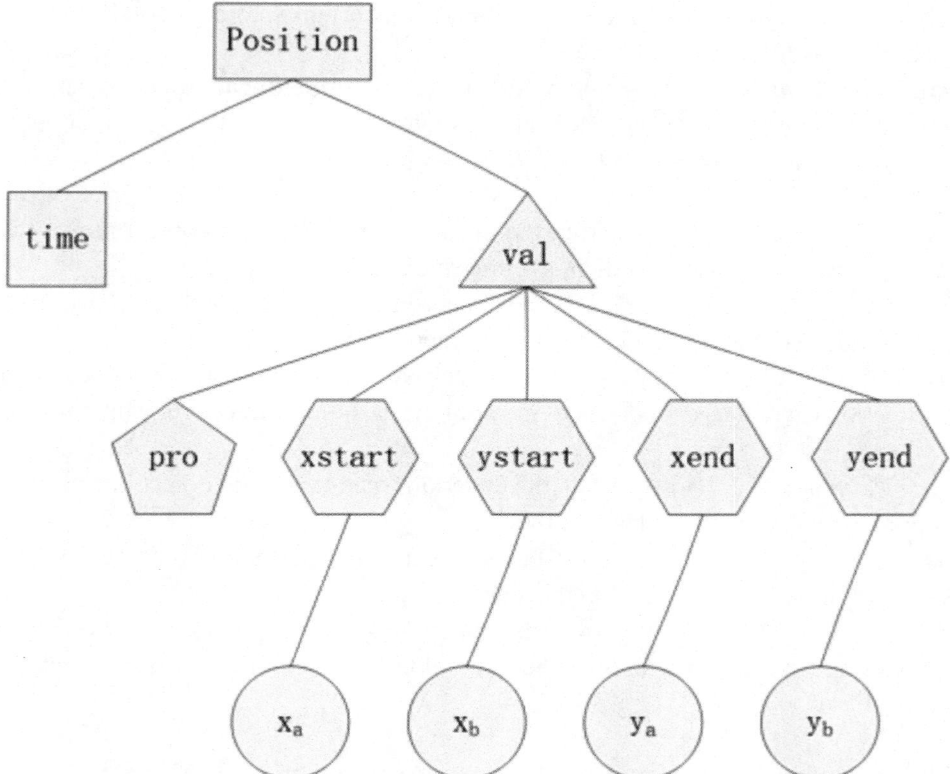

Applying the cold snap example mentioned in 2.1 to this model yields the following XML document:

XML

XML Document(.xml)

```
<?xml version="1.0" encoding="UTF-8"?>
<Position>
   <t-start>t1</t-start> <t-end>t2</t-end>
  <val pro="0.8">
   <xstart>30oE</xstart> <ystart> 50oN</ystart>
   <xend>60oE</xend> <yend>60oN</yend>
  </val>
</Position>
```

Definition 8. (Motion-Motion of uncertain spatiotemporal data) Motion can be expressed as a triple, *Motion = {time, end, range}*, where:

(1) *time* denotes the time of motion.
(2) *tend* denotes the motion trend of an uncertain spatiotemporal object.
(3) *range* denotes the range of motion of an uncertain spatiotemporal object.

In Definition 7, we already mentioned using the lower left corner and the upper right corner of the smallest outbound rectangle to describe the position of uncertain spatiotemporal objects, so we can define end and range as follows:

Definition 9. (tend-the trend of motion of uncertain spatiotemporal objects) *tend= {xaxis, yaxis, pro}*, assuming that the position of the uncertain spatiotemporal object is $\{(x_a, y_a), (x_b, y_b)\}$ at time t_1 and$\{(x_c, y_c),(x_d, y_d)\}$ at time t_2, we can get:

(1) If $xaxis = 1/2(x_a + x_b) - 1/2(x_c + x_d) > 0$, the uncertain spatiotemporal object moves to the left (in real case, it moves to the west), which is represented by L.
(2) If $xaxis = 1/2(x_a + x_b) - 1/2(x_c + x_d) < 0$, the uncertain spatiotemporal object moves to the right (in real case, it moves to the east), which is represented by R.
(3) If $xaxis = 1/2(x_a + x_b) - 1/2(x_c + x_d) = 0$, the uncertain spatiotemporal object does not move in the X-axis direction (in real case, it does not move in the east-west direction), which is represented by B.
(4) If $yaxis = 1/2(y_a + y_b) - 1/2(y_c + y_d) > 0$, the uncertain spatiotemporal object moves upward (in real case, it points north), which is denoted by U.
(5) If $yaxis = 1/2(y_a + y_b) - 1/2(y_c + y_d) < 0$, the uncertain spatiotemporal object moves downward (moving south in real situation), which is denoted by D.
(6) If $yaxis = 1/2(y_a + y_b) - 1/2(y_c + y_d) = 0$, the uncertain spatiotemporal object does not move in the Y-axis direction (in the real situation, the guide does not move in the north direction), which is represented by A.

Definition 10. (Range-Range of motion of uncertain spatiotemporal objects) *range = {xgra, ygra, pro}* Assuming that the position of the uncertain spatiotemporal object is $\{(x_a, y_a), (x_b, y_b)\}$at time t_1 and $\{(x_c, y_c), (x_d, y_d)\}$ at time t_2, we can get:

(1) The change of motion on the X-axis is expressed as $xgra = (x_d - x_c) / (x_b - x_a)$
(2) The change of motion on the Y-axis is $ygra = (y_d - y_c) / (y_b - y_a)$

Therefore, the motion of uncertain spatiotemporal data can be expressed by the following data model: Applying the cold snap example mentioned in 2.1 to this model yields the following XML document:

Figure 5. Motion of Uncertainty spatiotemporal data

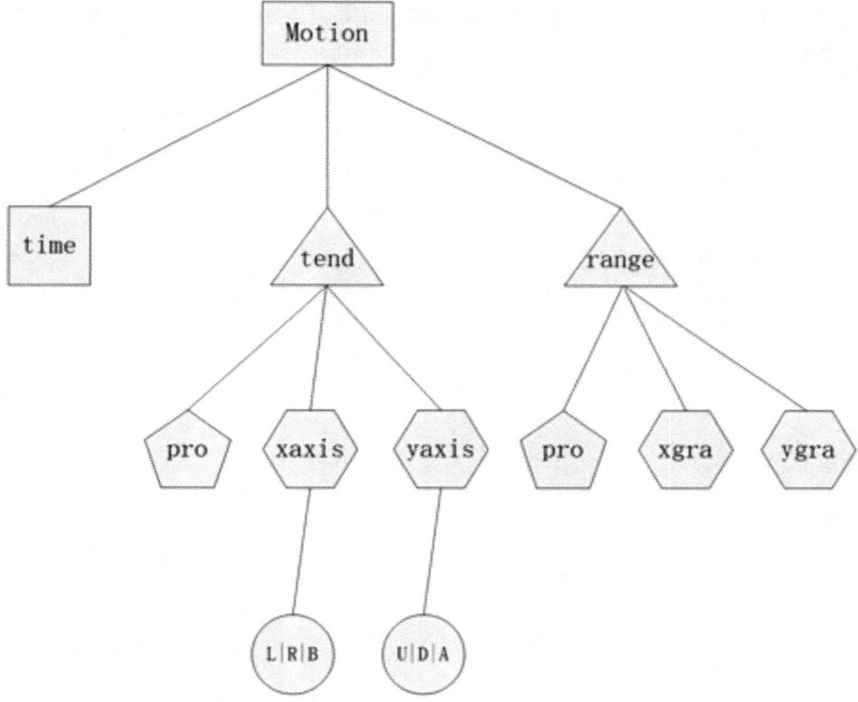

XML

XML Document(.xml)

```
<?xml version="1.0" encoding="UTF-8"?>
<Motion>
  <time>
    <t-start>t1</t-start>
    <t-end>t2</t-end>
  </time>
  <tend pro="0.8">
    <xaxis>R</xaxis> <!--1/2(30°E +40°E)-1/2(60°E +70°E)<0-->
    <yaxis>D</yaxis> <!--1/2(50°N +70°N)-1/2(60°N +80°N)<0-->
  </tend>
  <range pro="0.6">
    <xgra>1</xgra> <!--(70°E -60°E)/(40°E -30°E)=1-->
    <ygra>1</ygra> <!--(80°N -60°N)/(70°N -50°N)=1-->
  </range>
</Motion>
```

2.4 Overall Structure of Uncertain Spatio-Temporal Data Model Based on XML

According to the definition 1~10, an XML-based overall model of uncertain spatiotemporal data with the following structure can be obtained, which is described as follows:

In this model, uncertainty is that spatiotemporal data is further divided into change history (*OID*), The element time for time (*time*), (*pro*) representing uncertainty, and attribute element (*ATTR*) according to Definition 1 and Definition 2. According to Definitions 3 ~ 10, it can be known that attribute elements can be further divided into *General* and *spatial attributes*, and *spatial attributes* can be further divided into *Motion* and *Position*. Then we integrate the four parts of concrete models introduced in definition 3 ~ 10, and we can get the concrete structure model of uncertain spatiotemporal data based on XML. As shown in Figure 6.

Figure 6. Overall diagram of spatiotemporal data model based on XML

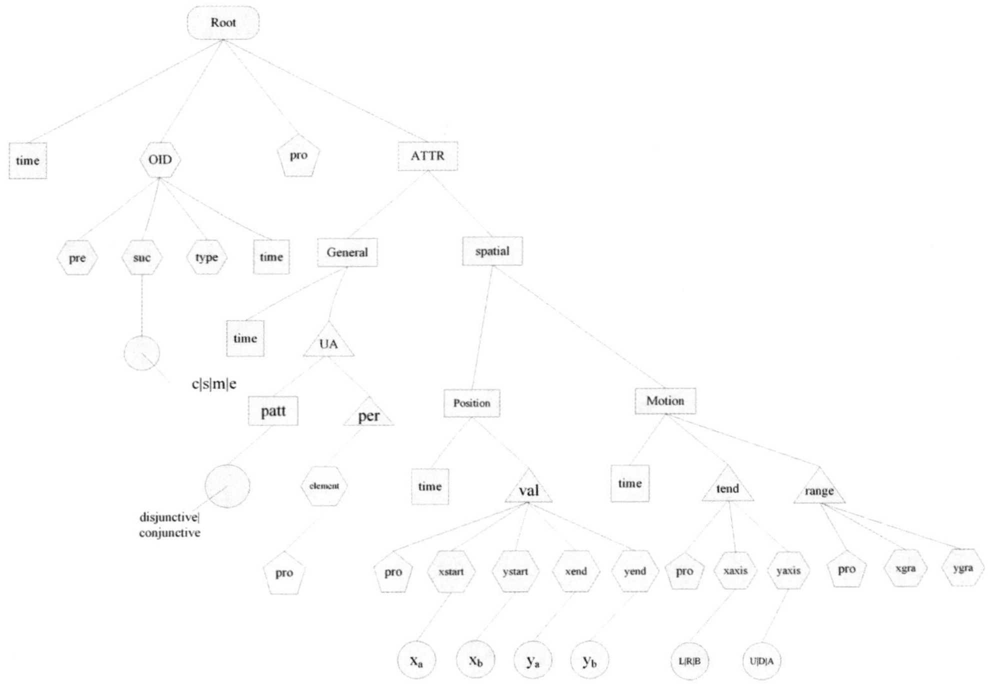

3 XML SCHEMA SPECIFICATION BASED ON UNCERTAIN SPATIOTEMPORAL DATA

XML Schema is more and more widely used to verify the validity of data. This section will represent uncertain spatiotemporal data models based on XML Schema, as specified by the W3C Schema Working Group. In this chapter, the basic definition method of XML Schema specification is introduced firstly, and then the uncertain spatiotemporal data model established in section 2 is represented according to the specification definition method introduced. In the introduction of the basic definition method of XML Schema specification, the method of classification introduction is adopted. This chapter first introduces the definition of the basic document declaration that a standard XML Schema specification document should have. Then, it is introduced according to the classification of elements, types and attributes. Here, the element category can be further divided into root element, complex element, time element and enumeration type element; Type categories can be further divided into basic data types, global complex types and extended complex types. Attribute categories are divided into general attributes and enumeration class attributes. The following diagram shows the structure of the XML Schema specification in Figure 7:

Figure 7. Structure of introduction about XML schema specification

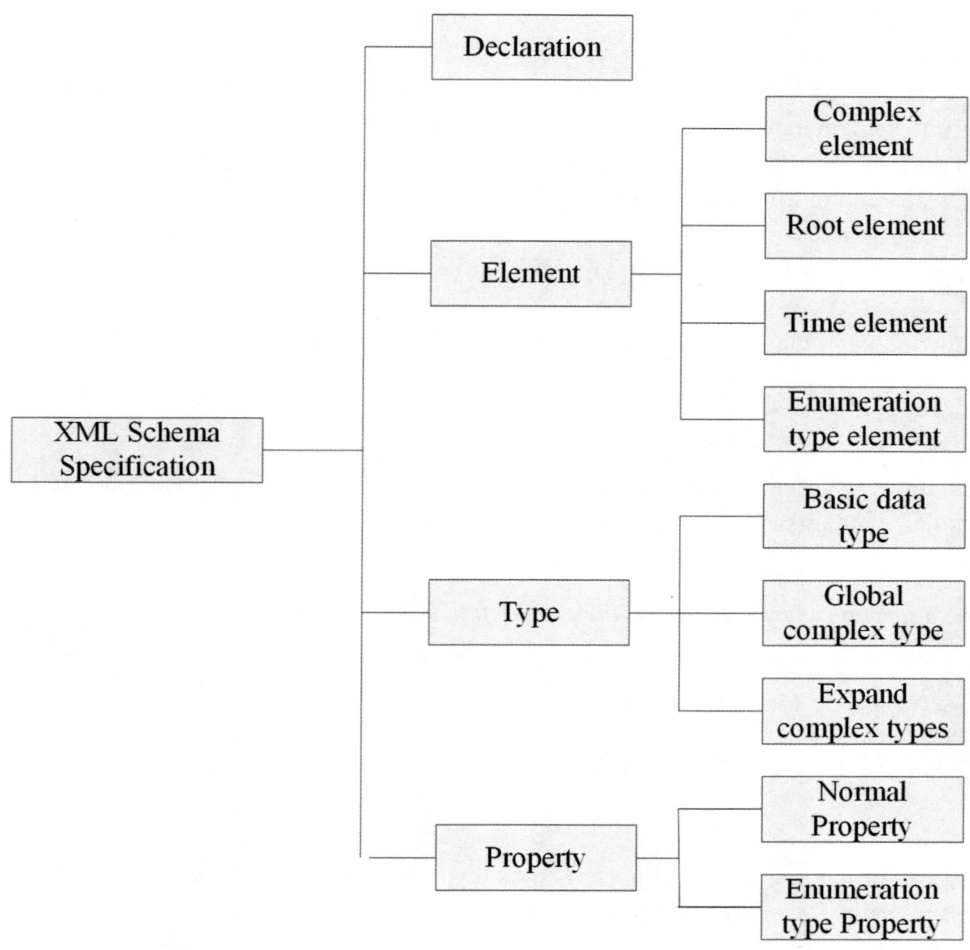

3.1 Introduction of XML Schema Definition Specification

3.1.1 Document Declaration Definition

In an XML Schema document, the declaration of the document has a fixed format, which is as follows:

```
<?xml version="…" encoding="…"?>
```

For example, in an XML document that chooses the 1.0 standard and the "UTF-8" encoding, declare the following:

```
<?xml version="1.0" encoding="UTF-8"?>
```

3.1.2 Element Definition

(1) Root element:

The root element of an XML Schema document consists of its root element name and namespace. Where the root element name can only use schema, and the namespace is one of the attributes of the root element. In other words, the root element schema must be defined under this namespace, which cannot be omitted. The general format is as follows:

```
<xs:schema xmlns:xs="…" elementFormDefault="…" >
```

The following examples are given to deepen our understanding:

```
<xs:schema xmlns:xs="https://www.w3.org/2001/XMLSchema">
```

In the example, the schema is defined under the namespace https://www.w3.org/2001/XMLSchema.

(2) Complex elements:

For complex elements of tree structure, they are defined as follows:

```
<xs:element name="..."/>
   <xs:complexType/>
      <xs:sequence/>
         <xs:element name="..." minOccurs="..." maxOccurs="..."/>
```

In the above format, the name of the element is represented as an attribute of the element. complexType indicates that the element is of type complex and contains one or more child elements. sequence indicates the order in which its children are represented. Then there is the definition of child elements, which is consistent with the above element definitions. minOccurs and maxOccurs represent the minimum and maximum number of times the element can occur.

Here is an example to illustrate:

```
<xs:element name="OID">
   <xs:complexType>
      <xs:sequence>
         <xs:element name="time" /> <xs:element name="pre" />
         <xs:element name="suc" /> <xs:element name="type"/>
      </xs:sequence>
   </xs:complexType>
</xs:element>
```

In the above example, a complex element named OID is defined, which contains four child elements and is defined in the following order: "time"→"pre"→" suc"→"type". There is no special limit on the number of appearances.

(3) Time element:

Because the time element is very important for spatiotemporal data, this chapter gives a special description of the time element here.

The definition of time element follows the following format strictly:

```
<xs:element name="time"/>
   <xs:simpleType/>
      <xs:restriction base="xs:dateTime"/>
         <xs:minInclusive value="1000-01-01T00:00:00"/>
            <xs:maxInclusive value="9999-12-31T23:59:59"/>
```

The element name is "time", the type is simple element type, and there are no child elements. The restriction states that the time element is defined based on the base element type "dateTime". minInclusive and maxInclusive describe the minimum and maximum values of the time element, and determine the range of values. In this example, we can know that the value of time is between "1000-01-01T00: 00:00" and "9999-12-31T23: 59:59".

(4) Enumerate type elements:

Enumeration types are important in XML Schema documents. In an element definition, the name and type of the element must be defined. At the same time, the basic data type must be defined with the time element. Enumeration value indicates that only one result can be selected from all enumeration values when an element is valued.

The detailed enumeration element type definition format is as follows:

```
<xs:element name="..."/>
   <xs:simpleType/>
      <xs:restriction base=" "/>
         <xs:enumeration value="..."/>
```

This chapter introduces an example to further illustrate in detail:

```
<xs:element name="xaxis">
   <xs:simpleType>
      <xs:restriction base="xs:string">
         <xs:enumeration value="L"/>
         <xs:enumeration value="R"/>
         <xs:enumeration value="B"/>
      </xs:restriction>
   </xs:simpleType>
</xs:element>
```

In this example, the simple element "xaxis" is defined based on the basic element type "xs: string". At the same time, the element defines three enumerated values "L", "R" and "B". Only one of the three can be taken in the value.

3.1.3 Type Definition

Types include simple types and complex types, where elements with child elements or attributes are complex types, and elements with only text content are simple types.

(1) Basic data types:

Basic data types, such as string, bool, date, datetime, time, integer, etc., need not be defined and can be used directly.

(2) Global complex types:

The format of complex type definitions is as follows:

```
<xs:complexType name="..."/>
   <xs:sequence/>
      <xs:element name="..."/>
```

The first line defines the name of the global complex type. sequence is used to define the order in which its child elements are defined. The child elements are then defined.

The following example is used to illustrate in detail:

```
<xs:complexType name="UAType">
   <xs:sequence>
      <xs:element name="per"/>
   </xs:sequence>
</xs:complexType>
```

In this example, the global complex type is "UAType", and it has only one child element called "per".

(3) Extensive complex type:

Extended types are defined on the basis of globally complex types.

The format is as follows:

```
<xs:complexType name="... "/>
    <xs:complexContent/>
        <xs:extension base="..."/>
            <xs:attribute name="..."/>
```

The global extension type is also a complex type. complexType indicates the name of the type. complexContent describes what the extension type contains, including what type definition the extension type is based on, expressed in extension, and the attributes that the extension type can contain.

The following examples are cited to illustrate:

```
<xs:complexType name="extendUAType">
    <xs:complexContent>
        <xs:extension base="UAType">
<xs:attribute name="patt"/>
        </xs:extension>
    </xs:complexContent>
</xs:complexType>
```

In this example, the name of the extended complex type is "extendUAType", and the content indicates that the global complex type used to define is "UAType" and an attribute named "patt".

3.1.4 Property Definition

Property definition is a specific description of an element or attribute. In general, the general format of general attribute definition is as follows:

```
<xs:attribute name="…" type="…" use="…" default="…"/>
```

First, define the attribute name, and then define the basic data type of the attribute value. use is used to mark whether this attribute is a necessary attribute of the element and whether it can be omitted. default indicates the original data of the attribute value, that is, the initial value or the default value. Example:

```
<xs:attribute name="pro" type="xs:float" use="optional" default="1.0"/>
```

Property "pro", whose value is of type "float" and whose default value is 1.0.

Here is a special property: enumeration type property. Attributes of enumerated types are also generic attributes, which are special in that there are multiple selectable values in their attribute values, and the final result can only be one of them.

The definition is as follows:

```
<xs:attribute name="..."/>
  <xs:simpleType/>
    <xs:restriction base="..."/>
      <xs:enumeration value="..."/>
```

First, define the attribute name and attribute type, and use restriction to point out the basic data type of attribute value. The enumeration represents all the value selections.

The following examples are given to understand:

```
<xs:attribute name="patt">
  <xs:simpleType>
    <xs:restriction base="xs:string">
      <xs:enumeration value="disjunctive"/>
      <xs:enumeration value="conjunctive"/>
    </xs:restriction>
  </xs:simpleType>
</xs:attribute>
```

In this example, the simple type attribute is named "patt", and the basic data type of its value is "string". And the value can only be one of "disjunction" and "conjunction".

The following is a detailed description of XML Schema specification writing for spatiotemporal data with uncertainty.

3.2 XML Schema Specification for Uncertain Spatiotemporal Data

The basic rules of the XML Schema specification definition are outlined in 3.1. Next, this chapter will define the uncertain spatiotemporal data model established in section 2 by XML Schema. According to Definition 1~10 and Figure 6, the uncertain spatiotemporal data is a tree structure. So this article will be defined according to the hierarchical structure of tree. Following the basic definition of XML Schema described in 3.1, you first define declarations that indicate namespaces and standards. At the same time, the root element name is defined as Schema. In this chapter, the uncertain spatiotemporal data model is divided into four main parts (OID, General, Position, Motion).

3.2.1 XML Schema Specification for Uncertain Spatiotemporal Object Change History (OID)

Rule 1: XML Schema specification constraints for uncertain spatiotemporal object evolution are specification constraints for complex elements and consist of specification constraints for simple elements and enumerated type elements.

The details are as follows:

According to definition 2, *OID = {pre, suc, type, time}* of uncertain spatiotemporal objects. According to element category, OID is a complex element, which can be defined according to the method defined by complex elements in 3.1.2. When defining four child elements:

(1) "*pre*" and "*suc*" are simple elements, defined in the general element format.
(2) As a special element, "*time*" refers to the definition of time element in 3.1.2, and the range of time value is specified from "1000-01-01T00: 00:00" to "9999-12-31T23: 59:59".
(3) Because "*type*" has four candidate values, it can be defined by enumeration element definition in 3.1.2.

This leads to the following XML Schema specification:

XML Schema (part1-evolution.xsd)

```
<?xml version="1.0" encoding="UTF-8"?>
<xs:schema xmlns:xs="https://www.w3.org/2001/XMLSchema"
elementFormDefault="qualified">

<xs:element name="OID">
<xs:complexType>
      <xs:sequence>
        <xs:element name="time" />
            <xs:element name="pre" />
            <xs:element name="suc" />
            <xs:element name="type"/>
    </xs:sequence>
</xs:complexType>
</xs:element>

<xs:element name="time">
<xs:simpleType>
 <xs:restriction base="xs:dateTime">
      <xs:minInclusive value="1000-01-01T00:00:00"/>
       <xs:maxInclusive value="9999-12-30T23:59:59"/>
    </xs:restriction>
    </xs:simpleType>
</xs:element>

<xs:element name="type" >
    <xs:simpleType>
         <xs:restriction base="xs:string">
         <xs:enumeration value="c"/>
         <xs:enumeration value="s"/>
         <xs:enumeration value="m"/>
         <xs:enumeration value="e"/>
    </xs:restriction>
    </xs:simpleType>
</xs:element>

</xs:schema>
```

3.2.2 XML Schema Specification for General Attributes of Uncertain Spatiotemporal Objects

In this section, we will introduce the basic rules of XML Schema specification writing for General attributes of uncertain spatiotemporal objects. According to the following rules 2 and 3, we can get generalized XML Schema specification documents for General attributes of uncertain spatiotemporal objects.

Rule 2: The schema specification constraint of General of uncertain spatiotemporal objects specifies complex elements, which is composed of complex elements, time elements and complex attribute specification constraints.

The details are as follows:

(1) According to the definition 3 ~ 4 about the General attribute (General) and the uncertain attribute (unknown attribute), we can know that the *General = {time, unknown attribute}*. The General attribute General contains child elements, so "General" is an element of a complex type.
(2) "*time*" is a time element. Considering the actual situation and significance of general attributes in the real world, the time element is taken as a period of time, so the time element can be defined as a complex type element, which includes two sub-elements, namely "t-start" and "t-end". At the same time, these two sub-elements must be defined separately according to the definition of time element in section 3.1.2.

(3) *Uncertain attribute = {patt, per}*, we can know that this attribute is a complex type attribute. Based on XML Schema, we can define the data type by ourselves, and the type of Uncertain attribute needs to be defined by ourselves.

Rule 3: The schema specification constraint of Uncertain attribute of Uncertain Spatiotemporal Objects is to standardize complex attributes, which is composed of enumerated class attributes and multiple child elements.

The details are as follows:

(1) *Uncertain attribute = {patt, per}*, the type is self-defined.

(2) The attribute "*patt*" is an enumerated attribute that can be defined according to Section 3.1.4. The definition process is as follows: First, define the global complex type "UAType", and then define the extended complex type "extendUAType" based on the already defined "UAType" type to indicate the type of attribute "*patt*".

(3) There is no limit to the number of occurrences of the sub-element "*per*", which can be one or more. At the same time, in order to express the uncertainty of spatiotemporal data, it contains the probability attribute "pro". In order to explain the value type of "per", a global complex type is defined as "elementType", and on this basis, the specific XML Schema specification of the extended complex type "extendelementType" is defined as follows:
XML Schema

XML Schema (part2-general.xsd)

```
<?xml version="1.0" encoding="UTF-8"?>
<xs:schema xmlns:xs="https://www.w3.org/2001/XMLSchema"
elementFormDefault="qualified">
<xs:element name="General">
  <xs:complexType>
   <xs:sequence>
   <xs:element name="time"/>
   <xs:element name="UA"/>
    </xs:sequence>
   </xs:complexType>
</xs:element>

<xs:element name="time">
  <xs:complexType>
   <xs:sequence>
   <xs:element name="t-start"/>
   <xs:element name="t-end"/>
     </xs:sequence>
  </xs:complexType>
</xs:element>
<xs:element name="t-start">
<xs:simpleType>
  <xs:restriction base="xs:dateTime">
    <xs:minInclusive value="1000-01-01T00:00:00"/>
   <xs:maxInclusive value="9999-12-30T23:59:59"/>
  </xs:restriction>
</xs:simpleType>
</xs:element>

<xs:element name="t-end">
  <xs:simpleType>
    <xs:restriction base="xs:dateTime">
   <xs:minInclusive value="1000-01-01T00:00:00"/>
   <xs:maxInclusive value="9999-12-30T23:59:59"/>
    </xs:restriction>
  </xs:simpleType>
</xs:element>
<xs:complexType name="UAType">
   <xs:sequence>
   <xs:element name="per"/>
  </xs:sequence>
</xs:complexType>

<xs:element name="per">
   <xs:complexType>
   <xs:sequence>
      <xs:element name="element" minOccurs="0"
maxOccurs="unbounded"/>
    </xs:sequence>
   </xs:complexType>
</xs:element>

<xs:complexType name="extendUAType">
 <xs:complexContent>
   <xs:extension base="UAType">
    <xs:attribute name="patt"/>
   </xs:extension>
  </xs:complexContent>
</xs:complexType>

<xs:attribute name="patt">
 <xs:simpleType>
   <xs:restriction base="xs:string">
    <xs:enumeration value="disjunctive"/>
    <xs:enumeration value="conjunctive"/>
   </xs:restriction>
  </xs:simpleType>
</xs:attribute>

<xs:complexType name="elementType"/>
    <xs:complexType name="extendelementType">
   <xs:complexContent>
     <xs:extension base="elementType">
         <xs:attribute name="pro" type="xs:float" use="optional"
default="1.0"/>
     </xs:extension>
    </xs:complexContent>
</xs:complexType>
</xs:schema>
```

3.2.3 XML Schema Specification for Position of Uncertain Spatiotemporal Objects

Rule 4: Pattern specification constraints of uncertain location of uncertain spatiotemporal objects are specifications of complex elements, which are composed of time elements and complex element specification constraints. The details are as follows:

(1) *position= {time, val}*, which is a complex element.
(2) The time element "*time*" is defined according to 3.1.1, and its range is specified from "1000-01-01T00: 00:00" to "9999-12-31T23: 59:59".
(3) *val= {xstart, ystart, xend, yend}*, and the type of value is integer. Customize the global complex type "valType", and on this basis, define the extended complex type "extendvalType", including the attribute "pro", which can be defined according to the general attribute definition in 3.1.4. This leads to the following XML Schema specification:
XML Schema

XML Schema (part3-position.xsd)

```
<?xml version="1.0" encoding="UTF-8"?>
<xs:schema xmlns:xs="https://www.w3.org/2001/XMLSchema"
elementFormDefault="qualified">
  <xs:element name="position">
 <xs:complexType>
   <xs:sequence>
<xs:element name="time"/>
<xs:element name="val"/>
   </xs:sequence>
 </xs:complexType>
</xs:element>
  <xs:element name="time">
 <xs:simpleType>
  <xs:restriction base="xs:dateTime">
    <xs:minInclusive value="1000-01-01T00:00:00"/>
    <xs:maxInclusive value="9999-12-30T23:59:59"/>
  </xs:restriction>
  </xs:simpleType>
</xs:element>
<xs:complexType name="valType">
  <xs:sequence>
<xs:element name="xstart" type="xs:int"/>
<xs:element name="ystart" type="xs:int"/>
<xs:element name="xend" type="xs:int"/>
<xs:element name="yend" type="xs:int"/>
  </xs:sequence>
</xs:complexType>
<xs:complexType name="extendvalType">
  <xs:complexContent>
  <xs:extension base="valType">
  <xs:attribute name="pro" type="xs:float" use="optional" default="1.0"/>
  </xs:extension>
   </xs:complexContent>
</xs:complexType>
</xs:schema>
```

3.2.4 XML Schema Specification for Motion of Uncertain Spatiotemporal Objects

Rule 5: The pattern specification constraint of uncertain spatiotemporal object motion is to standardize complex elements, which is composed of time element and two complex element specification constraints. The details are as follows:

(1) *Motion= {time, end, range}* is a complex element.
(2) The "*time*" element is defined as in section 3.2.3 and ranges from "1000-01-01T00: 00:00" to "9999-12-31T23: 59:59".
(3) "*end*" is a complex element, *tend= {xaxis, yaxis, pro}*. The elements of "xaxis" and "yaxis" are of enumerated type, and the definition of probability attribute is similar to 3.2.3 according to 3.1.1 definition.
(4) "*range*" is a complex element, *range= {xgra, ygra, pro}*. Among them, the types of "xgra" and "ygra" are integers, which can be defined according to basic elements. This leads to the following XML Schema specification:

XML Schema

XML Schema (part4-position.xsd)

```
<?xml version="1.0" encoding="UTF-8"?>
<xs:schema xmlns:xs="https://www.w3.org/2001/XMLSchema"
elementFormDefault="qualified" >
<xs:element name="motion">
  <xs:complexType>
     <xs:sequence>
        <xs:element name="time"/>
        <xs:element name="tend"/>
        <xs:element name="range"/>
     </xs:sequence>
  </xs:complexType>
</xs:element>
<xs:element name="time">
  <xs:simpleType>
   <xs:restriction base="xs:dateTime">
        <xs:minInclusive value="1000-01-01T00:00:00"/>
        <xs:maxInclusive value="9999-12-30T23:59:59"/>
   </xs:restriction>
</xs:simpleType>
</xs:element>
<xs:complexType name="tendType"> <xs:sequence>
      <xs:element name="xaxis"/>
      <xs:element name="yaxis"/>
  </xs:sequence>
</xs:complexType>
<xs:complexType name="extendtendType">
   <xs:complexContent>
     <xs:extension base="tendType">
          <xs:attribute name="pro" type="xs:float" use="optional" default="1.0"/>
     </xs:extension>
</xs:complexContent>
</xs:complexType>
<xs:element name="xaxis">
  <xs:simpleType>
 <xs:restriction base="xs:string">
 <xs:enumeration value="L"/>
 <xs:enumeration value="R"/>
 <xs:enumeration value="B"/>
</xs:restriction>
</xs:simpleType>
</xs:element>
<xs:element name="yaxis">
 <xs:simpleType>
 <xs:restriction base="xs:string">
 <xs:enumeration value="U"/>
 <xs:enumeration value="D"/>
 <xs:enumeration value="A"/>
</xs:restriction>
</xs:simpleType>
</xs:element>
<xs:complexType name="rangeType">
   <xs:sequence>
<xs:elementname="xgra" type="xs:int"/>
<xs:element name="ygra" type="xs:int"/>
   </xs:sequence>
   </xs:complexType>
   <xs:complexType name="extendrangeType">
 <xs:complexContent>
    <xs:extension base="rangeType">
   <xs:attribute name="pro" type="xs:float" use="optional" default="1.0"/>
      </xs:extension>
</xs:complexContent>
</xs:complexType>
</xs:schema>
```

4 APPLICATION EXAMPLE

In this section, taking Typhoon "Cyclone Matthew" as an example, we discuss the representation of uncertain spatiotemporal data based on XML and the application of XML Schema specification document in concrete examples. The chart of Typhoon Cyclone Matthew is as follows:

In order to further analyze the typhoon "Cyclone Matthew", the detailed basic data of "Cyclone Matthew" are introduced here. In the basic data table 1, the current occurrence time, current location, wind force, air pressure and typhoon type of typhoon "Cyclone Matthew" are included. According to the data in this table, this chapter will study the typhoon "Cyclone Matthew" to prove the correctness and effectiveness of the XML-based spatiotemporal data model mentioned in section 2 and 3 and the XML Schema normalized representation document of spatiotemporal data.

The specific data are shown in the following table:

According to Table 1, the time data and spatial data of typhoon (i.e., its longitude and latitude) are separated from each other, so it can be regarded as a spatiotemporal object, which is suitable for the research object of this chapter. In this chapter, according to the XML-based uncertain spatiotemporal data model introduced in section 2 and the XML representation of uncertain spatiotemporal data, the typhoon "Cyclone Matthew" is constructed and represented in detail. Then, according to the rules of XML Schema specification for uncertain spatiotemporal data given in section 3, the typhoon "Cyclone Matthew" will be represented in XML Schema normalization to verify the correctness and effectiveness of the methods introduced in section 2 and 3 of this chapter.

Figure 8. The run chart of "Cyclone Matthew"

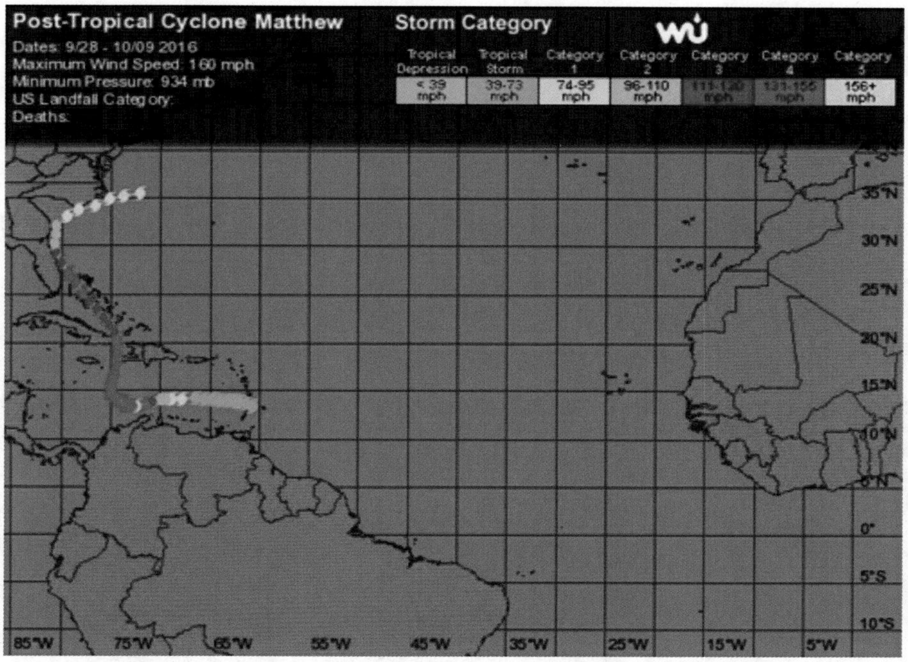

Table 1. Basic data of typhoon "Cyclone Matthew"

DateTime(GTM)	Lat(oN)	Lon(oW)	Wind (mph)	Pressure	Storm Type
9/28/2016 15	13.4	-60.7	60	1008	Tropical Storm
9/28/2016 18	13.6	-61.3	60	1008	Tropical Storm
9/28/2016 21	13.8	-62.0	60	1008	Tropical Storm
9/29/2016 00	13.9	-62.4	65	1004	Tropical Storm
9/29/2016 03 9/29/2016 06 9/29/2016 09 9/29/2016 12 9/29/2016 15 9/29/2016 21 9/30/2016 03 9/30/2016 06 9/30/2016 09 9/30/2016 15 9/30/2016 21 10/01/2016 03 10/01/2016 09 10/01/2016 15 10/01/2016 21 10/02/2016 03	13.9	-63.1	65	1004	Tropical Storm
	13.9	-64.0	65	1002	Tropical Storm
	14.0	-64.7	65	1002	Tropical Storm
	14.1	-65.5	70	995	Tropical Storm
	14.2	-66.3	70	996	Tropical Storm
	14.1	-67.8	75	993	Category 1 Hurricane
	14.1	-68.8	80	983	Category 1 Hurricane
	14.1	-69.3	100	979	Category 2 Hurricane
	14.0	-69.9	100	979	Category 2 Hurricane
	13.7	-70.8	115	968	Category 3 Hurricane
	13.5	-71.6	140	949	Category 4 Hurricane
	13.3	-72.3	160	941	Category 5 Hurricane
	13.3	-72.8	155	942	Category 4 Hurricane
	13.4	-73.4	145	947	Category 4 Hurricane
	13.5	-73.4	150	940	Category 4 Hurricane
	13.8	-73.6	150	940	Category 4 Hurricane

4.1 XML Representation of Typhoon "Cyclone Matthew"

4.1.1 XML Representation of Change Course of Typhoon "Cyclone Matthew"

In the study of the changing process of uncertain spatiotemporal objects, only when the research object is unique can we talk about its changing process. When the original spatiotemporal object is changed into other spatiotemporal objects, it no longer exists, so its changing process does not need to be studied again. Here, we choose the starting point of typhoon "Cyclone Matthew" to study, and the change course of its starting point is as follows:

Figure 9. The evolution history of "Cyclone Matthew"

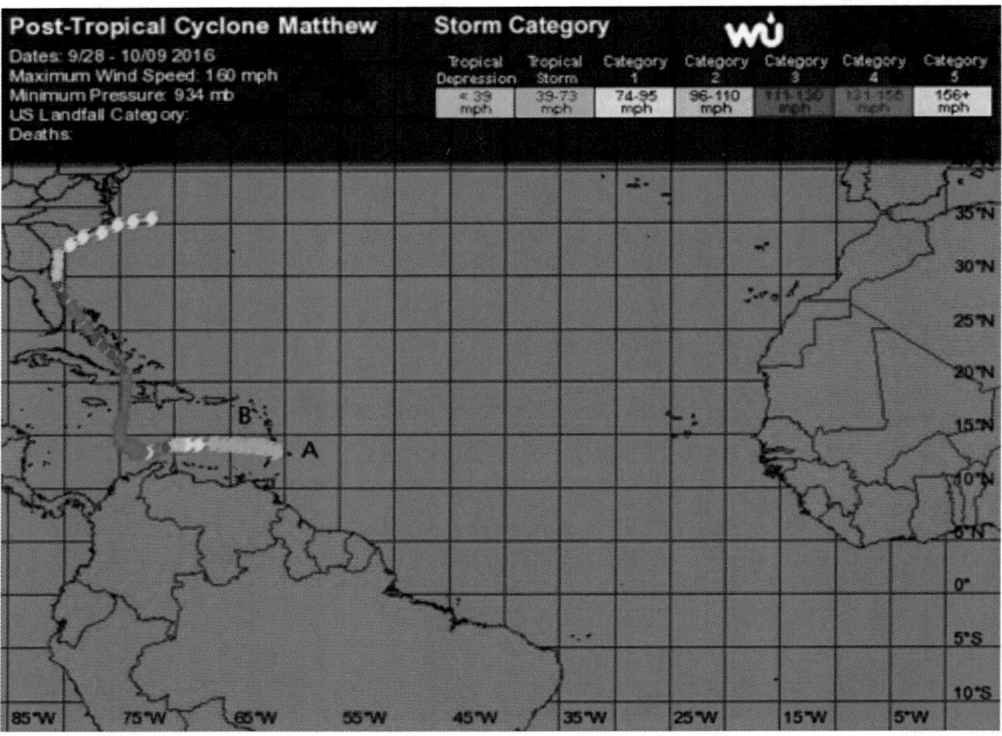

The specific structure of the course of change for creating Typhoon "Cyclone Matthew" according to definition 2 is as follows:

For convenience of expression, the starting point of typhoon is indicated by A. As you can see from the above figure, the "*pre*" of A is ∅, and it will evolve into B after a series of changes, that is, "*suc*" = B and "type" = create, so we can get the following XML document:

Figure 10. The evolution history of "Cyclone Matthew"

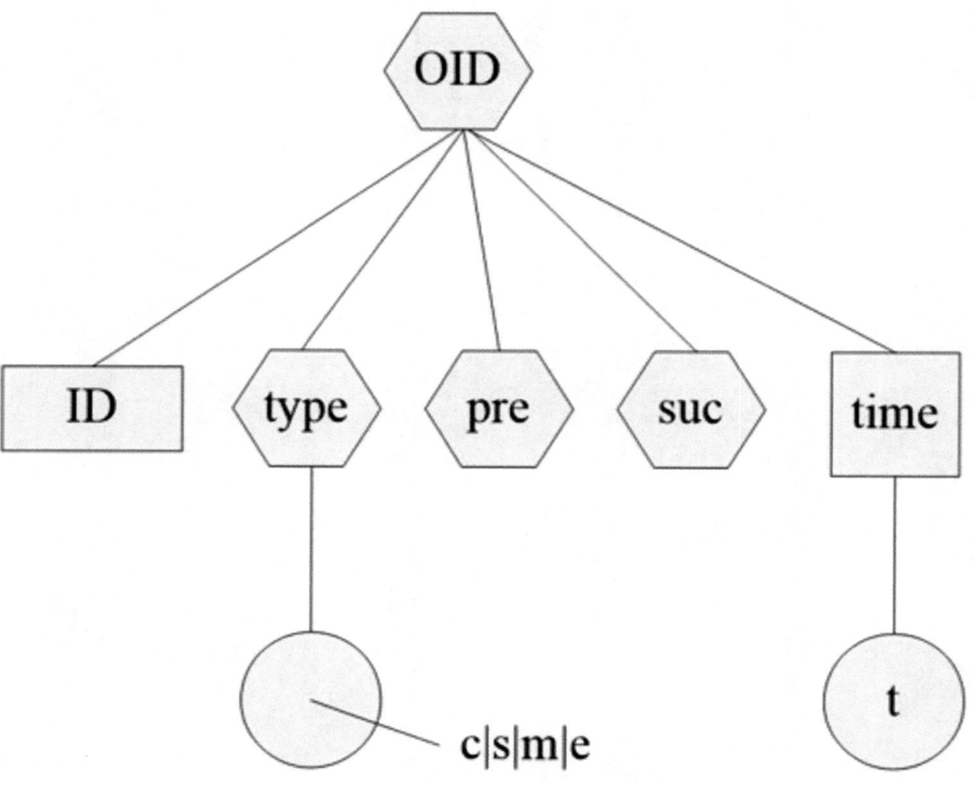

XML

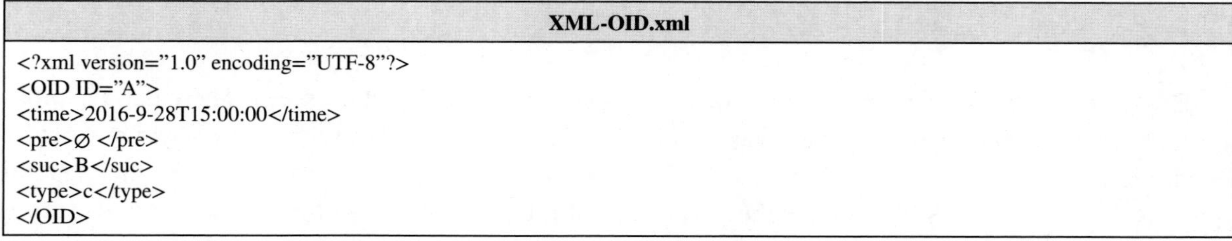

XML-OID.xml

```
<?xml version="1.0" encoding="UTF-8"?>
<OID ID="A">
<time>2016-9-28T15:00:00</time>
<pre>∅ </pre>
<suc>B</suc>
<type>c</type>
</OID>
```

4.1.2 XML Representation of General Attributes of Typhoon "Cyclone Matthew"

By analyzing the basic data of typhoons in Table 1, we can know that among the attributes of typhoons, the determined attributes are "wind", "pressure" and "Storm type", while the uncertain attributes include the coverage of typhoons and the probability of encountering typhoons at this position. According to definitions 3 ~ 4, the specific structure of the general attributes for creating typhoons "Cyclone Matthew" is as follows:

Figure 11. The general attribute structure of "Cyclone Matthew"

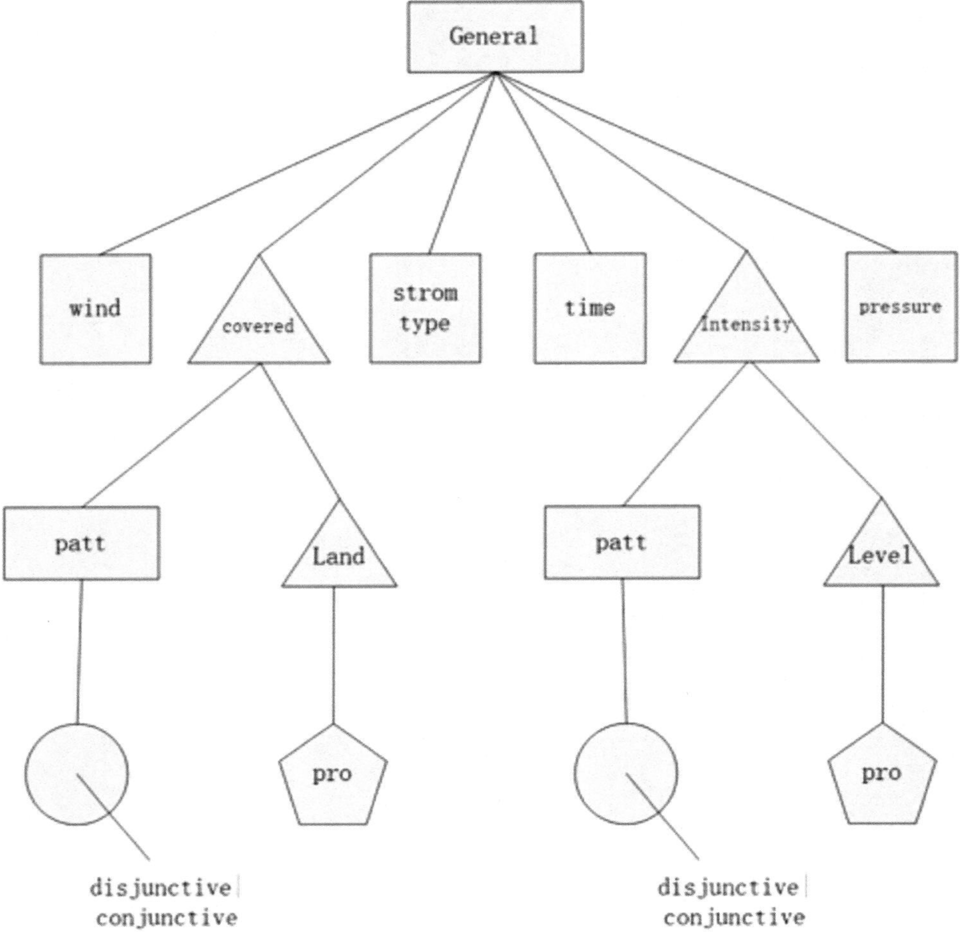

This section focuses on point B. Based on the data shown in Table 1, it is assumed here that the probability of typhoon occurring in Area 1 (land1) is 0.5 and the probability of typhoon occurring in Area 2 (land2) is 0.8. According to definition 4, since a typhoon can cover both land1 and land2, the value of "patt" is "conjunctive". Similarly, for the expression of typhoon intensity, it is assumed that the probability of typhoon intensity being strong is 0.5, and the probability of typhoon intensity being weak is 0.7. Since only one of the typhoon strengths can be selected, the value of "patt" is "disjunction". Taking the typhoon state at 0:00 on September 26, 2016 as an example, looking up Table 1, we can know that the wind is 65mph, the air pressure is 1004hp, and the typhoon type is Tropical Storm. You can get the following XML document:

XML

XML-General.xml

```
<?xml version="1.0" encoding="UTF-8"?>
<General>
<time>2016-9-29T00:00:00</time>
<wind>65</wind>
<pressure>1004</pressure>
<Storm type>Tropical Storm</Storm type>
<covered patt1="conjunctive">
<land pro="0.5">land1</land> <land pro="0.8">land2</land>
</covered>
<intensity patt2="disjunctive">
<level pro="0.6">strong</level> <level pro="0.7">weak</level>
</intensity>
</General>
```

4.1.3 XML Representation of the Position of Typhoon "Cyclone Matthew"

In section 2, in order to express the position of spatiotemporal data objects conveniently, this chapter adopts the minimum outer rectangle to represent the position of uncertain spatiotemporal objects. Here, two planar rectangular coordinate systems are used to calculate the spatial position of typhoons at two different times, for example:

Figure 12. Example of typhoon location in different time

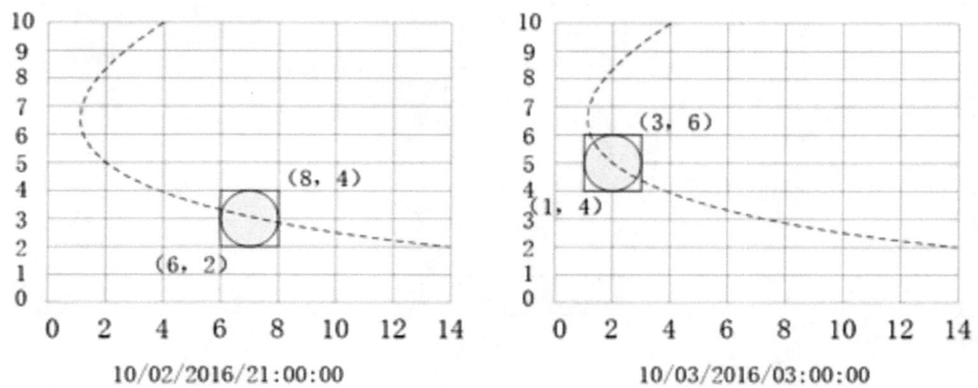

According to the location representation of the uncertain spatiotemporal data model based on XML mentioned in definitions 6 ~ 7, the spatiotemporal data model for the location of typhoon "Cyclone Matthew" is created as follows:

According to the data in Figure 12 and the specific structure in Figure 13, it is assumed that the probability of typhoon appearing at this position at two moments is 0.8 and 0.6 respectively; Get:

(1) At 21:00:00 on 2016-10-02T21, "xstart" = 6, "ystart" = 2, "xend" = 8, "yend" = 4;
(2) At 03:00 on 2016-10-03T03, "xstart" = 1, "ystart" = 4, "xend" = 3, "yend" = 6;

Figure 13. Structure of typhoon "Cyclone Matthew" position

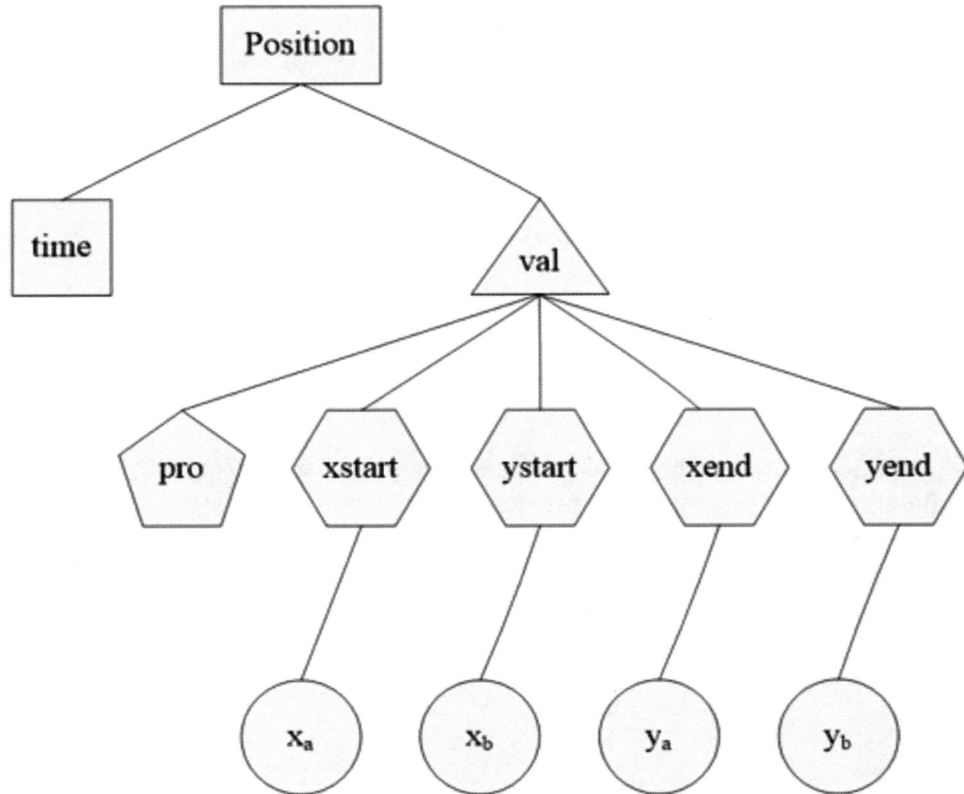

You can get the following XML document:

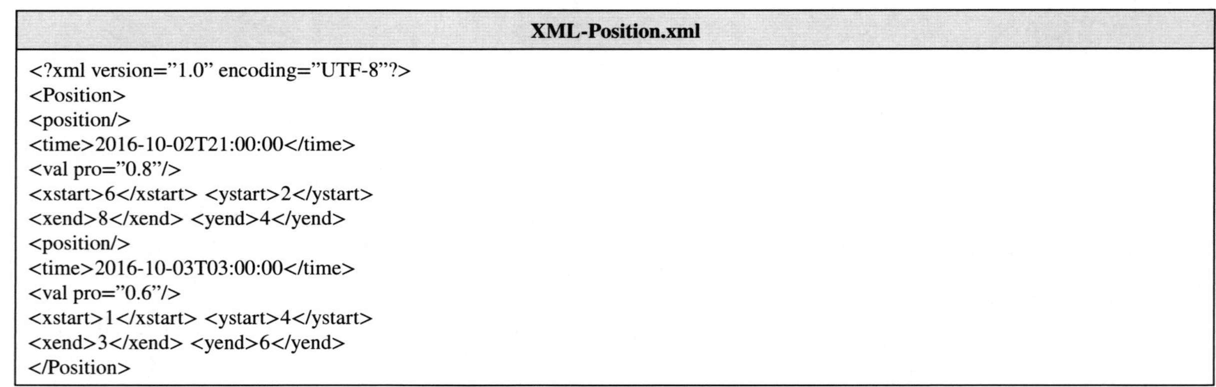

XML-Position.xml

```
<?xml version="1.0" encoding="UTF-8"?>
<Position>
<position/>
<time>2016-10-02T21:00:00</time>
<val pro="0.8"/>
<xstart>6</xstart> <ystart>2</ystart>
<xend>8</xend> <yend>4</yend>
<position/>
<time>2016-10-03T03:00:00</time>
<val pro="0.6"/>
<xstart>1</xstart> <ystart>4</ystart>
<xend>3</xend> <yend>6</yend>
</Position>
```

4.1.4 XML Representation of the Motion of Typhoon "Cyclone Matthew"

Typhoons are in motion at all times, and their trajectories can be seen in Figure 8. For convenience of expression, this subsection is still illustrated by the examples in Figure 12. According to Definitions 8 ~ 10, the specific structure of spatiotemporal data object motion can be obtained as follows:

Figure 14. Structure of typhoon "Cyclone Matthew" motion

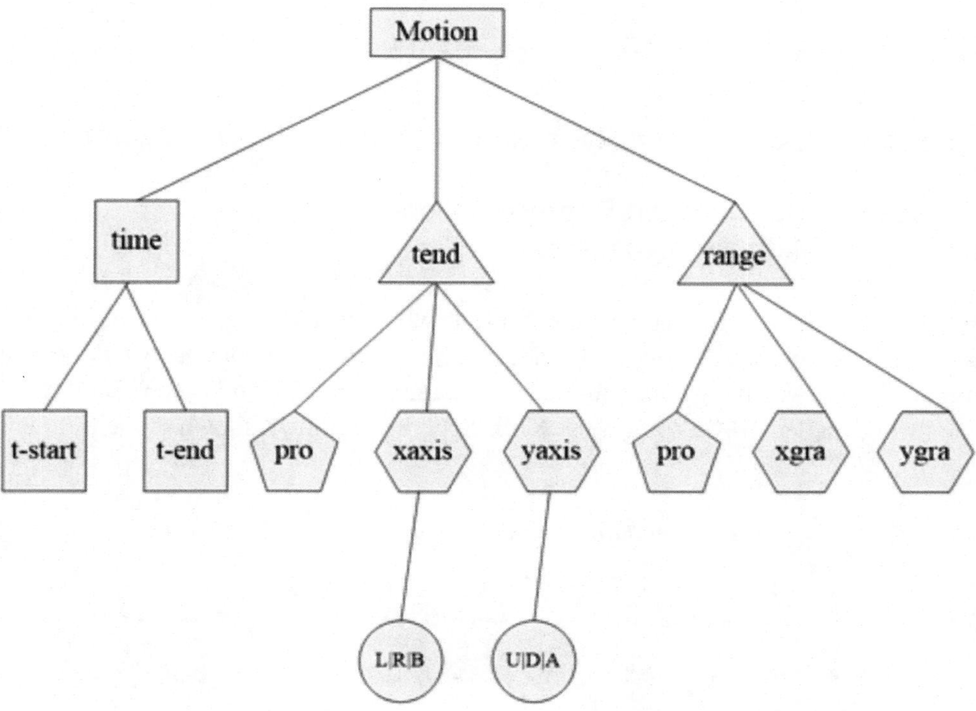

According to the data in Figure 12 and the specific structure in Figure 14, the following data are obtained:

(1) xaxis = 1/2 (6 +8)-1/2 (1 +3) = 5 > 0, so "xaxis" = "L";
(2) yaxis=1/2 (4 +2)-1/2 (4 +6) =-1 < 0, so "yaxis" = "U";
(3) xgra= (3-1)/ (8-6) = 1;
(4) ygra= (6-4)/ (4-2) = 1;

You get the following XML document:

XML-Motion.xml

```
<?xml version="1.0" encoding="UTF-8"?>
<Motion>
<time/>
<t-start>2016-10-02T21:00:00</t-start>
<t-end>2016-10-03T03:00:00</t-end>
<tend> <xaxis>L</xaxis>
<yaxis>U</yaxis>
</tend>
<range>
<xgra>1</xgra>
<ygra>1</ygra>
</range>
</Motion>
```

4.2 XML Schema Specification Representation of Typhoon "Cyclone Matthew"

4.2.1 XML Schema Specification Representation of Typhoon "Cyclone Matthew" Evolution

According to Rule 1, analyze the basic data of Table 1, which is the same as 4.1.1. This part still takes point A as the research object. According to the specific structure of typhoon "Cyclone Matthew", as shown in Figure 10, OID contains four sub-elements, namely "time", "pre", "suc" and "type", and also contains an attribute called "ID". You get the XML Schema document shown in the following figure:

Figure 15. Verification of XML schema document about typhoon "Cyclone Matthew" evolution

Looking at Figure 9, according to the change of point A, that is, point A changes to point B, and its change type is create type. You can then use the following XML document to verify the correctness and validity of the XML Schema document above.

The validation documentation is as follows:

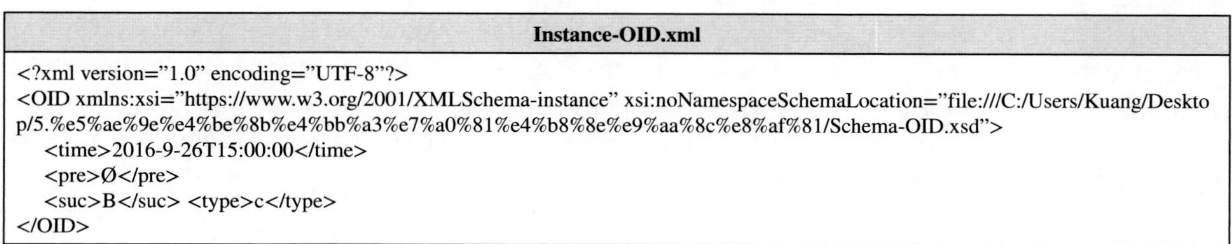

Instance-OID.xml

```
<?xml version="1.0" encoding="UTF-8"?>
<OID xmlns:xsi="https://www.w3.org/2001/XMLSchema-instance" xsi:noNamespaceSchemaLocation="file:///C:/Users/Kuang/Deskto
p/5.%e5%ae%9e%e4%be%8b%e4%bb%a3%e7%a0%81%e4%b8%8e%e9%aa%8c%e8%af%81/Schema-OID.xsd">
    <time>2016-9-26T15:00:00</time>
    <pre>Ø</pre>
    <suc>B</suc> <type>c</type>
</OID>
```

Using the XML validation document above, a screenshot of the validation results for the evolving XML Schema document, that is, the Schema-OID.xsd document, is shown in Figure 16 below:

Figure 16. Verification of Schema-OID.xsd about typhoon "Cyclone Matthew"

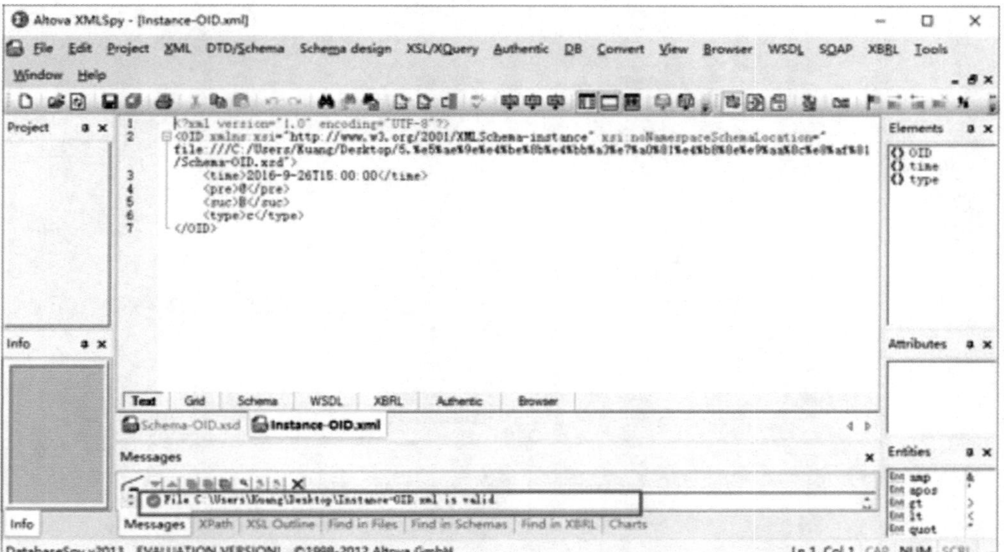

According to the red border line in Figure 16, we can know that the specific spatiotemporal data model of typhoon "Cyclone Matthew" created in this chapter according to the XML-based uncertain spatiotemporal model introduced in section 2, that is, Figure 10, is correct and valid, and the XML Schema document of typhoon "Cyclone Matthew" obtained according to the XML Schema document writing specification of uncertain spatiotemporal data change history introduced in section 3 is correct and valid.

4.2.2 XML Schema Specification Representation of Typhoon "Cyclone Matthew" General Attributes

According to the XML Schema specification writing rules on the General attributes of uncertain spatiotemporal data mentioned in Rule 2, analyzing the basic data contained in Table 1, and according to the specific data model structure of the General attributes of Typhoon "Cyclone Matthew" shown in Figure 11, it can be known that General contains four certain sub-elements, namely wind force, typhoon type, time, pressure, and two uncertain sub-elements, namely typhoon coverage and typhoon intensity. Therefore, according to Rule 2 mentioned in section 3, the XML Schema specification writing rules about the general attributes of uncertain spatiotemporal data can be applied to the example of Typhoon "Cyclone Matthew", and the following XML Schema document is obtained:

Figure 17. Verification of XML Schema Document about "Cyclone Matthew" general attributes

As in section 4.1.2, take the typhoon state at 0:00 on September 26, 2016 as an example, and look up the basic data in table 1. At this time, the wind force “wind” is 65mph, the air pressure “pressure” is 1004hp, and the typhoon type “strom type” is “Tropical Storm”. You can then use the following XML document to verify the correctness and validity of the XML Schema document above. The validation documentation is as follows:

Validation

Instance-General.xml

```
<?xml version=”1.0” encoding=”UTF-8”?>
<General xmlns:xsi=”https://www.w3.org/2001/XMLSchema-instance” xsi:noNamespaceSchemaLocation=”file:///C:/Users/Kuang/Desktop/5.%e5%ae%9e%e4%be%8b%e4%bb%a3%e7%a0%81%e4%b8%8e%e9%aa%8c%e8%af%81/Schema-General.xsd”>
<time>2016-9-26T00:00:00</time>
<wind>65</wind> <pressure>1004</pressure>
<Stormtype>Tropical Storm</Stormtype>
<covered patt=”conjunctive”/>
<per1/>
<land pro=”0.5”>land1</land> <land pro=”0.8”>land2</land>
<intensity patt=”disjunctive”/>
<per2/>
<level pro=”0.6”>strong</level> <level pro=”0.7”>weak</level>
</General>
```

A screenshot of the validation results for the Schema-General.xsd document is as follows:

Figure 18. Verification of Schema-General.xsd about typhoon “Cyclone Matthew”

As can be seen from the red border in Figure 18, the XML Schema document for the general attributes of Typhoon "Cyclone Matthew" obtained according to the XML Schema document writing specification for general attributes of uncertain spatiotemporal data introduced in section 2 is correct and valid.

4.2.3 XML Schema Specification Representation of Typhoon "Cyclone Matthew" Position

According to Rule 3 and Figure 13, Position contains two child elements, one is the time element, and the other is the element val with uncertainty. val also contains four sub-elements representing its specific spatial position, which are "xstart", "ystart", "xend" and "yend". At the same time, a "pro" attribute is used to express the probability of typhoon appearing in this position area. You get the following XML Schema document:

Figure 19. Verification of XML Schema Document about "Cyclone Matthew" position

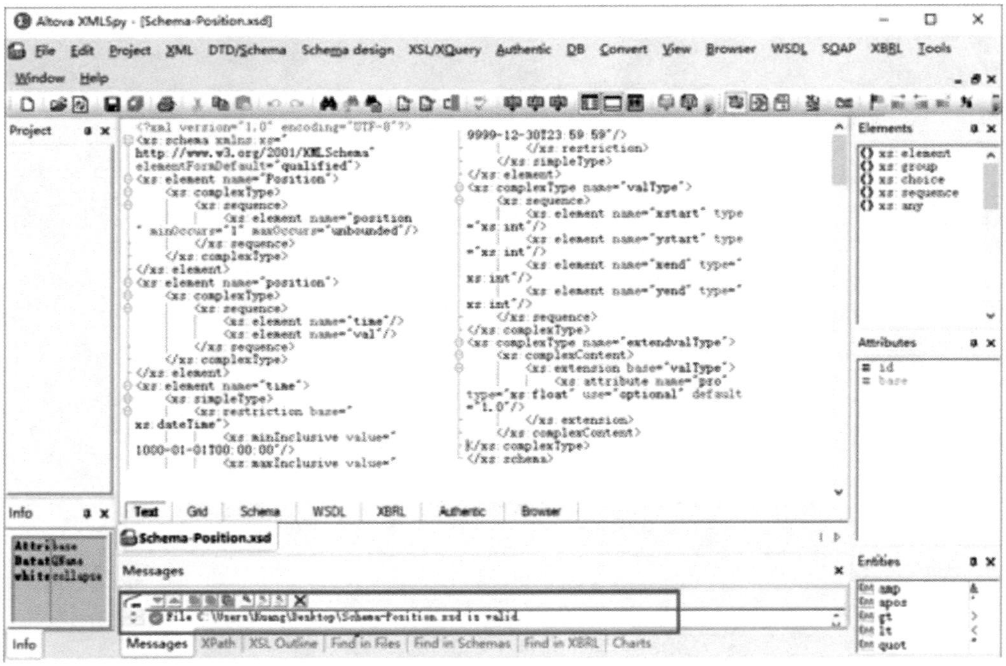

Using the spatial position of typhoons at two different times in Figure 12, write the following XML document:

XML document

Instance-Position.xml

```
<?xml version="1.0" encoding="UTF-8"?>
<Position xmlns:xsi="https://www.w3.org/2001/XMLSchema-instance" xsi:noNamespaceSchemaLocation="file:///C:/Users/Kuang/Desktop/5.%e5%ae%9e%e4%be%8b%e4%bb%a3%e7%a0%81%e4%b8%8e%e9%aa%8c%e8%af%81/Schema-Position.xsd">
<position/>
<time>2016-10-02T21:00:00</time>
<val pro="0.8"/>
<xstart>6</xstart> <ystart>2</ystart> <xend>8</xend> <yend>4</yend>
<position/>
  <time>2016-10-03T03:00:00</time>
<val pro="0.6"/>
<xstart>1</xstart> <ystart>4</ystart> <xend>3</xend> <yend>6</yend>
</Position>
```

Using the XML validation document above, a screenshot of the validation result for the moving XML Schema document, that is, the Schema-Position.xsd document, is shown in Figure 20 below:

Figure 20. Verification of Schema-Position.xsd about typhoon "Cyclone Matthew"

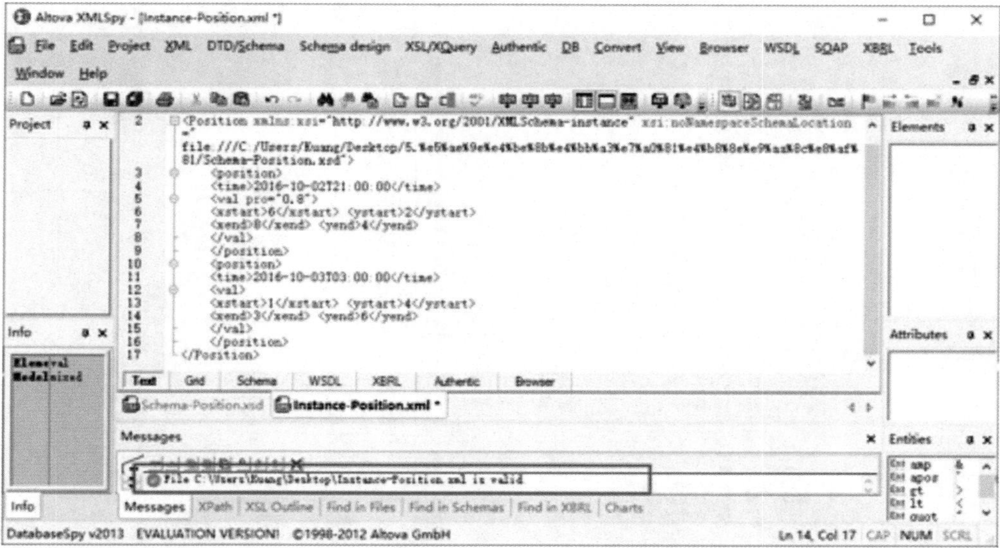

According to the red border line in Figure 20, the specific spatiotemporal data model for the location of Typhoon "Cyclone Matthew" created in this chapter based on the XML-based uncertain spatiotemporal model introduced in section 2, namely Figure 13, is correct and valid, and the XML Schema document for the location of Typhoon "Cyclone Matthew" obtained according to the XML Schema document writing specification for uncertain spatiotemporal data location introduced in section 3 is correct and valid.

4.2.4 XML Schema Specification Representation of Typhoon "Cyclone Matthew" motion

According to the XML Schema specification writing rules about the movement of uncertain spatiotemporal data mentioned in Rule 4 and the specific structure of the movement of Typhoon "Cyclone Matthew" introduced in Figure 14, it can be known that Motion contains three sub-elements, including a time element. According to the actual situation, the time element here is set as a complex type element, including two sub-elements, which are the start time "t-start" of the described motion course and the end time "t-end" of the described motion course. In addition, Motion also contains two sub-elements with uncertain attributes, namely "tend" representing Motion trend and "range" representing Motion change range. You can then get the following XML Schema document:

Figure 21. Verification of XML Schema document about "Cyclone Matthew" motion

Using the example of typhoon movement between two different moments described in Figure 12, write the following XML document to verify the correctness and effectiveness of Schema-Motion.xsd:

XML

instance-motion.xml

```
<?xml version="1.0" encoding="UTF-8"?>
</Motion xmlns:xsi="https://www.w3.org/2001/XMLSchema-instance" xsi:noNamespaceSchemaLocation="file:///C:/Users/Kuang/Desktop/5.%e5%ae%9e%e4%be%8b%e4%bb%a3%e7%a0%81%e4%b8%8e%e9%aa%8c%e8%af%81/Schema-Motion.xsd">
</time>
   <t-start>2016-10-02T21:00:00</t-start> <t-end>2016-10-03T03:00:00</t-end>
<tend/> <xaxis>L</xaxis> <yaxis>U</yaxis>
<range/> <xgra>1</xgra> <ygra>1</ygra>
```

A screenshot of the validation results for the Schema-Motion.xsd document is as follows:

Figure 22. Verification of Schema-Motion.xsd about typhoon "Cyclone Matthew"

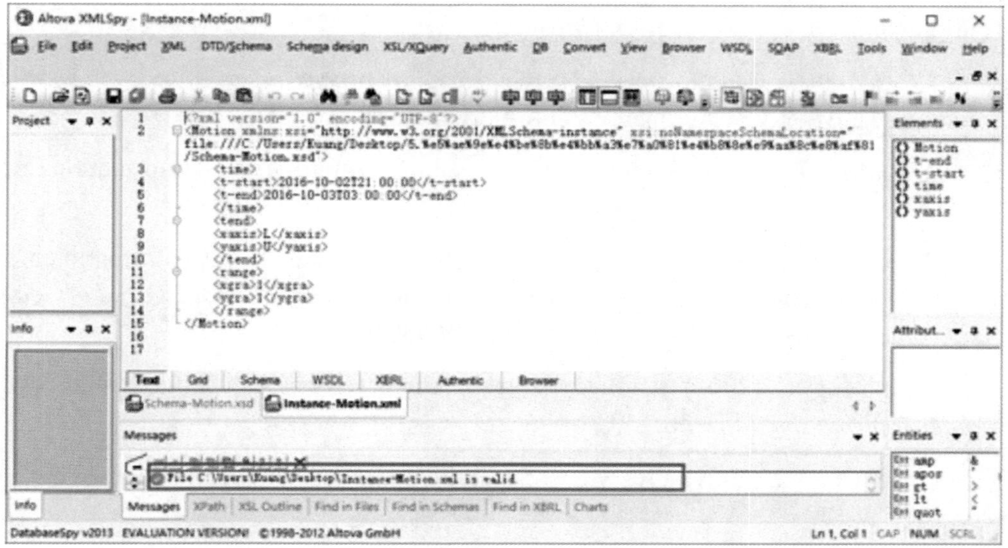

According to the red line in Figure 22, we can know that the specific spatiotemporal data model of typhoon "Cyclone Matthew" created in this chapter according to the XML-based uncertain spatiotemporal model introduced in section 2, that is, Figure 14, is correct and valid, and the XML Schema document of typhoon "Cyclone Matthew" obtained according to the XML Schema document writing specification of uncertain spatiotemporal data movement introduced in section 3 is correct and valid.

5 SUMMARY

Spatiotemporal database can effectively support and manage Spatiotemporal data. However, in the real world, in the process of transmitting and processing Spatiotemporal data, it is inevitable to encounter data loss and delay, which leads to unavoidable uncertainty. Therefore, it is necessary to deal with the Spatiotemporal data reasonably, so that the transmission and processing of Spatiotemporal data can be carried out accurately. XML itself has the advantages of good self-definition, completeness, standardization and clear structure, which is more conducive to the management of uncertain Spatiotemporal data. In the process of constructing uncertain Spatiotemporal data model based on XML, different types of nodes are created for further expression, and probability attributes are quoted to express the uncertainty of Spatiotemporal data. Based on the proposed model, XML Schema normalization is defined, and generalized XML Schema constraint documents for uncertain Spatiotemporal data are obtained. Finally, the typhoon "Cyclone Matthew" is cited as an example, which proves the correctness and effectiveness of the model and XML Schema document, and can express and manage Spatiotemporal data well.

REFERENCES

Bai, L. (2010). *Research on XML modeling method of spatiotemporal data*. Northeastern University.

Bai, L., Yan, L., Ma, Z., & Xu, C. (2015). Research on fuzzy spatiotemporal XML data Schema. [Natural Science Edition]. *Journal of Northeastern University*, (05), 622–625.

Bao, L. (2006). *Research on some key problems of uncertainty processing technology in spatiotemporal database*. Nanjing University of Aeronautics and Astronautics.

Cao, W. (2011). *Spatiotemporal data model and its application research*. PLA Information Engineering University.

Chen, B. Y., Yuan, H., Li, Q., Shaw, S. L., Lam, W. H. K., & Chen, X. (2016). Spatiotemporal data model for network time geographic analysis in the era of big data. *International Journal of Geographical Information Science*, *30*(6), 1041–1071. doi:10.1080/13658816.2015.1104317

Chen, L., Ji, Y., & Deng, C. (2006). An indexing technique based on extended temporal XML model. *Microcomputer Information, (15)*, 301-303 +69.

Chen, X., Zhu, J., & Chen, J. (2009). Overview of spatiotemporal data models. *Advances in Geographical Sciences*, (01), 9–17.

Chen, Z., Zhao, T., & Liu, W. (2021). Time-aware collective spatial keyword query. *Computer Science and Information Systems*, *28*(3), 1077–1100. doi:10.2298/CSIS200131034C

Gao, M. (2015). *Some studies on the propagation of spatiotemporal uncertainty*. Changan University.

Guo, Y., & Wu, Y. (2011). An XML index based on XML Schema. [Natural Science Edition]. *Journal of Huaqiao University*, (01), 43–47.

Hao, C., & Zou, J. (2006). XML storage based on XML Schema. *Computer Engineering and Application, (11)*, 173-175 +204.

Liu, D., Chen, H., Qi, H., & Yang, B. (2013). Research progress of spatiotemporal data mining. *Jisuanji Yanjiu Yu Fazhan*, (02), 225–239.

Ma, Y., Xiong, Q., Yang, J., Li, Y., Xiang, L., & Peng, F. (2006). Research on the design method of W3C XML Schema schema. *Computer Application Research*, (05), 80–82.

Pelekis, N., Theodoulidis, B., Kopanakis, I., & Theodoridis, Y. (2004). Literature review of Spatiotemporal database models. *The Knowledge Engineering Review*, *19*(3), 235–274. doi:10.1017/S026988890400013X

Rizzolo, F., & Vaisman, A. A. (2008). Temporal XML: Modeling, indexing, and query processing. *The VLDB Journal*, *17*(5), 1179–1212. doi:10.100700778-007-0058-x

Wang, X., Zhou, X., & Lu, S. (2000). Spatiotemporal data modelling and management: a survey. In *Proceedings of the 36th IEEE international conference on technology of object-oriented languages and systems*, (pp. 202-211). IEEE.

Ye, X., Chen, Z., Tang, Y., Tang, N., & Hu, S. (2007). Temporal XML indexing technology. *Journal of Computational Science*, (07), 1074–1085.

Ye, X. P., Chen, Z. Y., & Tang, Y. (2007). Temporal XML indexing technology. *Journal of Computational Science*, (07), 1074–1085.

Yu, Z., Yuan, L., Hu, Y., Li, Y., & Zong, Z. (2012). Expression and modeling method of vector spatio-temporal data based on geometric algebra. *Journal of Geo-Information Science*, (01), 67–73. doi:10.3724/SP.J.1047.2012.00067

Yuan, L., Yu, Z., Chen, S., Luo, W., Wang, Y., & Lü, G. (2010). CAUSTA: Clifford algebra-based unified Spatiotemporal analysis. *Transactions in GIS*, *14*(s1), 59–83. doi:10.1111/j.1467-9671.2010.01221.x

Zhang, Y., Wang, X., & Zhang, Y. (2009). Labeling Scheme for Temporal XML. *Web Information Systems and Mining, 2009. WISM 2009. International Conference on*, (pp. 277-279). IEEE.

Chapter 15
Determining Topological Relations of Uncertain Spatiotemporal Data

ABSTRACT

Determining topological relations has proved to be one of the most important operations on spatiotemporal data, which still merits further attention. In this chapter, the authors propose a valid and efficient topological relationship mechanism that allows identification of topological relations of uncertain spatiotemporal data over time. This approach adopts polygon approximation and triangulation to represent uncertain spatiotemporal data. The unique feature is that this approach not only considers the polygon approximation of a spatiotemporal region, but also takes the number of the salient points into account. Moreover, determining topological relations of uncertain spatiotemporal data is detailed investigated based on counter-clock-wisely directed triangle. Finally, the authors apply this approach to meteorological events and experiments are run to validate our approach and show its performance advantages.

1 INTRODUCTION

Spatiotemporal data typically include both spatial and temporal phenomena (Santos et al., 2014). Since spatiotemporal application domains manipulate a volume of such spatiotemporal data, research on managing spatiotemporal data have received much attention and extensively proposed (Liu et al., 2017; Pelekis et al., 2004; Sözer et al., 2015). In particular, determining topological relations has proved to be one of the most important operations on spatiotemporal data (Erwig & Schneider, 2002) because topological relations can be employed to manage and query spatiotemporal data (Li et al., 2017).

In determining topological relations of crisp spatiotemporal data, discrete approaches (Chirigati et al., 2016; Grumbach et al., 2001) and continuous approaches (Bai et al., 2012; Cheng, 2016; Le et al., 2013) are frequently used. The discrete approaches represent discrete topological relations of spatiotemporal data, and regard time as an added dimension. The continuous approaches indicate continuous topological relations of spatiotemporal data over time, and consider time as the whole coordinate system. In addi-

DOI: 10.4018/978-1-6684-9108-9.ch015

tion, the well known 4-Intersection approach (Guo et al., 2003), the 9-Intersection approach (Chen et al., 2001), and the Intersection and Difference (ID) model (Deng et al., 2007) is proposed to formalize topological relations of crisp spatiotemporal data. What's more, several other efforts have been made for determining topological relations of crisp spatiotemporal data, such as point-set topology (Muller, 2002), motion-based topology (Xie & Shibasaki, 2005), dimensional-extended topology (Bennett et al., 2002), and event-based topology (Doraiswamy et al., 2014), etc.

In the real world applications, spatiotemporal data is not always crisp but with features of uncertainty and fuzziness (Plewe, 2002; Sözer et al., 2008), which leads to accompanying studies on representing uncertain spatiotemporal regions (Abul et al., 2008; Cheung et al., 2004; Pfoser et al., 2005; Trajcevski et al., 2004; Tao et al., 2004; Xu et al., 2016; Boulila et al., 2011). In (Trajcevski et al., 2004), a moving object is modeled as a polyline with an implicit function in three-dimensional space, in which two dimensions for geography, and one for time. The work of Abul et al. (Abul et al., 2008) regards a moving object as a cylindrical volume where its radius represents the possible location imprecision. More specifically, a polygon in three dimensional space is represented as a sequence of spatiotemporal polylines at a constant speed with an uncertainty threshold. Pfoser et al. (Pfoser et al., 2005) split the underlying spatiotemporal regions into three parts, which are the core of the area, the boundary region, and the outside. Thus, an uncertain spatiotemporal region can be described using a membership function. In (Cheung et al., 2004), the uncertain polygons with uncertainty distribution are described by the cases where the vertices of the polygon are either correlated or uncorrelated. The uncertainty distribution of a polygon is derived from the uncertainty distributions of all the points located inside the polygon and there are an infinite number of these points in the polygon.

Topological relations of uncertain spatiotemporal data describe spatial intersection or relationships between indeterminate regions in space, which have been extensively proposed (Bao et al., 2016; Liu & Schneider, 2011; Roy & Stell, 2001). Liu and Schneidewe (Liu & Schneider, 2011) define a concept called *spatio-temporal uncertainty predicate* (*STUP*) which expresses the development of topological relationships between moving objects with uncertainty as a binary predicate. The benefit of this approach is that the predicates can be used as selection conditions in query languages and integrated into databases. In (Bao et al., 2016), Bao et al. extends the 2D Egg/Yolk model into the third dimension that can describe the approximate topological relations for indeterminate evolving regions. Then the correspondence between spatiotemporal relations and the 3D topological relations and presents a relation analysis model for indeterminate evolving 2D regions. The work of Roy and Stell (Roy & Stell, 2001) presents two new methods for extending the relations based on the RCC from crisp regions to indeterminate regions. As a formal context for these two methods, a generalization of the "egg-yolk" model of indeterminate regions is provided. In addition to those topological relations of uncertain spatiotemporal data, topological relations of fuzzy spatiotemporal data can also be experienced such as Bai et al. (Bai et al., 2013), Cheng (Cheng, 2016), and Tang et al. (Tang et al., 2010). However, the described methods studying the evolution of topological relations over time do not give quantitative evaluations, and the described methods aiming at modeling efficient topological relations do not consider continuous change of the topological relations.

The motivation of our research is the development of a valid and efficient topological relationship mechanism that allows identification of topological relations of uncertain spatiotemporal data over time. In this chapter, types of spatiotemporal regions are defined firstly. On this basis, we propose approaches for polygon approximation and triangulation. In succession, topological relations between (uncertain) spatiotemporal regions (over time) are detailed investigated. Subsequently, we apply our approach to meteorological events. Finally, the experimental results demonstrate the performance advantages of our approach.

The rest of the chapter is organized as follows. Section 2 defines types of spatiotemporal region. After proposing approaches for polygon approximation and triangulation in Section 3, Section 4 investigates topological relations of spatiotemporal data and Section 5 investigates topological relations of uncertain spatiotemporal data. In Section 6, we apply our approach to meteorological events. Section 7 presents the experimental results and Section 8 concludes the chapter.

2 TYPES OF SPATIOTEMPORAL REGION

The types of a spatiotemporal region can be divided into point, line, triangle, and polygon (it is easily confused at representing point and polygon because the first word of point and polygon are both p. As a result, we use region to indicate polygon in this chapter).

Definition 1. For a point of a spatiotemporal region, we have Point p (x, y), where x and y are x-coordinate and y-coordinate of the point.

Definition 2. For a line of a spatiotemporal region, we have Line $l <p_1, p_2>$, where Point p_1 (x, y) and Point p_2 (x, y) are the ending points of the line.

Definition 3. For a triangle of a spatiotemporal region, if

$$x(p_1) = \min\{x(p_1), x(p_2), x(p_3)\} \ \& \ y(p_1) = \min\{y(p_1), y(p_2), y(p_3)\} \ \& \ \begin{vmatrix} x_1 & y_1 & 1 \\ x_2 & y_2 & 1 \\ x_3 & y_3 & 1 \end{vmatrix} > 0,$$

then we have Triangle $t <p_1, p_2, p_3>$, where p_1 (x, y), p_2 (x, y), and p_3 (x, y) are the ending points of the triangle in reverse order. It is called counter-clock-wisely directed triangle, abbreviated as CDT.

Definition 4. For a region of a spatiotemporal region, if $x(p_1) = \min\{x(p_1), x(p_2), \ldots, x(p_n)\}$ & $y(p_1) = \min\{y(p_1), y(p_2), \ldots, y(p_n)\}$, then we have Region $r <p_1, p_2, \ldots, p_n>$, where p_1 (x, y), p_2 (x, y), $\ldots$, p_n (x, y) are the ending points of the region in reverse order.

3 POLYGON APPROXIMATION AND TRIANGULATION

In this section, we will propose approaches for polygon approximation and triangulation. Firstly, we propose an approach for polygon approximation of a spatiotemporal region. The key difference from the previous effort (Cheung et al., 2004) is that our approach not only considers the polygon approximation of a spatiotemporal region but also takes number of the salient points into account.

The approach is listed in the following:

Polygon approximation of a spatiotemporal region
Set points as salient points from the contour line
While (hasNextDomainantPoint)
If $P_{i-1}.x = P_i.x = P_{i+1}.x$ or $P_{i-1}.y = P_i.y = P_{i+1}.y$
P_i is eliminated
Else P_i.status = 1
Select initial point as P_0,and the last two dominant points as P_1 and P_2 and the rest be done in the same manner
Repeat
If P_0,P_1 and P_2 are at the same straight line then
P_1 is eliminated and $P_i \leftarrow$ NextDominantPoint
else
$P_0 \leftarrow P_1$, $P_i \leftarrow$ NextDominantPoint
End-if Until all points have been examined
End repeat

Our approach operates in three phases. In the first phase, we set salient points from the contour line of the spatiotemporal region according to the required degree of accuracy (01). In the second phase, we delete the in-between salient points, which are with the same *x*-coordinate or *y*-coordinate as the ending salient points (02-05). In the last phase, we delete the in-between salient points at the same straight line (06-13).

Example 1. Consider a polygon of a spatiotemporal region shown in Figure 1. Firstly, according to the required degree of accuracy, the salient points of the polygon are obtained and represented by the black dots shown as Figure 1(a). Secondly, the in-between salient points are deleted after checking whether the *x*-coordinate or *y*-coordinate is the same as the ending salient points. The deleted salient points are represented by adding a cross shown as Figure 1(b). Finally, an initial salient point with the minimum *x*-coordinate and *y*-coordinate is selected as P_0,and then other salient points are selected as P_1 to P_5 in reverse order, shown as Figure 1(b). In succession, because P_0, P_1, P_2, and P_3 are at the same straight line, the in-between salient points P_1 and P_2 are deleted. As a result, the polygon approximation of a spatiotemporal region is obtained shown as Figure 1(c).

Figure 1. Polygon approximation of a spatiotemporal region

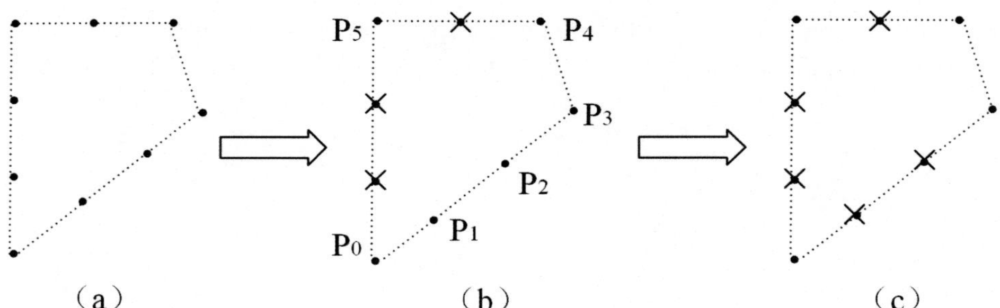

In the following, we propose an approach for polygon triangulation of a spatiotemporal region inspired by (Amato et al., 2001). Firstly, for Region $r <p_1, p_2, \ldots, p_n>$ ($n > 3$), select V_i from p_i with the minimum value of x. If V_{i1} and V_{i2} are with the same value of x, select V_i with the minimum value of y. V_0 is selected for initial consideration. Secondly, in a counterclockwise direction, select the point after V_0 as V_1 and the point before V_0 as V_2. Connect V_0, V_1, and V_2, then the triangle T_1 will be found. Thirdly, if T_1 is not a CDT or T_1 contains a point of *Points*, T_1 will be neglected and V_2 will be regarded as V_0. Else, T_1 will be inserted into *Triangulation* (Region *r*), and V_0 will be deleted from *Points*. Repeat step 2 in a counterclockwise direction. Finally, the set *Triangulation* (Region *r*) with (n-2) CDTs can be found. It is noted that Region $r <p_1, p_2, \ldots, p_n>$ has (n-2) vertices.

The approach is listed in the following:

Polygon triangulation of a spatiotemporal region
Make all feature points up as *Points*
Make all triangles up as *Triangulation* (Region *r*)
Repeat
$V_0 \leftarrow$ the first point in *Points*
V_0's last point $+V_0+V_0$'s next point$=T_1$
If (T_1 is CDT & nonePoints $\in T_1$)
Add T_1 into *Triangulation* (Region *r*)
Delete V_0 from Region *r*
Else
$V_0 \leftarrow V_0$'s next point
End if
End repeat;

Example 2. For a Region $r_a <P_1, P_2, P_3, P_4, P_5, P_6>$ shown in Figure 2(a), select p_1 as V_0 because $x(p_1) = \min x\{p_1, p_2, p_3, p_4, p_5, p_6\}$ shown in Figure 2(b). Then, P_1 is regarded as V_1 and P_6 is regarded as V_2. In the direction of V_0, V_1, V_2, triangle T_1 will be found shown in Figure 2(c). According to Definition 3, T_1 is CDT. As a result, T_1 is inserted into *Triangulation* (Region *r*) and delete P_1 from *Points*. Follow the above steps, in the direction of P_6, P_2, P_5, T_2 will be found shown in Figure 2(d). However, T_2 is not CDT according to Definition 3. As a result, T_2 will be neglected and P_5 will be regarded as V_0. Repeat step 2 in a counterclockwise direction, the new T_2 is CDT according to Definition 3 and is inserted into Triangulation (Region r_a) shown in Figure 2(e). Repeat the above 4 steps, T_3 and T_4 are found and inserted into Triangulation (Region r_a) shown in Figure 2(f) and Figure 2(g). The final result is shown in Figure 2(h).

Figure 2. Polygon triangulation of a spatiotemporal region

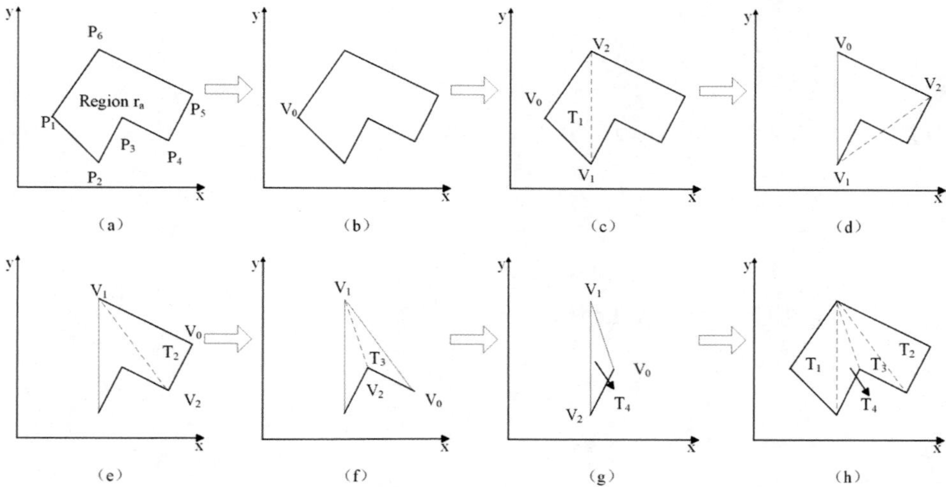

4 TOPOLOGICAL RELATIONS BETWEEN SPATIOTEMPORAL REGIONS

4.1 Determination of Spatiotemporal Regions

In this section, we study representations of spatiotemporal topological relations from four aspects, which are point, line, triangle, and polygon.

The spatiotemporal topological relations between two points contain two cases, which are *equal* and *disjoint*.

Definition 5. For two points of a spatiotemporal region Point p_1 (x, y) and Point p_2 (x, y), we have:

Equal (Point p_1, Point p_2): iff $(x\,(p_1) = x\,(p_2)) \wedge (\mathrm{y}\,(p_1) = \mathrm{y}\,(p_2))$.
Disjoint (Point p_1, Point p_2): iff $(\mathrm{x}\,(p_1) \neq (\mathrm{x}\,(p_2)) \vee (\mathrm{y}\,(p_1) \neq (\mathrm{y}\,(p_2))$.

The spatiotemporal topological relations between a line and a point contain three cases, which are *contain*, *meet*, and *disjoint*.

Definition 6. For a line of a spatiotemporal region Line l $<p_1, p_2>$ and a point of a spatiotemporal region Point p (x, y), we have:

Contain (Line l, Point p): iff

$$\begin{vmatrix} x_1(l) & y_1(l) & 1 \\ x_2(l) & y_2(l) & 1 \\ x(p) & y(p) & 1 \end{vmatrix} = 0 \wedge (min\,(x_1\,(l), x_2\,(l)) < x\,(p) < \max\,(x_1\,(l), x_2\,(l))).$$

Meet (Line l, Point p): iff Equal (p, p_1) $\vee$Equal (p, p_2).

Disjoint (Line l, Point p): iff

$$\begin{vmatrix} x_1(l) & y_1(l) & 1 \\ x_2(l) & y_2(l) & 1 \\ x(p) & y(p) & 1 \end{vmatrix} <> 0, \text{ while Left (Point } p\text{, Line } l\text{) if}$$

$$\begin{vmatrix} x_1(l) & y_1(l) & 1 \\ x_2(l) & y_2(l) & 1 \\ x(p) & y(p) & 1 \end{vmatrix} > 0; \text{ Right (Point } p\text{, Line } l\text{) if}$$

$$\begin{vmatrix} x_1(l) & y_1(l) & 1 \\ x_2(l) & y_2(l) & 1 \\ x(p) & y(p) & 1 \end{vmatrix} < 0.$$

The spatiotemporal topological relations between two lines contain six cases, which are *intersect*, *equal*, *contain*, *overlap*, *meet*, and *disjoint*.

Definition 7. For two lines of spatiotemporal regions Line $l_1 = <p_1, p_2>$ and Line $l_2 = <p_3, p_4>$, we have:

Intersect (Line l_1, Line l_2): iff ((Left (p_1, l_2) ∧ Right (p_2, l_2)) ∨ (Left (p_2, l_2) ∧ Right (p_1, l_2))) ∧ ((Left (p_3, l_1) ∧ Right (p_4, l_1)) ∨ (Left (p_4, l_1) ∧ Right (p_3, l_1))).
Equal (Line l_1, Line l_2): iff Meet (p_1, l_2) ∧ Meet (p_2, l_2).
Contain (Line l_1, Line l_2): iff (Contain (l_1, p_3) ∧ ¬ Disjoint (p_4, l_1)) ∨ (Contain (l_1, p_4) ∧ ¬ Disjoint (p_3, l_1)).
Overlap (Line l_1, Line l_2): iff (Contain (l_1, p_3) ∨ Contain (l_1, p_4)) ∧ Contain (l_2, p_1) ∨ Contain (l_2, p_2)).
Meet (Line l_1, Line l_2): iff (Contain (l_1, p_3) ∨ Contain (l_1, p_4) ∨ Contain (l_2, p_1) ∨ Contain (l_2, p_2) ∨ Meet (l_1, p_3) ∨ Meet (l_1, p_4) ∨ Meet (l_2, p_1) ∨ Meet (l_2, p_2)) ∧ ¬ (Equal (l_1, l_2) ∨ Contain (l_1, l_2) ∨ Contain (l_2, l_1) ∨ Overlap (l_2, l_1)).
Disjoint (Line l_1, Line l_2): iff Disjoint (p_1, l_2) ∧ Disjoint (p_2, l_2) ∧ Disjoint (p_3, l_1) ∧ Disjoint (p_4, l_1) ∧ ¬ (Intersect (l_1, l_2) ∨ Contain (l_1, l_2) ∨ Contain (l_2, l_1)).

The spatiotemporal topological relations between a point and a triangle contain three cases, which are *contain*, *meet*, and *disjoint*.

Definition 8. For a point of a spatiotemporal region Point p (x, y) and a triangle of a spatiotemporal region Triangle $t = <p_1, p_2, p_3>$, we have:

Contain (Triangle t, Point p): iff (Contain (l_1, p) ∨ Contain (l_2, p) ∨ Contain (l_3, p)).
Meet (Point p, Triangle t) | Meet (Triangle t, Point p): iff (Meet (p, l_1) ∨ Meet (p, l_2) ∨ Meet (p, l_3) ∨ Contain (l_1, p) ∨ Contain (l_2, p) ∨ Contain (l_3, p)).

Disjoint (Point p, Triangle t) | Disjoint (Triangle t, Point p): iff ($\neg$ ((Left (p, l_1) $\wedge$ Left (p, l_2) $\wedge$ Left (p, l_3)) $\vee$ (Right (p, l_1) $\wedge$ Right (p, l_2) $\wedge$ Right (p, l_3)).

The spatiotemporal topological relations between a line and a triangle contain three cases, which are *contain*, *intersect*, and *disjoint*.

Definition 9. For a line of a spatiotemporal region Line $l = <p_1, p_2>$ and a triangle of a spatiotemporal region Triangle $t = <p_1, p_2, p_3>$, we have:

Contain (Triangle t, Line l): iff (Contain (t, p_1) $\wedge \neg$ Disjoint (t, p_2)) $\vee$ (Contain (t, p_2) $\wedge \neg$ Disjoint (t, p_1)).
Intersect (Triangle t, Line l) | Intersect (Line l, Triangle t): iff (Contain (t, p_1) $\wedge$ Disjoint (t, p_2)) $\vee$ (Contain (t, p_1) $\wedge$ Disjoint (t, p_1)).
Disjoint (Triangle t, Line l) | Disjoint (Line l, Triangle t): iff Disjoint (t, p_1) $\wedge$ Disjoint (t, p_2)).

The spatiotemporal topological relations between two triangles contain 5 cases, which are *equal*, *contain*, *overlap*, *meet*, and *disjoint*.

Definition 10. For two triangles of spatiotemporal regions Triangle $t_1 = <p_1, p_2, p_3>$ and Triangle $t_2 = <p_4, p_5, p_6>$, where $l_1 = <p_1, p_2>$, $l_2 = <p_2, p_3>$, $l_3 = <p_3, p_1>$, $l_4 = <p_4, p_5>$, $l_5 = <p_5, p_6>$, $l_6 = <p_6, p_4>$, then we have:

Equal (Triangle t_1, Triangle t_2): iff (Equal (p_1, p_4) $\wedge$ Equal (p_2, p_5) $\wedge$ Equal (p_3, p_6)).
Contain (Triangle t_1, Triangle t_2): iff ($\neg$ Equal (t_1, t_2) $\wedge$ (Contain (t_1, p_4) $\vee$ Meet (t_1, p_4)) $\wedge$ (Contain (t_1, p_5) $\vee$ Meet (t_1, p_5)) $\wedge$ (Contain (t_1, p_6) $\vee$ Meet (t_1, p_6))).
Overlap (Triangle t_1, Triangle t_2): iff (Intersect (t_1, l_1) $\vee$ Intersect (t_1, l_2) $\vee$ Intersect (t_1, l_3)).
Meet (Triangle t_1, Triangle t_2): iff ((Meet (p_1, t_2) $\vee$ Meet (p_2, t_2) $\vee$ Meet (p_3, t_2) $\vee$ Meet (p_4, t_1) $\vee$ Meet (p_5, t_1) $\vee$ Meet (p_6, t_1)) $\wedge \neg$ (Equal (t_1, t_2) $\vee$ Overlap (t_1, t_2) $\vee$ Contain (t_1, t_2) $\vee$ Contain (t_2, t_1))).
Disjoint (Triangle t_1, Triangle t_2): iff (Disjoint (t_1, l_4) $\wedge$ Disjoint (t_1, l_5) $\wedge$ Disjoint (t_1, l_6)).

The spatiotemporal topological relations between two triangles are shown in Figure 3. It is noted that Figure 3(d) and Figure 3(e) are both Meet (Triangle t_1, Triangle t_2), while the former meets at a line and the latter meets at a point.

The spatiotemporal topological relations between two regions (polygons) contain 5 cases, which are *disjoint*, *equal*, *contain*, *overlap*, and *meet*.

Definition 11. For two spatiotemporal regions (polygons) Region $r_1 = <M_1, M_2, \ldots, M_m>$ and Region $r_2 = <N_1, N_2, \ldots, N_n>$, when $(Tr_1 \neq \varnothing) \wedge (Tr_2 \neq \varnothing)$, then we have:

Disjoint (Region r_1, Region r_2): iff ($\forall$ ($T_p \in Tr1 \wedge t_q \in Tr2$), Disjoint ($T_p$, t_q).
Equal (Region r_1, Region r_2): iff $\forall (m = n) \wedge (0 < i \leq m, T_i = t_i)$.
Contain (Region r_1, Region r_2): iff ($\neg$ Equal (Region r_1, Region r_2)) $\wedge$ (for $\forall$ N_j (x_j, y_j) $\in$ Region r_2, $\exists$ $T \in Tr1$, Contain (Triangle T, Point N_j) $\vee$Meet (Triangle T, Point N_j)).
Overlap (Region r_1, Region r_2): iff ($\neg$ (Equal (Region r_1, Region r_2) $\vee$ Contain (Region r_1, Region r_2) $\vee$ Contain (Region r_2, Region r_1))) $\wedge$ ($\exists$ $T_p \in Tr_1$, $t_q \in Tr_2$, Overlap (T_p, t_q) $\vee$ Equal (T_p, t_q) $\vee$ Contain (T_p, t_q) $\vee$ Contain (T_p, t_q)).

Figure 3. The spatiotemporal topological relations between two triangles

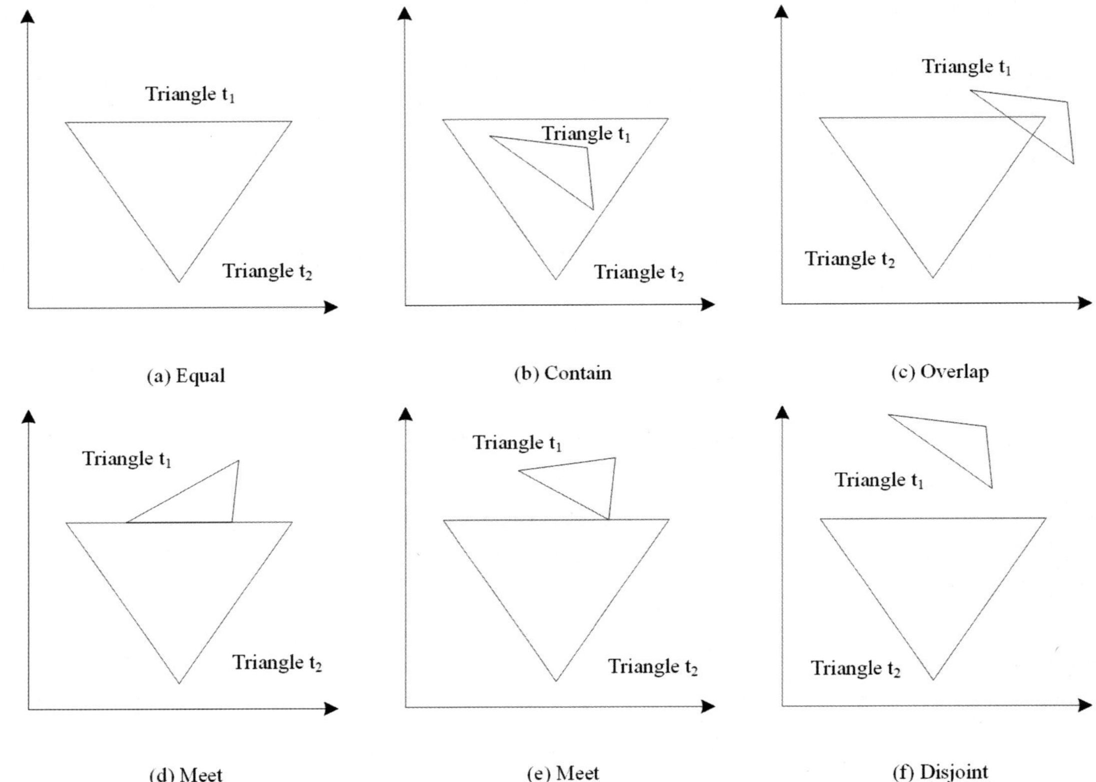

Meet (Region r_1, Region r_2): iff ($\neg$ (Equal (Region r_1, Region r_2) $\vee$ Contain (Region r_1, Region r_2) $\vee$ Contain (Region r_2, Region r_1) $\vee$ Overlop (Region r_1, Region r_2))) $\wedge$(($\exists$ M_i (x_i, y_i) $\in$ Region r_1, Meet (M_i, Region r_2)) $\vee$ ($\exists$ N_j (x_j, y_j) $\in$ Region r_2, Meet (N_j, Region r_1))).

Example 3. The spatiotemporal topological relations between two regions (polygons) are shown in Figure 4. In Figure 4(a), the spatiotemporal topological relation is *disjoint* because ($\forall$ ($T_p \in Tr1 \wedge t_q \in Tr2$), Disjoint ($T_p$, t_q) is true. In Figure 4(b), because $m = n = 6$ and $T_i = t_i$ for $0 < i \leq m$, the spatiotemporal topological relation is *equal*. In Figure 4(c), Region r_1 and Region r_2 are not equal because Equal (Region r_1, Region r_2) is not true. Furthermore, since (Contain (Triangle T_{r1}, Point N_0) $\wedge$ Contain (Triangle T_{r2}, Point N_1) $\wedge$ Meet (Triangle T_{r2}, Point N_2 | Point N_3)), the spatiotemporal topological relation is *contain*. In Figure 4(d), Region r_1 and Region r_2 are not equal nor contain because (Equal (Region r_1, Region r_2) $\vee$ Contain (Region r_1, Region r_2) is not true. Furthermore, we can obtain that the spatiotemporal topological relation is *overlap* because (Equal (T_1, t_1) $\wedge$ Contain (T_1, t_2) $\wedge$ Overlap (T_2, t_3) $\wedge$ Overlap (T_2, t_4)). In Figure 4(e), (Equal (Region r_1, Region r_2) $\vee$ Contain (Region r_1, Region r_2) $\vee$ Contain (Region r_2, Region r_1) $\vee$ Overlop (Region r_1, Region r_2)) is not true, firstly. Then, because (Meet (N_0, Region r_1) $\wedge$ Meet (N_1, Region r_1) $\wedge$ Meet (M_4, Region r_2)), the spatiotemporal topological relation is *meet*.

4.2 Determination of Spatiotemporal Regions Over Time

In this subsection, we investigate topological relations of spatiotemporal regions over time, which may remain one or more topological relations throughout the whole time. The former is regarded as *always* while the latter is regarded as *sometimes*.

In the time interval $<t_1, t_2>$ (t_1 and t_2 are starting and ending time point of the relation, respectively), the *always* topological relations of spatiotemporal regions can be represented as Relation $((r_1, r_2), <t_1, t_2>)$.

Definition 12. For two spatiotemporal regions (polygons) Region $r_1 = <M_1, M_2, \ldots, M_m>$ and Region $r_2 = <N_1, N_2, \ldots, N_n>$, then we have the *always* topological relations of spatiotemporal regions over time Relation $((r_1, r_2), <t_1, t_2>$:

Disjoint $((r_1, r_2), < t_1, t_2 >)$: iff Disjoint (r_1, r_2) when $t = < t_1, t_2 >$.
Equal $((r_1, r_2), <t_1, t_2 >)$: iff Equal (r_1, r_2) when $t = <t_1, t_2 >$.
Contain $((r_1, r_2), <t_1, t_2>)$: iff Contain (r_1, r_2) when $t = <t_1, t_2>$.
Overlap $((r_1, r_2), <t_1, t_2>)$: iff Overlap (r_1, r_2) when $t = <t_1, t_2>$.
Meet $((r_1, r_2), <t_1, t_2>)$: iff Meet (r_1, r_2) when $t = <t_1, t_2>$.

The *always* topological relations of spatiotemporal regions over time are shown in Figure 5, among which Figure 5(a) to Figure 5(e) are *disjoint*, *equal*, *contain*, *overlap*, and *meet*.

In the time interval $<t_1, t_2, t_3>$ (t_1 and t_3 are starting and ending time point of the relation, and t_2 is the time point of the relation changed), the *sometimes* topological relations of spatiotemporal regions can be represented as Relation_1-Relation_2 $((r_1, r_2), <t_1, t_2, t_3>)$, where Relation_1 $((r_1, r_2), <t_1, t_2>) \wedge \text{Relation}_2$ $((r_1, r_2), <t_2, t_3>)$.

Definition 13. For two spatiotemporal regions (polygons) Region $r_1 = <M_1, M_2, \ldots, M_m>$ and Region $r_2 = <N_1, N_2, \ldots, N_n>$, then we have the *sometimes* topological relations of spatiotemporal regions over time Relation_1-Relation_2 $((r_1, r_2), <t_1, t_2, t_3>)$:

Disjoint-Meet $((r_1, r_2), <t_1, t_2, t_3>)$: iff Disjoint $((r_1, r_2), <t_1, t_2>) \wedge$ Meet $((r_1, r_2), <t_2, t_3>)$.
Meet-Disjoint $((r_1, r_2), <t_1, t_2, t_3>)$: iff Meet $((r_1, r_2), <t_1, t_2>) \wedge$ Disjoint $((r_1, r_2), <t_2, t_3>)$.
Overlap-Meet $((r_1, r_2), <t_1, t_2, t_3>)$: iff Overlap $((r_1, r_2), <t_1, t_2>) \wedge$ Meet $((r_1, r_2), <t_2, t_3>)$.
Meet-Overlap $((r_1, r_2), <t_1, t_2, t_3>)$: iff Meet $((r_1, r_2), <t_1, t_2>) \wedge$ Overlap $((r_1, r_2), <t_2, t_3>)$.
Overlap-Equal $((r_1, r_2), <t_1, t_2, t_3>)$: iff Overlap $((r_1, r_2), <t_1, t_2>) \wedge$ Equal $((r_1, r_2), <t_2, t_3>)$.
Equal-Overlap $((r_1, r_2), <t_1, t_2, t_3>)$: iff Equal $((r_1, r_2), <t_1, t_2>) \wedge$ Overlap $((r_1, r_2), <t_2, t_3 >)$.
Overlap-Contain $((r_1, r_2), <t_1, t_2, t_3>)$: iff Overlap $((r_1, r_2), <t_1, t_2>) \wedge$ Contain $((r_1, r_2), <t_2, t_3 >)$.
Contain-Overlap $((r_1, r_2), <t_1, t_2, t_3>)$: iff Contain $((r_1, r_2), <t_1, t_2>) \wedge$ Overlap $((r_1, r_2), <t_2, t_3 >)$.
Contain-Equal $((r_1, r_2), <t_1, t_2, t_3>)$: iff Contain $((r_1, r_2), <t_1, t_2>) \wedge$ Equal $((r_1, r_2), <t_2, t_3>)$.
Equal-Contain $((r_1, r_2), <t_1, t_2, t_3>)$: iff Equal $((r_1, r_2), <t_1, t_2>) \wedge$ Contain $((r_1, r_2), <t_2, t_3>)$.

The *sometimes* topological relations of spatiotemporal regions over time are shown in Figure 6, among which Figure 6(a) to Figure 6(j) are the topological relations defined in Definition 13. It is noted that the topological relations of spatiotemporal regions cannot be changed from one topological relation to any topological relation defined in Definition 13 throughout the whole time. Accordingly, the *sometimes* topological relations of spatiotemporal regions over time have change order, shown in Figure 7.

Figure 4. The spatiotemporal topological relations between two regions

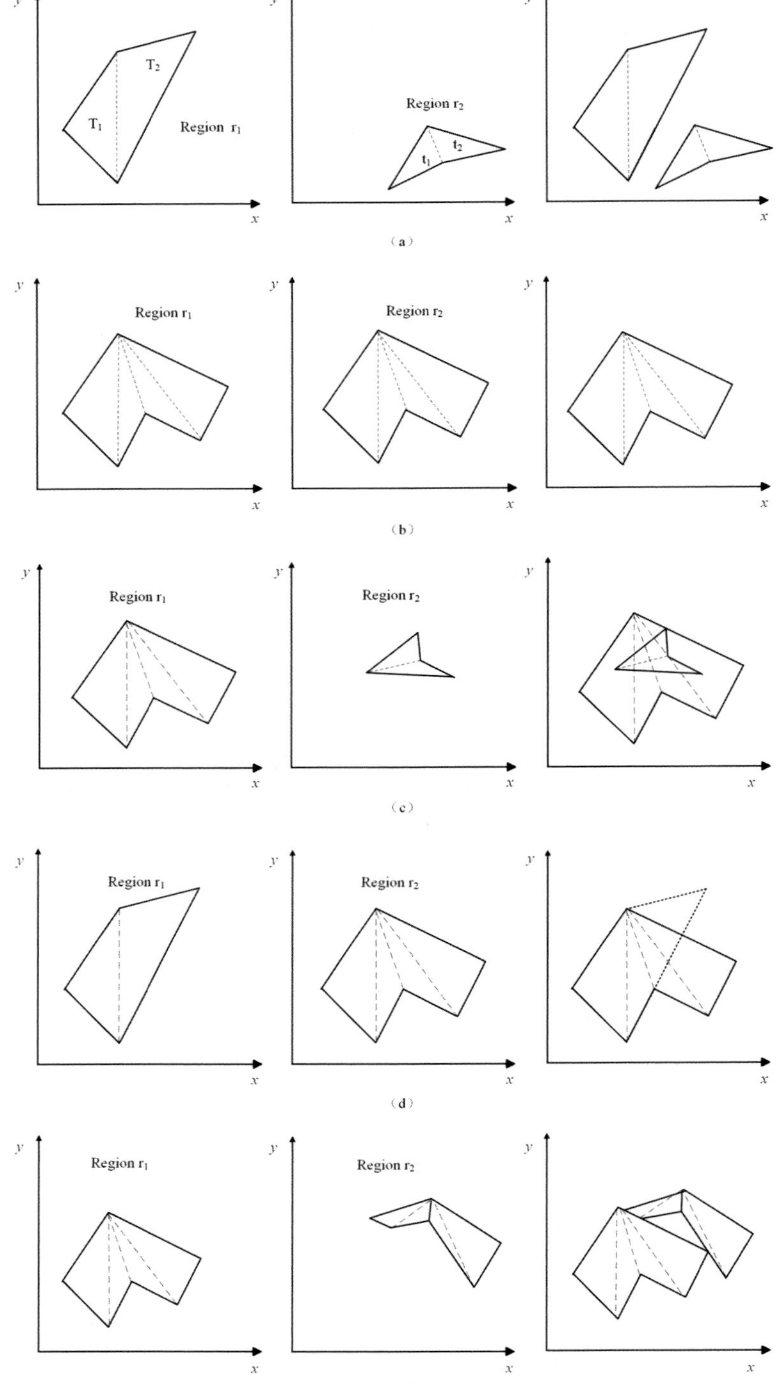

Figure 5. The always topological relations of spatiotemporal regions over time

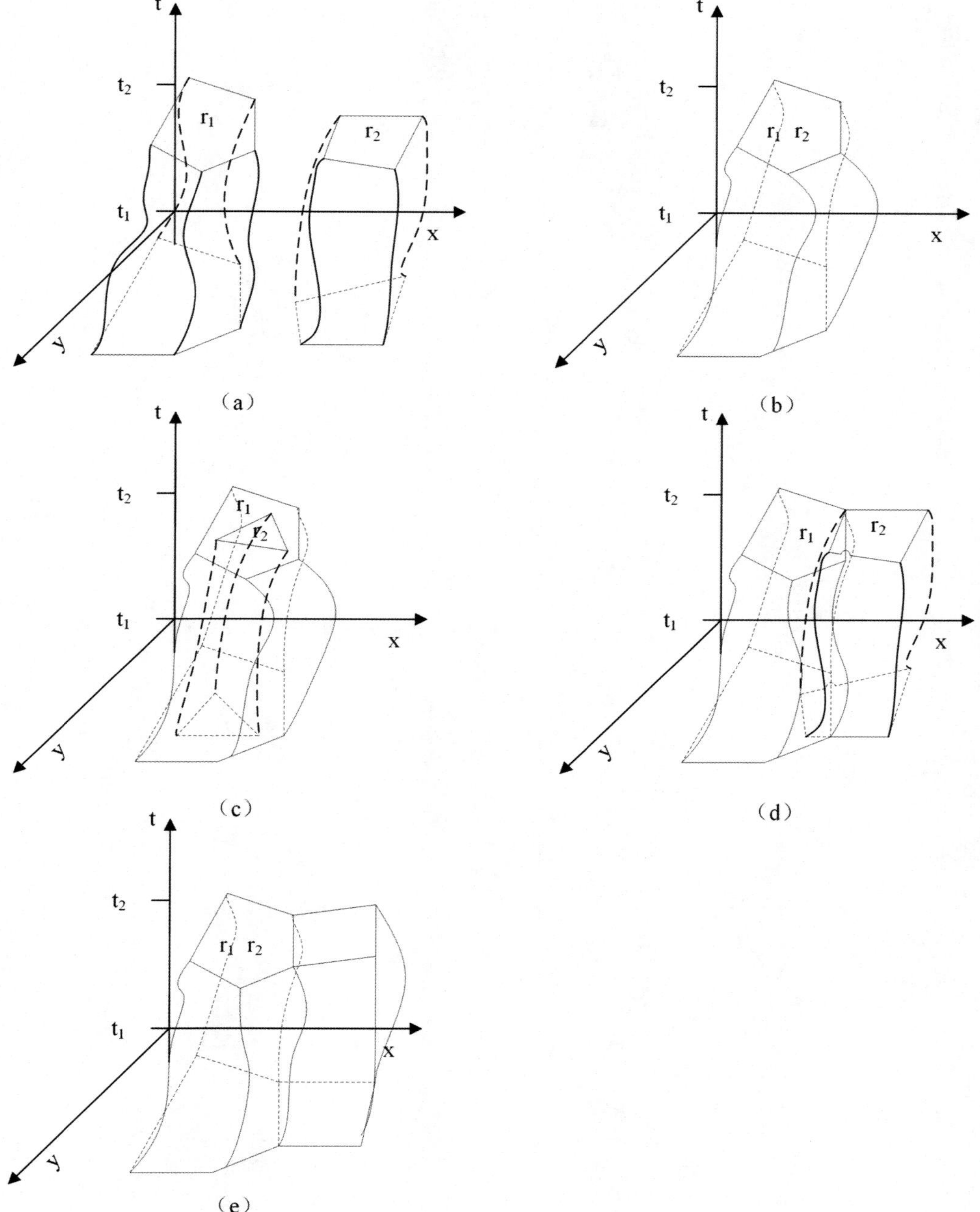

Figure 6. The sometimes topological relations of spatiotemporal regions over time

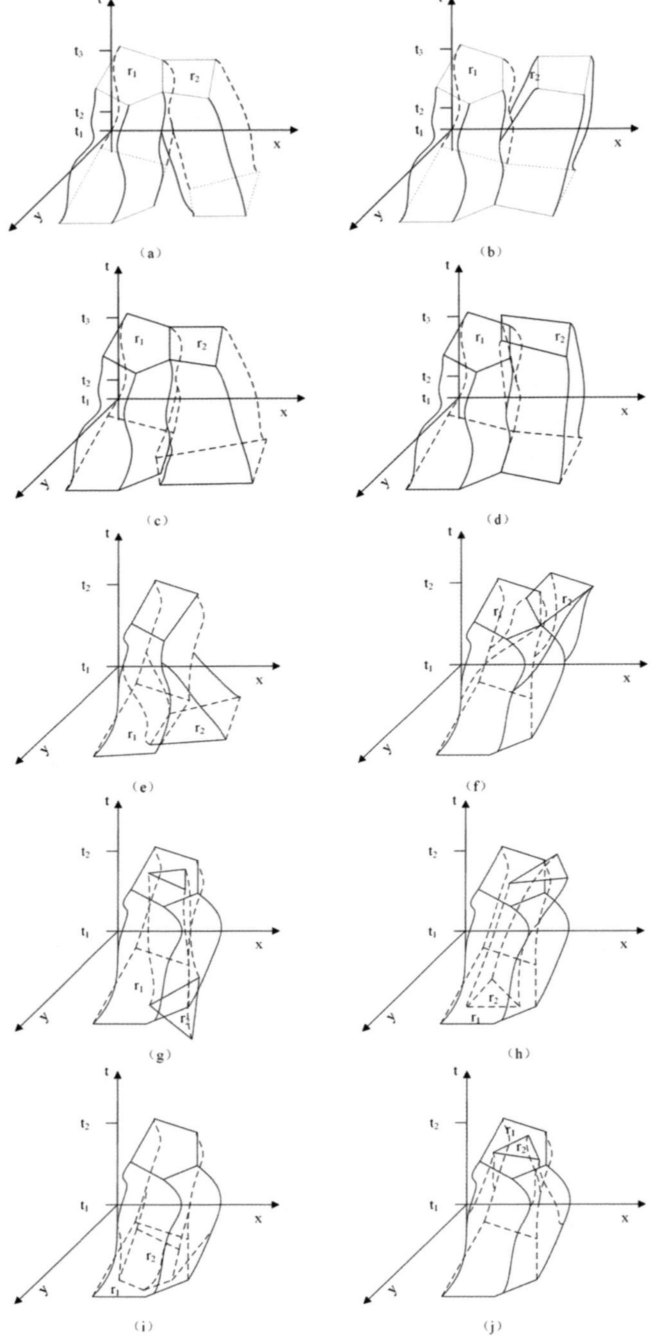

Figure 7. The change order of sometimes topological relations of spatiotemporal regions over time

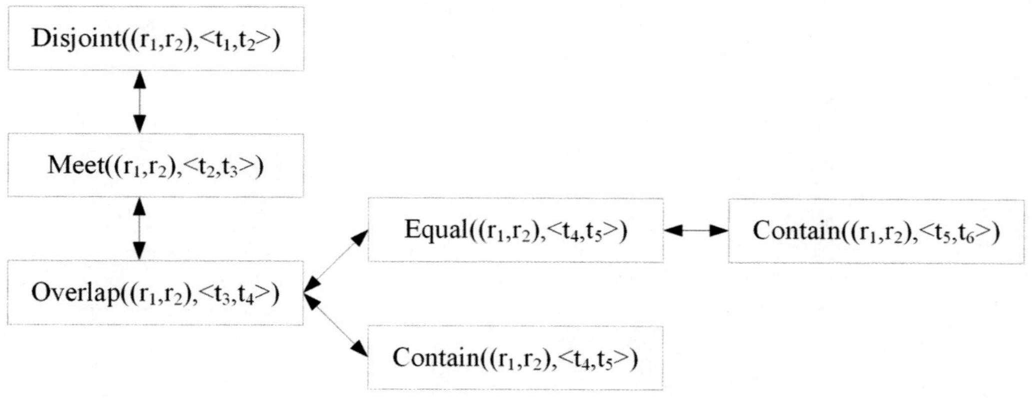

5 TOPOLOGICAL RELATIONS BETWEEN UNCERTAIN SPATIOTEMPORAL REGIONS

On the basis of Section 4, in this section, we investigate topological relations of uncertain spatiotemporal regions over time.

Definition 14. For an uncertain spatiotemporal region over time, then we have its type:

Uncertain point: U-Point $p\ (x, y)$.
Uncertain line: U-Line $l\ (p_1\ (x_1, y_1), p_2\ (x_2, y_2))$.
Uncertain triangle: U-Triangle $t\ (p_1\ (x_1, y_1), p_2\ (x_2, y_2), p_3\ (x_3, y_3))$.
Uncertain region: U-Region $r\ (p_1\ (x_1, y_1), p_2\ (x_2, y_2), p_3\ (x_3, y_3), \ldots, p_n\ (x_n, y_n))$.

where $p_i\ (x_i, y_i)$ $(0 < i \leq n)$ is an uncertain point with possibility distribution.

Although an uncertain point can be located in several possible locations, it cannot change the shape of the uncertain spatiotemporal region dramatically. As a result, uncertain polygon triangulation is regarded as the same manner as polygon triangulation in this chapter.

Example 4. Figure 8 shows a polygon triangulation of an uncertain polygon. In Figure 8(a), because each vertex $(P_1, P_2, P_3, P_4, P_5, P_6)$ of U-Region $r\ (P_1\ (x_1, y_1), P_2\ (x_2, y_2), P_3\ (x_3, y_3), P_4\ (x_4, y_4), P_5\ (x_5, y_5), P_6\ (x_6, y_6))$ has two possible locations, the uncertain polygon has several possible shapes. Figure 8(b) and Figure 8(c) show two possible shapes. According to the polygon triangulation approach, connect P_2 and P_6, P_3 and P_6, P_4 and P_6, the polygon in Figure 8(b) and Figure 8(c) can be triangulated. It can be observed that the processes of polygon triangulation of Figure 8(b) and Figure 8(c) are the same. They are triangulated by means of the vertices $(P_1, P_2, P_3, P_4, P_5, P_6)$.

Figure 8. Polygon triangulation of an uncertain polygon

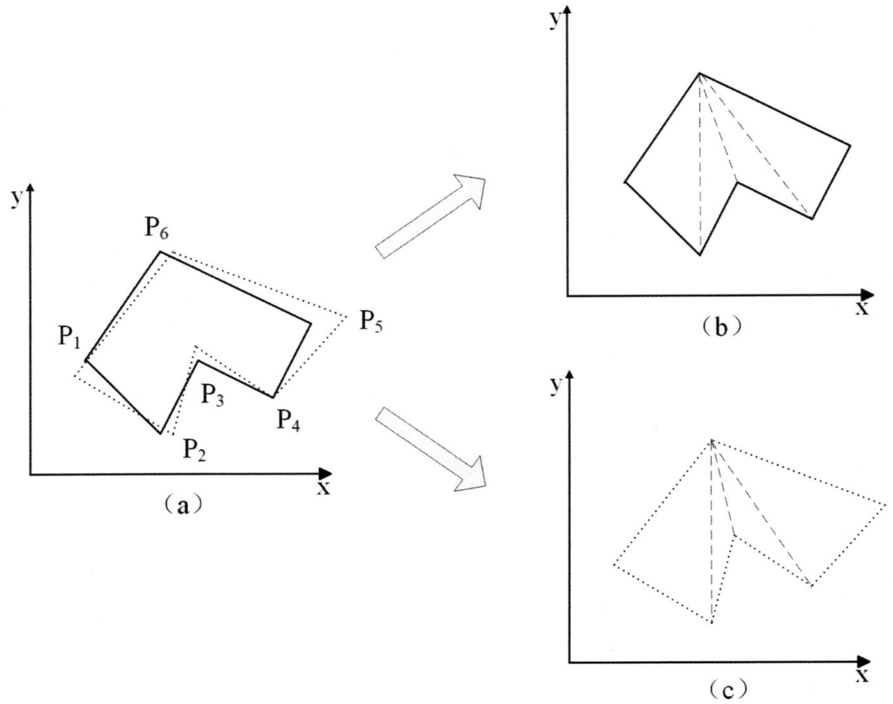

5.1 Determination of Uncertain Spatiotemporal Regions

Definition 15. For two uncertain triangles of spatiotemporal regions U-Triangle t_1 (p_1 (x_1, y_1), p_2 (x_2, y_2), p_3 (x_3, y_3)) and U-Triangle t_2 (p_1 (x_1, y_1), p_2 (x_2, y_2), p_3 (x_3, y_3)), then we have:

Disjoint (U-Triangle t_1, U-Triangle t_2): iff ∀ Disjoint (Triangle t_{1i}, Triangle t_{2j}).
Overlap (U-Triangle t_1, U-Triangle t_2): iff ∀ Overlap (Triangle t_{1i}, Triangle t_{2j}).
Contain (U-Triangle t_1, U-Triangle t_2): iff ∀ Contain (Triangle t_{1i}, Triangle t_{2j}).
D/M/O (U-Triangle t_1, U-Triangle t_2): iff ∃ (Disjoint (Triangle t_{1i}, Triangle t_{2j}) ∨ Meet (Triangle t_{1i}, Triangle t_{2j}) ∨ Overlap (Triangle t_{1i}, Triangle t_{2j})).
O/E/C (U-Triangle t_1, U-Triangle t_2): iff ∃ (Overlap (Triangle t_{1i}, Triangle t_{2j}) ∨ Equal (Triangle t_{1i}, Triangle t_{2j}) ∨ Contain (Triangle t_{1i}, Triangle t_{2j})).
O/C (U-Triangle t_1, U-Triangle t_2): iff ∃ (Overlap (Triangle t_{1i}, Triangle t_{2j}) ∨ Contain (Triangle t_{1i}, Triangle t_{2j})).

where $t_{1i} \in t_1$ and $t_{2j} \in t_2$.

Definition 16. For two uncertain spatiotemporal regions (polygons) U-Region $r_1 = <M_1, M_2, \ldots, M_m>$ and U-Region $r_2 = <N_1, N_2, \ldots, N_n>$, then we have:

Disjoint (U-Region r_1, U-Region r_2): iff ∀ Disjoint (Region r_{1i}, Region r_{2j}).

Overlap (U-Region r_1, U-Region r_2): iff ∀ Overlap (Region r_{1i}, Region r_{2j}).
Contain (U-Region r_1, U-Region r_2): iff ∀ Contain (Region r_{1i}, Region r_{2j}).
C/E/O (U-Region r_1, U-Region r_2): iff ∃ (Overlap (Region r_{1i}, Region r_{2j}) ∨ Equal (Region r_{1i}, Region r_{2j}) ∨ Contain (Region r_{1i}, Region r_{2j})).
C/O (U-Region r_1, U-Region r_2): iff ∃ (Overlap (Region r_{1i}, Region r_{2j}) ∨ Contain (Region r_{1i}, Region r_{2j})).
O/M/D (U-Region r_1, U-Region r_2): iff ∃ (Disjoint (Region r_{1i}, Region r_{2j}) ∨ Meet (Region r_{1i}, Region r_{2j}) ∨ Overlap (Region r_{1i}, Region r_{2j})).

where $r_{1i} \in r_1$ and $r_{2j} \in r_2$.

On the basis of Definition 16, we will propose an approach for determining topological relations of uncertain spatiotemporal regions (polygons) as follows:

Determination

Determination of uncertain spatiotemporal topological relations between regions
If ($\forall l_1 \in r_1, \forall l_2 \in r_2, l_1 \cap l_2 = \varnothing$)
If ($\forall$ ($T_p \in Tr_1 \wedge t_q \in Tr_2$), Disjoint ($T_p$, t_q))
Return Disjoint (U-Region r_1, U-Region r_2);
Else if ($\forall N_j (x_j, y_j) \in$ Region r_2, $\exists T \in Tr_1$, (N_j is contained by T) ∨ (N_j is meet with T))
Return Contain (U-Region r_1, U-Region r_2);
Else If ($\exists l_1 \in r_1, \exists l_2 \in r_2, l_1 \cap l_2 \neq \varnothing$)
If (($\exists l_1 \in r_1, \exists l_2 \in r_2, l_1 \cap l_2 =$ Points) ∧ ($\forall l_1 \in r_1, \forall l_2 \in r_2, l_1 \cap l_2 \neq$ Lines))
If (($\exists l_1 \in r_1, \exists l_2 \in r_2, l_1 \cap l_2 =$ Points) ∧ ($\forall l_1 \in r_1, \forall l_2 \in r_2, l_1 \cap l_2 \neq$ Lines))
Return Overlap (U-Region r_1, U-Region r_2);
If ($\exists l_1 \in r_1, \exists l_2 \in r_2, l_1 \cap l_2 =$ Lines)
If (the other lines are in the same side)
If ($\forall l_1 \in r_1, \exists l_2 \in r_2, l_1 \cap l_2 =$ Lines)
Return C/E/O (U-Region r_1, U-Region r_2)
Else
Return C/O (U-Region r_1, U-Region r_2);
If (the other lines are in the different side)
Return O/M/D (U-Region r_1, U-Region r_2);
End

Example 5. Figure 9 shows topological relations between uncertain regions. Firstly, determine whether Disjoint (U-Region r_1, U-Region r_2) or Contain (U-Region r_1, U-Region r_2) is true (01-05). Secondly, determine whether Overlap (U-Region r_1, U-Region r_2) is true (06-09). Thirdly, determine whether C/E/O (U-Region r_1, U-Region r_2) is true (10-13). Fourthly, determine whether C/O (U-Region r_1, U-Region r_2) is true (14-15). Finally, determine whether O/M/D (U-Region r_1, U-Region r_2) is true (16-18).

Figure 9. Topological relations between uncertain regions

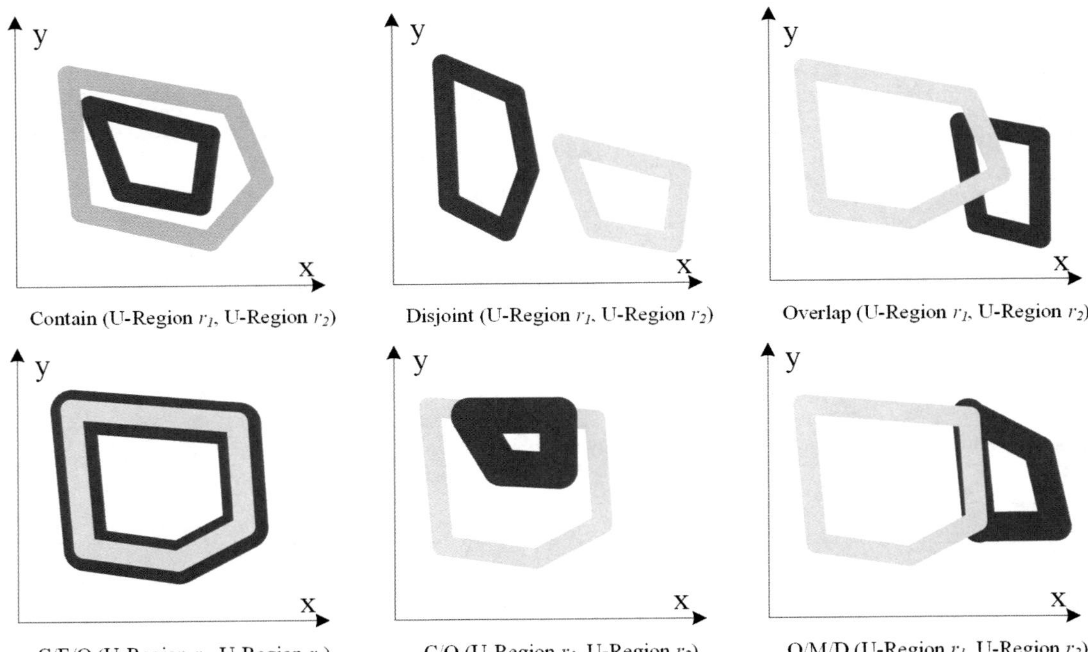

5.2 Determination of Uncertain Spatiotemporal Regions Over Time

Similar as topological relations of spatiotemporal regions over time, we investigate topological relations of uncertain spatiotemporal regions over time in two viewpoints, which are *always* topological relations and *sometimes* topological relations.

In the time interval $<t_1, t_2>$ (t_1 and t_2 are starting and ending time point of the relation, respectively), the *always* topological relations of uncertain spatiotemporal regions can be represented as Relation ((U-Region r_1, U-Region r_2), $<t_1, t_2>$. According to Definition 12 and Definition 16, *always* topological relations and their conditions are given, shown in Table 1.

Table 1. Always topological relations and their conditions

always **topological relations**	**conditions**
Disjoint ((U-Region r_1, U-Region r_2), $<t_1, t_2>$)	Disjoint (U-Region r_1, U-Region r_2) when $t = < t_1, t_2 >$
Contain ((U-Region r_1, U-Region r_2), $<t_1, t_2>$)	Contain (U-Region r_1, U-Region r_2) when $t = < t_1, t_2 >$
Overlap ((U-Region r_1, U-Region r_2), $<t_1, t_2>$)	Overlap (U-Region r_1, U-Region r_2) when $t = < t_1, t_2 >$
C/E/O ((U-Region r_1, U-Region r_2), $<t_1, t_2>$)	C/E/O (U-Region r_1, U-Region r_2) when $t = < t_1, t_2 >$
C/O ((U-Region r_1, U-Region r_2), $<t_1, t_2>$)	C/O (U-Region r_1, U-Region r_2) when $t = < t_1, t_2 >$
O/M/D ((U-Region r_1, U-Region r_2), $<t_1, t_2>$)	O/M/D (U-Region r_1, U-Region r_2) when $t = < t_1, t_2 >$

Example 6. Figure 10 shows two *always* topological relations. Figure 10(a) is Overlap ((U-Region r_1, U-Region r_2), $<t_1, t_2>$) and Figure 10(b) is C/O ((U-Region r_1, U-Region r_2), $<t_1, t_2>$) according to the conditions of *always* topological relations shown in Table 1.

Figure 10. Samples always topological relations

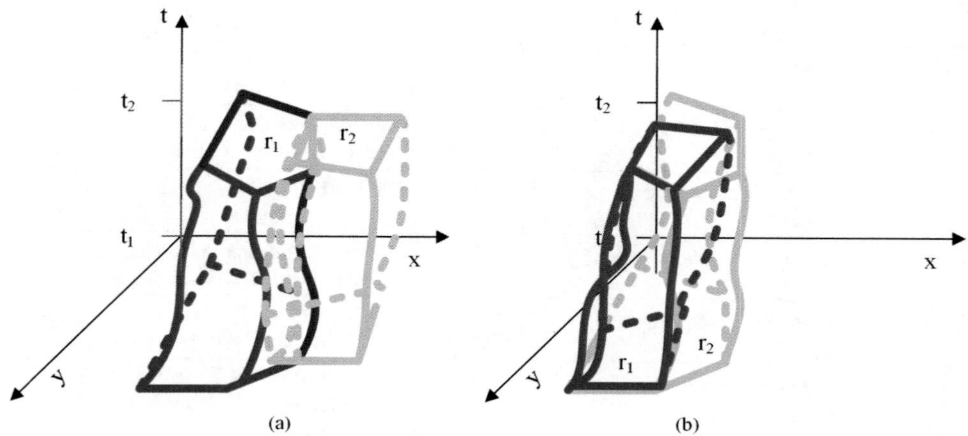

In the time interval $<t_1, t_2, t_3>$ (t_1 and t_3 are starting and ending time point of the relation, and t_2 is the time point of the relation changed), the *sometimes* topological relations of spatiotemporal regions can be represented as Relation_1-Realtion_2 ((U-Region r_1, U-Region r_2), $<t_1, t_2, t_3>$), where Relation_1 ((U-Region r_1, U-Region r_2), $<t_1, t_2>$) $\wedge$ Relation_2 ((U-Region r_1, U-Region r_2), $<t_2, t_3>$). According to Definition 13 and Definition 16, *sometimes* topological relations and their conditions are given, shown in Table 2.

Example 7. Figure 11 shows two *sometimes* topological relations. Figure 11(a) is O/M/D-Overlap ((U-Region r_1, U-Region r_2), $<t_1, t_2, t_3>$) and Figure 11(b) is Overlap-O/M/D ((U-Region r_1, U-Region r_2), $<t_1, t_2, t_3>$) according to the conditions of *sometimes* topological relations shown in Table 2.

Figure 11. Samples sometimes topological relations

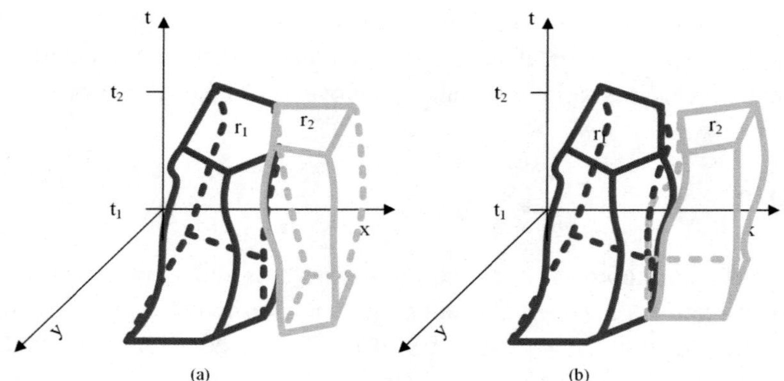

Table 2. Sometimes topological relations and their conditions

sometimes **topological relations**	**conditions**
Disjoint-O/M/D ((U-Region r_1, U-Region r_2), $<t_1, t_2, t_3>$)	Disjoint ((U-Region r_1, U-Region r_2), $<t_1, t_2>$) ∧ O/M/D ((U-Region r_1, U-Region r_2), $<t_2, t_3>$)
O/M/D-Disjoint ((U-Region r_1, U-Region r_2), $<t_1, t_2, t_3>$)	O/M/D ((U-Region r_1, U-Region r_2), $<t_1, t_2>$) ∧ Disjoint ((U-Region r_1, U-Region r_2), $<t_2, t_3>$)
Overlap-O/M/D ((U-Region r_1, U-Region r_2), $<t_1, t_2, t_3>$)	Overlap ((U-Region r_1, U-Region r_2), $<t_1, t_2>$) ∧ O/M/D ((U-Region r_1, U-Region r_2), $<t_2, t_3>$)
O/M/D-Overlap ((U-Region r_1, U-Region r_2), $<t_1, t_2, t_3>$)	O/M/D ((U-Region r_1, U-Region r_2), $< t_1, t_2 >$) ∧ Overlap ((U-Region r_1, U-Region r_2), $< t_2, t_3 >$)
Overlap-C/E/O ((U-Region r_1, U-Region r_2), $<t_1, t_2, t_3>$)	Overlap ((U-Region r_1, U-Region r_2), $<t_1, t_2>$) ∧ C/E/O ((U-Region r_1, U-Region r_2), $<t_2, t_3>$)
C/E/O-Overlap ((U-Region r_1, U-Region r_2), $<t_1, t_2, t_3>$)	C/E/O ((U-Region r_1, U-Region r_2), $<t_1, t_2>$) ∧ Overlap ((U-Region r_1, U-Region r_2), $<t_2, t_3>$)
Overlap-C/O ((U-Region r_1, U-Region r_2), $<t_1, t_2, t_3>$)	Overlap ((U-Region r_1, U-Region r_2), $<t_1, t_2>$) ∧ C/O ((U-Region r_1, U-Region r_2), $<t_2, t_3>$)
C/O-Overlap ((U-Region r_1, U-Region r_2), $<t_1, t_2, t_3>$)	C/O ((U-Region r_1, U-Region r_2), $<t_1, t_2>$) ∧ Overlap ((U-Region r_1, U-Region r_2), $<t_2, t_3>$)
C/E/O-C/O ((U-Region r_1, U-Region r_2), $<t_1, t_2, t_3>$)	C/E/O ((U-Region r_1, U-Region r_2), $<t_1, t_2>$) ∧ C/O ((U-Region r_1, U-Region r_2), $<t_2, t_3>$)
C/O-C/E/O ((U-Region r_1, U-Region r_2), $<t_1, t_2, t_3>$)	C/O ((U-Region r_1, U-Region r_2), $<t_1, t_2>$) ∧ C/E/O ((U-Region r_1, U-Region r_2), $<t_2, t_3>$)
Contain-C/O ((U-Region r_1, U-Region r_2), $<t_1, t_2, t_3>$)	Contain ((U-Region r_1, U-Region r_2), $<t_1, t_2>$) ∧ C/O ((U-Region r_1, U-Region r_2), $<t_2, t_3>$)
C/O-Contain ((U-Region r_1, U-Region r_2), $<t_1, t_2, t_3>$)	C/O ((U-Region r_1, U-Region r_2), $<t_1, t_2>$) ∧ Contain ((U-Region r_1, U-Region r_2), $<t_2, t_3>$)
Contain-C/E/O ((U-Region r_1, U-Region r_2), $<t_1, t_2, t_3>$)	Contain ((U-Region r_1, U-Region r_2), $<t_1, t_2>$) ∧ C/E/O ((U-Region r_1, U-Region r_2), $<t_2, t_3>$)
C/E/O-Contain ((U-Region r_1, U-Region r_2), $<t_1, t_2, t_3>$)	C/E/O ((U-Region r_1, U-Region r_2), $<t_1, t_2>$) ∧ Contain ((U-Region r_1, U-Region r_2), $<t_2, t_3>$)
Overlap-Contain ((U-Region r_1, U-Region r_2), $<t_1, t_2, t_3>$)	Overlap ((U-Region r_1, U-Region r_2), $<t_1, t_2>$) ∧ Contain ((U-Region r_1, U-Region r_2), $<t_2, t_3>$)
Contain-Overlap ((U-Region r_1, U-Region r_2), $<t_1, t_2, t_3>$)	Contain ((U-Region r_1, U-Region r_2), $<t_1, t_2>$) ∧ Overlap ((U-Region r_1, U-Region r_2), $<t_2, t_3>$)

It is noted that the topological relations of uncertain spatiotemporal regions cannot be changed from one topological relation to any topological relation throughout the whole time. Accordingly, the *sometimes* topological relations of uncertain spatiotemporal regions over time have change order, shown in Figure 12.

6 APPLICATIONS

In this section, we apply our approach to meteorological events and show how to use our approach to determine topological relations between two uncertain spatiotemporal regions. Figure 13 shows track probability forecast map for tropical cyclone NESAT on 27 July 2017. It provides the probability that NESAT will pass over a given location in the coming days. The probability represents the chance of a tropical cyclone crossing within 120 kilometers of that location. Such chances are represented by colors such as reddish for higher chance, yellow for medium chance, and bluish for lower chance. In the following, we will show how to use our approach to determine topological relations in this application in detail.

Figure 12. The change order of sometimes topological relations of uncertain spatiotemporal regions over time

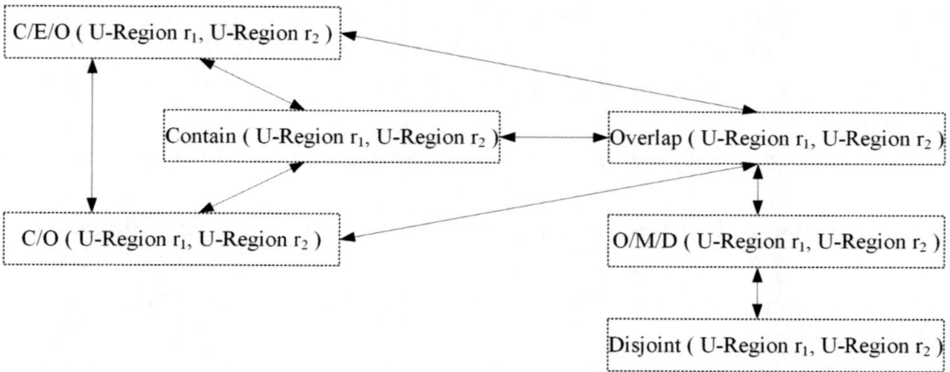

Figure 13. Track probability forecast map for tropical cyclone NESAT

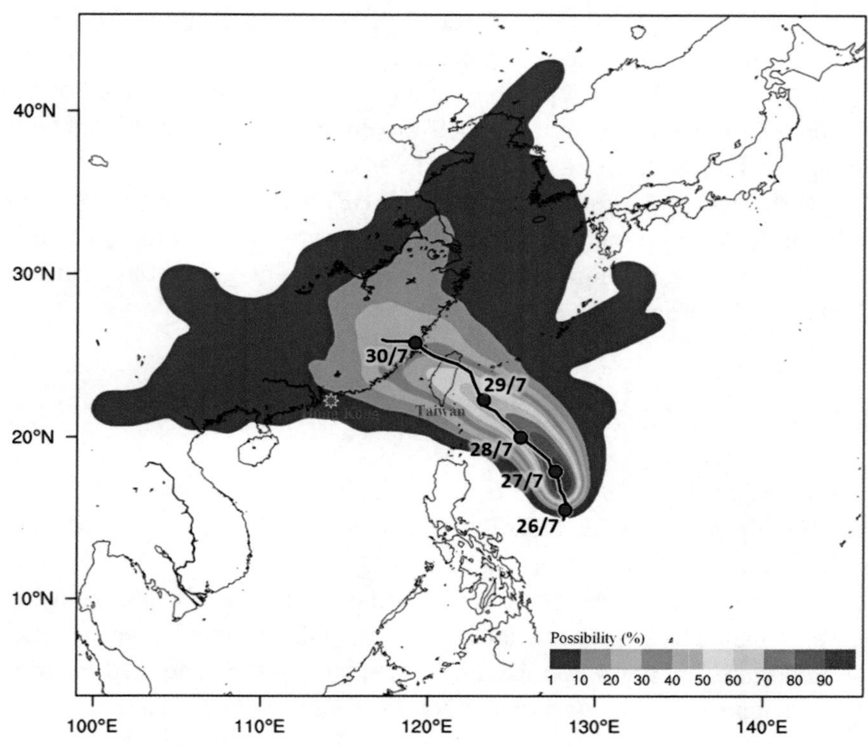

Step 1: Polygon approximation of spatiotemporal regions according to the approach proposed in Section 3.

Figure 14(a) to Figure 14(d) show spatiotemporal regions for representing approximately areas, including R1 and R2 in Figure 14(a), R1 and R3 in Figure 14(b), R1 and R4 in Figure 14(c), and R1 and R5 in Figure 14(d). Five spatiotemporal regions (R1 to R5) are with different roughly sizes. In particular, R1 correspond in size roughly to Taiwan, and R2 to R5 correspond in size roughly to approximately areas with different possibilities. Note that the red labels of R1 and black labels of R2 to R5 are added manually to clarify the figure. The polygons of R1 to R4 are generated according to the proposed approach in Section 3. The numbers of the salient points of R1 to R4 are 8, 10, 13, and 10, which not only considers the polygon approximation of a spatiotemporal region but also takes number of the salient points into account.

Step 2: Polygon triangulation of spatiotemporal regions according to the approach proposed in Section 3.

In Figure 14(a) to Figure 14(d), R1 to R4 can be triangulated according to the proposed approach in Section 3. Considering the clear and intuitive observation in Fig 14, the detailed polygon triangulations of R1 to R4 are not depicted because it does not affect the results of topological relations but the performances.

Step 3: Determination of uncertain spatiotemporal regions according to Definition 16 and the approach for determining topological relations of uncertain spatiotemporal regions proposed followed Definition 16.

In Figure 14(a) to Figure 14 (c), the topological relations between two uncertain spatiotemporal regions can be determined according to Definition 16 and the approach for determining topological relations of uncertain spatiotemporal regions proposed followed Definition 16. In Figure 14(a), R1 and R2 is Disjoint; in Figure 14 (b), R1 and R3 is Overlap; in Figure 14(c), R1 and R4 is C/O.

Step 4: Determination of uncertain spatiotemporal regions over time according to Table 1 and Table 2.

The process of Step 4 is to repeat Step 1 to Step 3 at different required time. For the determination of uncertain spatiotemporal regions over time, their topological relations can be obtained according to their corresponding conditions shown in Table 1 and Table 2.

In order to show the accuracy of our approach to MBR, we further depict MBR of R4 (shown in Figure 14(c)) in Figure 14(d) represented by R5. It can be observed that the topological relation between R1 and R5 is Contain. However, the topological relation of the two uncertain spatiotemporal regions can be either Contain or Overlap.

7 EXPERIMENTS

We implemented all the evaluations in Microsoft Visual Studio 10.0, and performed on Windows 7 system with 3.2 GHz i7 processor with 4 GB RAM. On the other hand, we used MATLAB to generate random shapes for evaluations.

To present evaluations of our approach, we performed three groups of experiments. In the first group of experiments, we evaluated the approximation of spatiotemporal shapes between MBR (Cobb & Petry, 1998) and Polygon. Figure 15 shows average area percentage of the generated random shapes, which indicate the degree of approximation of spatiotemporal shapes. For the area of real shape A_r and the area of approximated shape A_a, the area percentage $A = A_r / A_a$. It is obvious that the higher area percentage is, the higher degree of approximation is. It can be observed from Figure 15 that the Polygon has higher approximation of spatiotemporal shapes. It is noted that an immediate observation of the degree of approximation is not high enough. Actually, it is subjective to the shapes (including the best and worst cases), and Figure 15 only presents the average results.

Figure 14. Spatiotemporal regions for representing approximately areas

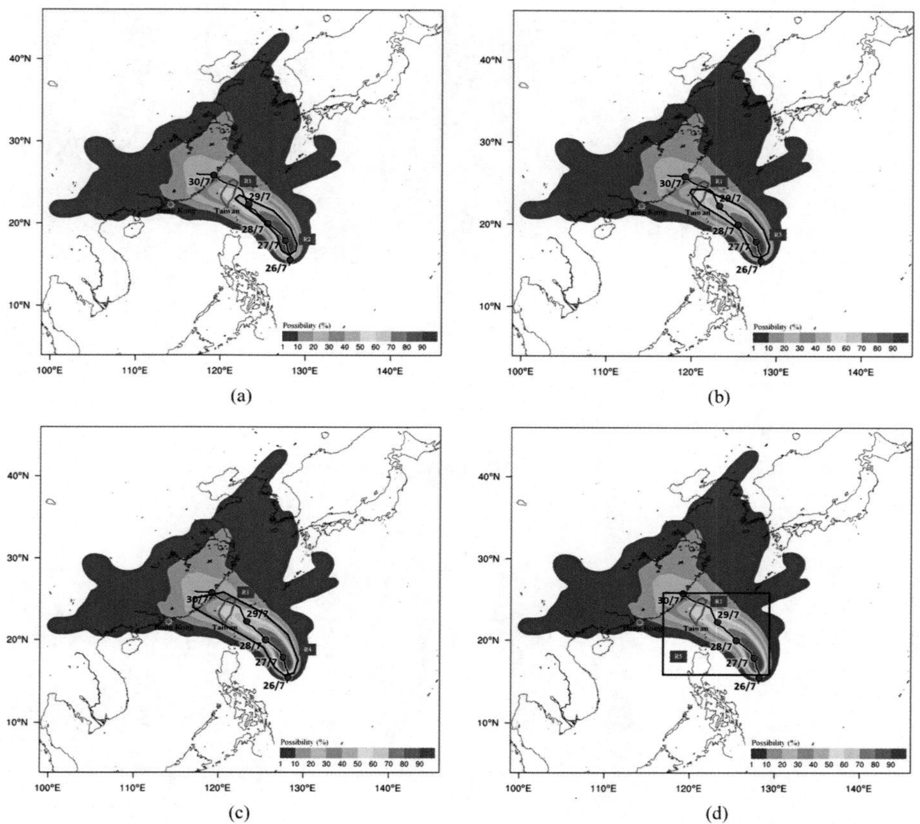

In the second group of experiments, we evaluate the effectiveness. The experiments are conducted to evaluate the polygon approximation and the polygon triangulation. Figure 16(a) shows the execution time of polygon approximation with different number of shapes between the approach (Cheung et al., 2004) (abbreviated as PB) and our approach (abbreviated as PA); Figure 16(b) shows the execution time of polygon triangulation with different number of polygons between the approach (Amato et al., 2001) (abbreviated as PR) and our approach (abbreviated as PT). It can be observed that the execution time of PA and PT have performance advantages for both polygon approximation and polygon triangulation. This can be explained by the fact that our approach not only considers the polygon approximation of a spatiotemporal region but also takes number of the salient points into account. Figure 17(a) shows the memory usage of polygon approximation with different number of shapes, and Figure 17(b) shows the memory usage of polygon triangulation with different number of polygons. It can be observed that PA and PT tend to use less memory, which is consistent with their execution time.

Figure 15. Average area percentage of the original shapes

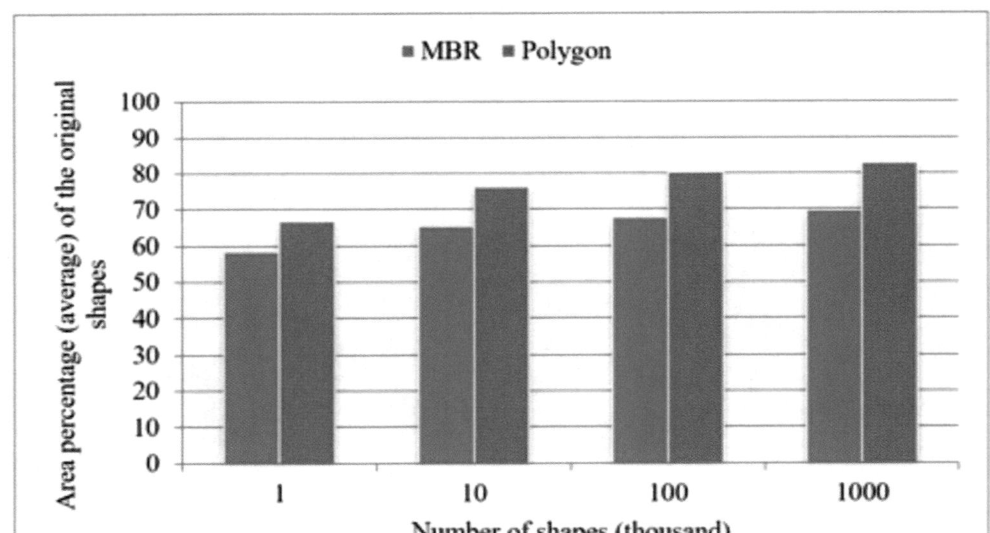

Figure 16. Execution time with different number of shapes or polygons

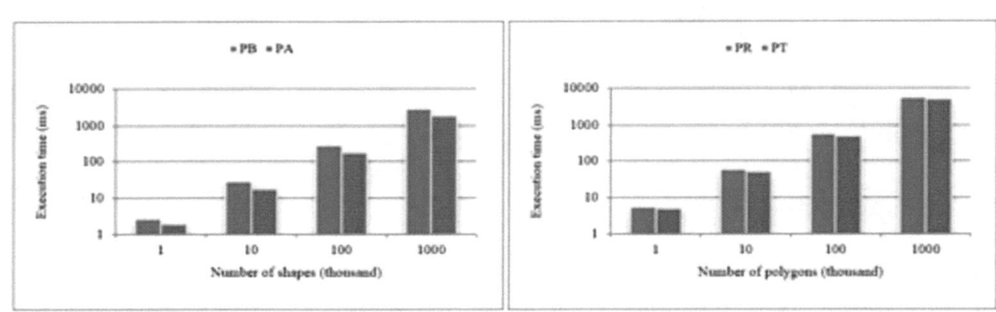

Figure 17. Memory usage with different number of shapes or polygons

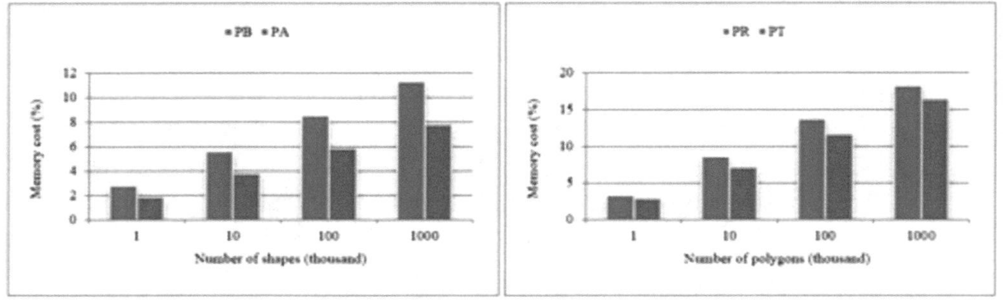

In the last group of experiments, we present the execution time of topological relations over time. Figure 18 shows the execution time of *always* topological relations, including Disjoint, Contain, Overlap, C/E/O, C/O, and C/M/D. It can be observed that C/M/D has the most execution time and Disjoint has the least execution time, which is affected by the condition of each *always* topological relation. Figure 19 shows the execution time of *sometimes* topological relations, including Disjoint-O/M/D, O/M/D-Disjoint, Overlap-O/M/D, O/M/D-Overlap, Overlap-C/E/O, C/E/O-Overlap, Overlap-C/O, C/O-Overlap, C/E/O-C/O, C/O-C/E/O, Contain-C/O, C/O-Contain, Contain-C/E/O, C/E/O-Contain, Overlap-Contain, and Contain-Overlap. It can be observed that C/E/O-C/O has the most execution time and Contain-Overlap has the least execution time, which is affected by not only the condition of each *sometimes* topological relation but also the change order of *sometimes* topological relations. It is noted that the execution time of Relation$_1$-Realtion$_2$ ((U-Region r_1, U-Region r_2), $<t_1, t_2, t_3>$) is different from the execution time of Relation$_2$-Realtion$_1$ ((U-Region r_1, U-Region r_2), $<t_1, t_2, t_3>$). This can be explained by the fact that Relation$_1$ ((U-Region r_1, U-Region r_2), $<t_1, t_2>$) and Relation$_2$ ((U-Region r_1, U-Region r_2), $<t_1, t_2>$) have different change orders to Relation$_2$ ((U-Region r_1, U-Region r_2), $<t_2, t_3>$) and Relation$_1$ ((U-Region r_1, U-Region r_2), $<t_2, t_3>$). According to Figure 18 and Figure 19, the average execution time of *always* and *sometimes* topological relations over time is shown in Figure 20.

8 SUMMARY

In this chapter, we propose a valid and efficient topological relationship mechanism that allows identification of topological relations of uncertain spatiotemporal data over time. We study the evolution of topological relations over time and give quantitative evaluations. The experimental evaluations show that the approaches of polygon approximation and polygon triangulation have performance advantages.

Figure 18. Execution time of always topological relations over time

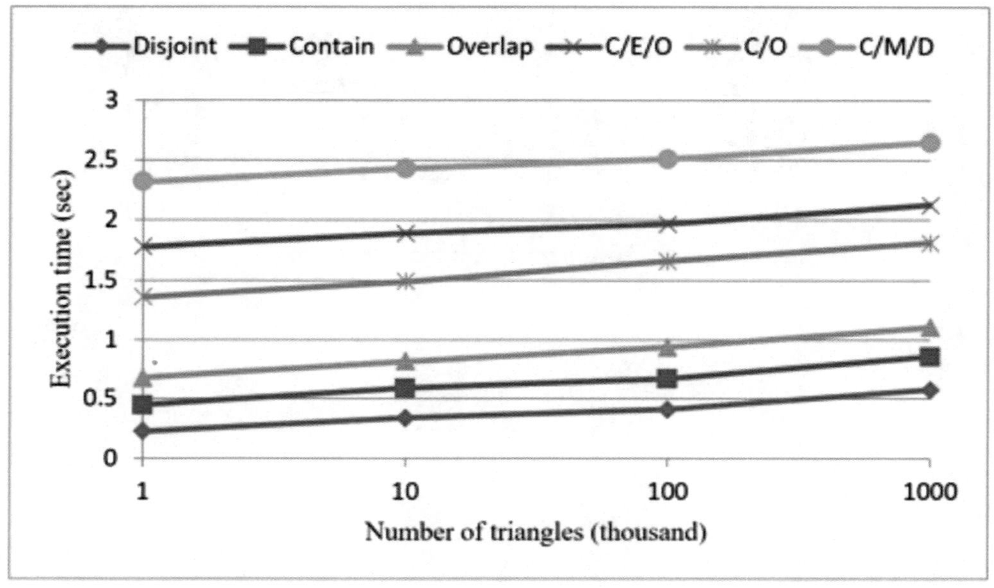

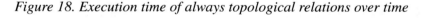

Figure 19. Execution time of sometimes topological relations over time

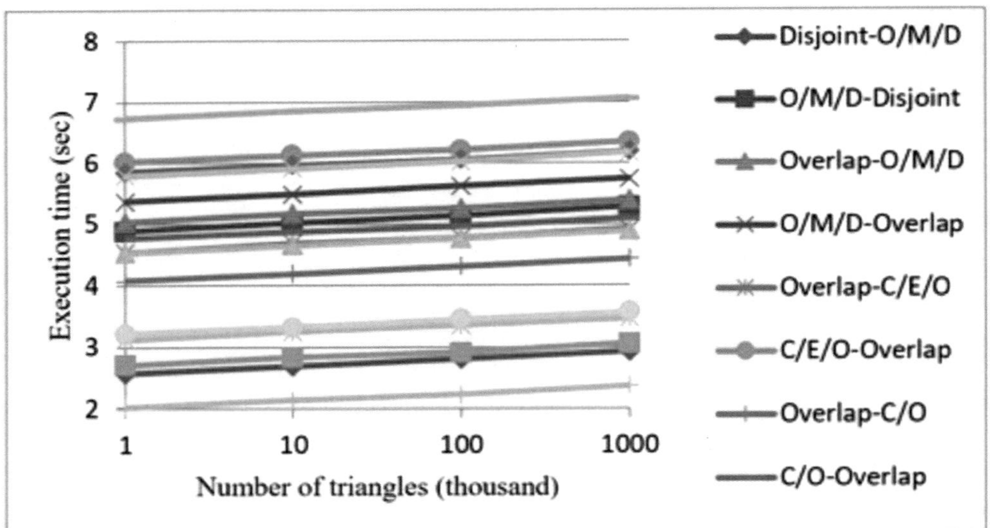

Figure 20. Average execution time of always and sometimes topological relations over time

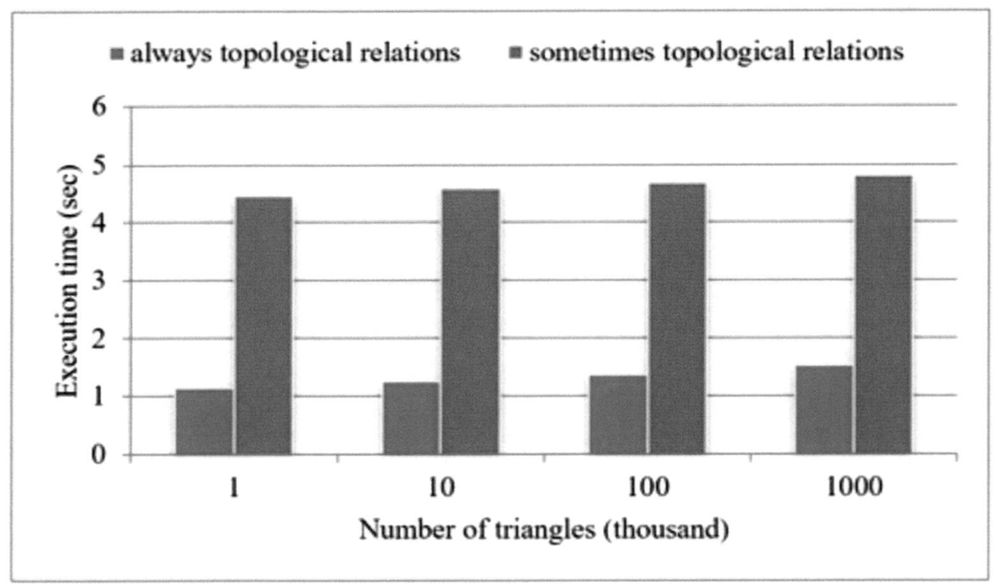

REFERENCES

Abul, O., Bonchi, F., & Nanni, M. (2008). Never walk alone: uncertainty for anonymity in moving objects databases. In proceedings of ICDE, (pp. 376-385) IEEE. doi:10.1109/ICDE.2008.4497446

Amato, N. M., Goodrich, M. T., & Ramos, E. A. (2001). A randomized algorithm for triangulating a simple polygon in linear time. *Discrete & Computational Geometry*, *26*(2), 245–265. doi:10.100700454-001-0027-x

Bai, L., Yan, L., & Ma, Z. M. (2012). Modeling topological relations between fuzzy spatiotemporal regions over time. In *Proceedings of IEEE International Conference on Fuzzy Systems*, (pp. 1-8). IEEE.

Bai, L., Yan, L., & Ma, Z. M. (2013). Determining topological relationship of fuzzy spatiotemporal data integrated with XML twig pattern. *Applied Intelligence*, *39*(1), 75–100. doi:10.100710489-012-0395-3

Bao, L., Qin, X., & Zhang, J. (2006). Reasoning the spatiotemporal relations between time evolving indeterminate regions. In D. S. Yeung, Z. Q. Liu, X. Z. Wang, & H. Yan (Eds.), *Advances in Machine Learning and Cybernetics*. Lecture Notes in Computer Science. Springer. doi:10.1007/11739685_47

Bennett, B., Cohn, A. G., Wolter, F., & Zakharyaschev, M. (2002). Multi-dimensional modal logic as a framework for spatio-temporal reasoning. *Applied Intelligence*, *17*(3), 239–251. doi:10.1023/A:1020083231504

Boulila, W., Farah, I. R., & Saheb Ettabaa, K. (2011). A data mining based approach to predict spatio-temporal changes in satellite images. *International Journal of Applied Earth Observation and Geoinformation*, *13*(3), 386–395. doi:10.1016/j.jag.2011.01.008

Chen, J., Li, C., Li, Z., & Gold, C. (2001). A Voronoi-based 9-intersection model for spatial relations. *International Journal of Geographical Information Science*, *15*(3), 201–220. doi:10.1080/13658810151072831

Cheng, H. (2016). Modeling and querying fuzzy spatiotemporal objects. *Journal of Intelligent & Fuzzy Systems*, *31*(6), 2851–2858. doi:10.3233/JIFS-169167

Cheung, C. K., Shi, W., & Zhou, X. (2004). A probability-based uncertainty model for point-in-polygon analysis in GIS. *GeoInformatica*, *8*(1), 71–98. doi:10.1023/B:GEIN.0000007725.41038.03

Chirigati, F., Doraiswamy, H., & Damoulas, T. (2016). Data polygamy: the many-many relationships among urban spatio-temporal data sets. In proceedings of SIGMOD, (pp. 1011-1025). ACM. doi:10.1145/2882903.2915245

Cobb, M. A., & Petry, P. E. (1998). Modeling spatial relationships within a fuzzy framework. *Journal of the Association for Information Science and Technology*, *49*(3), 253–266.

Deng, M., Cheng, T., Chen, X., & Li, Z. (2007). Topological relations between spatial regions based upon topological invariants. *GeoInformatica*, *11*(2), 239–267. doi:10.100710707-006-0004-x

Doraiswamy, H., Ferreira, N., Damoulas, T., Freire, J., & Silva, C. T. (2014). Using topological analysis to support event-guided exploration in urban data. *IEEE Transactions on Visualization and Computer Graphics*, *20*(12), 2634–2643. doi:10.1109/TVCG.2014.2346449 PMID:26356977

Erwig, M., & Schneider, M. (2002). Spatio-temporal predicates. *IEEE Transactions on Knowledge and Data Engineering*, *14*(4), 881–901. doi:10.1109/TKDE.2002.1019220

Grumbach, S., Rigaux, P., & Segoufin, L. (2001). Spatio-temporal data handling with constraints. *Geo-Informatica*, *5*(1), 95–115. doi:10.1023/A:1011464022461

Guo, P., Tao, H., & Luo, Y. (2003). Research on the relationship between 4-intersection and classifying invariant based on the simple regions. In *proceedings of 2003 International Conference on Machine Learning and Cybernetics*, (pp. 1642-1647). IEEE.

Le, H. H., Gabriel, P., Gietzel, J., & Schaeben, H. (2013). An object-relational spatio-temporal geoscience data model. *Computers & Geosciences*, *57*(4), 104–115. doi:10.1016/j.cageo.2013.04.014

Li, Z., Hu, F., Schnase, J. L., Duffy, D. Q., Lee, T., Bowen, M. K., & Yang, C. (2017). A spatiotemporal indexing approach for efficient processing of big array-based climate data with MapReduce. *International Journal of Geographical Information Science*, *31*(1), 17–35. doi:10.1080/13658816.2015.1131830

Liu, H., & Schneider, M. (2011). Querying moving objects with uncertainty in spatio-temporal databases. In *proceedings of the 2011 International Conference on Database Systems for Advanced Applications*, (pp. 357-371). ACM. 10.1007/978-3-642-20149-3_27

Liu, Y., Ester, M., Qian, Y., Hu, B., & Cheung, D. W. (2017). Microscopic and macroscopic spatio-temporal topic models for check-in data. *IEEE Transactions on Knowledge and Data Engineering*, *29*(9), 1957–1970. doi:10.1109/TKDE.2017.2703825

Muller, P. (2002). Topological spatio-temporal reasoning and representation. *Computational Intelligence*, *18*(3), 1–46. doi:10.1111/1467-8640.00196

Pelekis, N., Theodoulidis, B., Kopanakis, I., & Theodoridis, Y. (2004). Literature review of spatio-temporal database models. *The Knowledge Engineering Review*, *19*(3), 235–274. doi:10.1017/S026988890400013X

Pfoser, D., Tryfona, N., & Jensen, C. S. (2005). Indeterminacy and spatiotemporal data: Basic definitions and case study. *GeoInformatica*, *9*(3), 211–236. doi:10.100710707-005-1282-4

Plewe, B. (2002). The nature of uncertainty in historical geographic information. *Transactions in GIS*, *6*(4), 431–456. doi:10.1111/1467-9671.00121

Roy, A. J., & Stell, J. G. (2001). Spatial relations between indeterminate regions. *International Journal of Approximate Reasoning*, *27*(3), 205–234. doi:10.1016/S0888-613X(01)00033-0

Santos, M., Bateira, C., Soares, L., & Hermenegildo, C. (2014). Hydro-geomorphologic GIS database in Northern Portugal, between 1865 and 2010: Temporal and spatial analysis. *International Journal of Disaster Risk Reduction*, *10*, 143–152. doi:10.1016/j.ijdrr.2014.08.003

Sözer, A., Yazici, A., & Oğuztüzün, H. (2015). Indexing fuzzy spatiotemporal data for efficient querying: A meteorological application. *IEEE Transactions on Fuzzy Systems*, *23*(5), 1399–1413. doi:10.1109/TFUZZ.2014.2362121

Sözer, A., Yazici, A., Oğuztüzün, H., & Taş, O. (2008). Modeling and querying fuzzy spatiotemporal databases. *Information Sciences*, *178*(19), 3665–3682. doi:10.1016/j.ins.2008.05.034

Tang, X., Kainz, W., & Wang, H. (2010). Topological relations between fuzzy regions in a fuzzy topological space. *International Journal of Applied Earth Observation and Geoinformation*, *12*(S2), 151–165. doi:10.1016/j.jag.2010.01.004

Tao, Y. F., Kollios, G., Considine, J., Li, F., & Papadias, D. (2004). Spatio-temporal aggregation using sketches. In *Proc. 20th International Conference on Data Engineering*. ACM.

Trajcevski, G., Wolfson, O., Hinrichs, K., & Chamberlain, S. (2004). Managing uncertainty in moving objects databases. *ACM Transactions on Database Systems*, *29*(3), 463–507. doi:10.1145/1016028.1016030

Xie, R., & Shibasaki, R. (2005). A unified spatiotemporal schema for representing and querying moving features. *SIGMOD Record*, *34*(1), 45–50. doi:10.1145/1058150.1058159

Xu, Z., Luo, X. F., & Liu, Y. H. (2016). From Latency, through Outbreak, to Decline: Detecting Different States of Emergency Events Using Web Resources. *IEEE Transactions on Big Data*.

Chapter 16
Predicting Uncertain Spatiotemporal XML Data Integrated With Grey Dynamic Model

ABSTRACT

In this chapter, the authors propose an approach to predict uncertain spatiotemporal data. This approach is unique in the predicting element nodes which are integrated into the position element node in uncertain spatiotemporal XML data tree. At the same time, the other element nodes do not need to make any changes. In addition, the authors apply this method to meteorological applications and established a series of experimental models for testing. PGX (predictive model with grey model based on XML), which is applied to uncertain spatiotemporal objects, is able to achieve the minimum mean accuracy of 0.5% in a short time. The experimental results show that PGX can effectively improve the efficiency of information storage and retrieval. The experimental prediction accuracy is guaranteed (the relative error is between 0.5% and 5%) and the query time based on XML is 89.2% shorter than that of SQL Server.

1 INTRODUCTION

Spatiotemporal data are featured by spatial and temporal phenomena (Santos et al., 2015). Previous efforts started with separate research in temporal and spatial database areas. Along with the development of Mobile Devices and the advance of geographic information systems, a great deal of geoscientific data has been generated. These data lie in continuous space and change with time and space, so they have a high degree of particularity and complexity (Jeon et al., 2010). Hence, spatiotemporal data management is becoming more and more important, especially spatiotemporal data prediction.

The spatial and temporal uncertainty exists widely in the complex and variational real world. For instance, the incompleteness of knowledge, the fuzziness of concepts and the derivation of data make the entity possess the feature of uncertainty. Therefore, uncertainty is absolute while certainty is relative.

DOI: 10.4018/978-1-6684-9108-9.ch016

Recently, studies on predicting uncertain spatiotemporal objects have made great progress (Tao et al., 2004). Jeung et al. (Jeung et al., 2008) presented an approach which forecasted an object's future locations in a hybrid manner by using motion function and movement patterns. Cheng et al. (Cheng & Wang, 2008) used a dynamic recurrent neural network for spatial prediction, which is applied to forest fire. The trajectory of moving target, which is limited by traffic network, can be predicted accurately. (Jeung et al., 2010). The work of Boulila et al. (Boulila et al., 2011) takes imperfection into account, relating to the spatiotemporal mining process in satellite imaging. The particularity and complexity of the spatiotemporal data are enhanced. Because spatiotemporal data have been applied increasingly and widely in the field of transportation, meteorology, earthquake rescue, criminal analysis, web applications, public health and medical services (Xu et al., 2016). Therefore, it is urgent to improve the predicted technology of uncertain spatiotemporal data.

Coz et al. (Le Coz et al., 2014) developed a method with a statistical representation of uncertainties. In (McMillan et al., 2010), McMillan et al. provided a comprehensive review of the uncertain values for gauging and rating curves. However, in the field of XML, there are few researches on the prediction of uncertain spatiotemporal data. Additionally, compared with the certain spatiotemporal data, uncertainty enhances spatiotemporal data particularity and complexity, making it more challenging to predict uncertain spatiotemporal data accurately. Therefore, a new modeling technology of predicting uncertain spatiotemporal data is required. Researches on grey dynamic model have been investigated widely in recent years. Original data in grey dynamic model are composed of both certain and uncertain information. By obtaining part of the data, the correlation of all factors is measured, the data are preprocessed, and finally the differences and similarities of the development trend of all factors are obtained. The predicted sequence can be obtained by processing the current information. Meanwhile, the predicted results are accepted when the accuracy of the predicted meets the reliability requirement. In this case, the grey dynamic model can accurately predict the changing trend of the uncertain state of the spatiotemporal data. Therefore, the grey dynamic model is integrated into the prediction of uncertain spatiotemporal data. There is a series of efforts to improve the perception of the grey theory (Liu et al., 2012; Yang et al., 2014). In (Hamzacebi & Es, 2014), Hamzacebi and Es show the superiority of Optimized Grey Modeling (1, 1) when compared with the results in literature. The grey relational analysis of the fuzzy sets also takes an important occupation in the fuzzy measure field (Sun et al., 2018). Furthermore, Zhang et al. (Zhang et al., 2013) propose a grey relational projection method for the MADM problems with intuitionistic trapezoidal fuzzy number attribute. However, the grey theory is studied on combination with other techniques rather than itself (Kuang et al., 2015; Yang et al., 2014). In addition, it has been applied to other applications such as the electricity consumption. Actually, the theoretical basis of grey dynamic model is more beneficial to predict uncertain spatiotemporal data (Bai et al., 2017).

Extensible Markup Language (XML) has been applied to handle spatiotemporal data in the past few years. There is a growing interest in the research of uncertain XML data (Ma & Yan, 2016). In the field of uncertain spatiotemporal database, there are also several researchers modeling fuzzy spatiotemporal data based on XML and exploring algorithms for fixing inconsistencies of it in XML documents caused by changing operations (Ma et al., 2017). Then Li et al. (Li & Ma, 2017) introduce the object-stack algorithm that outperformed the traditional XML keyword query algorithms significantly, which could get high quality of query results with high search efficiency on the fuzzy XML document.

In the field of spatiotemporal prediction, researches have been put forward which take advantages of grey dynamic model and XML. For example, Bai et al. (Bai et al., 2017) investigated spatiotemporal XML data with the grey dynamic model and presented an algorithm for interpolation and prediction of spatiotemporal data based on XML. Unfortunately, the work only considers certain spatiotemporal data, and the prediction of uncertain spatiotemporal data has not been further studied in their work. They also ignored the memory performance and other relevant problems on relational database and XML.

In this chapter, a model is proposed that enables the accurate prediction of the uncertain spatiotemporal data. Besides, this model can be used to predict uncertain spatiotemporal data. For instance, the typhoon experiment can be strong proof to our theory. Our approach makes the following main contributions: Firstly, we integrate the grey dynamic model into XML to predict uncertain spatiotemporal data on the basis of previous achievement. In succession, the proposed predicted model (PGX) can be applied to reducing the uncertainty generated by the volatility of original data. Subsequently, our model can predict the motion of the uncertain spatiotemporal objects in the given time precisely. For example, in the meteorological experiments, this model can predict the future location region at a relatively accurate degree according to the center information of the hurricane. Finally, we make comparisons between relational database and XML to evaluate the effectiveness of storing uncertain spatiotemporal data. The experimental results demonstrate the performance advantages of our approach.

The rest of this chapter is organized as follows. Section 2 presents related work. Section 3 proposes an approach for predicting uncertain spatiotemporal data and the model definition. Section 4 gives a discussion. In Section 5, our approach is applied to meteorological applications and the experimental results are presented. Section 6 concludes the chapter.

2 RELATED WORK

2.1 Uncertain Spatiotemporal XML Data Model

In the field of spatiotemporal prediction, there was an early nonparametric regression method which used multivariate nonparametric regression to process spatiotemporal data by predicting traffic flow (Clark, 2003). Through development, a non-parametric regression model was developed to discuss spatiotemporal prediction under the absence of data (Haworth & Cheng, 2012). At the same time, the Markov model, which exhibits many years' superiority in predicted performance, also appears in the field of spatiotemporal prediction. Predicting future locations with Hidden Markov Model (Mathew et al., 2012), using variable Hidden Markov Model (Yang et al., 2014), and modifying Hidden Markov Model to produce adaptive parameter selection trajectory predicted methods (Qiao et al., 2015) are produced gradually.

In recent years, with the hot of artificial intelligence, in the field of spatiotemporal data prediction, the researches of neural network and in deep learning also occupy a territory. Some researchers have proposed convolution LSTM to construct the training model of end-to-end precipitation in spatiotemporal data prediction from the machine learning viewpoint (Shi et al., 2015). In the latest research, a kind of deep convolution neural network model is used to deal with traffic network speed prediction (Ma et al., 2017). Similarly, in deep learning, some scholars have raised the predicted problem of spatiotemporal data series (Chen & Wang, 2017). Some scholars considered the correlation between space and time and used stack automatic encoder model to learn general traffic flow features in the field of deep learning. They trained the model in a greedy hierarchical manner and proposed a deep architecture model to represent the characteristics of the traffic flow used for prediction (Lv et al., 2015).

In recent years, the study of spatiotemporal data has shown a trend of combining with other methods and other fields. Trajectory prediction is one of the hot topics in the research of spatiotemporal data prediction. In the last ten years, more and more scholars have studied the trajectory prediction of moving objects. The problems of frequent and uncertain trajectory prediction of moving objects (Morzy, 2007) and the spatiotemporal trajectory model (Lei et al., 2011) have been explored. Besides, the spatiotemporal behavior model-based method (Zolotukhin et al., 2013) for the prediction of moving position has been studied with the help of hidden Markov model (Qiao et al., 2015), which shows that predicted methods have been applied to the research of spatiotemporal data continuously.

2.2 Other Recommendations

Significant effectiveness of grey model in time series forecasting in small samples has been widely concerned (Ma & Liu, 2018). One of the most important aspects of grey system theory is the grey predicted model which is represented by the GM (1, 1) model with one order and one variable (Zeng et al., 2016). As a lot of methods have been put forward to improve the precision of grey model, some researchers begin to study the parameters in generation of grey model, shown in Table 1. The pre-processing of raw sequence $X^{(0)}$.

- The improvement of grey accumulating generation sequence $X^{(1)}$.
- Optimization of grey model background value $z^{(1)}(k)$.
- Optimization of grey model initial value $X^{(0)}$ (1).
- The residual error correction of grey predicted model $\varepsilon = \dot{x}^{(0)}(k) - x^{(0)}(k)$.

In Table 1, $X^{(0)}$ is generated by function transformation (Wei & Hu, 2009) and buffer operators (Liu et al., 2014). Wei and Hu (Wei & Hu, 2009) proposed adjustable parameters to compute the relative optimal modeling parameters automatically, and the concept of the new smooth degree of the first-class grey model was studied (Liu et al., 2014). $X^{(1)}$, the accumulating generation methods, was improved by the non-homogenous discrete grey model (NDGM) (Wu et al., 2014). The methods of generating $z^{(1)}(k)$ include convolution integral (Wang & Hao, 2016) and box plot (Chang et al., 2015). $X^{(0)}$ (1) is comprised of the first and the last item of a defined sequence. The residual error correction ε, which is used to judge the reasonability of prediction, is one of the most essential parts of grey model. Many scholars have examined the performance of ε (Wang et al., 2010; Yao & Liu, 2009). Besides, there are also other methods to regenerate the parameters (Ma & Liu, 2018; Wu et al., 2012; Wu et al., 2013; Xie & Liu, 2009).

As can be seen in Table 1, many researchers studied some parameters in the generation of grey models which are essential to build an accurate predicting model.

In addition, some related work on grey model have combined it with other methods, such as Markov (Ye et al., 2018; Kumar & Jain, 2010), fuzzy mathematics (Wong & Shiu, 2012; Froelich & Salmeron, 2014) and neural network (Wang, 2009; Zeng et al., 2016; Hu & Jiang, 2017). Markov chain is suitable for long-term data sequences with large random fluctuations (Ye et al., 2018), fuzzy mathematics can deal with multivariable situation, and neural network has been applied when the raw series has the big fluctuation (Zeng et al., 2016). Those are presented in the following shown in Table 2.

Table 1. Study on grey model parameters

Grey Model	Methods	Ref.	Highlights
$X^{(0)}$	Function transformation	(Wei & Hu, 2009)	The consistency of the new comparison criterion of the smooth degree with the prevision criterion is proved.
	Buffer operators	(Liu et al., 2014)	Under the axiomatic system of buffer operator, strengthening buffer operators whose buffer intensity can be adjusted are constructed.
$X^{(1)}$	Accumulating generation	(Wu et al., 2014)	A new NDGM with the fractional-order accumulation is put forward.
$z^{(1)}(k)$	-	(Wang et al., 2014)	The sequences of exponential distribution are predicted through optimization of background value in grey differential equation.
	Convolution integral	(Wang & Hao, 2016)	GMC (1, *n*) has a control parameter ***u***. ***n*** unknown interpolation coefficients are input into the background values of *n* variables so as to improve the adaptability of GMC (1, *n*).
	Box plot	(Chang et al., 2015)	Determine the background values by the box-plot membership function
$X^{(0)}$ (1)	-	(Wang et al., 2010)	The new initial condition is comprised of first and last items of a sequence generated from applying the first-order accumulative generation operator on sequence of raw data.
$\mathring{a}=\dot{x}^{(0)}(k)-x^{(0)}(k)$	-	(Yao & Liu, 2009)	Use the error sequence to remedy the original model to improve the accuracy.
	Neural network	(Hu & Jiang, 2017)	Replace the traditional GM (1, 1) model with the NN-GM (1, 1) model for a grey residual modification model.
Regenerating parameter	Discrete equations	(Xie & Liu, 2009)	Generate the new parameter through Grey-Model-based discrete operation (DGM).
	Grey Lotka–Volterra model	(Wu et al., 2012)	A linear programming method is used to estimate the parameters of the grey Lotka–Volterra model under the criterion of the minimization of MAPE.
	Fractional order accumulation	(Wu et al., 2013)	The function of new pieces of information is greater than that of old pieces of information.
	Kernel-based	(Ma& Liu, 2018)	The KGM (1, *n*) model is introduced to do with nonlinear multivariate model.

Table 2. Grey model with other methods

Methods	Ref	Highlights
Grey-Markov predicted model	(Ye et al., 2018)	Grey-Markov forecasting model is a combination of grey predicted model and Markov chain which show obvious optimization effects for data sequences with characteristics of non-stationary and volatility.
	(Kumar & Jain, 2010)	Grey-Markov model is used to time series models to forecast the consumption of conventional energy in India.
Fuzzy mathematics	(Wong & Shiu, 2012)	The predicted performance of FTS- heuristic model, two-factor model, Markov model and GM-GM (1, 1), GM-Markov, GM-Fourier is investigated. The comparison of the models is based on forecasting error of time series.
	(Froelich & Salmeron, 2014)	Predicted of multivariate interval-valued time series. Evolutionary algorithm for learning Fuzzy Grey Cognitive Maps (FGCMs).
Neural network	(Wang, 2009)	Combining the grey forecasting model with the GARCH to improve the estimated ability, the empirical evidence shows that the new hybrid GARCH model outperforms the other approaches in the neural network option-pricing model.
	(Zeng et al., 2016)	Introducing the BP neural network to amend TFGM (1, 1) and propose NNTFGM (1, 1), the amendment to TFGM (1, 1) through the BP neural network or SVM is effective after the experiments.
	(Wang et al., 2010)	The NN-GM(1, 1) model is able to directly determine the developing coefficient and control variable using a SLP without requiring the background value.

3 UNCERTAIN SPATIOTEMPORAL XML DATA PREDICTION

3.1 Uncertain Spatiotemporal Data

Uncertain spatiotemporal objects can be studied from space and time. Moreover, the uncertainty of them is independent. As a result, temporal types of uncertain spatiotemporal data can be divided into uncertain time point and uncertain time interval while spatial types of uncertain spatiotemporal data can be divided into uncertain point, uncertain line and uncertain region, shown in Table 3.

Definition 1. Temporal types of uncertain spatiotemporal data can be divided into uncertain time point $X_{tinstant}$ and uncertain time interval $X_{tinterval}$, where

- $X_{tinstant} = \{t, p_{tt} \mid \forall\, t \in R, p_{tt} \in (0, 1)\}$.
- $X_{tinterval} = \{t_s, t_e, p_{tl} \mid \exists\, t_s, t_e \in X_{tinstant}, p_{tl} \in (0, 1)\}$.

In Definition 1, p_{tt} represents the probability of $X_{tinstant}$'s existence, t_s and t_e represent the starting time and ending time of the event; $X_{tinterval}$ represents the interval between two time points and p_{tl} represents the existent probability of $X_{tinterval}$'s. In this chapter, the time point $X_{tinstant}$ is not regarded as the moment of reality, but the smallest fraction of discretized time.

Definition 2. Spatial types of uncertain spatiotemporal data can be divided into uncertain point X_{spoint}, uncertain line X_{sline}, and uncertain region $X_{sregion}$, where

- X_{spoint}={patt, x_l, y_l, x_r, y_r, x, y}.
- X_{sline}={p_l, ubound, lbound | $\exists$ $p_l \in X_{spoint}$}.
- $X_{sregion}$={p_r, x_l, y_l, x_r, y_r | $\exists$ $p_r \in X_{spoint}$ }.

In Definition 2, the value of *patt* is [0, 1], indicating the possibility of the point. When *patt* $\in$ [0, 1], the point is within *MBR* (minimum bounding rectangle) bounded by x_l, y_l, x_r, y_r, as shown in Figure 1(a); p_l is a set of uncertain points within a strip area, and *ubound* and *lbound* are the two boundary lines which descript where the uncertain line lies, as shown in Figure 1(b); p_r represents the set of uncertain points within a region, and (x_l, y_l) and (x_r, y_r) are the coordinates of the bottom left corner and the top right corner of the *MBR* as shown in Figure 1(c).

Definition 3. Uncertain spatiotemporal type set T_u is defined as

$$T_u = X_{tu} \times Y_{su} \tag{1}$$

where X_{tu} and X_{su} depict the uncertain temporal type and uncertain spatial type respectively.

According to Definition 3, uncertain spatiotemporal objects can be divided into six types as shown in Table 4 and Figure 2, including uncertain point in uncertain time point, uncertain line in uncertain time point, uncertain region in uncertain time point, uncertain point in uncertain time interval, uncertain line in uncertain time interval, and uncertain region in uncertain time interval.

Figure 1. Uncertain spatial types of point, line and region

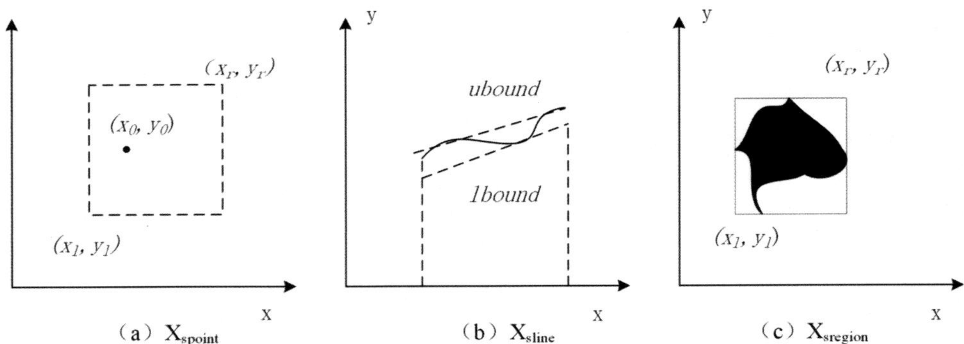

Table 3. Types of time and types of space

Types of time	Types of space
uncertain time point Xtinstant	uncertain point Xspoint
uncertain time interval Xtinterval	uncertain line Xsline
	uncertain region Xsregion

Table 4. Types of uncertain spatiotemporal objects

	Point	Line	Region
Time point	U_{IP}	U_{IL}	U_{IR}
Time interval	U_{LP}	U_{LL}	U_{LR}

Figure 2. Types of uncertain spatiotemporal object

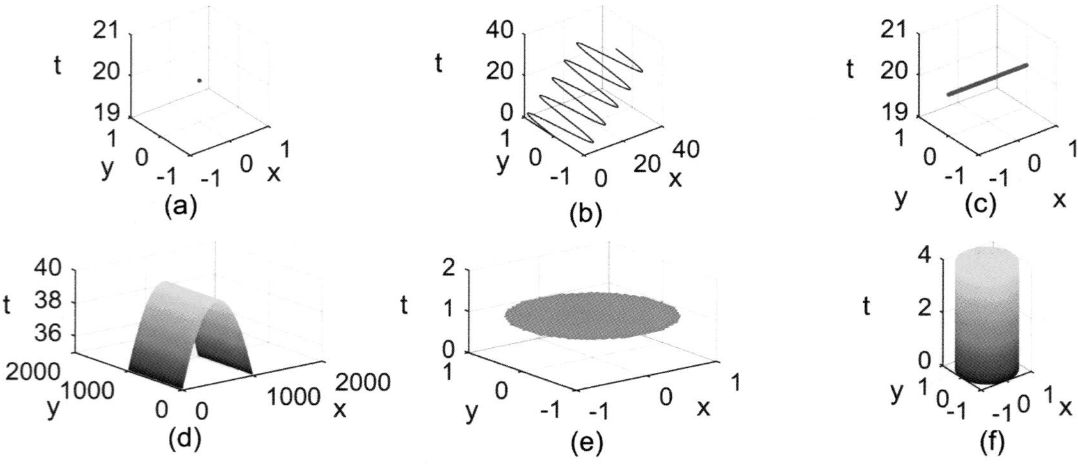

Definition 4. Types of uncertain spatiotemporal objects are U_{IP}, U_{LP}, U_{IL}, U_{LL}, U_{IR}, and U_{LR}, where

- $U_{IP} = (X_{tinstant}, X_{spoint})$ where $X_{tinstant} = t$ ($t \in R$) and $X_{spoint} = (patt, x_l, y_l, x_r, y_r, x, y)$.
- $U_{LP} = (X_{tinterval}, X_{spoint})$ where $X_{tinterval} = (t_s, t_e)$, $\exists\, t_s, t_e \in X_{tinstant}$ and $X_{spoint} = (patt, x_l, y_l, x_r, y_r, x, y)$.
- $U_{IL} = (X_{tinstant}, X_{sline})$ where $X_{tinstant} = t$ ($t \in R$) and $X_{sline} = (p_l, ubound, lbound)$, $\exists\, p_l \in X_{spoint}$.
- $U_{LL} = (X_{tinterval}, X_{sline})$ where $X_{tinterval} = (t_s, t_e)$, $\exists\, t_s, t_e \in X_{tinstant}$ and $X_{sline} = (p_l, ubound, lbound)$, $\exists\, p_l \in X_{spoint}$.
- $U_{IR} = (X_{tinstant}, X_{sregion})$ where $X_{tinstant} = t$ ($t \in R$) and $X_{sregion} = (p_r, x_l, y_l, x_r, y_r)$, $\exists\, p_r \in X_{spoint}$.
- $U_{LR} = (X_{tinterval}, X_{sregion})$ where $X_{tinterval} = (t_s, t_e)$, $\exists\, t_s, t_e \in X_{tinstant}$ and $X_{sregion} = (p_r, x_l, y_l, x_r, y_r)$, $\exists\, p_r \in X_{spoint}$.

According to the nature of spatiotemporal data, we give the definition of uncertain spatiotemporal data in the following.

Definition 5. The uncertain spatiotemporal (*USP*) data is a 4-tuple, *USP* = (*P*, *T*, *OID*, *ATTR*), where

- *P* is the probability that an uncertain spatiotemporal object exists in the current situation.
- *T* is the time that an uncertain spatiotemporal object exists in the current situation.
- *OID* is the changing history of an uncertain spatiotemporal object.
- *ATTR* is the attributes of an uncertain spatiotemporal object.

Definition 6. The changing history of a spatiotemporal object is a 4-tuple, *OID* = (*type*, *pre*, *suc*, *T*), where

- *type* is the type of the object's spatiotemporal change.
- *pre* is precursor.
- *suc* is successor.
- *T* is the changing time.

In Definition 6, *type* can represent *create*, *split*, *mergence*, *keep*, *expand*, *shrink*, *transform*, and *disappear*; *pre* and *suc* depict the changing state of a spatiotemporal object; *T* is the changing time, which can be time point or time interval.

Definition 7. Attribute of an uncertain spatiotemporal object is a 3-tuple, *ATTR* = (*general*, *spatial*, *forecast*), where

- *general* denotes the general attribute.
- *spatial* denotes the spatial attribute.
- *forecast* denotes the forecast attribute.

As for Definition 7, firstly, *general* attribute contains (*num*, *val*), where *num* is the number of the *USP* and *val* is the value of the *USP*. Secondly, *Spatial* attribute contains *position* and *motion* which are position and movement trend of *USP* respectively. In particular, the *position* attribute represents the location of the spatiotemporal object in the form of *MBR*; *motion* represents the movement trend, having three attributes (*T*, *tend*, *range*). *T* is the time, *tend* is the direction, and *range* is the speed of the moving trend associated with a node *pro* to represent the probability of the trend, denoted by X_a and Y_a whose value can be *l*, *r* and *k*. *l* means that the spatiotemporal objects move left or down and *r* means that the spatiotemporal objects move right or up. *k* means that the spatiotemporal objects keep its position and will not move. X_g and Y_g represent the length on *x-axis* and length on *y-axis*. Lastly, *Forecast* attribute uses data from *general* attribute and *spatial* attribute to predict and store the predicted results by grey dynamic model.

From Definition 1 to Definition 7, the spatiotemporal data model can be represented as shown in Figure 3.

Figure 3. Spatiotemporal object model

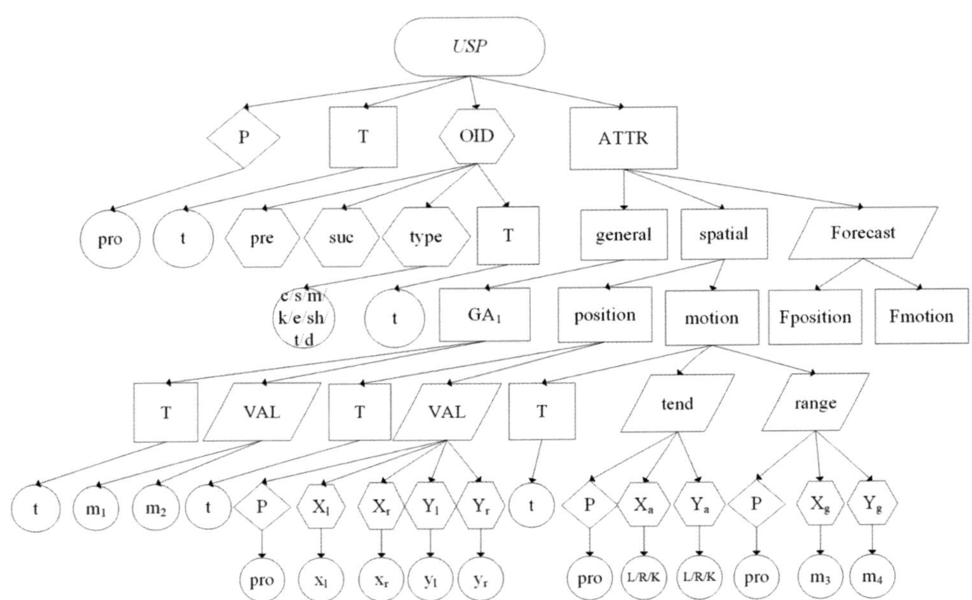

As we can see from Figure 3, USP has three attributes as described from Definition 1 to Definition 7, where *Fposition* and *Fmotion* represent the forecast position and motion respectively.

3.2 Uncertain Spatiotemporal XML Data for Prediction

3.2.1 The Structure of USP Based on XML and Grey Model

In XML data tree, every attribute is regarded as a node whose types are uncertain. With the unique feature of XML (extension and customize identification), we can develop custom models according to the characteristics of spatiotemporal data. In addition, the *forecast*, which has a special node called *patt*, has the ability to store the predicted results of other attributes. And *patt* describes the result of the prediction and has an uncertain type. This node represents the predicted results, and its value could be disjunctive (only one result from many possible ones) or conjunctive (two or more, or even the whole set of the possible results).

Based on the seven definitions above, the subsection will develop an uncertain spatiotemporal XML data model for prediction. The structure of constructing uncertain spatiotemporal XML data model integrated by grey dynamic model is shown in Figure 4.

For a spatiotemporal object, the dynamic grey model and XML are used to study the existing form and predict its future changes. Firstly, we store uncertain spatiotemporal data in XML. Then we use grey dynamic model to process data in order to make predictions. Finally, we store the predicted results in XML database. Uncertain spatiotemporal XML data is quite flexible and can be updated based on the storage of the uncertain spatiotemporal objects. As a result, the storage of uncertain spatiotemporal objects here is an irregular multi-tree. This may inevitably cause troubles when querying data, so we encode it as a binary tree before processing it by using grey model.

3.2.2 Prepare USP Before Prediction

Example. In the typhoon clouds' covering area, we can use *MBR* to describe the cloud area. Our model defines two pairs of coordinate values to describe the cloud area at a certain time point, which are at the lower left corner (x_l, y_l) and at the upper right corner (x_r, y_r). In the predicting model, XML is an irregular multiway tree. Querying multiway tree is rather complicated, so we transform the original data model into a binary tree before querying. The data model is transformed into binary tree for practical use so that two pairs of the coordinates are divided into four groups. Considering the actual operation, the data model is converted into a binary tree when uncertain spatiotemporal data is processed, and two groups of coordinates of the delineated position are divided into four groups based on the time (x_l, t), (y_l, t), (x_r, t), (y_r, t), respectively. After combining digital form for prediction with the grey dynamic model, the results show the accuracy is able to meet the requirements of the next prediction. A set of data is obtained during data extracting process each time. The time is defined as t_m, where m represents any value from 1 to n. Each query corresponds to a time t_m, this time node is the value of the left sub-tree of VAL's father node. The transforming processes are: take the part of the XML storage structure which stores the coordinates of the *MBR*; keep the leftmost line; delete the rest of the right lines (for example, delete the dotted lines in the figure as shown in Figure 5(a).); connect the sibling node from left to right; and finally converted into a binary tree. As a result, when querying for the coordinates of the position nodes (x_l, y_l, x_r, y_r), the information is within the binary tree at the root of *VAL*, the subtree of whose left child's right child has the value, as shown in Figure 5(b). We create stack *VAL1*, *VAL2*, *VAL3* and *VAL4* to store the value (x_l, y_l, x_r, y_r) and their corresponding time information of each query. After the results of grey prediction are calculated, the predicted value of possibility is returned to the XML database to be stored. Each time the information is updated, the grey dynamic model will predict the next time point information and update the XML database in the real time.

The problem of predicting the position of uncertain spatiotemporal objects is the core issue to be solved in this chapter. Based on the above definitions and descriptions, the structure of uncertain spatiotemporal XML data model integrated with grey dynamic model is shown in Figure 6.

In Figure 6, *Conjunctive* indicates that the predicted type of the spatiotemporal objects is coincident. Besides, a set of *original data* is involved to get the *forecast data*.

Figure 4. The structure of constructing uncertain spatiotemporal XML data model integrated by grey dynamic model

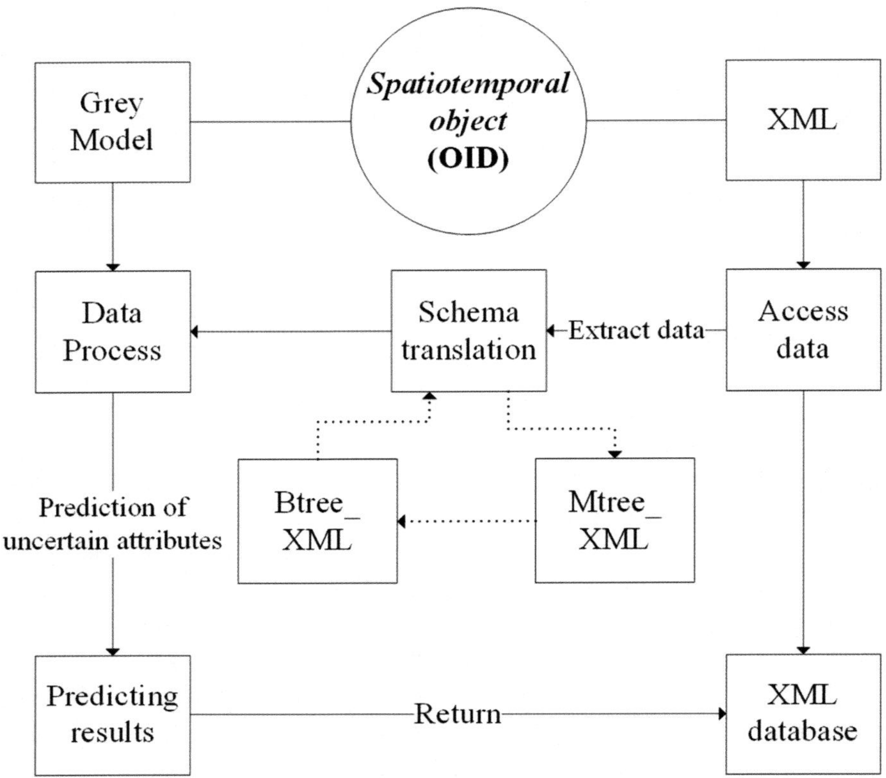

Lemma 1. The bottom left corner (X_l, Y_l, f_x, t_l) and the top right corner (X_r, Y_r, f_x, t_l) can be operated as (X_l, f_x, t_l), (X_r, f_x, t_l) and (Y_l, f_x, t_l), (Y_r, f_x, t_l).

Proof. Because the grey model is to deal with a single sequence, we need to deal with (x, y) separately in this model. Since X_l, X_r, Y_l, Y_r are relatively independent, we process them with grey dynamic model on the time sequence when predicting the positions of uncertain spatiotemporal objects by the proposed model. Now the tuples are (X_l, f_x, t_l), (X_r, f_x, t_l), (Y_l, f_x, t_l), (Y_r, f_x, t_l) where f_x represents the function of processing uncertain spatiotemporal data using grey dynamic model.

Suppose $X_l = 0$, $Y_l \neq 0$, then (X_l, Y_l, f_x, t_l) is equal to (Y_l, f_x, t_l); suppose $X_r \neq 0$, $Y_r = 0$, then (X_r, Y_r, f_x, t_l) is equal to (X_r, f_x, t_l); suppose $X_r \neq 0$, $Y_l \neq 0$, vector $\vec{X}$ and vector $\vec{Y}$ are represented as the current node, which is actually one of the coordinates, with grey model in Fig.7, and vector $\vec{Z}$ is represented as the node of the next time point. Since

$$\vec{Z} = \vec{X} + \vec{Y} \tag{2}$$

thus

$$(\vec{Z}, f_x, t_l) = (\vec{X}_l, f_l, t_l) + (\vec{Y}, f_x, t_l) \tag{3}$$

Figure 5. (a) Transform multi-tree into binary tree (b) Data structure of binary tree

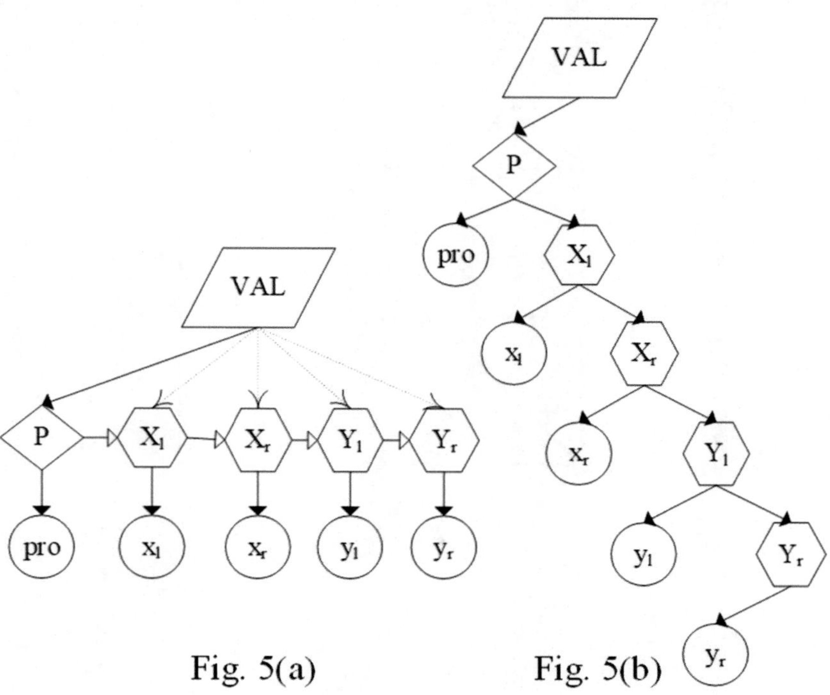

Figure 6. Structure of forecast node with grey dynamic model

```
<?xml version="1.0" encoding="ISO-8859-1"?>
<Forecast>
<patt>Conjunctive</patt>
<model>Grey Model</model>
<original data>23.1, 23.5, 23.8, 24, 24.5</original data>
<forecast data>24.5</forecast data>
</Forecast>
```

In the grey dynamic model, we use the latest data to predict the trajectory of uncertain spatiotemporal objects in real-time, so we can get accurate results.

Definition 8. Merge *n* time points into a group, the time sequence from t_{i-n+1} to t_i is following:

(Xli-n+1, ti-n+1) (Xli-n+2, ti-n+2) … (Xli, ti)

(Yli-n+1, ti-n+1) (Yli-n+2, ti-n+2) … (Yli, ti)

Figure 7. The corner of MBR

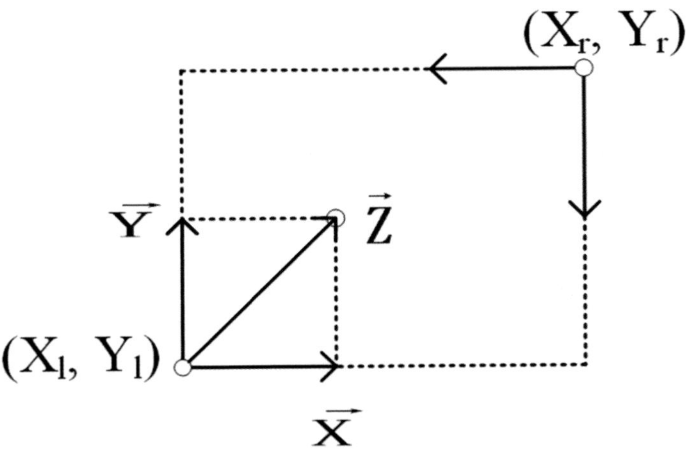

(Xri-n+1, ti-n+1) (Xri-n+2, ti-n+2) … (Xri, ti)

(Yri-n+1, ti-n+1) (Yri-n+2, ti-n+2) … (Yri, ti)

In Definition 8, each row represents a set of predicted sequences, the subscripts represent ordinal numbers, *l* represents the coordinates of lower left corner, and *r* represents the coordinates of upper right corner. There are *n* pairs of points, (X_l, Y_l) and (X_r, Y_r), representing position coordinates, and each line of the data is predicted by the grey dynamic model. Suppose the current time is t_i, then the next time is t_{i+1}. Therefore the grey dynamic model chooses *n* data from t_{i-n+1} to t_i to predict the uncertain spatiotemporal data. The predicted results correspond to (X_l, X_r, Y_l, Y_r) as position coordinates.

Only when the structure of the prediction and the actual value match with the requirement of accuracy, will we consider if the prediction is formula valid. At the end of this round of prediction, the oldest data is discarded, namely the data at t_{i-n+1}. Then update *n* sets of data from t_{i-n+2} to t_{i+1} to predict again, and update the original sequence and the predicted results in the real time. If one group of time changes too shortly, the updated uncertain spatiotemporal data cannot generate the grey equation. In that case, we can use the first prediction to obtain the predicted formula. After collecting *m* sets of data, we can update the formula with the time length of *m*. In this situation, the data keep changing.

When predicting the properties of an uncertain spatiotemporal object, we make predictions based on the types of the uncertain spatiotemporal objects. When the properties of uncertain spatiotemporal objects can be described in terms of data such as predicting the annual rainfall in a region, we can develop formula to predict. In particular, according to h_i, which represents the annual rainfall of one of the past few years, the sequence equations of (h_i, f_x, t_i) can be developed to predict the rainfall h_{i+1} of the next year. In this equation, f_x represents the function of *GM(1, 1)*.In this chapter, we only focus on *GM(1, 1)* used in predicting the spatial information of the uncertain spatiotemporal objects.

Because the predictions of uncertain spatiotemporal data may enhance the uncertainty, the similarity of the single result with the actual value cannot meet the requirement of prediction. Therefore, we expand the predicting range, taking the original uncertain spatiotemporal data into consideration.

Definition 9. A model called *REPM*. Define *R* as the predicted result of each group, $\Delta\varepsilon$ represents the mean residual error of m groups which is from (hi, $fx_{i,}$ ti) to (h$i_{+m-1,}$ $fx_{i+m-1,}$ $ti_{+m-1)}$, and then the residual error in the range of (hi ~ h$i_{+m-1)}$ called uncertain range by prediction of grey models is:

$$R_p(t) = R_o(t) \pm \Delta\varepsilon \tag{4}$$

where $R_p(t)$ is the function which predicts the range of uncertain spatiotemporal data, and $R_o(t)$ is the function in grey dynamic model calculates a sequence o f *n* numbers within one group, as shown in Figure 8.

Definition 10. A model called *URGM*, which varies over time *T*:

- URGM = MBR{(min-x, max-x)∪(min-y, max-y)}, when T = t_i.
- URGM = $\cup_i^{i+n}$MBR$_i${(min-x, max-x)∪(min-y, max-y)}, when T = t_i, t_{i+1}, …, t_{i+n}.

In Definition 10, when *T* is a time point, the grey predicted region is a *MBR* (denoted as *M*) whose coordinates are represented as (*min-x*, *min-y*) and (*max-x*, *max-y*). When *T* is a time series which is an assemble of *n* time points t_0, t_1, t_2, …, t_n, M_0, M_1, M_2, …, M_n represent the central positions of the real typhoon.

First of all, we consider (*min-x*, *max-x*) when *y* is constant as shown in Figure 9 (a). As described in Definition 9, five groups of *x* is predicted by the sequence when *t* is between t_{i-n+1} and t_i, and then the predicted coordinate of *x* is x_i when *t* is t_{i+1}. Similarly when *x* is constant, the (*min-y*, *max-y*) is shown in Figure 9 (b). Lastly, the region of prediction is a series of *MBRs* when *x* and *y* is variable at the same time, as shown in Figure 9(c).

As we can see in Figure 9, the sequence of t_0, t_1, t_2, t_3, t_4, …, t_n is represented as the time series. The black spots are predicted based on the previous five groups of data as shown in Figure 9(a) and Figure 9(b). In Figure 9(c), the yellow spots represent the coordinates of the *MBR* for each time moment, and the red spots M_0, M_1, M_2, M_3, M_4, …, M_n represent the true positions of spatiotemporal objects.

3.2.3 Predicted Steps

On the basis of the above definitions and investigations, we have the steps of predicting uncertain spatiotemporal XML data using the grey dynamic model in the following:

Step 1: Extract data information. First of all, query the predicted information and use it to make prediction.

Step 2: Process the information. Transform the structure of the data model from multiway tree into binary tree.

Step 3: Use grey dynamic model (f_x) to process data where f_x represents the function in grey dynamic model. The original sequence $x^{(0)}$ is extracted from each group (X, f_x, t) or (h_i, f_x, t_i). *GM(1, 1)* model of the winterization equation is developed by accumulated sequence $x^{(1)}$ in the grey dynamic model. List the undetermined coefficients. The matrix *B* and the data vector Y_n are transformed by the accumulated sequence $x^{(1)}$. After calculating the coefficients, the time responding equation can be obtained.

Step 4: Analyze the accuracy and make the next prediction. The residual $E_{(k)}$ and the relative error $e_{(k)}$ are calculated at each time, and the post-test error ratio is calculated based on these two values. After the prediction is assessed, if the evaluation turns out to be ideal, take the coefficient of the solution as the coefficient of the time response formulation equation and predict the next unknown time moment based on the corresponding time response formulation.

Step 5: Return the predicting results. The grey dynamic model returns the calculated probability of the prediction, and stores it in the XML database under the *forecast* node. Each time the data is updated, the grey dynamic model will predict the next time point and updates the XML database in real time.

Figure 8. Predicted range of f(t)

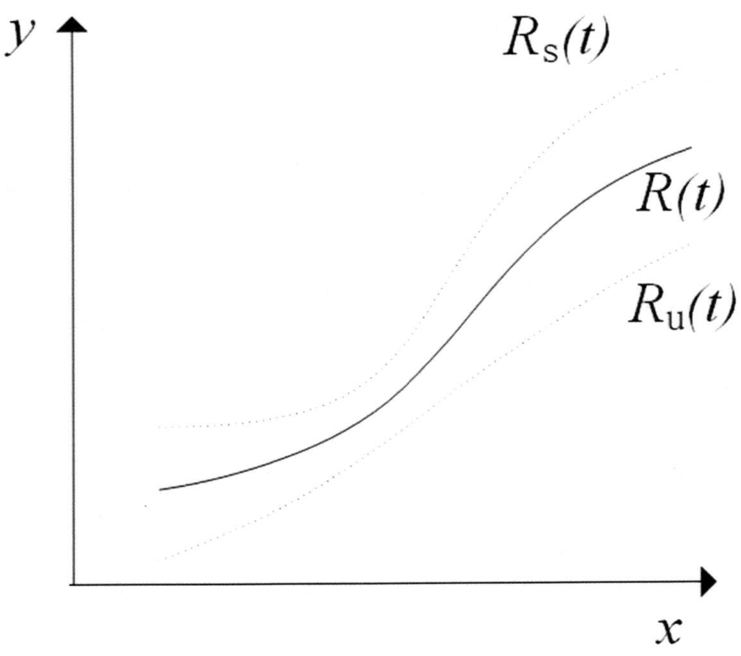

Figure 9. (a) The series of (min-x, max-x) (b) The series of (min-y, max-y) (c) The series of MBRs when x and y is variable at the same time

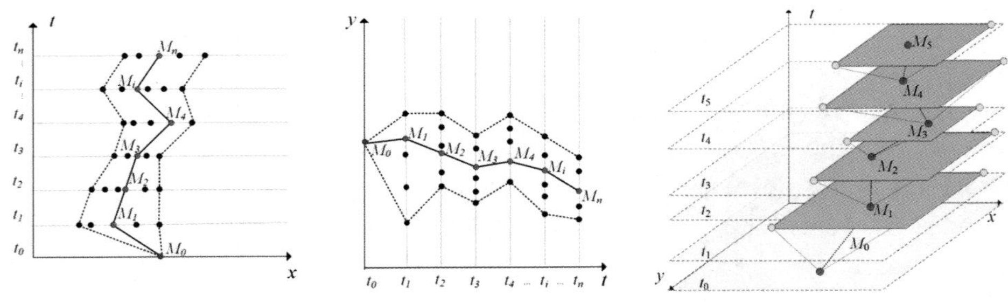

3.2.4 Algorithm of Prediction With Grey Model Based on XML(PGX)

A new algorithm of prediction with grey model based on XML (called PGX) has been represented. It is used to process spatiotemporal data and return predicted results. Grey model algorithm is redefined and applies to spatiotemporal datasets in PGX. Additionally, in order to compare Markov model with PGX, some modification is done as shown in the following.

The algorithmic PGX is used to predict attributes of spatiotemporal objects. It will return the predicted results and updated XML database when the input is USP. PGX processes USP with five steps.

Step 1. Initialize USP, an uncertain spatiotemporal object. And the initial values will be given in this step. This step is shown in line 01.

Step 2. Access data of USP with XML scheme, where P, T, OID, ATTR are the basic attributes of USP according to Definition 5. In this step, PGX can access different attributes of USP or ATTR. And the selected attributes will be stored as XML scheme, a multi tree which is represented as Mtree_XML in line 05. For example, selecting spatial of ATTR can work well when predicting the trajectory of USP. This step is shown from line 02 to 06.

Step 3. Scheme transformation. In order to read data easily, the Mtree_XML needs to be transformed to binary tree, which is represented as Btree_XML in line 08. And this step is shown from line 07 to 10.

Step 4. Data process. In this step, algorithm such as grey model or Markov model will be selected to predict the attributes of USP. This step is shown from line 11 to 15.

Step 5. Update XML database. The experimental results from step 4 will be input to update XML database. This step is shown from line 16 to 18.

The algorithm, grey model, is used to process data in PGX. In line 01, the grey model function is defined; From line 02 to 05, the Btree_XML is divided into different arrays, the consequences of Xr, Xl, Yr, Yl is used to make prediction by grey model; From line 06 to 11, do grey model method for predicting. Each array denotes Array_Xr[], Array_Xl[], Array_Yr[], Array_Yl[], and n is the length of each predicted results. And in line 9, fx is the grey model's predicting function which is used to process data; From line 12 to 13, results are returned to PGX.

The algorithm, Markov, is also used to process data in PGX. In line 01, define the Markov model function; From line 02 to 05, divide the Btree_XML into different arrays, the results of Xr, Xl, Yr, Yl, which is used to make prediction by Markov model; From line 06 to 17, the state_transition matrix of ATTR.attributes is initialized. Here, we choose spatial position to be discussed. And in line 10, total represents the amount of transition from Array[i] to Array[i+1]; From line 18 to 20, make prediction with Markov model method. And in line 19, m[k,j] is needed in Mx which is the predicting function of Markov model.

4 DISCUSSION

Markov Model is a statistical model. In order to compare it with PGX proposed in this chapter, we define the state variable of Markov, and give the definition of Markov hit rate.

Definition 11. Define the state variable and the initial state in the Markov model as increment and (x_0, y_0) respectively, then the increments of x_0 or y_0 are:

$$\begin{aligned} \Delta x &= x_i - x_{i-1} \\ \Delta y &= y_i - y_{i-1} \end{aligned} \tag{5}$$

where each Δx or Δy is set as an increment.

For example, suppose Δx = 0.1, and Δy = -0.2, the state partition and prediction of Markov model is shown in Figure 10. The state vector of Δx is (0, 1, 1, 1, 0, 0, 1, 0, 0, …, n) and the state vector of Δy is (0, 0, 1, 1, 0, 1, …, m), and then the checkered range represents the Δx range, the diagonal range represents the Δy range, and the shaded range (*DPR*) represents the junction of Δx and Δy, shown as (1), (2), (3), (4) in the Figure 10.It is noted that the state vector in Fig.10 is the increments vector. The initial state value should add Δx and Δy, and then we can get the next predictive position.

Algorithm of prediction with grey model based on XML (PGX)

```
Input: Uncertain spatiotemporal object---USP
Output: Predicting results and updated XML database
initialize_USP();
//access data of USP with XML scheme.
define access_data(OriginalData){
input P, T, OID;
access ATTR.property as Access_data;
return Access_data as Mtree_XML;
}
define schema_transformation(Mtree_XML) {
Btree_XML <-- Mtree_XML;
return Btree_XML;
}
//prediction with grey model or markov model.
define data_process (Btree_XML) {
doubel result = Grey_Model();
double result = Markov_Model();
return predicting_results;
}
define Update_Forecast(predicting_results){
return update XML database;
}
```

Grey Model algorithm

```
Input: Btree_XML
Output: Prediction by grey model
define Grey_Model() {
group(Btree_XML){
get Array_X_r[], Array_X_l[], Array_Y_r[], Array_Y_l[];
return X_r[], X_l[], Y_r[], Y_l[];
}
for(i=0; i<Array[].length-n; i++) {
from i to i+n-1{
for (each array in Array_X_r[], Array_X_l[], Array_Y_r[], Array_Y_l[]) {
do(Array,f_x,t_j);
}
}
return results;
}
```

Markov Model algorithm

```
Input: Btree_XML
Output: Prediction by Markov_Model
define Markov_Model() {
group(Btree_XML){
get Array_Xr[], Array_Xl[], Array_Yr[], Array_Yl[];
return Xr[], Xl[], Yr[], Yl[];
}
initialize IMatrix() {
set threshold;
group m[0,j] and m[k,0] states by threshold;
int g=0;
int sum=total;
for (each array in Array_Xr[], Array_Xl[], Array_Yr[], Array_Yl[]) {
when Array[i+1]-Array[i] is in m[0,j] and Array[i]-Array[i-1] is in m[k,0] {
g++;
}
return m[k,j]=(g/sum)*100%;
}
}
for (each array in Array_Xr[], Array_Xl[], Array_Yr[], Array_Yl[]) {
do(Array,Mx,tj);
}
}
```

Markov model divides the predicting range according to the state partition, which affected by the selection of the threshold. As a result, the predicting range results using Markov model cannot indicate the actual useful performance because it contains extra range by the selection of the threshold. Accordingly, we further define unit area hit rate in the following.

Definition 12. Overall Hit Rate of Markov Model (*OHRM*) is represented as:

$$OHRM = \frac{\min s}{mouts + \min s} \times 100\% \tag{6}$$

where *mins* and *mouts* are the times when predictive value is in the *DPR* or not, respectively.

Definition 13. Unit Area Hit Rate of Markov Model (*UHRM*) is represented as:

$$UHRM = \frac{\min s}{S \times (mouts + \min s)} \times 100\% \tag{7}$$

where *S* is the predicting range.

5 EXPERIMENT

5.1 Experimental Setup

All the evaluations have been implemented in MATLAB2016b, Dev C++, SQL Server2016, and performed on a system with 2.4 GHz Intel Core i5 processor with 8 GB RAM running on a Windows 7 system.

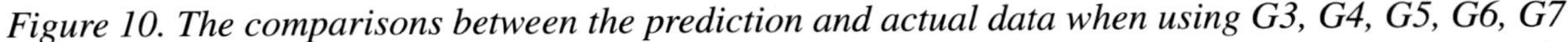

Figure 10. The comparisons between the prediction and actual data when using G3, G4, G5, G6, G7

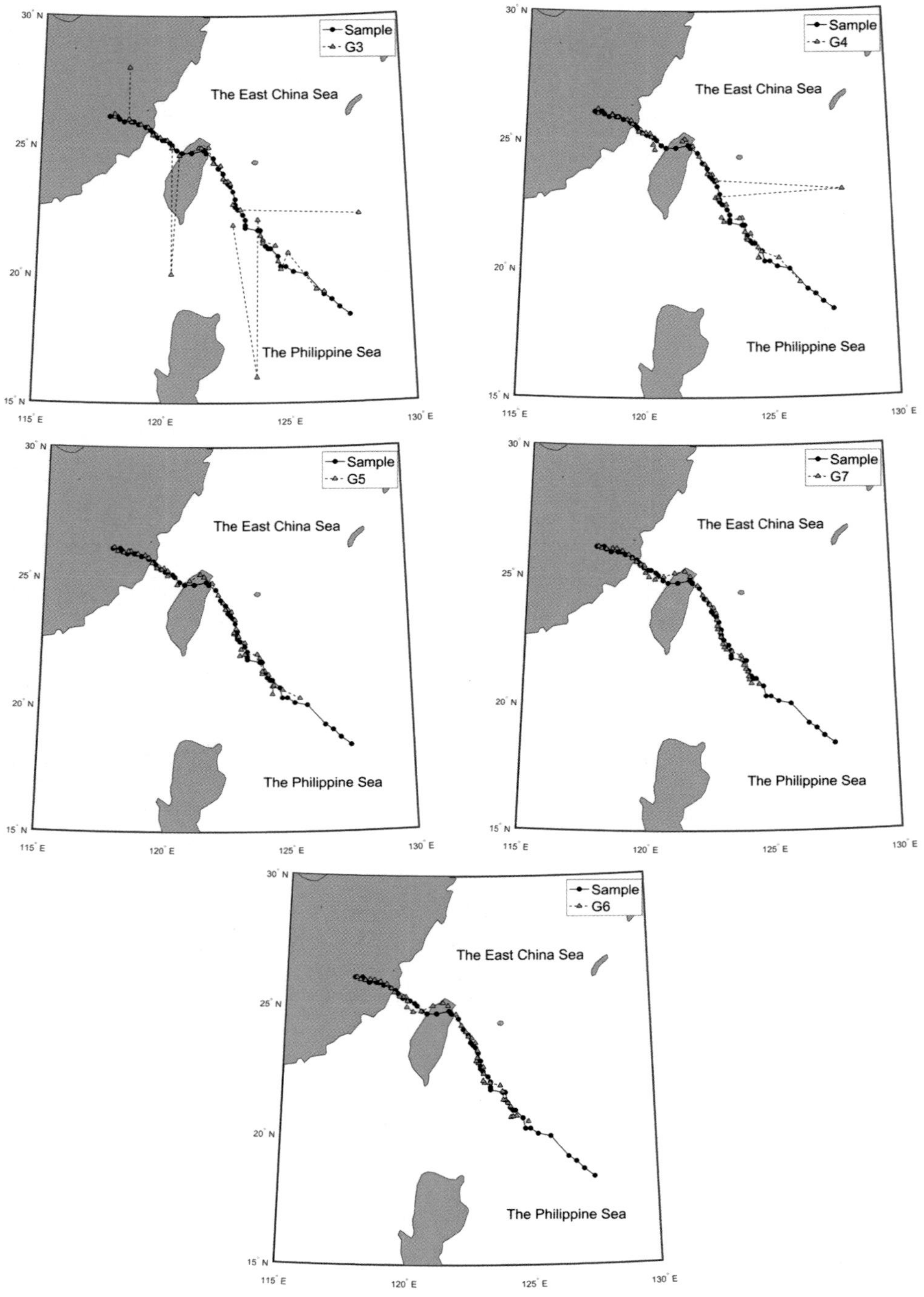

Figure 11. State partition and prediction of Markov model

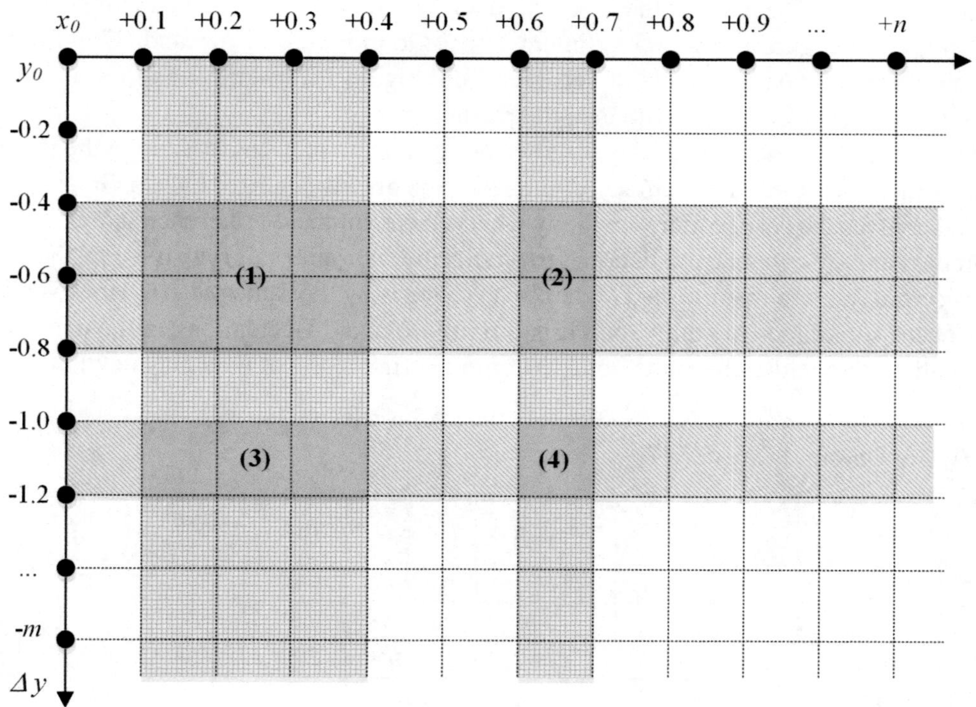

To evaluate our method, we use typhoon data to make prediction (http://typhoon.weather.com.cn/). The most common features of a typhoon are locations (latitude and longitude) at a particular time. So we measured these three elements in the experiments, including time, latitude and longitude. In order to simplify the experiments, we used the typhoon center's position to replace the MBR (Xl, Yl), (Xr, Yr) in our model. The experimental data is shown in Table 5 and explanation on symbols is shown in Table 6.

5.2 Evaluations

In the experiments, we took longitude and latitude data as X and Y respectively. In order to facilitate the experiments, we replaced MBR with the center position of typhoon. The predicted results are the moving curve of the typhoon's center that corresponds to time. In order to obtain the appropriate predicted method by which the predicted result is the most consistent with the actual data, n pairs of the data in ti-n+1-ti are used as original data and the results are compared with the actual data (the value n ranges from 3 to 7). We compared them in five aspects (accuracy, relative error, posterior difference, Data fitting and response time).

5.2.1 Accuracy

The accuracy of the results can be drawn from the comparison between the predicted results and the actual values as shown in Figure 11, where the black thin solid line is actual data and the dotted line represents the predicted data. Since each time we take n positions of typhoon for prediction, each result of the prediction is a subsequent of the (n + 1)th data. When data G3 is taken, the results are shown in Figure 11 (a), G4 in Figure 11 (b), G5 in Figure 11 (c), G6 in Figure 11 (d), and G7 in Figure 11 (e).

We can observe that on the aspect of accuracy from Figure 11, when G3 and G4 are taken into the experiments, there are serious distortions in the prediction.

When the experiment data is G5, there is a serious distortion of a single value in the prediction. The prediction is more volatile. The accuracy of the results is greatly improved when G6 and G7 are used, and the predicted results change more smoothly when a large number of reference samples are consulted.

The process of grey dynamic prediction is to predict the data value of group n + 1 by the pattern of the first n data sets, assuming that the data (data n + 1) changes by the same pattern. However, unexpected situations occur sometimes in reality, and it is difficult to avoid fluctuations in the data trend. In that kind of situation, the predicted results obtained from the first n sets of data may be biased.

Table 5. Typhoon nesat on July 2017

Y/M/D	Time	Serial number	Latitude N	Longitude E	Y/M/D	Time	Serial number	Latitude N	Longitude E
2017/7/27	17:00	1	18.4	127.5	2017/7/29	15:00	26	23.5	122.7
2017/7/27	20:00	2	18.7	127.1	2017/7/29	16:00	27	23.6	122.6
2017/7/27	23:00	3	19	126.8	2017/7/29	17:00	28	23.9	122.5
2017/7/28	2:00	4	19.2	126.5	2017/7/29	18:00	29	24.1	122.3
2017/7/28	5:00	5	20	125.8	2017/7/29	19:00	30	24.5	122.1
2017/7/28	8:00	6	20.1	125.3	2017/7/29	20:00	31	24.7	121.8
2017/7/28	11:00	7	20.3	125	2017/7/29	21:00	32	24.8	121.7
2017/7/28	14:00	8	20.3	124.8	2017/7/29	22:00	33	24.7	121.2
2017/7/28	17:00	9	20.7	124.7	2017/7/29	23:00	34	24.7	120.8
2017/7/28	19:00	10	21	124.4	2017/7/29	0:00	35	24.8	120.6
2017/7/28	20:00	11	21	124.3	2017/7/30	1:00	36	25	120.4
2017/7/28	21:00	12	21.1	124.2	2017/7/30	2:00	37	25.1	120.3
2017/7/28	22:00	13	21.3	124.1	2017/7/30	3:00	38	25.2	120.1
2017/7/28	23:00	14	21.7	124	2017/7/30	4:00	39	25.2	120
2017/7/29	1:00	15	21.7	123.9	2017/7/30	5:00	40	25.3	119.8
2017/7/29	4:00	16	21.8	123.4	2017/7/30	6:00	41	25.5	119.6
2017/7/29	6:00	17	21.9	123.4	2017/7/30	7:00	42	25.6	119.5
2017/7/29	7:00	18	22.1	123.4	2017/7/30	8:00	43	25.7	119.3
2017/7/29	8:00	19	22.3	123.3	2017/7/30	9:00	44	25.8	119
2017/7/29	9:00	20	22.5	123.1	2017/7/30	10:00	45	25.9	118.8
2017/7/29	10:00	21	22.6	123	2017/7/30	11:00	46	25.9	118.7
2017/7/29	11:00	22	22.7	123	2017/7/30	12:00	47	25.9	118.4
2017/7/29	12:00	23	22.9	123	2017/7/30	13:00	48	26	118.2
2017/7/29	13:00	24	23.2	122.9	2017/7/30	14:00	49	26.1	118.1
2017/7/29	14:00	25	23.4	122.8	2017/7/30	17:00	50	26.1	117.8

Table 6. Explanation on symbols

Symbols	Explanations
N3	3 serial numbers of latitude as a group, so n = 3
N4	4 serial numbers of latitude as a group, so n = 4
N5	5 serial numbers of latitude as a group, so n = 5
N6	6 serial numbers of latitude as a group, so n = 6
N7	7 serial numbers of latitude as a group, so n = 7
E3	3 serial numbers of longitude as a group, so n =3
E4	4 serial numbers of longitude as a group, so n =4
E5	5 serial numbers of longitude as a group, so n =5
E6	6 serial numbers of longitude as a group, so n =6
E7	7 serial numbers of longitude as a group, so n =7
G3	Use 3 typhoon positions in the model
G4	Use 4 typhoon positions in the model
G5	Use 5 typhoon positions in the model
G6	Use 6 typhoon positions in the model
G7	Use 7 typhoon positions in the model

Figure 12. (a) Comparisons on average relative error of latitudes (b) Comparisons on average relative error of longitudes

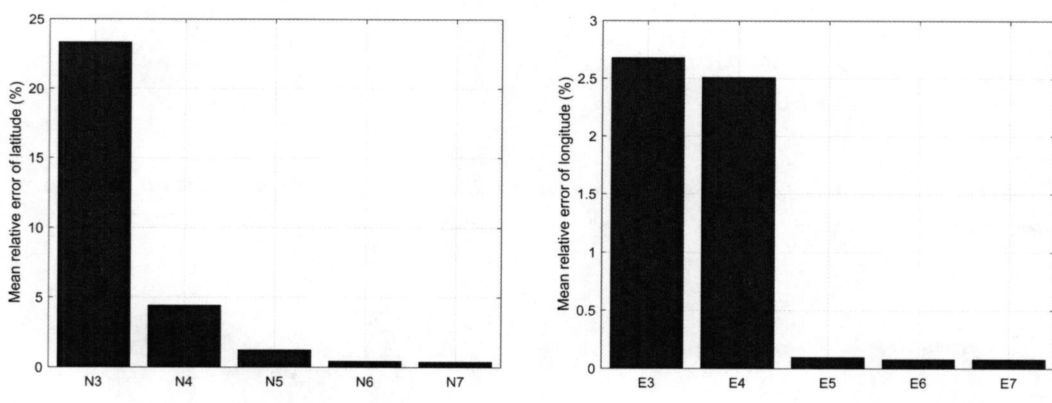

5.2.2 Relative Error

In this group of experiments, relative error is used to measure the deviation degree of predicted data from the actual data. We calculate the relative error in each prediction. When n equals to 4, average relative error of latitudes longitudes are shown in Figure 12(a) and Figure 12(b). The relative error of each group's latitude and longitudes are shown in Figure 13(a) and Figure 13(b).

Figure 13. (a) Diagram of relative error of latitudes (b) Diagram of relative errors of longitude

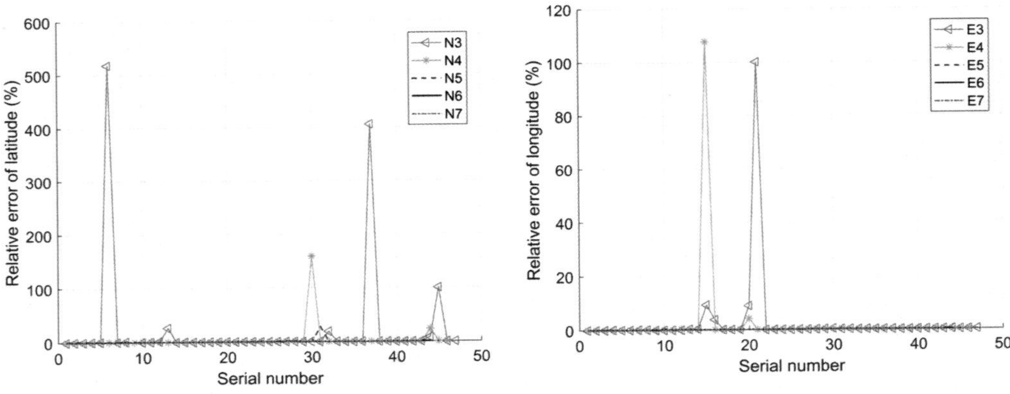

Figure 14. (a) Diagram of relative error of latitudes (b) Diagram of relative error of longitudes

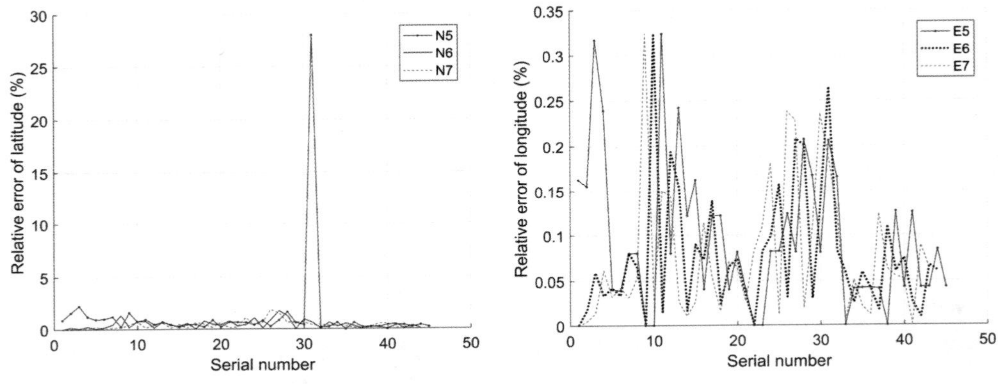

Figure 15. (a) Comparisons on average relative error of latitudes (b) Comparisons on average relative error of longitudes

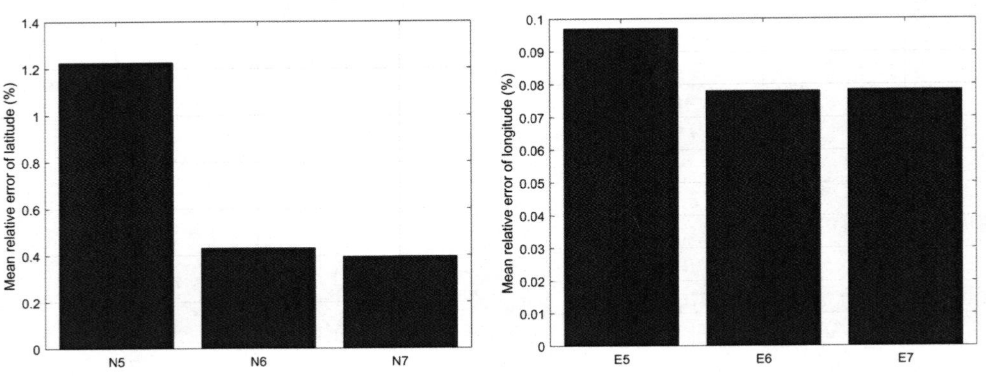

It can be observed that average relative errors of G5, G6 and G7 are all less than 0.02 from Figure 15. Generally speaking, the predicted errors of these three groups are small. From Figure 14, it can be concluded that the relative errors of N6 and N7 are stable within the range of 0.05, while the relative error of N5 group is less than 0.05 except for one data having a large deviation. The relative errors of E5, E6 and E7 are stable within the range of 0.0035.

5.2.3 Posterior Difference

The posterior difference C represents the degree of reliability of the $(n + 1)^{th}$ value calculated by the predictive equation.

$$C = \frac{S_2}{S_1} \times 100\% \tag{8}$$

$$S_1 = \sqrt{\frac{1}{N} \sum_{K=1}^{N} [x_{(k)}^{(0)} - \bar{x}]^2} \tag{9}$$

$$S_2 = \sqrt{\frac{1}{N-1} \sum_{K=2}^{N} [E_{(k)} - \bar{E}]^2} \tag{10}$$

where S_2 is the variance of the standard deviation of the residual error, S_1 denotes the standard deviation of the original data, and $x_{(k)}^{(0)}$ is the data of sequence 0 and k^{th}, and $E_{(k)}$ is the residual error.

We recalculate n sets of predicted data based on the equation compared with the actual data. When the data distribution is relatively stable, the posterior variance can be used as a very important measurement of predictive reliability. When the posterior variance is less than 0.35, it is considered that the predicted data is quite accurate. When the data is not stable enough, it may appear that the $(n + 1)^{th}$ predicted data is still close to the actual data, even if the posterior variance is large. This is also a normal phenomenon because the $(n + 1)^{th}$ data is not taken into account when calculating the posterior variance. So in either case, the posterior variance is an important criterion to measure the reliability of the prediction.

As the posterior difference is calculated by comparing the predicted data of the first n groups with the actual data respectively, which is shown in Figure 16(a). According to the predicted equation, when the posterior variance is less than 0.35, the prediction is considered accurate. Therefore, those values under 1 should be only concern. By showing only this kind of predicted results, we have Figure 16(b). It can be seen that posterior differences of *N6* and *N7* is the smallest ones. The *N3* and *N4* are the two largest ones, followed by *N5* group. In that case, we can draw a figure to reflect the number of each group's posterior difference elements and the proportion of elements above 0.35, as shown in Figure 16. We can see that with the increase of the number of groups, the proportion of the posterior difference greater than 0.35 decreases gradually, indicating that the reliability of data prediction increases gradually. After removing group *N3*, *N4* and redrawing the figure, we have Figure 17.

Figure 16. (a) Distribution on posterior difference of latitude (b) Distribution on posterior difference of latitude under 1

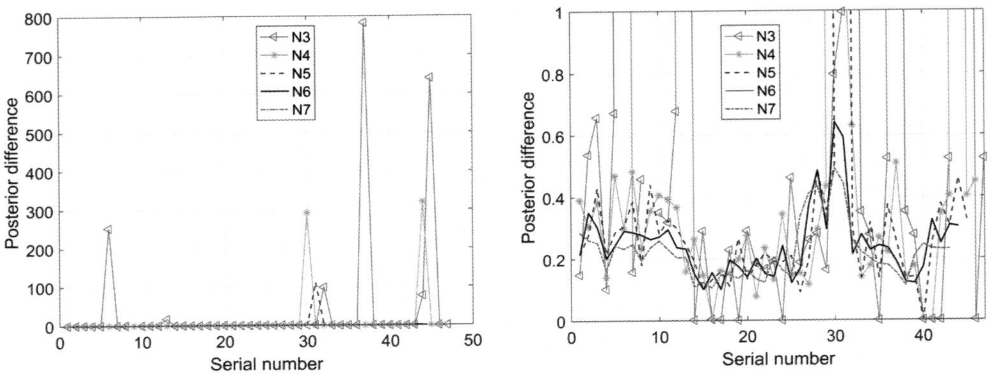

Figure 17. Distribution of latitudes' posterior difference on N5, N6, N7

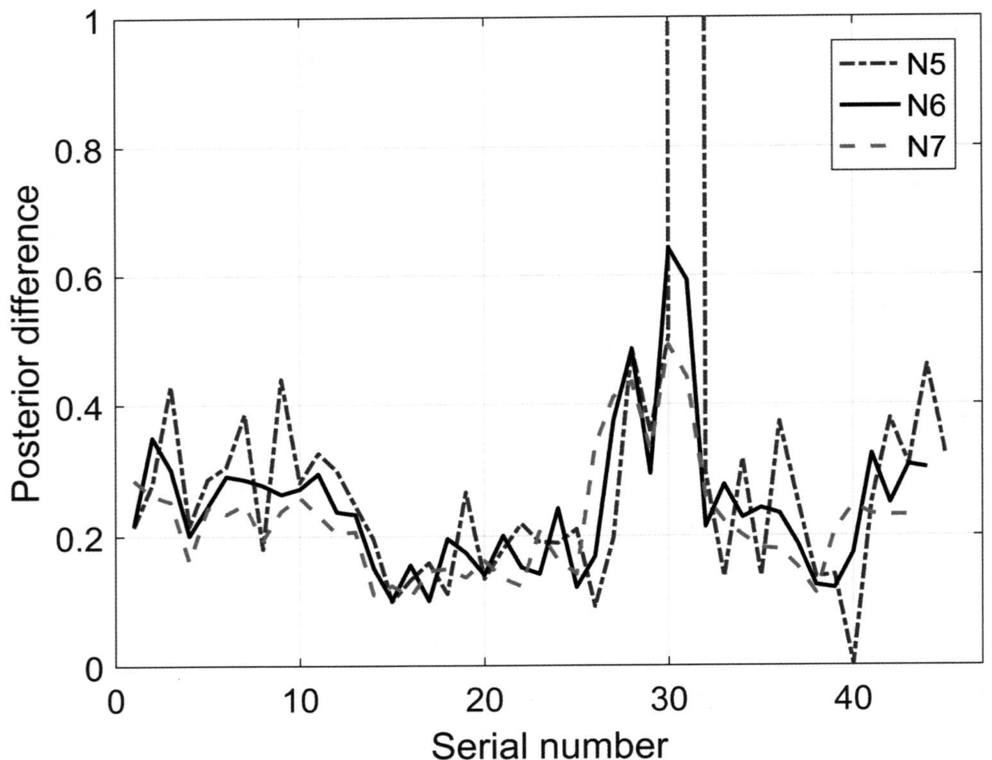

Figure 18. Posterior difference on latitudes of each group and the proportion of those above 0.35

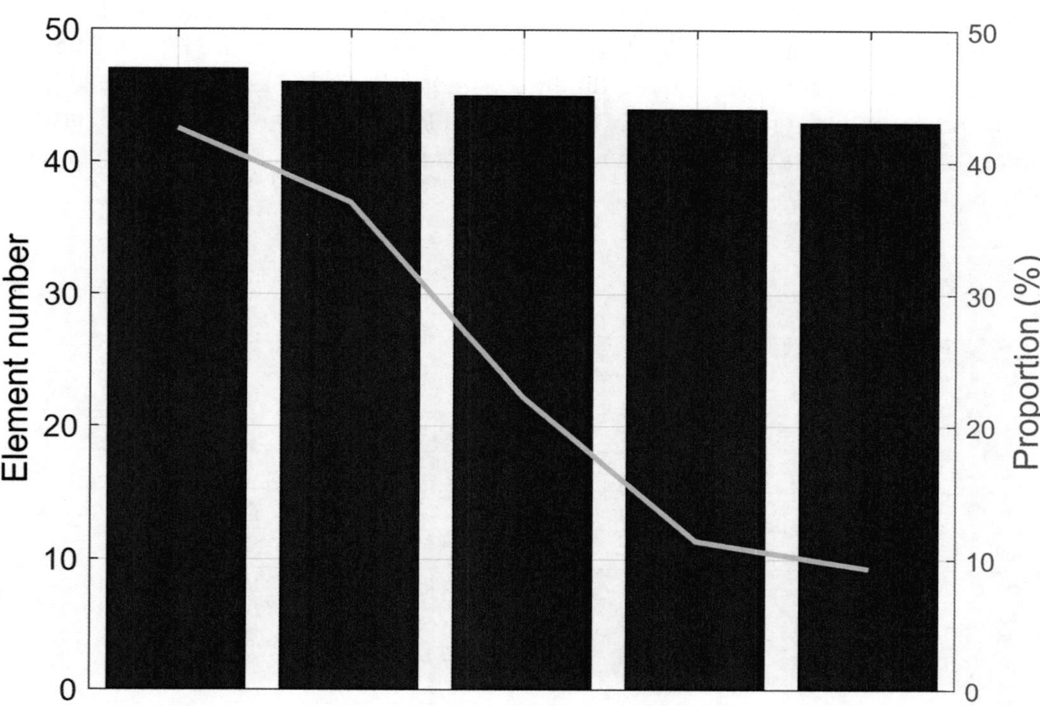

In Figure 18, the blue histogram represents the number of elements included in each groups' latitude data matrix, and the yellow line represents the proportion of elements whose posterior difference exceeds 0.35 in each set of data. We can see that the proportion of posterior difference above 0.35 decreases as the amounts of groups increases, thus indicating that the reliability of data forecasting grows When we remove group *N3*, *N4* and redraw the figure as shown in Figure 17, the posterior difference trends basically the same although the grouping among N5, N6 and N7 differs from each other. The posterior difference is relatively large from serial 1 to 14, and the posterior difference from groups 15 to 25 is smaller, followed by two peaks, which are more obvious in *N5* and *N6*, whereas the trend of *N7* is steadier, while it has a smaller value. We can draw a conclusion that as the grouping (sequence number) increases, changes in the posterior difference also tend to be stable. These characteristics are due to the distribution of the original data, as detailed data is shown in Table 7, Table 8, and Table 9.

It can be found that a number of a posteriori difference peaks occur when the original data has the same value, such as group 31 of *N5*, group 30 of *N6*, group 30 of *N7*, where 24.7 and 24.8 occurred multiple times. These data tend to become both larger and smaller, which is a great disadvantage for the prediction. But at the same time, according to the figure and table above, it can be concluded that larger group number *n* can be well compatible with these kinds of data distribution. Therefore, we can conclude that in order to improve the accuracy of prediction, we should obtain differently valued original data. If this is unavoidable, it's a good way to maximize *n* groups.

The posterior difference is calculated by comparing the predicted data of the first *n* groups with the real data, distribution on posterior difference of longitude in shown in Figure 19(a). When the posterior variance is less than 0.35, it is considered that the prediction is quite accurate, so we only care about those values under 1. By only showing this kind of predicted results, we have Figure 19(b).

Similarly, it can be seen that posterior differences in group *E3* and *E4* are the two largest ones, *E5* follows the posterior difference of E6 and E7 are the smallest ones, so we can draw a figure that reflects the number of each group's posterior difference elements and the proportion of elements above 0.35 as shown in Figure 20

Table 7. N=5 and posterior difference of latitude > 0.35

Group i	Posterior difference	Predicted sequence
3	0.4301	19, 19.2, 20, 20.1, 20.3
7	0.3855	20.3, 20.3, 20.7, 21, 21
9	0.4401	20.7, 21, 21, 21.1, 21.3
28	0.4863	23.9, 24.1, 24.5, 24.7, 24.8
29	0.3569	24.1, 24.5, 24.7, 24.8, 24.7
30	0.5054	24.5, 24.7, 24.8, 24.7, 24.7
31	111.4036	24.7, 24.8, 24.7, 24.7, 24.8
36	0.3732	25, 25.1, 25.2, 25.2, 25.3
42	0.3776	25.6, 25.7, 25.8, 25.9, 25.9
44	0.4604	25.8, 25.9, 25.9, 25.9, 26

Table 8. N=6 and posterior difference of latitude > 0.35

Group i	Posterior ifference	Predicted sequence
2	0.3505	18.7, 19, 19.2, 20, 20.1, 20.3
27	0.3742	23.6, 23.9, 24.1, 24.5, 24.7, 24.8
28	0.4845	23.9, 24.1, 24.5, 24.7, 24.8, 24.7
30	0.6409	24.5, 24.7, 24.8, 24.7, 24.7, 24.8
31	0.5917	24.7, 24.8, 24.7, 24.7, 24.8, 25

Table 9. N=7 and posterior difference of latitude > 0.35

Groupi	Posterior difference	Predicted sequence
27	0.4110	23.6, 23.9, 24.1, 24.5, 24.7, 24.8, 24.7
28	0.4352	23.9, 24.1, 24.5, 24.7, 24.8, 24.7, 24.7
30	0.4921	24.5, 24.7, 24.8, 24.7, 24.7, 24.8, 25

We can see that the proportion of posterior difference above 0.35 decreases as the amount of groups increases, thus indicating that the reliability of data forecasting grows. After removing group *E3*, *E4* and redrawing the figure, we have Figure 21.

Figure 19. (a) Distribution on posterior difference of longitude (b) Distribution on posterior difference under 1

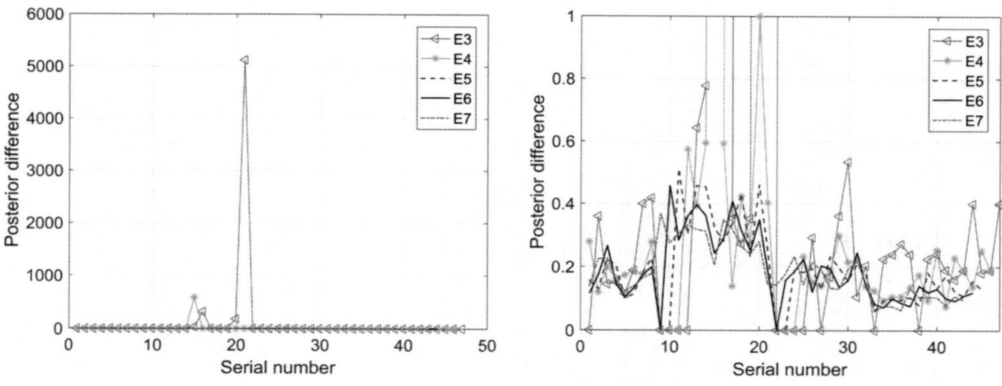

Figure 20. Posterior difference on longitude of each group and the proportion of those above 0.35

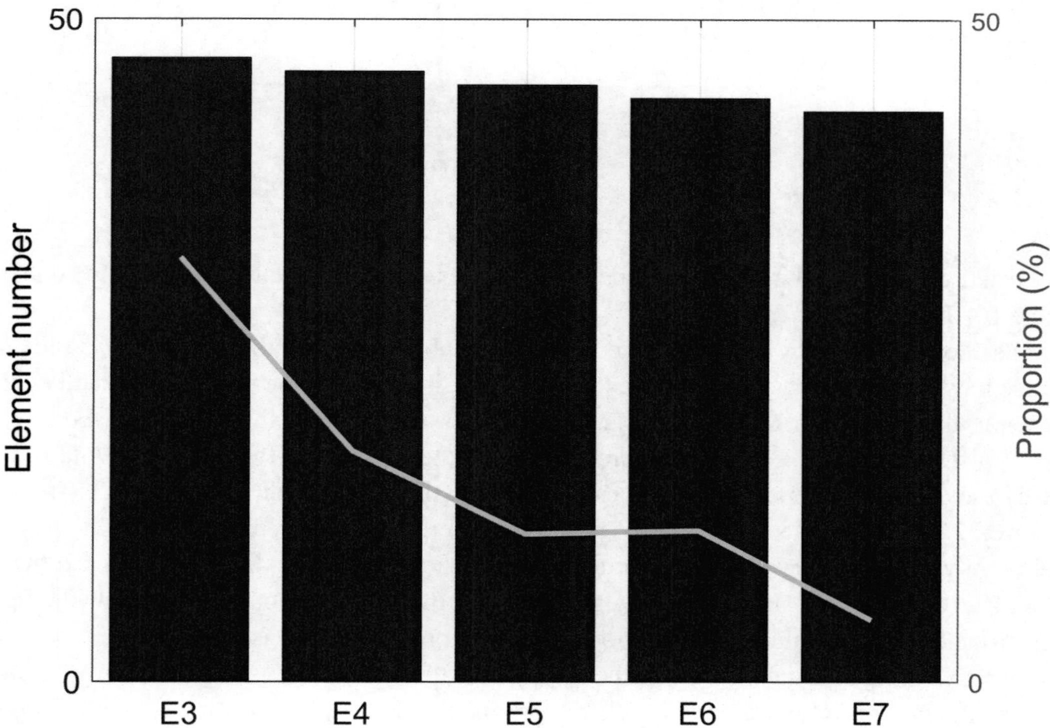

Figure 21. Distribution of latitudes' posterior difference on E5, E6, E7

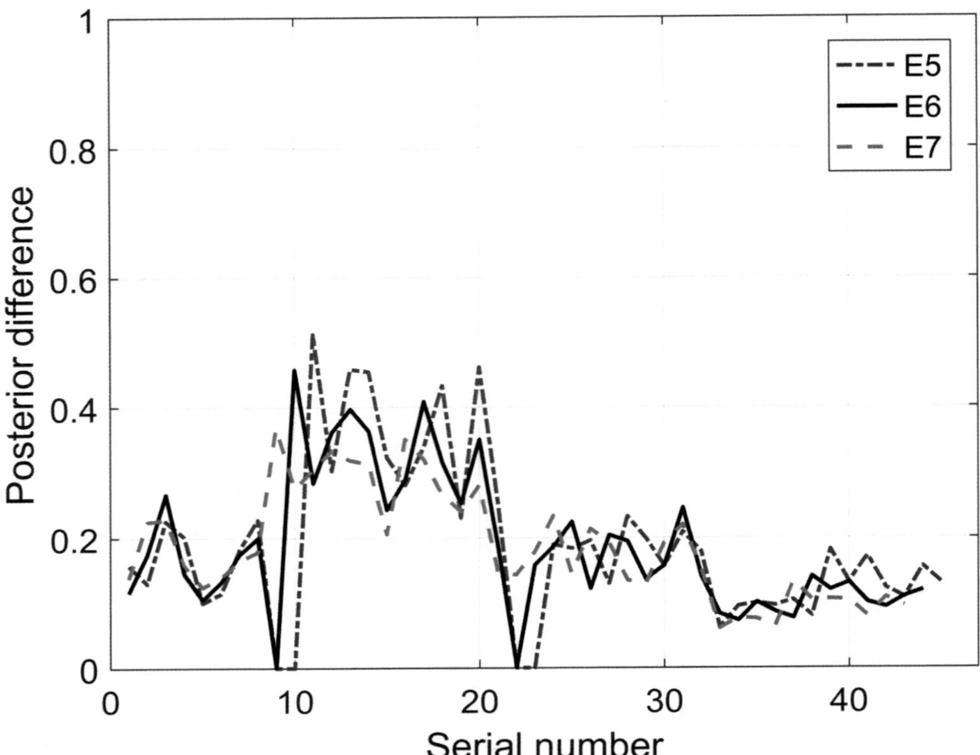

We can use similar analysis on longitudes which have been done on latitudes. Detailed data is shown in Table 10, Table 11, and Table 12.

Similar conclusions can be drawn from Table 10, Table 11, and Table 12 that when the data in a sequence have the similar or same values, the posterior difference of the prediction would be too large. In addition, the larger portion the same data has, the less satisfactory the results are. For example, in group 13 of *E6*, the data 123.4 appears three times and the posterior difference is 0.3965. In the group *E6* of *E7* the data 123.4 appears three times, resulting in the posterior difference of 0.3504.

Figure 22 shows the average values of posterior difference. The prediction made by grey dynamic model is only reliable when the posterior difference is no greater than 0.35. We can see from Figure 22(a) and 22(b) that group *G3* and *G4* have not met with this requirement. So we redraw the figure only on *G5*, *G6* and *G7*. The value of a posteriori difference on the group 5 is far above 0.35, which means that taking five groups of sample data as the original data for prediction is less reliable. While values of the group E6 and group E7 are both less than 0.35, the predictions have a stronger reliability. Here we have the number of elements that don't meet the requirement. We can see from the Figure 22(e) that the prediction is more reliable when group number is G7.

Table 10. E=5 and posterior difference of latitude > 0.35

Group i	Posterior difference	Predicted sequence
11	0.5124	124.3, 124.2, 124.1, 124, 123.9
13	0.4580	124.1, 124, 123.9, 123.4, 123.4
14	0.4544	124, 123.9, 123.4, 123.4, 123.4
18	0.4327	123.4, 123.3, 123.1, 123, 123
20	0.4611	123.1, 123, 123, 123, 122.9

Table 11. E=6and posterior difference of latitude > 0.35

Group i	Posterior difference	Predicted sequence
10	0.4572	124.4, 124.3, 124.2, 124.1, 124, 123.9
12	0.3611	124.2, 124.1, 124, 123.9, 123.4, 123.4
13	0.3965	124.1, 124, 123.9, 123.4, 123.4, 123.4
14	0.3628	124, 123.9, 123.4, 123.4, 123.4, 123.3
17	0.4080	123.4, 123.4, 123.3, 123.1, 123, 123

Table 12. E=7 and posterior difference of latitude > 0.35

Group i	Posterior difference	Predicted sequence
9	0.3681	124.7, 124.4, 124.3, 124.2, 124.1, 124, 123.9
16	0.3504	123.4, 123.4, 123.4, 123.3, 123.1, 123, 123
30	0.4921	24.5, 24.7, 24.8, 24.7, 24.7, 24.8, 25

Figure 22. (a) Average values of latitude's posterior difference (b) Average values of longitude's posterior difference (c) Mean values of latitude's posterior difference on N5 N6 N7 (d) Mean values of longitude's posterior difference on N5 N6 N7 (e) Numbers of data that doesn't meet the requirement of accuracy

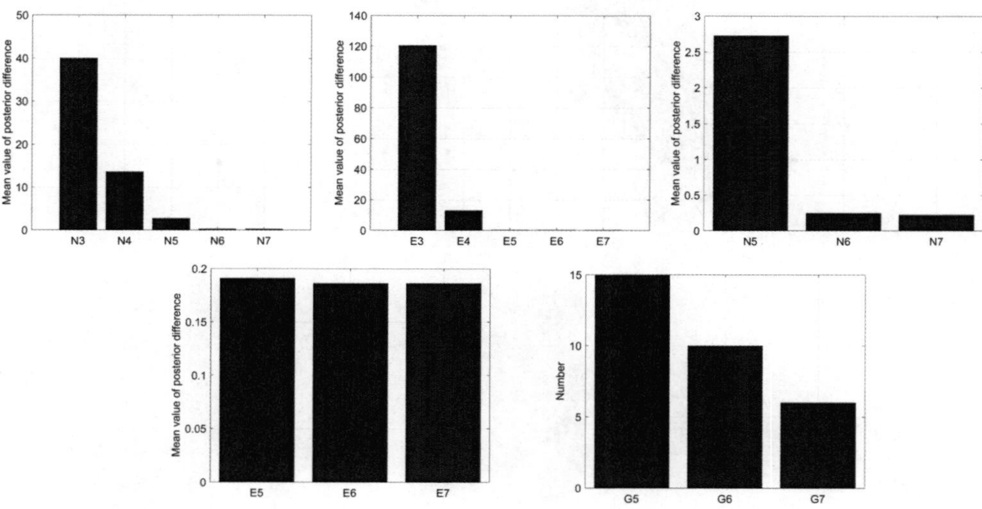

Figure 23. Uncertain regions of G3, G4, G5, G6, G7 predicted by REPM

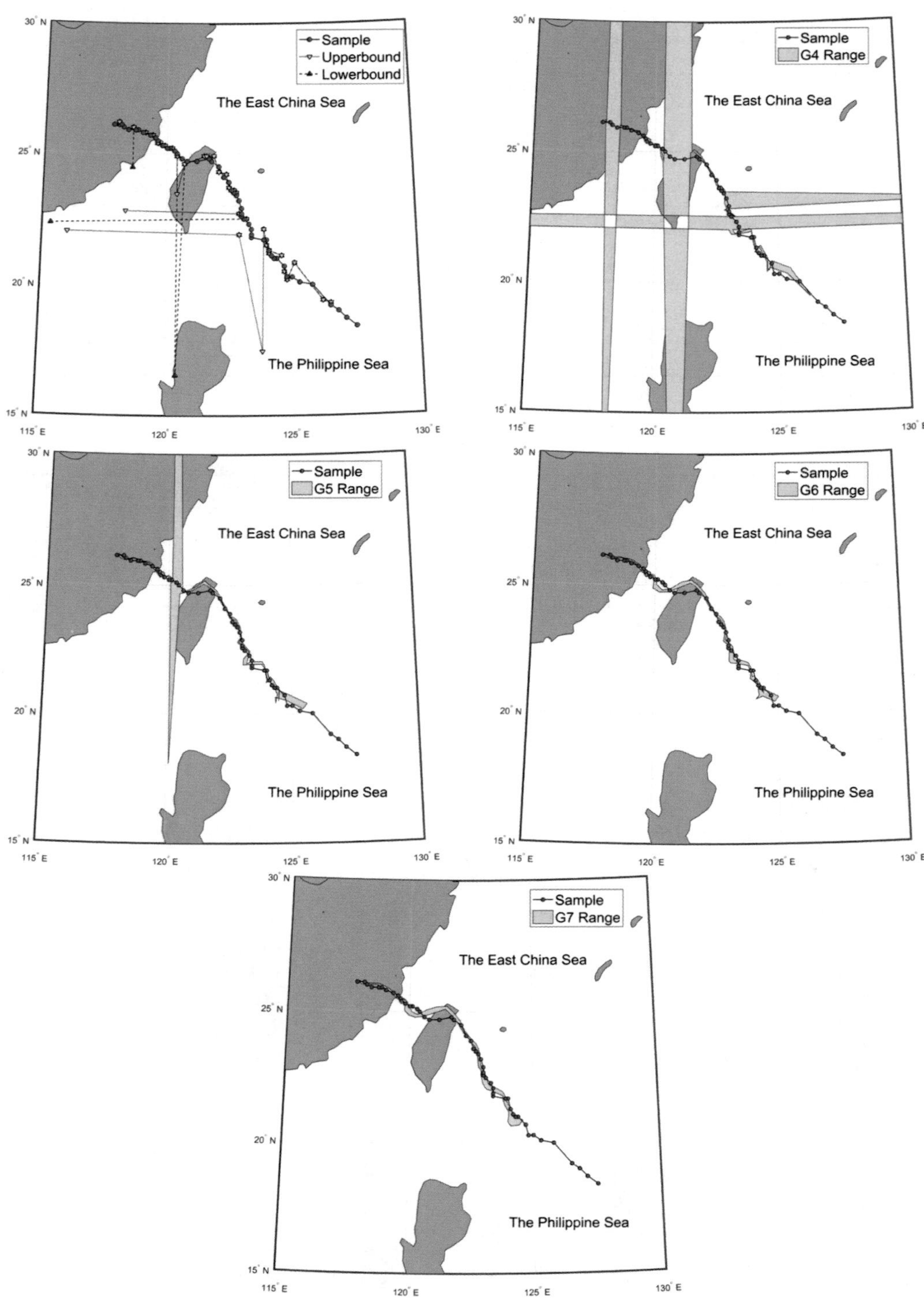

5.2.4 Data fitting

Figure 11(a), (b), (c), (d) and (e) show the actual trajectory of the typhoon on the map and the trajectory predicted by the grey dynamic model. As the amount of reference groups for prediction increases, the predicted value of the trajectory becomes closer to the actual value and the fitting degree becomes higher. But no matter how well they fit, there are still some gaps between the predicted points and the actual points. When considering an actual situation, suppose that a typhoon is about to occur in a place, the relevant departments need to predict the future location of the typhoon quickly, so that evacuation and protection can be organized in advance. Therefore, this prediction should be as comprehensive as possible and should be able to predict a regional scope, in order to maximize the safety of the residents' lives and property.

In order to evaluate the degree of fitting, our model uses the predicted value and the sample to calculate the relative error, which means that the sample should be located in the area whose center is the predicted data and the radius is the relative error. We calculate the average residual errors of the first n groups and then combine them with the predicted data. So we have the range calculated by Definition 10 as the upper bound and the lower bound of the predicted latitude and longitude. Theoretically, this range of prediction should include the trajectory of the moving typhoon. The experimental results are shown in Figure 23

The red dotted line in Figure 23 is the actual value of the sample data, that is, the path of the moving typhoon, and the grey area is the closed area enclosed by the predicted upper and lower bounds of the latitude and longitude. As seen from Figure 23(a), due to the small number of reference sample, the extreme values in the predicted data are excessive, making it too dispersed in the map and unable to form a closed area. For Figure 23(b) and 23(c), there are still large gaps between the predicted area and the sample value because of extreme values. In Figure 23(d) and 23(e), there is no extreme value and the inclusion of actual data in the predicted area has improved greatly compared with the first three images, but the results are still not satisfactory. The trajectory of the typhoon is affected by uncertainty in the process of movement, especially some of these factors only happen at a specific time. They should not be included in our model as the accuracy of the predicted range may be interfered.

Based on the analysis above, we propose a new way to predict the range denoted as Largest Region Predicted Method or LRPM. According to the characteristics of grey dynamic predicted model, we can select different values of sample as prediction reference group which may increase the uncertainty in the predictive model. Therefore, we remove the extreme values in the predicted results of G4, G5, G6, G7, and select the maximum and minimum values from the rest of the predicted data as the border of the region, shown in Figure 24.

We use *G3*, *G4*, *G5*, *G6*, *G7* to obtain the maximum and minimum values, and use these values as the upper and lower bounds of the range. As seen from Figure 24, we have greatly increased the actual sample value inclusion in this way.

Figure 24. Uncertain regions predicted by LRPM

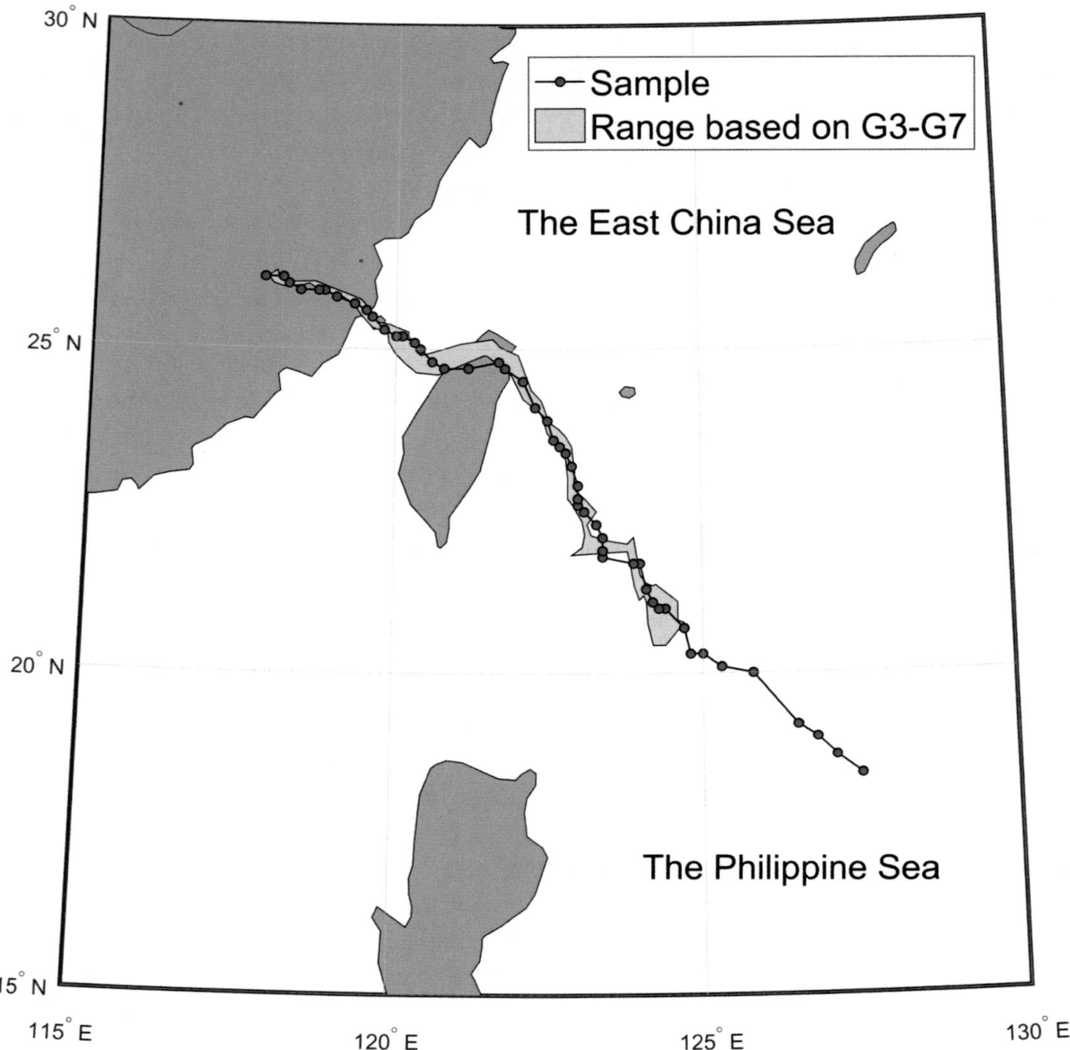

5.2.5 Response Time

For data storage and query, the traditional way is to use a relational database, and in this chapter, we use improved XML to do this. The comparison between these two methods on time efficiency is shown in Figure 25. As seen from the histogram, XML is far superior to the relational database in terms of the efficiency of the storage and query, and it is proved that XML is a better way to store and query predictive data. In order to get the effect of the grouping number on predicted time, we present the combined data in longitude and latitude to show the average predicted time of *G3*, *G4*, *G5*, *G6* and *G7*, as shown in Figure 26. It can be seen that the predicted time of these five groups are at most the degree of 10^{-3}, which also ensure the efficiency of the actual predicted application. By comparison, it can be concluded that it will cost more time querying data than predicting the results in XML structures.

Figure 25. Query times of relational database and XML

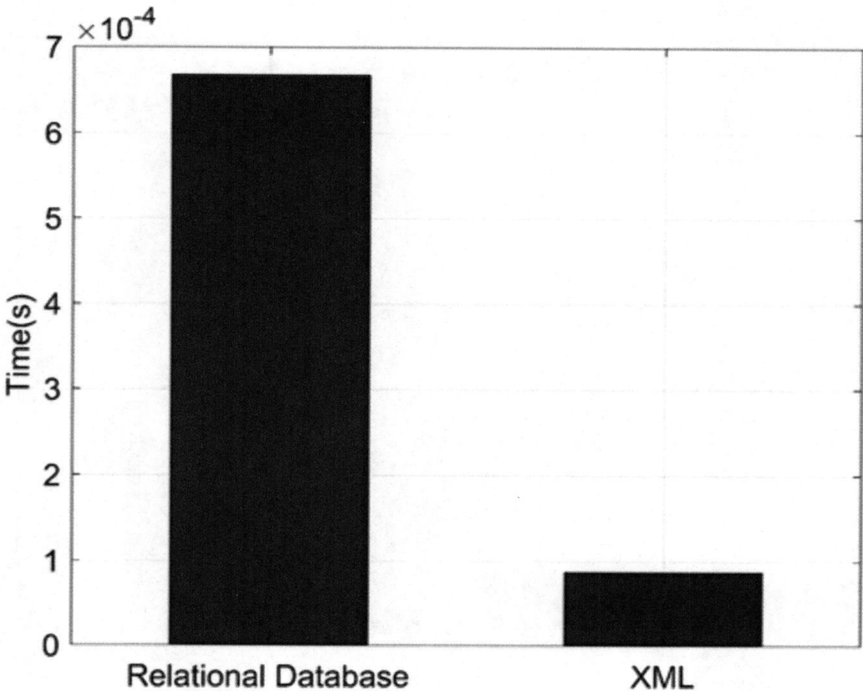

Figure 26. Average sums of time used to predict latitude and longitude

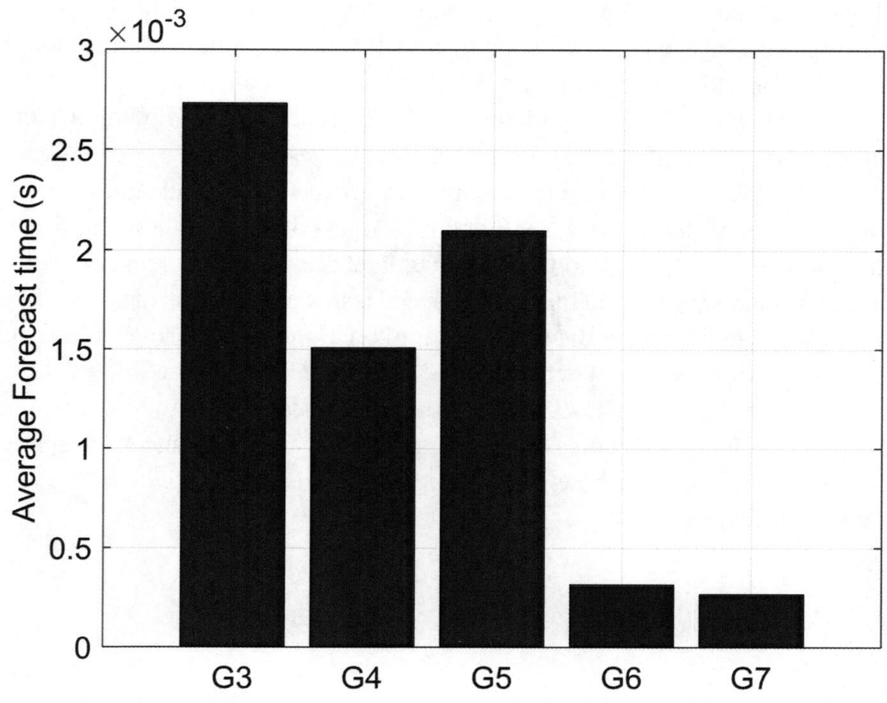

Figure 27. Query time of EModel and Xmodel

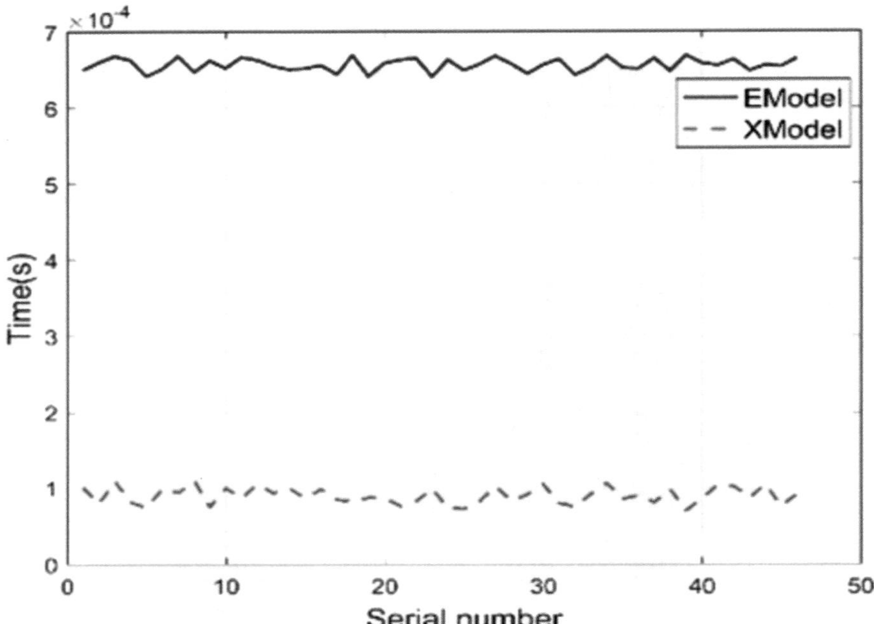

The experimental data is totally 50 couples which is divided into several groups. Therefore, the total number is certain, and the predicted time decreases as the number of groups increases. Theoretically, as the number of groups increases, the predicted time is usually shorter.

In the following, we compare XML with relational database model in query time. When querying predicted data, it is necessary to convert the multi-tree data model built by XML into a binary tree data model, and it is necessary to convert and establish the binary tree data model. The total conversion time and the total query time in the XModel add up to 0.00008718s. Compared with the storage structure of spatiotemporal data in relational database[56], EModel queries the same set of experimental data and for an average time of 0.0006674s. From the comparison, we can see the advantages of storage based on XML. The query time of each group by XML and relational database is shown in Figure 27.

Compared with XML, using traditional relational database is better in generalization, data storage, data persistence and query service. But the reading speed is low in relational database. In our experiment, the only thing needed is to transform the multi tree into binary tree by storing uncertain spatiotemporal data integrated XML. The experiment demonstrates that the transform time is less than that of querying database. The time of querying XML database is only 0.001 percent of transformation, which is negligible. Hence, XML is the better choice in the storage and querying of uncertain spatiotemporal data. At the same time, we are studying how to combine relational database with XML to store uncertain spatiotemporal data effectively.

5.3 Evalution on Markov Model

In combination with State and Probability of data in the last 20 groups predicted in experiment, the results show that minimum value was 0.1 and maximum value was 0.5, as shown in Table 13 and Table 14.

And the States in Table 13 and Table 14 is the States divided by threshold according to Definition 11. It is used to confirm the state-transition matrix which is an essential parameter in Markov Model. In combination with other probabilities, the values could be divided into eight segments: [0, 0.1], (0.1, 0.12], (0.12, 0.125], (0.125, 0.23], (0.23, 0.25], (0.25, 0.375], (0.35, 0.5] and (0.5, 1]. In addition, when the Probability value is not less than 0.5, it is considered that this state is more likely to occur, so the threshold value should be less than 0.5. Therefore, the threshold values of 0.1, 0.12, 0.125, 0.23, 0.25 and 0.375 can be selected. Similarly, in the longitude predicting results, the minimum value is 0.1 and the maximum value is 0.72. According to the same principle above, the Probability values can be divided into six segments, which are [0, 0.1], (0.1, 0.14], (0.14, 0.17], (0.17, 0.3], (0.3, 0.43], (0.43, 0.67] and (0.67, 0.72]. Then the thresholds are 0.1, 0.12, 0.15, 0.17, 0.35 and 0.43 in the range less than 0.5.

According to the Probability range of latitude and longitude, 10 sets of common thresholds are selected, which are 0.1, 0.12, 0.125, 0.15, 0.17, 0.23, 0.25, 0.35, 0.375 and 0.43 following the discussion above. And these thresholds will be used to select the group when the probability is equal or greater than corresponding threshold. Experimental results will be displayed in the following discussion according to different thresholds.

Table 13. The state partition of latitude

Group num.	State 1	State 2	State 3	State 4	State 5	State 6
31	0.5	0	0	0.5	0	0
32	0.1	0.2	0.2	0.1	0.2	0.1
33	0	0.375	0.5	0.125	0	0
34	0	0.5	0	0.25	0.25	0
35	0	0.5	0	0.25	0.25	0
36	0	0.375	0.5	0.125	0	0
37	0.1	0.2	0.2	0.1	0.2	0.1
38	0	0.375	0.5	0.125	0	0
39	0	0.375	0.5	0.125	0	0
40	0	0.5	0	0.25	0.25	0
41	0	0.375	0.5	0.125	0	0
42	0.1	0.2	0.2	0.1	0.2	0.1
43	0	0.375	0.5	0.125	0	0
44	0	0.375	0.5	0.125	0	0
45	0	0.375	0.5	0.125	0	0
46	0	0.375	0.5	0.125	0	0
47	0	0.5	0	0.25	0.25	0
48	0	0.5	0	0.25	0.25	0
49	0	0.375	0.5	0.125	0	0
50	0	0.375	0.5	0.125	0	0

Table 14. The state partition of longitude

Group num.	State 1	State 2	State 3	State 4	State 5
31	0.14	0	0.43	0.43	0
32	0.14	0	0.43	0.43	0
33	0	0.1	0.17	0.72	0
34	0	0	0.67	0.3	0
35	0	0	0.67	0.3	0
36	0.14	0	0.43	0.43	0
37	0.14	0	0.43	0.43	0
38	0	0.1	0.17	0.72	0
39	0.14	0	0.43	0.43	0
40	0	0.1	0.17	0.72	0
41	0.14	0	0.43	0.43	0
42	0.14	0	0.43	0.43	0
43	0	0.1	0.17	0.72	0
44	0.14	0	0.43	0.43	0
45	0.14	0	0.43	0.43	0
46	0.14	0	0.43	0.43	0
47	0	0.1	0.17	0.72	0
48	0.14	0	0.43	0.43	0
49	0.14	0	0.43	0.43	0
50	0	0.1	0.17	0.72	0

5.3.1 Predicted Time

We test the predicted time under different thresholds. When the threshold is equal to 0.1, the predicted time is about 0.025s, while the predicted time under other thresholds is close to 0.02s. The consumption time in the first experiment is obviously more than that in the other groups, because matrixs need to be created and data need to be loaded. As a result, we select the average time of the last nine sets of predicted time as the final prediction of Markov model, as shown in Figure 28.

5.3.2 Memory Consumption

Memory consumption of Markov Model is shown in Figure 29. The experimental results show that there is no significant relationship between memory consumption and the selected threshold. Since we employ the same experimental method, and the data we used was independent in the prediction, the detailed memory usage maintained about 26416 Byte fluctuate up and down shown in Table 15.

Figure 28. Predicted time of Markov model

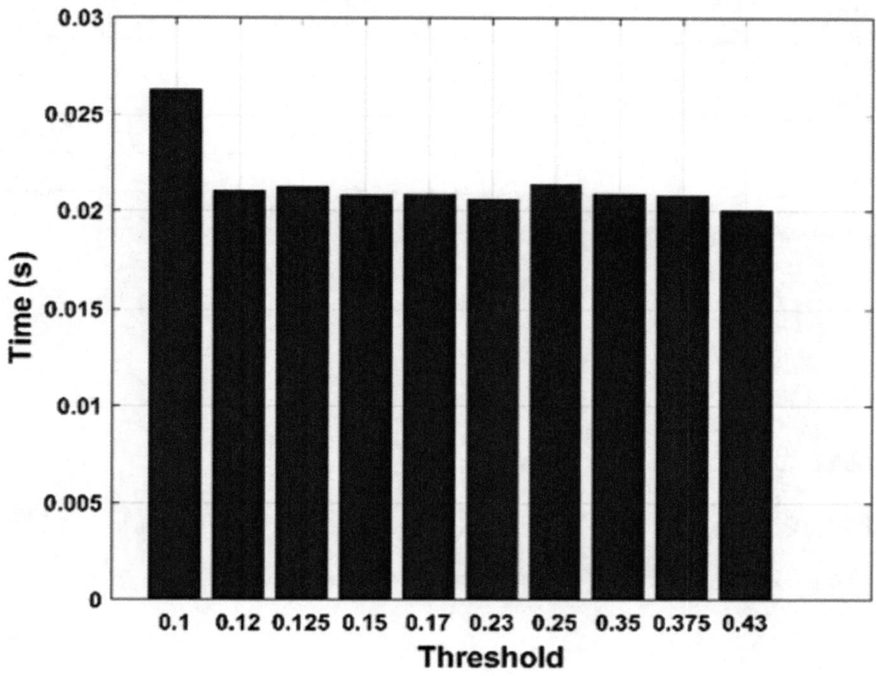

Figure 29. Memory consumption of Markov model

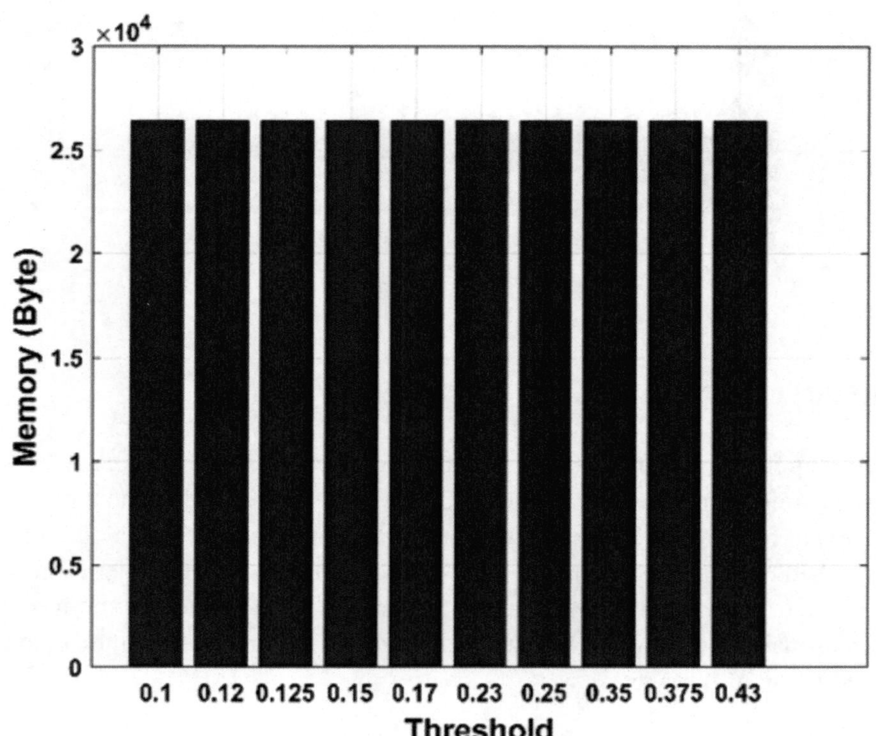

Table 15. The data of memory consumption using Markov model

Memory(Byte)	Threshold	Memory(Byte)	Threshold
26430	0.1	26412	0.23
26390	0.12	26421	0.25
26420	0.125	26418	0.35
26423	0.15	26415	0.375
26416	0.17	26416	0.43

Figure 30. Area and hit rate

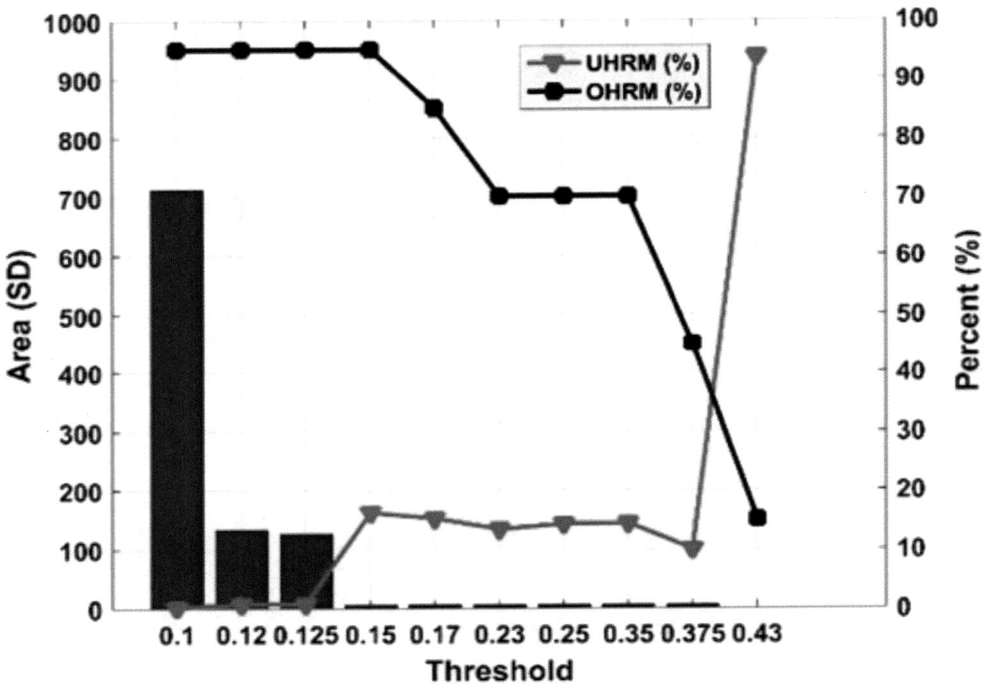

5.3.3 Unit Area Hit Rate

The variables used in this experiment are latitude and longitude, so the predicting Area is S = Δlatitude × Δlongtitude.. Therefore, the concept of Square Degree (SD) is defined as the unit of S. A unit SD is defined as the area of a rectangle with two sides' length of a unit latitude and a unit longitude.

In Figure 30, the histogram represents the Area of the range predicted under each threshold. From Figure 30, we can see that the maximum Area is more than 700 SD and the minimum is less than 10 SD. The results are reasonable, because when the selected thresholds increase, the State range may decrease, leading to the reduction of the Area.

According to Definition 13, Overall Hit Rate of Markov Model (OHRM) is the percentage of the predicted points as shown in Figure 30, the maximum OHRM is 95%, and the minimum is 15%. With the increase of thresholds, the OHRM shows a downward trend.

Specifically, when the threshold is less than 0.15, OHRM remains at 95%. Analyzing the reason, on the one hand, OHRM is stable because the increments of thresholds are small. On the other hand, OHRM is high because the smaller threshold of this segment, the more states is selected. So the predicted range has been extended, which contains more actual values. OHRM decreases when the thresholds are selected at [0.15, 0.23], because the threshold gradient is higher than before (0.02, 0.06 to 0.02, 0.05, 0.025). What's more, some data points are filtered out with the threshold increasing in this range. When the thresholds are selected at [0.23, 0.35], OHRM remains the same. Within this range, the forecast range of latitude has a certain impact, while the forecast range of longitude is the same as the threshold value of 0.15. When the thresholds are selected at [0.35, 0.43], OHRM always drops, and the falling speed is accelerated. The reason is that there are more data points of latitude and longitude filtered out by high threshold value. It is concluded that when the selection of thresholds can affect both latitude and longitude predicted range, OHRM will change dramatically.

According to the analysis of the Area and OHRM of Markov predicted range above, it is necessary to reduce the threshold and expand the predicted range in order to improve OHRM of Markov model. In actual situation, the typhoon forecast needs the request of accurate and moderate scope, which ensures that people can carry on the protection more quickly, accurately and effectively before typhoon comes. Therefore, considering the size of predicted range on the effect is important. So we defined the concept of unit area hit rate (UHRM) according to Definition 14, that is, the ratio of the OHRM to the Area of predicted range.

As shown in Figure 30, when the thresholds are in [0.1, 0.125], the Area of prediction is large and OHRM is remained at a high level of 95%, so UHRM remains below 1%. When the threshold is 0.15, UHRM is improved to 16% due to deduction of Area, while OHRM is still 95%. When the thresholds are in [0.15, 0.375], UHRM fluctuates down because Area doesn't change significantly, and OHRM decreases. When the threshold increases to 0.43, OHRM also reduces, but UHRM still improves greatly, reaching more than 90%. From the analysis above, we can see that UHRM is a more favorable indicator to measure the advantages and disadvantages of the methods.

According to Figure 30, OHRM is 95% when the thresholds are 0.12 and 0.125, and Area is only 1/5 comparing with area when threshold is 0.1. OHRM is more than 70% when the thresholds are 0.15, 0.17, 0.23, 0.25, and 0.35. Area is less than 10, and UHRM is about 15%. So we select these eight sets of thresholds to count again, as shown in Figure 31, which shows that when the threshold is 0.15, the area is the smallest, and OHRM and UHRM reach the maximum of these groups. So the threshold of 0.15 is the most appropriate choice for this experiment.

5.4 Comparisons

5.4.1 Predicted Time

In Grey model and Markov's multi-group experiments, the predicted time is calculated as shown in Figure 32. The predicted time of the Grey model is less than 0.015s, and that of Markov model is more than 0.02s. Therefore, we can conclude that the Grey model is superior to the Markov model in terms of memory consumption.

5.4.2 Memory Consumption

By comparing the memory usage in Matlab between Grey model and Markov model, their memory consumptions are shown in Figure 33. The memory consumption of the Grey model is about 8,000 byte, while that of the Markov model is about 26,000 byte, nearly 3.25 times as much as that of the Grey model. Thus, the performance of Grey model is obviously better than that of Markov model in memory consumption.

The memory consumption seems negligible due to its only MB degree. But it is worth mentioning that our dataset is small with only 50 series of data. Small static datasets are not enough to estimate their memory consumption such as our dataset. But dynamic datasets will be pervasive in the long run. In this situation, estimating the memory consumption makes sense.

5.4.3 Unit Area Hit Rate (UHRM)

Comparisons on *UHRM* are between the G7 group with the best performance in Grey model and the best performed group with threshold equals to 0.15 in Markov model, shown in Figure 34. The results show that *UHRM* in Markov model is better about 1.5% higher than that in Grey model.

Analyzing the reason, the location of the typhoon at the next time should be predicted firstly when Grey model is used to predict range, and then the scope should be extended outwards as the center of the circle. The scope of Markov model is determined by *State*, and probabilities of different *States* are generated by prediction. As a result, the scope of the prediction is wider, and then the *UHRM* is also higher. However, it is worth noting that the *State* matrix of Markov model needs to be changed dynamically according to different data sets, and Grey model doesn't need these transformations

Figure 31. Area and hit rate

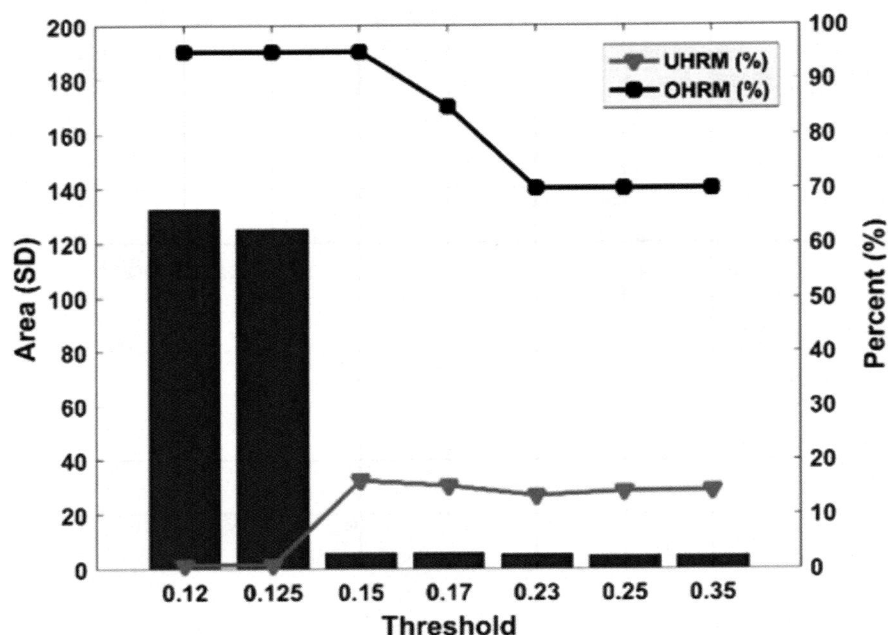

Figure 32. Predicted time of Grey model and Markov model

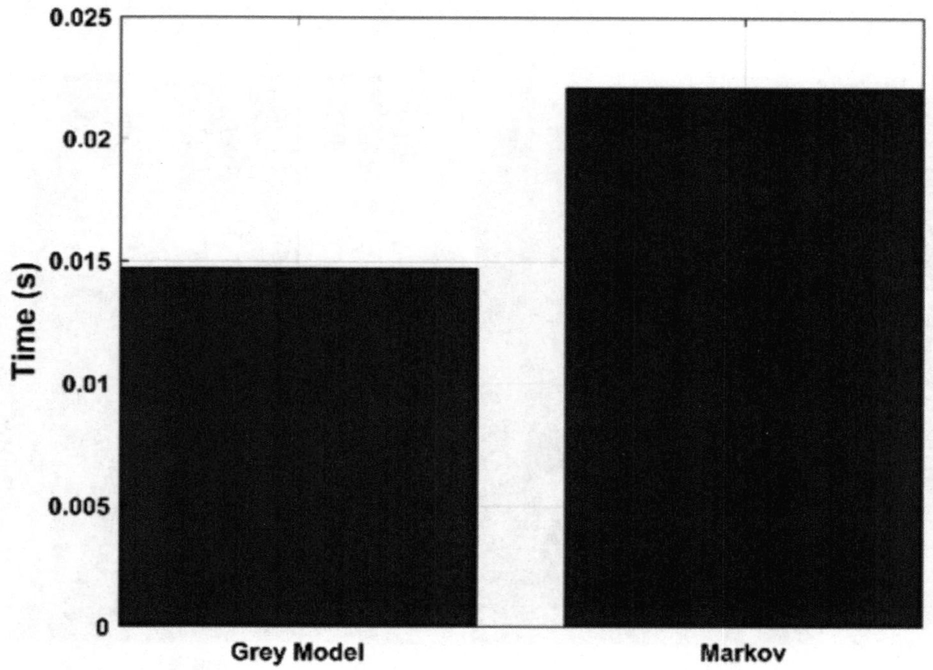

Figure 33. Memory consumption of Grey model and Markov model

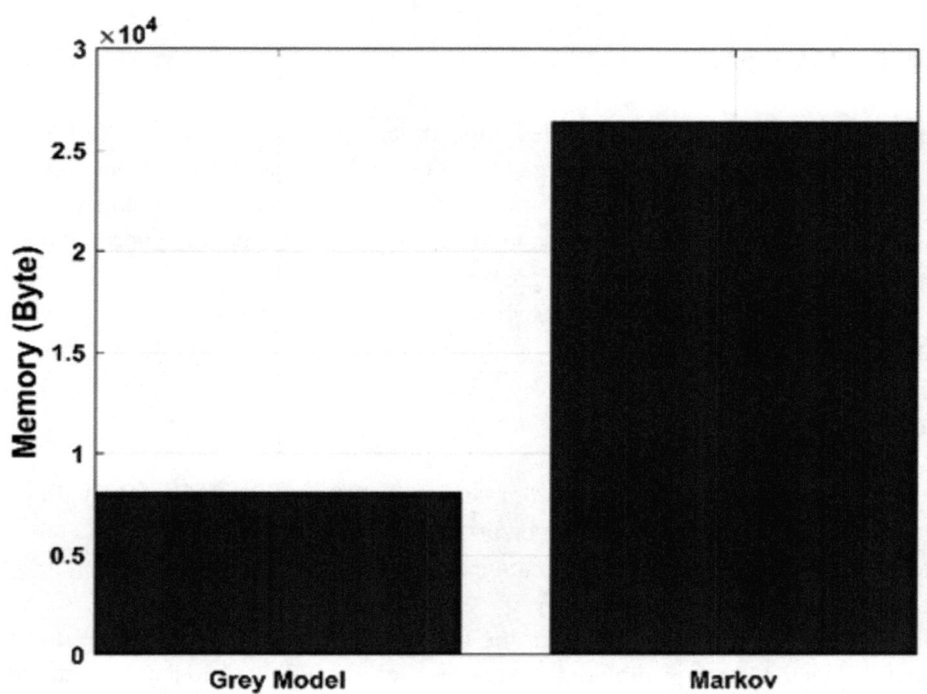

Figure 34. Unit area hit rate of Grey model and Markov model

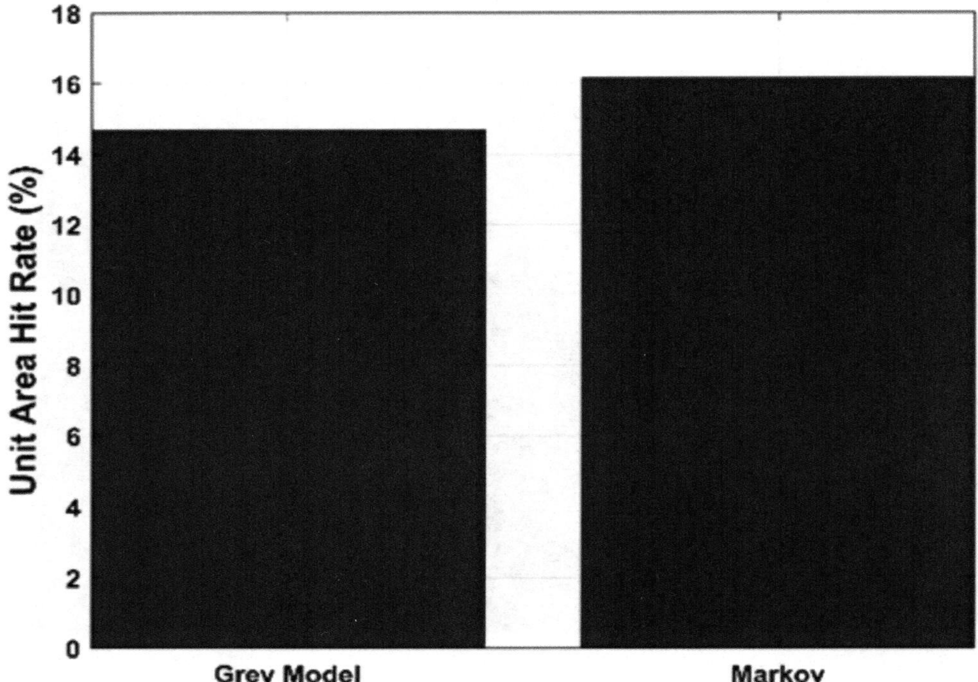

5.5 Experimental Conclusion

5.5.1 Query Performance

Query performance is mainly measured by response time. Through the statistical analysis of data, we can see that most time is taken up by the storage and query in the actual situation, and the calculation of prediction takes much less time than the former two. At the same time, by comparing the traditional relational database and the proposed approach in this chapter, it is proved that querying uncertain space-time data in XML has higher efficiency and greater advantages.

5.5.2 Predicted Performance

- Grey model with XML(PGX)

Accuracy and relative error: From the comparisons between predicted results with the actual data and numerical analysis, we can conclude that bizarre error would occur when the data are divided into 3 or 4 groups, and when the group number is 5, some data have greater errors, but when the group number is 6 or 7, the predicted results are satisfactory.

Posterior Difference: In the evaluation of the predicted reliability, we conclude that posterior difference is not only related to the group number, but also relies on the original data's smoothness. When the data do not change significantly, all original data should be treated with caution. And such data may be deleted if necessary. When the data distribution is suitable for prediction, the posterior difference will increase if the number of groups is too small. So selecting the appropriate grouping number is the key factor. In this chapter, group 7 is the most appropriate choice.

- Markov model

Accuracy: With the increase of threshold, the predicted range of Markov model method is shrinking. At the same time, OHRM is decreasing due to the reduction of the forecast range. In particular, OHRM will greatly change when the selection of threshold can affect the predicting range of latitude and longitude at the same time. UHRM is the ratio of OHRM to the area of the predicted range, which is also a key measure of the appropriate threshold selection. UHRM increases with the increasing of thresholds. The smaller the threshold is, the greater the impact of predicted area on UHRM is. When the threshold is larger, the impact of OHRM on UHRM is stronger. The results show that OHRM or UHRM is the most appropriate one when the threshold is 0.15.

- The comparisons between PGX and Markov model

Through the comprehensive experiments, Grey model and Markov model are used to predict the trajectory of typhoon, respectively. The results show that Grey model is superior obviously to Markov model in both time consumption and the memory consumption. What's more, Markov model is slightly better than Grey model in UHRM. However, it's necessary to consider the division of States and threshold selection according to different situations when applying the Markov model into practice. As a consequence, it's more complicated than the Grey model. Therefore, Grey model is better than Markov model on the prediction of uncertain spatiotemporal data.

To sum up, we can draw the following conclusions:

i. PGX, the more predicted groups, the smaller consistency and the relative errors are;
ii. PGX, the distribution of the original data has a great impact on the posterior difference. When selecting the original data, we should pay attention to the unregulated data and select the appropriate group number;
iii. In Markov model, the selection of the thresholds has a great impact on UHRM which is dataset oriented. The thresholds should not be too large or too small when setting a threshold.
iv. Markov model is slightly better than Grey model in UHRM, while Grey model is superior to Markov model significantly in terms of time consumption and memory usage. Therefore, Grey model method has excellent performance in the prediction of uncertain spatiotemporal data.
v. PGX can ensure the predicted accuracy and at the same time improve the storage and query performance of uncertain spatiotemporal data effectively.

6 SUMMARY

This chapter proposes an approach called PGX which predicts uncertain spatiotemporal data by integrating grey dynamic model with XML. Considering the multilayered information of uncertain spatiotemporal data as well as its hierarchical representation, we establish several groups of experiments to show its advantages. Firstly, uncertain spatiotemporal XML model grows fast and has a large storage capacity, which makes it adaptable to acclimatize to the long-term expansion of database. Secondly, experimental results show that PGX achieves a minimum mean accuracy of 0.5% in a short time. Markov' *UHRM* is better about 1.0% than that in PGX, but the *State* of matrix of Markov needs to be changed dynamically as memory consumption increases, while PGX doesn't need any transformation. Finally, compared with the traditional database storage, PGX has the advantages in querying time over relational database. The experimental results show that PGX can effectively improve the efficiency of information storage and retrieval when the experimental predicted accuracy (with a relative error between 5% and 0.5%) is guaranteed. What's more, the query time based on XML is 86.94% shorter than SQL Server. In conclusion, PGX performed well in the prediction of uncertain spatiotemporal data in our study.

REFERENCES

Bai, L. Y., Yan, L., & Ma, Z. M. (2017). Interpolation and Prediction of Spatiotemporal Data Based on XML Integrated with Grey Dynamic Model. *ISPRS International Journal of Geo-Information*, *6*(4), 1–14. doi:10.3390/ijgi6040113

Boulila, W., Farah, I. R., & Saheb Ettabaa, K. (2011). A data mining based approach to predict spatio-temporal changes in satellite images. *International Journal of Applied Earth Observation and Geoinformation*, *13*(3), 386–395. doi:10.1016/j.jag.2011.01.008

Chang, C. J., Li, D. C., Huang, Y. H., & Chen, C.-C. (2015). A novel gray forecasting model based on the box plot for small manufacturing data sets. *Applied Mathematics and Computation*, *265*, 400–408. doi:10.1016/j.amc.2015.05.006

Chen, Y. F., & Wang, L. (2017). Traffic Flow Prediction with Big Data: A Deep Learning based Time Series Model. In *Proceedings of the 2017 IEEE Conference on Computer Communications*, (pp. 1-2). IEEE. 10.1109/INFCOMW.2017.8116535

Cheng, T., & Wang, J. Q. (2008). Integrated Spatio-temporal Data Mining for Forest Fire Prediction. *Transactions in GIS*, *12*(5), 591–611. doi:10.1111/j.1467-9671.2008.01117.x

Clark, S. (2003). Traffic prediction using multivariate nonparametric regression. *Journal of Transportation Engineering*, *129*(2), 161–168. doi:10.1061/(ASCE)0733-947X(2003)129:2(161)

Froelich, W., & Salmeron, J. L. (2014). Evolutionary learning of fuzzy grey cognitive maps for the forecasting of multivariate, interval-valued time series. *International Journal of Approximate Reasoning*, *55*(6), 1319–1335. doi:10.1016/j.ijar.2014.02.006

Hamzacebi, C., & Es, H. A. (2014). Forecasting the annual electricity consumption of Turkey using an optimized grey model. *Energy*, *70*, 165–171. doi:10.1016/j.energy.2014.03.105

Haworth, J., & Cheng, T. (2012). Non-parametric regression for space–time forecasting under missing data. *Computers, Environment and Urban Systems*, *36*(6), 538–550. doi:10.1016/j.compenvurbsys.2012.08.005

Hu, Y. C., & Jiang, P. (2017). Forecasting energy demand using neural-network-based grey residual modification models. *The Journal of the Operational Research Society*, *68*(5), 556–565. doi:10.105741274-016-0130-2

Jeon, G., Jung, M. Y., Anisetti, M., Bellandi, V., Damiani, E., & Jeong, J. (2010). Specification of the geometric regularity model for fuzzy if-then rule-based deinterlacing. *Journal of Display Technology*, *6*(6), 235–243. doi:10.1109/JDT.2009.2037524

Jeung, H., Liu, Q., & Shen, H. T. (2008). A hybrid prediction model for moving objects. In *Proceedings of the ICDE*, (pp. 70-79). IEEE. 10.1109/ICDE.2008.4497415

Jeung, H., Yiu, M. L., Zhou, X. F., & Jensen, C. S. (2010). Path prediction and predictive range querying in road network databases. *The VLDB Journal*, *19*(4), 585–602. doi:10.100700778-010-0181-y

Kuang, H. B., Bashar, M. A., & Hipel, K. W. (2015). Grey-based preference in a graph model for conflict resolution with multiple decision makers. *IEEE Transactions on Systems, Man, and Cybernetics. Systems*, *45*(9), 1254–1267. doi:10.1109/TSMC.2014.2387096

Kumar, U., & Jain, V. K. (2010). Time series models (Grey-Markov, Grey Model with rolling mechanism and singular spectrum analysis) to forecast energy consumption in India. *Energy*, *35*(4), 1709–1716. doi:10.1016/j.energy.2009.12.021

Le Coz, J., Renard, B., Bonnifait, L., Branger, F., & Le Boursicaud, R. (2014). Combining hydraulic knowledge and uncertain gaugings in the estimation of hydrometric rating curves: A Bayesian approach. *Journal of Hydrology (Amsterdam)*, *509*, 573–587. doi:10.1016/j.jhydrol.2013.11.016

Lei, P. R., Shen, T. J., & Peng, W. C. (2011). Exploring spatial-temporal trajectory model for location prediction. In *Proceedings of the 12th IEEE International Conference on Mobile Data Management (MDM)*, (pp. 58-67). IEEE. 10.1109/MDM.2011.61

Li, T., & Ma, Z. M. (2017). Object-stack: An object-oriented approach for top-k keyword querying over fuzzy XML. *Information Systems Frontiers*, *19*(3), 669–697. doi:10.100710796-017-9748-0

Liu, J. F., Liu, S. F., & Fang, Z. G. (2014). New strengthening buffer operators based on adjustable intensity and their applications. *Journal of Grey System*, *26*(3), 117–126.

Liu, S. F., Forrest, J., & Yang, Y. J. (2012). A brief introduction to grey systems theory. *Grey Systems: Theory and Application*, *2*(2), 89–104. doi:10.1108/20439371211260081

Lv, Y. H., Duan, Y. J., & Kang, W. W. (2015). Traffic flow prediction with big data: A deep learning approach. *IEEE Transactions on Intelligent Transportation Systems*, *16*(2), 865–873.

Ma, X., & Liu, Z. B. (2018). The kernel-based nonlinear multivariate grey model. *Applied Mathematical Modelling*, *56*, 217–238. doi:10.1016/j.apm.2017.12.010

Ma, X. L., Dai, Z., He, Z. B., Ma, J., Wang, Y., & Wang, Y. (2017). Learning traffic as images: A deep convolutional neural network for large-scale transportation network speed prediction. *Sensors (Basel)*, *17*(4), 818. doi:10.339017040818 PMID:28394270

Ma, Z. M., Bai, L. Y., Ishikawa, Y., & Yan, L. (2017). Consistencies of fuzzy spatiotemporal data in XML documents. *Fuzzy Sets and Systems.*

Ma, Z. M., & Yan, L. (2016). Modeling fuzzy data with XML: A survey. *Fuzzy Sets and Systems*, *301*, 146–159. doi:10.1016/j.fss.2015.09.016

Mathew, W., Raposo, R., & Martins, B. (2012). Predicting future locations with hidden Markov models. In *Proceedings of the 2012 ACM conference on ubiquitous computing* (pp. 911-918). ACM. 10.1145/2370216.2370421

McMillan, H., Freer, J., Pappenberger, F., Krueger, T., & Clark, M. (2010). Impacts of uncertain river flow data on rainfall-runoff model calibration and discharge predictions. *Hydrological Processes*, *24*(10), 1270–1284. doi:10.1002/hyp.7587

Morzy, M. (2007). Mining frequent trajectories of moving objects for location prediction. In *Proceedings of International Workshop on Machine Learning and Data Mining in Pattern Recognition* (pp. 667-680). ACM. 10.1007/978-3-540-73499-4_50

Qiao, S. J., Shen, D. Y., Wang, X. T., Han, N., & Zhu, W. (2015). A self-adaptive parameter selection trajectory prediction approach via hidden Markov models. *IEEE Transactions on Intelligent Transportation Systems*, *16*(1), 284–296. doi:10.1109/TITS.2014.2331758

Santos, M., Santos, J. A., & Fragoso, M. (2015). Historical damaging flood records for 1871–2011 in Northern Portugal and underlying atmospheric forcings. *Journal of Hydrology (Amsterdam)*, *530*, 591–603. doi:10.1016/j.jhydrol.2015.10.011

Shi, X. J., Chen, Z. R., & Wang, H. (2015). Convolutional LSTM network: A machine learning approach for precipitation nowcasting. In Proceedings of Advances in Neural Information Processing Systems (pp. 802-810). ACM.

Sun, G. D., Guan, X., Yi, X., & Zhou, Z. (2018). Grey relational analysis between hesitant fuzzy sets with applications to pattern recognition. *Expert Systems with Applications*, *92*, 521–532. doi:10.1016/j.eswa.2017.09.048

Tao, Y. F., Kollios, G., Considine, J., & Li, F. (2004). Spatio-temporal aggregation using sketches. In *Proceedings of the 20th International Conference on Data Engineering*. ACM.

Wang, Y. H. (2009). Using neural network to forecast stock index option price: A new hybrid GARCH approach. *Quality & Quantity*, *43*(5), 833–843. doi:10.100711135-008-9176-9

Wang, Y. H., Dang, Y. G., Li, Y. Q., & Liu, S. (2010). An approach to increase prediction precision of GM (1, 1) model based on optimization of the initial condition. *Expert Systems with Applications*, *37*(8), 5640–5644. doi:10.1016/j.eswa.2010.02.048

Wang, Y. H., Liu, Q., Tang, J. R., Cao, W., & Li, X. (2014). Optimization approach of background value and initial item for improving prediction precision of GM (1, 1) model. *Journal of Systems Engineering and Electronics*, *25*(1), 77–82. doi:10.1109/JSEE.2014.00009

Wang, Z. X., & Hao, P. (2016). An improved grey multivariable model for predicting industrial energy consumption in China. *Applied Mathematical Modelling*, *40*(11), 5745–5758. doi:10.1016/j.apm.2016.01.012

Wei, Y., & Hu, D. H. (2009). Deficiency of the smoothness condition and its remedy. *Systems Engineering-Theory & Practice*, *29*(8), 165–170. doi:10.1016/S1874-8651(10)60066-X

Wong, H. L., & Shiu, J. M. (2012). Comparisons of fuzzy time series and hybrid Grey model for non-stationary data forecasting. *Applied Mathematics & Information Sciences*, *4*, 409–416.

Wu, L. F., Liu, S. F., Cui, W., Liu, D.-L., & Yao, T.-X. (2014). Non-homogenous discrete grey model with fractional-order accumulation. *Neural Computing & Applications*, *25*(5), 1215–1221. doi:10.100700521-014-1605-1

Wu, L. F., Liu, S. F., & Wang, Y. N. (2012). Grey Lotka-Volterra model and its application. *Technological Forecasting and Social Change*, *79*(9), 1720–1730. doi:10.1016/j.techfore.2012.04.020

Wu, L. F., Liu, S. F., Yao, L. G., Yan, S., & Liu, D. (2013). Grey system model with the fractional order accumulation. *Communications in Nonlinear Science and Numerical Simulation*, *18*(7), 1775–1785. doi:10.1016/j.cnsns.2012.11.017

Xie, N. M., & Liu, S. F. (2009). Discrete grey forecasting model and its optimization. *Applied Mathematical Modelling*, *33*(2), 1173–1186. doi:10.1016/j.apm.2008.01.011

Xu, Z., Luo, X. F., & Liu, Y. H. (2016). From Latency, through Outbreak, to Decline: Detecting Different States of Emergency Events Using Web Resources. *IEEE Transactions on Big Data*.

Yang, J., Xu, J., & Xu, M. (2014). Predicting next location using a variable order Markov model. In *Proceedings of the 5th ACM SIGSPATIAL International Workshop on GeoStreaming* (pp. 37-42). ACM. 10.1145/2676552.2676557

Yang, Y. J., Liu, S. F., & John, R. (2014). Uncertainty representation of grey numbers and grey sets. *IEEE Transactions on Cybernetics*, *44*(9), 1508–1517. doi:10.1109/TCYB.2013.2288731 PMID:25137681

Yao, T. X., & Liu, S. F. (2009). Characteristics and optimization of discrete GM (1, 1) model. *Systems Engineering: Theory and Practice*, *29*(3), 142–148.

Ye, J., Dang, Y. G., & Li, B. J. (2018). Grey-Markov prediction model based on background value optimization and central-point triangular whitenization weight function. *Communications in Nonlinear Science and Numerical Simulation*, *54*, 320–330. doi:10.1016/j.cnsns.2017.06.004

Zeng, B., Meng, W., & Tong, M. Y. (2016). A self-adaptive intelligence grey predictive model with alterable structure and its application. *Engineering Applications of Artificial Intelligence*, *50*, 236–244. doi:10.1016/j.engappai.2015.12.011

Zeng, X. Y., Shu, L., Huang, G. M., & Jiang, J. (2016). Triangular fuzzy series forecasting based on grey model and neural network. *Applied Mathematical Modelling*, *40*(3), 1717–1727. doi:10.1016/j.apm.2015.08.009

Zhang, X., Jin, F., & Liu, P. D. (2013). A grey relational projection method for multi-attribute decision making based on intuitionistic trapezoidal fuzzy number. *Applied Mathematical Modelling*, *37*(5), 3467–3477. doi:10.1016/j.apm.2012.08.012

Zolotukhin, M., Ivannikova, E., & Hamalainen, T. (2013). Novel method for the prediction of mobile location based on temporal-spatial behavioral patterns. In *Proceedings of IEEE International Conference on Information Science and Technology (ICIST)* (pp. 761-766). IEEE. 10.1109/ICIST.2013.6747655

Chapter 17
Querying Uncertain Spatiotemporal Data Based on XML Twig Pattern

ABSTRACT

Query management of uncertain spatiotemporal data has become a hot spot nowadays. In the existing research, there are plenty of research works on general data, uncertain data, and spatiotemporal data query, but there are relatively few research results on uncertain spatiotemporal data query. Based on uncertain data, this chapter proposes Usd-Twig algorithm, which can query uncertain spatiotemporal data. By extending interval coding, the authors add spatiotemporal elements of uncertain data to represent uncertain spatiotemporal information, establish uncertain spatiotemporal data document tree, and redefine the relationship between father and son and ancestor-descendant among nodes. At the same time, the query process is discussed in detail by an example, which proves its feasibility and correctness. Finally, the complexity of the algorithm is analyzed.

1 INTRODUCTION

With the explosive growth of spatiotemporal information data, there are more and more researches on spatiotemporal data and the research on related technologies in spatiotemporal field develops rapidly. Spatiotemporal data have the semantic features of space (Balbiani et al., 2002), (Hu et al., 2013) and time (Claramunt et al., 1999), (Obeid et al., 2005). In the development of spatiotemporal data, several spatiotemporal data models have been proposed (Langran et al., 1992), (Pelekis et al.,2004), (Sözer et al., 2008), such as spatiotemporal composite data model, object-relational model and spatiotemporal object-oriented data model. Nowadays, there are a lot of imprecise and uncertain information in the concrete application of many fields in the society. With the wide application of uncertain spatiotemporal data, the traditional data (i.e., conventional data) model is poor and powerless in dealing with related problems (Bai, 2013). At present, the modeling of uncertain spatiotemporal data (Emrich et al., 2012), (Senellart et al., 2007), (Emrich et al., 2012) has also been studied.

DOI: 10.4018/978-1-6684-9108-9.ch017

XML query technology has been the focus of many international and domestic research. At present, a large number of XML query theories have been proposed (Bruno et al., 2002), (Liu et al., 2011), (Liu et al., 2013), (Liu et al., 2014), (Liu et al., 2013), such as global matching theory, binary structure join theory and approximate query processing theory. In addition, some researchers focus on querying temporal data with XML (Nørvag et al.,2002), (Rizzolo et al., 2008), but there is little research on spatiotemporal query (Bai et al., 2014). The temporal data model based on XML can process the temporal data well and manage the temporal data effectively (Ye et al., 2007). In the literature (Ye et al., 2007), (Zhang et al., 2009), (Rizzolo et al., 2008) the research results of XML-based temporal data model by domestic and foreign researchers in recent years are fully displayed. For querying tree-like data like XML, many kinds of XML query languages have been proposed, such as XML-QL, Lorell, Quilt, XPath and XQuery. Although these query languages have their own characteristics, a common feature is that they take path expression as their core content, and users can use path expression to describe their positioning in XML data hierarchy. Path expressions in XML queries can be expressed as tree queries that independently describe query requirements. XML data query is mainly divided into single path query and multi-branch path query. In both of these path queries, XML queries can be represented as twig pattern queries. Due to the semi-structured and ordered characteristics of XML data, the application of complex Twig Query for XML data is more and more, and it has been paid more and more attention by researchers. In (Bai et al., 2013), Bai et al. measured fuzzy spatiotemporal XML data through five dimensions: OID, ATTR, FP, FT and FM. On this basis, Bai et al. (Bai et al., 2017) proposed a fast Twig query of leaf root based on XML spatiotemporal data.

In this chapter, firstly, we use extended interval coding to add spatiotemporal attributes on the basis of uncertain data, so as to combine the uncertainty and spatiotemporal characteristics of data. On this basis, aiming at how to quickly extract the information required by users from massive data streams, this chapter proposes a new algorithm based on the previous Twig query of uncertain data, which can query uncertain spatiotemporal data.

The rest contents of this chapter are as follows: Section 2 based on uncertain data through extended interval coding, and established the relevant document tree. A seven-tuple (DocId, LPos: RPos, LNum, Uncertain, Time, Space, Sequence) is used to represent the coding information of Uncertain spatiotemporal data nodes, In section 3, the Usd-Twig algorithm is proposed on the basis of extended interval coding and connected stack. This algorithm performs root traversal on the document tree, filters some node combinations with low probability through probability threshold after generating intermediate results, and finally outputs results conforming to Twig motion. In section 5, the correctness and possibility of the algorithm are proved in detail by an example, and the complexity of the algorithm is simply analyzed. Finally, this chapter is concluded.

2 NODE CODING OF UNCERTAIN SPATIOTEMPORAL DATA

In this chapter, the research of uncertain spatiotemporal data query method is mainly focused on Twig query problem. The core operation of the Twig query problem is to query a document fragment from uncertain spatiotemporal data that is consistent with Twig schema, contains multiple query nodes and satisfies a certain structural relationship.

Usually, we use Twig mode to express the nodes and the structural relationship between nodes. The key of Twig query is to encode the uncertain spatiotemporal data, because the structural relationship between nodes can be directly judged by using the encoded information. Based on the extended coding mode, the structural relationship among nodes in the uncertain spatiotemporal data document tree can be determined.

Interval coding is usually used to represent general data, also called conventional data, that is, certain general data without spatiotemporal attributes. Interval coding is mainly used for retrieval, which traverses the document tree first, and then every node in the document tree is represented by a set of integer values. At this time, this integer interval contains the coding range of the descendants of the node, and the structural relationship between nodes can be judged by the information contained in its integer interval.

Generally, a triple (Start, End, Depth) is used to represent the interval coding information of nodes, where:

Start is the sequence number information generated when the node is accessed for the first time during the first root traversal of the document tree;

End is the order value when the node is visited for the second time when the root first traverses a subtree of the document tree and then continues to trace back to the subtree;

Depth indicates the number of layers at which the nodes are located (the root node is Level 1).

Definition 1. Let the interval coding information of nodes A and B be known. At this time,

1. If A.End < B.Start, then A comes before B;
2. If A.Start < B.Start and A.End > B.End, then A is the ancestor node of B;
3. If A.Start < B.Start, A.End > B.End and A.depth+1=B.depth, then A is the parent node of B;
4. If A.Start > B.Start and A.End < B.End, then A is the descendant node of B;
5. If A.Start > B.Start A.End < B.End and A.depth-1=B.depth, then A is a child node of B;
6. If A.Start > B.End, then A is after B.

Figure 1. Relationships of region schemes of nodes

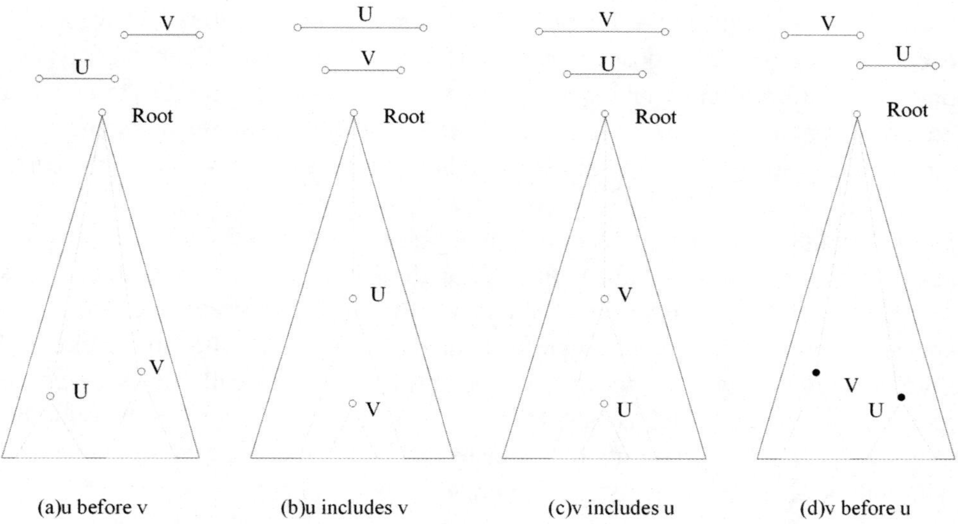

As shown in Figure 1, the relationship between any two nodes has two cases: completely disjoint and completely inclusive. Figures 1 (a) and (d) indicate that the relationship between any two nodes is completely disjoint, and Figures 1 (b) and (c) indicate that the relationship between any two nodes is completely inclusive.

In uncertain spatiotemporal data, the above region coding mode cannot effectively support Twig query of location nodes in uncertain spatiotemporal model tree, so it has great limitations. For example, because the above-mentioned region coding mode does not contain the uncertainty and spatiotemporal information of data, it is impossible to effectively distinguish conventional nodes, possible nodes and uncertain spatiotemporal nodes by this interval coding. Therefore, an extended region coding scheme is proposed in this chapter, which adds new attribute segments to represent node information and node properties on the basis of the original interval coding, so as to support Twig query of uncertain spatiotemporal data. Specifically, a seven-tuple (DI, LPos: RPos, LNum, Uncertain, Time, Space, Sequence) is used to represent the coding information of Uncertain spatiotemporal data nodes.

1. DI is the identity of the document;
2. LPos and RPos number the document tree in strict order. LPos is the sequence number information generated when the node is accessed for the first time when the document tree is accessed sequentially by using the method of first root traversal, and RPos is the sequence number information generated when the node is accessed again according to the retrospective order after traversing all the descendants of the node. Let the values of leaf node LPos and RPos be equal, that is, LPos = RPos;
3. LNum identifies the number of layers in which nodes are located. The root node is the first layer, and LNum will be added by 1 every next layer;
4. Uncertain identifies the properties of nodes (distinguishing deterministic nodes from uncertain nodes). If Uncertain=1, it means that the node is an Uncertain node. If Uncertain=0, it means that the node is deterministic.
5. Time identifies the time nature of a node and is a Boolean information. If Time=1, it means that the node has Time attribute; If Time=0, it means that the node does not have Time attribute;
6. Space identifies the spatial properties of nodes and is a Boolean information. If Space=1, it means that the node has spatial attributes; If Space=0, it means that the node does not have spatial attributes;
7. Sequence is an ordered set of possible nodes, which is used to store the names, types and spatiotemporal information of uncertain spatiotemporal nodes passing through the path from the root node to the current node when the first root traverses the document tree. Sequence is empty when there are no uncertain spatiotemporal nodes in the path from the root node to the current node.

Figure 2 is an example of extended interval coding based on uncertain spatiotemporal data, in which circles represent conventional node information; Triangle denotes the information of nodes with only uncertain quality, and calls such nodes uncertain nodes; Rectangle represents the information of nodes with both uncertain and spatiotemporal properties, and such nodes are called uncertain spatiotemporal nodes. The tag value beside the line between the parent node and the child node represents the probability value of the child node, which is called the path probability. If the path probability between CV_0 and T_1 is 0.5, it means that the probability of T_1 existence is 0.5. What needs to be explained here is that the default sibling nodes in this chapter are independent relationships.

Figure 2. An extended region labeling tree

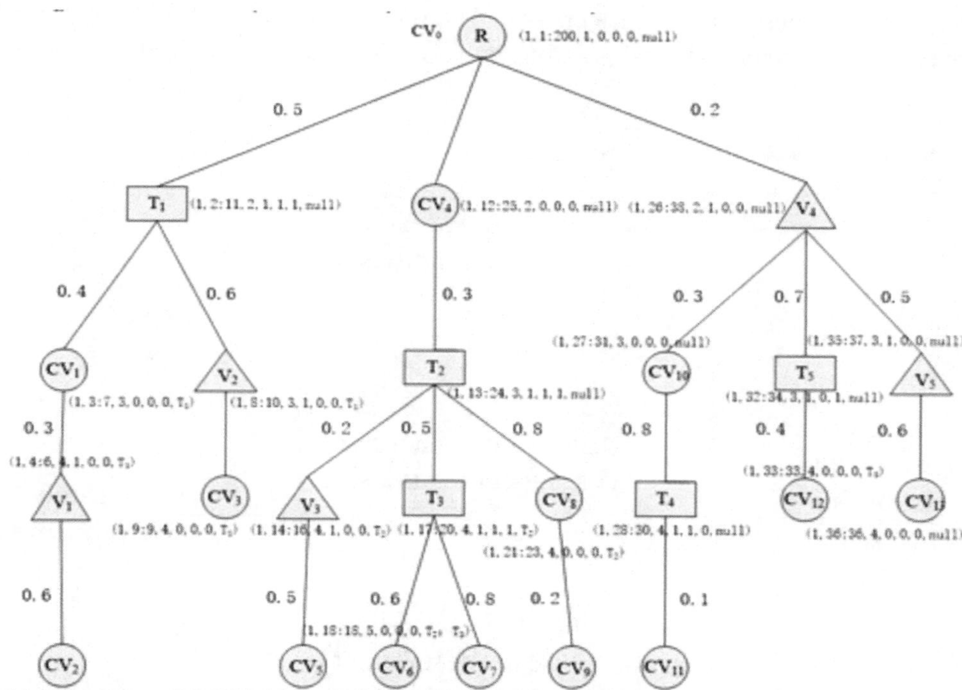

Because the document tree contains both uncertain nodes and uncertain spatiotemporal nodes, the structural relationship between nodes can no longer be simply limited to the relationship between conventional nodes, but needs to be refined. Therefore, we redefine and refine all kinds of relationships on the basis of extending interval coding, so as to judge the structural relationships among nodes in the new document tree. The following is the definition of the structural relationship between nodes:

Definition 2. Let $Node_1$, $Node_i$ and $Node_n$ represent different nodes respectively, and the specific coding information of the three nodes is as follows:

$$Node_1\left(D_1, L_1 : R_1, LN_1, U_1, UT_1, US_1, Sq_1\right)$$

$$Node_i\left(D_i, L_i : R_i, LN_i, U_i, UT_i, US_i, Sq_i\right)$$

$$Node_n\left(D_n, L_n : R_n, LN_n, U_n, UT_n, US_n, Sq_n\right)$$

$1 \leq i \leq n$, denoting node coding information in an uncertain spatiotemporal document tree given an extended region coding mode, respectively. The following are definitions of various relationships.

(1) Ancestor- descendant relationship A

In the uncertain spatiotemporal data document tree, due to the different attributes of nodes, the ancestor-descendant relationship can be further divided into conventional ancestor-descendant relationship, uncertain ancestor-descendant relationship and uncertain spatiotemporal ancestor-descendant relationship.

Figure 3. Ancestor-descendant relationship diagram

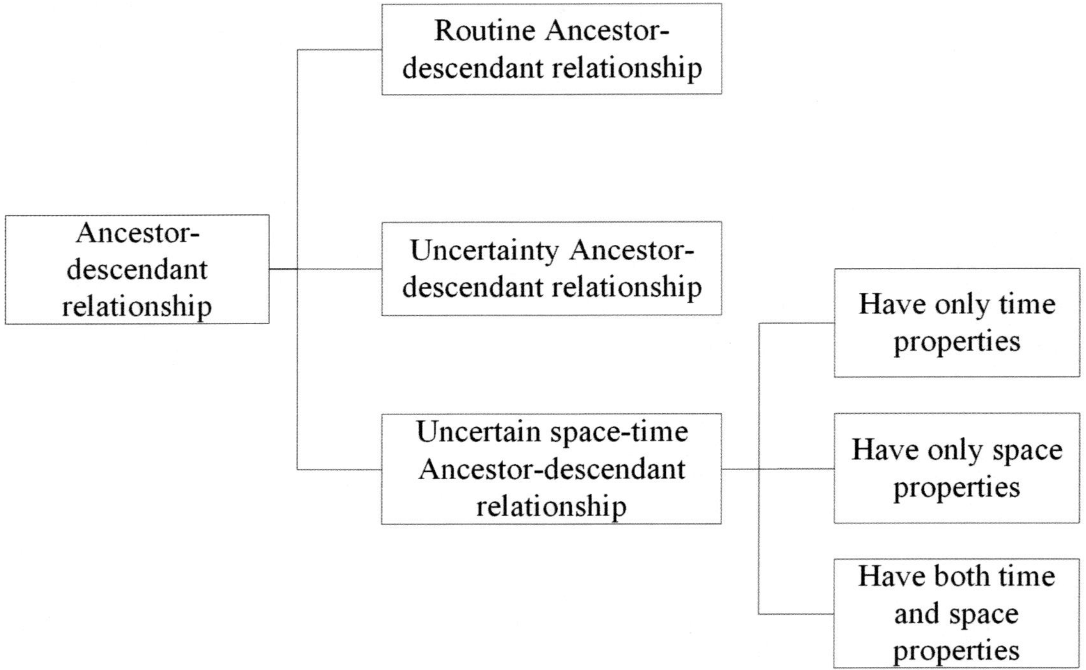

1. If $D_1=D_i$, $L_1<L_i$, $R_i<R_1$, $U_2\cap U_k\cap U_{i-1}=0$ $(2 \le k \le i\text{-}1)$, $U_1\cup U_i=1$, $UT_1\cup UT_i=0$, $US_1\cup US_i=0$, then $Node_i$ is the descendant node of $Node_1$, and there is a conventional ancestor-descendant relationship (RAD) between them;
2. If $D_1=D_i$, $L_1<L_i$, $R_i<R_1$, $U_2\cap U_k\cap U_{i-1}=0$ $(2 \le k \le i\text{-}1)$, $U_1\cup U_i=1$, $UT_1\cup UT_i=0$, $US_1\cup US_i=0$, then $Node_i$ is the descendant node of $Node_1$, and there is an uncertain ancestor-descendant relationship (UAD) between them;
3. If $D_1=D_i$, $L_1<L_i$, $R_i<R_1$, $U_2\cap U_k\cap U_{i-1}=0$ $(2 \le k \le i\text{-}1)$, $U_1\cup U_i=1$, $(UT_1\cup UT_i=1) \cup (US_1\cup US_i=1)$, then $Node_i$ is the descendant node of $Node_1$, and there is an uncertain spatiotemporal ancestor-descendant relationship (SAD) between them, which can be subdivided into the following three types:
    1) If $D_1=D_i$, $L_1<L_i$, $R_i<R_1$, $U_2\cap U_k\cap U_{i-1}=0$ $(2 \le k \le i\text{-}1)$, $U_1\cup U_i=1$, $UT_1\cup UT_i=1$, $US_1\cup US_i=0$, then $Node_i$ is the descendant node of $Node_1$, and there is an uncertain spatiotemporal ancestor-descendant relationship between them only with time attributes;
    2) If $D_1=D_i$, $L_1<L_i$, $R_i<R_1$, $U_2\cap U_k\cap U_{i-1}=0$ $(2 \le k \le i\text{-}1)$, $U_1\cup U_i=1$, $UT_1\cup UT_i=0$, $US_1\cup US_i=1$, then $Node_i$ is the descendant node of $Node_1$, and there is an uncertain spatiotemporal ancestor-descendant relationship between them only with spatial attributes;

3) If $D_1=D_i$, $L_1<L_i$, $R_i<R_1$, $U_2 \cap U_k \cap U_{i-1}=0$ $(2 \leq k \leq i\text{-}1)$, $U_1 \cup U_i=1$, $UT_1 \cup UT_i=1$, $US_1 \cup US_i=1$, then $Node_i$ is the descendant node of $Node_1$, and there is an uncertain spatiotemporal ancestor-descendant relationship between them with both temporal and spatial attributes;

It can be seen that there are three kinds of uncertain spatiotemporal ancestor-descendant relations: uncertain ancestor-descendant relations with only temporal attributes, uncertain ancestor-descendant relations with only spatial attributes and uncertain ancestor-descendant relations with both temporal and spatial attributes, which are collectively called uncertain spatiotemporal ancestor-descendant relations.

(2) Parent-child relationship

Parent-child relationship (PC) in uncertain spatiotemporal data document tree can be further divided into real parent-child relationship (RPC), uncertain parent-child relationship (UPC) and uncertain spatiotemporal parent-child relationship (SPC).

The uncertain spatiotemporal parent-child relationship can be subdivided into:

① Uncertain father-son relationship with only time attribute;
② Uncertain father-son relationship with spatial attribute only;
③ Uncertain parent-child relationship with both temporal and spatial attributes.

The specific classification is shown in Figure 4 on the following page.

Figure 4. Parent and child relationship diagram

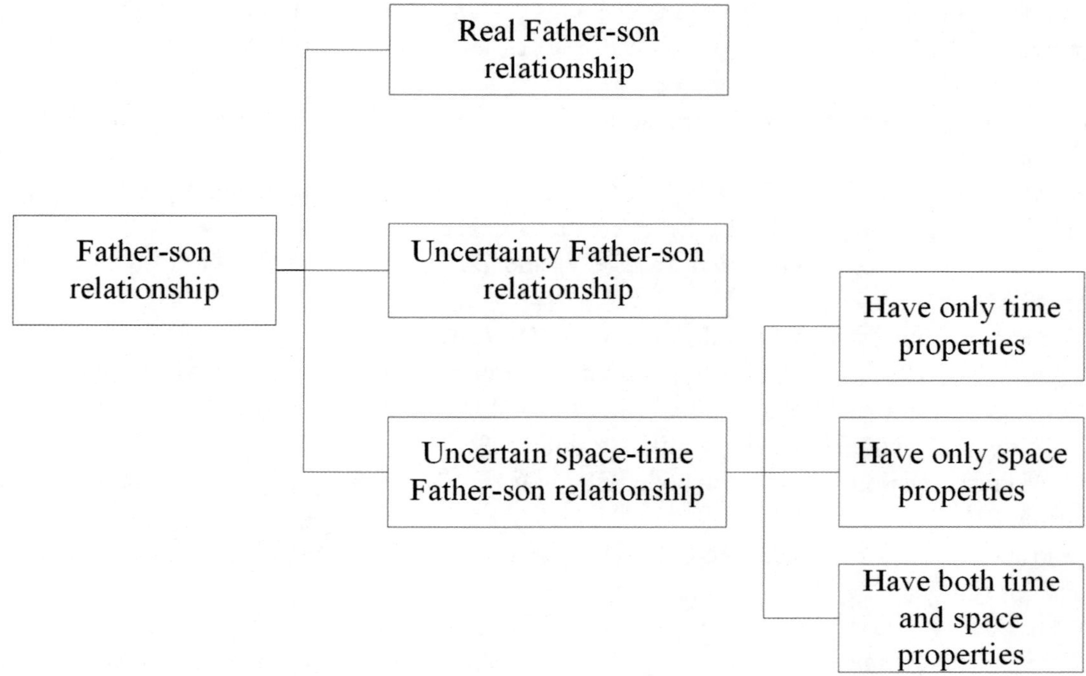

1. If $D_1=D_i$, $L_1<L_i$, $R_i<R_1$, $U_1 \cup U_i=0$, $LN_1+1=LN_i$, then $Node_1$ is the regular parent node of $Node_i$, and the real parent-child relationship (RPC) between them;
2. If $D_1=D_n$, $L_1<L_n$, $R_n<R_1$, $U_1 \cup U_n=0$, $LN_1+i=LN_n$, then $Node_1$ is the regular parent node of $Node_n$, and the real parent-child relationship (RPC) between them is established;
3. If $D_1=D_i$, $L_1<L_i$, $R_i<R_1$, $U_1 \cup U_i=1$, $LN_1+1=LN_i$, $UT_1 \cup UT_i=0$, $US_1 \cup US_i=0$, then $Node_1$ is the uncertain parent node of $Node_i$, and there is an uncertain parent-child relationship (UPC) between them;
4. If $D_1=D_i$, $L_1<L_i$, $R_i<R_1$, $U_1 \cup U_i=1$, $(UT_1 \cup UT_i=1) \cup (US_1 \cup US_i=1)$, $LN_1+1=LN_i$, then Node1 is the uncertain spatiotemporal parent node of $Node_i$, and there is an uncertain spatiotemporal parent-child relationship (SPC) between them, which can be subdivided into the following three types:
   1) If $D_1=D_i$, $L_1<L_i$, $R_i<R_1$, $U_1 \cup U_i=1$, $UT_1 \cup UT_i=1$, $US_1 \cup US_i=0$, $LN_1+1=LN_i$, then $Node_1$ is the uncertain spatiotemporal parent node of $Node_i$, and there is an uncertain spatiotemporal parent-child relationship between them only with time attributes;
   2) If $D_1=D_i$, $L_1<L_i$, $R_i<R_1$, $U_1 \cup U_i=1$, $UT_1 \cup UT_i=0$, $US_1 \cup US_i=1$, $LN_1+1=LN_i$, then $Node_1$ is the uncertain spatiotemporal parent node of $Node_i$, and there is an uncertain spatiotemporal parent-child relationship between them only with spatial attributes;
   3) If $D_1=D_i$, $L_1<L_i$, $R_i<R_1$, $U_1 \cup U_i=1$, $UT_1 \cup UT_i=1$, $US_1 \cup US_i=1$, $LN_1+1=LN_i$, then $Node_1$ is the uncertain spatiotemporal parent node of $Node_i$, and there is an uncertain spatiotemporal parent-child relationship between them with both temporal and spatial attributes;

From the above definitions, we can see that there are three kinds of uncertain spatiotemporal parent-child relationships: uncertain parent-child relationships with only temporal attributes, uncertain parent-child relationships with only spatial attributes and uncertain parent-child relationships with both temporal and spatial attributes. Of course, the three are collectively referred to as uncertain time-space parent-child relationship.

An example is given to illustrate the structural relationship between the above extended coding scheme and nodes:

According to definition 2, nodes CV_0, …, CV_{13} are conventional nodes, nodes V_1, V_2, V_3, V_4, V_5 are uncertain nodes, and nodes T_1, T_2, T_3, T_4, T_5 are uncertain space-time nodes;

The structural relationship between nodes CV_0 and CV_9 is conventional ancestor-descendant relationship (RAD).

CV_0 and V_3 are uncertain ancestral-progeny (UAD) relationships;

CV_0 and T_3 are uncertain spatiotemporal ancestral-progeny relationships (SAD), CV_0 and T_4 are uncertain ancestral-progeny relationships with temporal attributes only, and CV_0 and T_5 are uncertain ancestral-progeny relationships with spatial attributes only.

The structural relationship between nodes $CV_1 \leftrightarrow CV_2$, $CV_4 \leftrightarrow CV_5$, $CV_8 \leftrightarrow CV_9$ is real parent-child relationship (RPC) respectively.

The structural relationships between nodes $CV_1 \leftrightarrow V_1$, $V_2 \leftrightarrow CV_3$, $V_4 \leftrightarrow V_5$ are uncertain parent-child relationships (UPC);

The structural relationships among nodes $T_1 \leftrightarrow CV_1$, $CV_4 \leftrightarrow T_2$, $T_2 \leftrightarrow V_3$, $T_2 \leftrightarrow T_3$, $V_4 \leftrightarrow T_5$, $CV_{10} \leftrightarrow T_4$ are respectively uncertain spatiotemporal parent-child relationships (TPC), in which $V_4 \leftrightarrow T_5$ is an uncertain parent-child relationship with only spatial attributes and $CV_{10} \leftrightarrow T_4$ is an uncertain parent-child relationship with only temporal attributes.

3 TWIG QUERY FOR UNCERTAIN SPATIOTEMPORAL DATA

This section will focus on the Twig query of uncertain spatiotemporal data based on extended interval coding. The extended interval coding can directly judge the ancestral-descendant relationship between two nodes, without traversing other unrelated nodes between these two nodes, which is as easy as judging the parent-child relationship and can be completed in a constant time. The following first introduces the related foundation involved in the query algorithm, and then gives the algorithm implementation.

For the convenience of the following description, some basic terms are explained first. For each query node in the Twig mode query, it is denoted as q. The stack corresponding to the query node q is denoted as S_q, and the node stream corresponding to the query node q is denoted as T_q. The node stream T_q is an interval-coded ordered list of all data nodes corresponding to the query node q in the data stream T of the uncertain spatiotemporal data document. The data nodes here include element nodes and attribute nodes in the uncertain spatiotemporal data document tree. The interval code of data node extension is (DocId, LPos: RPos, LNum, Uncertain, Time, Space, Sequence), and all data nodes of node stream T_q are arranged in ascending order of (DocId, LPos).

3.1 Connected Stack

Connected stacks refer to multiple stacks connected to form a chain structure. The algorithm associates a stack for each node in Twig. The algorithm always satisfies during execution:

(1) Each node in the stack satisfies the predicate of the corresponding node on the Twig pattern.
(2) Every node in the stack, from the bottom of the stack to the top of the stack, appears in a path from the root node to the leaf node in an uncertain spatiotemporal data document tree.
(3) Only when there are directly connected edges between nodes in Twig mode can there be connections between corresponding stacks. Moreover, the connection always points from the stack corresponding to the child node to the stack corresponding to the parent node.
(4) If there is a connection from node B1 in stack S_B to node A1 in stack S_A, it means that A1 is the nearest ancestor node satisfying the predicate A in uncertain spatiotemporal data documents.

Figure 5. Overall and partial of the Twig pattern

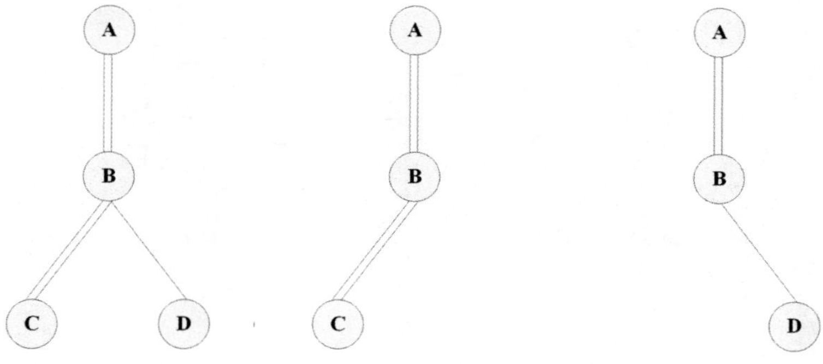

(a) twig mode (b) Left part of twig mode (c) Right part of twig mode

Through such a set of connected stacks, along the stack-to-stack connections, you can get an intermediate result that matches the path from the root node to the leaf node in Twig pattern.

As shown in Figure 5, Figure (a) shows a Twig pattern, and Figure (b) and Figure (c) show a path in the Twig of Figure (a), which are called left part and right part respectively. In the process of query processing, according to Figure (b) and Figure (c), the results matched by query are intermediate results, which need to be merged and connected through certain principles to get the final results. The principle of merging connection is to merge and connect the generated intermediate results according to their same common nodes, that is, nodes that exist in both paths. It should be noted that because there are many paths in a Twig pattern, it is necessary to merge and join in pairs. After several such processes, the final result matches the whole Twig pattern.

As shown in Figure 6, during Twig query processing of a simple document tree, the intermediate results are compressed and stored in the connected stack. Figure (a) is a path from root node to leaf node of uncertain spatiotemporal data document tree, and Figure (b) is similar. A1 denotes a node that satisfies the predicate for Node A in Figure 5, and B1, B2, C1, C2, D1 are similar. As shown in the above figure (b), it is the stack connected at a certain time during the left local processing of Twig mode in Figure 5. The relationship between node elements in the two stacks connected by arrows is ancestor-descendant relationship, the relationship between node elements in the two stacks connected by dotted lines is parent-child relationship, and the relationship between two adjacent node elements in each stack is also parent-child relationship. The connected stack contains one query result: (A1, B2, C2). Similarly, Figure (d) is the connected stack at a certain time during the right part processing of Twig mode in Figure 5, and the connected stack contains one query result: (A1, B2, D1).

Figure 6. An example of linked stacks

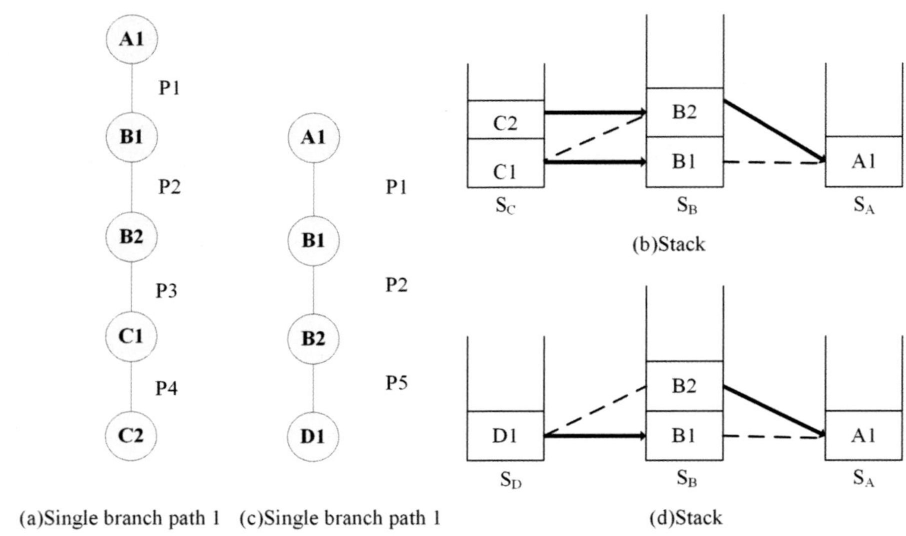

Take (A1, B2, D1) as an example, it is obtained in this way. C1 is the predicate that satisfies C in the Twig schema shown in Figure 5, so D1 is placed in the stack S_D. B1 and B2 are predicates that satisfy B in the Twig schema, so B1 and B2 are placed in the stack S_B, and because B1 is the ancestor of B2, B1 is below B2. Similarly, A1 is a predicate that satisfies A in Twig schema, so A1 is placed in stack S_A. A1 is the closest ancestor node to B2, so B2 points to A1 in S_A with an arrow. D1 points to B1 in S_B with an arrow, indicating that B1 is the nearest ancestor node that satisfies the predicate of B. A1 is the parent node of B1, so connect A1 and B1, B2 and D1 with a dotted line, similar. Therefore, A1, B2 and D1 are predicates satisfying A, B and C respectively, and the pairwise satisfy the structural relationship of Twig schema, so they are a correct query result.

Through each set of connected stacks, along the stack-to-stack connections, the result that matches the path from root node to leaf node in Twig pattern is only an intermediate result. If (A1, B2, C2) and (A1, B2, D1) are only the intermediate results of the Twig pattern that the user wants to query in Figure (a), they need to be connected to form the final result. It can be seen that the common nodes of (A1, B2, C2) and (A1, B2, D1) are A1 and B2, so the two sets of results are connected into (A1, B2, C2, D1) through the common node, that is, the final result.

3.2 Probability Calculation of Twig Query

Let $P_{whole} = \prod_{k=1}^{n} p_k$, P_{whole} be the probability of combining a group of nodes after Twig query, and pk be the relative probability between two element nodes, just like the probability on the path in Figure (b) and Figure (c). For example, the probability of node combination (A1, B2, C2) is $P_{(A1, B2, C2)} = p_1 \times p_2 \times p_3 \times p_4$, and the probability of (A1, B2, D1) is similar.

Attention should be paid to the calculation of repeated paths when calculating the probability of connecting intermediate results to form a final result. The probability calculation method of two connectable intermediate result connections is $P_{whole} = P(a) \times P(b)/P(com)$. Where a and b are two intermediate results to be connected respectively, P (a) and P (b) are their path probabilities respectively, com is the node element common to the two intermediate results a and b, and P (com) is its path probability.

For example, when calculating the probability of (A1, B2, C2, D1), it can be calculated by the formula $P_{whole} = \prod_{k=1}^{n} p_k$, that is, $P_{(A1, B2, C2, D2)} = p_1 \times p_2 \times p_3 \times p_4 \times p_5$, or by the probability of two intermediate results, that is, $P_{(A1, B2, C2)}$ and $P_{(A1, B2, D1)}$: $P_{(A1, B2, C2, D2)} = P_{(A1, B2, C2)} \times P_{(A1, B2, D1)} / P_{(A1, B2)}$.

3.3 Probability Threshold

In a document tree with uncertain information, some results obtained by querying according to a certain Twig pattern are of little use to users because of their low possibility, that is to say, even if these results are queried, users do not need them. Then which result probability value will satisfy the user and keep the result, and which result probability value will be discarded because it is lower than the user's expected probability value, at this time, it needs quantitative judgment. This quantization standard is the probability threshold. The definition of probability threshold is given below.

Definition 3. (Probability Threshold) In the Twig mode query for documents with uncertain information, the user sets an expected probability value for the query results to express his need for the probability value of the results. The results below this expected value are discarded because they cannot meet the user's needs, and only those above this expected probability value can be retained as the final results, so the expected probability value for the query results is called probability threshold.

In addition, it should be noted that, in addition to discarding the final results lower than the probability threshold given by the user, that if the probability of some intermediate results is lower than the probability threshold given by the user, they can be discarded directly without waiting for connection. Because even if they are connected to the final result, the probability of the final result will be less than the probability threshold, so such intermediate results can be discarded before connection.

Probability threshold is very helpful to solve the problem of choosing or rejecting Twig query results of documents with uncertain information, because the query results of documents with uncertain information are not as certain as those of ordinary documents, but have certain probability values. Therefore, the user filters the results according to the probability threshold, and retains those results that are likely to meet the user's requirements. Probability threshold makes some results with low probability value be discarded even if they are obtained. Discarding these results in advance in the algorithm can save the processing time of the algorithm and improve the query efficiency of the algorithm. Therefore, probability threshold is very important for the process of probability filtering in the query processing algorithm.

3.4 Twig Query Algorithm

Every node of ordinary document is determinate, and the result of twig query processing is also determinate. However, uncertain spatiotemporal documents contain not only uncertain information, but also spatiotemporal information. Therefore, the result of twig query processing is firstly uncertain with probability value, and secondly contains spatiotemporal nodes with spatiotemporal attributes.

First of all, these results with probability values can be filtered by the quantitative standard of probability threshold, and some results that cannot meet the requirements of users due to low probability values can be discarded. From 3.4.2, we can see that discarding these results in advance can save the processing time of the algorithm and improve the query efficiency of the algorithm. Usd-Twig algorithm sets up a two-dimensional dynamic character array to store the combination of query results and their probability values.

Secondly, the intermediate results of twig query processing can be judged by 2.3 extended interval coding, and then the conventional nodes, uncertain nodes and uncertain spatiotemporal nodes can be discarded or retained.

Based on Holistic Twig query processing algorithm and TwigStack query processing algorithm for uncertain data, this chapter proposes Usd-Twig algorithm on the basis of extended interval coding and connected stack.

The algorithm assumes that each node in the twig schema has been associated with a node stream, which includes the interval codes of all data nodes satisfying the twig schema in the uncertain spatiotemporal data document tree, and is arranged in ascending order of LPos.

Definition 4. (First Root Traversal of Tree) The first root traversal of a tree refers to accessing the root node first, then accessing each subtree of the root node in the order from left to right, and accessing other subtrees only after the traversal of one subtree is completed, which is similar to the depth-first traversal of a graph.

3.4.1 Data Structure for Usd-Twig Query Algorithm

1. Stack: It is used to express the order of node traversal, and according to twig mode, it carries out stack-out and stack-in operations on nodes, and records the ancestor node order of leaf nodes in twig mode.
2. Dynamic two-dimensional character array: used to store the intermediate results generated by the algorithm. Because the number of intermediate results and the number of nodes contained in the intermediate results have not yet been determined, the array does not specify the size. Using dynamic arrays, the size of the array is dynamically adjusted to save space.

3.4.2 The Idea of Algorithm

The idea of Usd-Twig query algorithm is based on TwigStack algorithm proposed in (Bruno et al., 2002) . However, because TwigStack algorithm is only suitable for Twig query on ordinary document trees (i.e., nodes in document trees are all conventional nodes), once there are uncertain nodes and nodes with spatiotemporal attributes in document trees, if we continue to query according to TwigStack algorithm, it will produce inconsistent results with users' needs. Therefore, the Usd-Twig query algorithm first traverses the document tree in Figure 2, and stores the nodes in the document tree that conform to the Twig query pattern into the connected stack. At this stage, the query result of a single path in the Twig pattern is obtained, that is, the local matching result. In this stage, Usd-Twig query algorithm adds three sections: probability calculation, probability filtering and judgment of node properties, in order to discard some inconsistent combinations in advance and ensure that the matching results of these single paths can form a final result with other results; After that, the local matching results obtained in the previous stage are combined and connected, and then the newly generated node combinations are calculated and filtered, and finally the final matching results of Twig query are obtained.

3.4.3 Basic Flow of Usd-Twig Algorithm

1. Firstly, the uncertain spatiotemporal data document is traversed by root, and each node is encoded according to the priority order of traversing tree nodes, and each node is read in turn according to the encoding size.
2. Different twig query modes correspond to different algorithms, but the common algorithm basis is to find the generated nodes corresponding to matching document nodes and store them in the corresponding stack. In the process of reading a certain node X, the nodes in the connection stack that have no ancestor-descendant relationship with this node need to be removed from the stack.
3. First of all, it is necessary to judge whether node X is on the stack. If the parent stack corresponding to X is not empty, X is on the stack, and a parent-child connection is established with the top node of the stack in the parent stack. Perform Step 4.
4. Determine whether this node is a leaf node in Twig mode
   a) is a leaf node, this node X is out of the stack, and the out-of-stack includes the ancestor nodes of the node X in the connection stack. Calculate whether the probability of this set of nodes is greater than the given probability threshold:

If it is greater than the probability threshold, continue to judge whether this group of nodes satisfy the spatiotemporal attribute (Uncertain=1, Time=1∪Space=1), and if so, add this group of nodes to the two-dimensional dynamic character array. Otherwise, this match result is discarded.

If it is less than the probability threshold, it will be discarded directly.

b) If it is not a leaf node, the algorithm continues to execute.

5. Loop through Step 2 until all node flows end.
6. Merge the intermediate results stored in the two-dimensional character array, find the common ancestor nodes of the nodes, and conform to the Twig pattern (it is necessary to judge whether it conforms to the Twig pattern according to the given structural relationship between nodes in the Twig pattern, combined with the extended interval coding and construction conditions of Figure 2), and generate the matching results.
7. Calculate the probability of a matching result every time, judge whether the probability is greater than a given probability threshold, if it is less than a given threshold, discard the result and return to step 6; If it is greater than the given threshold, this result is output. Until all the matching results have passed the test in Step 7, the Twig algorithm is finished.

The above algorithm can be divided into several steps, 1-5 in the algorithm flow corresponds to the following four steps:

① the root traverses the document tree to get the intermediate result
② Calculate the probability of intermediate results
③ Compared with probability threshold
④ Judge the properties of each node of the intermediate result

6-7 in the algorithm flow corresponds to the following four steps:

① Merge the intermediate results of connection
② Calculate the probability of the newly generated result set
③ Continue to compare with probability threshold
④ Output the final result

4 EXAMPLE VALIDATION

4.1 Twig Pattern

As shown in Figure 7, there are at least four situations in which uncertain spatiotemporal nodes exist in the document tree shown in Figure 2:

The first is that it only exists on a single path;
The second one exists in binary tree;
The third one exists in a trigeminal tree;
The fourth one exists in complex trees.

Figure 7. Exist situation of uncertain spatiotemporal information

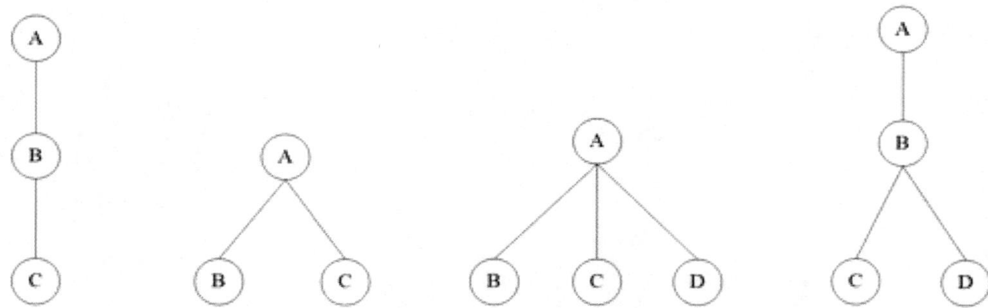

Corresponding to the four cases of the existence of uncertain spatiotemporal nodes in Figure 7, the existence of uncertain spatiotemporal nodes (which exist in rectangular form in section 2 and are represented by T_i) in the document tree shown in Figure 2 is shown in Figure 8, which can be seen from Figure 8:

Uncertain spatiotemporal node T_4 only exists on a single path.

Uncertain spatiotemporal node T_1 exists in binary tree.

Uncertain spatiotemporal node T_3 exists in binary tree.

The uncertain spatiotemporal node T_2 exists in both trigeminal tree and complex tree: T_2 exists in trigeminal tree in the third graph, and T_2 exists in complex tree in the fourth graph, that is, from another point of view, T_2 exists in complex tree.

Figure 8. Examples of uncertain spatiotemporal information in Figure 2

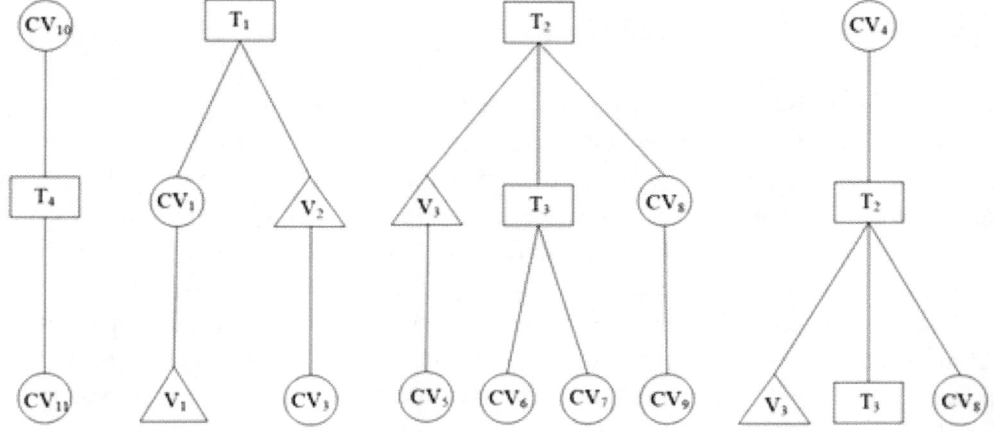

4.2 Twig Schema Query Instance

Corresponding to the four cases in which uncertain spatiotemporal information exists in Figure 7, there are four Twig patterns, as shown in Figure 9.

Figure 9. Twig pattern of uncertain spatiotemporal information

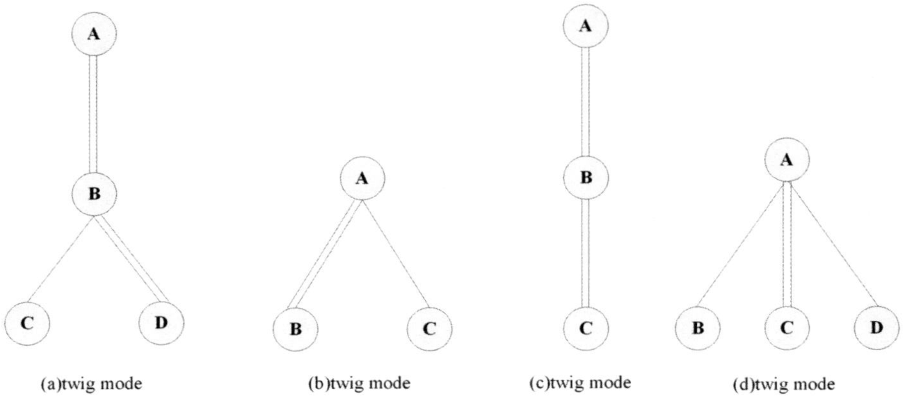

(a)twig mode (b)twig mode (c)twig mode (d)twig mode

Let's first look at the query results for Figure 2 according to the Twig schema in Figure 9 (a):

Table 1. Twig pattern of search result in Figure 9 (a)

Query results	Probability calculation	Probability judgment	Node judgment	Retain or not
(CV_0,T_2,V_3,CV_7)	0.2×0.3×0.5×0.8=0.024	yes	yes	yes
(CV_0,T_2,T_3,CV_9)	0.3×0.5×0.8×0.2=0.024	yes	yes	yes

Note: Figure (a) The probability threshold in Twig mode is set to 0.02.

Description of the above query process:

Step 1: Traverse the root of the document tree first and get the intermediate result.

According to the left part (A//B/C) of Twig pattern corresponding to Figure (a), the document tree in Figure 2 is traversed first, which means to find the elements matching with A in the document tree in the ascending order of LPos, and there is a descendant node B in A, while node B must have a child node C. According to 3.1, the traversed nodes are put into the corresponding stack, and the intermediate results are obtained by query. For example, root traversal first traverses the single path of the document tree from root node CV_0 to leaf node CV_2, and obtains intermediate results (CV_0, CV_1, V_1), (CV_0, V_1, CV_2), (T_1, V_1, CV_2). Similarly, this intermediate result is obtained when traversing other single paths of the document tree. Similarly, traverse the document tree in Figure 2 according to the right part (A//B/D) of Twig schema corresponding to Figure (a). However, in the query, the three single paths like CV_0 to CV_3, CV_0 to CV_{12}, and CV_0 to CV_{13} cannot query the appropriate intermediate results because there are too few layers and there are not enough extended solutions.

Step 2: Calculate the probability of each intermediate result according to the idea mentioned in 3.2. If the probability of the intermediate result is less than the given probability threshold, it is discarded without the third step; If the probability of the intermediate result is greater than the given probability threshold, it is temporarily reserved and continues to the third step.

Step 3: Judge whether there are uncertain spatiotemporal nodes in the result combination retained in the second step. Nodes whose properties have been identified by the attribute segments on the extended interval code of section 2 can be judged as Uncertain spatiotemporal nodes as long as the conditions of "Uncertain=1, Time=1∪Space=1" are met, that is, retained, otherwise, discarded.

The results obtained in the first three steps are as follows:

(1) The intermediate result of matching the document tree in Figure 2 according to Twig pattern A//B/C is called the first group, and it is numbered as follows:

1. (CV_0, CV_1, V_1) P=0.5×0.4×0.3=0.06 (no definite space-time node T, abandon it)
2. (CV_0, V_1, CV_2) P=0.5×0.4×0.3×0.6=0.036 (no definite space-time node T, abandon it)
3. (CV_0, V_2, CV_3) P=0.5×0.6=0.3 (no definite space-time node T, abandon it)
4. (T_1, V_1, CV_2) P=0.4×0.3×0.6=0.072
5. (CV_0, T_2, V_3) P=0.3×0.2=0.06
6. (CV_0, T_2, T_3) P=0.3×0.5=0.15
7. (CV_0, T_2, CV_8) P=0.3×0.8=0.24
8. (CV_4, V_3, CV_5) P=0.3×0.2×0.5=0.03 (no definite space-time node T, abandon it)
9. (CV_4, T_3, CV_6) P=0.3×0.5×0.6=0.09
10. (CV_4, T_3, CV_9) P=0.3×0.5×0.8=0.12
11. (CV_4, CV_8, CV_9) P=0.3×0.8×0.2=0.048(no definite space-time node T, abandon it)
12. (CV_0, CV_{10}, T_4) P=0.2×0.3×0.8=0.048
13. (CV_0, T_4, CV_{11}) P=0.2×0.3×0.8×0.1=0.0048 (probability less than 0.02, discard)
14. (V_4, T_4, CV_{11}) P=0.3×0.8×0.1=0.024
15. (CV_0, T_5, CV_{12}) P=0.2×0.7×0.4=0.056
16. (CV_0, T_5, CV_{13}) P=0.2×0.5×0.6=0.06

(2) The intermediate results generated by matching the document tree in Figure 2 according to Twig pattern A//B/D are called the second group, and they are also numbered. The results of intermediate result combination and its probability are as follows:

1. (CV_0, CV_1, CV_2) P=0.5×0.4×0.3×0.6=0.036 (no definite space-time node T, abandon it)
2. (CV_0, T_2, CV_5) P=0.3×0.2×0.5=0.03
3. (CV_0, T_2, CV_6) P=0.3×0.5×0.6=0.09
4. (CV_0, T_2, CV_7) P=0.3×0.5×0.8=0.12
5. (CV_0, T_2, CV_9) P=0.3×0.8×0.2=0.048
6. (CV_0, CV_{10}, CV_{11}) P=0.2×0.3×0.8×0.1=0.0048 (probability less than 0.02, discard)

Step 4: Connect the intermediate results. Join according to the merge join principle in 3.1. The process is as follows:

(1) The maximum common node combination of the first group and the second group is (CV_0, T_2). In the first group, the combination sequence numbers satisfying the maximum common node combination (CV_0, T_2) are 5, 6 and 7. Renumber as follows:

1. (CV_0, T_2, V_3) P=0.3×0.2=0.06
2. (CV_0, T_2, T_3) P=0.3×0.5=0.15

3. (CV_0, T_2, CV_8) P=0.3×0.8=0.24

(2) In the second group, the combination sequence numbers satisfying the maximum common node combination (CV_0, T_2) are 2, 3, 4, 5. Renumber as follows:

1. (CV_0, T_2, CV_5) P=0.3×0.2×0.5=0.03
2. (CV_0, T_2, CV_6) P=0.3×0.5×0.6=0.09
3. (CV_0, T_2, CV_7) P=0.3×0.5×0.8=0.12
4. (CV_0, T_2, CV_9) P=0.3×0.8×0.2=0.048

(3) Merge joins: It should be noted here that some final results obtained after merging joins according to this principle do not conform to the structure of the overall Twig pattern, so they are discarded. At this time, it is necessary to judge according to the given structural relationship among nodes in Twig pattern, combined with section 2 extended interval coding and construction conditions. In the Twig mode of Figure (a), C and D must satisfy the conditions "LNum of C is less than LNum of D, LPos of C is less than LPos of D, and RPos of C is less than RPos of D", so that the combined node combination can be preserved. Therefore, after merging and connecting, it is necessary to judge the relationship between C and D through section 2 extended interval coding, and then choose to abandon or keep it. The specific process is as follows:

1. (CV_0, T_2, V_3, CV_5) (RPos of V_3 is greater than that of CV_5, does not meet the condition, discarded)
2. (CV_0, T_2, V_3, CV_6)
3. (CV_0, T_2, V_3, CV_9)
4. (CV_0, T_2, V_3, CV_7)
5. (CV_0, T_2, T_3, CV_5) (LPos of T_3 is greater than that of CV_5, RPos of V_3 is greater than that of CV_5, does not meet the condition, discarded)
6. (CV_0, T_2, T_3, CV_6) (RPos of V_3 is greater than that of CV_6, does not meet the condition, discarded)
7. (CV_0, T_2, T_3, CV_7) (RPos of T_3 is greater than that of CV_6, does not meet the condition, discarded)
8. (CV_0, T_2, T_3, CV_9)
9. (CV_0, T_2, CV_8, CV_5) (LPos of CV_8 is greater than that of CV_5, RPos of CV_8 is greater than that of CV_5, does not meet the condition, discarded)
10. (CV_0, T_2, CV_8, CV_6) (LPos of CV_8 is greater than that of CV_6, RPos of CV_8 is greater than that of CV_6, does not meet the condition, discarded)
11. (CV_0, T_2, CV_8, CV_7) (LPos of CV_8 is greater than that of CV_7, RPos of CV_8 is greater than that of CV_7, does not meet the condition, discarded)
12. (CV_0, T_2, CV_8, CV_9) (RPos of CV_8 is greater than that of CV_9, does not meet the condition, discarded)

Step 5: Calculate the probability of the selected four groups of nodes, compare them with the probability threshold, and then choose to keep or discard them. The results are as follows:

1. (CV_0, T_2, V_3, CV_6) P=0.2×0.3×0.5×0.6=0.018 (probability less than 0.02, discard)
2. (CV_0, T_2, V_3, CV_7) P=0.2×0.3×0.5×0.8=0.024
3. (CV_0, T_2, V_3, CV_9) P=0.3×0.2×0.8×0.2=0.0096 (probability less than 0.02, discard)

4. (CV_0, T_2, T_3, CV_9) P=0.3×0.5×0.8×0.2=0.024
5. To sum up, only (CV_0, T_2, V_3, CV_7) and (CV_0, T_2, T_3, CV_9) are returned.

The following is the query result for Figure 2 according to the Twig schema of Figures (b), (c) and (d):

Table 2. Twig pattern of search result in Figure 9 (b)

Query results	Probability calculation	Probability judgment	Node judgment	Retain or not
(CV_0, CV_1, CV_4)	0.5×0.4=0.2	yes	no	no
(CV_0, T_2, V_4)	0.2×0.3=0.06	no	yes	no
(T_1, V_1, V_2)	—	—	—	no
(V_4, T_4, T_5)	0.3×0.8×0.7=0.168	yes	yes	yes
(V_4, CV_{11}, T_5)	0.3×0.8×0.1×0.7=0.0168	no	—	no
(V_4, CV_{12}, V_5)	0.7×0.4×0.5=0.14	yes	no	no

Note: Figure (b) The probability threshold in Twig mode is set to 0.1.

Table 3. Twig pattern of search result in Figure 9 (c)

Query results	Probability calculation	Probability judgment	Node judgment	Retain or not
(CV_0, CV_1, CV_2)	0.5×0.4×0.3×0.6=0.036	no	—	no
(CV_0, T_2, CV_5)	0.3×0.2×0.5=0.03	no	—	no
(CV_0, T_2, CV_6)	0.3×0.5×0.6=0.09	yes	yes	yes
(CV_0, T_2, CV_7)	0.3×0.5×0.8=0.12	yes	yes	yes
(CV_0, T_2, CV_8)	0.3×0.8×0.2=0.048	yes	yes	yes
(CV_0, CV_{10}, CV_{11})	0.2×0.3×0.8×0.1=0.0048	no	—	no

Note: Figure (c) The probability threshold in Twig mode is set to 0.04.

Table 4. Twig pattern of search result in Figure 9 (d)

Query results	Probability calculation	Probability judgment	Node judgment	Retain or not
(CV_0, T_1, T_2, V_4)	0.5×0.3×0.2=0.03	yes	yes	yes
(CV_0, T_1, V_3, V_4)	0.5×0.3×0.2×0.2=0.006	no	—	no
(CV_0, T_1, T_3, V_4)	0.5×0.3×0.5×0.2=0.015	yes	yes	yes
(CV_0, T_1, CV_8, V_4)	0.5×0.3×0.8×0.2=0.024	yes	yes	yes
(CV_0, T_1, CV_5, V_4)	0.5×0.3×0.2×0.5×0.2=0.003	no	—	no
(CV_0, T_1, CV_6, V_4)	0.5×0.3×0.5×0.6×0.2=0.009	no	—	no
(CV_0, T_1, CV_7, V_4)	0.5×0.3×0.5×0.8×0.2=0.012	yes	yes	yes
(CV_0, T_1, CV_9, V_4)	0.5×0.3×0.8×0.2×0.2=0.0048	no	—	no

Note: Figure (d) The probability threshold in Twig mode is set to 0.01.

The first column in the above tables is the partial result of the root traversal query on the uncertain spatiotemporal document tree according to the corresponding Twig schema, and the relationship between each group of node combinations exists one-to-one mapping with the nodes on the corresponding Twig schema of each table.

The second column in the above tables is the probability calculated for each node combination according to 3.4.2.

The third column of the list is the result of quantization judgment according to the set probability threshold. If the probability threshold set in Table 2 is 0.1, the probabilities of the second and fourth groups are discarded because they are less than 0.1.

The fourth column in the above tables is to determine whether the node combination retained after the third step of screening contains at least one uncertain spatiotemporal data node, and then choose to retain or discard it. For example, the first group, the second group and the sixth group in Table 3 have been discarded in the judgment of the probability threshold in the second step, so they no longer participate in the judgment of the third step, and only need to judge whether there is at least one uncertain spatiotemporal data node in each group node combination in the third group, the fourth group and the fifth group, if there is one, then retain it, and if there is no one, then discard it. The third group, the fourth group and the fifth group are all retained because they all contain uncertain spatiotemporal data nodes marked with "T_i".

4.3 Algorithm Complexity

In the worst case, such as the Twig pattern corresponding to graph (c) in Figure 9, which only contains ancestor-descendant relationship, the time complexity of the algorithm is linearly related to the sum of the number of nodes and the number of matching results. Let the number of nodes be n and the number of matching results be m, and the time complexity of the algorithm is O (m + n). For Twig queries with parent-child relationships, the algorithm will produce redundant intermediate matching results, that is, it cannot merge and join with other intermediate matching results.

5 SUMMARY

For the representation of Uncertain spatiotemporal data, this chapter uses a seven-tuple (DocId, LPos: RPos, LNum, Uncertain, Time, Space, Sequence) to represent the coding information of Uncertain spatiotemporal data nodes through extended interval coding based on Uncertain data, and establishes the related document tree. The parent-child relationship and ancestor-descendant relationship among nodes in the document tree can be judged by node coding. For the query of uncertain spatiotemporal data, based on previous query processing algorithms for uncertain data, this chapter proposes Usd-Twig algorithm on the basis of extended interval coding and connected stack. This algorithm performs root traversal on the document tree, filters some node combinations with low probability through probability threshold after generating intermediate results, and discards some node combinations without uncertain spatiotemporal nodes to reduce redundancy. Then, by merging and connecting intermediate results, filters some newly generated node combinations with low probability through probability threshold again, and finally outputs results conforming to Twig mode. The correctness and possibility of the algorithm are proved in detail by an example, and the complexity of the algorithm is simply analyzed.

REFERENCES

Bai, L. Y., Li, Y., & Liu, J. M. (2017). *Fast Leaf-to-Root Holistic Twig Query on XML Spatiotemporal Data* [In Chinese]. Northeastern University. doi:10.17706/jcp.12.6.534-542

Bai, L. Y., Yan, L., & Ma, Z. M. (2013). Determining topological relationship of fuzzy spatiotemporal data integrated with XML twig pattern. *Applied Intelligence*, *39*(1), 75–100. doi:10.100710489-012-0395-3

Bai, L. Y., Yan, L., & Ma, Z. M. (2014). Querying fuzzy spatiotemporal data using XQuery. *Integrated Computer-Aided Engineering*, *21*(2), 147–162. doi:10.3233/ICA-130454

Balbiani, P., & Condotta, J. F. (2002). Spatial reasoning about points in a multidimensional setting. *Applied Intelligence*, *17*(3), 221–238. doi:10.1023/A:1020079114666

Bruno, N., Koudas, N., & Srivastava, D. (2002). Holistic twig joins: Optimal XML pattern matching. *Proceedings of the 2002 ACM SIGMOD International Conference on Management of Data*, (pp. 310-321). ACM. 10.1145/564691.564727

Claramunt, C., Parent, C., Spaccapietra, S., et al. (1999). Database modelling for environmental and land use changes. *Proceedings of Geographical Information and Planning*. Springer Berlin Heidelberg.

Emrich, T., Kriegel, H. P., & Mamoulis, N. (2012). Indexing uncertain spatiotemporal data. *Proceedings of the 21st ACM International Conference on Information and Knowledge Management (CIKM)*, Sheraton, 395-404.

Emrich, T., Kriegel, H. P., & Mamoulis, N. (2012). Querying uncertain spatiotemporal data. *Proceedings of the 28th International Conference on Data Engineering (ICDE)*, Washington D.C., 354-365.

Hu, L., Ku, W. S., Bakiras, S., & Shahabi, C. (2013). Spatial query integrity with voronoi neighbors. *IEEE Transactions on Knowledge and Data Engineering*, *25*(4), 863–876. doi:10.1109/TKDE.2011.267

Langran, G., & Chrisman, N. (1992). A framework for temporal geographic information. *Cartographica*, *40*(1), 1–14.

Liu, G., Yao, M., & Wang, D. (2011). A novel three-phase XML twig pattern matching algorithm based on version tree. *Proceedings of the Eighth International Conference*, (pp. 1678-1688). IEEE. 10.1109/FSKD.2011.6019809

Liu, J., Ma, Z. M., & Ma, R. (2013). Efficient processing of twig query with compound predicates in fuzzy XML. *Fuzzy Sets and Systems*, *229*(2), 33–53. doi:10.1016/j.fss.2012.11.004

Liu, J., Ma, Z. M., & Qv, Q. L. (2014). Dynamic querying possibilistic XML data. *Information Sciences*, *261*(4), 70–88.

Liu, J., Ma, Z. M., & Yan, L. (2013). Querying and ranking incomplete twigs in probabilistic XML. *World Wide Web (Bussum)*, *16*(3), 325–353. doi:10.100711280-011-0149-x

Nørvag, K. (2002). Temporal query operators in XML database. *Proceedings of the 2002 ACM Symposium on Applied Computing*, (pp. 02-406). ACM. 10.1145/508791.508868

Obeid, N. (2005). A formalism for representing and reasoning with temporal information, event and change. *Applied Intelligence, 23*(2), 109–119. doi:10.100710489-005-3416-7

Pelekis, N., Theodoulidis, B., Kopanakis, I., & Theodoridis, Y. (2004). Literature review of spatiotemporal database models. *The Knowledge Engineering Review, 19*(3), 235–274. doi:10.1017/S026988890400013X

Rizzolo, F., & Vaisman, A. A. (2008). Temporal XML: Modeling, indexing, and query processing. *The VLDB Journal, 17*(5), 1179–1212. doi:10.100700778-007-0058-x

Sözer, A., & Yazici, A. (2008). Modeling and querying fuzzy spatiotemporal databases. *Information Sciences, 178*(19), 3665–3682. doi:10.1016/j.ins.2008.05.034

Senellart, S., & Abiteboul, S. (2007). On the complexity of managing probabilistic XML data. *Proceedings of the 26th ACM SIGACT-SIGMOD-SIGART Symposium on Principles of Database Systems*, (pp. 283-292). ACM. 10.1145/1265530.1265570

Ye, X. P., Chen, Z. Y., & Tang, Y. (2007). Temporal XML indexing technology. *Journal of Computational Science*, (07), 1074–1085.

Zhang, Y. P., Wang, X. J., & Zhang, Y. (2009). Labeling Scheme for Temporal XML. *Web Information Systems and Mining, WISM 2009. International Conference on, IEEE*, (pp. 277-279). IEEE.

Chapter 18
Keyword Query of Uncertain Spatiotemporal XML Data

ABSTRACT

As an increasing volume of data objects in the real world has spatial features and temporal features, spatiotemporal data emerge in more and more spatiotemporal applications. Although keyword query has been studied on spatiotemporal data in traditional database, relatively little work has been carried out to investigate keyword query of uncertain spatiotemporal data. In this chapter, the authors investigate uncertain spatiotemporal data representation based on XML. Building upon this, they propose a keyword query approach for uncertain spatiotemporal XML data, which includes the data structure of a dynamic keyword data warehouse, probability calculation, keyword query algorithm, as well as pruning and sorting algorithms for keyword query. Finally, the experimental results demonstrate the performance advantages of this approach. Such approach optimizes the structure of spatiotemporal XML data, which facilitates its keyword query.

1 INTRODUCTION

Recently, with the explosive growth of spatiotemporal data, the demand for spatiotemporal data modeling and querying is increasing. For spatiotemporal data modeling, Chen et al. (Chen et al., 2016) propose a spatiotemporal data model based on a compressed linear reference to transform network time geographic entities in 3D space to 2D compressed linear reference space. The advantage of this model is that spatiotemporal operations and index structures can be utilized to implement spatiotemporal operations and queries directly. The event-driven spatiotemporal data model (Li et al., 2014) is proposed to dynamically express and simulate the spatiotemporal processes of spatiotemporal phenomena. Cheng et al. (Cheng et al., 2021) propose a dynamic spatiotemporal logic for representing and reasoning dynamic spatiotemporal knowledge. For spatiotemporal data querying, Kim et al, (Kim et al., 2000) present a spatiotemporal data model that supports a bitemporal concept for spatial objects and designs a spatiotemporal database query language denoted as STQL. Guan et al. (Guan et al., 2017) present a trajectory

DOI: 10.4018/978-1-6684-9108-9.ch018

indexing method to accelerate time-consuming spatiotemporal queries of massive trajectory data by extending GeoHash algorithm to satisfy the requirements for both high-frequent updates and common trajectory query operations.

At the same time, XML has good self-descriptiveness and extensibility and has become an international standard for representation and exchange in the Web (An et al., 2005). Therefore, some efforts have been made in modeling and querying spatiotemporal data based on XML (Yuan et al., 2010). Zipf and Krüger (Zipf & Krüger, 2001) propose a self-consistent framework to describe temporal data by an XML schema, which is combined with GML schema to realize spatiotemporal XML schema. Liu and Wan (Liu & Wan, 2010) use XML to describe a feature-based spatiotemporal data model, which can use Native XML Database to store the spatiotemporal data. Chen and Revesz (Chen & Revesz, 2003) study a query language for spatiotemporal data based on XML, which supports spatiotemporal data heterogeneity at the language level. Bai et al. (Bai et al., 2016) study spatiotemporal operations using XQuery, and investigate query result processing by listing query examples. In addition to those spatiotemporal data modeling and querying approaches based on XML, there are also several further achievements on fuzzy or uncertain spatiotemporal data modeling and querying based on XML (Jeung et al., 2008; Cheng & Wang, 2008; Boulila et al., 2011; Bai et al., 2015; Xu et al., 2016; Ma et al., 2018; Bai et al., 2018; Chen et al., 2018; Bai et al., 2018; Bai et al., 2017; Bai et al., 2021).

Keyword query is one of the most important queries on spatiotemporal data. Mehta et al. (Mehta et al., 2015) address the problem of efficient evaluation of queries that perform spatiotemporal keyword-based filtering on spatiotemporal objects, combining two hybrid indexes for concepts and techniques for spatiotemporal queries. Nepomnyachiy et al. (Nepomnyachiy et al., 2014) study a framework for spatiotemporal data, which exploits the structure of spatiotemporal data to shrink the temporal search space dramatically and use a shallow tree to search spatiotemporal data. Chen et al. (Chen et al., 2021) propose a time-aware collective spatial keyword query approach, which considers the positional relevance, textual relevance, and temporal relevance between spatiotemporal objects. Bai et al. (Bai et al., 2022) study the intra-coupling logic relationship and the inter-coupling logic relationship, and then propose a calculation method for keyword coupled similarity based on XML. Although keyword query approaches of spatiotemporal data have received attention in relational database, the study of keyword query of spatiotemporal data has received relatively little attention and still merits further attention. In addition, some core ideas of data query methods such as SLCA (Lakshmanan et al., 1997) and PrList (Li et al., 2011) can also be experienced in XML.

In this chapter, we study uncertain spatiotemporal data representation based on XML. On the basis of it, we further propose a keyword query approach for uncertain spatiotemporal XML data, including data structure of dynamic keyword data warehouse, probability calculation, and a keyword query algorithm. Finally, we perform two groups of experiments to show the performance advantages of our approach from efficiency and effectiveness viewpoints.

The rest of this article is organized as follows. Section 2 introduces a keyword query method for uncertain spatiotemporal XML data. After the keyword query method of uncertain spatiotemporal XML data is proposed in Section 3, the pruning and sorting algorithm of keyword query is proposed in Section 4, the experimental evaluation is carried out in Section 5, and the conclusion of this chapter is in Section 6.

2 UNCERTAIN SPATIOTEMPORAL DATA REPRESENTATION BASED ON XML

In this section, we present uncertain spatiotemporal data representation and uncertain spatiotemporal XML tree. Then, we give a definition for minimum meaningful tree. Finally, we present the structure of an uncertain spatiotemporal XML tree.

Definition 1. The uncertain spatiotemporal data can be represented as a 5-tuple *USP* = (*OID*, *ATTRI*, *USP*, *USM*, *UST*), where:

- *OID* represents the change history of uncertain spatiotemporal data. A type that represents the change of uncertain spatiotemporal objects in a time interval or time point and its values are *created* (*c*), *split* (*s*), *merger* (*m*), and *eliminate* (*e*). Precursor of it is *pre*, successor of it is *suc*.
- *ATTRI* contains general attributes and spatiotemporal attributes.
- *USP* indicates the location of the uncertain spatiotemporal data, which is represented by MBR.
- *USM* represents the motion of uncertain spatiotemporal data. It shows the trend and the change in the movement of spatiotemporal objects in a time interval or time point. The trend of change is divided into *x*-axis direction and *y*-axis direction.
- *UST* indicates the time of the uncertain spatiotemporal data.

Definition 2. Uncertain spatiotemporal XML tree can be represented by an 8-tuple *USXT* = {*D*, *U*, *E*, *R*, *Label*, α, β, γ}, where:

- *D is a set which stores the normal node.*
- *U* is a set of uncertain nodes, including normal uncertain nodes and uncertain spatiotemporal nodes.
- *E* is the edge set, E_i is the edge connecting D_j and *Uk* in *USXT*.
- *R* is the root node, $R \subseteq D$.
- *Label* is the text label set for normal nodes.
- α is a function that returns the text label of a node.
- β is a function that returns the probability of occurrence of a node.
- γ is a function whose return value is *mux* or *ind*.

Definition 3: For an uncertain spatiotemporal XML document Tree *USXT* and a set of query keywords $Key = \{k_1, k_2,..., k_i\}$, a minimum meaningful tree (*MMT*) is a subtree of *USXT*.

In Definition 3, *W* is contained in *D*. The tag set for all nodes on *W* contains all the elements in the key set *Key*. For any two elements in *K*, the smallest and lowest common ancestor *LCA* node belongs to the common node set *D* or the uncertain spatiotemporal node set *U*, and the return value of γ function of this *LCA* node is *ind*. For an *MMT*, the root node is the *SLCA* node and contains all of the *Key* sets. The *MMT* is a possible world that contains all the elements of the *Key* collection. Such an *MMT* contains no other redundant information, it has good query semantics and extracts the content of the original XML file that is meaningful to the user. However, *MMT* is not necessarily *USXT*, because the root node of an *MMT* may be uncertain. In this case, the lowest determined ancestor node is added to *MMT*, and then *MMT* can be regarded as *USXT* subtree.

Figure 1 shows the structure of an uncertain spatiotemporal XML tree, where:

(1) Root node: The XML document tree has only one root node, which is the parent node of all elements and is represented by ellipses in the model.
(2) Element node: Element node can be the parent node of other nodes, while the parent node of element node can only be the element node or root node. Element nodes are represented by hexagons.
(3) Attribute node: To be used with its parent element node, it is represented as a rectangle. Temporal attribute is represented as a square.
(4) Value node: It is a leaf node, which can be a number or text and is represented by a circle.
(5) Uncertain node: For the relationship between uncertain spatiotemporal data, it is defined as an element and represented by a triangle. Uncertain spatiotemporal nodes are divided into independent nodes and mutually exclusive nodes, and their values are *ind* and *mux*, that is, the values of triangles are *ind* or *mux*. In the uncertain spatiotemporal data model, the uncertainty of data is expressed by probability *p*, and the probability value is placed on the edge of XML document tree. The value range of probability *p* is [0, 1].

Figure 1. The structure of an uncertain spatiotemporal XML tree

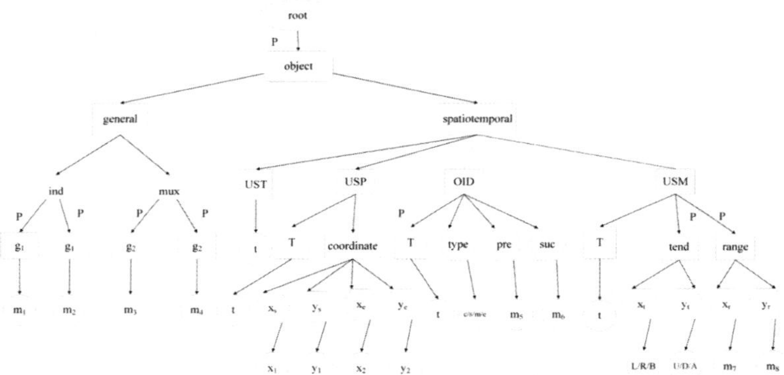

3 KEYWORD QUERY FOR UNCERTAIN SPATIOTEMPORAL XML DATA

3.1 Data Structure of Dynamic Keyword Data Warehouse

If the XML document tree has m layers, the dynamic keyword data warehouse needs an m*1-dimensional array to represent the layer information. For example, the first element in this array holds the layer number of the first layer and a pointer. This pointer points to a linked list of information from all nodes in the first tier. The m-layer XML document tree needs m linked lists, and the linked list nodes are called UK nodes. In order to distinguish the nodes in the XML document tree, the nodes in the linked list are called nodes. Generally, the nodes in the XML document tree correspond to the nodes in the dynamic keyword data warehouse one by one. In the special case, multiple nodes correspond to one node. When initializing the dynamic keyword data warehouse, UK node is used to represent the nodes containing query keywords in the XML document tree.

UK node consists of five parts: code, number, probability, keyword information contained, and node label. Node labels are introduced to deal with uncertain spatiotemporal data. The coding information of *UK* node generally refers to the prefix coding-Dewey coding of the current node. The numbering sequence of *UK* node is composed of the numbers of each node traversed from the root node of the uncertain spatiotemporal XML document tree to the previous root of the current node, and the conditional probability of the path from the root node of the uncertain spatiotemporal XML document tree to the current node is composed of the probability sequence.

Definition 4. Keyword Information (KI) can be represented by a 2-tuple BP = $\{b, p\}$, where

- b is a binary bit string consisting of n binary bits, where n is the number of keywords in the current query, and each binary bit corresponds to a keyword.
- p is the probability of binary bit string b.

In Definition 4, If the i-th binary bit is 1, it means that the current node contains the i-th keyword, and if it is 0, it means that it does not contain this keyword. If there are currently n keywords, the KI consists of 2^n BP. It is generally considered that b in BP binary group of SLCA nodes is "11111 …" and p is a nonzero constant. In fact, the BP binary group of the SLCA node and the logical predicate of the query keyword are OR-NOT related. Assuming the query keyword *Key*= {K1, K2}, if the query logic is "K1, not K2", *B* in the BP binary group of the SLCA node is "01" and *P* is a nonzero constant. If the query logic is "K1 or K2", *B* in the BP binary group of SLCA nodes can be "01", "10" or "11", corresponding to *P* being a nonzero constant. If the query logic is "K1 and K2", *B* in the BP binary group of SLCA nodes are "11" and *P* is a nonzero constant. The general model of dynamic keyword data warehouse is shown in Figure 2, and the model of the *UK* node is shown in Figure 3.

Figure 2. The general model of dynamic keyword data warehouse

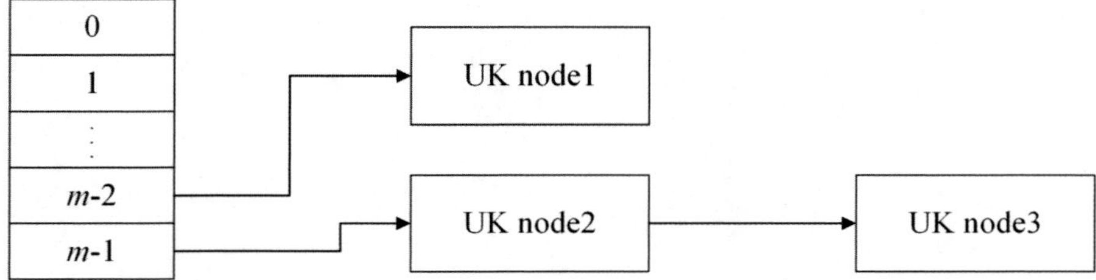

Figure 4 is an uncertain spatiotemporal XML document tree composed of part of cloud information. The information in "()" is the first root traversal number of the XML document tree node, and the sequence in the form of "0.0.1..." is the encoding of the XML document tree node. If the query keyword is (9: 00, A), the initialized keyword data warehouse is shown in Figure 5.

For example, in the fourth layer *UK* node 2, < 01, 1 >, 1 means that a keyword 9:00 appears, 0 means that the first keyword A does not appear, and the second 1 means that the probability of this happening in *UK* node 2 is 1.

Figure 3. The model of UK node

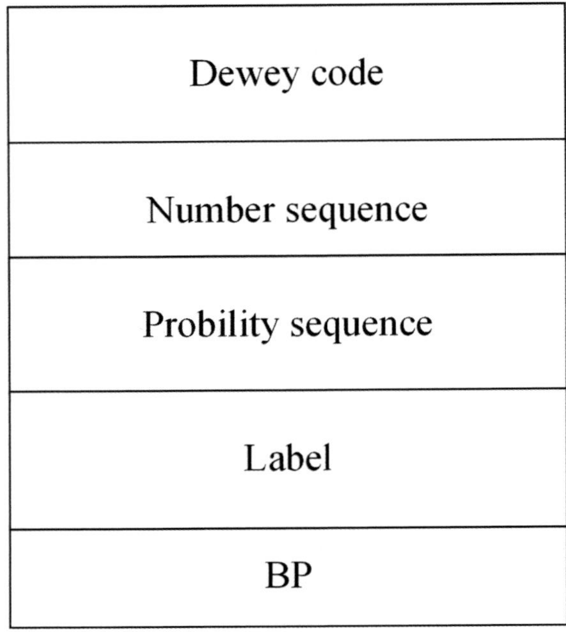

Figure 4. The uncertain spatiotemporal data model with partial cloud1 information

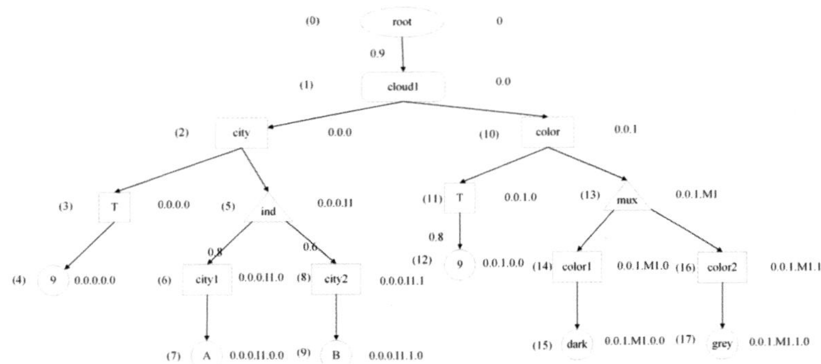

Figure 5. Initialized model of dynamic keyword data repository

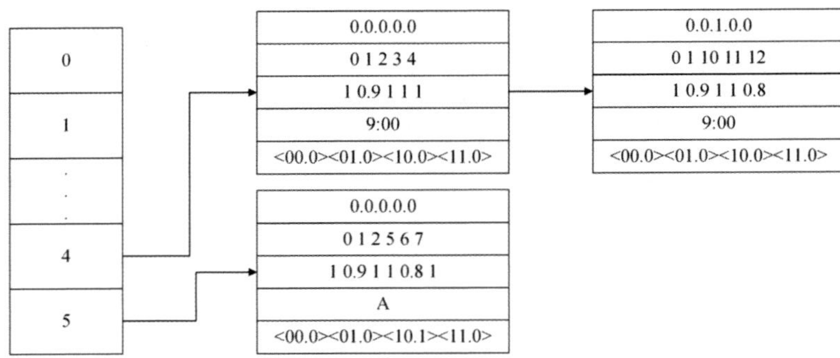

(1) Arrangement of *UK* nodes.

The corresponding *UK* nodes of XML nodes in the same layer are in the same linked list in the dynamic keyword data warehouse, and the arrangement order of nodes in the linked list is the same as that of the previous root traversal of nodes in the corresponding XML document tree. For example, both Node A and Node B are located in the 6th layer linked list of keyword data warehouses. The 6th bit of the numbering sequence of Node A is i, and the 6th bit of the numbering sequence of Node B is j. If i is greater than j, A is greater than B; if i is equal to j, A is equal to B; if i is less than j, A is less than B. Obviously, *UK* Node 1 is larger than *UK* Node 2 in the graph.

(2) Parent-child relationship of *UK* node.

The dynamic keyword data warehouse uses the number sequence of nodes in the linked list to determine the parent-child relationship. If node A is in the fourth layer linked list, node B is in the fifth layer linked list, and the fourth digit of the number sequence of node B is equal to the fourth digit of the number sequence of node A, then node A is the father of node B. This method makes use of the comparison of a certain bit in the integer sequence to judge the father-son relationship, avoids the string comparison in the traditional method and the stack-out and stack-in operation during the comparison, thus greatly improving the time utilization rate and space utilization rate, and further improving the efficiency of judging the father-son relationship.

(3) Many-to-one *UK* nodes.

When querying uncertain spatiotemporal data, the keyword query form is mostly "the location of spatiotemporal object D from time A to time B", instead of the keyword query form of ordinary uncertain data "Time A, location $\{(x_1, y_1), (x_2, y_2)\}$". Note that the location of uncertain spatiotemporal data query directly matches only the XML document tree is the location attribute node. What it needs to return is the value node of the location attribute. The query position matching of common uncertain data is directly the value node of the position attribute of XML document tree. The query time of uncertain spatiotemporal data is a time interval, and the time value node is required to be within the time interval range. The query time of common uncertain data is a time, and the time value node is required to be equal to the time value.

As a result, this section studies the corresponding relationship between uncertain spatiotemporal data nodes and *UK* nodes. If the value node of the queried spatiotemporal attribute can be represented only by one node, the relationship between uncertain spatiotemporal data node and *UK* node is one-to-one, and the processing mode is the same as that of ordinary uncertain data. If the value node of the queried spatiotemporal attribute can be represented by two or more nodes, the uncertain spatiotemporal data node and *UK* node are many-to-one. For example, when querying the changes of spatiotemporal objects at a certain time, the time value can be represented by a value node t_1, then t_1 has a one-to-one relationship with the corresponding *UK* node. When querying the changes of spatiotemporal objects in a certain time interval, the time interval (t_2, t_3) is represented by two value nodes t_2 and t_3. When querying the position of a certain spatiotemporal object, the position $\{(x_s, y_s), (x_e, y_e)\}$ is represented by the minimum adjacency matrix, and four value nodes are needed, then (t_2, t_3), the position $\{(x_s, y_s), (x_e, y_e)\}$ and the corresponding *UK* node are many-to-one. Our approach abstracts several value nodes of position and time interval information in the original uncertain spatiotemporal XML tree into a *UK* node, so that the keyword query method of dynamic keyword data warehouse is suitable for querying uncertain spatiotemporal data, and the processing of *UK* node in general.

If the value node of the spatiotemporal attribute is represented by two or more nodes, then:

(1) Merge the text labels in several value nodes as the text labels in the new *UK* node.
(2) The coding sequence takes the coding sequence of the leftmost node of the query keyword in the attribute subtree.
(3) Number sequence takes the number sequence of the leftmost node of the query keyword in the attribute subtree.
(4) After calculating the probability of the merged node hierarchically, it is marked on the edge of connecting the new node with its parent node as the conditional probability of the new node.
(5) The number of layers of the new *UK* node in the dynamic data warehouse is the number of layers of the leftmost node in the XML document tree.

If the query time interval is (t_2, t_3) when the value node corresponding to attribute T in the uncertain spatiotemporal XML document tree is time t_4 and satisfies that t_4 is greater than or equal to $t_2$and less than or equal to t_3, the corresponding *UK* node is generated by t_4 node. For example, if the query time interval is (8:00, 10:00) when the value node of attribute T in the uncertain spatiotemporal XML document tree is "9:00", the corresponding *UK* node can be generated with the value node 9:00.

If the query time interval is (t_2, t_3) and the value node corresponding to the attribute T in the uncertain spatiotemporal XML document tree is of interval type, set to (t_5, t_6) if one of the following two conditions is satisfied:

(1) t_5 is less than or equal to t_2 and t_6 is greater than or equal to t_3.
(2) t_5 is greater than or equal to t_2 and t_6 is less than or equal to t_3.

Aggregate the nodes T_s, T_e, t_5, t_6 (note $T_s = t_5$, $T_e = t_6$) into a *UK* node, which is a many-to-one node. For example, when querying the position of cloud1 in time interval (t_1, t_2), the processing of time interval nodes and spatial position attribute coordinate value nodes is as shown in Figure 6.

Suppose that t_5 is less than or equal to t_2 and t_6 is greater than or equal to t_3 in Figure 6, where $P_{xy} = p_1 \times p_2 \times p_3 \times p_4$.

If the *UK* node is in the *n*-th layer, the Dewey code of the node in the XML document tree corresponding to the *UK* node is the first *n* bits of the code sequence of the *UK* node, the probability sequence of the corresponding node is the first *n* bits of the probability sequence of the *UK* node, and the number of the node in the XML document tree corresponding to the *UK* node is the first *n* bits of the number sequence of the *UK* node. For one-to-one *UK* nodes, the actual text label of the *UK* node at the *n*-th level is the text label of the XML node corresponding to the first *n* bits of the coding sequence, and has nothing to do with the text label of the *UK* node. If and only if the number of layers *n* is equal to the number of bits of the coding sequence of the *UK* node, the actual text label of the XML node corresponding to the *UK* node is the text label of the *UK* node. The text label of a many-to-one *UK* node is a collection of the actual text labels of all the XML value nodes it corresponds to.

If the *UK* node A does not have a parent node on its upper layer, it will be moved from *UK* node A to the upper layer to generate a parent node, and only the BP binary group of *UK* nodes can be changed in this process. Then SLCA nodes are generated, and finally, the *MMT* is generated. Then solving *MMT* of uncertain spatiotemporal data can be transformed into solving SLCA nodes. If there are only two keywords to be queried, a *UK* node is considered to be a SLCA node when the *b* value of a *UK* node is "11" and the probability *p* is non-zero.

Figure 6. Generation of the many-to-one UK node

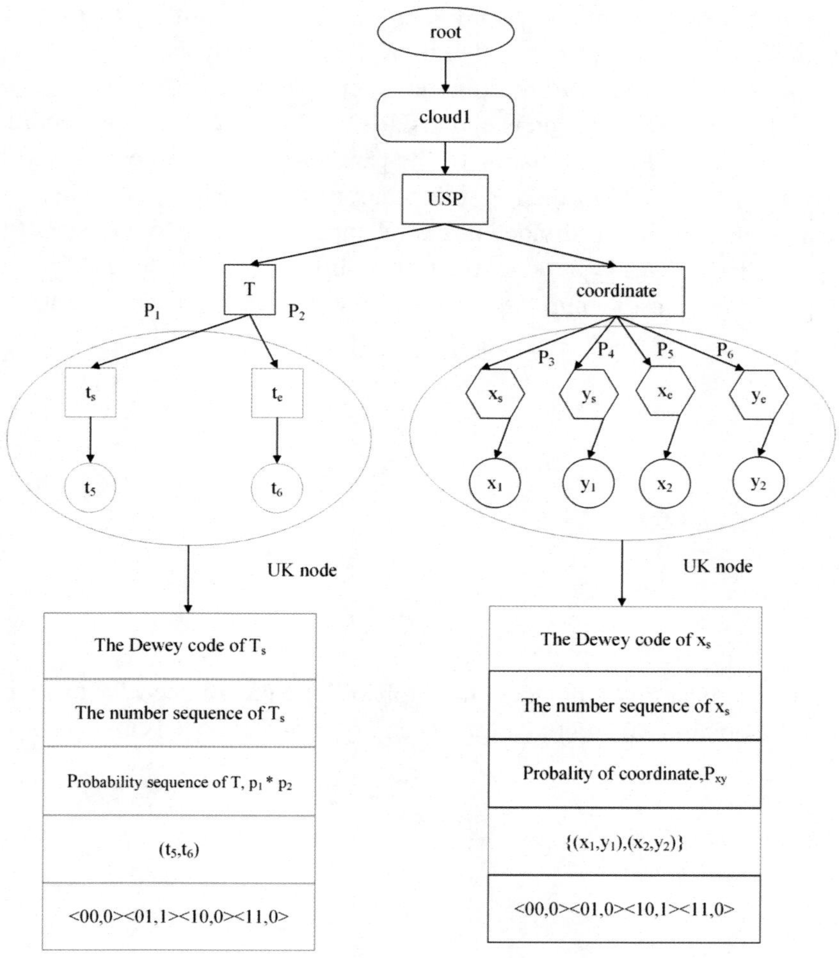

3.2 Probability Calculation

If n nodes in an XML document tree correspond to a many-to-one UK node, then the n nodes must not be mutually exclusive. Pi is used to denote the probability of the i-th node, and P is used to denote the probability that n nodes exist at the same time, that is, the conditional probability of many-to-one UK nodes

$$P = P_1 \times \ldots \times P_n \tag{1}$$

P_{rs} denotes the product of the path probabilities from the root node to the current *SLCA* node, and that is the probability sequence of the *UK* node corresponding to the *SLCA* node, P_{ts} denotes the probability of the *SLCA* node becoming an *SLCA* node in an XML subtree, and P_s denotes the final probability of the *SLCA* node.

$$P_s = P_{rs} \times P_{ts} \tag{2}$$

The calculation process of P_{ts} is the process of passing the keyword containing the case to the parent node at the bottom of the dynamic keyword data warehouse. Assuming that the child node of the parent node F is m, the child node is represented by K_i $(1 \leq i \leq m)$. If there are n query keywords, the BP information of K_i is 2^n, and each BP information is represented by BP_{ij} $(1 \leq j \leq 2^n)$, the probability value P_{ij} $(1 \leq j \leq 2^n)$ of the BP_{ij} information is updated to P^*_{ij} $(1 \leq j \leq 2^n)$, and the conditional probability of the child node K_i is f_i. Each BP information of the parent node F is represented by BP_{Fj} $(1 \leq j \leq 2^n)$ the probability value P_{Fj} $(1 \leq j \leq 2^n)$ of the BP_{Fj} information is updated to probability value P^*_{Fj} $(1 \leq j \leq 2^n)$. Probability calculation method is divided into three kinds according to the type of the parent node:

(1) If the parent node is a *mux* type node, the probability value of each *BP* of its all child nodes is updated according to Equation (3). *mux* type parent node is updated according to Equation (4) and Equation (5).

$$P^*_{ij} = P_{ij} \times f_i \ (1 \leq i \leq m,\ 1 \leq j \leq 2^n) \tag{3}$$

$$P^*_{Fj} = P_{Fj} + P^*_{ij} \ (1 \leq i \leq m,\ 2 \leq j \leq 2^n) \tag{4}$$

$$P^*_{F1} = 1 - \sum f_i \ (1 \leq i \leq m) \tag{5}$$

(2) If the parent node is an *ind* type node, the probability value of each *BP* of all its child nodes is updated according to Equation (6) and Equation (7). *ind* type parent node is updated according to Equation (8)

$$P^*_{ij} = P_{ij} \times f_i \ (1 \leq i \leq m,\ 2 \leq j \leq 2^n) \tag{6}$$

$$P^*_{i1} = 1 - f_i \times (1 - P_{i1}) \ (1 \leq i \leq m) \tag{7}$$

$$P^*_{Fj} = P_{Fj} \times (\sum P^*_{ij}) \ (1 \leq i \leq m,\ 2 \leq j \leq 2^n) \tag{8}$$

(3) If the parent node is a common type of *UK* node, calculate the probability according to the parent node of *ind* type. Unlike an *ind* type node, if the parent node is an ordinary type of the *UK* node, when the last item of its *BP* (The last term is the BP term where the binary bit string is all 1) is not zero, then this *UK* node is a *SLCA* node. The final probability of the *SLCA* node is calculated using Equation (2) and compared with the final probability of the other *SLCA* nodes. Finally, the *SLCA* node is output according to the order of final probability from large to small.

3.3 USlist Algorithm

In this subsection, we propose an algorithm denoted as USlist. Firstly, the spatiotemporal XML document tree is preorder traversal. According to the keyword set of the user query, the UK nodes of the matched XML document tree nodes are generated correspondingly and stored in the Dynamic Keyword Data

Warehouse. The USlist algorithm divides the UK nodes into many-to-one UK nodes and one-to-one UK nodes, and introduces generation algorithm of many-to-one UK nodes, which can be used to query the uncertain spatiotemporal XML data. From the leftmost UK node of the node list at the bottom of the Dynamic Keyword Data Warehouse, traverse all the UK nodes from the bottom to up and left to right. For an UK node with a parent node, use a certain integer of the number sequence of the UK node to determine the parent-child relationship, and the keyword inclusion case of the UK node is passed to the parent node. For an UK node without a parent node, use this UK node to generate its parent node. Considering the user's desire to return a higher probability of the query results, USlist set up the list to store SLCA nodes. Each node of the list stores the final probability of an SLCA node and its Dewey code. The order of the nodes in the list is arranged according to the value of the final probability. Only when all the UK nodes have been traversed, the Dewey code of the SLCA node with the highest K-bit probability value and its probability are output. The *USlist* algorithm can be performed in four steps.

USlist algorithm

***USlist* algorithm**

```
Create UKDR{ //Initialize Dynamic Keyword Data Warehouse
while(node.next!=root){
If (node.value=single) // Create one-to-one UK nodes
If (node.value=multi)// Create many-to-one UK nodes
Create MUKnode; }}
for (int i = UKDR. The size (); i >= 1, i --){
makeSLCA (UKDR, i) {// Acquire the SLCA node at the i-th layer
q1 = UKDR. get (j) first; //q1 points to the first element of the i-th linked list
q2 = UKDR. get (j - 1); //q2 points to the header of (i-1)-th linked list
while (q1! =null){// If there is a UK node at the i-th layer
if(q1 = SLCA) // If the UK node is SLCA node
insertSort (SLCAline, q1.Dewey, q1.BP.P);
updatenodeinfo (q1); // Update the node which q1 point to
if(q2. Next =null) // If the i-1 layer has no elements
{remove (q1);}
else {// If the first layer has UK nodes
while (q2.next< q1.parent)
q2= q2.next;// the q2pointer moves backwards
if (q2.next > q1.parent)
{remove (q1);}
else {
nodeinfoParent (q2.next, q1
}}
zeroSLCA (UKDR, 0) {// Get the SLCA nodes at layer 0
if (q1 =SLCA)
insertSort (SLCAline, q1); }
for (int i = 0; i < k; i++) {
printf (SLCAnode. Dewey, SLCAnode. BP. P);
SLCAnode = SLCAnode. Next;}
```

Step 1: In the first step, traversing the uncertain spatiotemporal XML document tree, the nodes containing query keywords correspond to the *UK* nodes in the dynamic keyword data warehouse

(1) If the accessed node is the root node in the uncertain spatiotemporal XML document tree, 0 is taken as the initial number sequence of the root node, and 1 is taken as the initial probability sequence

of the root node. For other nodes, the number of the node is combined with the number sequence of its parent node as its number sequence, and the conditional probability of the node is combined with the probability sequence of its parent node as its probability sequence.

(2) If an indeterminate spatiotemporal XML node is a query keyword and is the i-th of the keyword set $Key = \{k_1, k_2, \ldots, k_i\}$, the probability sequence, number sequence and Dewey coding sequence of the node are stored in the *UK* node corresponding to the *UK* node generating the dynamic keyword data warehouse, where the i-th bit of the binary bit string b in the *BP* is 1 and the probability p is 1. If the accessed node is a keyword, but more than one node is needed to represent its value node, these nodes are correspondingly generated into a *UK* node, and this *UK* node is a many-to-one *UK* node.

(3) If the node in the indeterminate spatiotemporal XML document tree is in the j-level of the document tree and matches a certain keyword, the *UK* node corresponding to this node is placed at the end of the j-level linked list in the dynamic keyword data warehouse.

Step 2: From left to right, we traverse the nodes of the k level of the dynamic keyword data warehouse, notice that k is not equal to 0, and finally get the *SLCA* nodes of the current level

(1) Pointer q_1 is used to point to the first element of the linked list at the current level j, and pointer q_2 is used to point to the head node of the linked list at the j-1 level.

(2) If the probability P of the last 2-tuple of the *UK* node pointed by q_1 is not 0, the first j bits of the Dewey coding sequence of the *UK* node and the final probability value of its *SLCA* node are stored in a node of the *SLCA* node linked list, and the linked list nodes are inserted into the *SLCA* node linked list according to the order of probability value from large to small. Note that the binary bit string of the last 2-tuple is in the form of "11111 ...", and then set the probability value of this 2-tuple to 0.

(3) If the node pointed to q_2 has no successor node, which means that the node pointed to q_1 has no parent node in its upper linked list, then the parent node of the node pointed to q_1 is generated. If its parent node becomes the successor of the node pointed to q_2, and then the q_1 pointer is moved backward.

(4) Otherwise, in the first case, the q_2 pointer is moved backward until the next field of the node pointed by q_2 points to the parent node of the node pointed by q_1. At this time, the *BP* binary group of the parent node pointed by q_1 is changed by using the proposed probability calculation method, and the keyword containing information of the node pointed by q_1 is transmitted to its parent node. In the second case, the next field where q_2 points to the node points to a node larger than the parent node where q_1 points to the node. At this point, the parent node of the q_1-pointing node is generated and placed after the q_2-pointing node, and then the q_1 pointer is moved backward.

(5) If the q_1 pointer is not empty, (2) of this step is executed; Otherwise, the K layer becomes the K+1 layer, and (2) of this step is performed on the K+1 layer.

Step 3: The nodes of layer 0 linked list are accessed from left to right to solve *SLCA* nodes.

Step 4: The probability values and Dewey codes of *SLCA* nodes whose probability values rank in the first K bits in the list of *SLCA* nodes are outputted

The time complexity and space complexity of *USlist* algorithm are analyzed from three stages: initialization process of dynamic keyword data warehouse, *SLCA* node solving process and *SLCA* node sorting process. Assuming that the number of uncertain spatiotemporal XML nodes is D, the number of queried keywords is K, the number of nodes containing queried keywords in uncertain spatiotemporal XML documents is M, the number of layers of dynamic keyword data warehouse is B, the number of *UK* nodes in layer *i* is M_i, and the number of *SLCA* nodes is L.

Time complexity: the initialization of dynamic keyword data warehouse is to generate corresponding *UK* nodes with uncertain spatiotemporal XML nodes containing keywords, and this process needs to traverse all uncertain spatiotemporal XML nodes, so the time complexity of this stage is O(D). In the process of solving *SLCA* nodes, each node of *UK* nodes in layer *i* should be compared with the bit *i* of the numbering sequence of UK nodes in layer *i*-1. If the parent node of *UK* node M_{ij} is not found in layer *i*-1, M_{ij} is used to generate the parent node, and the number of *UK* nodes in layer *i*-1 is increased by 1. In the worst case, the minimum common ancestor of every two keyword-containing nodes is the root node of the uncertain spatiotemporal XML tree, and the time complexity of this case is $O(\sum^{L}_{j=2}(B-j+1)*M_j+B+M)$. In the best case, M *UK* nodes are all in the same layer and the parent nodes are the same, and the time complexity of this case is O (2(M+B)-1). The *SLCA* nodes are sorted using insert sorting, and in the best case the *SLCA* nodes are already ordered (from large to small) with a time complexity of O(L). In the worst case, the *SLCA* nodes are in reverse order and the time complexity is $O(L^2)$.

Space complexity: The space complexity is related to the number of layers of dynamic keyword data warehouse and the number of *UK* nodes, and the space complexity is O(M+B).

3.4 Example

Figure 7 shows the location information of the cloud named cloud2. If the keyword query is (8: 00-12: 00, the location of the cloud), the corresponding information of the dynamic keyword data warehouse is as follows:

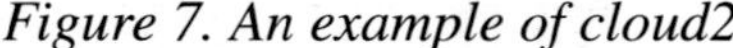

Figure 7. An example of cloud2

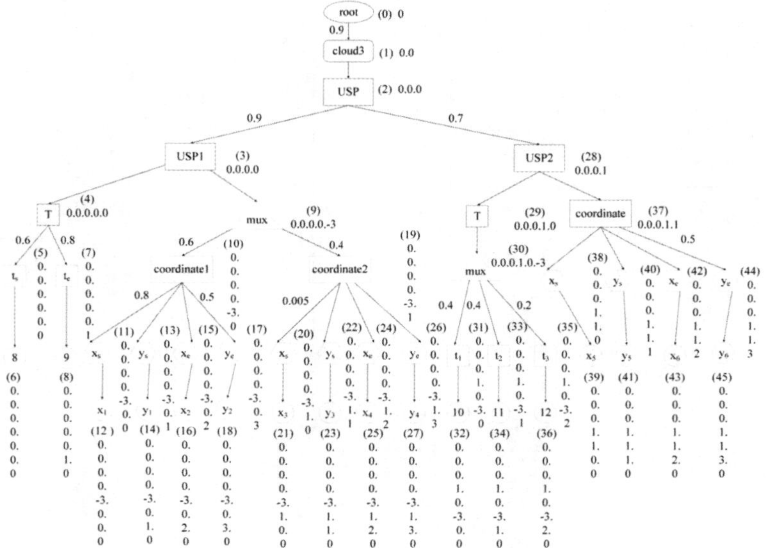

(1) Initialize the dynamic keyword data warehouse according to (8: 00-12: 00, cloud position). Because the time interval (8:00, 9:00) is included in the query time interval (8:00, 12:00), a many-to-one *UK* node is generated. The conditional probability of many-to-one *UK* nodes is the product of the conditional probabilities of all merged nodes, that is, 0.6 × 0.8 = 0.48. Other information of this many-to-one *UK* node is generated. Because time information is the first key to be queried, the corresponding probability of *BP* information binary bit string "01" of many-to-one *UK* node is 1. Finally, the generated *UK* node is placed at the fifth layer. Then, three many-to-one *UK* nodes with position information are generated, where the conditional probability of $\{(x_1, y_1), (x_2, y_2)\}$ is 0.5 × 0.8 = 0.4, the conditional probability of $\{(x_3, y_3), (x_4, y_4)\}$ is 0.5 × 0.6 = 0.3, and the conditional probability of $\{(x_5, y_5), (x_6, y_6)\}$ is 0.5. The corresponding probability of the three *BP* information binary bit strings "10" of the dynamic keyword data warehouse is 1, which are located at the 7th, 6th and 5th layers of dynamic keyword data warehouse respectively. Time information of cloud2 between 10:00 and 11:00 is also in the query time interval (8:00, 12:00), then the corresponding one-to-one *UK* nodes are generated, which are in the 7th layer of the dynamic keyword data warehouse. The specific initialization information are shown in Figure 8, Figure 9, and Figure 10.

Figure 8. Initialize the 7th layer of the UK node

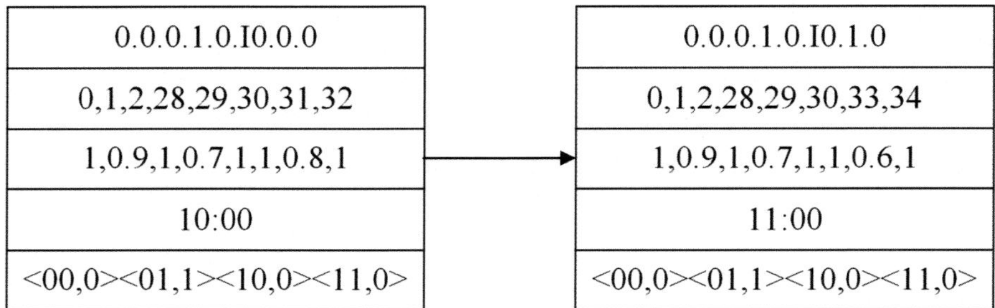

Figure 9. Initialize the 6th layer of the UK node

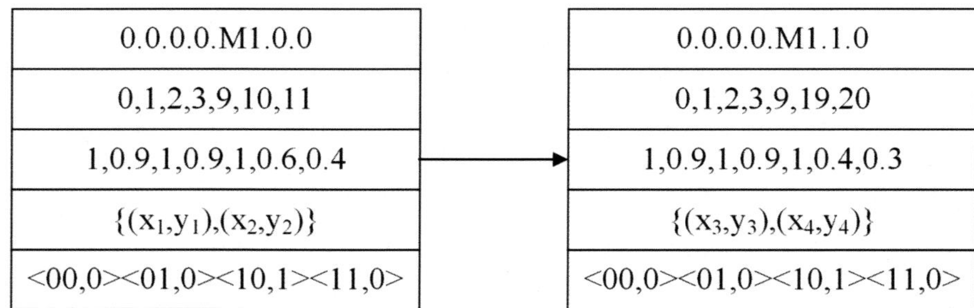

Figure 10. Initialize the 5th layer of the UK node

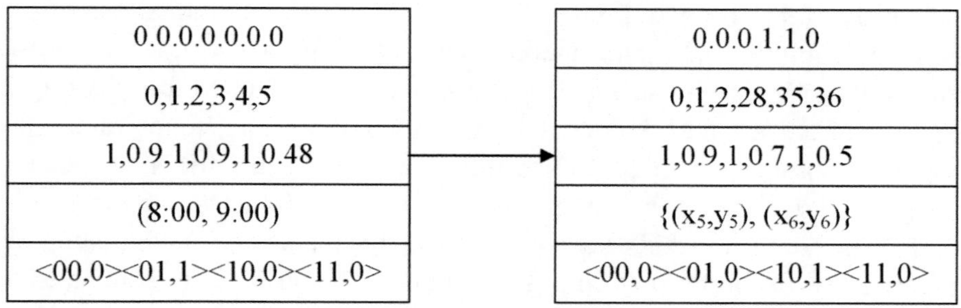

(2) Pass the keyword of the 7th layer to the 6th layer. Because the 7th bit (starting from 0) of the probability sequence of both *UK* nodes in the 7th layer is 1, that is, the conditional probability is 1, update the *BP* information according to the probability calculation formula, and the updated *UK* node of the 7th layer is the same as Figure 8. Because there is no parent node of the 7th layer *UK* node in the 6th layer, *UK* node of the 7th layer should be used to generate its parent node according to the algorithm. Finally, the *UK* node of the 6th layer in the dynamic keyword data warehouse is updated as shown in Figure 11.

Figure 11. Updated UK nodes of the sixth layer

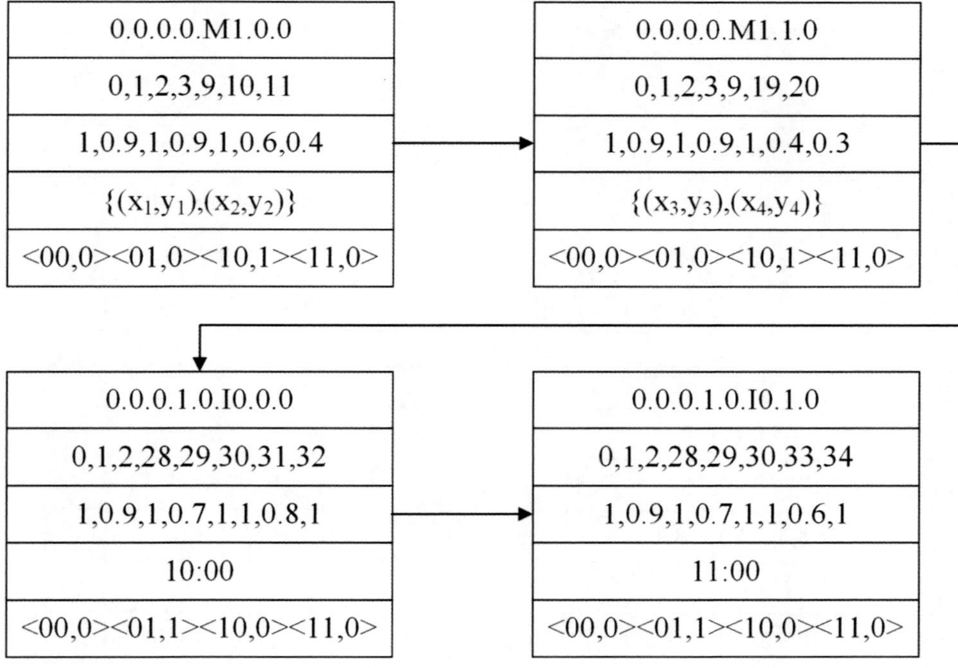

(3) Pass the keyword of the 6th layer to the 5th layer. The 6th bit (starting from 0) of the probability sequence of the first *UK* node in layer 6 is 0.4, that is, the conditional probability is 0.4, then the corresponding probability of *BP* information binary bit string "10" is updated to 0.4, and the corresponding probability of binary bit string "00" is updated to 0.6. The 6th bit (starting from 0) of the probability sequence of the second *UK* node in layer 6 is 0.3, that is, the conditional probability is 0.3, then the corresponding probability of *BP* information binary bit string "10" is updated to 0.3, and the corresponding probability of binary bit string "00" is updated to 0.7. The 6th bit (starting from 0) of the probability sequence of the third *UK* node in layer 6 is 0.8, that is, the conditional probability is 0.8, then the corresponding probability of *BP* information binary bit string "01" is updated to 0.8, and the corresponding probability of binary bit string "00" is updated to 0.2. The 6th bit (starting from 0) of the probability sequence of the fourth *UK* node in the 6th layer is 0.6, that is, the conditional probability is 0.4, then the corresponding probability of *BP* information binary bit string "01" is updated to 0.8, and the corresponding probability of binary bit string "00" is updated to 0.2. The final update result of all *UK* nodes in the 6th layer is shown in Figure 12. The first two *UK* nodes in the 6th layer of the dynamic keyword data warehouse have no parent node in the 5th layer of the dynamic data warehouse, so they need to generate their own parent nodes. If the fourth *UK* node and the third *UK* node in the 6th layer are the same parent node and the parent node is an *ind* type node, the parent node of the third *UK* node and the fourth *UK* node is generated by the method of dealing with *ind* type nodes. The *UK* node in the 5th layer of the final dynamic keyword data warehouse is shown in Figure 13.

Figure 12. Update all the UK nodes of the six layer

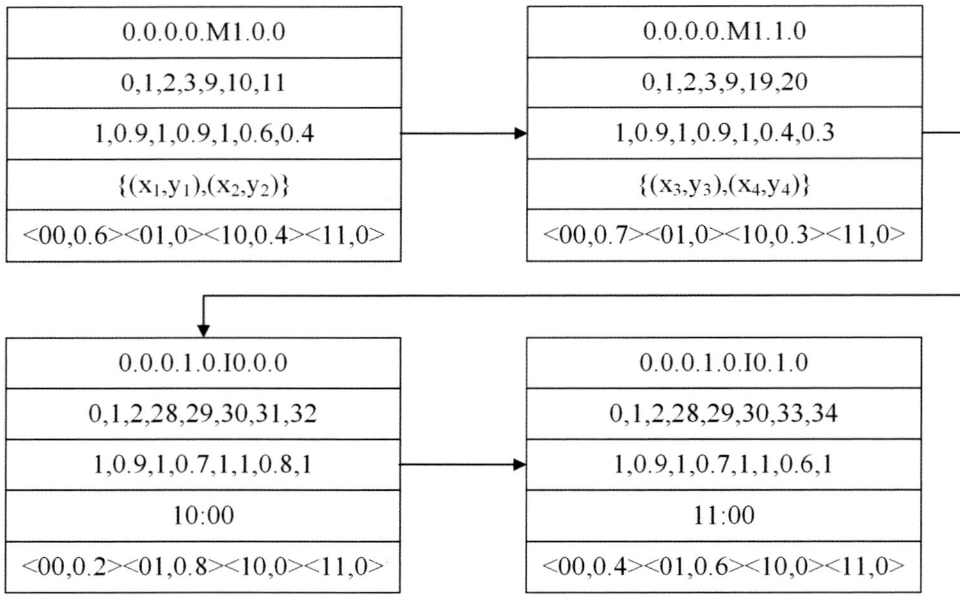

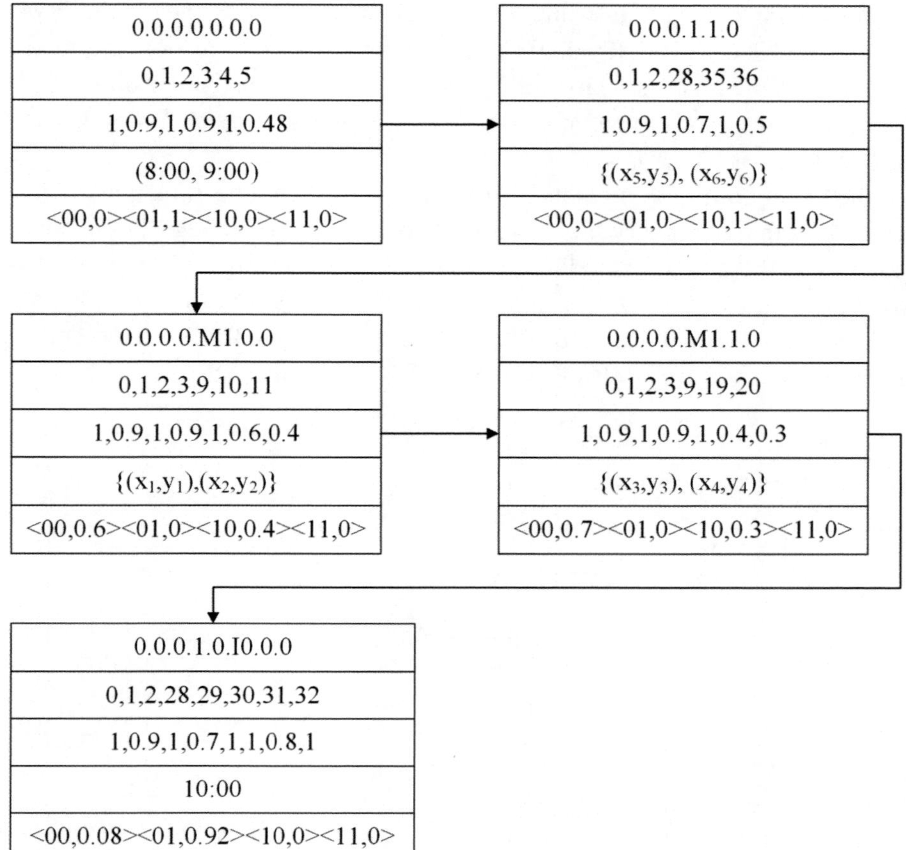

Figure 13. Updated UK nodes of the five layer

(4) Pass the keyword of the 5th layer to the 4th layer. Because the *UK* node in Figure 13 has no parent node in the 4th layer, it is necessary to update the *BP* information of each *UK* node according to the fifth bit of the probability sequence, and then generate a parent node respectively. Taking the fourth *UK* node in Figure 13 as an example, the fifth bit of its probability sequence is 0.4, and the probability corresponding to *BP* information "10" is 0.3, then the probability corresponding to updated *BP* information "10" is $0.3 \times 0.4 = 0.12$, and the probability corresponding to "00" is $1 - 0.12 = 0.88$. The updated *UK* node of the 5th layer is shown in Figure 14. The parent node of the 2nd and 3rd *UK* nodes in layer 5 is *mux* type. According to the generation method of *mux* type parent node, the common parent node of the 2nd and 3rd *UK* nodes is generated, and the final 4th *UK* node is shown in Figure 15.

(5) Pass the keyword of *UK* node of the 4th layer to the 3rd layer. Since the 4th bit (starting from 0) of the probability sequence of *UK* nodes in the 4th layer is all 1, that is, the conditional probabilities from *UK* nodes of the 4th layer to their parent nodes are all 1, the updated *BP* information of *UK* nodes of the 4th layer has not changed, as shown in Figure 15. Use the *UK* node in Figure 15 to generate its parent node. The first and third *UK* nodes have the same parent node, and the second and fourth *UK* nodes have the same parent node. In the 4th layer, taking the generation process of the parent node of the first *UK* node and the third *UK* node as an example. Firstly, the first *UK* node is used to generate

its parent node, and then the third *UK* node is used to update the *BP* information of its parent node: the probability corresponding to binary bit string "11" is 0.36 $\times$ 0.48=0.1728, the probability corresponding to binary bit string "01" is 0.64 $\times$ 0.48=0.3072, and the probability corresponding to binary bit string "10" is 0.36 $\times$ 0.52 = 0.1872, and the probability corresponding to the binary bit string "00" is 0.64 $\times$ 0.52 = 0.3328. In the same way, the parent nodes of the second and fourth *UK* nodes can be obtained. The final *UK* node of the 3rd layer is shown in Figure 16.

(6) Find out the *SLCA* node and calculate the final probability of it becoming a *SLCA* node. The corresponding probability that the binary bit string of the two *UK* nodes being "11" is not 0, so the XML nodes corresponding to these two *UK* nodes are *SLCA* nodes. According to Formula (1), the final probability of the first *SLCA* node is 1 $\times$ 0.9 $\times$ 1 $\times$ 0.9 $\times$ 0.1728 = 0.139968, and the final probability of the second *SLCA* node is 1 $\times$ 0.9 $\times$ 0.7 $\times$ 0.46 = 0. 2898. The code "0.0.0.1" of the second *SLCA* node is first output, and then the code "0.0.0.0" of the first *SLCA* node is output.

Figure 14. Update all the UK nodes of the fifth layer

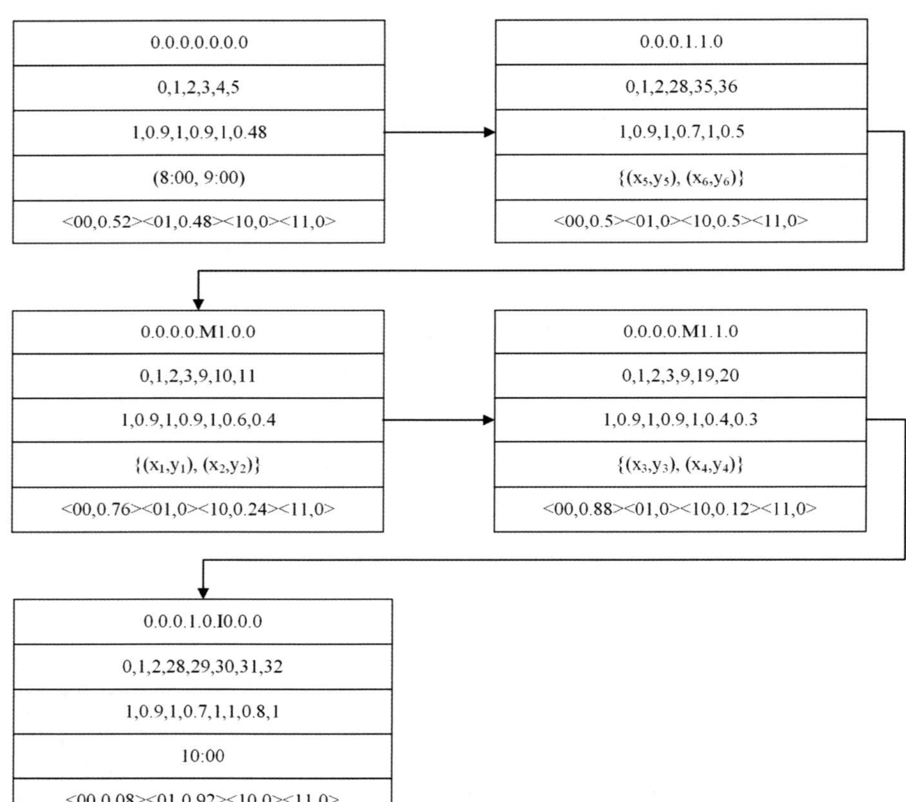

Figure 15. Updated UK nodes of the fourth layer

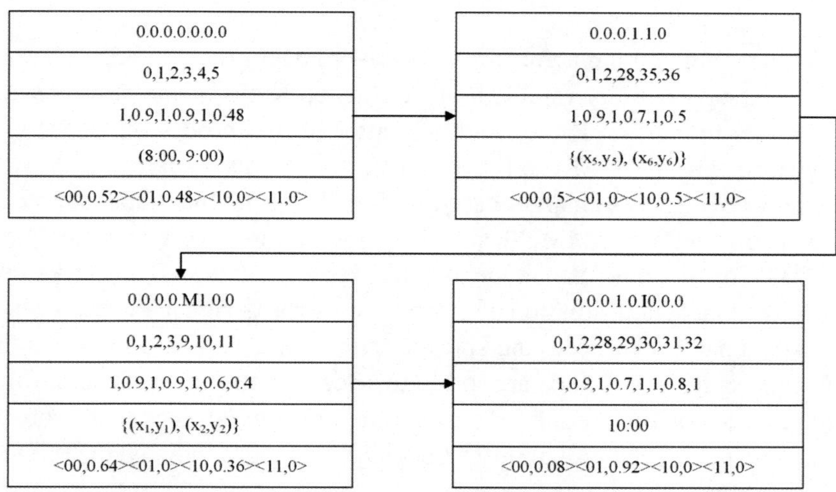

Figure 16. Updated UK nodes of the third layer

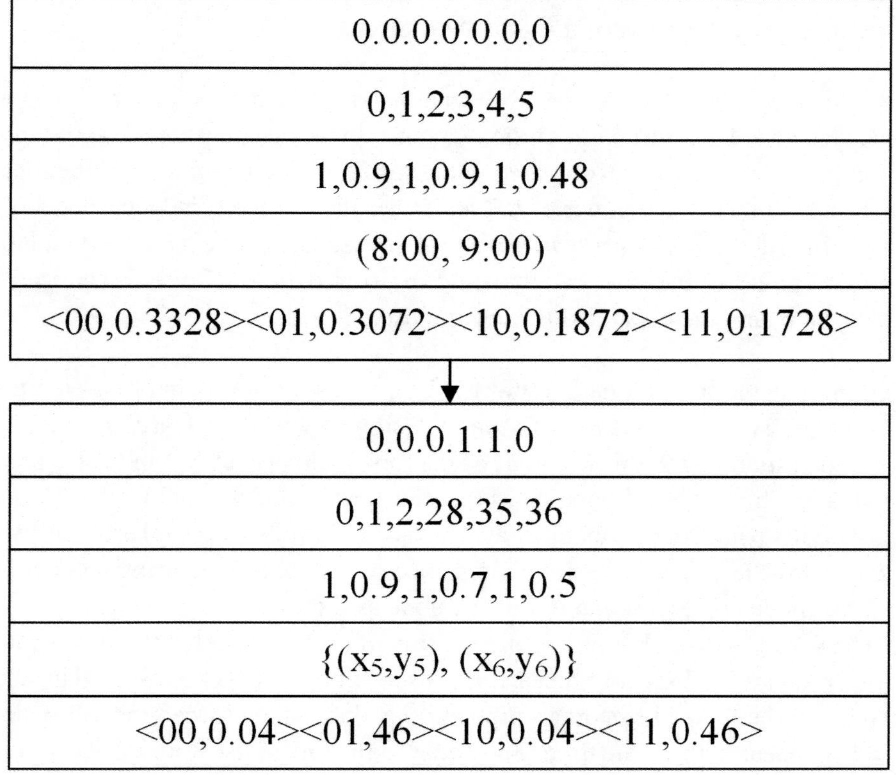

4 PRUNING AND SORTING ALGORITHM OF KEYWORD QUERY

Top-K algorithm is the main ranking algorithm for keyword query results. Top-K algorithm can return the query results with the probability value ranking in the top K bits. Generally, Top-K algorithm only returns the SLCA nodes in the first K bits, and only after further processing can it return the subtree containing all keywords. However, SRCT-Top-k in directly returns a subtree with SLCA node as the root node and all keywords. In this chapter, based on SRCT-Top-k, uncertain spatiotemporal elements are added to form a sort algorithm-MMT-Top-k for keyword query of uncertain spatiotemporal data based on XML. MMT-Top-k should extend the dynamic keyword data warehouse, extend the method of transferring the keyword inclusion situation of UK node upward, design a screening strategy, screen out the query results with small probability, and sort the remaining returned results. Firstly, the minimum meaningful trees in the same SLCA node are sorted to select the minimum meaningful trees with probability value in the first K position, remove the minimum meaningful trees with probability value after the K position, and update the total probability value of SLCA nodes. Finally, the minimum meaningful trees in different SLCA nodes are sorted to return the minimum meaningful trees MMT of K groups. In particular, a return group contains all the smallest meaningful tree MMT with the same SLCA node as the root node.

4.1 Extended Dynamic Keyword Data Warehouse

In order to facilitate the MMT-Top-k query, the dynamic keyword data warehouse proposed in section 3.1 will be expanded. The basic structure of the dynamic keyword data warehouse will not be changed, only the UK node will be expanded. Compared with the UK node in Section 3.1, the meaning of probability sequence and numbering sequence of *UK* nodes has not changed, and Dewey coding has become *PEDewey* coding. In order to deal with spatiotemporal nodes, this chapter changes text labels into a part of BP information. The BP of the extended dynamic keyword data warehouse is changed from a binary group to a triple group, and the expanded BP is composed as follows:

(1) Assuming that the number of query keywords is n, the binary bit string b has n bits, each bit represents a queried keyword, and records the inclusion of query keywords in the subtree with the XML node corresponding to this *UK* node as the root. A binary bit of 1 indicates that this keyword is included, and a binary bit of 0 indicates that this keyword is not included.

(2) Divide probability p into total probability and partial probability. The total probability represents the probability that the keyword inclusion represented by the binary bit string b occurs in the subtree with the XML node corresponding to the *UK* node as the root.

(3) There can be several sub-probabilities, and the sum of each sub-probability is the total probability, and the total probability does not exceed 1. Each sub-probability is represented by a linked list, and the head node of the linked list stores a probability value, which is the probability that all nodes in the linked list appear at the same time. The nodes in the linked list store *PEDewey* codes and node labels corresponding to uncertain time and space nodes, and the labels of many-to-one UK nodes are still generated according to the label generation method defined in Definition 5. All *PEDewey*-encoded corresponding nodes in the same linked list constitute an instance of the current binary bit string b keyword inclusion.

The expanded BP information structure is shown in Figure 17:

Figure 17. The extended BP structure

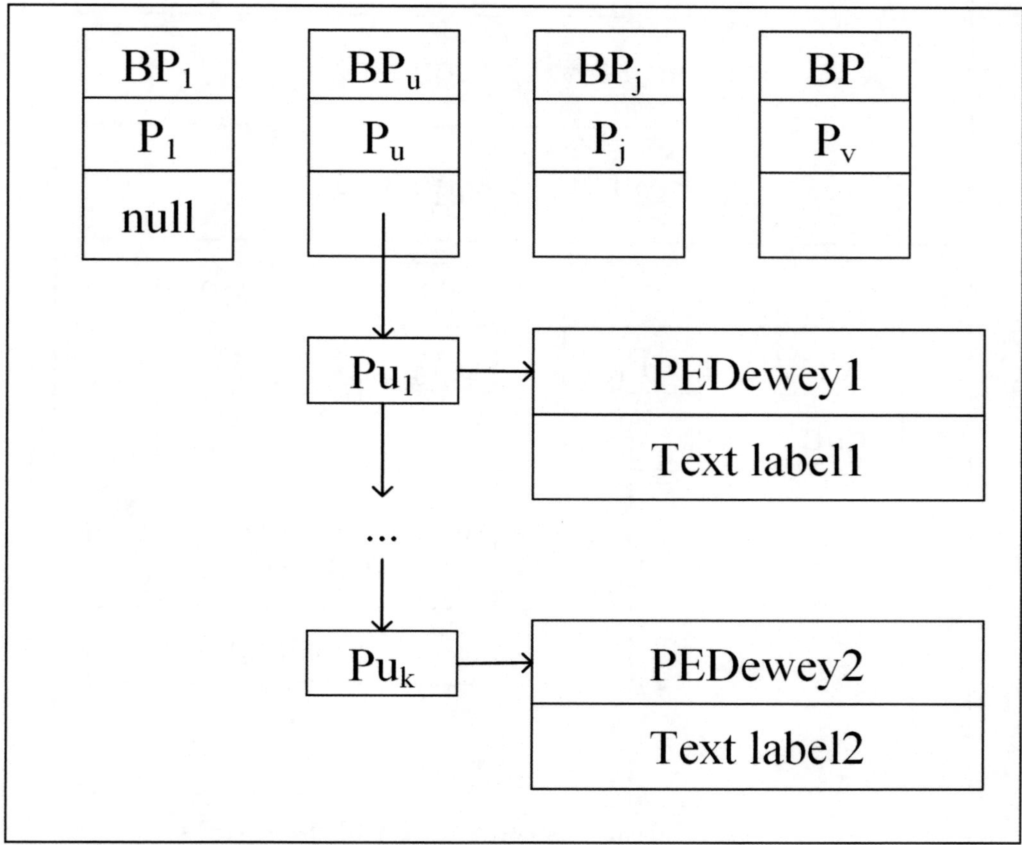

For extended dynamic keyword data warehouses, many-to-one *UK* nodes are still generated as defined 5. In order to support the MMT-Top-k algorithm, the dynamic keyword data warehouse should be initialized by adding the probability value and probability linked list. During initialization, the nodes of the probability link list are composed of *PEDewey* code and text label of the *UK* node, and the probability value is the total probability value.

The extended dynamic keyword data warehouse is shown in Figure 18:

4.2 Probability Calculation of Extended UK Nodes

Considering that MMT-Top-k algorithm needs to update the total probability information of SLCA nodes in order to delete the minimum meaningful tree with lower probability value when sorting the minimum meaningful tree of the same SLCA node within a group, this chapter divides the calculation of probability value into before sorting within a group and during sorting within a group.

Figure 18. The extended dynamic keyword data repository

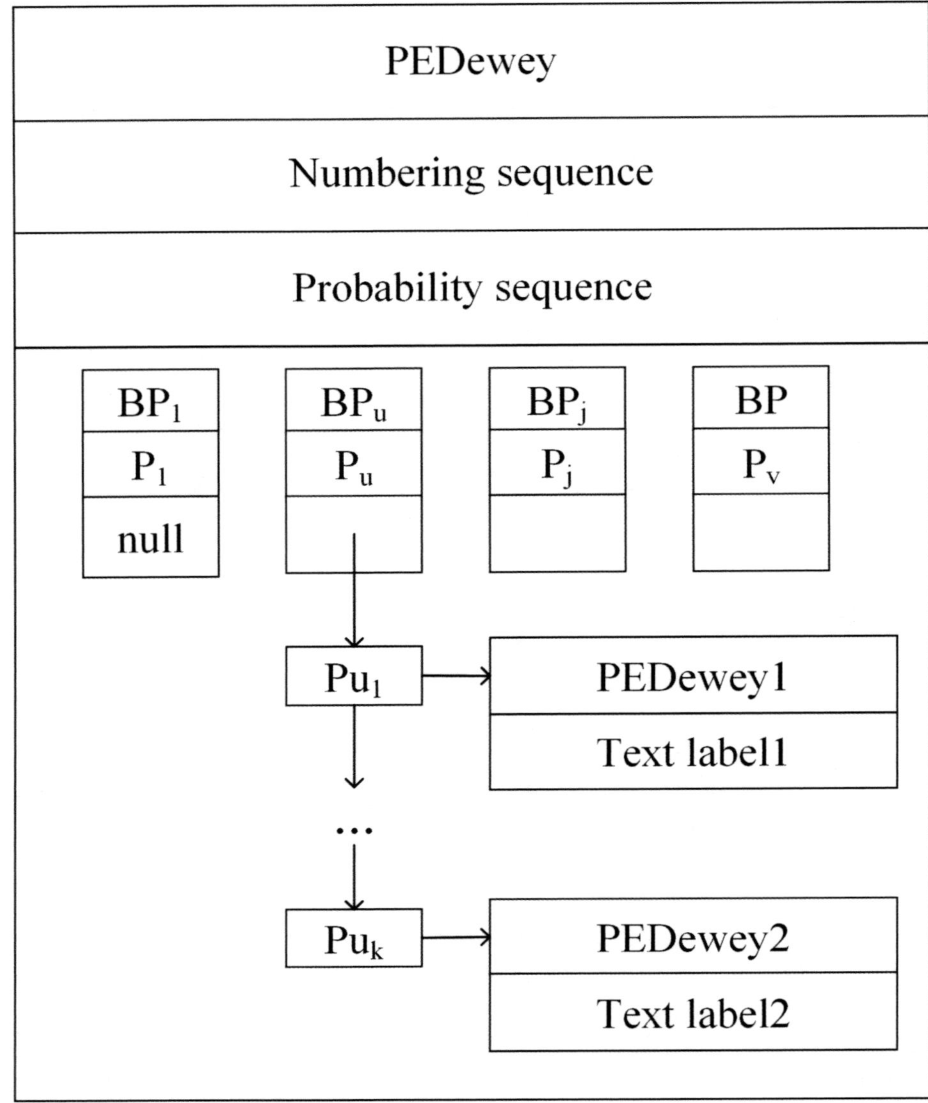

4.2.1 Probability Calculation Before Sorting Within a Group

When the MMT-Top-k algorithm is initialized, the probability calculation of many-to-one *UK* nodes is the same as 3.2.

Similar to the initialized operation of *USlist* algorithm, MMT-Top-k algorithm also traverses the *UK* node of dynamic keyword data warehouse, and passes up the keyword inclusion of the underlying *UK* node, that is, updates the BP information of its parent node according to the underlying *UK* node. The specific methods are as follows:

Suppose the keyword set $Key=\{w_1, w_2, w_3 ... w_n\}$, the parent node of *UK* node is *FU*, the total probability of the i ($1 \leq i \leq 2^n$) item of *BP* information of *FU* node is p_i, the binary bit string is b_i, the number of linked lists of corresponding partial probabilities is M_i, and the partial probability value of each linked list of partial probabilities is p_{ij} ($1 \leq j \leq M_i$). The *FU* node has x child nodes, each child node K_k ($0 \leq k \leq x$), the value of conditional probability is f_k, the total probability of the $u(1 \leq u \leq 2^n)$ item of BP information of the node K_k is p_u, the binary bit string is b_u, the number of linked lists of corresponding partial probabilities is M_u, and the partial probability value of each linked list of partial probabilities is p_{uv} ($1 \leq v \leq M_u$).

(1) If the *FU* node is of mux type, the *BP* information of its child node K_k is updated using formulas 9 and 10.

$$p_u = p_u \times f_k (1 \leq u \leq 2^n) \tag{9}$$

$$p_{uv} = p_{uv} \times f_k \ (2 \leq u \leq 2^n, 1 \leq v \leq M_u) \tag{10}$$

The total probability p_i and the partial probability value p_{ij} of the term $i(1 \leq i \leq 2^n\text{-}1)$ of the *BP* information of the parent node *FU* are then updated as follows: p_i is the sum of the total probability values of the term i of the *BP* information of all the child nodes. For all child nodes K_k, if the partial probability value of item i of *BP* information of a child node is not empty, all the partial probability linked lists of item i of the child node are added to the partial probability information of item i of BP information of the parent node *FUK*. Finally, the total probability value of the first term of the parent node *FUK* is updated by using Formula 11.

$$P_1 = f_k + (1 - \sum^{x}_{k=2} f_k) \tag{11}$$

(2) If the parent node *FU* is type of ind, the *BP* information of its child node K_k is updated by using Formula 12, Formula 13and Formula 14.

$$p_u = p_u \times f_k (1 \leq u \leq 2^n) \tag{12}$$

$$p_u = p_{1\text{-}} f_k \times (1 - p_u)(u=1) \tag{13}$$

$$p_{uv} = p_{uv} \times f_k (2 \leq u \leq 2^n, 1 \leq v \leq M_u) \tag{14}$$

Thereafter, the total probability p_i and the partial probability value p_{ij} of the term $i(1 \leq i \leq 2^n\text{-}1)$ of the *BP* information of the parent node *FU* are updated according to the following method: each binary bit string b_i of the *BP* information of the parent node *FU* is logically "and" operated with the binary bit strings of all its child nodes K_k ($0 \leq k \leq x$), and if the binary bit strings b_u of the child nodes are the same as the binary bit strings b_i of the parent node *UK*, the partial probability information corresponding to the binary bit strings b_u of these child nodes is arranged and combined. Thereafter, the permutation and combination result is placed in the i-th sub-probability information of the *BP* information of the parent node *UK*, and the total probability information p_i of the i-th item of the parent node is equal to the product of the total probability information of these child nodes, and the sub-probability value of each item of the parent node is equal to the product of the sub-probability values of these child nodes. The linked list node of each sub-probability linked list of the parent node is composed of the linked list nodes of the corresponding sub-probability linked list of these child nodes.

(3) If the parent node *FU* is an ordinary XML node, it is treated in the same way as if the parent node *FU* is of type ind. Note that if the parent node *FU* is a normal XML node, it may be the root node of the smallest meaningful tree *MMT*. At this time, if the total probability value of the last item of the parent node *BP* information is not 0, the minimum meaningful tree *MMT* can be obtained from the partial probability linked list of the last item of the parent node *BP* information (the item with all binary bit strings is the last item of *BP* information), and the product of the partial probability and the path probability of the parent node is the probability of the minimum meaningful tree *MMT*, and then the total probability value of the item is changed to 0, and the partial probability information is changed to null.

4.2.2 Probability Calculation of Intra-Group Sorting

In order to sort the minimum meaningful tree in the same *SLCA* node, the minimum meaningful tree whose probability value is after the *K*-th bit should be removed, that is, in the dynamic keyword data warehouse, the sub-probability linked list whose probability value is after the *K*-th bit should be removed, and the sub-probability linked lists are mutually exclusive. The total probability value of the updated *SLCA* node is the original total probability value minus the sub-probability value of the sub-probability linked list. Assuming that the *UK* node corresponding to this *SLCA* node has *u* sub-linked lists, the total probability is expressed as *p*, and the updated total probability is expressed as *p**.

$$p^{*}=p-\sum\nolimits^{u}_{j=k+1}p_{j} \tag{15}$$

4.3 Screening Strategy of MMT-Top-k

MMT-Top-K only returns the smallest meaningful tree *MMT* whose probability values rank in the first *K* positions. However, *MMT* with low probability value always occupies a lot of space to store the updated sub-probability linked list in the process of its generation. In view of the above situation, this chapter puts forward the following strategies:

Let p_i be the total probability value of item *i* of *BP* information at *UK* node, p_{ij} be the *j*-th partial probability value of item *i*, and min store the probability boundary value, indicating that the return result below min is unacceptable. Therefore, the probability values of the first *K* groups of minimum meaningful trees returned by MMT-Top-K are all greater than or equal to min. If too many minimum meaningful trees are returned, the value of min can be appropriately increased, and if too few minimum meaningful trees are returned, the value of min can be appropriately reduced to obtain more minimum meaningful trees higher than the probability boundary value.

(1) When initializing the dynamic keyword data warehouse, if it is a many-to-one *UK* node, it is necessary to correspond multiple uncertain spatiotemporal XML nodes to a *UK* node. At this time, the conditional probability of this *UK* node is calculated according to the probability formula of 3.2. If the conditional probability is less than min, the generation of this many-to-one *UK* node is abandoned.

(2) If p_i is less than min, then p_i becomes 0, and all the sub-probability linked lists of item *i BP* information are deleted, and the sub-probability information becomes null, then all the sub-probability linked lists of item *i BP* information do not participate in generating parent node *FU*.

(3) If p_i is not less than min, the *BP* information of the *UK* node is updated. If the total probability of item *i* of the *BP* information of the *UK* node is less than min, the total probability p_i of item *i* of the *BP* information of the *UK* node is changed to 0, and the partial probability information is changed to null.

(4) If p_i is not less than min, the *BP* information of the *UK* node is updated. If the total probability of item *i* of the *BP* information of the *UK* node is greater than or equal to min, the partial probability value p_{ij} of item *i* of the *BP* information of the *UK* node is checked. If p_{ij} is less than min, delete the *j*-th partial probability linked list of the *i*-th BP information, and update the total probability value to make the total probability value p_i - p_{ij}. If the final total probability value p_i of item *i* of *BP* information of *UK* node is less than min after processing all the linked lists of sub-probability, then p_i becomes 0, all the linked lists of sub-probability of *BP* information of item *i* are deleted, and the sub-probability information becomes null.

(5) Refer to section 4.2: When the parent node *FU* is an ind type or an ordinary XML node, each binary bit string b_i in the *BP* information of the parent node *FU* is logically "and" operated with the binary bit strings of all its child nodes K_k (0≤k≤x). If the binary bit strings b_u of the child node are the same as the binary bit strings b_i of the parent node *UK*, the probability information corresponding to the binary bit strings b_u of these child nodes is arranged and combined. After adopting the screening strategy:

①If the total probability product of the *i*-th *BP* information of two child nodes is less than min, the partial probability information corresponding to the binary bit string b_u of these two child nodes will not be permutated and combined, and will not participate in the generation of the parent node *FU*.

②If the total probability product of the first item *BP* information of two child nodes is greater than or equal to min, and the product of the partial probability value of the first item *BP* information of two child nodes is less than min, the corresponding partial probability linked list of the first item *BP* information of these two child nodes does not participate in permutation and combination, and does not participate in the generation of parent node *FU*.

4.4 Ranking Strategy of Query Results Based on MMT-Top-k

After the screening strategy in section 4.3, MMT-Top-k first obtains all the minimum meaningful trees *MMT* whose probability value is higher than the probability boundary value min. The sorting method of *MMT* whose probability value is higher than the probability boundary value min is as follows:

First, the *MMT* of the same *SLCA* node is sorted, and then the *MMT* of different *SLCA* nodes is sorted.

4.4.1 MMT Sorting of the Same SLCA Node

If the total probability value of the last item of the *BP* information of the *UK* node is not 0, then its corresponding XML node is the *SLCA* node. The *MMT* of the same *SLCA* node is stored in the same *UK* node. Each partial probability information of the last *BP* information of the *UK* node corresponds to a different minimum meaningful tree *MMT*, and each partial probability value corresponds to the probability of a minimum meaningful tree *MMT*. If the number *N* of the minimum meaningful tree *MMT* with the same *SLCA* node as the root node is greater than *K*, the probability of the minimum meaningful tree *MMT* is taken from *K* probability linked lists with the first *K* position of the probability value, all the probability linked lists with the probability value after the *K* position are deleted, and the total probability of the *UK* node where the *MMT* is located is updated so as not to contain the deleted probability; If the number of the minimum meaningful tree *MMT* with the same *SLCA* node as the root node *N* is less than *K*, the *UK* node will not be changed. In this way, the *MMT* sorting of the same *SLCA* node is obtained, and then the *MMT* sorting of different *SLCA* nodes is carried out.

4.4.2 MMT Sorting of Different SLCA Nodes

(1) Defining non-partitionable sets

The minimum meaningful trees *MMT* of different *SLCA* nodes are stored in different *UK* nodes. For each *UK* node, we introduce probability boundary 1 and probability boundary 2 as an unpartitioned set. By comparing the probability boundary 1 and probability boundary 2 of each *UK* node, we continue to reduce the size of *UK* nodes, and finally get *K* groups of minimum meaningful trees *MMT* with the first *K* probability values.

Definition 7. Inseparable Set is defined as a non-separable set for all the smallest meaningful trees *MMT* with the same *SLCA* node as the root node. We take the product of the total probability of the last *BP* information of *SLCA* node corresponding to *UK* node and the path probability of *SLCA* as the probability boundary 1 of the unpartitionable set, and the product of the path probability of *SLCA*, which is the maximum partial probability of the last *BP* information, as the probability boundary 2 of the unpartitionable set. Note that probability boundary 1 is greater than or equal to probability boundary 2. A table tb1 is obtained by ordering a plurality of non-partitionable sets from large to small according to a probability boundary 1 and a table tb2 is obtained by ordering a plurality of non-partitionable sets from large to small according to a probability boundary 2.

(2) Top-k strategy

If the inseparable sets represented by the first *K* entries of table tb1 are the same as the inseparable sets represented by the first *K* entries of table tb2, then *K* inseparable sets are returned in the order in which they are arranged in table tb2.

If the inseparable set represented by the first *K* entries of table tb1 and the inseparable set represented by the first *K* entries of table tb2 are only partially identical, the inseparable set represented by the first *K* entries of table tb1 is returned.

If the inseparable set represented by the first *K* entries of table tb1 is completely different from the inseparable set represented by the first *K* entries of table tb1, the inseparable set represented by the first *K* entries of table tb1 is returned.

4.5 MMT-Top-k Algorithm

The MMT-Top-k algorithm firstly performs root traversal on uncertain spatiotemporal XML documents, and according to the keyword set queried by users, generates extended *UK* nodes corresponding to the matched XML document tree nodes and stores them in the corresponding positions of the extended dynamic keyword data warehouse. MMT-Top-k algorithm also divides extended *UK* nodes into many-to-one *UK* nodes and one-to-one *UK* nodes in order to query the spatiotemporal attributes of uncertain spatiotemporal data whose values can only be expressed by multiple value nodes. After that, we start from the leftmost *UK* node of the lowest linked list of the extended dynamic data warehouse, traverse the *UK* node from bottom to top and from left to right, and pass the keyword inclusion of the *UK* node to the parent node of the *UK* node. Finally, the MMT-Top-K algorithm first obtains all the minimum meaningful trees which are higher than the probability boundary value min selected by the screening strategy, and then uses the sorting algorithm to select *K* groups of minimum meaningful trees *MMT* with probability values in front of *K* bits, that is, *K* unpartitionable sets.

The MMT-Top-k algorithm is implemented as follows:

MMT-Top-k algorithm

```
createUKDR{ // Initialize the dynamic keyword data warehouse
while(node.next!=root){// Root traversal of uncertain spatiotemporal XML document tree
if(node.value=single) // If it is a single-valued node
create OUKnode;// Generate one-to-one UK nodes
if(node.value=multi)// If it is a multi-valued node, whether the conditional probability is greater than the probability boundary value min is judged
create MUKnode;}}// If the conditional probability is greater than the probability boundary value min, a many-to-one UK node is generated according to definition 6
for(int i=UKDR.layer();i>=1,i--){// Traverse the data warehouse from bottom to top and from left to right (except layer 0), find all SLCA nodes, sort the minimum meaningful trees in the same SLCA node first, and then sort the minimum meaningful trees in different SLCA nodes
makeSLCA(UKDR,i){// Get the Layer i SLCA Node
q1=UKDR.get(j).first;// q1 points to the first element of the i-level linked list
q2=UKDR.get(j-1);// q2 points to the head node of Layer i-1 linked list
while(q1!=null){// If there are UK nodes in Layer i
If(q1=SLCA){// If the XML node corresponding to the UK node is an SLCA node higher than the probability boundary min
Sort(q1);// Call the sort function to sort within this SLCA node group: all the sub-linked lists of this SLCA node are removed from the sub-linked lists below the k-th bit according to the order of probability value from large to small, and the total probability of the last BP information of this SLCA node is modified
InsertLine1(q1. p1, q1);// p1 is the product of the total probability of SLCA nodes and the path probability, that is, probability boundary 1. Insert sorting function Insert1 is called to sort SLCA nodes according to the size of probability boundary 1, and the address of this SLCA node in the data warehouse is stored in Line1
InsertLine2(q1. p2, q1);// p2 is the maximum partial probability value of the SLCA node, that is, the probability boundary 2 calls the insert sorting function Insert2 to sort the SLCA nodes according to the size of the probability boundary 2, and stores the address of the SLCA node in the data warehouse in Line2
updateNodeInfo(q1);}// Update q1 Points to Node
If(q2.next=null) // If there are no elements in the i-1 layer
{updateP(q1);// First update the probability information of q1 according to section 4.2, and then filter the BP information greater than the probability boundary value min according to section 4.3
remove(q1);}// If the q1 pointing node has BP information greater than min, the q1 pointing node is moved up to the i-1 layer to generate its parent node, and the q1 pointer moves backward; Otherwise, the q1 pointer moves directly backward
else {// If there are UK nodes in layer i-1
while (q2.next< q1.parent)// q2 points to the successor of the node less than q1 points to the parent of the node
q2= q2.next;// q2 Pointer moves backward
if(q2.next> q1.parent)// q2 points to the successor of the node greater than q1 points to the parent of the node
{ updateP(q1);// First update the probability information of q1 according to section 4.2, and then filter the BP information greater than the probability boundary value min according to section 4.3
remove(q1);}// If the q1 pointing node has BP information greater than min, the q1 pointing node is moved up to the i-1 layer to generate its parent node, and the q1 pointer moves backward; Otherwise, the q1 pointer moves directly backward
else {// If q2 points to the node's successor is equal to q1 points to the node's father
nodeinfoParent(q2.next, q1);}// The BP information of q1 node greater than the probability boundary value min is transmitted to the successor of the node indicated by q2 pointer, and then the p1 pointer moves backward
} } }
ZeroSLCA(UKDR,0){// Get the SLCA node in Layer 0
q1=UKDR.get(0).first;// q1 points to the first element of the Layer 0 linked list
if(q1=SLCA){// If the XML node corresponding to the UK node is a SLCA node higher than the probability boundary min
Sort(q1);// Call the sort function to sort within this SLCA node group: all the sub-linked lists of this SLCA node are removed from the sub-linked lists below the k-th bit according to the order of probability value from large to small, and the total probability of the last BP information of this SLCA node is modified
InsertLine1(q1. p1, q1);// p1 is the probability boundary 1 of SLCA node. Insert sorting function InsertLine1 is called to sort SLCA nodes according to the size of probability boundary 1, and the address of this SLCA node in data warehouse is stored in Line1
InsertLine2(q1. p2, q1);}// p2 is the maximum partial probability value of SLCA node, that is, probability boundary 2. Insert sorting function InsertLine2 is called to sort SLCA nodes according to the size of probability boundary 2, and the address of this SLCA node in data warehouse is stored in Line2
Selectnode(Line1,Line2);// According to Line1 and Line2, K groups of minimal meaningful subtrees are selected by Selectnode function and stored in SLCNode chain table
while(SLCAnode.next!=null){// Traversing SlaRnode linked list
Printf (SLCAnode.MMT);// K groups of minimal meaningful trees with the output probability value ranked in the first K bits, that is, K unpartitionable sets
SLCAnode=SLCAnode.next;}
```

The MMT-Top-k algorithm is divided into the following three steps:

Step 1: (lines 1-6) In the traversal process, if the uncertain spatiotemporal XML node contains keywords, the *UK* node of the extended dynamic keyword data warehouse is generated by using the information of the uncertain spatiotemporal XML node. If the accessed node is a keyword, but more than one node is needed to represent its value node, the conditional probability of these nodes is calculated according to formula 2 by using the method in definition 5. If it is greater than the probability boundary value min, a *UK* node is generated correspondingly, and this *UK* node is a many-to-one *UK* node.

Step 2: (lines 5-34) All the minimum meaningful tree *MMTs* above the probability boundary value min are screened out, and all the *MMTs* in the same *SLCA* node are sorted first, and then the *MMTs* in different SLCA nodes are sorted according to section 4.4.2.

The extended dynamic keyword data warehouse is traversed from bottom to top and from left to right. If the *UK* node has a parent node, the *BP* information of the parent node is updated. If the *UK* node has no parent node, the *UK* node is used to generate its parent node and update the *BP* information of the parent node.

The updating method of parent node *BP* information is related to the node type of the parent node: if the parent node is mux type, use (1) in section 4.2 to get the parent node *BP* information; If the parent node is of type ind, use (2) in section 4.2 to get the parent node *BP* information; If the parent node is of type ind, use (2) in section 4.2 to get the parent node *BP* information; If the parent node is an ordinary uncertain spatiotemporal XML node type, use (3) in section 4.2 to obtain the parent node *BP* information. In the process of generating the parent node, according to the screening strategy in Section 4.3, pruning the probabilistic linked list below min, and screening out the smallest meaningful tree above the probability boundary value min.

Among them, (lines 13-15) and (lines 31-34) sort the filtered smallest meaningful trees. The function sort is used to sort the minimum meaningful trees of the same *SLCA* node. The number of the minimum meaningful trees of the same *SLCA* node is relatively small, and they are arranged directly according to the probability value from large to small. After that, the minimum meaningful trees of different *SLCA* n odes are sorted. All the minimal meaningful trees of the same *SLCA* node are regarded as an unpartitionable set, and the unpartitionable sets are sorted by the function InsertLine1 according to the probability boundary 1 of the unpartitionable set, and the sorting result exists in line 1. The function InsertLine1 is used to sort the unpartitionable sets according to the probability boundary 2 of the unpartitionable sets, and the sorting result exists in line 2.

Step 3: (lines 33-38) All the non-partition sets in the top *K* bits are selected, and all the minimal meaningful trees of these non-partition sets are output. Using the Top-K strategy in section 4.4.2, *K* non-partition sets are screened out in line 1 and line 2, and all the minimal meaningful trees of *K* non-partition sets are output.

4.6 Algorithm Complexity Analysis

The time complexity and space complexity of MMT-Top-k algorithm are analyzed from three stages: initialization of dynamic keyword data warehouse, solution of *SLCA* nodes and ordering of *SLCA* nodes. Assuming that the number of uncertain spatiotemporal XML nodes is *D*, the number of queried keywords is *K*, the number of nodes containing queried keywords in uncertain spatiotemporal XML documents is *M*, the number of layers of dynamic keyword data warehouse is *B*, the number of *UK* nodes in layer *i* is M_i, all the probability linked lists of M_i are ML_i, the *j* node in layer *i* is M_{ij}, the probability linked lists of

M_{ij} are ML_{ij}, the number of *SLCA* nodes greater than the probability boundary value min is L, and the probability linked lists of the last *BP* information in each *SLCA* node are L_i.

Time complexity of the algorithm:

The initialization of dynamic keyword data warehouse is to generate the corresponding *UK* node with uncertain spatiotemporal XML nodes containing keywords. This process needs to traverse all uncertain spatiotemporal XML nodes, so the time complexity of this stage is *O(D)*.

In the process of solving *SLCA* nodes, each node of *UK* nodes in layer *i* should be compared with the bit *i* of the numbering sequence of *UK* nodes in layer *i*-1. If the parent node of *UK* node M_{ij} is not found in layer *i*-1, M_{ij} is used to generate the parent node, and the number of *UK* nodes in layer *i*-1 is increased by 1.

In the worst case, the minimum common ancestor of every two keywords containing nodes is the root node of the uncertain spatiotemporal XML tree, and all the sub-probability linked lists participate in the whole process of generating the sub-probability information of the parent node. In this case, the time complexity of the algorithm MMT-Top-k is $O(\sum^{L}_{j=2}(B-j+1)*ML_j+B+ML)$. In the best case, *M UK* nodes are in the same layer, the parent nodes are the same, and all the sub-probability linked lists do not participate in generating the sub-probability information of the parent node. All the time complexity of this case is O(2(ML+B)-1);

The minimum meaningful tree sorting within the same *SLCA* node uses insertion sorting, and the best case is that the *MMT* within all *SLCA* nodes has been ordered (from large to small), and the time complexity is $O(\sum^{L}_{i=2} L_i)$. In the worst case, the MMT in all SLCA nodes is in reverse order and the time complexity is $O(\sum^{L}_{i=1} L_i^2)$.

Sort among different *SLCA* nodes using insertion sort, using probability upper bound and probability lower bound each sort, the best case is that the *SLCA* nodes have been ordered (from large to small), the time complexity is O(2L). In the worst case, the SLCA nodes are in reverse order and the time complexity is $O(2L^2)$.

Spatial complexity of the algorithm:

The spatial complexity is related to the number of layers of dynamic keyword data warehouse, the number of UK nodes and the number of SLCA nodes, and the spatial complexity is O (M+B+2L).

4.7 Examples

Figure 19 shows the location information of the cloud layer named cloud3. If the query keyword is (8: 00-12: 00, the location of the cloud layer) and 0.0006 is specified as the probability boundary value min, the corresponding information of the dynamic keyword data warehouse is as follows:

(1) Initialize the dynamic keyword data warehouse according to (8: 00-12: 00, cloud position). Where the time interval (8:00, 9:00) is included in the query time interval (8:00, 12:00), the corresponding many-to-one *UK* node is generated, and the conditional probability of the many-to-one *UK* node is the product of the conditional probabilities of all merged nodes, that is, 0.6×0.8=0.48. Other information of this many-to-one *UK* node is generated according to Definition 5, Definition 6 and 7. Because time information is the first key to be queried, the corresponding total probability of *BP* information binary bit string "01" of many-to-one *UK* node is 1, and the sub-probability is also 1. Finally, the generated *UK* node is placed in Layer 5. Then, according to the methods of definition 5 and definition 6, two many-to-one *UK* nodes with position information are generated, where the conditional probability of {(x1, y1), (x2, y2)} is 0.5×0.8=0.4, which is greater than the probability boundary value min0.0006,

then the corresponding many-to-one UK node is generated and stored in the sixth layer of the extended dynamic keyword data warehouse; However, the conditional probability of positions {(x3, y3), (x4, y4)} is 0.0005, which is lower than the probability boundary value min0.0006. According to the screening strategy (1), positions {(x3, y3), (x4, y4)} do not generate corresponding many-to-one *UK* nodes; If the conditional probability of {(x5, y5), (x6, y6)} is 0.5, which is greater than the probability boundary value min0.0006, the corresponding many-to-one *UK* node is generated and exists in the fifth layer of the extended dynamic keyword data warehouse. The corresponding total probability of *BP* information binary bit string "10" of these two many-to-one *UK* nodes is 1, and the partial probability is also 1. When the time information of cloud3 is also within the query time interval (8:00, 12:00) at 10:00, 11:00 and 12:00, the corresponding one-to-one *UK* nodes are generated. The corresponding total probability of *BP* information binary bit string "01" of these three *UK* nodes is 1, and the partial probability is also 1, which is in the 7th layer of the extended dynamic keyword data warehouse. The specific initialization information is as follows:

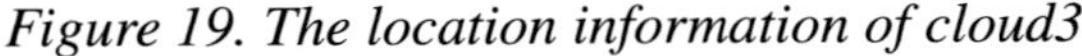

Figure 19. The location information of cloud3

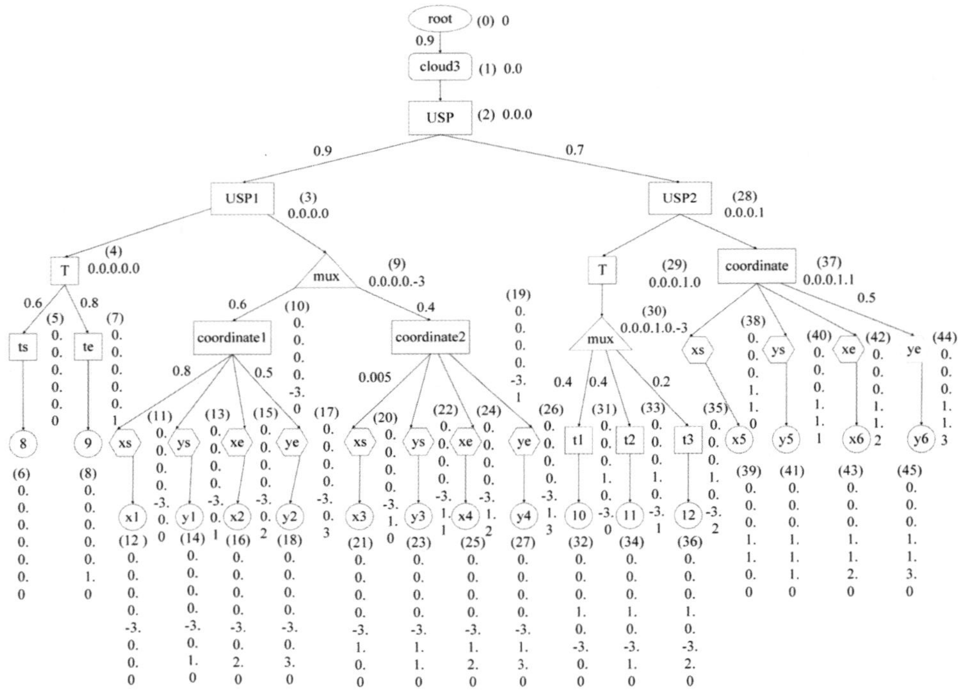

(2) Pass the keyword inclusion of Layer 7 to Layer 6: Because the 7th bit (starting from 0) of the probability sequence of the three *UK* nodes in Layer 7 is 1, that is, the conditional probability is 1, update the *BP* information according to the probability calculation formula in Section 4.2, and the updated Layer 7 *UK* nodes are the same as Figure 22. Because Layer 6 does not have a parent of the Layer 7 *UK* node, the Layer 7 *UK* node is used to generate its parent node, and finally the Layer 6 *UK* node is updated as shown in Figure 23.

Figure 20. Initialize the fifth floor of the UK node

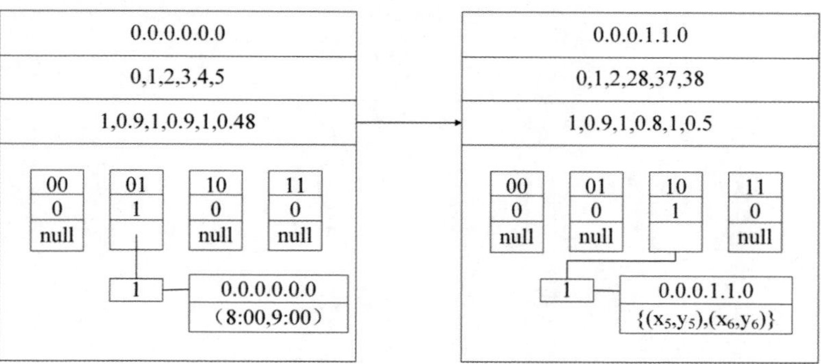

Figure 21. Initialize the sixth floor of the UK node

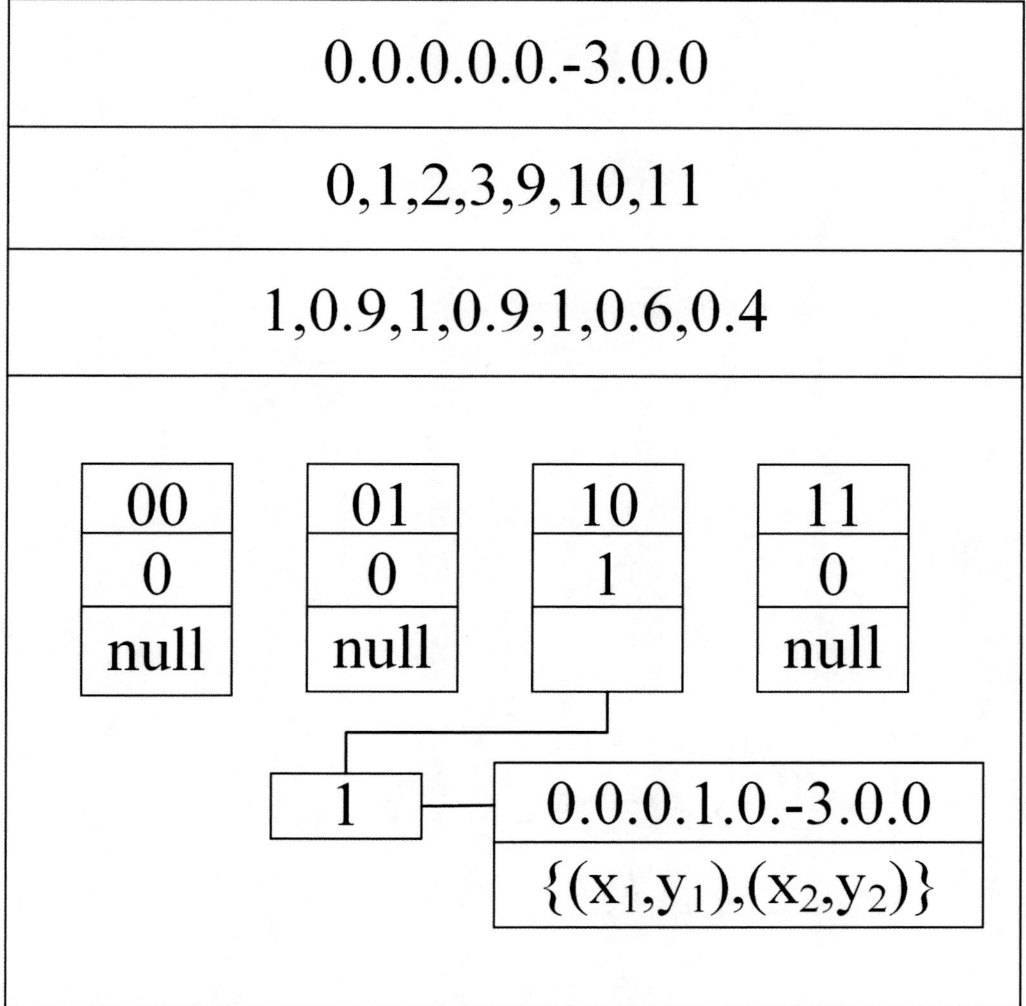

Figure 22. Initialize the seventh floor of the UK node

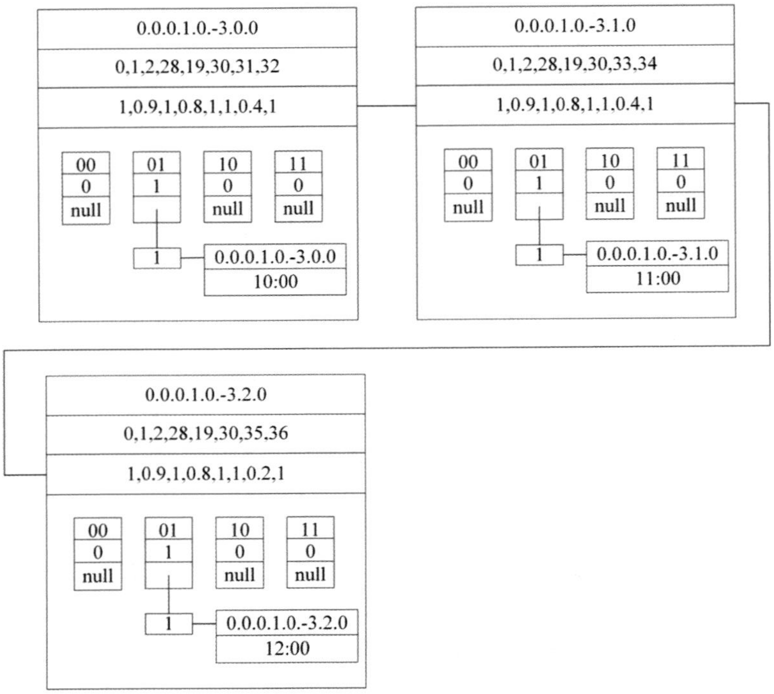

Figure 23. Update the seventh floor of the UK node

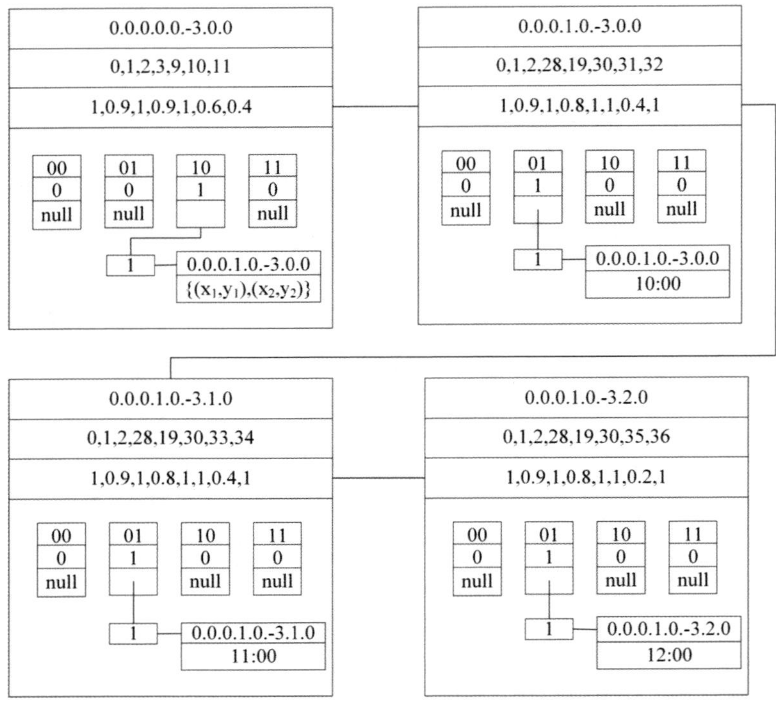

(3) Pass Layer 6 keyword inclusion to Layer 5. The sixth bit (starting from 0) of the probability sequence of the first *UK* node in layer 6 is 0.4, that is, the conditional probability is 0.4, the corresponding total probability of *BP* information binary bit string “10” is updated to 0.4, the partial probability is also updated to 0.4, and the corresponding total probability of binary bit string “00” is updated to 0.6. Other *UK* nodes in Layer 6 of the extended dynamic keyword data warehouse also update the probability part of *BP* information in this way. The final update results of all *UK* nodes in Layer 6 are shown in Figure 24. Because the *UK* nodes in Layer 6 of the extended dynamic keyword data warehouse have no parent nodes in Layer 5 of the dynamic data warehouse, they need to generate their own parent nodes. The second *UK* node, the third *UK* node and the fourth *UK* node in the sixth layer have the same parent node, and the parent node is a mux node in the XML document tree, then the *BP* information of the parent nodes of these three *UK* nodes is generated by the probability calculation method of mux parent node in section 4.2, and then a common parent node is generated. The *UK* node of Layer 5 of the final dynamic keyword data warehouse is shown in Figure 25.

Figure 24. Update the sixth floor of the UK node

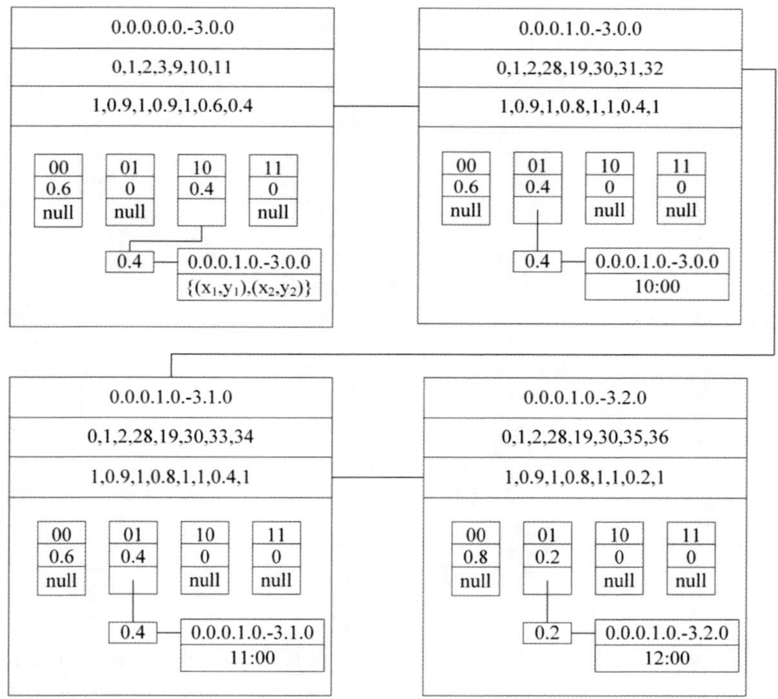

(4) Pass Layer 5 keyword inclusion to Layer 4. The *UK* node in Figure 25 has no parent node at the 4th layer, so it is necessary to update the *BP* information of each *UK* node according to the 5th bit of the probability sequence, and then generate the parent node respectively. Taking the first *UK* node in Figure 25 as an example, the fifth bit of its probability sequence is 0.48, and the probability corresponding to *BP* information “01” is 1, then the total probability corresponding to updated *BP* information “01” is 1×0.48=0.48, the split probability is 0.48, and the total probability corresponding to “00” is 1-0.48=0.

52. The parent node of the third *UK* node in layer 5 is mux type. According to the generation method of mux type parent node in section 4.2, the third *UK* node is updated first to generate the parent node of the third *UK* node. The final Layer 4 *UK* node is shown in Figure 26.

Figure 25. Update the fifth floor of the UK node

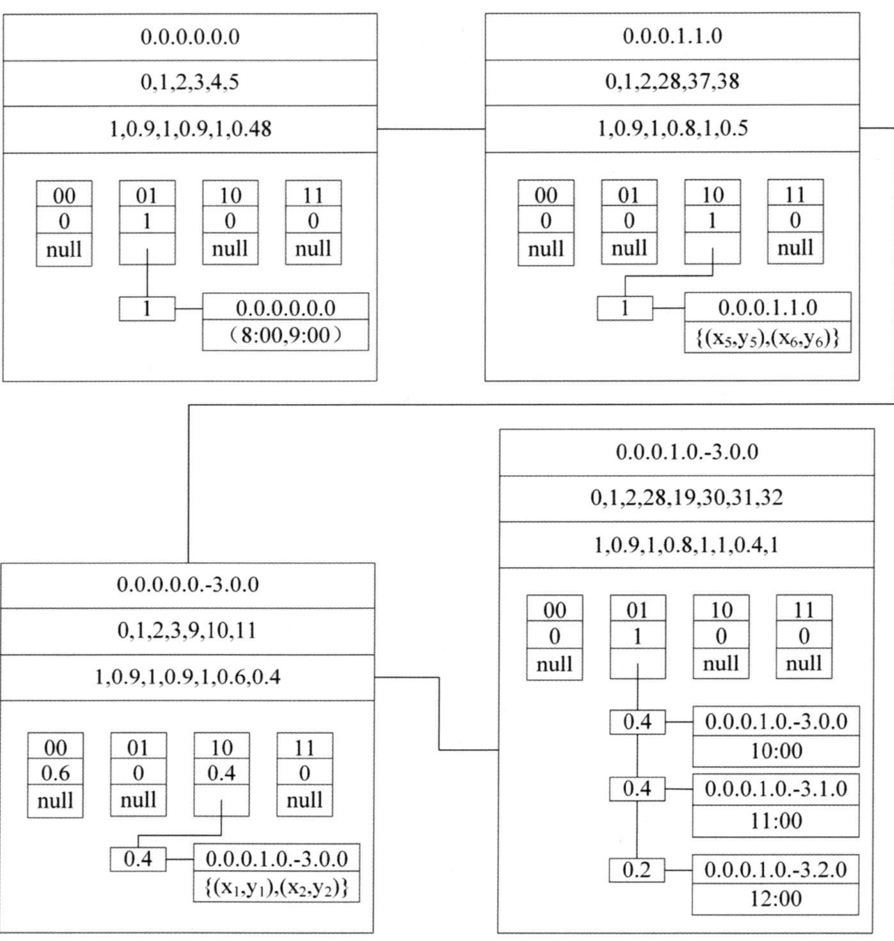

(5) Pass Layer 4 *UK* node keyword inclusion to Layer 3. Since the 4th bit (starting from 0) of the probability sequence of Layer 4 *UK* nodes is all 1, that is, the conditional probabilities from Layer 4 *UK* nodes to their parent nodes are all 1, the updated *BP* information of Layer 4 *UK* nodes has not changed, as shown in Figure 25. Use the *UK* node in Figure 25 to generate its parent node. The first and third *UK* nodes have the same parent node, and the second and fourth *UK* nodes have the same parent node. The fourth layer takes the generation process of the parent node of the first *UK* node and the third *UK* node as an example. First, the first *UK* node is used to generate its parent node, and then the third *UK* node is used to update the *BP* information of its parent node: the probability corresponding to the binary bit string "11" is 0.24×0.48=0.1152, the probability corresponding to the binary bit string "01" is 0.76×0.48=0.3648, the probability corresponding to the binary bit string "10" is 0.24×0.52=0.1248,

and the probability corresponding to the binary bit string "00" is 0.76×0.52=0.3952. In the same way, the parent nodes of the second and fourth *UK* nodes can be obtained. The final Layer 3 *UK* node is shown in Figure 27.

(6) Find out the *SLCA* nodes, calculate the final probability of becoming *SLCA* nodes, and sort them according to the sorting method. The corresponding probability that the binary bit string of the two *UK* nodes shown in the figure is "11" is not 0, so the XML nodes corresponding to these two *UK* nodes are *SLCA* nodes. According to Formula 1, the final probability of the first *SLCA* node, that is, the upper bound of probability, is 1×0.9×1×0.9×0.1152=0.093312, the product of the maximum partial probability value and the path probability, that is, the lower bound of probability, is 1×0.9×1×0.9×0.1152=0.093312, and the upper bound of probability of the second *SLCA* node is 1×0.9×1×0.7×0.5=0.315 and the lower bound of probability is 1×0.9×1×0.7×0.2=0.126. Sort by probability upper bound is the same as that by probability lower bound. According to the query result sorting strategy of MMT-Top-k, the code of the second SLCA node "0.0.0.1" is output first, and then the code of the first *SLCA* node "0.0.0.0" is output.

Figure 26. The fourth floor of the UK node

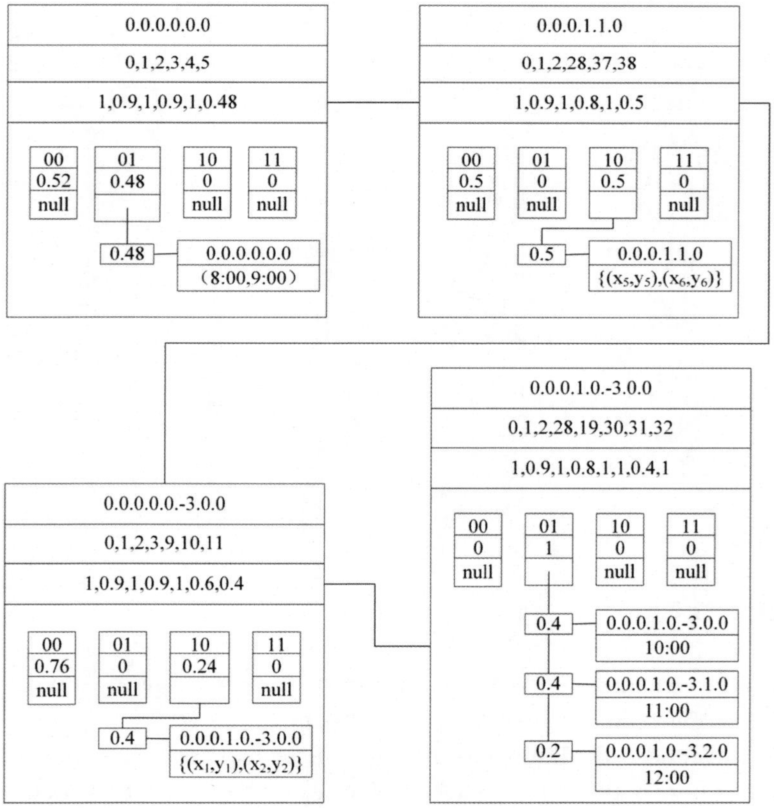

Figure 27. The third floor of the UK node

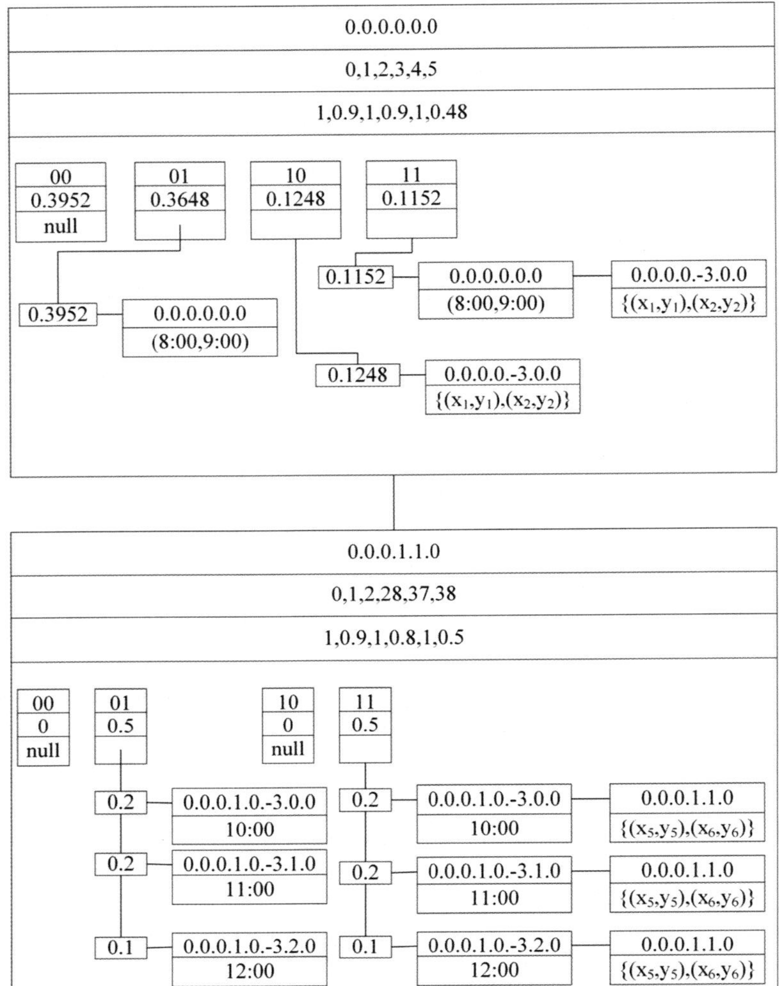

5 EXPERIMENTS

5.1 Experimental Setup

The experiments are implemented in Pycharm, and performed on a system with 2.5 GHz Intel Core i7 processor with 8 GB RAM running on Windows 10 system.

For the evaluations, time (yagoDateFacts), geographical location (yagoGeonamesOnlyData), and facts (yagoFacts) subsets are extracted from YAGO. The extracted real data subsets are combined into a total dataset containing temporal and spatial information. The dataset has 64928 triples, 138592 nodes, and 53967 edges. On the other hand, we perform the evaluations from four types of queries as shown in Table 1. Evaluations are performed according to its structure, coding method, traversed method, and query approach in the experiments.

Table 1. Original fuzzy spatiotemporal data

Query type	Query condition
Q1	The query contains text attributes only
Q2	The query contains temporal attributes
Q3	The query contains spatial attributes
Q4	The query contains spatiotemporal attributes

5.2 Experimental Results

We perform two groups of experiments. The first group of experiments focus on efficiency of the approach and the second group of experiments focus on effectiveness of the approach. In terms comparisons, TCoSKQ (Chen et al., 2021) and KQ (Bai et al., 2022) are performed to compare.

In the first group of experiments, execution time comparisons and memory cost comparisons are evaluated, which are shown in Figure 17 and Figure 18. We can observe from Figure 17 that TCoSKQ has the largest execution time for Q1 to Q4, KQ is the second, and USlist has the smallest execution time. On the other hand, we can observe from Figure 18 that TCoSKQ has the largest memory cost for Q1 to Q4, KQ is the second, and USlist has the smallest memory cost. The reason why KQ and USlist perform better than TCoSKQ can be explained by the fact that KQ and USlist are both based on XML, which has structural advantages. Furthermore, the reason why USlist perform better than KQ can be explained by the fact that we further optimize its structure based on XML.

Figure 28. Execution time comparisons

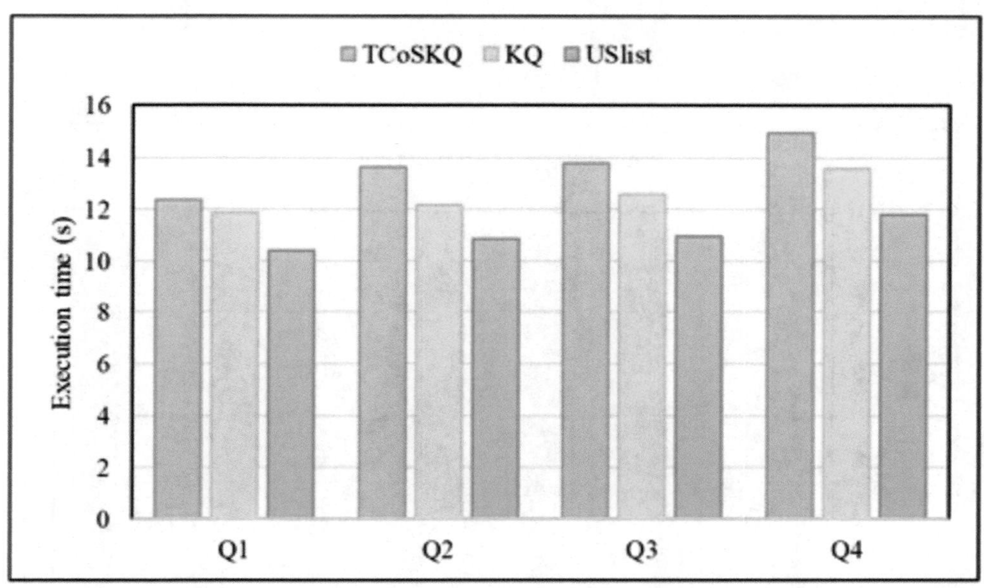

Figure 29. Memory cost comparisons

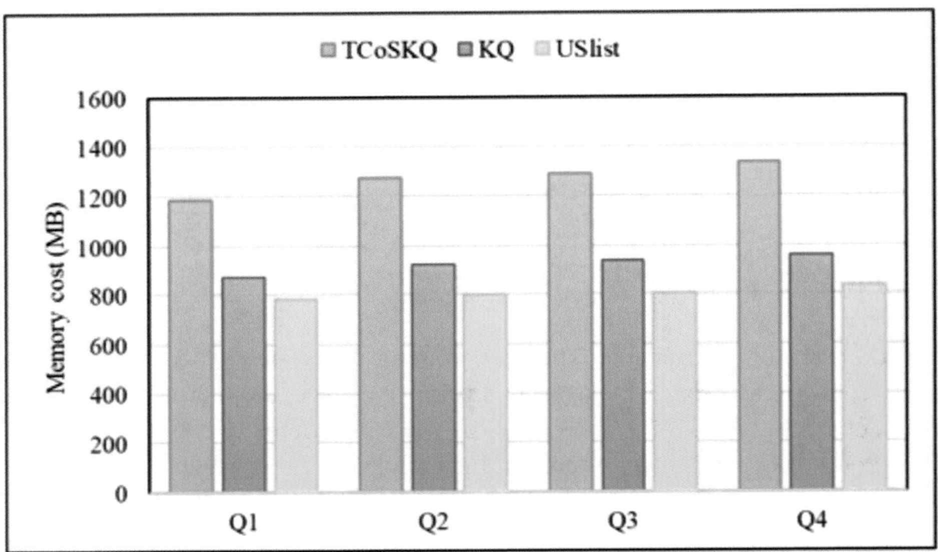

In the second group of experiments, Recall, Precision, and F-Score comparisons are evaluated, which are shown in Figure 19, Figure 20, and Figure 21. We can observe from Figure 19 to Figure 21 that USlist has the highest Recall, Precision, and F-Score for Q1, Q2, and Q4, KQ is the second, and TCoSKQ has the lowest Recall, Precision, and F-Score. In other words, TCoSKQ and KQ only have slight performance differences for Q1, Q2, Q3, and Q4, and USlist has the best but also slight better performance advantages.

Figure 30. Recall comparisons of different query type

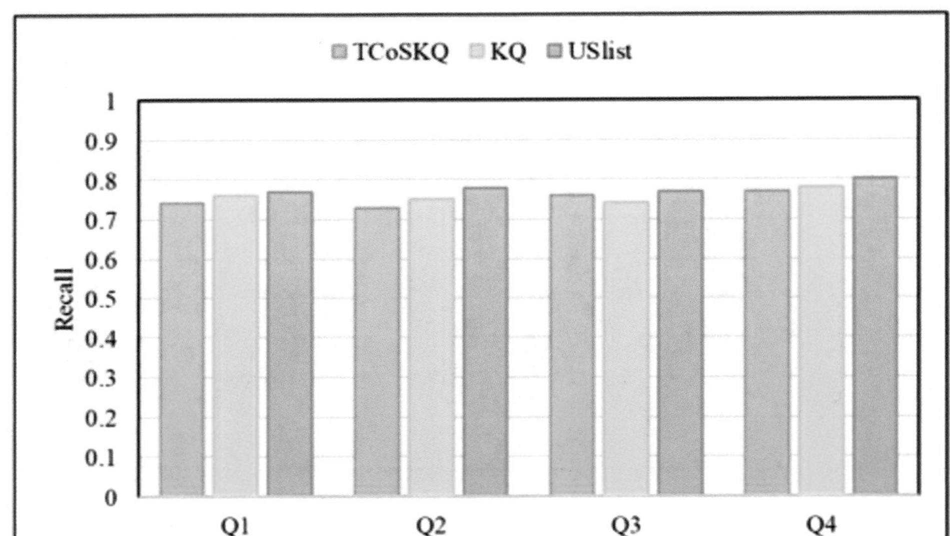

Figure 31. Precision comparisons of different query type

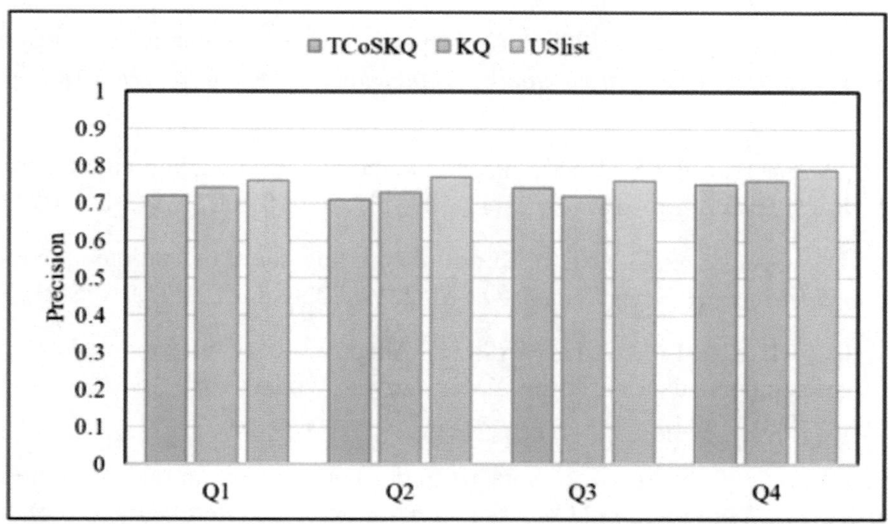

Figure 32. F-Score comparisons of different query type

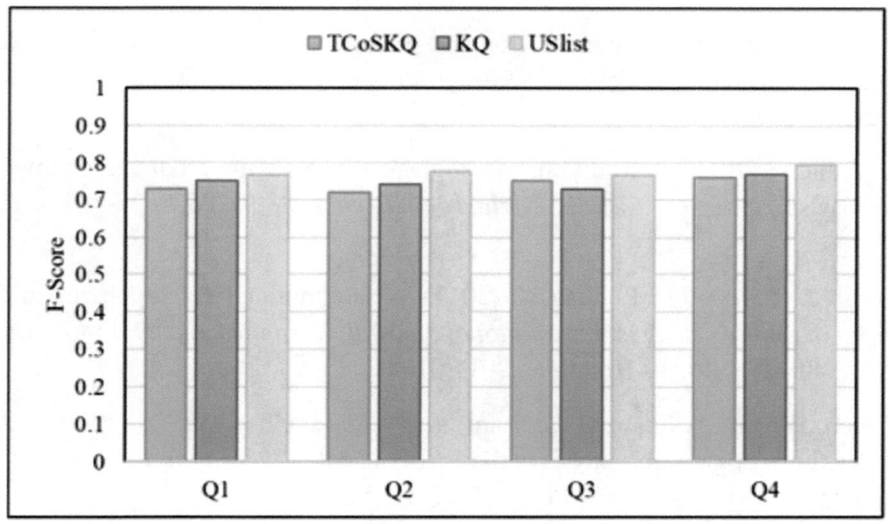

6 SUMMARY

This chapter investigates uncertain spatiotemporal data representation based on XML. Based on this, we explore the data structure of a dynamic keyword data warehouse, probability calculation, and a keyword query algorithm. We propose a keyword query approach for uncertain spatiotemporal XML data, along with pruning and sorting algorithms for keyword query. Experimental results show that the effectiveness of our approach has slight performance advantages, and the efficiency of our approach as performance advantages.

REFERENCES

An, Y., Borgida, A., & Mylopoulos, J. (2005). Constructing complex semantic mappings between XML data and ontologies. In *Proceedings of the International Semantic Web Conference* (pp. 6-20). Springer. 10.1007/11574620_4

Bai, L., Cao, X., & Jia, W. (2018). Uncertain spatiotemporal data modeling and algebraic operations based on XML. *Earth Science Informatics*, *11*(1), 109–127. doi:10.100712145-017-0322-6

Bai, L., Cui, Z., Duan, X., & Fu, H. (2022). Keyword coupling query of spatiotemporal data based on XML. *Journal of Intelligent & Fuzzy Systems*, *42*(3), 2219–2228. doi:10.3233/JIFS-211537

Bai, L., He, A., Liu, M., Zhu, L., & Xing, Y. (2021). Adaptive query relaxation and result categorization of fuzzy spatiotemporal data based on XML. *Expert Systems with Applications*, *168*, 114222. doi:10.1016/j.eswa.2020.114222

Bai, L., Lin, Z., & Xu, C. (2016). Spatiotemporal operations on spatiotemporal XML data using XQuery. In *Proceedings of the 12th International Conference on Natural Computation, Fuzzy Systems and Knowledge Discovery* (pp. 13-15). IEEE. 10.1109/FSKD.2016.7603362

Bai, L., Yan, L., & Ma, Z. (2015). Fuzzy spatiotemporal data modeling and operations in XML. *Applied Artificial Intelligence*, *29*(3), 259–282. doi:10.1080/08839514.2015.1004615

Bai, L., Yan, L., & Ma, Z. (2017). Interpolation and prediction of spatiotemporal data based on XML integrated with grey dynamic model. *ISPRS International Journal of Geo-Information*, *6*(4), 113. doi:10.3390/ijgi6040113

Bai, L., Zhu, L., & Jia, W. (2018). Determining topological relations of uncertain spatiotemporal data based on counter-clock-wisely directed triangle. *Applied Intelligence*, *48*(9), 2527–2545. doi:10.100710489-017-1100-3

Boulila, W., Farah, I. R., & Saheb Ettabaa, K. (2011). A data mining based approach to predict spatiotemporal changes in satellite images. *International Journal of Applied Earth Observation and Geoinformation*, *13*(3), 386–395. doi:10.1016/j.jag.2011.01.008

Chen, B. Y., Yuan, H., Li, Q., Shaw, S. L., Lam, W. H. K., & Chen, X. (2016). Spatiotemporal data model for network time geographic analysis in the era of big data. *International Journal of Geographical Information Science*, *30*(6), 1041–1071. doi:10.1080/13658816.2015.1104317

Chen, X., Yan, L., Li, W., & Zhang, F. (2018). Fuzzy spatio-temporal data modeling based on XML schema. *Filomat*, *32*(5), 1663–1677. doi:10.2298/FIL1805663C

Chen, Y., & Revesz, P. (2003). Querying spatiotemporal XML using DataFoX. In *Proceedings of the IEEE/WIC International Conference on Web Intelligence* (pp. 70-79). IEEE.

Chen, Z., Zhao, T., & Liu, W. (2021). Time-aware collective spatial keyword query. *Computer Science and Information Systems*, *28*(3), 1077–1100. doi:10.2298/CSIS200131034C

Cheng, H., Li, P., Wang, R., & Xu, H. (2021). Dynamic spatio-temporal logic based on RCC-8. *Concurrency and Computation*, *33*(22), 1–12. doi:10.1002/cpe.5900

Cheng, T., & Wang, J. Q. (2008). Integrated spatio-temporal data mining for forest fire prediction. *Transactions in GIS*, *12*(5), 591–611. doi:10.1111/j.1467-9671.2008.01117.x

Guan, X., Bo, C., Li, Z., & Yu, Y. (2017). ST-hash: An efficient spatiotemporal index for massive trajectory data in a NoSQL database. In *Proceedings of the 25th International Conference on Geoinformatics*. IEEE. 10.1109/GEOINFORMATICS.2017.8090927

Jeung, H., Liu, Q., & Shen, H. T. (2008). A hybrid prediction model for moving objects. In *Proceedings of the ICDE* (pp. 70-79). 10.1109/ICDE.2008.4497415

Kim, D. H., Ryu, K. H., & Kim, H. S. (2000). A spatiotemporal database model and query language. *Journal of Systems and Software*, *55*(2), 129–149. doi:10.1016/S0164-1212(00)00066-2

Lakshmanan, L. V. S., Leone, N., Ross, R., & Subrahmanian, V. S. (1997). ProbView: A flexible database system. *ACM Transactions on Database Systems*, *22*(3), 419–469. doi:10.1145/261124.261131

Li, J., Liu, C., Zhou, R., & Wang, W. (2011). Top-k keyword search over probabilistic XML data. In *Proceedings of the 27th International Conference on Data Engineering* (pp. 1104-1115). IEEE. 10.1109/ICDE.2011.5767875

Li, X., Yang, J., Guan, X., & Wu, H. (2014). An event-driven spatiotemporal data model (E-ST) supporting dynamic expression and simulation of geographic processes. *Transactions in GIS*, *18*(1), 76–96. doi:10.1111/tgis.12127

Liu, X., & Wan, Y. (2010). Storing spatio-temporal data in XML native database. In *Proceedings of the 2nd International Workshop on Database Technology and Applications* (pp. 45-49). IEEE. 10.1109/DBTA.2010.5659107

Ma, Z., Bai, L., Ishikawa, Y., & Yan, L. (2018). Consistencies of fuzzy spatiotemporal data in XML documents. *Fuzzy Sets and Systems*, *343*, 97–125. doi:10.1016/j.fss.2017.03.009

Mehta, P., Skoutas, D., & Voisard, A. (2015). Spatio-temporal keyword queries for moving objects. In *Proceedings of the 23rd SIGSPATIAL International Conference on Advances in Geographic Information Systems* (pp. 1-10). IEEE.

Nepomnyachiy, S., Gelley, B., Jiang, W., & Minkus, T. (2014). What, where, and when: keyword search with spatio-temporal ranges. In *Proceedings of the 8th Workshop on Geographic Information Retrieval* (pp. 15-22). ACM. 10.1145/2675354.2675358

Xu, Z., Luo, X. F., & Liu, Y. H. (2016). From latency, through outbreak, to decline: Detecting different states of emergency events using web resources. *IEEE Transactions on Big Data*.

Yuan, L., Yu, Z., Chen, S., Luo, W., Wang, Y., & Lü, G. (2010). CAUSTA: Clifford Algebra-based Unified Spatio-Temporal Analysis. *Transactions in GIS*, *14*(s1), 59–83. doi:10.1111/j.1467-9671.2010.01221.x

Zipf, A., & Krüger, S. (2001). TGML: extending GML by temporal constructs - a proposal for a spatio-temporal framework in XML. In *Proceedings of the 9th ACM International Symposium on Advances in Geographic Information Systems* (pp. 39-42). ACM.10.1145/512161.512183

Chapter 19
Flexible Query of Uncertain Spatiotemporal XML Data

ABSTRACT

Query, as an important part of spatiotemporal database operation, has become a research hotspot and focus. This chapter mainly studies the flexible query method of uncertain spatiotemporal XML data. This chapter proposes an uncertain spatiotemporal data representation model based on XML, and a T-List structure has been proposed based on this model. On this basis the chapter proposes a flexible query method. According to the different number of relaxing attributes, the query relaxation can be divided into single attribute relaxation and the combining attribute relaxation. This chapter proposes a single-relaxation algorithm for single attribute relaxation and a multiple-relaxation algorithm for combining attribute relaxation. In order to facilitate the user to check the results, the chapter presents the RSort algorithm for sorting accurate results and extended results.

1 INTRODUCTION

With the continuous development and popularization of science and technology, the users of spatiotemporal databases have gradually changed, and a large number of ordinary users can access spatiotemporal databases and obtain information through various channels. Most ordinary users do not know the actual situation of the data, often can not accurately define the query conditions. Therefore, users want to access the database in a flexible query way.

In recent years, with the rapid growth of spatiotemporal data, the demand for spatiotemporal data modeling and query is increasing. For spatiotemporal data modeling, Chen et al. (Chen et al., 2015) proposed a spatiotemporal data model based on compressed linear reference, which transformed network temporal geographical entities in three-dimensional space into two-dimensional compressed linear reference space. Cheng et al. (Cheng et al., 2021) proposed a dynamic spatiotemporal logic, which is used to represent and reason dynamic spatiotemporal knowledge. Guan et al. (Guan et al., 2017) proposed a trajectory index method, which extended *GeoHash* algorithm to meet the requirements of high-frequency update and common trajectory query operations, thus accelerating the time-consuming spatiotemporal

DOI: 10.4018/978-1-6684-9108-9.ch019

query of massive trajectory data. What's more, spatiotemporal query technology mainly includes the following aspects: Simple Temporal Query (Hao, 2011) mainly studies how to query the state of an object at a certain time. Furthermore, Ma et al. (Ma, 2012) proposes selective query, which mainly queries all spatiotemporal data objects passing through a certain area within a certain time interval. On this basis, join query (Li, 2012) is proposed, which queries objects that are at a certain distance from a certain data object in a certain time interval. Que et al. (Que et al.,2014) proposes spatiotemporal nearest neighbor query, which queries the data object closest to an object or region within a certain time interval.

Because XML has good self-description and extensibility, people have made some efforts in spatiotemporal data modeling and query relaxation based on XML. Some researchers have proposed an adaptive query relaxation method based on XML (Liu et al., 2010). This method returns only the results related to the query results. Dfgdfg et al. (Dfgdfg et al., 2011) put forward XPath query relaxation method. This method uses rewriting rules to relax query conditions. Bai et al. (Bai et al., 2016) used XQuery to study spatiotemporal operations, and studied query result processing by listing query examples. In addition, Bai et al. (Bai et al., 2021) has made some achievements in modeling and querying fuzzy or uncertain spatiotemporal data based on XML.

Due to the uncertainty of real information, most of them use fuzzy sets and fuzzy logic form to model language for query. The main idea of this work is to extend the SQL language and add an additional classical DBMS layer to evaluate fuzzy predicates ((Kandel et al., 1984); (Galindo et al., 2006); (Mama et al., 2019); (Mama et al., 2019); (Mama et al., 2019)). In addition, Meng et al. (Meng et al., 2009) proposed a query relaxation method based on semantic similarity to solve the problem that the results returned by Web database queries are empty or the number of results returned is small. Based on another idea, the query relaxation method with context preference (Yan et al., 2012) is generated to meet the user's personalized query needs. This method stores context preference by constructing interest tree. Although the research on flexible query technology of Web database has developed to a certain extent, the related research on flexible query of uncertain spatiotemporal data is still lacking.

In this chapter, we propose a flexible query method of uncertain Spatiotemporal XML Data, and give the corresponding ranking method of results. Based on this model, this chapter proposes a *T-List* structure which can quickly locate nodes that meet the time range of query conditions, and reduces the time required for query matching. This chapter proposes a method of relaxing initial query and general attribute query on uncertain spatiotemporal data model and a flexible query method of relaxing spatiotemporal attribute on *T-List* structure. Single-Relaxation algorithm is proposed for single attribute relaxation, and Multiple-Relaxation algorithm is proposed for combined attribute relaxation. In order to facilitate users to view the query results, this chapter proposes a *RSort* algorithm to sort the exact results and the extended results.

The rest of this article is organized as follows. In the section 2, a flexible query method of uncertain spatiotemporal data based on XML is proposed. *T-List* structure is proposed to facilitate query expansion. Section 3 mainly studies the method of sorting query results. For the convenience of users to view the results, the accurate results and extended results are sorted separately. Section 4 is an example analysis, and the conclusion of this chapter is in Section 5.

2 FLEXIBLE QUERY METHOD OF UNCERTAIN SPATIOTEMPORAL DATA BASED ON XML

In this Section, we propose a flexible query method for uncertain spatiotemporal data based on XML. *T-List* structure is proposed to facilitate query expansion. This section also divides flexible query into single attribute relaxation and combined attribute relaxation, and proposes Single-Relaxation algorithm and Multiple-Relaxation algorithm respectively. In addition, in order to facilitate the sorting of results, a method of storing query results with result set is proposed.

2.1 Uncertain Spatiotemporal Data Model Based on XML

Due to the limitation of equipment, technology and natural factors, the uncertainty of spatiotemporal data is difficult to avoid. Therefore, it is particularly important to build a model that can express the uncertainty of spatiotemporal data. Uncertain spatiotemporal data model needs to meet many requirements: first, uncertain spatiotemporal data model needs to be able to store and express massive high-dimensional spatiotemporal data; Secondly, the model needs to express the possibility of the real world on the basis of ensuring less data redundancy; Finally, the model should be able to express the movement trend of spatiotemporal data well, which not only reflects the uncertainty of data, but also does not affect the operation and processing of spatiotemporal data. In order to meet the above requirements, this section proposes an XML-based uncertain spatiotemporal data model on the basis of XML-based spatiotemporal data model and P-document model, and adds *ind* and *mux* nodes on the basis of the original XML-based uncertain spatiotemporal data model.

Definition 1. Use triples to represent uncertain spatiotemporal data based on XML, USP= {ID, General, Spatial}.

Where the ID represents a code that uniquely identifies the identity of the data. General represents a set of General attributes, which is composed of a series of fixed attributes. For example, in *CarDB*, manufacturer, power type, production date, etc. are all included in the General set. Spatial represents a collection of spatiotemporal attributes. Spatiotemporal attribute set should not only express the uncertainty of data, but also express the information such as the probability of data occurrence. In *CarDB*, position and speed are all spatiotemporal data, which can change with time and have certain uncertainty. For a certain time, the vehicle can only be located at one position, so the position information is a mux type node.

Definition 2. The Minimum Bounding Rectangle (MBR) is used to represent the spatial position information of uncertain spatiotemporal data. Each dimension has a boundary interval. Assuming that the boundary interval of the *i*-th dimension is $I_i(o)=[l_i, u_i]$, the representation of the smallest enclosing rectangle of dimension d is as follows:

$$I^d(o) = I_1(o) \times I_2(o) \ldots \times I_d(o) \# (\text{AUTONUM} \setminus {*}\text{Arabic})$$

The range of possible positions of a data object at a given moment or time period is not a regular graph parallel to an axis, and its shapes may be varied. When judging irregular shapes, we need to compare and judge figures point by point, which will undoubtedly prolong the data processing time. On the contrary, the geometry judgment for rectangle is very simple, so the minimum outer rectangle is used to represent the position information. For a two-dimensional position information can be expressed as $\{x_1, x_2, y_1, y_2\}$. Taking the vehicle information database *CarDB* as an example, the uncertain spatio-temporal data structure diagram based on XML is given, as shown in Figure 1:

Figure 1. A model for uncertain spatiotemporal data based on XML

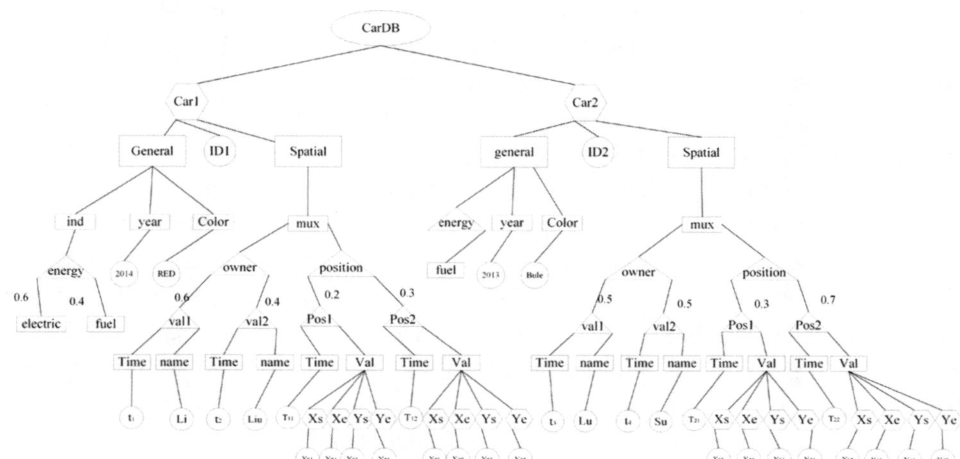

2.2 T-List Structure

When executing the query operation, the first step is to carry out accurate query, that is, to find the data object that conforms to it strictly according to the initial query conditions. At this time, if the number of returned results is enough, flexible query will not be carried out; The query condition is relaxed when the number of results returned by the query is empty or small. This means that if the conditions are relaxed, there will be a second or even more queries, which will undoubtedly increase the query waiting time of users. In order to quickly locate potential matching objects and reduce the matching time of flexible queries, this chapter proposes a *T-List* structure based on time division. The *T-List* structure uses the method of equal depth histogram to divide the whole time of XML document tree into several time periods with different lengths. A linked list is used to store the node information belonging to each time period, and the related information of data objects belonging to or intersecting with this time period is composed of information points and stored in the corresponding linked list. The length of time period is different because of the uneven distribution of data information. The *T-List* structure is described in detail below.

2.2.1 Data Structure

The basic structure of *T-List* is shown in Figure 2. *T-List* structure is mainly used to store the temporal and spatial positions of potential matching nodes and some necessary information. The structure consists of an array of *n*3* and n linked lists. The first column of the array stores the initial time of the time period represented by the linked list, the second column stores the upper time limit of the time period represented by the linked list, and the third column stores the pointer *P** to the linked list. Thus, the first two columns of each row of the array represent a time period, and the third column stores the head pointer of a linked list, and the time range of information points stored in the linked list contains the time period represented by the first two columns of the array of the row or intersects with the time period represented by the linked list. When querying node information belonging to a certain time period, we only need to quickly find one or more time periods related to the time period in the array of *T-List* structure, then find the designated linked list according to the corresponding linked list pointer stored in the third column of the array, and then find the data nodes strictly meeting the time period requirements from the linked list.

The time attribute is divided into several time periods, and each linked list represents a time period. The linked list is composed of information nodes, and the basic structure of information points is shown in Figure 3. The information node consists of *EDewey* code, time attribute, space attribute and probability sequence. The probability values in the probability sequence include all the probability values on the path from the root node of the XML document tree to the current node. At the same time, the probability sequence also records the node type, because different node types have different calculation methods when calculating the overall return probability of probability. The probability sequence is actually composed of several tuples with the structure <P_1, …, P_n, Type>. The purpose of this recording is to facilitate the calculation of the return probability of the results when the results are finally sorted. For example, if the parent node of a node is a *mux* type node and the probability from the parent node to the node is 0.3, then this short path is stored in the probability sequence in a manner of < 0.3, 0.7 *mux* >. In this way, when seeking the path probability, we can clearly understand the node type and probability value.

Figure 2. A structure for T-List

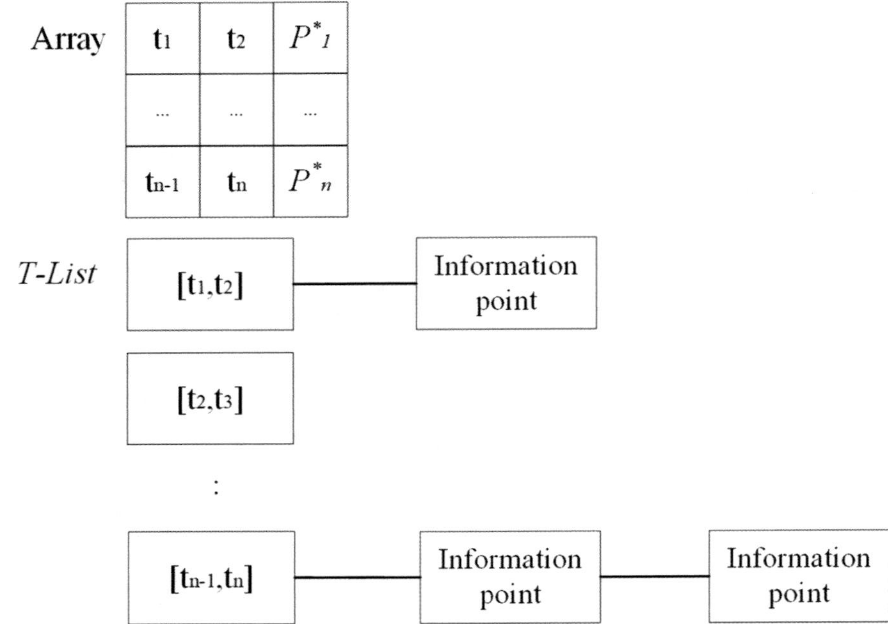

Figure 3. Basic structure of information points

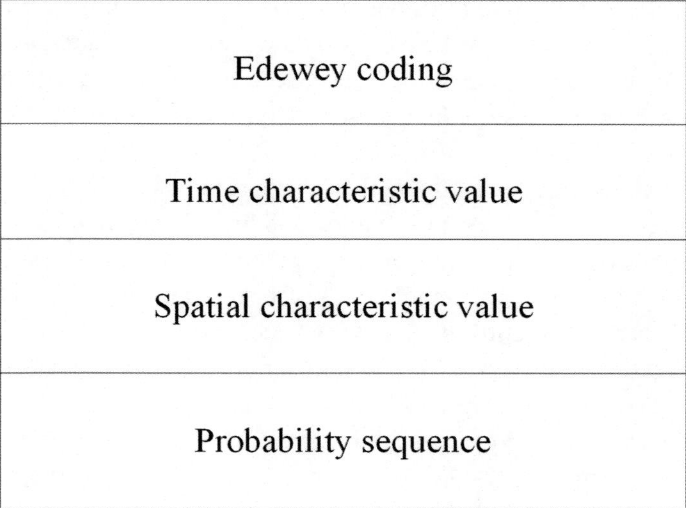

2.2.2 Creation of *T-List* Structure

If an XML document tree stores a lot of contents, in order to reduce the number of comparisons and locate the time period quickly, a multi-layer nesting strategy can be adopted, that is, the total historical time is divided into several time intervals with large span first, and then segmented in detail within the time period. Here, only a small range of time period is taken as an example to divide the time period in detail. For the division of time periods, the isometric histogram method is used to make the number of information points contained in each time period basically the same.

The following details the method of dividing time periods for XML document trees and creating *T-List* structures

Algorithm1. Algorithm for Creating T-List Structure of XML Document Tree

```
Input:XML document tree to be queried
Output:T-List Structure

Make the number of information points stored in each linked list m
The total number of possible locations of all objects in the spatiotemporal database is Z and the time range of this document tree is [t_low, t_up]
Calculate n=Z/m
Initializes an n*3 array for each time division point and a pointer to the corresponding linked list
Let the lower bound of time period low=t_low,Upper bound of time period up=t_up
while(low<t_up)
Execute Q: {t∈[low,up]}, record the number of nodes a traversed during the query
if(a<=m)
Save the values of low and up in order in the array U
Let low=up,up=t_up
else
Modify the value of up,let up=low+(up-low)/2
end while
Initialize n linked lists to form T-List structure,Store the head node pointer of each linked list in the third column of array U
return T-List
```

Algorithm 1 needs to set the number of information points stored in each linked list. Because the linked list can only traverse one by one from beginning to end, if the linked list is too long, it will increase the traversal time; If the length of linked list is too short, it will increase the number of linked lists and occupy more space, so the number of information points can be determined according to the size of the document tree, but because ordinary users don't know the relevant knowledge, the value is specified by the system.

The main purpose of algorithm 1 is to divide the time period and initialize the *T-List* structure. First, create an $n*3$ array for storing time period information and linked list pointers (line 04). Then, the maximum and minimum values of the time range are used as conditions for query. If the number of query results is greater than the number of information points m stored in each linked list, the range of query conditions (lines 06-13) is reduced until the number of query results is less than or equal to m, and the values of low and up are stored in the first two columns of array U in sequence. Modify the values of low and up (line 12) and continue to divide the next point in time.

Algorithm 1 uses the method of equal depth histogram partition, so the time interval is not divided evenly, and the length of the time interval depends on the number of possible positions in the time interval. There are many reasons for the difference in time interval length, such as geographical location, economic development, special festivals and so on. For example, when inquiring about vehicles passing through a scenic spot in Qinhuangdao in a certain period of time, when the set value of linked list length is the same, the length of time interval varies greatly at different times. On special holidays, such as May Day, the divided time interval will be very small, because the traffic volume in holiday scenic spots will be significantly higher than that on ordinary days.

In addition, the *T-List* structure of each tree can be dynamically updated. When the XML document tree has insertion, deletion or modification operations, the *T-List* structure will be updated according to the actual situation.

2.2.3 Application of *T-List* Structure

A group of time periods are obtained by the periods partition algorithm, and these time points are used to partition time periods, so that each linked list corresponds to a time period, and the values conforming to the time period are stored. When executing the query operation, firstly, the *T-List* structure is initialized, and according to the time of each possible position of each stored object, it is stored in the linked list of corresponding time period in the form of information points. Of course, this time division method cannot perfectly include the uncertain time range of each storage object. It is possible that the possible time range of a query object in a certain position is not completely contained in the time period represented by any linked list, and the time range spans two-time division intervals and intersects with two adjacent time periods. In this case, the information point is stored in two linked lists with time intersection at the same time. This storage method ensures the possibility of every information point in every possible time period at the cost of sacrificing storage space.

Example 1. Assume that the three-time intervals that have been divided are [2015.3.5 08:00,2015.3.6 10:00], [2015.3.6 10:00,2015.3.6 18:00], [2015.3.6 18:00,2015.3.7 14:00]. The possible time range for discovering a range of locations in a document when traversing the XML document tree is [2015.03.06 09:56, 2015.03.06 10:08]. This time range does not completely satisfy any one of the three -time intervals, so it is impossible to store the information points corresponding to this position in a linked list, because the object may meet the query conditions within the possible time interval. If only stored in a linked list, the accuracy of query results will be reduced. Therefore, the corresponding information with the time range of [2015.03.06 09:56 and 2015.03.06 10:08] should be stored at the same time, indicating that the time intervals are [2015.03.05 08:00, 2015.03.06 10:00] and [2015.3.6 10:00, 2015.03.06 18:00].

2.3 Flexible Query Method for Uncertain Spatiotemporal Data

In order to better meet the query requirements of users, reduce the number of repeated input of query conditions, and provide potential objects in line with user preferences, a flexible query method for uncertain spatiotemporal data is proposed in this section. In this section, the definition of relaxation query for uncertain spatiotemporal data is given, and the algorithm ideas and steps are described in detail.

2.3.1 Spatiotemporal Attribute Query Relaxation Definition

Definition 3. Time attribute relaxation. Time is a one-dimensional attribute, and time with uncertainty is expressed in an interval $[t_{i1}, t_{i2}]$ in an XML document. Nodes that meet the time condition should satisfy $[t_{i1}, t_{i2}] \subseteq [t_s, t_e]$. When the attribute to be relaxed is time attribute, the relaxation with time condition range is completed in rounds. When other query conditions are satisfied, the nodes that intersect with the query time are expanded first. When expanding, calculate and save the time satisfaction degree of this node, and record it as T_s. The calculation formula is:

$$T_s = \frac{[t_{i1}, t_{i2}] \cap [t_s, t_e]}{[t_{i1}, t_{i2}]} \#(\text{AUTONUM}\backslash*\text{Arabic})$$

If the number of query results is still small at this time, the second round of time relaxation is carried out, and the query scope is expanded in the second round of relaxation, and nodes that intersect with the new query scope are added to the results. In the second and every relaxation round, the time range in the initial query condition is enlarged, and a new time query range $[t_s-\delta, te_+\delta]$ is obtained. δ calculates the time sub-relaxation threshold φT th$_r$ough the weight of time attribute in the query condition and the given relaxation threshold S, a*n*d then further calculates it. After expanding the time range, it is necessary to modify the relaxation threshold S for subsequent relaxation steps. The specific calculation formula is shown in Equation 3.

$$[t_s, t_e] \leftarrow \left[t_s - h\sqrt{\frac{1-\varphi_T}{\varphi_T}}, t_e + h\sqrt{\frac{1-\varphi_T}{\varphi_T}} \right] \#(\text{AUTONUM}\backslash*\text{Arabic})$$

Therefore, the calculated value of δ mentioned above is $\delta = \text{h}\sqrt{\frac{1-\varphi_T}{\varphi_T}}$. In this case, the formula for T_s is:

$$T_s = \frac{t_e - t_s}{t_e - t_s + 2\delta} \times \frac{[t_{i1}, t_{i2}] \cap [t_s - \delta, t_e + \delta]}{[t_{i1}, t_{i2}]} \#(\text{AUTONUM}\backslash*\text{Arabic})$$

Time satisfaction T_s is mainly used when sorting the final query results. In the calculation formula of T_s in the second expansion, there is one more coefficient $\frac{t_e - t_s}{t_e - t_s + 2\delta}$ than that in the calculation formula of the first expansion. Because the time period expanded in the second round has no intersection with the scope of the initial query condition, the satisfaction degree with the initial query condition is lower than that returned by the first expansion.

At this time, two rounds of conditional relaxation have been carried out on the time attribute. If the number of returned results is still small at this time, the third round of time relaxation can be continued, and the relaxation mode of the third round and subsequent rounds is similar to that of the second round.

As shown in Figure 4, only the time period T_2 satisfies the condition and meets the initial query time period. When relaxing the time condition, the node T_1, which intersects the time interval with the query time, is first added to the result set, when $T_s=(T_1 \cap T)/T_1$. If the total number of returned results is still small at this time, the second round of time range relaxation will continue. When the time range is expanded to T', T_3 intersects with T', and the time period T_3 is added to the result set, a coefficient T/T' (T/T' must be less than 1) is added to the calculation formula of time satisfaction, because after the time range is expanded, the newly added results are less satisfied with the initial query conditions.

Figure 4. The relaxation of time range

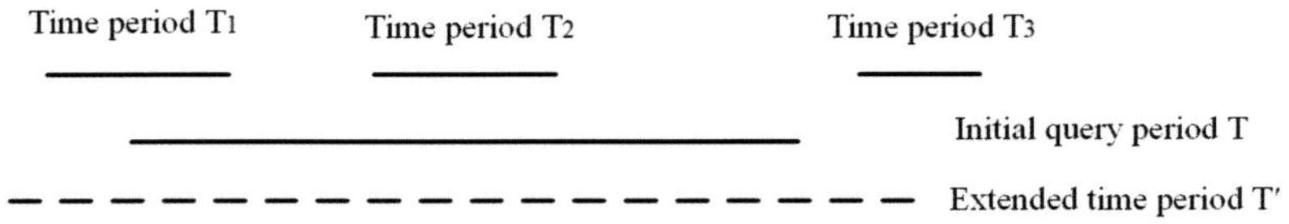

Time period T1   Time period T2   Time period T3

Initial query period T

Extended time period T′

Definition 4. Spatial Attribute Relaxation. The minimum outbound rectangle (MBR) is used to represent the given spatial location range in the query condition Q, which is denoted as MBR_Q. When querying precisely, the minimum outbound rectangle of the returned node is contained in the given minimum outbound rectangle if other conditions are satisfied. For spatial range relaxation, first add nodes that overlap with MBRQ spatiotemporal to the query results, as shown in R_3 and R_4 in Figure 5 (a). As shown in the figure, when expanding, calculate and save the space satisfaction degree L_s at this time. The calculation formula is:

$$L_s = \frac{MBR_i \cap MBR_Q}{MBR_i} \#(\text{AUTONUM} \setminus *\text{Arabic})$$

If the number of query results is still small at this time, the second round of spatial condition relaxation is needed, that is, expanding the MBR_Q range. The new query range is represented as $MBR_{Q'}$, and then new results contained in or intersecting with the new query range are added to the query results, as shown in R_5 and R_6 in Figure 5 (b). The process is similar to time conditional relaxation, and the sub-relaxation threshold of spatial attributes is calculated according to the weight and relaxation threshold of spatial attributes, and the spatial range is modified by using the sub-relaxation threshold. The scope expansion of the third and subsequent rounds is similar to that of the second round, and the relaxation threshold is modified after each modification of the query scope. The formula for expanding the spatial range is:

$$\{x_s,x_e,y_s,y_e\}\leftarrow\left\{x_s-h\sqrt{\frac{1-\varphi_L}{\varphi_L}},x_e+h\sqrt{\frac{1-\varphi_L}{\varphi_L}},y_s-h\sqrt{\frac{1-\varphi_L}{\varphi_L}},y_e+h\sqrt{\frac{1-\varphi_L}{\varphi_L}}\right\}$$

#(AUTONUM *Arabic)

At this time, the calculation formula of L_s is:

$$L_s=\frac{MBR_Q}{MBR_{Q'}}\times\frac{MBR_i\cap MBR_{Q'}}{MBR_i}$$ #(AUTONUM *Arabic)

Figure 5. (a) The initial spatial query range and (b) the extended spatial range(b)

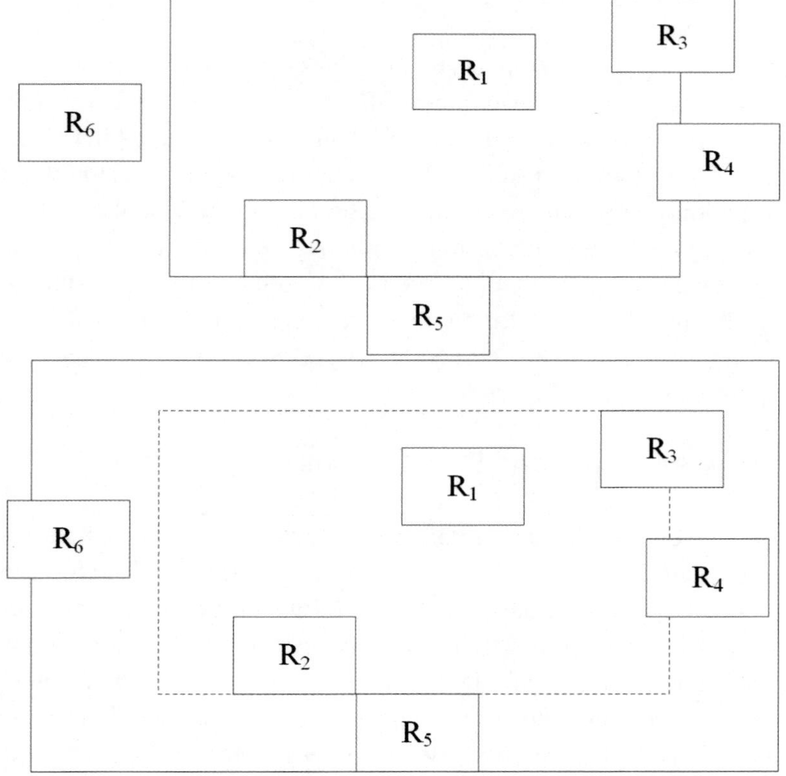

The rectangular box in Figure 5 (a) is the query scope. In the exact query, only R_1 and R_2 fully meet the query criteria and can be returned to the user. At this time, the number of returned results is small, so flexible query method is used to relax spatial attributes, and the relaxation process is carried out in rounds. In the first round, nodes that overlap with the initial query scope in space, namely R_3 and R_4, are added to the result. At this time, $L_{s,R3}=(S_{R3}\cap S_1)/S_{R3}$,$L_{s,R4}=(S_{R4}\cap S_1)/S_{R4}$. If the number of returned results is still small at this time, the second round of condition relaxation is performed. As shown in Figure 5 (b), the dotted box represents the original spatial query range. After the range is expanded, the query range is expanded to the outer solid rectangle. The calculation formula is shown in Equation 6. After each round of expansion, the relaxation threshold should be modified (for example, each round decreases by step size of 0.1). At this point, R_5 and R_6 can also be added to the result. If the number of results is still small at this time, the third round and subsequent rounds of relaxation will continue, and the calculation method is the same as that of the second round of relaxation.

Definition 5. Single Attribute Relaxation. Single Attribute Relaxation is to find the attribute with the smallest weight (least important) among the keywords defined by query conditions for condition relaxation, while other attribute conditions remain unchanged.

Definition 6. Combination Attribute Relaxation. In Combination Attribute Relaxation, the condition of each attribute in the initial query condition is relaxed. According to the weight of each attribute, the degree of relaxation is different. The greater the weight, the smaller the degree of relaxation of attributes.

2.3.2 Result Set

In the process of query, we need a structure to store the query results, so we propose a result set structure, which consists of two linked lists, representing result set 1 and result set 2 respectively. Result set 1 is used to store the results that accurately meet the initial query conditions; After condition relaxation, all the newly added results are stored in result set 2. The qualified results are stored in the result set in the form of result information points. The result information points include the node's *EDewey* code, the temporal satisfaction degree T_s, the spatial satisfaction degree L_s and the general attribute satisfaction degree G_s, the path probability value that has been calculated from the probability sequence, and the final probability P_{fin} that has been used for the result ranking. The specific calculation method of path probability value is introduced in detail in Section 3.1 and Section 3.2 of Section 3. The result of the result information point is shown in Figure 6.

2.3.3 Flexible Query Algorithm and Basic Process

In the process of flexible query, the query relaxation for spatiotemporal attributes mainly involves the round relaxation introduced in section 2.3.1. The initial query criteria defined by users may include only general attributes, spatiotemporal attributes, or both general attributes and spatiotemporal attributes. When only general attributes are defined, the matching content does not include spatiotemporal attributes of data objects. Therefore, its query method is similar to the flexible query method of general Web database. In this chapter, the query relaxation method of a single general attribute is not discussed in detail. In view of the latter two cases, this chapter presents a flexible query method for uncertain spatiotemporal data.

Before performing a flexible query, determine the importance of each keyword in the initial query criteria and calculate the importance and assign weights to the attributes defined in the query criteria. After the weight allocation is completed, the query relaxation operation is carried out according to the weight value.

Figure 6. The structure of result information point

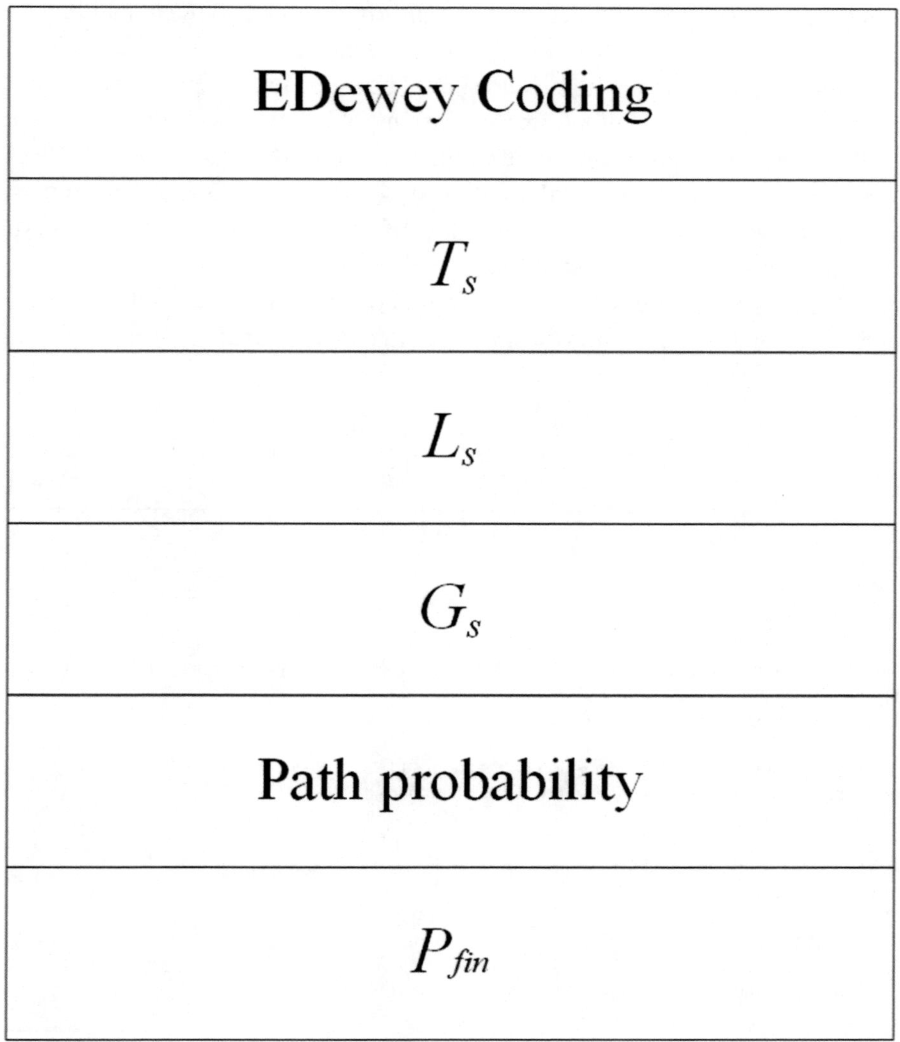

Query relaxation can be divided into single attribute relaxation and combined attribute relaxation according to the number of attributes that need to be relaxed. According to the number and type of user-defined query conditions, there are many situations of single attribute relaxation and combined attribute relaxation. According to the weight of attributes, the attributes of single attribute relaxation and expansion may be spatiotemporal attributes or general attributes. This chapter only introduces the single attribute relaxation for spatiotemporal attributes in detail. For general attributes, refer to the calculation method in the adaptive query relaxation method (Meng et al., 2009) based on semantic similarity of Web database. Combination attribute relaxation may relax that all attributes are general attributes, all are spatiotemporal attributes or have both general attributes and spatiotemporal attributes. The loosening method of spatiotemporal attributes is different from that of general attributes. In this chapter, the loosening method of spatiotemporal attributes is divided into different rounds. In the first round, the nodes that intersect with the query range of spatiotemporal attributes in the initial query condition are expanded, and in the second round and every subsequent round, the query range is expanded. After expanding the query range, the nodes that belong to or intersect with the new query range are found in the *T-List* structure. After each round of loosening, the loosening threshold should be modified so that the next round of loosening can modify the query scope. In addition, after each round of query relaxation, check whether the total number of results meets the requirements, and if so, stop the next round of query relaxation. Specific flexible query algorithms are given in detail in algorithm 2, algorithm 3 and algorithm 4.

Query relaxation is required only when the number of returned results is null or small, but not when there are enough query results. How much of this "less" concept is can be given by the system. Assume that the system sets query relaxation when the number of query results returned to the user is less than r.

Now a query condition Q is given, and the query results are provided for users through flexible query algorithm.

Algorithm2. Flexible query algorithm

```
Input:Initial query condition Q
Output:Query results

01. Initialize the result set;
02. Execute the initial query condition Q, traverse each position node in the XML document tree, and initialize the T-List structure;
03. if (Initial query criteria met)
04. Create a result information point, process related information, and save the result in result set 1;
05. else
06. Create an information point structure, process position information, and store the processing results in T-List;
07. if (The number of result information points in result set 1 is greater than r)
08. Perform Step 12
09. else
10. Calculate IDF values for each key defined in Q and assign weights
11. if (Single Attribute Relaxation)
12. Call the Single-Relaxation algorithm
13. else if (Combination Attributes Relaxation)
14. Call the Multiple-Relaxation algorithm
15. Call the result sorting algorithm // The result sorting algorithm is described in detail in section 3
16. return
```

Algorithm 2 is the whole step of flexible query. The first is the preparation stage of flexible query (line 01), which initializes two result sets. Result set 1 is used to store accurate results that meet the initial query conditions, while all newly added results after query relaxation are stored in result set 2. Because when the exact query returns null results or the number of results is too small, the condition relaxation will be carried out and potential matching objects will be added. Obviously, the matching degree between the loosened query results and the initial query conditions is lower than that obtained by the initial query. Therefore, in order to ensure that the user sees the accurate query results first when viewing the results, the loosened results of all queries should be ranked behind the accurate results that meet the initial query conditions in the final result sorting. Therefore, in order to ensure that all the exact results are ranked before the relaxed results, two result sets are used in algorithm 2. In the final result sorting stage, the results in result set 1 are returned first, and then the results in result set 2 are returned.

At the end of the preparation phase, traverse the XML document tree and initialize the *T-List* structure, storing the exact results in result set 1 (line 04). At the same time, there may be potential matching objects in the results that do not meet the initial query conditions. In order to reduce the loosened query time, *T-List* structure is used to store the temporal and spatial information of data objects (line 06). In this way, when loosening the query, we can directly locate the linked lists of several storage information points in the T-List structure, then find the nodes in these linked lists that meet the spatial conditions, and then check the correctness of the general attributes of nodes according to the *EDewey* codes of nodes. Before expanding the query, you need to check the number of exact results returned (line 07). If the number of results is not less than the specified value, the query relaxation is not needed, and the results are sorted directly. If the number of results is less than the specified value, flexible queries are needed to provide them with potential matching objects that may meet the needs of users. According to the number of relaxed attributes, flexible queries can be divided into two situations: single attribute relaxation and combined attribute relaxation. The Single-Relaxation method is called for single property relaxation (line 12), and the Multiple-Relaxation method is called for composite property relaxation (line 14). These two methods will be described in detail in the next section.

Finally, the result sorting stage. Sort the results in Result Set 1 and Result Set 2, respectively, and return the results to the user in the order of Sort Result Set 1 and Sort Result Set 2. The calculation method of the satisfaction degree between the query results and the initial query conditions, the calculation method of the return probability of the results and the final ranking method will be introduced in detail in Section 3.

2.3.4 Single-Relaxation Algorithm and Multiple-Relaxation Algorithm

According to the number of attributes that need to be relaxed, flexible query is divided into two ways: single attribute relaxation and combined attribute relaxation. According to the different query conditions defined by users, each query method can be divided into different situations. This section proposes Single-Relaxation algorithm for single attribute relaxation and Multiple-Relaxation algorithm for combined attribute relaxation. These two algorithms are based on calculating the weight of each keyword in the query condition, as shown in Algorithm 3 and Algorithm 4 in detail.

Algorithm 3 firstly selects the attribute with the smallest weight in the query conditions, calculates the sub-relaxation threshold φm of the attribute, and then relaxes the attribute. If the attribute is a typed attribute in the general attribute, add all the attribute values whose semantic similarity with the attribute does not exceed φm $_t$o the query condition (line 07); If the property is a numeric property in a generic property, expand its query scope (line 09). After the above operation, a new query condition $\tilde{Q}$ is formed, and the result is stored in the result set 2 by executing $\widetilde{Q}$.

If the attribute to be relaxed is a spatiotemporal attribute, query relaxation is divided into two steps. After initial query, *T-List* structure has been generated to store information based on time period, so when relaxing spatiotemporal attributes, all nodes conforming to time period can be located quickly, and then the spatiotemporal information stored in information points of *T-List* structure is compared, which saves a lot of query time. In the first round of relaxation, nodes that intersect the query criteria range and pass the correctness check are added to result set 2. If there are still few results at this time, the second and subsequent rounds of query relaxation are performed, that is, the query range is expanded according to the sub-relaxation threshold (lines 16 and 22), and the nodes that intersect the new query range and pass the correctness check are added to the result set 2. Correctness check is to find the node in XML document tree according to the *EDewey* code of the stored node in result set 2, and judge whether the node meets other attribute conditions. If not, the result object cannot be added to the query result. If the query result is still empty after the above relaxation steps, the relaxation threshold will be adjusted in incremental steps of 0.1 (lines 18 and 24).

Algorithm3. Single-Relaxation algorithm

01. min $=w_1$,m = 1; // The min denotes the minimum value of the keyword weight, and the m denotes the location of the minimum weight
02. for (i=1; i<=n; i++) //n is the number of keywords defined in the initial query criteria
03. if (w_i< min)
04. min $=w_i$,m = i;
05. if (Relaxation characteristics are general characteristics) do
06. if (A_m is a typed attribute)
07. Find keywords whose semantic similarity with A_m is higher than the sub-relaxation threshold in the tree and add them to the query conditions
08. if (A_m is a numeric attribute) // What is stored in a general property is a certain constant value
09. The query scope of attribute A_m become $\left[q-h\sqrt{\frac{1-\varphi_m}{\varphi_m}},q+h\sqrt{\frac{1-\varphi_m}{\varphi_m}}\right]$
10. A new query condition $\tilde{Q}$ is obtained, $\tilde{Q}$ is executed, and the result is put into result set 2;
11. S←S – 0.1;
12. while (The total number of results in result sets 1 and 2 is less than r)
13. if (The relaxation characteristic is time characteristic)
14. The first round of relaxation. Locating one or more linked lists in the array of *T-List* according to the time range defined in Q, traversing the linked lists, converting the information points intersecting with the time range of QT into result information points and checking the correctness of other attribute values, calculating Ts if they meet the conditions, and storing other relevant information in result set 2;
// Correctness check: According to the *EDewey* code of the stored node in the result set 2, find the node in the XML document tree, judge whether the node meets other conditions besides the time attribute, if so, add the information point to the result set 2
15. while (The total number of results in result sets 1 and 2 is less than r)
16. $\left[t_s,t_e\right]\leftarrow\left[t_s-h\sqrt{\frac{1-\varphi_t}{\varphi_T}},t_e+h\sqrt{\frac{1-\varphi_T}{\varphi_T}}\right]$;
17. Searching for nodes in T-List that meet the new time range, checking the correctness, calculating Ts if they meet the time range, and processing relevant information into result information points and adding them into result set 2;
18. S←S – 0.1;
19. else if (Relaxation attributes are spatial attributes)
20. Carry out the first round of spatial relaxation. Searching nodes in the corresponding linked list that meet the relaxed spatial range conditions, checking the correctness of other attributes, calculating L_s if they meet the conditions, processing related contents, and storing new results in result set 2;
21. while (The total number of results in result sets 1 and 2 is less than r)
22. $\left\{x_s,x_e,y_s,y_e\right\}\leftarrow\left\{x_s-h\sqrt{\frac{1-\varphi_L}{\varphi_L}},x_e+h\sqrt{\frac{1-\varphi_L}{\varphi_L}},y_s-h\sqrt{\frac{1-\varphi_L}{\varphi_L}},y_e+h\sqrt{\frac{1-\varphi_L}{\varphi_L}}\right\}$
23. In the *T-List* in accordance with the time range of the linked list continue to find the nodes that meet the expanded spatial conditions to check the correctness. If it matches, L_s is calculated, relevant contents are processed, and new results are stored in result set 2;
24. S←S – 0.1;
25. return Result Set 1, Result Set 2

According to different query conditions defined by users, the relaxation of combined attributes can be divided into three different situations: only general attributes, only spatiotemporal attributes, both general attributes and spatiotemporal attributes.

The specific algorithm operation is as follows:

Algorithm4 Multiple-Relaxation algorithm

01. if (Contains only generic attributes in the condition)
02. for each basic query attribute do
03. According to the sub-relaxation threshold and semantic correlation table, the query scope is modified;
04. obtained a new query condition $\tilde{Q}$, $\tilde{Q}$ is executed, and the result is put into result set 2;
05. S←S – 0.1;
06. while (The total number of results in result sets 1 and 2 is more than r)
07. else if (Include only spatiotemporal attributes)
08. Add the nodes that intersect the time condition and space condition in the initial query condition and pass the correctness check to the result set 2, and calculate L_s and T_s;
09. while (The total number of results in result sets 1 and 2 is less than r)
10. $[t_s, t_e] \leftarrow \left[t_s - h\sqrt{\frac{1-\varphi_T}{\varphi_T}}, t_e + h\sqrt{\frac{1-\varphi_T}{\varphi_T}} \right]$

$$\{x_s, x_e, y_s, y_e\} \leftarrow \left\{ x_s - h\sqrt{\frac{1-\varphi_L}{\varphi_L}}, x_e + h\sqrt{\frac{1-\varphi_L}{\varphi_L}}, y_s - h\sqrt{\frac{1-\varphi_L}{\varphi_L}}, y_e + h\sqrt{\frac{1-\varphi_L}{\varphi_L}} \right\}$$

11. In the *T-List*, we find the linked lists that meet the extended time conditions, and find the information points that intersect with the extended range of space in these linked lists. The correctness check is carried out, and if the correctness check is passed, T_s and L_s are calculated, and the related information is processed into result information points, which are stored in the result set 2;
12. S←S – 0.1;
13. else // There are both general attributes and spatiotemporal attributes in query conditions
14. for General attributes in each query condition
15. According to the sub-relaxation threshold and semantic correlation table, the query scope is modified;
16. Searching for nodes that intersect the time condition and space condition in the initial query condition in *T-List* to check the correctness (the check standard is the relaxed general attribute condition), processing the result information points through the checked calculation T_s and L_s, and adding them to the result set 2; //First round of query relaxation
17. while (The total number of results in result sets 1 and 2 is less than r)
18. $[t_s, t_e] \leftarrow \left[t_s - h\sqrt{\frac{1-\varphi_T}{\varphi_T}}, t_e + h\sqrt{\frac{1-\varphi_T}{\varphi_T}} \right]$

$$\{x_s, x_e, y_s, y_e\} \leftarrow \left\{ x_s - h\sqrt{\frac{1-\varphi_L}{\varphi_L}}, x_e + h\sqrt{\frac{1-\varphi_L}{\varphi_L}}, y_s - h\sqrt{\frac{1-\varphi_L}{\varphi_L}}, y_e + h\sqrt{\frac{1-\varphi_L}{\varphi_L}} \right\}$$

19. In *T-List* to find the new time range linked list, in the linked list to find the nodes in line with the expanded space range, to check the correctness. Calculate T_s, L_s and G_s from the checked nodes and add them to result set 2;
20. return Result Set 1, Result Set 2

In algorithm 4, each attribute defined in the query condition is relaxed, and the weight value of each attribute is different, and its relaxation degree is also different. When the query condition contains only general attributes (lines 02-06), the situation is similar to the flexible query of Web database, and the query relaxation method based on semantic similarity is used to relax the query. When only spatiotemporal attributes are included in the query criteria, in the first round of relaxation (line 08), locate the linked list involved in the relevant time period, and find out the nodes intersecting with the expanded time range or space range to add to the result set 2. In the second round of query relaxation, modify the temporal and spatial range (line 10), and once again find the node that intersects it in the T-List result and add it to result set 2. Because general attributes are not involved in the query criteria, there is no need to check the correctness of newly added nodes. When the query condition contains both general attributes and spatiotemporal attributes, the query method is the same as the query method that only contains spatiotemporal attributes, except that the result correctness check (line 19) is carried out at the end, that is, the object is found in the tree according to the EDewey code in the result information point, and then the general attributes are compared whether they meet the relaxed general attribute conditions, if not, they are not added to the result set.

3 SORTING ALGORITHM OF QUERY RESULTS

In this section, we propose a sorting method combining the satisfaction degree of results and the return probability, which sorts the query results completely. The sorting algorithm is helpful to save users' judgment time and facilitate users to view the results. The sorting method is described in detail below.

3.1 Calculation Method of Result Satisfaction Degree

The types of keywords defined in query criteria are uncertain, and may only have general attributes, spatiotemporal attributes, or both general attributes and spatiotemporal attribute conditions. There are different ways to calculate the satisfaction degree of general attributes and spatiotemporal attributes. According to the partition method of adaptive query method based on semantic similarity (Meng et al., 2009), general attributes are divided into numerical attributes and classified attributes. The calculation method of satisfaction degree for general attributes refers to the calculation formula in reference (Meng et al., 2009). The satisfaction degree of general attributes is defined as G_s. For the general attribute set $\{A_1, \ldots, A_n\}$ in the query result, the satisfaction degree of the initial query condition Q is evaluated as follows:

$$G_s\left(A_i, Q_{A_i}\right) = \sum_{i=1}^{n} w_i \times \begin{cases} VSim\left(A_i, Q_{A_i}\right) & \text{if } Domain\left(A_i\right) \text{ is a typed attribute} \\ VSim\left(A_i, Q_{A_i}\right) & \text{if } Domain\left(A_i\right) \text{ is a typed attribute} \end{cases} \#\left(\text{AUTONUM} \setminus {}^*\text{Arabic}\right)$$

Where n denotes the number of general attributes in the query condition Q, and w_i denotes the weight value of attribute A_i; $VSim(A_i, Q_{Ai})$ represents the semantic similarity between the value of the typed attribute A_i in the general attribute in the returned result and the corresponding keyword in the initial query condition; $VSim(A_i, Q_{Ai})$ represents the semantic similarity between the numeric attribute A_i in the general attribute in the returned result and the corresponding keyword in the initial query condition.

Because of the uncertainty of spatiotemporal attributes, some spatiotemporal objects may completely meet the query conditions, partially meet the query conditions and completely do not meet the query conditions. Table 1 summarizes the formulas for calculating the satisfaction of the temporal and spatial location attributes described in subsection 2.3.1.

Table 1. The calculation formulas of the satisfaction degree about the time and space attributes

Degree of satisfaction	Time characteristic	Spatial characteristics
Accurate result	$T_s=1$	$L_s=1$
first round of relaxation	$T_s = \frac{[t_{i1},t_{i2}] \cap [t_s,t_e]}{[t_{i1},t_{i2}]}$	$L_s = \frac{MBR_i \cap MBR_Q}{MBR_i}$
second round of relaxation	$T_s = \frac{t_e - t_s}{t_e - t_s + 2\delta} \times \frac{[t_{i1},t_{i2}] \cap [t_s - \delta, t_e + \delta]}{[t_{i1},t_{i2}]}$	$L_s = \frac{MBR_Q}{MBR_{Q'}} \times \frac{MBR_i \cap MBR_{Q'}}{MBR_i}$

Obviously, for the extended result, the values of T_s and L_s are both less than 1. This is because all the extended results are less satisfied with the initial conditions than the exact results, and different extended results have different satisfaction with the query conditions, and the extended results also need to be ranked according to their importance according to the satisfaction with the original query conditions. In addition, a coefficient less than 1 is added to the calculation formula of the satisfaction degree of conditional relaxation in the second round compared with that in the first round, that is, the initial query range is divided by the expanded query range. This is because there is no intersection between the spatiotemporal attribute value of the extended results in the second round and the query scope defined by the initial query conditions, so the satisfaction degree between the extended results in the second round and the initial query conditions is lower.

3.2 Calculation Mode of Probability Sequence

Different types of nodes in the XML document tree have been introduced in section 2.1. Different node types in the XML document tree result in different probability calculations.

For *mux* type nodes, their child nodes are mutually exclusive, and only one or all of these nodes can appear in a certain time range. Therefore, if the parent node of a node is a *mux* type node, the probability of passing through the node is the probability recorded on its connection with the parent node.

For an *ind* type node, the relationship between its child nodes is independent. Suppose a node of an *ind* type contains n child nodes, which are $\{x_1, x_2, \ldots, x_n\}$, and the corresponding probabilities are $\{P_{x1}, P_{x2}, \ldots, P_{xn}\}$. Then the probability of reaching the x_1 node through the parent node is $P_{x1} \times (1-P_{x2}) \times \ldots \times (1-P_{xn})$.

3.3 Sorting Thought and Algorithm

3.3.1 Sorting Thought

In algorithm 2, two result sets are used to store the exact results and the flexible query extension results respectively, so that all the exact results can be ranked before the extension results in the final sorting. Results in Result Set 1 and Result Set 2 are also sorted in their respective result sets by return probability and satisfaction with the initial query criteria.

3.3.2 Flexible Query Sorting Algorithm

After the operation of algorithm 2, all the results stored in result set 1 are accurate results, and all the results stored in result set 2 are query slack results. The results in result set 1 and result set 2 are sorted respectively. When returning the results to the user, the ordered result set 1 is returned first and then the ordered result set 2 is returned.

Algorithm5 RSort sorting algorithm

Input: Result Set 1, Result Set 2
Output: The ordered sequence of results returned to the user
01. Calculate the P_{path} according to the probability sequence $<P_1, \ldots, P_n, \text{Type}>$, $P_{fin}=L_s \times T_s \times G_s \times P_{path}$
02. Count the number of results n1 in result set 1 and the number of results n2 in result set 2;
03. for (i=0; $i<n_1$; i++) // Sort Result Set 1
04. for (j=0; $j<n_1$; j++)
05. if $(P_{fini}>P_{finj})$
06. temp = result information point $_i$ // temp is a blank result information point
07. Result information point $_i$ = result information point $_j$, result information point $_j$ = temp;
08. end for
09. end for
10. for (i=0; $i<$ n2; i++) // Sort Result Set 2
11. for (j=0; $j<n_2$; j++)
12. if $(P_{fini}>P_{finj})$
13. temp = result information point $_i$
14. Result information point $_i$ = result information point $_j$, result information point $_j$ = temp;
15. end for
16. end for
17. The exact data object is returned to the user according to the Dewey return in result set 1
18. Return the extended data object to the user according to the Dewey return in result set 2

Algorithm 5 sorts result set 1 and result set 2 separately. Firstly, the probability sequence in the result information points is calculated. Different node types have different calculation methods, and the path probability to the location of the information nodes is obtained after calculation. The result saved in result set 1 is the exact result, the values of T_s, L_s and G_s are all 1, and the value of P_{fin} is the value of path probability. Therefore, the result information points in result set 1 only need to be sorted according to the path probability of nodes (rows 04 to 12), and the higher the probability, the higher the position. Result Set 2 stores the expanded query results after condition relaxation, and the satisfaction degree of information needs to be considered when sorting. So T_s, L_s and G_s are all taken into account when calculating P_{fin} (line 01). Then sort according to the size of P_{fin} value (lines 14 to 21). When the results are returned to the user, the node details are returned based on the *EDewey* encoding of the nodes stored in the result set, and all the nodes stored in result set 1 are ranked before result set 2.

4 CASE ANALYSIS

In this section, three query instances are used to introduce the execution flow and calculation method of flexible query method for uncertain spatiotemporal data in detail, and the working conditions of *T-List* structure and result set structure are shown in detail when analyzing these three instances.

4.1 Calculation Example

Aiming at the relationship between time and position in uncertain spatiotemporal attributes, the process of loosening method and sorting method involved in this chapter is introduced in detail with an example. Three query criteria are defined: *Q1*, *Q2*, and *Q3*, where *Q2* uses a single attribute relaxation mode and *Q3* uses a combined attribute relaxation mode.

Q_1: CarDB{Model=Carmy}
Q_2: CarDB{Time∈ [2016.10.2 9:00, 2016.10.2 10:00]^Pos∈{20,50,20,50}}
Q_3: CarDB{Model=Carmy^Time∈ [2016.10.2 18:30, 2016.10.2 19:00]^ Pos∈{60,70,30,50}}

Among them, only one attribute is defined in the query condition *Q1*, that is, the vehicle whose vehicle type is Camry. Because only one general attribute is defined in this condition, there is no need to distinguish between single attribute relaxation and combined attribute relaxation. If flexible query is needed, it must be a single attribute relaxation of general attribute. Two attribute values are defined in the query condition *Q2*, and the query goal is to query the information of all vehicles passing through the coordinate area {20, 50, 20, 50} between 9:00 am and 10:00 am on October 2, 2016. These two attributes are spatiotemporal attributes, and *Q2* has been specified to relax single attribute before defining query conditions, so *Q2* performs single attribute relaxation of spatiotemporal attributes. The query condition *Q3* includes both general attributes and spatiotemporal attributes, and its query goal is to find the information of all vehicles with Camry models passing through the coordinate area {60, 70, 30, 50} between 18:30 and 19:00 on October 2, 2016.

The above query conditions involve three different documents as shown in Figure 7 (a), (b) and (c). Assuming that each document has two locations, the probability of vehicles being in different locations at a certain time or time period is different. Details are shown in Figure 7.

To facilitate viewing the data information recorded in the document tree, the contents of the XML document tree are summarized in Table 2. Detailed location information about the three documents is recorded in Table 2, and each location information is described as location, starting time and spatial range. Table 3 records the weight distribution of keywords defined in the three query criteria.

The semantic similarity table of the general attribute Camry in *Q1* is shown in Table 4.

Given the system relaxation threshold of 0.6, the sub-relaxation threshold of each query attribute is calculated, as shown in Table 5.

Figure 7. The branch (a) (b) (c) of XML document tree

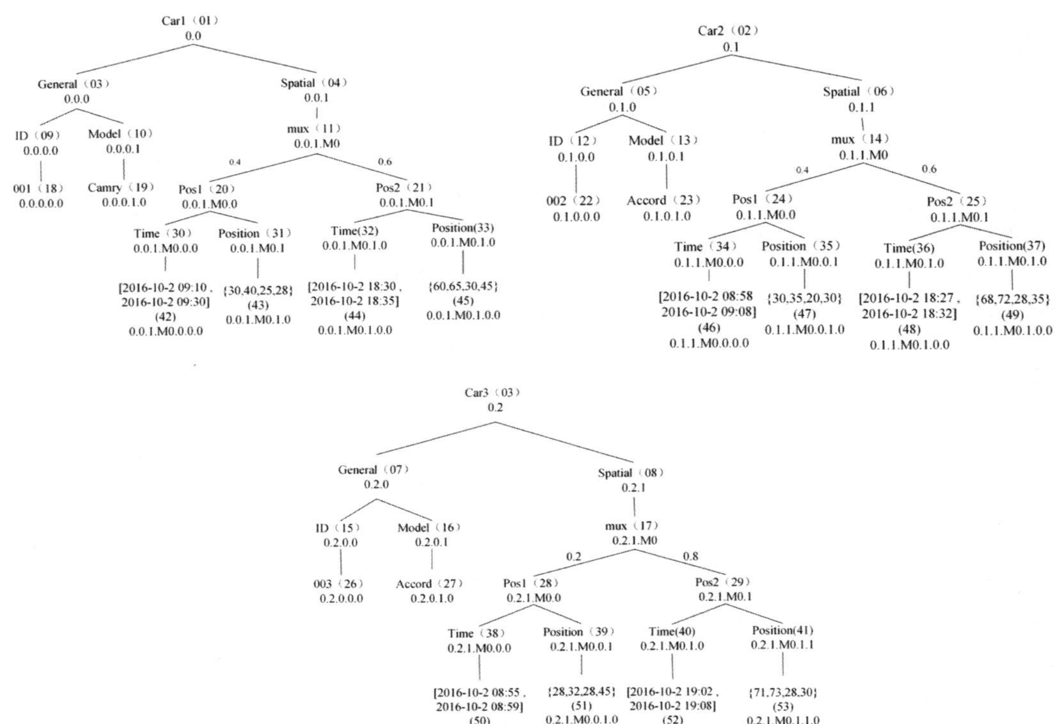

Table 2. Time and position information

Position	Begin time	End time	Spatial range
Car1.Pos1	2016.10.2 09:10	2016-10-2 09:30	{30,40,25,28}
Car2.Pos1	2016-10-2 08:58	2016-10-2 09:08	{30,35,20,30}
Car3.Pos1	2016-10-2 08:55	2016-10-2 08:59	{28,32,28,45}
Car1.Pos2	2016-10-2 18:30	2016-10-2 18:35	{60,65,30,45}
Car2.Pos2	2016-10-2 18:27	2016-10-2 18:32	{68,72,28,35}
Car3.Pos2	2016-10-2 19:02	2016-10-2 19:08	{71,73,28,30}

Table 3. Instance of specified attributes weight assignments

Characteristic	Characteristic value	Weight
Q_1.Model	Camry	1
Q_2.Time	[2016.10.2 9:00, 2016.10.2 10:00]	0.2
Q_2.Pos	{20,50,20,50}	0.8
Q_3.Model	Camry	0.4
Q_3.Time	[2016.10.2 18:30, 2016.10.2 19:00]	0.4
Q_3.Pos	{60,70,30,50}	0.2

Table 4. The results of semantic similarity computation

Classified characteristic value	Similarity characteristic value	Similarity
Camry	Accord Civic Altima	0.68 0.2 0.45

Table 5. Sub-relaxation threshold calculation results

Characteristic	Sub-relaxation threshold
Q_1.Model	0.6
Q_2.Time	0.18
Q_2.Pos	0.72
Q_3.Model	0.67
Q_3.Time	0.67
Q_3.Pos	0.33

For the query condition Q1, only one general attribute Model = Camry is included, and only Car1 meets the query condition after query. When loosening the query, according to the semantic similarity table, the semantic similarity between Accord and Camry is 0.68, which exceeds its sub-relaxation threshold of 0.6. Accord is added to the query condition to form a new query condition as follows:

$$\widetilde{Q_1} : \{Model = Camry \vee Accord\}$$

The meaning of the new query condition is to find vehicles with Camry or Accord model, and the query of vehicles with Accord model is added on the basis of the original query condition. When a new query condition is executed, both Car2 and Car3 are added to result set 2.

For query condition *Q2*, only two spatiotemporal attributes are defined in the condition, with weights of 0.2 and 0.8 respectively. It can be seen that temporal attributes are not as important as spatial attributes. The greater the attribute weight, the larger its sub-relaxation domain; The larger the sub-relaxation threshold, the smaller the change of query interval. When relaxing a single attribute, select the time attribute to relax. Execute the query condition *Q2*, only *Pos1* in *Car1* meets the query condition, and store the relevant information in the result information point and add it to the result set 1. The number of results is small, so query relaxation operation is carried out. At this point, the *T-List* result has been initialized, as shown in Figure 8 (the time period for storing information points in the figure belongs to October 2, 2016). Because the time range of Car2. Pos1 is not completely contained in any linked list, but intersects with both linked list 1 and linked list 2, the information points of *Car2. Pos1* are stored in both linked list 1 and linked list 2, similar to the situation of *Car2. Pos2*, which is stored in both linked list 3 and linked list 4.

Q2 loosens a single attribute. Because the weight of time attribute is small, time attribute is selected for query relaxation. In the first round of relaxation, find the node that intersects with the time period [2016.10.2 09:00, 2016.10.2 10:00], and *Car2.Pos1* time [2016.10.2 08:58, 2016.10.2 09:08] intersects with this. Check the spatial position of *Car2.Pos1*, whose position is {30, 35, 20, 30} exactly matches the initial query condition {20, 50, 20, 50}, so you can calculate the satisfaction degree of this node and store the relevant information in the result information point and add it to the result set 2. Time is not uniformly expressed in time division units, but automatically converts hours into minutes in the calculation process. After calculation, T_s=(9:08-9:00)/(9:08-8:58)=0.8,L_s=1, and because it does not involve general attributes, G_s defaults to 1, and the probability node type on path probability is *mux*, so the path probability is $P_{path} = 0.4$, $P_{fin}=L_s \times T_s \times G_s \times P_{path}=0.32$. At this point, there are only two results in the result set, and the number is still very small, so the second round of query relaxation is needed. In the second round of query relaxation, it is necessary to calculate the sub-relaxation threshold, and the calculation result may be decimal. However, because the values such as time and position are integers, the calculated new time range is rounded up in minutes, and the query conditions are modified by integers.

It can be seen from Table 5 that the sub-relaxation threshold of *Q2*. Time is 0.18, which is calculated by equation 2, in which $h=1.06\sigma n^{-1/5}$. For simple calculation, σ takes 10 and n takes 1000, and the expanded time range is [2016.10.2 08:54, 2016.10.2 10:06]. *Car3.Pos1* has a time range of [2016.10.2 08:55, 2016.10.2 08:59], is within the loosened query range, and is being checked for correctness. At this point, *Car3.Pos1* has a spatial range of {28, 32, 28, 45}, which meets the initial query criteria, so it can be added to result set 2. Calculate the satisfaction degree L_s=1,G_s =1,*Ts*=[(10:00-09:00)/(10:06-08:54)] × [(08:59-08:55)/(08:59-08:55)]=0.83, and the probability node type on the path probability is *mux*, so the path probability is $P_{path} = 0.2$, $P_{fin}=L_s \times T_s \times G_s \times P_{path}=0.166$. The result set is shown in Figure 9. At this time, the results are still few, so we need to modify the relaxation threshold and continue to expand the query scope.

The query condition *Q3* includes both general attributes and spatiotemporal attributes. When relaxing the combined attributes, the extended conditions of general attributes are used when checking the correctness. The weights of the three attributes are 0.4, 0.4 and 0.2 respectively, and the sub-relaxation thresholds are 0.67, 0.67 and 0.33 respectively. First, execute the query condition *Q3*, *Car1.Pos2* fully meets the query condition, and store the relevant information in result set 1. The number of results is small, so query relaxation is needed. According to the semantic similarity table, we can see that the semantic similarity between Camry and Accord exceeds its sub-relaxation threshold, and Accord is added to the query conditions for correctness check. The first round of relaxation of spatiotemporal attributes is carried out to find nodes that intersect the temporal or spatial range. *Car2.Pos2* intersects with the time and space ranges of the query condition, and *Car3.Pos3* does not intersect with the time and space ranges of the initial query condition, so *Car2.Pos2* may be an extended result, but it is still uncertain, and it is necessary to check the correctness of the general attributes of *Car2.Pos2*. After checking, it can be seen that the Model value of *Car2.Pos2* is Accord, which accords with the extended result range of general attributes, so *Car2.Pos2* is an extended result. After calculation, T_s=(18:32-18:30)/(18:32-18:27)=0.4,L_s=[(70-68) × (35-30)]/[(72-68) × (35-28)]=0.36. According to the semantic similarity table, G_s=0.68, and the probability node type on path probability is *mux*, so the solution process of path probability is $P_{path} = 0.4$, so $P_{fin}=L_s \times T_s \times G_s \times P_{path}=0.039168$. Save related results in result set 2.

Figure 8. The initialized T-List structure

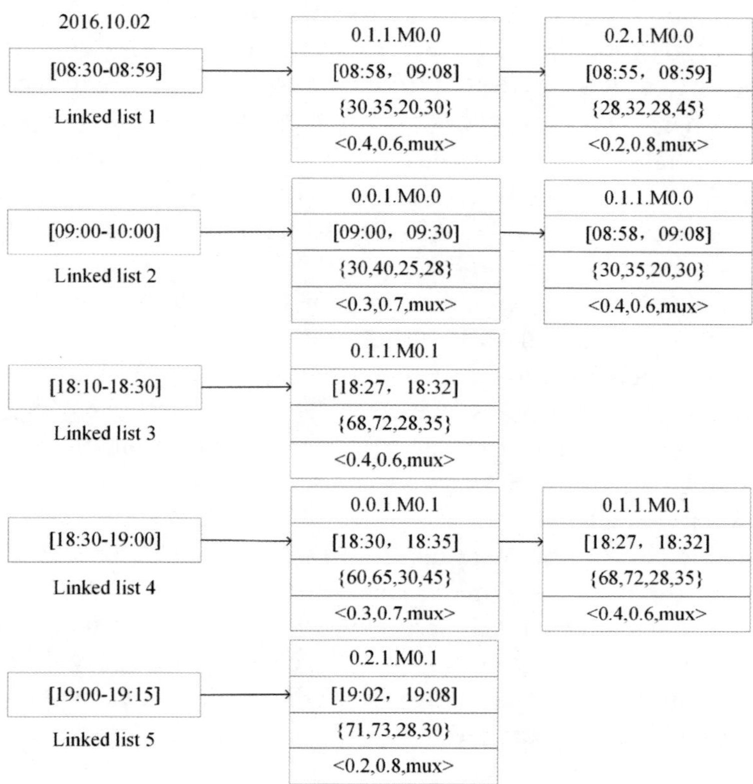

Figure 9. Single attribute relaxation for the Q2

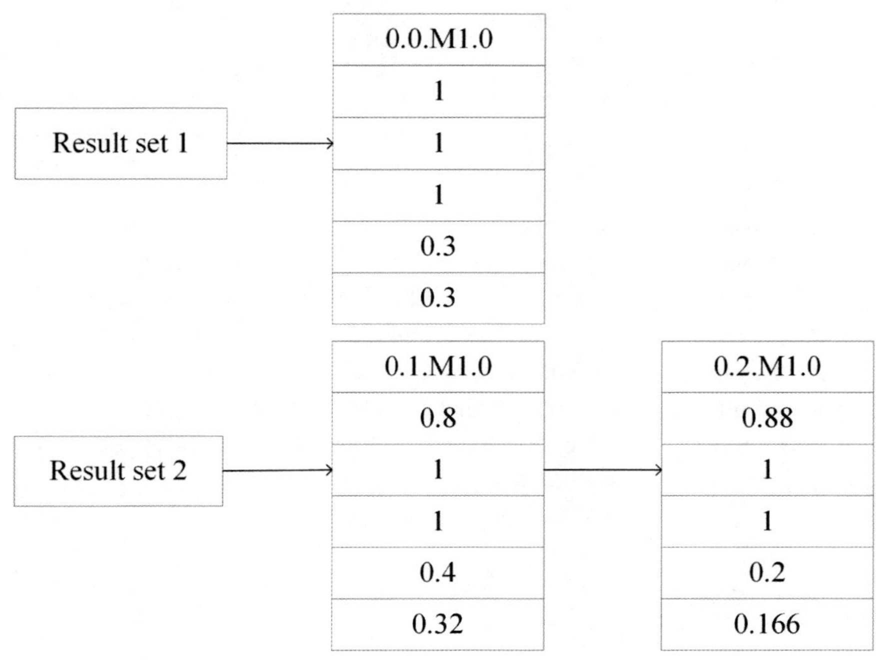

At this time, the results are still few, and the second round of query for spatiotemporal attributes is relaxed. The sub-relaxation thresholds of temporal and spatial attributes are 0.4 and 0.2, respectively. After calculation by formulas 2 and 5, the time range is expanded to [2016.10.2 18:27, 2016.10.2 19:03] and *Car3. Pos2*'s time range [2016.10.2 19:02, 2016.10.2 19:08]. The spatial range is extended to {56, 74, 26, 54} intersecting with the spatial range {71, 73, 28, 30} of *Car3. Pos 2*. *Car3.Pos2* is an extended node because the correctness of the general attribute is checked and found to conform to the relaxed range of the general attribute. Calculate T_s=[(19:00-18:30)/(19:03-18:27)] × [(19:03-19:02)/(19:08-19:02)]=0.139,L_s=((70-60) × (50-30))/((74-56) × (54-26))) × ((2×2)/(2×2))=0.397, G_s=0.68, so the probability node type on the path probability is mux, so the path probability is P_{path} =0.2, $P_{fin}=L_s \times T_s \times G_s \times P_{path}$=0.0075. At this time, the number of results is still small, so the third round of expansion is needed, and the relaxation threshold S=S-0.1 is adjusted, that is, the sub-relaxation threshold becomes 0.5 at this time. Modify the query scope, and the steps are similar to the second round of query expansion.

When sorting the query results, because the result set 1 stores accurate query results, in order to ensure the accuracy of the query, all the accurate results are ranked in front of the extended results, that is, all the results in result 1 are ranked in front of result set 2. Inside the two result sets, they are sorted according to P_{fin} values from high to low.

Sort the existing results of *Q3*. In the result set of *Q3*, there is only one result in result set 1 and two results in result set 2. In result set 2, the P_{fin} value of *Car2.Pos2* is 0.039168, and the P_{fin} value of *Car3.Pos2* is 0.0075, and the value with high probability ranks first. According to the *EDewey* code in the result information point, the storage document of the object is found, and the relevant information is extracted and returned to the user. The ranking of existing results for *Q3* is shown in Table 6. Table shows that one exact result and two extended results are obtained. The details are as follows:

Table 6. Existing result sort table for Q3

	id	Model	Time	Position
Accurate query results	001	Camry	[2016.10.2 18:30, 2016.10.2 18:35]	{60,65,30,45}
Query slack results	002	Accord	[2016.10.2 18:27, 2016.10.2 18:32]	{68,72,28,35}
	003	Accord	[2016.10.2 19:02, 2016.10.2 19:08]	{71,73,28,30}

The flexible query algorithm proposed in this chapter adopts the way of sacrificing space to reduce the time complexity of the algorithm. In the model proposed in this chapter, depth-first algorithm is used to traverse the document tree and generate *T-List* structure. When the data in the tree changes, the *T-List* structure will be updated automatically. When loosening the query, you need to do the second query, the third query, etc. until the number of results meets the requirements, that is to say, you need to traverse the XML document tree many times. After *T-List* structure is adopted, when loosening the query, the linked list in *T-List* structure is traversed first, which is equivalent to establishing index, pruning to a great extent, and significantly reducing the query time.

5 SUMMARY

Flexible Query of Uncertain Spatiotemporal XML Data can avoid the problem of insufficient selectivity caused by empty or few query results when users query uncertain spatiotemporal objects. Flexible query provides users with objects that approximately meet the requirements, and considers user preferences to provide users with acceptable potential matching objects. From the user's point of view, flexible query provides users with more possible results and useful information before they find satisfactory results, which saves the time of multiple queries and improves the efficiency. From the perspective of database, flexible query reduces the number of times users visit the system to a certain extent, and reduces the query burden.

REFERENCES

Bai, L., He, A., Liu, M., Zhu, L., & Xing, Y. (2021). *Adaptive query relaxation and result categorization of fuzzy spatiotemporal data based on XML*. Reseearch Gate.

Bai, L., Lin, Z., & Xu, C. (2016). Spatiotemporal operations on spatiotemporal XML data using XQuery. In *Proceedings of the 12th International Conference on Natural Computation, Fuzzy Systems and Knowledge Discover*, Changsha, China. 10.1109/FSKD.2016.7603362

Bin, Q. (2014). *Design and implementation of nearest neighbor search algorithm for uncertain data*. Heilongjiang University.

Chen, B. Y., Yuan, H., Li, Q., Shaw, S. L., Lam, W., & Chen, X. (2016). Spatiotemporal data model for network time geographic analysis in the era of big data. *International Journal of Geographical Information Science*, *30*(6), 1041–1071. doi:10.1080/13658816.2015.1104317

Chen, Z., Zhao, T., & Liu, W. (2021). Time-aware collective spatial keyword query. *Computer Science and Information Systems*, *28*(3), 1077–1100. doi:10.2298/CSIS200131034C

Dfgdfg, F., Flesca, S., & Furfaro, F. (2011). Xpath query relaxation through rewriting rules. *IEEE Transactions on Knowledge and Data Engineering*, *23*(10), 1583–1600. doi:10.1109/TKDE.2010.203

Galindo, J., Urrutia, A., & Piattini, M. (2006). *Fuzzy Databases: Modeling, Design and Implementation*. Idea Group Publishing Hershey. doi:10.4018/978-1-59140-324-1

Guan, X., Bo, C., Li, Z., & Yu, Y. (2017). ST-hash: An efficient spatiotemporal index for massive trajectory data in a NoSQL database. In *Proceedings of the 25th International Conference on Geoinformatics* (pp. 02–04). Buffalo, USA. 10.1109/GEOINFORMATICS.2017.8090927

Hao, Z. X. (2017). *New theory of spatiotemporal database*. Science Press.

Kandel, A., & Zemankova-Leech, M. (1984). *Fuzzy relational databases, a key to expert systems*. Verl. TÜV Rheinland.

Li, Z. C. (2012). *Research on complex query method of spatiotemporal database*. Huazhong University of Science and Technology.

Liu, X., & Wan, Y. (2010). Storing spatiotemporal data in XML native database. In *Proceedings of the 2nd International Workshop on Database Technology and Applications* (pp. 27–28). Wuhan, China.

Ma, C. Y. (2012). *Research on Complex Query Processing in Spatiotemporal Database*. Zhejiang University.

Mama, R., & Machkour, M. (2019). A study of fuzzy query systems for relational databases. In *Proceedings of the 4th International Conference on Smart City Applications* (pp. 1-5). ACM. 10.1145/3368756.3369105

Mama, R., & Machkour, M. (2019). A study on fuzzy interrogation systems of database. In *2019 International Conference of Computer Science and Renewable Energies (ICCSRE)* (pp. 1-6). IEEE. 10.1109/ICCSRE.2019.8807564

Mama, R., & Machkour, M. (2019). Fuzzy Questions for Relational Systems. In *Proceedings of the Third International Conference on Smart City Applications* (pp. 104-114) IEEE.

Meng, X. F. (2009). *Research on Key Technologies of Flexible Query in Web Database*. Northeastern University.

Yan, W. (2012). *Research on XML Flexible Query Technology*. Northeastern University.

Chapter 20
Query Relaxation for Uncertain Spatiotemporal XML Data

ABSTRACT

Users often cannot accurately give query constraints so that the query results may be empty or very few. Traditional algorithms cannot be used to deal with uncertain spatiotemporal data because they have no relaxation query on spatiotemporal attributes. Therefore, in this chapter, the authors propose new flexible query algorithms, which add query relaxation processing for uncertain spatiotemporal XML data. Considering that XML has great advantages in exchanging and representing spatiotemporal data, the authors propose an uncertain spatiotemporal data model based on XML. According to the different number of relaxing attributes, they give SingleRelaxation algorithm and MultipleRelaxation algorithm. In addition, a T-List structure is designed to quickly locate the nodes' positions of uncertain spatiotemporal data, and RSort algorithm is proposed to sort accurate query results and extended query results. The experimental results show the superiority of this approach.

1 INTRODUCTION

In real world applications, the uses of spatiotemporal data are very extensive, such as traffic monitoring (Chen et al., 2005), large urban network (Laharotte et al., 2014), and person recognition (Gheissari et al., 2006), etc. Furthermore, spatiotemporal data have both spatial attributes and temporal attributes, and may change with time or space leading to uncertainties (Emrich et al., 2012). There are a lot of efforts studying temporal data modeling (Ma et al., 2022; Hu et al., 2015), spatiotemporal data modeling (Ma et al., 2013), uncertain spatiotemporal data modeling (Bai, et al., 2018), uncertain spatiotemporal reasoning, (Bai, et al., 2018), uncertain spatiotemporal querying (Emrich et al., 2012), fuzzy spatiotemporal data constructing, (Cheng, et al., 2019), fuzzy spatiotemporal modeling (Bai, et al. 2021), fuzzy spatiotemporal data representing (Cheng, et al. 2019), and fuzzy spatiotemporal data reasoning (Cheng, et al. 2021)

Owing to the development and popularization of science and technology, a large number of Web ordinary users can access information through various ways through spatiotemporal queries. Considering spatiotemporal query methods, Navathe et al. (Navathe & Ahmed, 1989) and Gao et al. (Gao et al., 2018) use temporal data query method, which queries whether the object changes within a certain period and the

DOI: 10.4018/978-1-6684-9108-9.ch020

type of changes that have occurred. Dai et al. (Dai et al., 2005) and Sistla et al. (Sistla et al., 2015) apply the uncertain spatial data query, which queries the moving range of an object. Emrich et al. (Emrich et al., 2012) and Raghebi et al. (Raghebi & Banaei-Kashani, 2018) use the uncertain spatiotemporal data query technology, which queries the changes in a certain area within a certain time period. Wang et al. (Wang et al., 2013) utilize the join query method, which queries objects within a particular interval of time at a certain distance from a specific object. Furthermore, Wang et al. (Wang et al., 2013) use the spatiotemporal nearest neighbor query method, which queries an entity closest to the object or region under study within a specific time interval.

However, most users often cannot accurately give query constraints. In an exact query, the query results may be empty or very few. Therefore, the flexible query is necessary. At present, query relaxation mainly involves removing an attribute condition under the initial query condition or expanding the scope of the query to obtain more query results. Huh et al. (Huh et al., 2000) present a knowledge abstraction database that extracts semantic data relationships from the underlying database and supports relaxation query by using query generalization and specialization steps. However, it does not distinguish between the exact results and the extended results. Mottin et al. (Mottin et al., 2014) design a system *IQR* that reports the dynamic relaxation of the original query constraints to users at one time according to some optimization objectives, in which users respond by either accepting or declining the relaxation. Muslea et al. (Muslea & Lee, 2005) give a novel algorithm, *TOQR*, which uses a small dataset to determine the implicit relationships among the domain attributes before exploiting the domain knowledge to relax the failed query. The algorithm of relaxation query cannot be adjusted according to users' preferences. Zhang et al. (Zhang et al., 2017) present an *AQR* algorithm, which assigns a weight to each property through the data distribution in the database.

In recent years, XML has been widely used in the data storage and Web field. Researchers have begun to study query relaxation methods based on XML. Liu et al. (Liu et al., 2010) present an adaptive query relaxation method based on XML. This method only returns results related to the query conditions. Liu et al. (Liu & Yan, 2015) develop a novel top-k retrieval approach that can smartly generate the most promising answers in the order correlated with the ranking measure. Flesca et al. (Flesca & Furfaro, 2010) propose an XPath relaxation query method and use override rules to support XML relaxation query processing. However, the cost of query relaxation in these methods is invariable and cannot be adjusted according to users' preferences.

In order to solve the problem of meeting users' preferences, Meng et al. (Meng et al., 2017) propose a query relaxation method based on semantic similarity. The method firstly estimates the current users' preferences according to the initial query conditions and the original data distributions. Subsequently, it relaxes the initial query according to the semantic similarity between the relaxation threshold, the attribute weight, and the attribute value. Finally, the query results are sorted according to their satisfaction with the initial query. Yi et al. (Yi et al., 2005) give an approach of automatic elements matching between XML application schemas using similarity measure and relaxation labeling. The similarity measures consider element categories and their properties. Contextual constraints are used in the relaxation labeling to try to achieve an optimal matching. However, these methods cannot support uncertain spatiotemporal data very well. In addition, these methods increase the cost of query relaxation because single attribute relaxation and multiple attribute relaxation are not considered under these methods.

Ranking query results becomes the next challenge after query relaxation. Jones et al. (Jones et al., 2000) combine a comprehensive account of the probabilistic retrieval model with new systematic experiments on TREC Program material and present a ranking model called *PIR*. Agrawal et al. (Agrawal et al., 2006) present a *CPR* algorithm, which is based on the preference model without interest degree, say $\{i_1 > i_2 | X\}$, which means the item i_1 is preferred to i_2 in the context of X. However, these methods do not differentiate between the exact results and the extended results, which increases the complexity of the sorting algorithm.

In this chapter, based on the aforementioned advantages of XML, EDewey code (Li et al., 2011), and TF-IDF idea (Meng et al., 2017), we propose a query relaxation approach based on semantic similarity, and propose a result ranking approach for uncertain spatiotemporal data based on XML.

Consider the example in Table 1 that gives some temporal and spatial information of some cars. We define a query condition *Q*: "Find all cars' information with Camry models passing through the space range {60, 70, 30, 50} between 18:30 and 19:00", expressed as: *Q*: CarDB {Model = Carmy∩ Time∈[18:30, 19:00] ∩ Space ∈{60,70,30,50}}.

Table 1. Temporal and spatial information

	General	Spatiotemporal		
	Model	**Time**	**Space**	**Pos**
Car1	Camry	[18:30,18:35]	{60,65,30,45}	0.6
		[09:10,09:30]	{30,40,25,28}	0.4
Car2	Accord	[18:27,18:32]	{68,72,28,35}	0.6
		[08:58,09:08]	{30,35,20,30}	0.4
Car3	Accord	[19:02,19:08]	{71,73,28,30}	0.8
		[08:55,08:59]	{28,32,28,45}	0.2

Executing the query condition *Q*, and *Car1.Pos2* completely satisfies the query condition; however, the number of results is small. Therefore, the query condition needs to be relaxed. The query condition *Q* contains the general attribute and the spatiotemporal attributes, which need to be relaxed separately. During the relaxation process, if the satisfaction degrees of time, space, general attribute and path meet the query condition, the relaxation is appropriate. In view of this, we can see *Car2.Pos2* may be a result.

The main contributions can be divided as following.

- A representation model of uncertain spatiotemporal data based on XML is established. A *T-List* structure is constructed based on this model, which can quickly locate the nodes satisfying the query constraints, is designed.
- We propose flexible query algorithms, adding query relaxation processing for Uncertain Spatiotemporal XML Data.
- We propose *SingleRelaxation* algorithm and *MultipleRelaxation* algorithm for single and multiple attribute relaxation respectively.
- *RSort* algorithm is proposed to sort the exact results and the extended results.

The rest of the chapter is organized as follows: In Section 2, we propose a method based on XML for the flexible query of uncertain spatiotemporal data. A method for sorting query results is designed in Section 3. We show the experimental results in Section 4. Finally, Section 5 gives theoretical and practical contributions and Section 6 gives conclusions and directions for future work.

2 QUERY RELAXATION

2.1 Uncertain Spatiotemporal XML Data Model

An uncertain spatiotemporal XML data model is the basis of investigating queries on uncertain spatiotemporal data in an XML document. In this subsection, we give an uncertain spatiotemporal data model which adds the nodes of type *ind* and *mux*.

Definition 1. The uncertain spatiotemporal XML data is denoted as *USP* = {*ID, General, Spatial*}, where

- *ID* represents an encoding that uniquely identifies the identity of the data.
- *General* denotes a set of general attributes, comprising a group of definite and invariant attributes.
- *Spatial* is a collection of uncertain spatiotemporal attributes.

Definition 2. Suppose the boundary interval of ith dimension in n-dimensional space is $I_i(o) = [l_i, u_i]$, the Minimum Bounding Rectangle (MBR) with dimension n is represented by $I^d(o) = I_1(o) \times I_2(o) \times \ldots \times I_n(o)$.

Concerning uncertain spatiotemporal XML data, we propose an uncertain spatiotemporal data model based on XML, as shown in Figure 1.

Figure 1. A model for uncertain spatiotemporal data based on XML

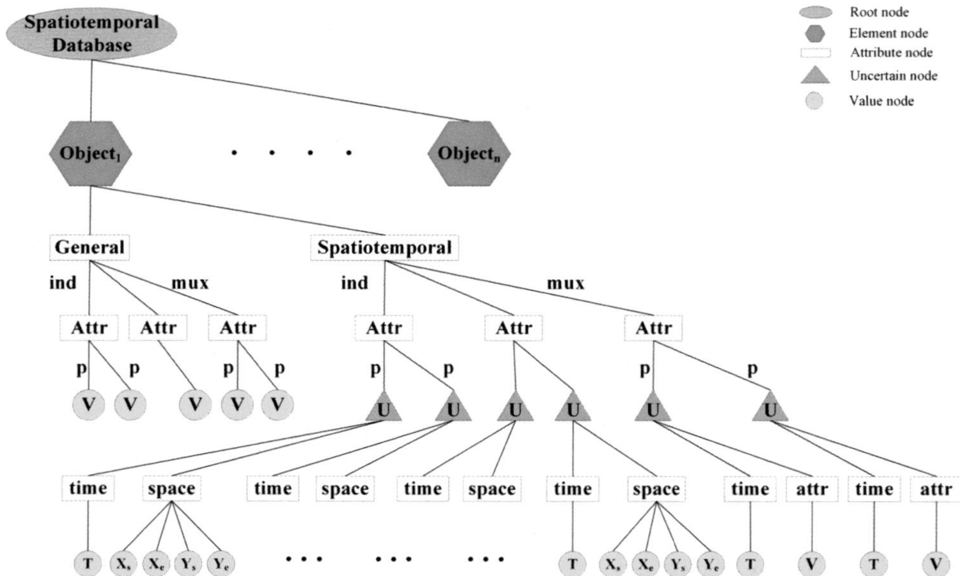

2.2 *T-List*

In order to locate potential matching objects quickly and reduce the time cost for flexible query matching, we propose a type of node storage structure *T-list* based on time segment partition which is used to reconstruct and optimize XML data document in our chapter. It uses the method of contour histogram to divide the whole timespan of the XML document tree into several time segments of different lengths according to the uniform node density. Hence, this subsection mainly introduces the data structure of *T-List*.

As shown in Figure 2, it shows the basic structure of *T-list* which consists of an array of n*3. The first two columns of the arrays represent the time segment, and the third column stores a header pointer *P** to a linked list which stores the data nodes that are contained in or intersected with the time segment corresponding to the linked list. Therefore, for the query conditions using time keywords, the nodes that meet the time will be quickly searched in the array of the *T-List*, and then the designated linked list can be found according to the corresponding linked list pointer in the third column of the array, which will greatly reduce the query sample and improve the query time. Finally, the Info nodes (information nodes) that strictly meet the requirements of the time segment can be searched in these linked lists.

Figure 2. A structure of T-List

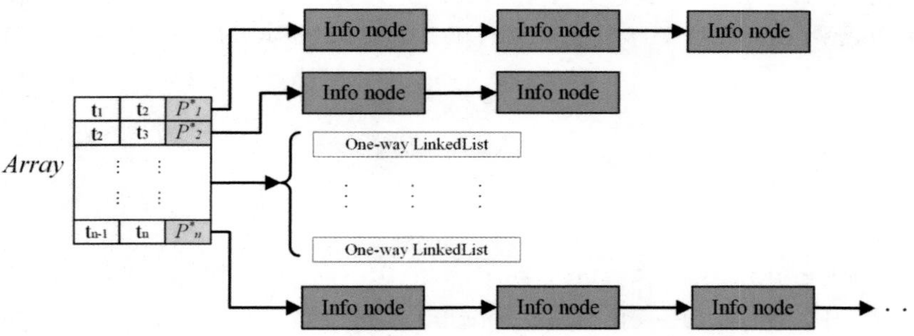

These data nodes are also called information nodes, which is composed of *EDewey* code, temporal attribute, spatial attribute and probability sequence. The probability sequence consists of a multiple of tuples structured as <P_1,..., P_n, *Type*>, including node types and all probability values from the root node of the XML document tree to the current node. It facilitates the calculation of the probability of the result when ranking the final results.

The node type in the probability sequence is divided into two types: *mux*-type and *ind*-type. For the *mux*-type nodes, the child nodes are mutually exclusive, and only one or none of them can appear during a certain time interval. Therefore, if the parent node of a node is a *mux*-type node, the probability of passing through this node is the probability recorded on the connection line between the parent node and itself. For *ind*-type nodes, the relationship between their child nodes is independent. Assuming that a *ind*-type node contains *n* child nodes $\{x_1, x_2, \ldots, x_n\}$ with probabilities $\{P_{x1}, P_{x2}, \ldots, P_{xn}\}$. The probability of reaching the x_1 node through the parent node is $P_{x1} \times (1-P_{x2}) \times \ldots \times (1-P_{xn})$.

2.3 Spatiotemporal Attribute Relaxation

The relaxation of spatiotemporal attributes in query conditions is mainly divided into two parts: the relaxation of temporal attributes and spatial attributes.

2.3.1 Relaxation of Temporal Attributes

Time is a one-dimensional attribute. If we need to relax the temporal condition, firstly find the node whose temporal information intersects with the temporal condition. Then add these nodes in the result set. Finally calculate the time satisfaction of the node, denoted as T_s. The calculation formula is shown in Equation (1) where $[t_{i1}, t_{i2}]$ denotes the length of the temporal range of the newly added node and $[t_s, t_e]$ signifies the length of temporal range in the query condition.

$$T_s = \frac{[t_{i1},\ t_{i2}] \cap [t_s,\ t_e]}{[t_{i1},\ t_{i2}]} \tag{1}$$

If one round of relaxation does not meet the requirements, a second round of relaxation would be required. During the second relaxation, the temporal range in the initial query condition is enlarged to obtain a new time query range $[t_s - \delta, t_e + \delta]$. The specific calculation formula is shown in Equation (2).

$$[t_s,\ t_e] \leftarrow [t_s - h\sqrt{\frac{1-\varphi_T}{\varphi_T}},\ t_e + h\sqrt{\frac{1-\varphi_T}{\varphi_T}}] \tag{2}$$

The formula forδ mentioned above is$\delta\ =\ h\sqrt{(1-\phi_T)/\phi_T}$ where φ_T denotes the sub-relaxation threshold of the time. Here the sub-relaxation threshold φ_i means the relaxation degree of a keyword whose formula is shown in Equation (3). In Equation (3), n denotes the number of the keywords, w_i represents the weight of the keyword, and S denotes the given relaxation threshold in the initial query condition Q.

$$\varphi_{i(i=1,\dots,n)} = \begin{cases} \frac{w_i}{\varphi_i} = ,\dots, = \frac{w_n}{\varphi_n} \\ S = \sum_{i=1}^{n} w_i \times \varphi_i \end{cases} \tag{3}$$

In this case, the Equation (4) for time satisfaction degree T_s of the second relaxation is as follows:

$$T_s = \frac{t_e - t_s}{t_e - t_s + 2\delta} \times \frac{[t_s,\ t_e] \cap [t_s - \delta,\ t_e + \delta]}{[t_{i1}, t_{i2}]} \tag{4}$$

In the formula of T_s of the second relaxation, there is a coefficient $\frac{t_e - t_s}{t_e - t_s + 2\delta}$ in addition to the calculation formula of the first relaxation. Compared with the first relaxation, the time interval of the second relaxation has no intersection with the range of the initial query condition. Thus, its satisfaction with the initial query condition is lower than the first relaxation.

At this point, two rounds of relaxation have been performed on the temporal attributes. If the returned results are still small, the third and subsequent relaxations can be continued similar to that in the second round.

As shown in Figure 3, in the initial query condition, only the time interval T_2 meets the conditions and conforms to the initial query time interval T. When the time condition is relaxed, the node whose time interval intersects with the time interval T_1, is firstly added to the result set. At this time, $T_s = (T_1 \cap T)/T_1$. If the total number of results returned is still small, the second round of relaxation is executed. The temporal range is expanded to T', and T_3 as well as T' are intersected. At this instance, T_3 is added to the result set, and a coefficient T/T' is added to the formula of the time satisfaction (T/T' value must be less than 1). Because the temporal range is expanded, the newly added results are less satisfied with the initial query conditions.

Figure 3. Temporal range relaxation

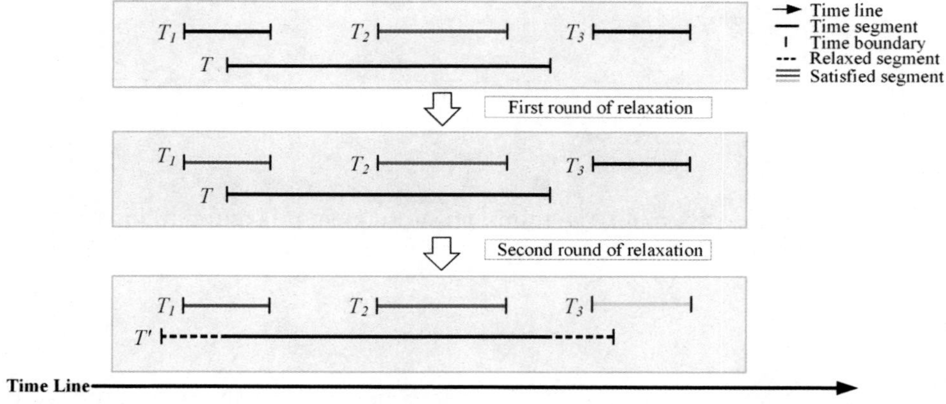

2.3.2 Relaxation of Spatial Attributes

MBR is used to denote the given spatial range in the query condition Q, represented by MBR_Q (Figure 4(a)). If the spatial condition needs to be relaxed, the node overlapping MBR_Q is firstly added to the query results as shown in R_3 and R_4 in Figure 4(b). Then, at the time of expansion, the space satisfaction L_s is calculated according to Equation (5).

$$L_s = \frac{MBR_i \cap MBR_Q}{MBR_i} \quad (5)$$

If a round of relaxation does not meet the requirement, a second round is required. First enlarge the new spatial query scope $\text{MBR}_{Q'}$ according to Equation (6), whose process is similar to temporal relaxation. Then, add new results that are included in or intersect with the new query scope, as shown in R_5 and R_6 in Figure 4(c).

$$\{x_s, x_e, y_s, y_e\} \leftarrow \{x_s - h\sqrt{\frac{1-\varphi_L}{\varphi_L}},\ x_e + h\sqrt{\frac{1-\varphi_L}{\varphi_L}},\ y_s - h\sqrt{\frac{1-\varphi_L}{\varphi_L}},\ y_e + h\sqrt{\frac{1-\varphi_L}{\varphi_L}}\} \tag{6}$$

Therefore, Equation (7) for calculating L_s of the second relaxation is as follows:

$$L_s = \frac{MBR_Q}{MBR_{Q'}} \times \frac{MBR_i \cap MBR_{Q'}}{MBR_i} \tag{7}$$

Figure 4. Relaxation of spatial attributes

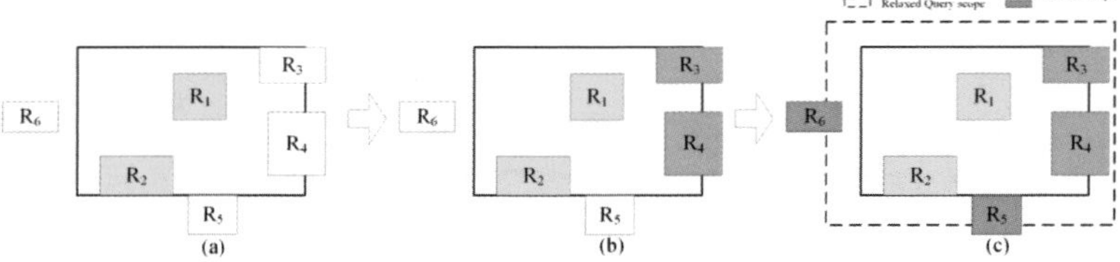

If the number of results is still small, the third and subsequent relaxation rounds can continue similarly to the second round.

2.3.3 Result Set

Because query results require a storage structure in a query process, a result set structure is proposed. This structure comprises two linked lists, which are represented by *Result Set1* and *Result Set2* respectively. *Result set1* is used to store the results that precisely meet the initial query condition, and the newly added results after relaxation are all stored in *Result Set2*. The results that meet the condition are stored in the result set as result information nodes. The result information nodes include the node's EDewey code, the time satisfaction T_s, the spatial satisfaction L_s and the general attribute satisfaction G_s, the path probability valueP_{path}, and the final probability P_{fin} which has been used for the result ranking. The specific calculation of the path probability value is described in detail under Subsection3.1.

2.4 Query Relaxation Algorithm

The query relaxation is divided into three types: only general attributes, only spatiotemporal attributes and both. When only contains general attributes, the query method is similar to the flexible query method of general Web database. In this chapter, we propose a flexible query method for uncertain spatiotemporal data only for the latter of the two cases.

Before raising the flexible query, determine the weight of each keyword in the initial query first. Here, $IDF_i(t) = \log(\frac{n}{F_i(t)})$ and $w_i = \frac{IDF_i(t)}{\sum_{i=1}^{k} IDF_i(t)}$ are used to calculate the importance and assign weights for the attributes defined under the query conditions. After the weight assignment is completed, the query relaxation is performed according to the size of the weight value.

Query relaxation can be divided into two cases: single attribute relaxation and multiple attribute relaxation. Single attribute relaxation is to find the attribute with the least weight (least important) in the keyword defined by the query condition to relax conditionally, while other attribute conditions are unchanged. We only discuss the single attribute relaxation for spatiotemporal attributes in detail. Multiple attribute relaxation is the conditional relaxation of multiple attributes that need to be relaxed according to the weight of each attribute. It may be only general attributes or only spatiotemporal attributes or both. Spatiotemporal attribute query relaxation method is different from the general attribute. The specific flexible query algorithm is given in detail in Algorithm 1, Algorithm 2 and Algorithm 3. Furthermore, these three algorithms are also collectively referred to as *SPQR* Algorithm.

Algorithm 1 Query relaxation algorithm

Input:Initial Query Condition *Q*, a XML document tree *XMLTree*, *T-ListU*, crisp result set *Result Set1* and relaxed result set *Result Set2*.
Output:*Result Set1*, *Result Set2*

```
while Traverse(XMLTree)!= null do
 if Match(XMLTree ->node,Q) then
   rnode= Create(XMLTree ->node); //create a result information node
   Add(Result Set1, rnode);
 else
   rnode= Create(XMLTree ->node);
   Add(U, rnode);
   if Count(Result Set1)>r then
 goto 17;
else
 Q->keyword.weight←Weight();
 if IsSingleRelaxation() then
    SingleRelaxation();
 else if IsMultiple Relaxation() then
    MultipleRelaxation();
RRank(); //Result ranking algorithm is introduced in Section 3
Return Result Set1, Result Set2;
```

Assume that the system sets the occurrence of query relaxation when the number of query results returned to the user is less than *r*. A query condition *Q* is given and the query result is provided to the user through the flexible query algorithm.

Algorithm 1 includes the entire process involved in the flexible query. Firstly, traverse the XML document tree and store the crisp results in *Result Set*1 (lines 1-4). At the same time, store the potential matching objects in *T-List* (lines 5-7). Then, check if the number of results in *Result Set1* is greater than the specified value *r*. If does, there is no need to perform query slack (lines 8-9) and directly sort the results (line 16). Otherwise, a flexible query is required to provide it with potential matches that may meet the users' needs. According to the number of relaxed attributes, flexible query can be divided into two situations: single attribute relaxation and multiple attribute relaxation. When a single attribute is relaxed, the *SingleRelaxation* method (lines 10-13) is called. And when the multiple attribute is relaxed, the *MultipleRelaxation* method is called (lines 14-15). Finally, in the result ranking phase, rank the results in *Result Set1* and *Result Set2* respectively and return the results to the users in the order of Ranked *Result Set1* and Ranked *Result Set2* (lines 16-17). The calculation method of the satisfaction of the query results and the initial query conditions, the calculation method of the return probability of the results, and the final result ranking method will be described in detail in Section 3.

In our chapter, the *SingleRelaxation* algorithm and *MultipleRelaxation* algorithm are based on the query relaxation rewriting algorithm proposed by *Meng* et al. (Meng et al., 2017).

Algorithm 2 gives an algorithm for single attribute query relaxation.

Algorithm 2 first selects the keyword with the minimum weight (lines 1-5), and then determines the property type of the keyword. If the attribute is a typed attribute in a general attribute, look for attributes in the XML tree whose semantic similarity to the keyword is upper than that of the φ_m and add them to the query condition (lines 6-11). If the attribute is a numeric attribute in a general attribute, expand its query scope and add it into Q(lines 12-13). Then, execute Q and store the result in *Result Set2* (line 14). If the keyword is a temporal or spatial attribute (lines 16 and 20), query relaxation should be divided into two parts: temporal and spatial attributes. During the relaxation, look in the *T-list* for nodes that intersect the initial range of query condition and pass the correctness check, and add them into *Result Set2* (lines 17-18 and 21-22). Then, calculate the new query range of the keyword and adjust relaxation threshold S in steps of 0.1(line 19 and 23) to proceed to the next round of relaxation until the number of returned results is greater than *r*. Correctness check is to find the node in XML document tree according to the stored node's EDewey code in *Result Set2*, and also to judge whether the node meets other conditions.

For multiple attribute relaxation, according to different user-defined query condition, it can be divided into three different situations: only general attributes, only spatiotemporal attributes, both general attributes and spatiotemporal attributes.

The algorithm is as follows:

In Algorithm 3, each keyword in the query condition is relaxed. Because each attribute has a different weight value, its degree of relaxation varies. When the keyword is a general attribute, its situation is similar to that of Web database flexible queries, and query relaxation is performed according to the semantic similarity based query relaxation method (lines 1-4). When the keyword is a temporal or spatial attribute, its relaxation is similar to that of the spatiotemporal relaxation in Algorithm 2 (lines 5-11). If the number of query results returned is upper than *r*, stop the relaxation.

Algorithm 2 SingleRelaxationAlgorithm

```
Input:Initial Query Condition Q, a XML document tree XML Tree, T-List U, crisp result set Result Set1 and relaxed result set Result Set2.
Output:Result Set1, Result Set2
min = w_1; //min denotes the minimum weight value of the keyword.
m = 1; // m denote(denotes) the location of the keyword whose weight is minimum.
   for i= 1 to n do //n is the number of keywords in the initial query condition.
      if w_i<min then
      min = w_1 ;m = i;
   If IsGeneralAttribute(Q->keyword_m) then
   while Count(Result Set1)+ Count (Result Set2) <r do
   if IsTypedAttribute(Q->keyword_m) then
      while Traverse(XMLTree)!= null do
         if Match(Q->keyword_m,XMLTree ->node)>φ_m then
            Add(Q, XMLTree ->node)
   if IsNumericAttribute(Q->keyword_m) then
      Q->keyword_m= [q - δ,q + δ] // qdenotes the initial query range of Q->keyword_m.
   Result Set2←Execute(Q)
   S = S – 0.1;
   if IsTemporalAttribute(Q->keyword_m) then
   while Count(Result Set1)+ Count (Result Set2) <r do
   callFunction Relaxation(U, Q->keyword_m, temporal);
      S = S - 0.1;
else if IsSpatialAttribute() then
   while Count(Result Set1)+ Count (Result Set2) <r do
      callFunction Relaxation(U, Q->keyword_m, spatial);
      S = S - 0.1;
   Return Result Set1, Result Set2
Function Relaxation(U, Q->keyword, attributetype)
headpointer[]←LocateIntersect(U, Q->keyword); //headpoint stores head pointers of link lists
   for i= 1 to Count(headpointer) do
   p = headpointer[i]->next;
   while p!= null do
     if LocateIntersect (p, Q->keyword) then
        while Traverse(XMLTree)!= null do
           if Check (XMLTree ->node,p) then
              satisfactiondegree= Calculate(p,attributetype)
              Add(Result Set2, p);
     p = p-> next;
   Q->keyword_m= [q - δ,q + δ];
```

Algorithm 3 MultipleRelaxation Algorithm

Input:Initial Query Condition *Q*, a XML document tree *XML Tree,T-List U*, crisp result set *Result Set1* and relaxed result set *Result Set2* and the number of relaxed keyword *m*.
Output:*Result Set1*, *Result Set2*
for $i = 1$ to m **do**
while Count(*Result Set1*)+ Count(*Result Set2*) <r **do**
if IsGeneralAttribute(*Q->keyword*$_i$) **then**
Q->keyword$_i$= [q_i - δ, q_i+ δ] // $q_i$denotes the initial query range of *Q->keyword*$_i$.
elseif IsSpatiotemporalAttribute(*Q->keyword*$_i$) **then**
if IsTemporalAttribute(*Q->keyword*$_i$) **then**
callFunction Relaxation(*U*, *Q->keyword*$_i$,*temporal*);
else
callFunction Relaxation(*U*, *Q->keyword*$_i$,*spatial*);
$S = S - 0.1$;
Return *Result Set1*, *Result Set2*;

3 QUERY RESULTS RANKING

In this section, we propose a result ranking method that combines the satisfaction degree with the returned probability, to rank the returned results. It is helpful to save the users' judgment time so that users can quickly get the results with a higher matching degree.

3.1 Result Satisfaction Degree

The type of keywords used in query conditions are mainly divided into two types: general and spatiotemporal attributes. The computational methods for their satisfaction are different. For general attributes, it is subdivided into numerical and typed attributes according to the classification of adaptive query method based on semantic similarity. Equation (8) shows the satisfaction degree G_s of the general attribute, where $\{A_1, \ldots, A_n\}$ denotes a general attribute set, n means the number of general attributes, and w_i denotes the weighted normal value of the attribute A_i. Note that $VSim(A_i, Q_{Ai})$ denotes the semantic similarity between the value of the typed attribute A_i of the returned result and the corresponding keyword in the initial query condition, $NSim(A_i, Q_{Ai})$ represents the semantic similarity between the numeric attribute A_i of returned result and the corresponding keyword in the initial query condition.

$$G_s(A_i, Q_{Ai}) = \sum_{i=1}^{n} w_i \times \begin{cases} VSim(A_i, Q_{Ai}) & A_i \in \textit{typed attribute} \\ NSim(A_i, Q_{Ai}) & A_i \in \textit{numeric attribute} \end{cases} \tag{8}$$

For spatiotemporal attributes, their satisfaction degree is calculated differently from that of general attributes due to their uncertainty. Table 2 summarizes the formulas for calculating the satisfaction degree of temporal and spatial attributes.

Table 2. The formulas for calculating satisfaction degrees of temporal and spatial attributes

Satisfaction Degree	Temporal Attributes	Spatial Attributes
Crisp Results	$T_s = 1$	$L_s = 1$
First Round of Relaxation	$T_s = \frac{[t_{i1}, t_{i2}] \cap [t_s, t_e]}{[t_{i1}, t_{i2}]}$	$L_s = \frac{MBR_i \cap MBR_Q}{MBR_i}$
Second Round of Relaxation	$T_s = \frac{t_e - t_s}{t_e - t_s + 2\delta} \times \frac{[t_s, t_e] \cap [t_s - \delta, t_e + \delta]}{[t_{i1}, t_{i2}]}$	$L_s = \frac{MBR_Q}{MBR_{Q'}} \times \frac{MBR_i \cap MBR_{Q'}}{MBR_i}$

As shown in Table 2, both T_s and L_s of relaxed results are less than 1. This is because the matching degree of relaxed results to the initial query condition is lower than that of the crisp results. In addition, compared with the first relaxation, the computational method for the satisfaction after the second conditional relaxation is increased by a factor less than 1, since the spatiotemporal attribute values of the results in the second relaxation and the query scope of the initial query conditions no longer intersect. Therefore, the satisfaction of relaxed results in the second round is lower than that of the first round's.

3.2 Result Ranking Algorithm

In Algorithm 1, *Result Set1* and *Result Set2* are used to store crisp results and relaxed results respectively to rank all the crisp results ahead of the relaxed results. They are also ranked in their respective result sets based on the returned probability and the satisfaction degree, respectively.

After the flexible query on uncertain spatiotemporal data by Algorithm 1, all the results in *Result Set1* are crisp results, and all the results in *Result Set2* are relaxed results. Then the results in *Result Set1* and *Result Set2* are ranked respectively, as detailed in Algorithm 4 (also called as *SPQRR* Algorithm). When the results are returned to the user, the ordered *Result Set1* is returned first and then the ordered *Result Set2* is returned.

Algorithm 4 ranks *Result Set1* and *Result Set2* separately. Firstly, we calculate the probability sequence of the result information node according to the node type. Then the path probability to the location of the information node is obtained. T_s, L_s and G_s of the results which are accurate and stored in *Result Set1* are all 1, and the value of P_{fin} is the value of path probability. Therefore, the result information nodes in *Result Set1* only need to be ranked according to the path probability of the node (lines 1-6), and the higher the calculated probability, the higher the rank position. *Result Set2* holds the query results expanded after the condition is relaxed. Therefore, the satisfaction of the information needs to be taken into account when ranking, i.e., T_s, L_s and G_s are all taken into account when calculating P_{fin}. Then, rank by the value of the P_{fin} (lines 7-12). When the result is returned to the user, the details of the node are returned according to the EDewey code of the node in the result set, and all the nodes in the Result Set1 are ranked ahead of the Result Set2.

Algorithm 4 RRank Algorithm (Result Set1, Result Set2)

```
Input: Result Set1, Result Set2
Output: the ranking Result Set1, the ranking Result Set2
    n_1 = Count(Result Set1);
P_fin ←call FunctionCal_Fin(Result Set1,n_1); // calculate the path probability
    for i=1 to n_1 do // RankResult Set1
    for j=1 to n_1 do
        if P_fini>P_finj then
            Swap(ResultInforPoint_i, ResultInforPoint_j);
    n_2 = Count(Result Set2);
    P_fin ←call FunctionCal_Fin(Result Set2,n_2);
    for i=1 to n_2 do // RankResult Set2
    for j=1 to n_2 do
        if P_fini>P_finj then
            Swap(ResultInforPoint_i, ResultInforPoint_j);
    Return Result Set1, Result Set2
Function Cal_Fin(Result Set,n)
for i= 1 tondo
    if Ismux(Type_i) then
        P_path = P_i ;
    else
        P_path = (1-P_1)×(1-P_2)×...×P_i×...×(1-P_n);
  P_fini = L_s×T_s×G_s×P_path
ReturnP_fin
```

4 EXPERIMENTS

4.1 Experimental Settings

The experiments are conducted on a computer running Windows 10 with Intel Core i5-4300U (dominant frequency 1.9GHz) CPU, 8 GB of RAM, and 480 GB of a solid state drive. We implemented all algorithms in Python3.6. For the experimental results, we used the Memory-Profiler plug-in for performance testing and Excel for cartographic analysis. We use the following dataset to evaluate the performance of our methods.

Dataset. The dataset in the experiment is derived from an open source hurricane dataset. The original dataset includes general attributes (say wind speed and type), and spatiotemporal attributes (such as time and position). Based on the spatiotemporal XML data model proposed in the chapter, it is reconstructed from the relational dataset to the XML dataset.

4.2 Query Relaxation Experiment

This experiment tests the performance of the algorithm in checking the recall, precision and comprehensive performance. The efficiency of checking the recall (Equation(9)) is the ratio of the number of relevant results queried to the total number of relevant results in the dataset, and is commonly used to evaluate the quality of the query results. The efficiency of checking the precision (Equation(10)) refers to the proportion of relevant results in the result set, and is used to evaluate the accuracy of the query results. F-score (Equation(11)) is a comprehensive consideration indicator to examine the query relaxation effect.

$$Precision = \frac{|\{relevant\ documents\} \cap \{retrieved\ documents\}|}{|\{retrieved\ documents\}|} \tag{9}$$

$$Recall = \frac{|\{relevant\ documents\} \cap \{retrieved\ documents\}|}{|\{relevant\ documents\}|} \tag{10}$$

$$F - Measure = (\frac{recall^{-1} + precision^{-1}}{2})^{-1} = 2 \cdot \frac{recall \cdot precision}{recall + precision} \tag{11}$$

Because the algorithm described in this chapter mainly considers the relaxation query for spatio-temporal attributes (space and time), the query conditions can be divided into three categories: simple temporal relaxation query ($Q1$), simple spatial relaxation query ($Q2$), and composite spatiotemporal relaxed query ($Q3$). The query structure and examples of each query condition are shown in Table 3. In order to perform a comprehensive and reasonable comparison and evaluation, it is necessary to carry out comparative experiments of the algorithms with three kinds of query conditions. To ensure the accuracy of the experiment, each condition will randomly generate multiple test samples to test the algorithms. Then take the average one as the final experimental results of the condition. Due to the different query requirements and preferences of users, the definitions for the content of *relevant documents* in recall and precision formulas vary from user to user. Therefore, the recall and precision of the result set obtained after each conditional query is calculated by different users and then the average value of the obtained data is considered to obtain a more realistic recall and precision.

Table 3. The query structure and practical examples of Q1, Q2, and Q3

Query Name	Type	Practical Example
Q1	SingleTime	Time ∈ [2017-03-11,2017-04-05] Time ∈ [2017-03-11,2017-04-05] ∩ Wind Type=1 Time ∈ [2017-03-11,2017-04-05] ∩ Wind Type=1 ∩ Wind Speed=100
Q2	SingleSpace	Longitude ∈ [43,45] ∩ Latitude ∈ [-16,-14] ∩Wind Type=1 Longitude ∈ [21,24] ∩ Latitude ∈ [33,34] ∩ Wind Type=1 Longitude ∈ [21,24] ∩ Latitude ∈ [33,34] ∩ Wind Type=1 ∩ Wind Speed=100
Q3	Multiple	Time ∈ [2017-03-11,2017-04-05] ∩ Longitude ∈ [21,24] ∩ Latitude ∈ [33,34] Time ∈ [2017-03-11,2017-04-05] ∩ Longitude ∈ [21,24] ∩ Latitude ∈ [33,34] ∩ Wind Type=1 Time ∈ [2017-03-11,2017-04-05] ∩ Longitude ∈ [21,24] ∩ Latitude ∈ [33,34] ∩ Wind Type=1 ∩ Wind Speed=100

In this chapter, we choose the *TOQR* algorithm and *AQR* algorithm which are commonly used in the previous web relational databases to compare with *SPQR* algorithm. The former starts with an empty query, then uses *TAN* algorithm to learn the topology and parameters of Bayesian network for each basic query condition in the failed query to predict whether the query condition can be satisfied or not. Finally, the query conditions in the failed query are added to the initial empty query according to the breadth priority order in the Bayesian network topology. The latter assigns the corresponding weight to each attribute according to its distribution in the database. Because the algorithms above are representative and similar to the *SPQR* algorithm, which all adopt some methods to relax the initial conditions to expand the result set. We select them as the comparative case of this group of experiment. As shown in Figure 5, it is a comparison diagram of *SPQR*, *AQR* and *TOQR* algorithms for the recall, precision, and *F-Score* under different query conditions.

Figure 5. The recall, precision, and F-Score of SPQR, AQRand TOQR under Q1, Q2, and Q3

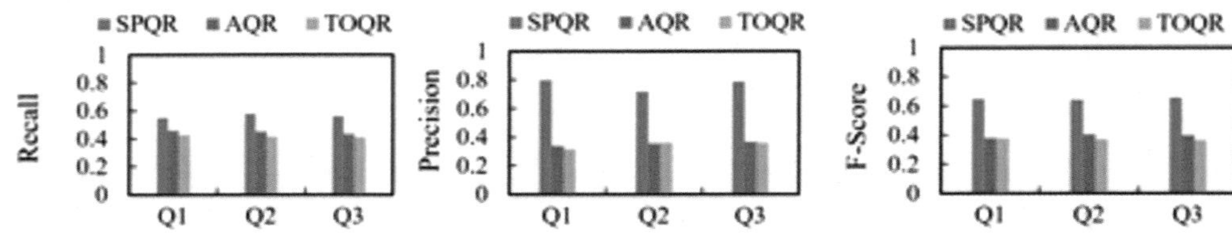

As shown in Figure 5, *SPQ*R is significantly superior to *AQR* and *TOQR* in terms of recall, precision and *F-Score*, while there is little difference between *AQR* and *TOQR* in terms of query relaxation performance. This is because the *SPQR* algorithm is based on a special XML spatiotemporal data model, which has a unique advantage in dealing with spatiotemporal attribute query relaxation based on XML. Although the other two algorithms can also be used in spatiotemporal data query, they are not optimized for spatiotemporal data model. Therefore, their ability of processing spatiotemporal data is not very good compared with SPQR.

4.3 Result Ranking Experiment

This experiment mainly tests the result sorting performance of the *SPQRR* algorithm proposed in this chapter, compared with that of the commonly used *CPR* algorithm and *PIR* algorithm. The *CPR* is based on the preference model without interest degree, and *PIR* focuses on researching the user preferences on unspecified attribute values by taking advantages of query history, which combines the global importance of unspecified attribute values and the correlation between unspecified and specified values. In this chapter, the top 10precision results within the result set is used as the evaluation standard to measure the ranking effect of each algorithm, and Equation(12) is given as follows.

$$Precision = \frac{|\,top\ 10\ relevant\ tuples\ retrieved \cap 10\ relevant\ tuples\,|}{10} \quad (12)$$

Figure 6 shows the comparison of the sorting results for the SingleSpace query($Q2$) and the Multiple query($Q3$) according to different algorithms. In order to ensure the accuracy and comprehensiveness of the results, we randomly generated 10 query conditions for each query group. The precision of the top 10 results of each condition are calculated by different users and then obtain the average precision of its condition. Finally, the average precision of this group of query is obtained. Whether $Q2$ or $Q3$, the effect of *SPQRR* algorithm is better than that of *CPR* and *PIR* in Figure 6. Unlide the latter of two algorithms based on single factor ranking, this algorithm combines the comprehensive consideration of time satisfaction degree, spatial satisfaction degree and uncertainty. Therefore, it is more suitable for ranking uncertain spatiotemporal results because it provides excellent performance in ranking obtained from spatiotemporal database query

Figure 6. The precision of SPQRR, CPR and PIR for the result ranking

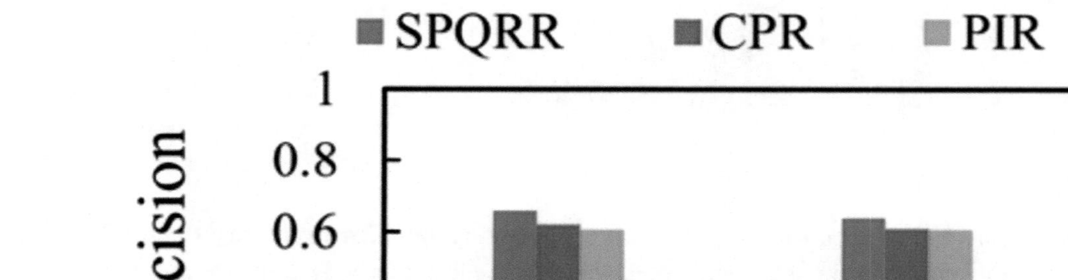

4.4 Query Performance Analysis

This experiment mainly tests the query execution time and memory consumption of *SPQR*. *SPQR* not only reconstructs and optimizes the relaxation algorithm of the traditional relational database according to the XML database model proposed in this chapter, but also adds *T-list*. In order to test the effect of *T-list* on the overall performance of the algorithm, we choose to test the execution time and memory cost of the algorithm with *T-list* and without *T-list* in different size of datasets. Figure 7 shows that execution time of the three types of query condition ($Q1$, $Q2$ and $Q3$) under a dataset size of 500, 1000 and 5000 respectively, when the T-*list* is used and not used. In order to ensure the accuracy of the data, each case is to take a number of test conditions under the average. Figure 8 compares the corresponding memory consumption.

Figure 7. The execution time of whether use T-list structure in different data set scale

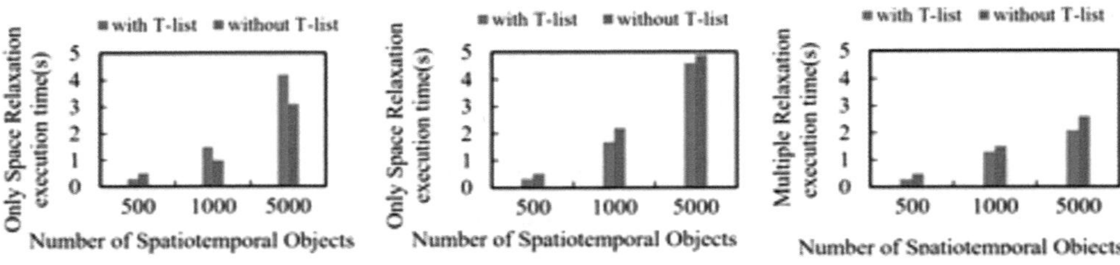

Figure 8. The memory footprint of whether use T-list structure in different data set scale

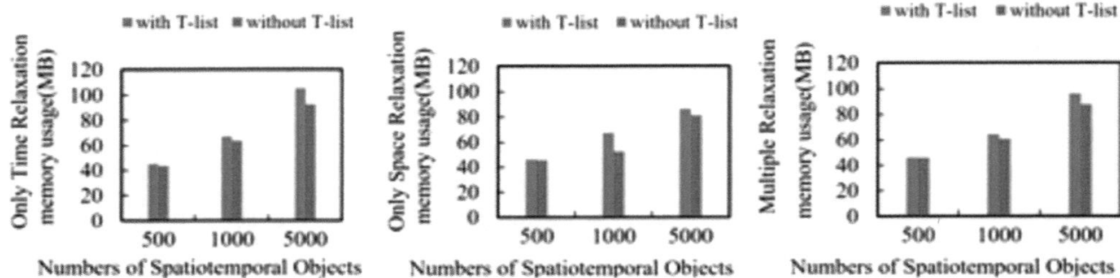

As shown in Figure 7, the execution time of the algorithm using the *T-list* structure is distinctly shorter under three different sizes of data set. It indicated that *T-list* can effectively improve the query speed regardless of the size of the data set, and is more suitable for operating a spatiotemporal database. This is because *T-list* automatically divides the dataset into groups based on temporal attributes, speeding up the execution of query conditions with temporal attributes. However, because of the addition of the *T-list*, the memory occupied will increase because the program will generate more intermediate variables and structures during the execution process. In Figure 8, the algorithm with the *T-list* always occupies more memory than the one without it. Its memory footprint increases as the database size increases. This effect is because of the reconstruction of the entire dataset by *T-list*. Most users are more sensitive to the increase in query time than that in memory usage. Hence, an increase in small amount of memory is necessary to achieve a considerable decrease in query time. Therefore, *T-list* is practical, necessary, and suitable for spatiotemporal data queries.

5 THEORETICAL AND PRACTICAL CONTRIBUTIONS

The first theoretical contribution is the proposed uncertain spatiotemporal data model based on XML. On the basis of it, a *T-List* structure is constructed to quickly locate the nodes satisfying the query constraints. In addition, we propose two algorithms for single and multiple attribute relaxation respectively.

The practical contribution of the chapter is providing valuable approach for spatiotemporal applications such as geographical and environmental information systems, etc.

6 SUMMARY

In this chapter we first developed a query relaxation method *SPQR* on uncertain spatiotemporal XML data to avoid the problem of selectivity shortage caused by empty or fewer query results. Then we present *SPQRR*, a result ranking approach based on satisfaction and path probability to rank the query results and provide better returned results for users. The experimental results show that our query relaxation and result ranking method can achieve both the relatively high Recall and high Precision compared with those of several common algorithms at the same time.

REFERENCES

Agrawal, R., Rantzau, R., & Terzi, E. (2006). Context-sensitive ranking. In *Proceedings of the 2006 ACM SIGMOD international conference on Management of data*. Association for Computing Machinery. 10.1145/1142473.1142517

Bai, L., Cao, X., & Jia, W. (2018). Uncertain spatiotemporal data modeling and algebraic operations based on XML. *Earth Science Informatics*, *11*(1), 109–127. doi:10.100712145-017-0322-6

Bai, L., Wang, J., Di, X., & Li, N. (2021). Fixing the inconsistencies in fuzzy spatiotemporal RDF graph. *Information Sciences*, *578*, 166–180. doi:10.1016/j.ins.2021.07.038

Bai, L., Zhu, L., & Jia, W. (2018). Determining topological relations of uncertain spatiotemporal data based on counter-clock-wisely directed triangle. *Applied Intelligence*, *48*(9), 2527–2545. doi:10.100710489-017-1100-3

Chen, S. C., Shyu, M. L., Peeta, S., & Zhang, C. (2005). Spatiotemporal vehicle tracking: The use of unsupervised learning-based segmentation and object tracking. *IEEE Robotics & Automation Magazine*, *12*(1), 50–58. doi:10.1109/MRA.2005.1411419

Cheng, H., Li, P., Wang, R., & Xu, H. (2021). Dynamic spatio-temporal logic based on RCC-8. *Concurrency and Computation*, *33*(22), 1–12. doi:10.1002/cpe.5900

Cheng, H., Wang, R., Li, P., & Xu, H. (2019). Representing and reasoning fuzzy spatio- temporal knowledge with description logics: A survey. *Intelligent Data Analysis*, *23*(S1), 113–132. doi:10.3233/IDA-192847

Cheng, H., Yan, L., Ma, Z., & Ribaric, S. (2019). Fuzzy spatio-temporal ontologies and formal construction based on fuzzy Petri nets. *Computational Intelligence*, *35*(1), 204–239. doi:10.1111/coin.12199

Dai, X., Yiu, M. L., Mamoulis, N., Tao, Y., & Vaitis, M. (2005). Probabilistic spatial queries on existentially uncertain data. In *Proceedings of International Symposium on Spatial and Temporal Databases*. Springer. 10.1007/11535331_23

Emrich, T., Kriegel, H. P., Mamoulis, N., Renz, M., & Zufle, A. (2012). Querying uncertain spatiotemporal data. In *Proceedings of 2012 IEEE 28th international conference on data engineering*. IEEE. 10.1109/ICDE.2012.94

Flesca, S., & Furfaro, F. (2010). XPath query relaxation through rewriting rules. *IEEE Transactions on Knowledge and Data Engineering*, *23*(10), 1583–1600.

Gao, J., Agarwal, P. K., & Yang, J. (2018). Durable top-k queries on temporal data. *Proceedings of the VLDB Endowment International Conference on Very Large Data Bases*, *11*(13), 2223–2235.

Gheissari, N., Sebastian, T. B., & Hartley, R. (2006). Person reidentification using spatiotemporal appearance. In *Proceedings of 2006 IEEE Computer Society Conference on Computer Vision and Pattern Recognition (CVPR'06)*. IEEE. 10.1109/CVPR.2006.223

Hu, Y., & Stefan, D. (2015). Temporal data management and processing with column oriented NoSQL databases. *Journal of Database Management*, *26*(3), 41–70. doi:10.4018/JDM.2015070103

Huh, S. Y., Moon, K. H., & Lee, H. (2000). A data abstraction approach for query relaxation. *Information and Software Technology*, *42*(6), 407–418. doi:10.1016/S0950-5849(99)00100-7

Jones, K. S., Walker, S., & Robertson, S. E. (2000). A probabilistic model of information retrieval: development and comparative experiments: Part 2. *Information Processing & Management*, *36*(6), 809–840. doi:10.1016/S0306-4573(00)00016-9

Laharotte, P. A., Billot, R., Come, E., Oukhellou, L., Nantes, A., & El Faouzi, N. E. (2014). Spatiotemporal analysis of bluetooth data: Application to a large urban network. *IEEE Transactions on Intelligent Transportation Systems*, *16*(3), 1439–1448. doi:10.1109/TITS.2014.2367165

Li, J., Liu, C., Zhou, R., & Wang, W. (2011). Top-k keyword search over probabilistic XML data. In *Proceedings of 2011 IEEE 27th International Conference on Data Engineering*. IEEE. 10.1109/ICDE.2011.5767875

Liu, C., Li, J., Yu, J. X., & Zhou, R. (2010). Adaptive relaxation for querying heterogeneous XML data sources. *Information Systems*, *35*(6), 688–707. doi:10.1016/j.is.2010.02.002

Liu, J., & Yan, D. L. (2015). Answering approximate queries over XML data. *IEEE Transactions on Fuzzy Systems*, *24*(2), 288–305. doi:10.1109/TFUZZ.2015.2453168

Ma, J., Zeng, D., Zhao, H., & Liu, C. (2013). Cross-correlation measure for mining spatio-temporal patterns. *Journal of Database Management*, *24*(2), 13–34. doi:10.4018/jdm.2013040102

Ma, R., Hu, Z., & Yan, L. (2022). A temporal JSON data model and its query languages. *Journal of Database Management*, *33*(1), 1–29. doi:10.4018/JDM.299556

Meng, X., Zhang, X., Tang, Y., & Bi, C. (2017). Adaptive query relaxation and top-k result ranking over autonomous web databases. *Knowledge and Information Systems*, *51*(2), 395–433. doi:10.100710115-016-0982-4

Mottin, D., Marascu, A., Basu Roy, S., Das, G., Palpanas, T., & Velegrakis, Y. (2014). IQR: an interactive query relaxation system for the empty-answer problem. In *Proceedings of the 2014 ACM SIGMOD international conference on Management of data*. Association for Computing Machinery. 10.1145/2588555.2594512

Muslea, I., & Lee, T. J. (2005). Online query relaxation via bayesian causal structures discovery. In *Proceedings of AAAI*. AAAI Press.

Navathe, S. B., & Ahmed, R. (1989). A temporal relational model and a query language. *Information Sciences*, *49*(1-3), 147–175. doi:10.1016/0020-0255(89)90026-1

Raghebi, Z., & Banaei-Kashani, F. (2018). Probabilistic reachability query in evolving spatiotemporal contact networks of moving objects. In *Proceedings of the 26th ACM SIGSPATIAL International Conference on Advances in Geographic Information Systems*. Association for Computing Machinery. 10.1145/3274895.3274976

Sistla, A. P., Wolfson, O., & Xu, B. (2015). Continuous nearest-neighbor queries with location uncertainty. *The VLDB Journal*, *24*(1), 25–50. doi:10.100700778-014-0361-2

Wang, Y., Li, X., Li, X., & Wang, Y. (2013). A survey of queries over uncertain data. *Knowledge and Information Systems*, *37*(3), 485–530. doi:10.100710115-013-0638-6

Yi, S., Huang, B., & Chan, W. T. (2005). XML application schema matching using similarity measure and relaxation labeling. *Information Sciences*, *169*(1-2), 27–46. doi:10.1016/j.ins.2004.02.013

Zhang, X., Meng, X., Tang, Y., & Bi, C. (2017). Adaptive query relaxation and result categorization based on data distribution and query context. *Journal of Information Science and Engineering*, *33*(5), 1375–1396.

Compilation of References

Abiteboul, S., Kimelfeld, B., Sagiv, Y., & Senellart, P. (2009). On the Expressiveness of Probabilistic XML Models. *The VLDB Journal, 18*(5), 1041–1064. doi:10.1007/s00778-009-0146-1

Abul, O., Bonchi, F., & Nanni, M. (2008). Never walk alone: uncertainty for anonymity in moving objects databases. In proceedings of ICDE, (pp. 376-385) IEEE. doi:10.1109/ICDE.2008.4497446

Aburas, M. M., Ho, Y. M., Ramli, M. F., & Ash'aari, Z. H. (2017). Improving the capability of an integrated CA-Markov model to simulate spatio-temporal urban growth trends using an Analytical Hierarchy Process and Frequency Ratio. *International Journal of Applied Earth Observation and Geoinformation, 59*, 65–78. doi:10.1016/j.jag.2017.03.006

Ademaj, F., Schwarz, S., Berisha, T., & Rupp, M. (2019). A Spatial Consistency Model for Geometry-Based Stochastic Channels. *IEEE Access : Practical Innovations, Open Solutions, 7*, 183414–183427. doi:10.1109/ACCESS.2019.2958154

Agrawal, R., Rantzau, R., & Terzi, E. (2006). Context-sensitive ranking. In *Proceedings of the 2006 ACM SIGMOD international conference on Management of data*. Association for Computing Machinery. 10.1145/1142473.1142517

Ahuja, A. G., & Gadicha, A. B. (2014). Answering XML query using tree based association rule. *International Journal of Applied Innovation in Engineering & Management, 3*(3), 143–146.

Akhter, I., Simon, T., Khan, S., Matthews, I., & Sheikh, Y. (2012). Bilinear Spatiotemporal Basis Models. *ACM Transactions on Graphics, 31*(2), 17–29. doi:10.1145/2159516.2159523

Alamri, S., Taniar, D., & Safar, M. (2014). A taxonomy for moving object queries in spatial databases. *Future Generation Computer Systems, 37*, 232–242. doi:10.1016/j.future.2014.02.007

Algergawy, A., Mesiti, M., Nayak, R., & Saake, G. (2011). XML data clustering: An overview. *ACM Computing Surveys, 43*(1), 1–41. doi:10.1145/1978802.1978804

Ali, K. (2017). A comparative study of well-known sorting algorithms. *International Journal of Advanced Research in Computer Science, 8*(1).

Al-sharif, A. A., & Pradhan, B. (2014). Monitoring and predicting land use change in Tripoli Metropolitan City using an integrated Markov chain and cellular automata models in GIS. *Arabian Journal of Geosciences, 7*(10), 4291–4301. doi:10.1007/s12517-013-1119-7

Amagasa, T., Yoshikawa, M., & Uemura, S. (2000). A Data Model for Temporal XML Documents. In *Proceedings of DEXA*, (pp. 334-344). ACM. 10.1007/3-540-44469-6_31

Amato, N. M., Goodrich, M. T., & Ramos, E. A. (2001). A randomized algorithm for triangulating a simple polygon in linear time. *Discrete & Computational Geometry, 26*(2), 245–265. doi:10.1007/s00454-001-0027-x

Amjadi, J., & Soroudi, M. (2018). Twin signed total Roman domination numbers in digraphs. *Asian-European Journal of Mathematics, 11*(3), 1850034. doi:10.1142/S1793557118500341

Analyti, A., & Pachoulakis, I. (2008). A survey on models and query languages for temporally annotated RDF. *International Journal of Advanced Computer Science and Applications, 1*(3), 28–35.

Antonić, O., Križanb, J., & Marki, A. (2001). Spatio-temporal interpolation of climatic variables over large region of complex terrain using neural networks. *Ecological Modelling, 138*(1-3), 255–263. doi:10.1016/S0304-3800(00)00406-3

An, Y., Borgida, A., & Mylopoulos, J. (2005). Constructing complex semantic mappings between XML data and ontologies. In *Proceedings of the International Semantic Web Conference* (pp. 6-20). ACM. 10.1007/11574620_4

Arenas, H., Aussenac-Gilles, N., Comparot, C., & Trojahn, C. (2018). Ontologie pour l'intégration de données d'observation de la Terre et contextuelles basée sur les relations topologiques [Ontology for the integration of Earth observation and contextual data based on topological relations]. In *Proc. IC*, Nancy, France.

Artale, A., & Franconi, E. (2005). Temporal Description Logics. Handbook of Temporal Reasoning in Artificial Intelligence, 1, 375-388.

Artale, A., Kontchakov, R., Lutz, C., Wolter, F., & Zakharyaschev, M. (2007). Temporalising tractable description logics. In *14th International Symposium on Temporal Representation and Reasoning (TIME'07)* (pp. 11-22). IEEE. 10.1109/TIME.2007.62

Augusto, J. C. (2003). A general framework for reasoning about change. *New Generation Computing, 21*(3), 209–246. doi:10.1007/BF03037474

Baazizi, M. A., Bidoit, N., & Colazzo, D. (2011). Efficient Encoding of Temporal XML Documents. In *Proceedings of the 18th IEEE International Symposium on Temporal Representation and Reasoning*, (pp. 15-22). IEEE.

Baazizi, M. A., Bidoit, N., & Colazzo, D. (2011). Efficient Encoding of Temporal XML Documents. In *Proceedings of the 18th International Symposium on Temporal Representation and Reasoning* (pp. 15-22). IEEE.

Babu, D. B., Prasad, R. S. R., & Santhosh, M. (2012). XML twig pattern matching algorithms and query processing [J] [IJERT]. *International Journal of Engineering Research & Technology (Ahmedabad), 1*(3), 1–6.

Bai, L. Y., Yan, L., & Ma, Z. M. (2015) Fuzzy Spatiotemporal Data Modeling and Operations in XML. Applied Artificial Intelligence, 29, pp,259-282. doi:10.1080/08839514.2015.1004615

Bai, L., He, A., Liu, M., Zhu, L., & Xing, Y. (2021). *Adaptive query relaxation and result categorization of fuzzy spatiotemporal data based on XML*. Reseearch Gate.

Bai, L. (2010). *Research on XML modeling method of spatiotemporal data*. Northeastern University.

Bai, L. Y., Li, Y., & Liu, J. M. (2017). *Fast Leaf-to-Root Holistic Twig Query on XML Spatiotemporal Data* [In Chinese]. Northeastern University. doi:10.17706/jcp.12.6.534-542

Bai, L. Y., Xu, C. M., & Liu, X. L. (2015). A Framework for Spatiotemporal Data Representation in XML. *Journal of Computer Information Systems, 11*(14), 5091–5098.

Bai, L. Y., Yan, L., & Ma, Z. M. (2013). Determining Topological Relationship of Fuzzy Spatiotemporal Data Integrated with XML Twig Pattern. *Applied Intelligence, 39*(1), 75–100. doi:10.1007/s10489-012-0395-3

Bai, L. Y., Yan, L., & Ma, Z. M. (2014). Querying fuzzy spatiotemporal data using XQuery. *Integrated Computer-Aided Engineering, 21*(2), 147–162. doi:10.3233/ICA-130454

Bai, L. Y., Yan, L., & Ma, Z. M. (2014). Spatiotemporal Operations Integrated with Functions in XML. *Journal of Computer Information Systems*, *10*(21), 9079–9086.

Bai, L. Y., Yan, L., & Ma, Z. M. (2017). Interpolation and Prediction of Spatiotemporal Data Based on XML Integrated with Grey Dynamic Model. *ISPRS International Journal of Geo-Information*, *6*(4), 1–14. doi:10.3390/ijgi6040113

Bai, L., Cao, X., & Jia, W. (2018). Uncertain spatiotemporal data modeling and algebraic operations based on XML. *Earth Science Informatics*, *11*(1), 109–127. doi:10.1007/s12145-017-0322-6

Bai, L., Cui, Z., Duan, X., & Fu, H. (2022). Keyword coupling query of spatiotemporal data based on XML. *Journal of Intelligent & Fuzzy Systems*, *42*(3), 2219–2228. doi:10.3233/JIFS-211537

Bai, L., He, A., Liu, M., Zhu, L., & Xing, Y. (2021). Adaptive query relaxation and result categorization of fuzzy spatiotemporal data based on XML. *Expert Systems with Applications*, *168*, 114222. doi:10.1016/j.eswa.2020.114222

Bai, L., Lin, Z., & Xu, C. (2016). Spatiotemporal operations on spatiotemporal XML data using XQuery. In *Proceedings of the 12th International Conference on Natural Computation, Fuzzy Systems and Knowledge Discovery* (pp. 13-15). IEEE. 10.1109/FSKD.2016.7603362

Bai, L., Liu, J., & Yu, C. (2016). *A spatiotemporal data model and marking dictionaries for sea surface meteorological data in XML*. In *Proc. ICNC-FSKD*, Huangshan, China. 10.1109/FSKD.2016.7603519

Bai, L., Wang, J., Di, X., & Li, N. (2021). Fixing the inconsistencies in fuzzy spatiotemporal RDF graph. *Information Sciences*, *578*, 166–180. doi:10.1016/j.ins.2021.07.038

Bai, L., & Xu, C. (2015). *Spatiotemporal Query Algebra Based on Native XML. Handbook of Research on Innovative Database Query Processing Techniques*. IGI Global.

Bai, L., & Xu, C. (2015). Spatiotemporal query algebra based on native XML. In L. Liu & M. T. Özsu (Eds.), *Handbook of Research on Innovative Database Query Processing Techniques* (pp. 275–293). IGI Global.

Bai, L., & Xu, C. (2015). Spatiotemporal Query Algebra Based on Native XML. In B. Sheng & X. Li (Eds.), *Handbook of Research on Innovative Database Query Processing Techniques* (pp. 275–293). IGI Global.

Bai, L., Yan, L., & Ma, Z. M. (2012). Modeling topological relations between fuzzy spatiotemporal regions over time. In *Proceedings of IEEE International Conference on Fuzzy Systems*, (pp. 1-8). IEEE.

Bai, L., Yan, L., Ma, Z., & Xu, C. (2015). Research on fuzzy spatiotemporal XML data Schema. [Natural Science Edition]. *Journal of Northeastern University*, (05), 622–625.

Bai, L., & Zhu, L. (2019). An Algebra for Fuzzy Spatiotemporal Data in XML. *IEEE Access : Practical Innovations, Open Solutions*, *7*, 22914–22926. doi:10.1109/ACCESS.2019.2898228

Bai, L., Zhu, L., & Jia, W. (2018). Determining topological relations of uncertain spatiotemporal data based on counter-clock-wisely directed triangle. *Applied Intelligence*, *48*(9), 2527–2545. doi:10.1007/s10489-017-1100-3

Balbiani, P., & Condotta, J. F. (2002). Spatial reasoning about points in a multidimensional setting. *Applied Intelligence*, *17*(3), 221–238. doi:10.1023/A:1020079114666

Balbiani, P., Condotta, J. F., & Del Cerro, L. F. (2002). Tractability results in the block algebra. *Journal of Logic and Computation*, *12*(5), 885–909. doi:10.1093/logcom/12.5.885

Bao, L. (2006). *Research on some key problems of uncertainty processing technology in spatiotemporal database*. Nanjing University of Aeronautics and Astronautics.

Bao, L., & Qin, X. (2005). The discrete representation of continuously moving indeterminate objects. *Chinese Journal of Aeronautics*, *18*(1), 59–64. doi:10.1016/S1000-9361(11)60283-5

Bao, L., Qin, X., & Zhang, J. (2006). Reasoning the spatiotemporal relations between time evolving indeterminate regions. In D. S. Yeung, Z. Q. Liu, X. Z. Wang, & H. Yan (Eds.), *Advances in Machine Learning and Cybernetics*. Lecture Notes in Computer Science. Springer. doi:10.1007/11739685_47

Bao, L., Zhou, M., & Li, Q. (2006). A histogram-based grey estimator for spatiotemporal selective queries. In *Proceedings of the 5th International Conference on Machine Learning and Cybernetics* (pp. 325-329). IEEE. 10.1109/ICMLC.2006.259127

Baratis, E., Petrakis, E. G. M., Batsakis, S., Maris, N., & Papadakis, N. (2009). TOQL: Temporal ontology querying language. In *Proceedings of the International Symposium on Spatial and Temporal Databases* (pp. 338-354). Springer. 10.1007/978-3-642-02982-0_22

Bartosz, C., Jakub, N., & Katarzyna, J. (2018). Machine learning modeling of plant phenology based on coupling satellite and gridded meteorological dataset. *International Journal of Biometeorology*, *62*(7), 1297–1309. doi:10.1007/s00484-018-1534-2 PMID:29644431

Batsakis, S., & Petrakis, E. G. M. (2011). Representing Temporal Knowledge in the Semantic Web: The Extended 4D Fluents Approach. In Combinations of intelligent methods and applications (4th ed., Vol. 8, pp. 55-69). Springer.

Batsakis, S., & Petrakis, E. G. M. (2010). SOWL: spatio-temporal representation, reasoning and querying over the semantic web. In *Proc. I-SEMANTICS*, Graz, Austria. 10.1145/1839707.1839726

Batsakis, S., & Petrakis, E. G. M. (2011). Representing temporal knowledge in the semantic web: The extended 4d fluents approach. In H. S. Nguyen, A. M. Tjoa, E. Weippl, & E. J. Neuhold (Eds.), *Combinations of Intelligent Methods and Applications* (pp. 55–69). Springer. doi:10.1007/978-3-642-19618-8_4

Batsakis, S., & Petrakis, E. G. M. (2011). SOWL: a framework for handling spatio-temporal information in OWL 2.0. In *International Workshop on Rules and Rule Markup Languages for the Semantic Web* (6th ed., Vol. 6826, pp. 242-249). Springer. 10.1007/978-3-642-22546-8_19

Battle, R., & Kolas, D. (2011). Geosparql: Enabling a geospatial semantic web. *Semantic Web Journal*, *3*, 355–370. doi:10.3233/SW-2012-0065

Belbaraka, M., & Stojmenović, I. (1994). On generating B-trees with constant average delay and in lexicographic order. *Information Processing Letters*, *49*(1), 27–32. doi:10.1016/0020-0190(94)90050-7

Bennett, B., Cohn, A. G., Wolter, F., & Zakharyaschev, M. (2002). Multi-dimensional modal logic as a framework for spatio-temporal reasoning. *Applied Intelligence*, *17*(3), 239–251. doi:10.1023/A:1020083231504

Bhalotia, G., Nakhe, C., & Hulgeri, A. (2002). Keyword searching and browsing in databases using BANKS. In *Proceedings of the 18th Conference on Data Engineering* (pp. 431–440). IEEE. 10.1109/ICDE.2002.994756

Billhardt, H., Borrajo, D., & Maojo, V. (2002). A context vector model for information retrieval. *Journal of the Association for Information Science and Technology*, *53*(3), 236–249.

Bin, Q. (2014). *Design and implementation of nearest neighbor search algorithm for uncertain data*. Heilongjiang University.

Blekas, K., Nikou, C., Galatsanos, N., & Tsekos, N. V. (2008). A regression mixture model with spatial constraints for clustering spatiotemporal data. *International Journal of Artificial Intelligence Tools*, *17*(06), 1023–1041. doi:10.1142/S0218213008004278

Bonnici, V., & Giugno, R. (2016). On the Variable Ordering in Subgraph Isomorphism Algorithms. *IEEE/ACM Transactions on Computational Biology and Bioinformatics*, *14*(1), 193–203. doi:10.1109/TCBB.2016.2515595 PMID:26761859

Boulila, W., Farah, I. R., & Saheb Ettabaa, K. (2011). A data mining based approach to predict spatiotemporal changes in satellite images. *International Journal of Applied Earth Observation and Geoinformation*, *13*(3), 386–395. doi:10.1016/j.jag.2011.01.008

Brickley, D., Guha, R. V., & Layman, A. (1998). *Resource description framework (RDF) schema specification*. W3C. http://www. w3. org/TR/PR-rdf-schema

Brodt, A., Nicklas, D., & Mitschang, B. (2010). Deep integration of spatial query processing into native RDF triple stores. In *Proc. ACM SIGSPATIAL*, San Jose, CA, USA. 10.1145/1869790.1869799

Broekstra, J., Kampman, A., & Van Harmelen, F. (2002). Sesame: A generic architecture for storing and querying rdf and rdf schema. In *International semantic web conference* (pp. 54-68). Berlin, Heidelberg: Springer Berlin Heidelberg.

Bruno, N., Koudas, N., & Srivastava, D. (2002). Holistic twig joins: optimal XML pattern matching. *Proceedings of the 2002 ACM SIGMOD International Conference on Management of Data* (pp. 310-321). ACM. 10.1145/564691.564727

Budak Arpinar, I., Sheth, A., Ramakrishnan, C., Lynn Usery, E., Azami, M., & Kwan, M. P. (2006). Geospatial ontology development and semantic analytics. *Transactions in GIS*, *10*(4), 551–575. doi:10.1111/j.1467-9671.2006.01012.x

Camossi, E., Bertolotto, M., & Bertino, E. (2003). A Multigranular Spatiotemporal Data Model. In *Proceedings of the 11th ACM International Symposium on Advances in Geographic Information Systems* (pp. 94-101). ACM.

Cao, W. (2011). *Spatiotemporal data model and its application research*. PLA Information Engineering University.

Carlo, A., & Alexandros, G. A. (2015). Preliminary Investigation of Reversing RML: From an RDF dataset to its Column-Based data source. *Biodiversity Data Journal*, *3*(3), e5464. PMID:26312054

Chakkarwar, V. A., Professor, A., & Joshi, A. A. (2016). Semantic Web Mining using RDF Data. *International Journal of Computer Applications (0975 - 8887)*, 133FDLh (10), 14-19.

Chakkarwar, V. A., Professor, A., & Joshi, A. A. (2016). Semantic Web Mining using RDF Data. *International Journal of Computer Applications*, *133FDLh*(10), 14-19.

Chang, C. J., Li, D. C., Huang, Y. H., & Chen, C.-C. (2015). A novel gray forecasting model based on the box plot for small manufacturing data sets. *Applied Mathematics and Computation*, *265*, 400–408. doi:10.1016/j.amc.2015.05.006

Chang, D. C., Dokos, S., & Lovell, N. H. (2011). Temporo-Spatial Model Construction Using the MML and Software Framework. *IEEE Transactions on Biomedical Engineering*, *58*(12), 3528–3531. doi:10.1109/TBME.2011.2168955 PMID:21947514

Chang, T. P., & Chen, S. Y. (2012). An efficient algorithm of frequent XML query pattern mining for ebXML applications in E-commerce. *Expert Systems with Applications*, *39*(2), 2183–2193. doi:10.1016/j.eswa.2011.07.011

Che, D., Ling, T. W., & Hou, W. C. (2011). Holistic boolean-twig pattern matching for efficient XML query processing. *IEEE Transactions on Knowledge and Data Engineering*, *24*(11), 2008–2024. doi:10.1109/TKDE.2011.128

Chen, L., Ji, Y., & Deng, C. (2006). An indexing technique based on extended temporal XML model. *Microcomputer Information, (15)*, 301-303 +69.

Chen, Y., & Revesz, P. (2003). Querying Spatiotemporal XML Using DataFox. In Proceedings of Web Intelligence (pp. 301-309). doi:10.1109/WI.2003.1241208

Chen, Y., Wang, W., Liu, Z., & Lin, X. (2009). Keyword search on structured and semi-structured data. In SIGMOD. doi:10.1145/1559845.1559966

Chen, B. Y., Yuan, H., Li, Q., Shaw, S. L., Lam, W. H. K., & Chen, X. (2016). Spatiotemporal data model for network time geographic analysis in the era of big data. *International Journal of Geographical Information Science*, *30*(6), 1041–1071. doi:10.1080/13658816.2015.1104317

Cheng, H. (2016). Modeling and querying fuzzy spatiotemporal objects. *Journal of Intelligent & Fuzzy Systems*, *31*(6), 2851–2858. doi:10.3233/JIFS-169167

Cheng, H., Li, P., Wang, R., & Xu, H. (2021). Dynamic spatio-temporal logic based on RCC-8. *Concurrency and Computation*, *33*(22), 1–12. doi:10.1002/cpe.5900

Cheng, H., & Ma, Z. (2017). f- ALL (D) - LTL: A Fuzzy Spatio-Temporal Description Logic. In *Proc. KSEM*, Melbourne, Australia.

Cheng, H., Ma, Z., & Li, P. (2020). A fuzzy spatial description logic for the semantic web. *Journal of Ambient Intelligence and Humanized Computing*.

Cheng, H., Wang, R., Li, P., & Xu, H. (2019). Representing and reasoning fuzzy spatio- temporal knowledge with description logics: A survey. *Intelligent Data Analysis*, *23*(S1), 113–132. doi:10.3233/IDA-192847

Cheng, H., Yan, L., Ma, Z., & Ribaric, S. (2019). Fuzzy spatio-temporal ontologies and formal construction based on fuzzy Petri nets. *Computational Intelligence*, *35*(1), 204–239. doi:10.1111/coin.12199

Cheng, R., Emrich, T., & Kriegel, H. P. (2014). Managing Uncertainty in Spatial and Spatio-Temporal Data. In *Proceedings of ICDE*, (pp. 1302-1305). IEEE. 10.1109/ICDE.2014.6816766

Cheng, T., & Wang, J. Q. (2008). Integrated Spatio-temporal Data Mining for Forest Fire Prediction. *Transactions in GIS*, *12*(5), 591–611. doi:10.1111/j.1467-9671.2008.01117.x

Chen, J., Li, C., Li, Z., & Gold, C. (2001). A Voronoi-based 9-intersection model for spatial relations. *International Journal of Geographical Information Science*, *15*(3), 201–220. doi:10.1080/13658810151072831

Chen, L., Gupta, A., & Kurul, M. E. (2005). *A semantic-aware RDF query algebra*. In *Proceedings of the International Conference on Management of Data (COMAD)* (pp. 1-12). Hyderabad, India.

Chen, S. C., Shyu, M. L., Peeta, S., & Zhang, C. (2005). Spatiotemporal vehicle tracking: The use of unsupervised learning-based segmentation and object tracking. *IEEE Robotics & Automation Magazine*, *12*(1), 50–58. doi:10.1109/MRA.2005.1411419

Chen, S., Li, H. G., & Tatemura, J. (2006). Twig2Stack: bottom-up processing of generalized-treepattern queries over XML documents. *Proceedings of the 32nd International Conference on Very Large Data Bases* (pp. 283-294). ACM.

Chen, X., Yan, L., Li, W., & Zhang, F. (2018). Fuzzy spatio-temporal data modeling based on XML schema. *Filomat*, *32*(5), 1663–1677. doi:10.2298/FIL1805663C

Chen, X., Zhu, J., & Chen, J. (2009). Overview of spatiotemporal data models. *Advances in Geographical Sciences*, (01), 9–17.

Chen, Y. F., & Wang, L. (2017). Traffic Flow Prediction with Big Data: A Deep Learning based Time Series Model. In *Proceedings of the 2017 IEEE Conference on Computer Communications*, (pp. 1-2). IEEE. 10.1109/INFCOMW.2017.8116535

Chen, Y., & Revesz, P. (2003). Query spatiotemporal XML using DataFox. *Proceedings of ACM Internal Conference on Web Intelligence* (pp. 301-309). ACM.

Chen, Y., & Revesz, P. (2003). Querying spatiotemporal XML using DataFoX. In *Proceedings of the IEEE/WIC International Conference on Web Intelligence* (pp. 70-79). IEEE.

Chen, Y., & Revesz, P. Z. (2003). Querying Spatiotemporal XML Using DataFoX. In *Proceedings of WI*, pp. 301-309.

Chen, Z., Zhao, T., & Liu, W. (2021). Time-aware collective spatial keyword query. *Computer Science and Information Systems*, *28*(3), 1077–1100. doi:10.2298/CSIS200131034C

Cheung, C. K., Shi, W., & Zhou, X. (2004). A probability-based uncertainty model for point-in-polygon analysis in GIS. *GeoInformatica*, *8*(1), 71–98. doi:10.1023/B:GEIN.0000007725.41038.03

Chirigati, F., Doraiswamy, H., & Damoulas, T. (2016). Data polygamy: the many-many relationships among urban spatio-temporal data sets. In proceedings of SIGMOD, (pp. 1011-1025). ACM. doi:10.1145/2882903.2915245

Choi, Y., & Chung, C. (2002). Selectivity estimation for spatio-temporal queries to moving objects. In *Proceedings of the ACM SIGMOD International Conference on Management of Data* (pp. 276-287). ACM. 10.1145/564691.564742

Christina, L., Panagiotis, P., & Anastasia, A. (2016). Radius-aware Approximate Blank Node Matching using Signatures. *Knowledge and Information Systems*, *50*(2), 1–38.

Claramunt, C., Parent, C., & Spaccapietra, S. (1999). Database modelling for environmental and land use changes. Proceedings of Geographical Information and Planning Springer Berlin Heidelberg (pp. 181-202). doi:10.1007/978-3-662-03954-0_10

Claramunt, C., Parent, C., Spaccapietra, S., et al. (1999). Database modelling for environmental and land use changes. *Proceedings of Geographical Information and Planning*. Springer Berlin Heidelberg.

Claramunt, C., & Theriault, M. (1995). Managing time in GIS: an event-oriented approach. In *Proceedings of the International Workshop on Temporal Databases* (pp. 32-45). ACM. 10.1007/978-1-4471-3033-8_2

Clark, S. (2003). Traffic prediction using multivariate nonparametric regression. *Journal of Transportation Engineering*, *129*(2), 161–168. doi:10.1061/(ASCE)0733-947X(2003)129:2(161)

Cobb, M. A., & Petry, F. E. (1998). Modeling Spatial Relationships within a Fuzzy Framework. *Journal of the American Society for Information Science*, *49*(3), 253–266. doi:10.1002/(SICI)1097-4571(199803)49:3<253::AID-ASI6>3.0.CO;2-F

Cobb, M. A., & Petry, P. E. (1998). Modeling spatial relationships within a fuzzy framework. *Journal of the Association for Information Science and Technology*, *49*(3), 253–266.

Cohen, S., Mamou, J., Kanza, Y., & Sagiv, Y. (2003). XSEarch: a semantic search engine for XML. In *Proceedings of the 29th International Conference on Very Large Data Bases* (pp. 45-46). ACM.

Condotta, J. F. (2004). A general qualitative framework for temporal and spatial reasoning. *Constraints*, *9*(2), 99–121. doi:10.1023/B:CONS.0000024047.02149.64

Consoli, S. (2015). A Smart City Data Model based on Semantics Best Practice and Principles. In *Proc. WWW*, Florence, Italy, 1395-1400. 10.1145/2740908.2742133

Consortium, O. G. (2012). *OGC GeoSPARQL - A geographic query language for RDF data*. OGC Candidate Implementat. Stand.

Córcoles, J. E., Garcia-Consuegra, J., & Peralta, J. (2000). *A Spatio-Temporal Query Language for a Data Model based on XML*. In *Proceedings of the 6th ECGI & GIS Workshop*, Lyon, France.

Córcoles, J. E., & González, P. (2001). A specification of a spatial query language over GML. In *Proceedings of the 9th ACM International Symposium on Advances in Geographic Information Systems*. Atlanta, GA, USA. 10.1145/512161.512186

Cordella, L. P., Foggia, P., Sansone, C., & Vento, M. (2004). A (Sub) Graph Isomorphism Algorithm for Matching Large Graphs. *IEEE Transactions on Pattern Analysis and Machine Intelligence*, *26*(10), 1367–1372. doi:10.1109/TPAMI.2004.75 PMID:15641723

Cost, S., & Salzberg, S. (1993). A weighted nearest neighbor algorithm for learning with symbolic features. *Machine Learning*, *10*(1), 57–78. doi:10.1007/BF00993481

Crouch, R., & Kalouli, A. L. (2018). Named Graphs for Semantic Representations. In Proc. *SEM@NAACL-HLT, New Orleans, Louisiana, USA, 113-118. doi:10.18653/v1/S18-2013

Crouch, R., & Kalouli, A. L. (2018). *Named Graphs for Semantic Representations*. In *Proceedings of the 2nd Joint Workshop on Semantic Parsing and Semantic Analysis* (pp. 113-118). New Orleans, Louisiana, USA.

Cui, Q., Wang, N. Z., & Haenggi, M. (2018). Vehicle distributions in large and small cities: Spatial models and applications. *IEEE Transactions on Vehicular Technology*, *67*(11), 10176–10189. doi:10.1109/TVT.2018.2865679

Cyganiak, R. (2005). *A relational algebra for SPARQL*. Digital Media Systems Laboratory HP Laboratories Bristol.

Dai, X., Yiu, M. L., Mamoulis, N., Tao, Y., & Vaitis, M. (2005). Probabilistic spatial queries on existentially uncertain data. In *Proceedings of International Symposium on Spatial and Temporal Databases*. Springer. 10.1007/11535331_23

Dautov, R., & Distefano, S. (2018). *Semantic Web Languages for Policy Enforcement in the Internet of Things*. In *Proc. HCC*, Mérida, Mexico. 10.1007/978-3-319-74521-3_21

de Farias, T. M., Roxin, A., & Nicolle, C. (2016). SWRL rule-selection methodology for ontology interoperability. *Data & Knowledge Engineering*, *105*, 53–72. doi:10.1016/j.datak.2015.09.001

De Virgilio, R., Maccioni, A., & Torlone, R. (2013). A similarity measure for approximate querying over RDF data. In *Proceedings of the Joint EDBT/ICDT 2013 Workshops* (pp. 205-213). ACM. 10.1145/2457317.2457352

Debruyne, C., & O'Sullivan, D. (2017). *Client-side Processing of GeoSPARQL Functions with Triple Pattern Fragments*. Presented at the 26th WWW, Perth, Australia.

Deerwester, S., Dumais, S., Furnas, G., Landauer, T. K., & Harshman, R. (1990). Indexing by latent semantic analysis. *Journal of the American Society for Information Science*, *41*(6), 391–407. doi:10.1002/(SICI)1097-4571(199009)41:6<391::AID-ASI1>3.0.CO;2-9

Deng, S. S., Xia, L. H., & Wang, F. (2009). Analysis of Spatio-Temporal Characteristics of Urban Land Cover and its Landscape Pattern: a Case Study in NanHai District of Foshan City. In Proceedings of Joint Urban Remote Sensing Event (pp. 1-9).

Deng, M., Cheng, T., Chen, X., & Li, Z. (2007). Topological relations between spatial regions based upon topological invariants. *GeoInformatica*, *11*(2), 239–267. doi:10.1007/s10707-006-0004-x

Dey, A., Pal, A., & Long, H. V. (2019). Fuzzy minimum spanning tree with interval type 2 fuzzy arc length: Formulation and a new genetic algorithm. *Soft Computing*, *23*, 1–12.

Dfgdfg, F., Flesca, S., & Furfaro, F. (2011). Xpath query relaxation through rewriting rules. *IEEE Transactions on Knowledge and Data Engineering*, *23*(10), 1583–1600. doi:10.1109/TKDE.2010.203

Ding, Z., Peng, Y., & Pan, R. (2006). BayesOWL: Uncertainty modeling in semantic web ontologies. *Soft computing in ontologies and semantic web*, 3-29.

Di, X., Wang, J., Cheng, S., & Bai, L. (2019). Pattern Match Query for Spatiotemporal RDF Graph. In *The International Conference on Natural Computation, Fuzzy Systems and Knowledge Discovery* (pp. 532-539). Berlin, Germany: Springer.

Dobra, A., Garofalakis, M., Gehrke, J., & Rastogi, R. (2004). Sketch-based multi-query processing over data streams. *Lecture Notes in Computer Science, 2992*, 621–622. doi:10.1007/978-3-540-24741-8_32

Doraiswamy, H., Ferreira, N., Damoulas, T., Freire, J., & Silva, C. T. (2014). Using topological analysis to support event-guided exploration in urban data. *IEEE Transactions on Visualization and Computer Graphics, 20*(12), 2634–2643. doi:10.1109/TVCG.2014.2346449 PMID:26356977

Duckham, M., Mason, K., Stell, J., & Worboys, M. (2001). A Formal Approach to Imperfection in Geographic Information. *Computers, Environment and Urban Systems, 25*(1), 89–103. doi:10.1016/S0198-9715(00)00040-5

Ďuračiová, R., & Faixová Chalachanová, J. (2018). Fuzzy spatio-temporal querying the PostgreSQL/PostGIS database for multiple criteria decision making. In *Dynamics in GIscience 4* (pp. 81–97). Springer International Publishing. doi:10.1007/978-3-319-61297-3_7

Du, Z., Jeong, Y. S., Jeong, M. K., & Kong, S. G. (2012). Multidimensional Local Spatial Autocorrelation Measure for Integrating Spatial and Spectral Information in Hyperspectral Image Band Selection. *Applied Intelligence, 36*(2), 542–552. doi:10.1007/s10489-010-0274-8

Elzein, N. M., Majid, M. A., Fakherldin, M., & Hashem, I. A. T. (2018). Distributed Join Query Processing for Big RDF Data. *Advanced Science Letters, 24*(10), 7758–7761. doi:10.1166/asl.2018.13013

Emrich, T., Kriegel, H. P., & Mamoulis, N. (2012). Indexing uncertain spatiotemporal data. *Proceedings of the 21st ACM International Conference on Information and Knowledge Management (CIKM)*, Sheraton, 395-404.

Emrich, T., Kriegel, H. P., & Mamoulis, N. (2012). Indexing uncertain spatio-temporal data. *Proceedings of the 21st ACM International Conference on Information and Knowledge Management* (pp. 395-404). ACM.

Emrich, T., Kriegel, H. P., & Mamoulis, N. (2012). Querying uncertain spatiotemporal data. *Proceedings of the 28th International Conference on Data Engineering (ICDE)*, Washington D.C., 354-365.

Emrich, T., Kriegel, H. P., Mamoulis, N., Renz, M., & Zufle, A. (2012). Querying uncertain spatio-temporal data. In *Proceedings of 2012 IEEE 28th international conference on data engineering*. IEEE. 10.1109/ICDE.2012.94

Eom, S., Shin, S., & Lee, K. H. (2015). Spatiotemporal query processing for semantic data stream. In *Proceedings of the 9th International Conference on Semantic Computing,* (pp. 7–9). IEEE. 10.1109/ICOSC.2015.7050822

Erwig, M., Guting, R. H., Schneider, M., & Vazirgiannis, M. (1999). Spatio-temporal data types: An approach to modeling and querying moving objects in databases. *GeoInformatica, 3*(3), 265–291. doi:10.1023/A:1009805532638

Erwig, M., & Schneider, M. (2002). Spatio-temporal predicates. *IEEE Transactions on Knowledge and Data Engineering, 14*(4), 881–901. doi:10.1109/TKDE.2002.1019220

Fernandez, M., Simeon, J., & Wadler, P. (2000). An Algebra for XML Query. In *Proceedings of the 2000 International Conference on Foundations of Software Technology and Theoretical Computer Science*, (pp. 11-45). IEEE.

Flesca, S., & Furfaro, F. (2010). XPath query relaxation through rewriting rules. *IEEE Transactions on Knowledge and Data Engineering, 23*(10), 1583–1600.

Fong, J. (1995). Mapping Extended Entity Relationship Model to Object Modeling Technique. *SIGMOD Record, 24*(3), 18–22. doi:10.1145/211990.212007

Fong, J. (2002). Translating Object-oriented Database Transactions into Relational Transactions. *Information and Software Technology*, *44*(1), 41–51. doi:10.1016/S0950-5849(01)00211-7

Fong, J., & Cheung, S. K. (2005). Translating Relational Schema into XML Schema Definition with Data Semantic Preservation and XSD Graph. *Information and Software Technology*, *47*(7), 437–462. doi:10.1016/j.infsof.2004.09.010

Fossati, M., Dorigatti, E., & Giuliano, C. (2018). N-ary relation extraction for simultaneous T-Box and A-Box knowledge base augmentation. *Semantic Web*, *9*(4), 413–439. doi:10.3233/SW-170269

Franceschet, M., Montanari, A., & Gubiani, D. (2007). Modeling and Validating Spatio-Temporal Conceptual Schemas in XML Schema. In *Proceedings of the 18th International Conference on DEXA* (pp. 25-29). ACM. 10.1109/DEXA.2007.106

Frank, A., Grumbach, S., Güting, R. H., Jensen, C. S., Koubarakis, M., Lorentzos, N., Manolopoulos, Y., Nardelli, E., Pernici, B., Schek, H.-J., Scholl, M., Sellis, T., Theodoulidis, B., & Widmayer, P. (1999). Chorochronos: A research network for spatiotemporal database systems. *SIGMOD Record*, *28*(3), 12–21. doi:10.1145/333607.333609

Frasincar, F., Houben, G. J., & Pau, C. (2002). XAL: An Algebra for XML Query Optimization. *Australian Computer Science Communications*, *24*(2), 49–56.

Frasincar, F., Houben, G. J., Vdovjak, R., & Barna, P. (2004). RAL: An algebra for querying RDF. *World Wide Web (Bussum)*, *7*(1), 83–109. doi:10.1023/B:WWWJ.0000015866.43076.06

Froelich, W., & Salmeron, J. L. (2014). Evolutionary learning of fuzzy grey cognitive maps for the forecasting of multivariate, interval-valued time series. *International Journal of Approximate Reasoning*, *55*(6), 1319–1335. doi:10.1016/j.ijar.2014.02.006

Galindo, J., Urrutia, A., & Piattini, M. (2006). *Fuzzy Databases: Modeling, Design and Implementation*. Idea Group Publishing Hershey. doi:10.4018/978-1-59140-324-1

Gao, J., Agarwal, P. K., & Yang, J. (2018). Durable top-k queries on temporal data. *Proceedings of the VLDB Endowment International Conference on Very Large Data Bases*, *11*(13), 2223–2235.

Gao, M. (2015). *Some studies on the propagation of spatiotemporal uncertainty*. Changan University.

Gheissari, N., Sebastian, T. B., & Hartley, R. (2006). Person reidentification using spatiotemporal appearance. In *Proceedings of 2006 IEEE Computer Society Conference on Computer Vision and Pattern Recognition (CVPR'06)*. IEEE. 10.1109/CVPR.2006.223

Gilberto, A. G., Gonzalo, N., & Andrea, R. (2005). A spatiotemporal access method based on snapshots and events. In *Proceedings of the 13th Annual ACM International Workshop on Geographic Information Systems* (pp. 115-124). ACM.

Goodhue, P., McNair, H., & Reitsma, F. (2015). Trusting crowdsourced geospatial semantics. *The International Archives of the Photogrammetry, Remote Sensing and Spatial Information Sciences*, *40*(W3), 25–28. doi:10.5194/isprsarchives-XL-3-W3-25-2015

Grandi, F., Mandreoli, F., & Tiberio, P. (2003). A Temporal Data Model and Management System for Normative Texts in XML Format. In *Proceedings of the 5th ACM International Workshop on Web Information and Data Management*, (pp. 29-36). ACM. 10.1145/956699.956706

Grumbach, S., Rigaux, P., & Segoufin, L. (2001). Spatio-temporal data handling with constraints. *GeoInformatica*, *5*(1), 95–115. doi:10.1023/A:1011464022461

Guan, D., Li, H., Inohae, T., Su, W., Nagaie, T., & Hokao, K. (2011). Modeling urban land use change by the integration of cellular automaton and Markov model. *Ecological Modelling*, *222*(20-22), 3761–3772. doi:10.1016/j.ecolmodel.2011.09.009

Guan, X., Bo, C., Li, Z., & Yu, Y. (2017). ST-hash: An efficient spatiotemporal index for massive trajectory data in a NoSQL database. In *Proceedings of the 25th International Conference on Geoinformatics*. IEEE. 10.1109/GEOINFORMATICS.2017.8090927

Guo, L. (2013). Pioneering GML deployment for NSDI—Case study of USTIGER/GML. *ISPRS International Journal of Geo-Information*, *2*(2), 82–93. doi:10.3390/ijgi2010082

Guo, L., Shao, F., Botev, C., & Shanmugasundaram, J. (2003). XRANK: ranked keyword search over XML documents. In *Proceedings of the ACM SIGMOD International Conference on Management of Data* (pp. 28-39). ACM. 10.1145/872757.872762

Guo, P., Tao, H., & Luo, Y. (2003). Research on the relationship between 4-intersection and classifying invariant based on the simple regions. In *proceedings of 2003 International Conference on Machine Learning and Cybernetics*, (pp. 1642-1647). IEEE.

Guo, Y., & Wu, Y. (2011). An XML index based on XML Schema. [Natural Science Edition]. *Journal of Huaqiao University*, (01), 43–47.

Gutierrez, C., Hurtado, C. A., & Vaisman, A. (2006). Introducing time into RDF. *IEEE Transactions on Knowledge and Data Engineering*, *19*(2), 207–218. doi:10.1109/TKDE.2007.34

Gutierrez, C., Hurtado, C., & Vaisman, A. (2005). *Temporal RDF*. In *Proc. ESWC*, Heraklion, Greece.

Gutierrez, C., Hurtado, C., & Vaisman, A. (2005). *Temporal RDF*. In *Proceedings of the European Semantic Web Conference*, Crete, Greece.

Güting, R. H., Behr, T., & Xu, J. (2010). Efficient k-nearest neighbor search on moving object trajectories. *The VLDB Journal*, *19*(6), 687–714. doi:10.1007/s00778-010-0185-7

Hadjieleftheriou, M., Kollios, G., & Tsotras, V. (2003). Performance evaluation of spatio-temporal selectivity estimation techniques. In *Proceedings of the 15th International Conference on Scientific and Statistical Database Management* (pp. 207-216). IEEE. 10.1109/SSDM.2003.1214981

Hadjieleftheriou, M., Kollios, G., Tsotras, V. J., & Gunopulos, D. (2002). Efficient Indexing of Spatiotemporal Objects. *Lecture Notes in Computer Science*, *2287*, 251–268. doi:10.1007/3-540-45876-X_17

Hakimpour, F., Aleman-Meza, B., Perry, M., & Sheth, A. (2009). Spatiotemporal-thematic data processing for the semantic web. In A. G. Cohn, D. M. Mark, & A. R. Frank (Eds.), *The Geospatial Web* (pp. 79–89). Springer.

Hallot, P., & Billen, R. (2016). Enhancing spatio-temporal identity: States of existence and presence. *ISPRS International Journal of Geo-Information*, *5*(5), 62. doi:10.3390/ijgi5050062

Hamzacebi, C., & Es, H. A. (2014). Forecasting the annual electricity consumption of Turkey using an optimized grey model. *Energy*, *70*, 165–171. doi:10.1016/j.energy.2014.03.105

Han, W. S., Lee, J., & Lee, J. H. (2013). Turboiso: Towards ultrafast and robust subgraph isomorphism search in large graph databases. In *Proceedings of the 2013 ACM SIGMOD International Conference on Management of Data*. ACM. 10.1145/2463676.2465300

Hao, C., & Zou, J. (2006). XML storage based on XML Schema. *Computer Engineering and Application, (11)*, 173-175 +204.

Hao, Z. X. (2017). *New theory of spatiotemporal database*. Science Press.

Haworth, J., & Cheng, T. (2012). Non-parametric regression for space–time forecasting under missing data. *Computers, Environment and Urban Systems*, *36*(6), 538–550. doi:10.1016/j.compenvurbsys.2012.08.005

Hayes, J. (2004). *A graph model for RDF. Darmstadt University of Technology: Darmstadt, Germany*. University of Chile.

He, H., & Singh, A. K. (2008). Graphs-at-a-time: Query language and access methods for graph databases. In *Proceedings of the 2008 ACM SIGMOD International Conference on Management of Data* (pp. 405-418). ACM. 10.1145/1376616.1376660

He, J., Liu, L. Y., Yu, F., & Han, Y. (2016). A Method of RDF Fuzzy Query Based on No Query Language Service with Permutated Breadth First Search Algorithm. *Procedia Computer Science*, *100*, 321–328. doi:10.1016/j.procs.2016.09.163

Hernández, D., Hogan, A., & Krötzsch, M. (2015). Reifying RDF: What Works Well With Wikidata? In *Proc. ISWC*, Bethlehem, PA, USA, 32-47.

Hernández, D., Hogan, A., & Krötzsch, M. (2015). Reifying RDF: What Works Well With Wikidata? In *Proceedings of the 11th International Workshop on Scalable Semantic Web Knowledge Base Systems* (pp. 23-31). Bethlehem, PA, USA.

Hoffart, J., Fabian, M. S., Berberich, K., & Weikum, G. (2013). YAGO2: A spatially and temporally enhanced knowledge base from Wikipedia. *Artificial Intelligence*, *194*, 28–61. doi:10.1016/j.artint.2012.06.001

Hoffart, J., Suchanek, F. M., Berberich, K., Lewis-Kelham, E., De Melo, G., & Weikum, G. (2011). Yago2: Exploring and querying world knowledge in time, space, context, and many languages. In *Proceedings of the 20th International Conference Companion on World Wide Web* (pp. 229-232). ACM. 10.1145/1963192.1963296

Ho, L. T., Arch-int, S., & Arch-int, N. (2017). Introducing Fuzzy Temporal Description Logic. In *Proc. ICIBE*, Sapporo, Japan.

Hristidis, V., Koudas, N., Papakonstantinou, Y., & Srivastava, D. (2006). Keyword proximity search in XML trees. *IEEE Transactions on Knowledge and Data Engineering*, *18*(4), 525–539. doi:10.1109/TKDE.2006.1599390

Hristidis, V., & Papakonstantinou, Y. (2002). Keyword Search in Relational Databases. In *Proceedings of the 28th International Conference on Very Large Data Bases* (pp. 670-681). ACM.

Huang, B., Yi, S. Z., & Chan, W. T. (2004). Spatio-Temporal Information Integration in XML. *Future Generation Computer Systems*, *20*(7), 1157–1170. doi:10.1016/j.future.2003.11.005

Huang, L., Hu, Y., Li, Y., Kishore Kumar, P. K., Koley, D., & Dey, A. (2019). A study of regular and irregular neutrosophic graphs with real-life applications. *Mathematics*, *7*(6), 551. doi:10.3390/math7060551

Hu, G. Z., & Hammad, R. (2005). Querying and indexing XML documents. *Journal of Computer and System Sciences*, *71*(4), 219–233.

Huh, S. Y., Moon, K. H., & Lee, H. (2000). A data abstraction approach for query relaxation. *Information and Software Technology*, *42*(6), 407–418. doi:10.1016/S0950-5849(99)00100-7

Hu, L., Ku, W. S., Bakiras, S., & Shahabi, C. (2013). Spatial query integrity with voronoi neighbors. *IEEE Transactions on Knowledge and Data Engineering*, *25*(4), 863–876. doi:10.1109/TKDE.2011.267

Hurtado, C., & Vaisman, A. (2006). Reasoning with temporal constraints in RDF. In *International Workshop on Principles and Practice of Semantic Web Reasoning* (pp. 164-178). Springer Berlin Heidelberg. 10.1007/11853107_12

Hu, Y. C., & Jiang, P. (2017). Forecasting energy demand using neural-network-based grey residual modification models. *The Journal of the Operational Research Society*, *68*(5), 556–565. doi:10.1057/s41274-016-0130-2

Hu, Y., & Stefan, D. (2015). Temporal data management and processing with column oriented NoSQL databases. *Journal of Database Management*, *26*(3), 41–70. doi:10.4018/JDM.2015070103

Jadidi, A., Mostafavi, M. A., Bédard, Y., & Shahriari, K. (2014). Spatial representation of coastal risk: A fuzzy approach to deal with uncertainty. *ISPRS International Journal of Geo-Information*, *3*(3), 1077–1100. doi:10.3390/ijgi3031077

Jagadish, H. V., Lakshmanan, L. V., & Srivastava, D. (2001). TAX: a Tree Algebra for XML. In *Proceedings of the 8th International Workshop on Database Programming Languages*, (pp. 149-164). IEEE.

Jamour, F., Abdelaziz, I., & Kalnisk, P. (2018). A demonstration of magiq: matrix algebra approach for solving RDF graph queries. In *Proceedings of the VLDB Endowment* (pp. 1978-1981). Rio de Janeiro, Brazil. 10.14778/3229863.3236239

Jeon, G., Anisetti, M., Kim, D., Bellandi, V., Damiani, E., & Jeong, J. (2009). Fuzzy rough sets hybrid scheme for motion and scene complexity adaptive deinterlacing. *Image and Vision Computing*, *27*(4), 425–436. doi:10.1016/j.imavis.2008.06.001

Jeon, G., Jung, M. Y., Anisetti, M., Bellandi, V., Damiani, E., & Jeong, J. (2010). Specification of the geometric regularity model for fuzzy if-then rule-based deinterlacing. *Journal of Display Technology*, *6*(6), 235–243. doi:10.1109/JDT.2009.2037524

Jeroen, A., Gilad, M., & Anjali, D. Z. (2018). A machine learning model to determine the accuracy of variant calls in capture-based next-generation sequencing. *BMC Genomics*, *19*(1), 263. doi:10.1186/s12864-018-4659-0 PMID:29665779

Jeung, H., Liu, Q., & Shen, H. T. (2008). A hybrid prediction model for moving objects. In *Proceedings of the ICDE*, (pp. 70-79). IEEE. 10.1109/ICDE.2008.4497415

Jeung, H., Yiu, M. L., Zhou, X. F., & Jensen, C. S. (2010). Path prediction and predictive range querying in road network databases. *The VLDB Journal*, *19*(4), 585–602. doi:10.1007/s00778-010-0181-y

Jiang, Z. (2020). Spatial Structured Prediction Models: Applications, Challenges, and Techniques. *IEEE Access : Practical Innovations, Open Solutions*, *8*, 38714–38727. doi:10.1109/ACCESS.2020.2975584

Jonathan, R. S., Peter, M., & Bruno, S. (2001). Dynamic Models for Spatiotemporal Data. *Journal of the Royal Statistical Society. Series A, (Statistics in Society)*, *63*(4), 673–689.

Jones, K. S., Walker, S., & Robertson, S. E. (2000). A probabilistic model of information retrieval: development and comparative experiments: Part 2. *Information Processing & Management*, *36*(6), 809–840. doi:10.1016/S0306-4573(00)00016-9

Kandel, A., & Zemankova-Leech, M. (1984). *Fuzzy relational databases, a key to expert systems*. Verl. TÜV Rheinland.

Kayacan, E., Ulutas, B., & Kaynak, O. (2010). Grey system theory-based models in time series prediction. *Expert Systems with Applications*, *37*(2), 1784–1789. doi:10.1016/j.eswa.2009.07.064

Khaled, T., & Afnan, B. (2013). A novel approach to the selection sort algorithm with parallel computing and dynamic programming concepts. *JKAU: Comp. IT*, *2*, 27-44.

Kim, D. H., Ryu, K. H., & Kim, H. S. (2000). A spatiotemporal database model and query language. *Journal of Systems and Software*, *55*(2), 129–149. doi:10.1016/S0164-1212(00)00066-2

Kimelfeld, B., Kosharovsky, Y., & Sagiv, Y. (2008). Query Efficiency in Probabilistic XML Models. In *Proceedings of the 2008 ACM SIGMOD International Conference on Management of Data*, (pp. 701-714). ACM. 10.1145/1376616.1376687

Kim, J. J., Shin, I. S., Lee, Y. S., & Moon, J.-Y. (2016). Spatio-Temporal Ontology Management Systems for Semantic Web. *Information (Basel)*, *19*, 4237–4254.

Kim, J., Shin, H., Han, W. S., Hong, S., & Chafi, H. (2015). Taming subgraph isomorphism for RDF query processing. *Proceedings of the VLDB Endowment International Conference on Very Large Data Bases*, *8*(11), 1238–1249. doi:10.14778/2809974.2809985

Kim, R. G., Doppa, J. R., Pande, P. P., Marculescu, D., & Marculescu, R. (2017). Machine Learning and Manycore Systems Design: A Serendipitous Symbiosis. *Computer*, *51*(7), 66–77. doi:10.1109/MC.2018.3011040

Klyne, G., Carroll, J. J. (2006). *Resource description framework (RDF): Concepts and abstract syntax.*

Kolas, D., Dean, M., & Hebeler, J. (2006). Geospatial Semantic Web: Architecture of Ontologies. In *Proceedings of the 2006 IEEE Aerospace Conference* (pp. 183–194). IEEE.

Kong, L. B., Gilleron, R., & Lemay, A. (2009). Retrieving meaningful relaxed tightest fragments for XML keyword search. In *Proceedings of the 12th International Conference on Extending Database Technology* (pp. 815-826). ACM. 10.1145/1516360.1516454

Koubarakis, M., & Kyzirakos, K. (2010). *Modeling and Querying Metadata in the Semantic Sensor Web: The Model stRDF and the Query Language stSPARQL.* In *Proc. ESWC*, Heraklion, Greece. 10.1007/978-3-642-13486-9_29

Kristensson, P. O., Dahlback, N., Anundi, D., Bjornstad, M., Gillberg, H., Haraldsson, J., Martensson, I., Nordvall, M., & Stahl, J. (2009). An evaluation of space time cube representation of spatiotemporal patterns. *IEEE Transactions on Visualization and Computer Graphics*, *15*(4), 696–702. doi:10.1109/TVCG.2008.194 PMID:19423892

Kuang, H. B., Bashar, M. A., & Hipel, K. W. (2015). Grey-based preference in a graph model for conflict resolution with multiple decision makers. *IEEE Transactions on Systems, Man, and Cybernetics. Systems*, *45*(9), 1254–1267. doi:10.1109/TSMC.2014.2387096

Kuijpers, B., & Othman, W. (2010). Trajectory Databases: Data models, Uncertainty and Complete Query Languages. *Journal of Computer and System Sciences*, *76*(7), 538–560. doi:10.1016/j.jcss.2009.10.002

Kumar, U., & Jain, V. K. (2010). Time series models (Grey-Markov, Grey Model with rolling mechanism and singular spectrum analysis) to forecast energy consumption in India. *Energy*, *35*(4), 1709–1716. doi:10.1016/j.energy.2009.12.021

Kuper, P. V., Breunig, M., & Al-Doori, M. (2016). Application of 3d spatiotemporal data modeling, management, and analysis in db4geo. *ISPRS Annals of the Photogrammetry, Remote Sensing and Spatial Information Sciences*, *4*, 63–170.

Kwan, M. P. (2004). GIS methods in time-geographic research: Geocomputation and geovisualization of human activity patterns. *Geografiska Annaler. Series B, Human Geography*, *86*(4), 267–280. doi:10.1111/j.0435-3684.2004.00167.x

Kyzirakos, K., Karpathiotakis, M., & Koubarakis, M. (2010). Developing registries for the semantic sensor Web using stRDF and stSPARQL. In *International Workshop on Semantic Sensor Networks*. ACM.

Kyzirakos, K., Karpathiotakis, M., & Koubarakis, M. (2012). Strabon. A semantic geospatial DBMS. In *Proceedings of ISWC* (pp. 362-376). IEEE.

Laharotte, P. A., Billot, R., Come, E., Oukhellou, L., Nantes, A., & El Faouzi, N. E. (2014). Spatiotemporal analysis of bluetooth data: Application to a large urban network. *IEEE Transactions on Intelligent Transportation Systems*, *16*(3), 1439–1448. doi:10.1109/TITS.2014.2367165

Lakshmanan, L. V. S., Leone, N., Ross, R., & Subrahmanian, V. S. (1997). ProbView: A flexible database system. *ACM Transactions on Database Systems*, *22*(3), 419–469. doi:10.1145/261124.261131

Langran, G. (1989). A review of temporal database research and its use in GIS applications. *International Journal of Geographical Information Systems*, *3*(1), 215–232. doi:10.1080/02693798908941509

Langran, G., & Chrisman, N. (1992). A framework for temporal geographic information. *Cartographica*, *40*(1), 1–14.

Langran, G., & Chrisman, N. R. (1988). A framework for temporal geographic information systems. *Cartographica*, *25*(3), 1–14. doi:10.3138/K877-7273-2238-5Q6V

Le Coz, J., Renard, B., Bonnifait, L., Branger, F., & Le Boursicaud, R. (2014). Combining hydraulic knowledge and uncertain gaugings in the estimation of hydrometric rating curves: A Bayesian approach. *Journal of Hydrology (Amsterdam)*, *509*, 573–587. doi:10.1016/j.jhydrol.2013.11.016

Lee, J., Han, W. S., Kasperovics, R., & Lee, J. H. (2012). An in-depth comparison of subgraph isomorphism algorithms in graph databases. *Proceedings of the VLDB Endowment International Conference on Very Large Data Bases*, *5*(7), 594–605. doi:10.14778/2535568.2448946

Lee, K. S., Lee, K. Y., Kim, Y. H., Choi, J. J., & Jang, G. S. (2015). Spatio-Temporal Ontology for the Semantic Web. *International Information Institute (Tokyo). Information (Basel)*, *18*, 329–334.

Le, H. H., Gabriel, P., Gietzel, J., & Schaeben, H. (2013). An object-relational spatio-temporal geoscience data model. *Computers & Geosciences*, *57*(4), 104–115. doi:10.1016/j.cageo.2013.04.014

Lehto, L., & Kilpeläinen, T. (2001). Generalizing XML-Encoded Spatial Data on the Web. In *Proceedings of the 20th International Cartographic Conference*, (pp. 2390-2396). IEEE.

Lei, P. R., Shen, T. J., & Peng, W. C. (2011). Exploring spatial-temporal trajectory model for location prediction. In *Proceedings of the 12th IEEE International Conference on Mobile Data Management (MDM)*, (pp. 58-67). IEEE. 10.1109/MDM.2011.61

Liagouris, J., Mamoulis, N., Bouros, P., & Terrovitis, M. (2014). An effective encoding scheme for spatial RDF data. *Proceedings of the VLDB Endowment International Conference on Very Large Data Bases*, *7*(12), 1271–1282. doi:10.14778/2732977.2733000

Li, C., Huang, J., Wang, B., Zhou, Y., Bai, Y., & Chen, Y. (2019). Spatial-Temporal Correlation Prediction Modeling of Origin-Destination Passenger Flow Under Urban Rail Transit Emergency Conditions. *IEEE Access : Practical Innovations, Open Solutions*, *7*, 162353–162365. doi:10.1109/ACCESS.2019.2951604

Lieberman, J., Singh, R., & Goad, C. (2007). W3c geospatial vocabulary. *Incubator group report*. W3C.

Li, G. L., Feng, J. H., Wang, J. Y., & Zhou, L. Z. (2007). Efficient keyword search for valuable LCAs over XML documents. In *Proceedings of the 16th ACM Conference on Information and Knowledge Management* (pp. 31–40). ACM.

Li, G., Yan, L., & Ma, Z. (2019). A method for fuzzy quantified querying over fuzzy resource description framework graph. *International Journal of Intelligent Systems*, *34*(6), 1086–1107. doi:10.1002/int.22087

Li, G., Yan, L., & Ma, Z. (2019). An approach for approximate subgraph matching in fuzzy RDF graph. *Fuzzy Sets and Systems*, *376*, 106–126. doi:10.1016/j.fss.2019.02.021

Li, J., Liu, C., Rui, Z., & Bo, N. (2009). Processing XML keyword search by constructing effective structured queries. In *Proceedings of the Joint International Conferences on Advances in Data and Web Management* (pp. 88–99). ACM. 10.1007/978-3-642-00672-2_10

Li, J., Liu, C., Zhou, R., & Wang, W. (2011). Top-k keyword search over probabilistic XML data. In *Proceedings of the 27th International Conference on Data Engineering* (pp. 1104-1115). IEEE. 10.1109/ICDE.2011.5767875

Li, S., & Xu, M. (2010). A Novel Approach of Computing XML Similarity based on Weighted XML Data Model. In *Proceedings of the 8th IEEE International Conference on Control and Automation*, (pp. 1157-1162). IEEE. 10.1109/ICCA.2010.5524091

Li, T., & M, Z. M. (2018). A structure-based approach of keyword querying for fuzzy XML data. *International Journal of Intelligent Systems*, *22*(2), 125–140.

Li, T., & Ma, Z. M. (2017). Object-stack: An object-oriented approach for top-k keyword querying over fuzzy XML. *Information Systems Frontiers*, *19*(3), 669–697. doi:10.1007/s10796-017-9748-0

Li, T., Xin, L., & Meng, X. F. (2012). Rtop-k: a keyword proximity search method based on semantic and structural relaxation. In *Proceedings of the IEEE International Conference on Systems, Man, and Cybernetics* (pp. 2079–2084). IEEE. 10.1109/ICSMC.2012.6378046

Liu, C., Li, J., Yu, J. X., & Zhou, R. (2010). Adaptive relaxation for querying heterogeneous XML data sources. *Information Systems*, *35*(6), 688–707. doi:10.1016/j.is.2010.02.002

Liu, C., Vincent, M. W., & Liu, J. (2006). Constraint Preserving Transformation from Relational Schema to XML Schema. *World Wide Web (Bussum)*, *9*(1), 93–110. doi:10.1007/s11280-005-4263-5

Liu, D., Chen, H., Qi, H., & Yang, B. (2013). Research progress of spatiotemporal data mining. *Jisuanji Yanjiu Yu Fazhan*, (02), 225–239.

Liu, G., Yao, M., & Wang, D. (2011). A novel three-phase XML twig pattern matching algorithm based on version tree. *Proceedings of the Eighth International Conference*, (pp. 1678-1688). IEEE. 10.1109/FSKD.2011.6019809

Liu, H., & Schneider, M. (2011). Querying moving objects with uncertainty in spatio-temporal databases. In *proceedings of the 2011 International Conference on Database Systems for Advanced Applications*, (pp. 357-371). ACM. 10.1007/978-3-642-20149-3_27

Liu, J. F., Liu, S. F., & Fang, Z. G. (2014). New strengthening buffer operators based on adjustable intensity and their applications. *Journal of Grey System*, *26*(3), 117–126.

Liu, J., & Ma, Z. M. (2013). Formal Transformation from Fuzzy Object-oriented Databases toFuzzy XML. *Applied Intelligence*, *39*(3), 630–641. doi:10.1007/s10489-013-0438-4

Liu, J., Ma, Z. M., & Feng, X. (2013). Formal Approach for Reengineering Fuzzy XML in Fuzzy Object-oriented Databases. *Applied Intelligence*, *38*(4), 541–552. doi:10.1007/s10489-012-0386-4

Liu, J., Ma, Z. M., & Ma, R. (2013). Efficient processing of twig query with compound predicates in fuzzy XML. *Fuzzy Sets and Systems*, *229*(2), 33–53. doi:10.1016/j.fss.2012.11.004

Liu, J., Ma, Z. M., & Qv, Q. L. (2014). Dynamic querying possibilistic XML data. *Information Sciences*, *261*(4), 70–88.

Liu, J., Ma, Z. M., & Yan, L. (2013). Efficient labeling scheme for dynamic XML trees. *Information Sciences*, *221*(2), 338–354. doi:10.1016/j.ins.2012.09.036

Liu, J., Ma, Z. M., & Yan, L. (2013). Querying and ranking incomplete twigs in probabilistic XML. *World Wide Web (Bussum)*, *16*(3), 325–353. doi:10.1007/s11280-011-0149-x

Liu, J., & Yan, D. L. (2015). Answering approximate queries over XML data. *IEEE Transactions on Fuzzy Systems*, *24*(2), 288–305. doi:10.1109/TFUZZ.2015.2453168

Liu, S. F., Forrest, J., & Yang, Y. J. (2012). A brief introduction to grey systems theory. *Grey Systems: Theory and Application*, *2*(2), 89–104. doi:10.1108/20439371211260081

Liu, S., & Lin, Y. (1998). *An Introduction to Grey Systems: Foundations, Methodology and Applications*. Emerald Publishing Limited.

Liu, X. H., & Wan, Y. C. (2010). Storing Spatio-Temporal Data in XML Native Database. In *Proceedings of the 2nd International Workshop on Database Technology and Applications* (pp. 1-4). IEEE. 10.1109/DBTA.2010.5659107

Liu, X., & Wan, Y. (2010). Storing spatiotemporal data in XML native database. In *Proceedings of the 2nd International Workshop on Database Technology and Applications* (pp. 27–28). Wuhan, China.

Liu, Y., Ester, M., Qian, Y., Hu, B., & Cheung, D. W. (2017). Microscopic and macroscopic spatio-temporal topic models for check-in data. *IEEE Transactions on Knowledge and Data Engineering*, *29*(9), 1957–1970. doi:10.1109/TKDE.2017.2703825

Li, X., Yang, J., Guan, X., & Wu, H. (2014). An event-driven spatiotemporal data model (E-ST) supporting dynamic expression and simulation of geographic processes. *Transactions in GIS*, *18*(1), 76–96. doi:10.1111/tgis.12127

Li, Y. Y., Yu, C., & Jagadish, H. V. (2004). Schema-free XQuery. In *Proceedings of the VLDB Conference* (pp. 72–83). ACM.

Li, Z. C. (2012). *Research on complex query method of spatiotemporal database*. Huazhong University of Science and Technology.

Li, Z., Hu, F., Schnase, J. L., Duffy, D. Q., Lee, T., Bowen, M. K., & Yang, C. (2017). A spatiotemporal indexing approach for efficient processing of big array-based climate data with MapReduce. *International Journal of Geographical Information Science*, *31*(1), 17–35. doi:10.1080/13658816.2015.1131830

Lo, A., Ozyer, T., Kianmehr, K., & Alhajj, R. (2010). VIREX and VRXQuery: Interactive Approach for Visual Querying of Relational Databases to Produce XML. *Journal of Intelligent Information Systems*, *35*(1), 21–49. doi:10.1007/s10844-009-0087-6

Lu, J. H., Chen, T., & Ling, T. W. (2005). Efficient processing of XML twig patterns with parent child edges: A look-ahead approach. *Proceedings of the 13th internal conference on very Large Data Bases* (pp. 193-204). ACM.

Lu, J. H., Chen, T., & Ling, T. W. (2005). From region encoding to extended dewey: on efficient processing of XML twig pattern matching. *Proceeding of the 31st ACM Internal Conference on very Large Data Bases* (pp. 533-542). ACM.

Luo, W., Yuan, L., Wu, M., & Yu, Z. (2010). Spatial-temporal data analysis with spacetime algebra: A case study with satellite altimetry data. In *2010 18th International Conference on Geoinformatics* (pp. 1-5). IEEE. 10.1109/GEOINFORMATICS.2010.5567880

Lutz, C., Wolter, F., & Zakharyashev, M. (2008). *Temporal Description Logics: A Survey*. In *Proc. TIME*, Montreal, Canada, 3-14.

Lu, X., Hu, T., & Yin, F. (2019). A novel spatiotemporal fuzzy method for modeling of complex distributed parameter processes. *IEEE Transactions on Industrial Electronics*, *66*(10), 7882–7892. doi:10.1109/TIE.2018.2877118

Lv, Y. H., Duan, Y. J., & Kang, W. W. (2015). Traffic flow prediction with big data: A deep learning approach. *IEEE Transactions on Intelligent Transportation Systems*, *16*(2), 865–873.

Ma, C. Y. (2012). *Research on Complex Query Processing in Spatiotemporal Database*. Zhejiang University.

Ma, J., Zeng, D., Zhao, H., & Liu, C. (2013). Cross-correlation measure for mining spatio-temporal patterns. *Journal of Database Management*, *24*(2), 13–34. doi:10.4018/jdm.2013040102

Mama, R., & Machkour, M. (2019). A study of fuzzy query systems for relational databases. In *Proceedings of the 4th International Conference on Smart City Applications* (pp. 1-5). ACM. 10.1145/3368756.3369105

Mama, R., & Machkour, M. (2019). A study on fuzzy interrogation systems of database. In *2019 International Conference of Computer Science and Renewable Energies (ICCSRE)* (pp. 1-6). IEEE. 10.1109/ICCSRE.2019.8807564

Mama, R., & Machkour, M. (2019). Fuzzy Questions for Relational Systems. In *Proceedings of the Third International Conference on Smart City Applications* (pp. 104-114) IEEE.

Mamoulis, N., Cao, H., & Kollios, G. (2004). Mining, Indexing, and Querying Historical Spatiotemporal data. In *Proceedings of the 10th ACM SIGKDD international conference on Knowledge Discovery and Data Mining* (pp. 236-245). ACM. 10.1145/1014052.1014080

Mandya, A., Bollegala, D., Coenen, F., & Atkinson, K. (2018). *Combining Long Short Term Memory and Convolutional Neural Network for Cross-Sentence n-ary Relation Extraction*. Department of Computer Science.

Mane, A., Babu, D. R., & Anand, M. C. (2004). XML Representation of Spatial Data. In *Proceedings of the 2004 IEEE India Annual Conference*, (pp. 490-493). IEEE.

Manola, F., Miller, E., & McBride, B. (2004). RDF primer. *W3C recommendation, 10*(1-107), 6.

Ma, R., Hu, Z., & Yan, L. (2022). A temporal JSON data model and its query languages. *Journal of Database Management, 33*(1), 1–29. doi:10.4018/JDM.299556

Mark, A. F., Stephen, L., & Gourab, K. S. (2019). Can Machine Learning Algorithms Predict Which Patients Will Achieve Minimally Clinically Important Differences From Total Joint Arthroplasty? *Clinical Orthopaedics and Related Research, 477*(6), 1267–1279. doi:10.1097/CORR.0000000000000687 PMID:31094833

Mashechkin, I. V., Petrovskiy, M. I., Tsarev, D. V., & Chikunov, M. N. (2019). Machine Learning Methods for Detecting and Monitoring Extremist Information on the Internet. *Programming and Computer Software, 45*(3), 99–115. doi:10.1134/S0361768819030058

Mathew, W., Raposo, R., & Martins, B. (2012). Predicting future locations with hidden Markov models. In *Proceedings of the 2012 ACM conference on ubiquitous computing* (pp. 911-918). ACM. 10.1145/2370216.2370421

Ma, X. L., Dai, Z., He, Z. B., Ma, J., Wang, Y., & Wang, Y. (2017). Learning traffic as images: A deep convolutional neural network for large-scale transportation network speed prediction. *Sensors (Basel), 17*(4), 818. doi:10.3390/s17040818 PMID:28394270

Ma, X., & Liu, Z. B. (2018). The kernel-based nonlinear multivariate grey model. *Applied Mathematical Modelling, 56*, 217–238. doi:10.1016/j.apm.2017.12.010

Ma, Y., Xiong, Q., Yang, J., Li, Y., Xiang, L., & Peng, F. (2006). Research on the design method of W3C XML Schema schema. *Computer Application Research*, (05), 80–82.

Ma, Z. M., Bai, L. Y., Ishikawa, Y., & Yan, L. (2017). Consistencies of fuzzy spatiotemporal data in XML documents. *Fuzzy Sets and Systems*.

Ma, Z. M., Liu, J., & Li, Y. (2010). Fuzzy data modeling and algebraic operations in XML. *International Journal of Intelligent Systems, 25*(9), 925–947. doi:10.1002/int.20424

Ma, Z. M., & Yan, L. (2016). Modeling fuzzy data with XML: A survey. *Fuzzy Sets and Systems, 301*, 146–159. doi:10.1016/j.fss.2015.09.016

Ma, Z. M., Zhang, W. J., Ma, W. Y., & Chen, G. Q. (2001). Conceptual Design of Fuzzy Object–Oriented Databases Utilizing Extended Entity-Relationship Model. *International Journal of Intelligent Systems*, *16*(6), 697–711. doi:10.1002/int.1031

Ma, Z., Li, G., & Yan, L. (2018). Fuzzy data modeling and algebraic operations in RDF. *Fuzzy Sets and Systems*, *351*, 41–63. doi:10.1016/j.fss.2017.11.013

Mazuran, M., Quintarelli, E., & Tanca, L. (2012). Data mining for XML query answering support. *IEEE Transactions on Knowledge and Data Engineering*, *24*(8), 1393–1407. doi:10.1109/TKDE.2011.80

McBride, B. (2004). The resource description framework (RDF) and its vocabulary description language RDFS. In *Handbook on ontologies* (pp. 51–65). Springer Berlin Heidelberg. doi:10.1007/978-3-540-24750-0_3

McMillan, H., Freer, J., Pappenberger, F., Krueger, T., & Clark, M. (2010). Impacts of uncertain river flow data on rainfall-runoff model calibration and discharge predictions. *Hydrological Processes*, *24*(10), 1270–1284. doi:10.1002/hyp.7587

Mehrotra, R., & Sharma, A. (2009). Evaluating Spatio-Temporal Representations in Daily Rainfall Sequences from Three Stochastic Multi-Site Weather Generation Approaches. *Advances in Water Resources*, *32*(6), 948–962. doi:10.1016/j.advwatres.2009.03.005

Mehta, P., Skoutas, D., & Voisard, A. (2015). Spatio-temporal keyword queries for moving objects. In *Proceedings of the 23rd SIGSPATIAL International Conference on Advances in Geographic Information Systems* (pp. 1-10). IEEE.

Mendelzon, A. O., Rizzolo, F., & Vaisman, A. (2004). Indexing Temporal XML Documents. In *Proceedings of the 30th International Conference on VLDB* (pp. 216-227). ACM.

Mendelzon, A. O., Rizzolo, F., & Vaisman, A. (2004). Indexing temporal XML documents. In *Proceedings of the Thirtieth international conference on Very large data bases-Volume 30* (pp. 216-227). IEEE.

Meng, X. F. (2009). *Research on Key Technologies of Flexible Query in Web Database*. Northeastern University.

Meng, X., Zhang, X., Tang, Y., & Bi, C. (2017). Adaptive query relaxation and top-k result ranking over autonomous web databases. *Knowledge and Information Systems*, *51*(2), 395–433. doi:10.1007/s10115-016-0982-4

Mennis, J. L., & Fountain, A. G. (2001). A spatio-temporal GIS database for monitoring alpine glacier change. *Photogrammetric Engineering and Remote Sensing*, *67*(8), 967–974.

Mishra, V. N., & Rai, P. K. (2016). A remote sensing aided multi-layer perceptron-Markov chain analysis for land use and land cover change prediction in Patna district (Bihar), India. *Arabian Journal of Geosciences*, *9*(4), 1–18. doi:10.1007/s12517-015-2138-3

Mitakos, T., & Almaliotis, I. (2009). Representing Geographic Information in Multidimensional XML: Applying Dimensions in Spatial Databases. In *Proceedings of the 16th IEEE International Conference on Systems, Signals and Image Processing*, (pp. 1-4). IEEE. 10.1109/IWSSIP.2009.5367760

Moffitt, V. Z., & Stoyanovich, J. (2017). *Temporal graph algebra*. In *Proceedings of the 16th International Symposium on Database Programming Languages* (pp. 10). Munich, Germany.

Mokhtar, H. M., & Su, J. (2004). Universal Trajectory Queries for Moving Object Databases. In *Proceedings of the 2004 IEEE International Conference on Mobile Data Management*, (pp. 133-144). IEEE. 10.1109/MDM.2004.1263051

Montgomery, L. D. (1995). *Temporal geographic information systems technology and requirements: where we are today.* [PhD thesis, Department of Geography, Ohio State University].

Morzy, M. (2007). Mining frequent trajectories of moving objects for location prediction. In *Proceedings of International Workshop on Machine Learning and Data Mining in Pattern Recognition* (pp. 667-680). ACM. 10.1007/978-3-540-73499-4_50

Motik, B. (2012). Representing and querying validity time in RDF and OWL: A logic-based approach. *Journal of Web Semantics*, *12*, 3–21. doi:10.1016/j.websem.2011.11.004

Mottin, D., Marascu, A., Basu Roy, S., Das, G., Palpanas, T., & Velegrakis, Y. (2014). IQR: an interactive query relaxation system for the empty-answer problem. In *Proceedings of the 2014 ACM SIGMOD international conference on Management of data*. Association for Computing Machinery. 10.1145/2588555.2594512

Muller, P. (2002). Topological spatio-temporal reasoning and representation. *Computational Intelligence*, *18*(3), 1–46. doi:10.1111/1467-8640.00196

Muslea, I., & Lee, T. J. (2005). Online query relaxation via bayesian causal structures discovery. In *Proceedings of AAAI*. AAAI Press.

Nalica, A. D. (2010). Spatial-Temporal Modeling of Growth in Rice Production in the Philippines. *The Philippine Statistician*, *59*, 15–25.

Nandal, R. (2013). Spatio-temporal database and its models: A review. *IOSR Journal of Computer Engineering*, *11*(2), 91–100. doi:10.9790/0661-11291100

Naser, T., Alhajj, R., & Ridley, M. J. (2009). Two-way Mapping Between Object-oriented Databases and XML. *Informatica (Vilnius)*, *33*(3), 297–308.

Navathe, S. B., & Ahmed, R. (1989). A temporal relational model and a query language. *Information Sciences*, *49*(1-3), 147–175. doi:10.1016/0020-0255(89)90026-1

Nepomnyachiy, S., Gelley, B., Jiang, W., & Minkus, T. (2014). What, where, and when: keyword search with spatio-temporal ranges. In *Proceedings of the 8th Workshop on Geographic Information Retrieval* (pp. 15-22). ACM. 10.1145/2675354.2675358

Nierman, A., & Jagadish, H. V. (2002). ProTDB: Probabilistic Data in XML. In *Proceedings of VLDB*, (pp. 646-657). IEEE.

Nierrman, A., & Jagadish, H. V. (2002). ProTDB: Probabilistic Data in XML. In: Proceedings of Very Large Data Bases, Pages 646–657.

Nikitopoulos, P., Vlachou, A., Doulkeridis, C., & Vouros, G. A. (2018). DiStRDF: Distributed Spatio-temporal RDF Queries on Spark. In EDBT/ICDT Workshops (pp. 125-132). ACM.

Nikitopoulos, P., Vlachou, A., Doulkeridis, C., & Vouros, G. A. (2021). Parallel and scalable processing of spatio-temporal RDF queries using Spark. *GeoInformatica*, *25*(4), 623–653. doi:10.1007/s10707-019-00371-0

Nitta, K., & Savnik, I. (2014). A Distributed Query Execution Method for RDF Storage Managers. In *Proceedings of the 10th International Workshop on Scalable Semantic Web Knowledge Base Systems* (pp. 7-18). Riva del Garda, Trentino, Italy.

Noh, S. Y., & Gadia, S. K. (2005). An XML-Based Framework for Temporal Database Implementation. In *Proceedings of the 12th International Symposium on Temporal Representation & Reasoning* (pp. 180-182). IEEE.

Nørvåg, K. (2002). Algorithms for Temporal Query Operators in XML Databases. In *Proceedings of the 2002 International Conference on Extending Database Technology*, (pp. 169-183). IEEE.

Nørvåg, K. (2002). Temporal query operators in XML database. *Proceedings of the 2002 ACM Symposium on Applied Computing* (pp. 402-406). ACM. 10.1145/508791.508868

Obeid, N. (2000). Towards a model of learning through communication. *Knowledge and Information Systems*, *2*(4), 498–508. doi:10.1007/PL00011655

Obeid, N. (2005). A formalism for representing and reasoning with temporal information, event and change. *Applied Intelligence*, *23*(2), 109–119. doi:10.1007/s10489-005-3416-7

Oliboni, B., & Pozzani, G. (2008). Representing Fuzzy Information by Using XML Schema. *In: Proceedings of the 19th International Conference on Database and Expert Systems Application*, (pp. 683–687). IEEE. 10.1109/DEXA.2008.44

Pan, F., & Hobbs, J. R. (2005). *Temporal Aggregates in OWL-Time*. In *Proceedings of the FLAIRS conference* (pp. 560-565). Clearwater Beach, Florida, USA.

Parent, C. S., Spaccapietra, S., & Zimanyi, E. (1999). Spatio-temporal conceptual models: data structures + space + time. In *Proceedings of the 7th ACM Symposium on Advances in Geographic Information Systems* (pp. 26-33). ACM. 10.1145/320134.320142

Parrott, L., Proulx, R., & Plante, X. T. (2008). Three-dimensional metrics for analysis of spatiotemporal data in ecology. *Ecological Informatics*, *3*(6), 343–353. doi:10.1016/j.ecoinf.2008.07.001

Pelekis, N., Theodoulidis, B., Kopanakis, I., & Theodoridis, Y. (2004). Literature Review of Spatio-Temporal Database Models. *The Knowledge Engineering Review*, *19*(3), 235–274. doi:10.1017/S026988890400013X

Peng, N., Poon, H., Quirk, C., Toutanova, K., & Yih, W. (2017). Cross-Sentence N-ary Relation Extraction with Graph LSTMs. *Transactions of the Association for Computational Linguistics*, *5*, 5. doi:10.1162/tacl_a_00049

Pereira, S., Zêzere, J. L., Quaresma, I., Santos, P. P., & Santos, M. (2016). Mortality patterns of hydro-geomorphologic disasters. *Risk Analysis*, *36*(6), 1188–1210. doi:10.1111/risa.12516 PMID:26616470

Perez, J., Arenas, M., & Gutierrez, C. (2006). Semantics and complexity of SPARQL. In *Proceedings of the 5th International Semantic Web Conference* (pp. 30-43). Athens, GA, USA.

Perry, M. S. (2008). A framework to support spatial, temporal and thematic analytics over semantic web data.

Perry, M., Herring, J. (2012). OGC GeoSPARQL-A geographic query language for RDF data. *OGC Implement. Standard*, 40.

Perry, M., Estrada, A., Das, S., & Banerjee, J. (2015). *Developing GeoSPARQL Applications with Oracle Spatial and Graph*. In *Proceedings of the ISWC* (pp. 57-61). Bethlehem, Pennsylvania, USA.

Perry, M., Jain, P., & Sheth, A. P. (2011). SPARQL-ST: Extending SPARQL to Support Spatiotemporal Queries. *Geospatial Semantics and the Semantic Web*, *12*, 61–86. doi:10.1007/978-1-4419-9446-2_3

Perry, M., Sheth, A. P., & Hakimpour, F. (2007). Supporting complex thematic, spatial and temporal queries over semantic web data. *International Conference on GeoSpatial Sematics*, (pp. 228-246). Springer, Berlin, Heidelberg. 10.1007/978-3-540-76876-0_15

Perry, M., Sheth, A., Arpinar, I. B., & Hakimpour, F. (2009). Geospatial and temporal semantic analytics. In *Handbook of Research on Geoinformatics* (pp. 161–170). IGI Global. doi:10.4018/978-1-59140-995-3.ch021

Peuquet, D. J. (2001). Making space for time: Issues in space-time data representation. *GeoInformatica*, *5*(1), 11–32. doi:10.1023/A:1011455820644

Peuquet, D. J., & Duan, N. (1995). An event-based spatio-temporal data model (ESTDM) for temporal analysis of geographical data. *International Journal of Geographical Information Systems*, *9*(1), 7–24. doi:10.1080/02693799508902022

Pfoser, D., & Tryfona, N. (2008). The Use of Ontologies in Location-based Services: The Space and Time Ontology in Protégé. *Research Academic Computer Technology Institute. Research Unit*, *3*, 15.

Pfoser, D., Tryfona, N., & Jensen, C. S. (2005). Indeterminacy and spatiotemporal data: Basic definitions and case study. *GeoInformatica*, *9*(3), 211–236. doi:10.1007/s10707-005-1282-4

Plewe, B. (2002). The nature of uncertainty in historical geographic information. *Transactions in GIS*, *6*(4), 431–456. doi:10.1111/1467-9671.00121

Powers, S. (2003). *Practical RDF: solving problems with the resource description framework.*

Psychas, I. D., Marinaki, M., Marinakis, Y., & Migdalas, A. (2017). Non-dominated sorting differential evolution algorithm for the minimization of route-based fuel consumption multi-objective vehicle routing problems. *Energy Systems*, *8*(4), 785–814. doi:10.1007/s12667-016-0209-5

Pugliese, A., Udrea, O., & Subrahmanian, V. S. (2008). *Scaling RDF with Time*. In *Proc. WWW*, Beijing, China.

Pugliese, A., Udrea, O., & Subrahmanian, V. S. (2008). Scaling RDF with time. In *Proceedings of the 17th International Conference on World Wide Web* (pp. 1365-1366). IEEE.

Pugliese, A., Udrea, O., & Subrahmanian, V. S. (2008). Scaling RDF with time. In *Proceedings of the 17th international conference on World Wide Web* (pp. 605-614). ACM. 10.1145/1367497.1367579

Qian, J., Li, X., Zhang, C., Chen, L., Jung, T., & Han, J. (2019). Social network de-anonymization and privacy inference with knowledge graph model. *IEEE Transactions on Dependable and Secure Computing*, *16*(4), 679–692. doi:10.1109/TDSC.2017.2697854

Qiao, S. J., Shen, D. Y., Wang, X. T., Han, N., & Zhu, W. (2015). A self-adaptive parameter selection trajectory prediction approach via hidden Markov models. *IEEE Transactions on Intelligent Transportation Systems*, *16*(1), 284–296. doi:10.1109/TITS.2014.2331758

Raghebi, Z., & Banaei-Kashani, F. (2018). Probabilistic reachability query in evolving spatiotemporal contact networks of moving objects. In *Proceedings of the 26th ACM SIGSPATIAL International Conference on Advances in Geographic Information Systems*. Association for Computing Machinery. 10.1145/3274895.3274976

Rathee, S., & Yadav, A. (2013). Survey on spatio-temporal database and data models with relevant features. *International Journal of Scientific and Research Publications*, *3*(1), 152–156.

Ravindra, P., Kim, H. S., & Anyanwu, K. (2011). *An intermediate algebra for optimizing RDF graph pattern matching on MapReduce*. In *Proceedings of the Extended Semantic Web Conference* (pp. 46-61). Berlin, Germany. 10.1007/978-3-642-21064-8_4

Reed, T. W., Reitsma, F., & McMeekin, D. A. (2015). Browsing spatial knowledge with linked ontologies. In *2015 11th International Conference on Innovations in Information Technology (IIT)* (pp. 196-200). IEEE. 10.1109/INNOVATIONS.2015.7381539

Renolen, A. (1996). *History graphs: conceptual modeling of spatio-temporal data.* [PhD thesis, in GIS Frontiers in Business and Science, International Cartographic Association].

Ribaric, S., & Hrkac, T. (2012). A model of fuzzy spatio-temporal knowledge representation and reasoning based on high-level Petri nets. *Information Systems*, *37*(3), 238–256. doi:10.1016/j.is.2011.09.010

Rizzolo, F., & Vaisman, A. A. (2008). Temporal XML: Modeling, Indexing, and Query Processing. *The VLDB Journal*, *17*(5), 1179–1212. doi:10.1007/s00778-007-0058-x

Robertson, E. L. (2004). *Triadic relations: An algebra for the semantic web*. In *Proceedings of the International Workshop on Semantic Web and Databases* (pp. 63-77). Toronto, Canada.

Roy, A. J., & Stell, J. G. (2001). Spatial relations between indeterminate regions. *International Journal of Approximate Reasoning*, *27*(3), 205–234. doi:10.1016/S0888-613X(01)00033-0

Sammatat, S., Boonsith, N., & Lekdee, K. (2016). *Generalized linear mixed models for spatio-temporal data with an application to leptospirosis in thailand*.

Sammatat, S., Boonsith, N., & Lekdee, K. (2020). *Estimation and detection of rice yields in Thailand using spatial and longitudinal data analysis*.

Santos, M., Bateira, C., Soares, L., & Hermenegildo, C. (2014). Hydro-geomorphologic GIS database in Northern Portugal, between 1865 and 2010: Temporal and spatial analysis. *International Journal of Disaster Risk Reduction*, *10*, 143–152. doi:10.1016/j.ijdrr.2014.08.003

Santos, M., Santos, J. A., & Fragoso, M. (2015). Historical damaging flood records for 1871–2011 in Northern Portugal and underlying atmospheric forcings. *Journal of Hydrology (Amsterdam)*, *530*, 591–603. doi:10.1016/j.jhydrol.2015.10.011

Sardar, Z., & Abdul, W. (2009). A new friends sort algorithm. In *2009 2nd IEEE International Conference on Computer Science and Information Technology*. IEEE. 10.1109/ICCSIT.2009.5234550

Sellis, T. (1999). Research issues in spatio-temporal database systems. In *International Symposium on Spatial Databases* (pp. 5-11). Springer Berlin Heidelberg.

Senellart, P., & Abiteboul, S. (2007). On the Complexity of Managing Probabilistic XML Data. In *Proceedings of the 26th ACM SIGACT-SIGMOD-SIGART Symposium on Principles of Database Systems* (pp. 283-292). ACM. 10.1145/1265530.1265570

Seqev, A., & Shoshani, A. (1987). Logical modeling of temporal data. In *Proceedings of the ACM SIGMOD International Conference on Management of Data* (pp. 114-121). IEEE.

Shang, H., Zhang, Y., Lin, X., & Yu, J. X. (2008). Taming verification hardness: An efficient algorithm for testing subgraph isomorphism. *Proceedings of the VLDB Endowment International Conference on Very Large Data Bases*, *1*(1), 730–741. doi:10.14778/1453856.1453899

Shaw, S. L., & Yu, H. (2009). A GIS-based time-geographic approach of studying individual activities and interactions in a hybrid physical–virtual space. *Journal of Transport Geography*, *17*(2), 141–149. doi:10.1016/j.jtrangeo.2008.11.012

Sheng, G. L., Su, Y. L., & Wang, W. D. (2019). A new fractal approach for describing induced-fracture porosity/permeability/compressibility in stimulated unconventional reservoirs. *Journal of Petroleum Science Engineering*, *179*, 855–866. doi:10.1016/j.petrol.2019.04.104

Shi, X. J., Chen, Z. R., & Wang, H. (2015). Convolutional LSTM network: A machine learning approach for precipitation nowcasting. In Proceedings of Advances in Neural Information Processing Systems (pp. 802-810). ACM.

Sicilia, M., & Barriocana, E. G. (2006). Extending Object Database Interfaces with Fuzziness Through Aspect-Oriented Design. *SIGMOD Record*, *35*(2), 4–9. doi:10.1145/1147376.1147377

Sistla, A. P., Wolfson, O., Chamberlain, S., & Dao, S. (1997). Modeling and querying moving objects. In *Proceedings of the 13th International Conference on Data Engineering* (pp. 422-431). IEEE. 10.1109/ICDE.1997.581973

Sistla, A. P., Wolfson, O., & Xu, B. (2015). Continuous nearest-neighbor queries with location uncertainty. *The VLDB Journal*, *24*(1), 25–50. doi:10.1007/s00778-014-0361-2

Smart, P. D., Abdelmoty, A. I., El-Geresy, B. A., & Jones, C. B. (2007). A framework for combining rules and geo-ontologies. In *International Conference on Web Reasoning and Rule Systems* (pp. 111-125). Springer. 10.1007/978-3-540-72982-2_10

Smeros, P., & Koubarakis, M. (2016). Discovering Spatial and Temporal Links among RDF Data. In LDOW@WWW.

Song, Q., Wu, Y., Lin, P., Dong, L. X., & Sun, H. (2018). Mining Summaries for Knowledge Graph Search. *IEEE Transactions on Knowledge and Data Engineering*, *29*(10), 1887–1900. doi:10.1109/TKDE.2018.2807442

Song, X. Y., Wang, Y. H., Wu, G., & Wang, S. J. (2011). Base state amendments spatio-temporal data model with dynamic selection of base state. In *Proceedings of the 4th International Congress on Image and Signal Processing* (pp. 15-17). IEEE. 10.1109/CISP.2011.6100782

Soutou, C. (2001). Modeling Relationships in Object-relational Databases. *Data & Knowledge Engineering*, *36*(1), 79–107. doi:10.1016/S0169-023X(00)00035-5

Sözer, A., Yazici, A., & Oğuztüzün, H. (2015). Indexing fuzzy spatiotemporal data for efficient querying: A meteorological application. *IEEE Transactions on Fuzzy Systems*, *23*(5), 1399–1413. doi:10.1109/TFUZZ.2014.2362121

Sözer, A., Yazici, A., Oğuztüzün, H., & Taş, O. (2008). Modeling and querying fuzzy spatiotemporal databases. *Information Sciences*, *178*(19), 3665–3682. doi:10.1016/j.ins.2008.05.034

Stefanakis, E. (2001). A unified framework for fuzzy spatio-temporal representation and reasoning. In *Proceedings of the 20th international cartographic conference* (pp. 2678-2687). ACM.

Sun, C., Chan, C. Y., & Goenka, A. K. (2007). Multiway SLCA-based keyword search in XML data. In *Proceedings of the World Wide Web Conference* (pp. 1043-1052). ACM. 10.1145/1242572.1242713

Sun, G. D., Guan, X., Yi, X., & Zhou, Z. (2018). Grey relational analysis between hesitant fuzzy sets with applications to pattern recognition. *Expert Systems with Applications*, *92*, 521–532. doi:10.1016/j.eswa.2017.09.048

Sun, J., Papadias, D., Tao, Y., & Liu, B. (2004). Querying about the past, the present, and the future in spatio-temporal databases. In *Proceedings of the 20th International Conference on Data Engineering* (pp. 433-444). IEEE. 10.1109/ICDE.2004.1319997

Sun, K., Zhu, Y., Pan, P., Hou, Z., Wang, D., Li, W., & Song, J. (2019). Geospatial data ontology: The semantic foundation of geospatial data integration and sharing. *Big Earth Data*, *3*(3), 269–296. doi:10.1080/20964471.2019.1661662

Takama, Y., & Hattori, S. (2007). Mining association rules for adaptive search engine based on RDF technology. *IEEE Transactions on Industrial Electronics*, *54*(2), 790–796. doi:10.1109/TIE.2007.891650

Tan, C., & Yan, S. (2017). Spatiotemporal data organization and application research. *The International Archives of the Photogrammetry, Remote Sensing and Spatial Information Sciences*, *42*(W7), 1363–1366. doi:10.5194/isprs-archives-XLII-2-W7-1363-2017

Tang, X., Kainz, W., & Wang, H. (2010). Topological relations between fuzzy regions in a fuzzy topological space. *International Journal of Applied Earth Observation and Geoinformation*, *12*(S2), 151–165. doi:10.1016/j.jag.2010.01.004

Tao, Y. F., Kollios, G., Considine, J., & Li, F. (2004) Papadias, D. Spatio-temporal aggregation using sketches. *Proc. 20th International Conference on Data Engineering*. IEEE.

Tao, Y. F., Kollios, G., Considine, J., Li, F., & Papadias, D. (2004). Spatio-temporal aggregation using sketches. In *Proc. 20th International Conference on Data Engineering*. ACM.

Tao, Y., Kollios, G., Considine, J., Li, F., & Papadias, D. (2004). Spatio-temporal aggregation using sketches. In *Proceedings of the 20th International Conference on Data Engineering* (pp. 632-643). IEEE.

Tao, Y., & Papadias, D. (2001). MV3R-tree: a Spatio-Temporal Access Method for Time-Stamp and Interval Queries. In *Proceedings of VLDB* (pp. 431-440). IEEE.

Tappolet, J., & Bernstein, A. (2009). Applied Temporal RDF: Efficient Temporal Querying of RDF Data with SPARQL. In *Proc. ESWC*, Heraklion, Greece. 10.1007/978-3-642-02121-3_25

Tathiane, M., Artem, S., & Andrew, J. G. (2018). Machine Learning Identifies Stemness Features Associated with Oncogenic Dedifferentiation. *Cell*, *173*(2), 338–354. doi:10.1016/j.cell.2018.03.034 PMID:29625051

Thakkar, H., Punjani, D., Auer, S., & Vidal, M. E. (2017). Towards an integrated graph algebra for graph pattern matching with Gremlin. In *Proceedings of the International Conference on Database and Expert Systems Applications* (pp. 81-91). Lyon, France. 10.1007/978-3-319-64468-4_6

Theodoridis, Y., Papadias, D., Stefanakis, E., & Sellis, T. (1998). Direction relations and two-dimensional range queries: Optimization techniques. *Data & Knowledge Engineering*, *27*(97), 313–336. doi:10.1016/S0169-023X(97)00060-8

Tian, Y., & Patel, J. M. (2008). Tale: A tool for approximate large graph matching. In *2008 IEEE 24th International Conference on Data Engineering* (pp. 963-972). IEEE. 10.1109/ICDE.2008.4497505

Tian, Z., Lu, J., & Li, D. (2011). A survey on XML keyword search. In APWeb. doi:10.1007/978-3-642-20291-9_52

Tong, H., Faloutsos, C., Gallagher, B., & Eliassi-Rad, T. (2007). Fast best-effort pattern matching in large attributed graphs. In *Proceedings of the 13th ACM SIGKDD international conference on Knowledge discovery and data mining* (pp. 737-746). ACM. 10.1145/1281192.1281271

Tong, Q. (2018). Mapping object-oriented database models into RDF (S). *IEEE Access : Practical Innovations, Open Solutions*, *6*, 47125–47130. doi:10.1109/ACCESS.2018.2867152

Tøssebro, E. (2002). *Representing Uncertainty in Spatial and Spatiotemporal Databases*. [Doctoral Thesis, Norwegian University of Science and Technology].

Tøssebro, E., & Güting, R. H. (2001). Creating representations for continuously moving regions from observations. In *Proceedings of the 7th International Symposium on Spatial and Temporal Databases* (pp. 158-175). ACM. 10.1007/3-540-47724-1_17

Tøssebro, E., & Nygård, M. (2002). Abstract and Discrete Models for Uncertain Spatiotemporal Data. In *Proceedings of the 14th IEEE International Conference on Scientific and Statistical Database Management*, (pp. 240-240). IEEE. 10.1109/SSDM.2002.1029727

Tøssebro, E., & Nygård, M. (2002). Uncertainty in Spatiotemporal Databases. *Advanced Information Systems*, 43–53.

Trajcevski, G., Wolfson, O., Hinrichs, K., & Chamberlain, S. (2004). Managing Uncertainty in Moving Objects Databases. *ACM Transactions on Database Systems*, *29*(3), 463–507. doi:10.1145/1016028.1016030

Tran, B. H., Plumejeaud-Perreau, C., & Bouju, A. (2018). A Web Interface for Exploiting Spatio-Temporal Heterogeneous Data. *Web and Wireless Geographical Information Systems*, 118-129.

Treur, J. (2018). Network Reification as a Unified Approach to Represent Network Adaptation Principles within a Network. In *International Conference on Theory and Practice of Natural Computing*. ACM. 10.1007/978-3-030-04070-3_27

Tryfona, N., & Hadzilacos, T. (1998). Logical data modeling of spatiotemporal applications: Definitions and a model. In *Proceedings. IDEAS'98. International Database Engineering and Applications Symposium (Cat. No. 98EX156)* (pp. 14-23). IEEE.

Tryfona, N., & Jensen, C. S. (1999). Conceptual data modeling for spatiotemporal applications. *GeoInformatica, 3*(3), 245–268. doi:10.1023/A:1009801415799

Tryfona, N., & Jensen, C. S. (2000). Using abstractions for spatio-temporal conceptual modeling. In *Proceedings of the 2000 ACM Symposium on Applied Computing* (pp. 313-322). ACM. 10.1145/335603.335775

Turowski, K., & Weng, U. (2002). Representing and Processing Fuzzy Information—An XML-based Approach. *Knowledge-Based Systems, 15*(1-2), 67–75. doi:10.1016/S0950-7051(01)00122-8

Vaisman, A., & Chentout, K. (2019). Mapping Spatiotemporal Data to RDF: A SPARQL Endpoint for Brussels. *ISPRS International Journal of Geo-Information, 8*(8), 353. doi:10.3390/ijgi8080353

Vatsavai, R. R., Ganguly, A., & Chandola, V. (2012). Spatiotemporal data mining in the era of big spatial data: Algorithms and applications. In *Proceedings of the 1st ACM SIGSPATIAL International Workshop on Analytics for Big Geospatial Data* (pp. 1–10). ACM. 10.1145/2447481.2447482

Vazirgiannis, M., & Wolfson, O. (2001). A Spatiotemporal Model and Language for Moving Objects on Road Networks. *Lecture Notes in Computer Science, 2121*, 20–35. doi:10.1007/3-540-47724-1_2

Velayutham, V., Chandrasekaran, S., & Mohan, S. (2018). Web user interface based on OGC standards for sensor cloud using big data. *International Journal of Communication Networks and Distributed Systems, 20*(4), 389. doi:10.1504/IJCNDS.2018.092143

Venkateswara, R.K. (2012). Spatiotemporal data mining: Issues, tasks and applications. *Int. J. Comput. Sci. Eng. Surv.*

Viqueira, J. R. R. (2000). Relational Algebra for Spatio-Temporal Data Management. In *Proceedings of the EDBT 2000 PhD Workshop*, (pp. 43-46). ACM.

Virgilio, R., & De. (2015). Approximate querying of RDF graphs via path alignment. *Distributed and Parallel Databases, 33*(4), 555–581. doi:10.1007/s10619-014-7142-1

Vlachou, A., Doulkeridis, C., Glenis, A., Santipantakis, G. M., & Vouros, G. A. (2019). *Efficient spatio-temporal RDF query processing in large dynamic knowledge bases.* In *Proc. SAC*, Limassol, Cyprus. 10.1145/3297280.3299732

Wang, D., Zou, L., & Zhao, D. (2014). gst-Store: An Engine for Large RDF Graph Integrating Spatiotemporal Information. Presented at the 17th EDBT, Athens, Greece, March 24-28.

Wang, H., & Aggarwal, C. C. (2010). A survey of algorithms for keyword search on graph data. In Managing and Mining Graph Data. doi:10.1007/978-1-4419-6045-0_8

Wang, C., Dong, X. J., Zhou, F., Cao, L., & Chi, C.-H. (2015). Coupled Attribute Similarity Learning on Categorical Data. *IEEE Transactions on Neural Networks and Learning Systems, 26*(4), 781–797. doi:10.1109/TNNLS.2014.2325872 PMID:25794382

Wang, C., Tao, L. B., & Wang, M. C. (2011). Coupled nominal similarity in unsupervised learning. In *Proceedings of the 20th ACM Conference on Information and Knowledge Management* (pp. 973-978). ACM. 10.1145/2063576.2063715

Wang, D., Zou, L., Feng, Y., Shen, X., Tian, J., & Zhao, D. (2013). S-store: An engine for large rdf graph integrating spatial information. In *International Conference on Database Systems for Advanced Applications* (pp. 31-47). ACM. 10.1007/978-3-642-37450-0_3

Wang, D., Zou, L., & Zhao, D. (2014). gst-Store: An Engine for Large RDF Graph Integrating Spatiotemporal Information. In *Proceedings of the 17th International Conference on Extending Database Technology* (pp. 79-90). ACM.

Wang, D., Zou, L., & Zhao, D. (2017). gst-store: Querying Large Spatiotemporal RDF Graphs. *Data and Information Management*, *1*(2), 84–103. doi:10.1515/dim-2017-0008

Wang, F., & Zaniolo, C. (2003). Temporal Queries in XML Document Archives and Web Warehouses. In *Proceedings of the 10th International Symposium on Temporal Representation and Reasoning and the 4th IEEE International Conference on Temporal Logic*, (pp. 47-55). ACM.

Wang, J., Di, X., Liu, J., & Bai, L. (2019). *A Constraint Framework for Uncertain Spatiotemporal Data in RDF Graphs.* In *The International Conference on Natural Computation, Fuzzy Systems and Knowledge Discovery*, Berlin, Germany, 727-735.

Wangni, J. (2017). Stochastic Orthant-Wise Limited-Memory Quasi-Newton Method. *Clinical Orthopaedics and Related Research.*

Wang, X. Y., Zhou, X. F., & Lu, S. Lu. (2000). Spatiotemporal Data Modeling and Management: A Survey. In *Proceedings of the 36th International Conference on Technology of Object-Oriented Languages and Systems* (pp. 202-211). ACM.

Wang, X., Zhou, X., & Lu, S. (2000). Spatiotemporal data modelling and management: a survey. In *Proceedings of the 36th IEEE international conference on technology of object-oriented languages and systems*, (pp. 202-211). IEEE.

Wang, X., Zhou, X., & Lu, S. (2000). Spatiotemporal Data Modelling and Management: a Survey. In *Proceedings of the 36th IEEE International Conference on Technology of Object-Oriented Languages and Systems*, (pp. 202-211). IEEE.

Wang, Y. H. (2009). Using neural network to forecast stock index option price: A new hybrid GARCH approach. *Quality & Quantity*, *43*(5), 833–843. doi:10.1007/s11135-008-9176-9

Wang, Y. H., Dang, Y. G., Li, Y. Q., & Liu, S. (2010). An approach to increase prediction precision of GM (1, 1) model based on optimization of the initial condition. *Expert Systems with Applications*, *37*(8), 5640–5644. doi:10.1016/j.eswa.2010.02.048

Wang, Y. H., Liu, Q., Tang, J. R., Cao, W., & Li, X. (2014). Optimization approach of background value and initial item for improving prediction precision of GM (1, 1) model. *Journal of Systems Engineering and Electronics*, *25*(1), 77–82. doi:10.1109/JSEE.2014.00009

Wang, Y., Li, X., Li, X., & Wang, Y. (2013). A survey of queries over uncertain data. *Knowledge and Information Systems*, *37*(3), 485–530. doi:10.1007/s10115-013-0638-6

Wang, Z. X., & Hao, P. (2016). An improved grey multivariable model for predicting industrial energy consumption in China. *Applied Mathematical Modelling*, *40*(11), 5745–5758. doi:10.1016/j.apm.2016.01.012

Watkins, E. R., & Nicole, D. A. (2006). Named Graphs as a Mechanism for Reasoning About Provenance. In Proc. APWeb, Harbin, China, 943-948. doi:10.1007/11610113_99

Wei, Y., & Hu, D. H. (2009). Deficiency of the smoothness condition and its remedy. *Systems Engineering-Theory & Practice*, *29*(8), 165–170. doi:10.1016/S1874-8651(10)60066-X

Wen, F., & Amir, A. (2017). Two-dimensional sorting algorithm for high-throughput K-best MIMO detection. *IET Communications*, *11*(6), 817–822. doi:10.1049/iet-com.2016.0790

Wikle, C. K. (2001). A kernel-based spectral approach for spatio-temporal dynamic models. In *Proceedings of the 1st Spanish Workshop on Spatio-Temporal Modelling of Environmental Processes (METMA)* (pp. 167-180). ACM.

Wilson, D., & Martinez, T. (1997). Improved heterogeneous distance functions. *Journal of Artificial Intelligence Research*, *6*(1), 1–34. doi:10.1613/jair.346

Wlodarczyk, T. W., Rong, C., O'Connor, M., & Musen, M. (2011). SWRL-F: a fuzzy logic extension of the semantic web rule language. In *Proc. WIMS*, Sogndal, Norway. 10.1145/1988688.1988735

Wolfson, O. (1998). Querying the uncertain position of moving objects. *Lecture Notes in Computer Science*, *1399*, 310–337. doi:10.1007/BFb0053708

Wong, H. L., & Shiu, J. M. (2012). Comparisons of fuzzy time series and hybrid Grey model for non-stationary data forecasting. *Applied Mathematics & Information Sciences*, *4*, 409–416.

Wong, S., Ziarko, W., & Wong, P. (1985). Generalized vector spaces model in information retrieval. In *Proceedings of the 8th Annual International ACM SIGIR Conference on Research and Development in Information Retrieval* (pp. 18–25). ACM. 10.1145/253495.253506

Wu, D., Zhou, H., Shi, J., & Mamoulis, N. (2020). Top-k relevant semantic place retrieval on spatiotemporal RDF data. *The VLDB Journal*, *29*(6), 893–917. doi:10.1007/s00778-019-00591-8

Wu, L. F., Liu, S. F., Cui, W., Liu, D.-L., & Yao, T.-X. (2014). Non-homogenous discrete grey model with fractional-order accumulation. *Neural Computing & Applications*, *25*(5), 1215–1221. doi:10.1007/s00521-014-1605-1

Wu, L. F., Liu, S. F., & Wang, Y. N. (2012). Grey Lotka-Volterra model and its application. *Technological Forecasting and Social Change*, *79*(9), 1720–1730. doi:10.1016/j.techfore.2012.04.020

Wu, L. F., Liu, S. F., Yao, L. G., Yan, S., & Liu, D. (2013). Grey system model with the fractional order accumulation. *Communications in Nonlinear Science and Numerical Simulation*, *18*(7), 1775–1785. doi:10.1016/j.cnsns.2012.11.017

Wu, X., Zhang, C., & Zhang, S. (2005). Database Classification for Multidatabase Mining. *Information Systems*, *30*(1), 71–88. doi:10.1016/j.is.2003.10.001

Wu, Y., Agrawal, D., & Abbadi, A. (2001). Applying the golden rule of sampling for query estimation. In *Proceedings of the ACM SIGMOD International Conference on Management of Data* (pp. 325-336). ACM. 10.1145/375663.375724

Xie, N. M., & Liu, S. F. (2009). Discrete grey forecasting model and its optimization. *Applied Mathematical Modelling*, *33*(2), 1173–1186. doi:10.1016/j.apm.2008.01.011

Xie, R., & Shibasaki, R. (2005). A unified spatiotemporal schema for representing and querying moving features. *SIGMOD Record*, *34*(1), 45–50. doi:10.1145/1058150.1058159

Xiong, X., Mokbel, M. F., & Aref, W. G. (2008). Spatio-Temporal Database. Encyclopedia of GIS, 1114-1115.

Xu, K., Wikle, C. K., & Fox, N. I. (2005). A kernel-based spatio-temporal dynamical model for nowcasting weather radar reflectivities. *Journal of the American Statistical Association*, *100*(472), 1133–1144. doi:10.1198/016214505000000682

Xu, L., Wong, A., & Clausi, D. A. (2017). A Novel Bayesian Spatial–Temporal Random Field Model Applied to Cloud Detection From Remotely Sensed Imagery. *IEEE Transactions on Geoscience and Remote Sensing*, *55*(9), 4913–4924. doi:10.1109/TGRS.2017.2692264

Xu, Y., & Papakonstantinou, Y. (2005). Efficient keyword Search for Smallest LCAs in XML Databases. In *Proceedings of the ACM SIGMOD International Conference on Management of Data* (pp. 527–538). ACM. 10.1145/1066157.1066217

Xu, Y., & Papakonstantinou, Y. (2008). Efficient LCA based keyword search in XML data. In *Proceedings of the ACM Conference on Conference on Information and Knowledge Management* (pp. 535–546). ACM. 10.1145/1353343.1353408

Xu, Z., Luo, X. F., & Liu, Y. H. (2016). From latency, through outbreak, to decline: Detecting different states of emergency events using web resources. *IEEE Transactions on Big Data*.

Xu, Z., Luo, X. F., & Liu, Y. H. (2016). From Latency, through Outbreak, to Decline: Detecting Different States of Emergency Events Using Web Resources. *IEEE Transactions on Big Data*.

Yang, J., Xu, J., & Xu, M. (2014). Predicting next location using a variable order Markov model. In *Proceedings of the 5th ACM SIGSPATIAL International Workshop on GeoStreaming* (pp. 37-42). ACM. 10.1145/2676552.2676557

Yang, Y. J., Liu, S. F., & John, R. (2014). Uncertainty representation of grey numbers and grey sets. *IEEE Transactions on Cybernetics*, *44*(9), 1508–1517. doi:10.1109/TCYB.2013.2288731 PMID:25137681

Yan, L., Zhao, P., & Ma, Z. (2019). Indexing temporal RDF graph. *Computing*, *101*(10), 1457–1488. doi:10.1007/s00607-019-00703-w

Yan, W. (2012). *Research on XML Flexible Query Technology*. Northeastern University.

Yan, Y., Wang, C., & Zhou, A. (2008). Efficiently querying rdf data in triple stores. In *Proceedings of the 17th international conference on World Wide Web* (pp. 1053-1054). ACM. 10.1145/1367497.1367652

Yao, T. X., & Liu, S. F. (2009). Characteristics and optimization of discrete GM (1, 1) model. *Systems Engineering: Theory and Practice*, *29*(3), 142–148.

Yazici, A., Zhu, Q., & Sun, N. (2001). Semantic data modeling of spatiotemporal database applications. *International Journal of Intelligent Systems*, *16*(7), 881–904. doi:10.1002/int.1040

Ye, J., Dang, Y. G., & Li, B. J. (2018). Grey-Markov prediction model based on background value optimization and central-point triangular whitenization weight function. *Communications in Nonlinear Science and Numerical Simulation*, *54*, 320–330. doi:10.1016/j.cnsns.2017.06.004

Ye, X., Chen, Z., Tang, Y., Tang, N., & Hu, S. (2007). Temporal XML indexing technology. *Journal of Computational Science*, (07), 1074–1085.

Yi, S., Huang, B., & Chan, W. T. (2005). XML application schema matching using similarity measure and relaxation labeling. *Information Sciences*, *169*(1-2), 27–46. doi:10.1016/j.ins.2004.02.013

Yuan, L., Lü, G., Luo, W., Yu, Z., Yi, L., & Sheng, Y. (2012). Geometric algebra method for multidimensionally-unified GIS computation. *Chinese Science Bulletin*, *57*(7), 802–811. doi:10.1007/s11434-011-4891-3

Yuan, L., Yu, Z., Chen, S., Luo, W., Wang, Y., & Lü, G. (2010). CAUSTA: Clifford algebra-based unified Spatiotemporal analysis. *Transactions in GIS*, *14*(s1), 59–83. doi:10.1111/j.1467-9671.2010.01221.x

Yuan, L., Yu, Z., Luo, W., Zhou, L., & Lü, G. (2011). A 3D GIS spatial data model based on conformal geometric algebra. *Science China. Earth Sciences*, *54*(1), 101–112. doi:10.1007/s11430-010-4130-9

Yu, H. (2006). Spatio-temporal GIS design for exploring interactions of human activities. *Cartography and Geographic Information Science*, *33*(1), 3–19. doi:10.1559/152304006777323136

Yu, H., & Shaw, S. L. (2004, August). Representing and visualizing travel diary data: A spatio-temporal gis approach. In *2004 ESRI International User Conference* (pp. 1-13). IEEE.

Yu, Z., Yuan, L., Hu, Y., Li, Y., & Zong, Z. (2012). Expression and modeling method of vector spatiotemporal data based on geometric algebra. *Journal of Geo-Information Science*, (01), 67–73. doi:10.3724/SP.J.1047.2012.00067

Zeng, B., Meng, W., & Tong, M. Y. (2016). A self-adaptive intelligence grey predictive model with alterable structure and its application. *Engineering Applications of Artificial Intelligence*, *50*, 236–244. doi:10.1016/j.engappai.2015.12.011

Zeng, X. Y., Shu, L., Huang, G. M., & Jiang, J. (2016). Triangular fuzzy series forecasting based on grey model and neural network. *Applied Mathematical Modelling*, *40*(3), 1717–1727. doi:10.1016/j.apm.2015.08.009

Zêzere, J. L., Pereira, S., Tavares, A. O., Bateira, C., Trigo, R. M., Quaresma, I., Santos, P. P., Santos, M., & Verde, J. (2014). DISASTER: A GIS database on hydro-geomorphologic disasters in Portugal. *Natural Hazards*, *72*(2), 503–532. doi:10.1007/s11069-013-1018-y

Zhang, Y. P., Wang, X. J., & Zhang, Y. (2009). Labeling Scheme for Temporal XML. *Web Information Systems and Mining, WISM 2009. International Conference on, IEEE*, (pp. 277-279). IEEE.

Zhang, Y., Wang, X., & Zhang, Y. (2009). Labeling Scheme for Temporal XML. *Web Information Systems and Mining, 2009. WISM 2009. International Conference on*, (pp. 277-279). IEEE.

Zhang, C., Chen, S. C., Shyu, M. L., & Peeta, S. (2003). Adaptive background learning for vehicle detection and spatio-temporal tracking. In *Fourth International Conference on Information, Communications and Signal Processing, 2003 and the Fourth Pacific Rim Conference on Multimedia. Proceedings of the 2003 Joint* (Vol. 2, pp. 797-801). IEEE. 10.1109/ICICS.2003.1292566

Zhang, F., Wang, K., Li, Z., & Cheng, J. (2019). Temporal Data Representation and Querying Based on RDF. *IEEE Access : Practical Innovations, Open Solutions*, *7*, 85000–85023. doi:10.1109/ACCESS.2019.2924550

Zhang, S., Li, S., & Yang, J. (2009). GADDI: Distance index based subgraph matching in biological networks. In *Proceedings of the 12th International Conference on Extending Database Technology* (pp. 1062-1065). ACM. 10.1145/1516360.1516384

Zhang, X., & Fong, J. (2000). Translating Update Operations From Relational to Object-oriented Databases. *Information and Software Technology*, *42*(3), 197–210. doi:10.1016/S0950-5849(99)00058-0

Zhang, X., Jin, F., & Liu, P. D. (2013). A grey relational projection method for multi-attribute decision making based on intuitionistic trapezoidal fuzzy number. *Applied Mathematical Modelling*, *37*(5), 3467–3477. doi:10.1016/j.apm.2012.08.012

Zhang, X., Meng, X., Tang, Y., & Bi, C. (2017). Adaptive query relaxation and result categorization based on data distribution and query context. *Journal of Information Science and Engineering*, *33*(5), 1375–1396.

Zhang, X., Yang, Q., Ding, J., & Wang, Z. (2020). Entity Profiling in Knowledge Graphs. *IEEE Access : Practical Innovations, Open Solutions*, *8*, 27257–27266. doi:10.1109/ACCESS.2020.2971567

Zhao, H., Xu, L., Guo, Z., Liu, W., Zhang, Q., Ning, X., Li, G., & Shi, L. (2019). A new and fast waterflooding optimization workflow based on INSIM-derived injection efficiency with a field application. *Journal of Petroleum Science Engineering*, *179*, 1186–1200. doi:10.1016/j.petrol.2019.04.025

Zhao, P., & Han, J. (2010). On graph query optimization in large networks. *Proceedings of the VLDB Endowment International Conference on Very Large Data Bases*, *3*(1-2), 340–351. doi:10.14778/1920841.1920887

Zhu, L., Li, N., & Bai, L. (2020). Algebraic operations on spatiotemporal data based on RDF. *ISPRS International Journal of Geo-Information*, *9*(2), 80. doi:10.3390/ijgi9020080

Zhu, L., Li, N., Bai, L., Gong, Y., & Xing, Y. (2020). stRDFS: Spatiotemporal Knowledge Graph Modeling. *IEEE Access : Practical Innovations, Open Solutions*, *8*, 129043–129057. doi:10.1109/ACCESS.2020.3008688

Zhu, L., Meng, X., & Mi, Z. (2022). Fuzzy Spatiotemporal Data Modeling and Operations in RDF. *Information (Basel)*, *13*(10), 503. doi:10.3390/info13100503

Zhu, L., Ng, W. K., & Cheng, J. (2011). Structure and attribute index for approximate graph matching in large graphs. *Information Systems*, *36*(6), 958–972. doi:10.1016/j.is.2011.03.009

Zipf, A., & Krüger, S. (2001). TGML: extending GML by temporal constructs - a proposal for a spatiotemporal framework in XML. In *Proceedings of the 9th ACM International Symposium on Advances in Geographic Information Systems* (pp. 39-42). ACM.10.1145/512161.512183

Zolotukhin, M., Ivannikova, E., & Hamalainen, T. (2013). Novel method for the prediction of mobile location based on temporal-spatial behavioral patterns. In *Proceedings of IEEE International Conference on Information Science and Technology (ICIST)* (pp. 761-766). IEEE. 10.1109/ICIST.2013.6747655

Zou, L., Chen, L., & Özsu, M. T. (2009). Distance-join: Pattern match query in a large graph database. *Proceedings of the VLDB Endowment International Conference on Very Large Data Bases*, *2*(1), 886–897. doi:10.14778/1687627.1687727

Zou, L., Mo, J. H., Chen, L., Özsu, M. T., & Zhao, D. (2011). gStore: Answering SPARQL queries via subgraph matching. *Proceedings of the VLDB Endowment International Conference on Very Large Data Bases*, *4*(8), 482–493. doi:10.14778/2002974.2002976

Zou, L., & Özsu, M. T. (2017). Graph-based RDF data management. *Data Science and Engineering*, *2*(1), 56–70. doi:10.1007/s41019-016-0029-6

Zuo, C., Pal, A., & Dey, A. (2019). New Concepts of Picture Fuzzy Graphs with Application. *Mathematics*, *7*(5), 470. doi:10.3390/math7050470

About the Authors

Luyi Bai received his PhD degree from Northeastern University, China. He is an academic visiting scholar at University of Leicester, UK. His current research interests include knowledge graph, spatio-temporal data management, uncertain databases, and fuzzy databases, etc. He has published over 40 papers in several Journals such as ACM Transactions on Knowledge Discovery from Data, World Wide Web Journal, Information Sciences, Knowledge-Based Systems, Neural Networks, and Expert Systems with Applications, etc. He has also published over 20 papers in several Conferences such as WWW, DASFAA, and KSEM, etc. He has authored one monograph published by Springer. He is a member of IEEE, ACM, CCF, and CAAI.

Lin Zhu, received her PhD degree from Liaoning Technical University, China. Her current research interests include knowledge graph and spatiotemporal database. She has published over 20 papers in several journals such as Expert Systems with Applications, Applied Soft Computing, and Applied Intelligence, etc. She is also a member of CAAI.

Index

O

P

Q

R

S

T

U

X

Printed in the United States
by Baker & Taylor Publisher Services